P9-AGK-815

151295

Engineering Mechanics: STATICS

Engineering Mechanics: STATICS

R. C. Hibbeler

Department of Engineering Mechanics
Illinois Institute of Technology

Macmillan Publishing Co., Inc.
New York
Collier Macmillan Publishers
London

Copyright © 1974, R. C. Hibbeler

Printed in the United States of America

All rights reserved. No part of this book may be reproduced or transmitted in any form or by any means, electronic or mechanical, including photocopying, recording, or any information storage and retrieval system, without permission in writing from the Publisher.

This book is the first part of *Engineering Mechanics: Statics and Dynamics,* copyright © 1974 by R. C. Hibbeler.

Macmillan Publishing Co., Inc.
866 Third Avenue, New York, New York 10022

Collier-Macmillan Canada, Ltd.

Library of Congress Cataloging in Publication Data

Hibbeler, R. C.
   Engineering mechanics: statics.

   Companion volume to Engineering mechanics: dynamics. These two works are also published together as Engineering mechanics: statics and dynamics.
   1. Statics.   I. Title.
TA351.H5   620.1'03   73-17147
ISBN 0-02-354070-0

Printing: 1 2 3 4 5 6 7 8   Year: 4 5 6 7 8 9 0

Preface

The purpose of this book is to provide the student with a clear and thorough presentation of the theory and application of engineering mechanics as it is currently required for the engineering curriculum. One of the major aims of the book is to help develop the student's ability to analyze problems—a most important skill for any engineer.

Although engineering mechanics is based upon relatively few principles, it is these principles which provide a necessary means for the solution of many problems relating to present-day engineering design and analysis. In this book, emphasis is given to both the understanding and the application of these principles, so that the student will have a firm basis for understanding how these principles are utilized both in more advanced courses of study and in engineering practice.

For teaching purposes, as each new principle is introduced, it is first applied to simple situations. Specifically, each principle is applied first to a particle, then to a rigid body subjected to a system of coplanar forces, and finally to the most general case of three-dimensional force systems acting on a rigid body. This presentation allows the instructor some flexibility for teaching the material, since each of the three cases is elaborated upon in separate chapters.

The contents of each chapter are separated into well-defined units. Each unit contains the development and explanation of a specific topic, illustrative example problems, and a set of problems designed to test the student's ability to apply the theory. In any set, the problems are generally arranged in order of increasing difficulty, and the answers to all even-numbered problems are given in the back of the book. Many of the problems depict realistic situations encountered in engineering practice. It is hoped that this realism will stimulate student interest in engineering mechanics and furthermore will help the student to develop his skills in reducing any such problem from its physical description to a model or symbolic representation whereby the principles of mechanics may be applied. All numerical problems are stated in terms of the currently used British system of units; however, if it is deemed necessary, some of the problems may be worked with metric units, using the table of conversion factors given in Appendix C.

Diagrams are used extensively throughout the book, since they provide an important means for obtaining a complete understanding of both the theory and its applications. By emphasizing the use of diagrams in the examples, the student is given a logical and orderly procedure for the solution of problems. Furthermore, when diagrams are included in the analysis, physical insight relating to the problem is maintained. For example, the free-body diagram is introduced early in the book, and it is used whenever a force analysis is required for a problem solution.

Mathematics provides a systematic means of applying the principles of mechanics. The student is expected to have prior knowledge of algebra, geometry, trigonometry, and some calculus. Vector analysis is introduced in this book at points where it is most applicable. Its use often provides a convenient means for presenting concise derivations of the theory, and it makes possible a simple and systematic solution of many complicated three-dimensional problems. Occasionally, the example problems are solved in several ways in an effort to compare the use of a vector analysis with other mathematical techniques based upon a conventional scalar approach. In this way, the student develops the ability to use mathematics as a tool whereby the solution of any problem may be carried out in the most direct and effective manner.

The contents of the book are divided into 11 chapters.* In particular, the fundamental concepts of rigid-body mechanics are outlined in Chapter 1. The notion of a vector and the properties of a concurrent force system are introduced in Chapter 2, and this theory is then applied to the equilibrium of particles in Chapter 3. Chapter 4 contains a general discussion of both concentrated and distributed force systems and methods used to simplify them. The principles of rigid-body equilibrium are developed in Chapter 5. These principles are applied to specific problems involving the equilibrium of trusses, frames, and machines in Chapter 6 and to the analysis of internal forces in beams and cables in Chapter 7. Applications to problems involving frictional forces are discussed in Chapter 8. By introducing the methods for reducing a distributed load to a concentrated resultant force early in Chapter 4, this theory may be incorporated with problems involving equilibrium. At the discretion of the instructor, however, this material may be covered later in conjunction with topics relating to centroids and center of gravity, given in Chapter 9. This can be done by simply omitting the problems involving

---

*This book is also available in a combined volume, *Engineering Mechanics: Statics and Dynamics.*

distributed force systems in the intervening chapters. On the other hand, since the theory in Chapter 9 does not depend upon the methods of equilibrium, this chapter may also be covered before rigid-body equilibrium (Chapter 5). If time permits, sections concerning more advanced topics, indicated by stars, may be studied. Some topics in Chapter 10 ("Moment of Inertia for an Area") and all of Chapter 11 ("Virtual Work") may be omitted without any loss of continuity from the basic course. (Note that this more advanced material also provides a suitable reference for basic principles when it is covered in more advanced courses.)

The author has endeavored to write a textbook that will appeal to both student and instructor alike. In doing so, it must be admitted that the development of this book was not accomplished singlehandedly. Through the years, many people have given both their support and their help. Although I cannot list them all, I wish to acknowledge the valuable suggestions and comments made by Professors G. Mavrigian, Youngstown State University; W. G. Plumtree, California State University at Los Angeles; M. E. Raville, Georgia Institute of Technology; A. Pytel, Pennsylvania State University; G. W. Washa, University of Wisconsin; R. Schaefer, University of Missouri at Rolla; and P. K. Mallick, Illinois Institute of Technology. Gratitude is extended to the engineering students at Youngstown State University and Illinois Institute of Technology for their assistance both in the preparation and classroom testing of the manuscript. I wish also to thank my secretaries, Bernadine and Judy, who tirelessly typed and retyped the manuscript. Lastly, I would like to praise the publishing staff for presenting the manuscript in such fine artistic form.

It is hoped that all instructors and students using this textbook will find it most suitable for the purpose for which it is intended. Since they can provide the most critical review of this work, the author welcomes and will gladly acknowledge any comments they make regarding its contents.

Russell C. Hibbeler

Contents

Engineering Mechanics: STATICS

1

General Principles

1-1. Definitions

Mechanics, in general, is that branch of the physical sciences concerned with the state of rest or motion of bodies which are subjected to the action of forces. The theory of mechanics forms the basis of most present-day engineering design and analysis. For example, a comprehensive study of the engineering sciences relating to structural members, machine elements, fluid flow, electrical instrumentation, and even molecular and atomic behavior requires a thorough knowledge of the principles of mechanics.

Besides being one of the most important physical sciences in engineering, mechanics is also considered one of the oldest physical sciences. Writings as early as those of Archimedes (287–212 B.C.) record how he developed the principle of buoyancy in hydrostatics, and explained the equilibrium of the lever. Simon Stevin (1548–1620) not only formulated the parallelogram law used to combine forces vectorally, but he is also recognized for the development of many important concepts in the subject of statics. Galileo Galilei (1564–1642) was one of the first major contributors to the field of dynamics. His work consisted of experiments made with pendulums and falling bodies. The most significant contributions to the field of mechanics, however, were made by Sir Isaac Newton (1642–1727). He is noted for his formulation of the laws of motion and the law of universal gravitational attraction. Some of the other notable pioneers in the science of mechanics who made important contributions were Bernoulli, Euler, Lagrange, and Hamilton.

Mechanics is generally subdivided into five branches: *rigid-body mechanics, deformable-body mechanics, fluid mechanics, relativistic mechanics,* and *quantum mechanics.* The subject of engineering mechanics as treated in this book is concerned with the laws of mechanics applicable to the study of rigid-body behavior. The basic laws governing the behavior of rigid bodies are formulated from the three laws of motion first postulated by Sir Isaac Newton. For this reason, rigid-body mechanics is sometimes referred to as *Newtonian* or *classical mechanics*. A thorough study of rigid-body mechanics is a necessary prerequisite for the study of the mechanics of deformable bodies and the mechanics of fluids.

In 1905 Albert Einstein presented his general theory of relativity which placed limitations on classical mechanics. In this regard, the findings of relativistic mechanics differ significantly from classical mechanics when the speed of the body approaches the speed of light (186,000 mi/sec or 3.0×10^8 m/sec). Hence, the theory of relativity is most often applied to study the motions of celestial bodies and subatomic size particles, which move at fantastically high rates of speed. The theory of quantum mechanics was developed during 1925 and 1926 after it was realized that classical mechanics failed to predict the behavior of particles moving within atomic distances of one another. Because man, however, is macroscopic in size, we directly observe and obey the laws of classical mechanics. Therefore, this science forms a suitable basis for the design and analysis of the majority of engineering problems, since the speed of the body studied is generally much smaller than the speed of light, and the body is many times greater than atomic size.

The study of rigid-body mechanics is generally divided into two subject areas: statics and dynamics. *Statics* deals with the equilibrium of bodies under the action of forces, while *dynamics* is concerned with the accelerated motion of bodies. Dynamics is further subdivided into *kinematics,* which is the study of the geometry of motion without reference to the forces which cause the motion, and *kinetics,* which relates the imposed forces to the resulting motions. Basically, statics can be considered as a special case of dynamics in which the body is in equilibrium and therefore is either at rest or moves with constant velocity. Most structures are designed with the intention that they remain in equilibrium. Furthermore, even structural members having small accelerations, such as some aircraft and machine components, can be designed under pseudoequilibrium conditions, provided these accelerations are neglected. Clearly, therefore, many engineers need a thorough working knowledge of the principles of statics.

1–2. Fundamental Quantities, Units

Four fundamental quantities commonly used in mechanics are length, time, force, and mass. In general, each of these quantities is defined on the basis of an arbitrarily chosen *unit* or standard. By applying a simple experimental process to compare quantities of the same kind to the standard unit, we can then form a basis for defining the standard quantities.

The concept of *length* is needed to locate the position of a point in space and thereby describe the size of a physical system. The unit of length measurement is the standard *meter* (m) which was originally defined by the distance between parallel lines marked on a platinum-iridium bar kept at standard pressure and temperature and located in the International Bureau of Weights and Measures at Sèvres, France. A more current definition of the meter,* which makes this unit readily accessible to scientists throughout the world, is taken to be 1,650,763.73 wave lengths in vacuum of the orange-red line of the spectrum of krypton-86. All other units of length are defined in terms of the standard meter. For example, 1 centimeter (cm) is equal to 0.01 m and 1 foot (ft) is equal to 0.3048m.

Time is conceived by a succession of events. Some convenient units for measurements of time are the second, minute, and hour. By international agreement, each of these measurements is a fraction of a standard unit of time measured by an atomic clock, having a time unit based upon the duration of 9,192,631,770 cycles of radiation associated with a specified transition of the isotope cesium-133.

Force is generally considered as a "push" or "pull" exerted by one body on another. A man pushing on a wall is exerting a force on the wall; the wall in turn is pushing back on the man with an equal, but opposite force. In the same manner, the man standing on a floor exerts a force on the floor, which is equal and opposite to the force of the floor on the man. Forces acting between objects always occur in equal and opposite pairs; no single force can act alone. This fact follows from Newton's third law of motion—for every action there is an equal and opposite reaction. Force interaction can occur when there is direct contact between bodies, such as a man pushing on a wall, or it can occur through a distance by which the bodies are physically separated. Examples of the latter type include gravitational, electrical, and magnetic forces. Engineers define the standard unit of force as being either the *pound* (lb) or the newton (N). Each of these two units is measured by the amount of pull exerted by the earth upon an object at a specified latitude and height above sea level. This force or gravitational attraction by the earth on a body is defined as the *weight* of the body. Comparison of weights can be made using a spring balance. Since the effect of gravity changes with respect to the distance from the center of the earth, it is important to make comparisons at a specified latitude and height above sea level.

Mass is regarded as a property which is used to determine the resistance of matter to a change in its motion. Unlike the concept of weight, *mass is constant regardless of position*. For this reason, comparison of masses

* 11th International Conference on Weights and Measures, Paris, 1960.

is usually made by means of a lever-arm balance. The international standard of mass, as adopted by the 11th International Conference on Weights and Measures, is the *kilogram* (kg) defined by a bar of platinum alloy kept at the International Bureau of Weights and Measures. Occasionally grams (g) are also used to measure mass, 1 g = 0.001 kg.

The four fundamental quantities, length, time, force, and mass are all related using Newton's law of motion—force is proportional to the product of mass and acceleration, i.e., $F = kma$. For convenience, if we select the constant of proportionality $k = 1$, the *units* used to define force, mass, length, and time cannot *all* be selected arbitrarily. Instead, the equality $F = ma$ is maintained if three of the four units (called *primary units*) are arbitrarily defined and the fourth unit is derived from the equation.

Five important systems of units used to describe the four fundamental quantities are listed in Table 1-1. In particular, the MKS, SI, and CGS systems are both defined using length, time, and mass as primary units. These three systems are called *absolute,* since the defined measurements of the primary units can be made at *any location.* For example, the meter has the same (or absolute) length regardless of where the measurement is made. The unit of force in these systems is a *derived* unit. Hence, in the MKS system, a *newton* is the amount of force needed to give 1 kg mass an acceleration of 1 m/sec^2 ($F = ma$). Whereas in the CGS system, a *dyne* is defined as the amount of force which gives a mass of 1 g an acceleration of 1 cm/sec^2. These two absolute systems of units are used almost universally by scientists throughout the world.

Table 1-1   System of Units

Type of System	Name of System	Length	Mass	Force	Time
Absolute	Metric (MKS) and Système International (SI)	meter (m)	kilogram (kg)	newton,* N $\left(\dfrac{\text{kg-m}}{\text{sec}^2}\right)$	second (sec)
Absolute	(CGS)	centimeter (cm)	gram (g)	dyne* $\left(\dfrac{\text{g-cm}}{\text{sec}^2}\right)$	second (sec)
Gravitational	Metric Gravitational (MKGFS)	meter (m)	metric slug* $\left(\dfrac{\text{kg}_f\text{-sec}^2}{\text{m}}\right)$	kilogram force (kg$_f$)	second (sec)
Gravitational	British Gravitational (FPS)	foot (ft)	slug* $\left(\dfrac{\text{lb-sec}^2}{\text{ft}}\right)$	pound (lb)	second (sec)

*Derived unit

Since most experiments involve a direct measurement of force, engineers prefer to use a *gravitational system* of units in preference to an absolute system. In a gravitational system, the three primary units are force, length, and time. Mass, therefore, becomes a derived unit, Table 1-1. In formulating the MKGFS system, the units of length (m) and time (sec) are the same as in the MKS system. The MKGFS system, however, is often confused with the MKS system since the unit of mass in the MKS system and the unit of force in the MKGFS system have the same name—the kilogram. Due to frequent misunderstanding in solving problems, it should therefore be kept firmly in mind that the kilogram (kg) is a unit of mass in the MKS system and the kilogram-force (kg_f) is a unit of force in the MKGFS system. Specifically, the unit of mass in the MKGFS system is the *metric slug* defined as the amount of mass to which a force of 1 kg_f imparts an acceleration of 1 m/sec^2. On the other hand, in the FPS system of units, the unit of mass is called a *slug*, which is equal to the amount of mass which is accelerated at 1 ft/sec^2 when acted upon by a force of 1 lb.

Currently the FPS system of units is predominantly used by American engineers; however, in the near future, the SI units of measurement are intended, in time, to replace the FPS system. By adopting the metric units, American engineers will be in a more suitable position to communicate in a quantitative sense with engineers located in other nations of the world. Although this change will come in due time, in this book we will use the FPS system of units as a means for applying the principles of mechanics to solving problems. If deemed necessary, the problems for solution may be worked in SI units using the appropriate conversion factors. See Appendix C.

1–3. Fundamental Idealizations

If a physical body is represented in its natural state, application of the principles of mechanics becomes exceedingly complex. In the physical world all matter is composed of atoms. Thus, when a force is applied to a solid body, a series of interatomic forces is established among all the atoms of the solid to prevent the body from collapsing. In an effort to find the actual amount of force resisted by the body, at some point inside the body, it would be necessary to analyze each of the atomic interactions to arrive at an answer—a nearly impossible task. To simplify this problem, we may view the body as having a macroscopic form and consider each element of the body to be made up of a continuous "spread" or *continuum* of matter, rather than a finite number of discrete atomic particles. The behavior of this assumed continuum can then be studied experimentally in order to find relations between deformations of the solid and the forces applied to it. This deformable-continuum model of a physical body is an important idealization used throughout the study of deformable-body mechanics and fluid mechanics.

We may further simplify the model representing the physical body by assuming the body to be entirely rigid. For a *rigid body* each small portion or particle of the body remains at a constant distance away from every other particle in the body both before and after applying a load to the body. This simplification eliminates the need for experimental testing, since the body cannot deform. The concept of the rigid-body assumption is an important idealization in the study of engineering mechanics. In solving problems, however, we should be clearly aware of its limitations, for, in reality, all bodies deform. Since many of the principles of engineering mechanics are related to the shape of the body, it is important to recognize problems where applied loadings might cause large deformations of the body. If the loads severely deform a body such that the orientation of the loading *after* it is applied is *not known,* the rigid-body model must be replaced by the deformable-continuum model. However, if the deformed shape of the body is *known,* so that the final position of the applied loads can be determined with sufficient accuracy, then the rigid-body assumption may be justified. In many cases the deformations occurring in engineering structures, machines, mechanisms, etc. are relatively small, and the rigid-body assumption is suitable for analysis. Thus, with the exception of springs, the principles of mechanics as discussed in this book will be based on the assumption that all materials are rigid.

If the size or shape of a body has no consequence in the problem solution, we may use a particle to represent a model of the body. A *particle* essentially has no size but has a mass. This idealization is useful in statics for studying the equilibrium of a body subjected to a concurrent force system. In dynamics its use is often justified in studying the motion of bodies having trajectories larger than the dimensions of the body, such as the motion of a planetary body about the sun. Since geometry of the body is not involved, the principles of mechanics reduce to a particularly simplified form when applied to a particle. For this reason, throughout this book specific principles of mechanics are first applied to a particle before they are applied to a rigid body.

Another important fundamental idealization used in mechanics is the concept of a concentrated force. When any external load is applied to the surface of a body, it is actually distributed over a finite surface area. The intensity of these *distributed forces* is measured in terms of pressure or force per unit area. In some cases, however, the distributed load can be simplified to a *concentrated force.* This can be done provided the area over which the load is applied is small compared to the finite dimensions of the body. When a distributed load can be represented as a concentrated force, computations regarding the effect of the load on the body are greatly simplified.

The entire structure of rigid-body mechanics is formulated on the basis of relatively few fundamental principles. These principles or laws were conceived on the basis of *experimental evidence*. We will briefly state these principles here and discuss them in greater detail at points in the book where they are needed.

Newton's Three Laws of Motion. In the late seventeenth century, Sir Isaac Newton formulated his three fundamental laws governing the motion of a particle. These laws are as follows:

First Law. A particle originally at rest, or moving at a constant velocity, will continue to remain at rest or move at constant velocity in a straight line, provided there is no unbalanced force acting on the particle.

Second Law. A particle acted upon by an unbalanced force **F** receives an acceleration **a** in the direction of the force. The acceleration is directly proportional to the force and inversely proportional to the particle mass *m*. This law is commonly expressed in mathematical terms as

$$\mathbf{F} = m\mathbf{a}$$

Third Law. For every force acting on a particle, the particle exerts an equal, opposite, and collinear reactive force.

Newton's Law of Gravitational Attraction. Shortly after formulating his three laws of motion for a particle, Newton postulated a law governing the mutual attraction between any two particles. In mathematical form this law can be expressed by the equation

$$F = G\frac{m_1 m_2}{r^2} \tag{1-1}$$

where

F = the force of attraction between the two particles

G = the universal constant of gravitation; according to experimental evidence $G = 3.44 \times 10^{-8}$ lb–ft²/slug² $(6.67 \times 10^{-11}$ m³/(kg–sec²))

m_1, m_2 = the masses of each of the two particles

r = the distance between the centers of both particles

Any two particles or bodies have a mutual attractive (gravitational) force acting between them. In the case of a particle located at or near the surface of the earth, however, the only attractive force having any sizable magnitude is that of the earth's gravitation. Thus, for our purpose, this will be the only gravitational force considered.

The Parallelogram Law for Finding the Force Resultant. Originally developed by Simon Stevin back in the late sixteenth century, the paral-

lelogram law is used to find a single resultant force equivalent to two forces acting at a point. This is done by constructing a parallelogram whose sides represent the given forces. The diagonal of the parallelogram then represents the magnitude of the resultant force.

The Principle of Transmissibility.   This principle states that a force, applied to a rigid body, may act at any point along its line of action without altering the conditions of equilibrium or the conditions of motion of the body.

1–5. Method of Problem Solution

One of the most effective ways of studying engineering mechanics is to work problems. Merely studying concepts or general principles about some theory will be of little use if this knowledge is not applied in a meaningful way. In working problems it is very important to present the work in a *logical* and *orderly* manner. It is strongly advised to follow these steps:

1. Read the problem carefully. List the data given and the results required.
2. Draw and label any necessary diagrams needed for the solution. In solving equilibrium problems, for example, this step will include drawing the necessary free-body diagrams.
3. List all the relevant principles, generally in mathematical form.
4. Think about the problem in terms of the actual *physical situation*. Try to correlate this knowledge with each mathematical expression that is written out.
5. Solve the necessary equations algebraically as far as is practical, then complete the solution numerically. For engineering work, a slide rule in most cases provides the desired degree of accuracy for solution.
6. Check through the problem making sure that the equations used are dimensionally homogeneous and that the units of the numerical data used in the solution are consistent.*
7. Study the answer with technical judgment and common sense to determine whether or not the answer seems reasonable.
8. Once the solution has been completed, review the problem. Try to think of other ways of obtaining the same solution.

---

*The terms of any equation used to describe a physical process must be dimensionally homogeneous, that is, each term must be expressed in the same units. Provided this is the case, all the terms of the equation can then be combined if numerical data is substituted for the variables. For later applications, the example on page 11 illustrates the method for converting from one set of units to another.

In applying the above procedure, do the work as neatly as possible the first time. Being neat generally stimulates clear and orderly thinking and vice versa.

Example

Given a speed of $v = 10$ ft/sec, convert the units to mi/hr.

Solution

Since 5,280 ft $= 1$ mi, 60 sec $= 1$ min, and 60 min $= 1$ hr, then

$$v = 10 \text{ ft/sec} = \frac{10 \text{ ft}}{1 \text{ sec}} \frac{60 \text{ sec}}{1 \text{ min}} \frac{60 \text{ min}}{1 \text{ hr}} \frac{1 \text{ mi}}{5,280 \text{ ft}}$$

$$= \frac{36,000}{5,280} \text{ mi/hr} = 6.82 \text{ mi/hr} \qquad\qquad Ans.$$

2

Force and Position Vectors

2-1. Scalars and Vectors

Many of the physical quantities in mechanics can be expressed mathematically by means of scalars and vectors. A quantity possessing only a magnitude is called a *scalar.* Some scalars are always positive—for example, mass, energy, or volume. Others, classified as algebraic scalars, such as temperature, may be either positive or negative. In this book scalars will be indicated by letters of ordinary type. The mathematical operations involving scalars follow the same rules as those of elementary algebra.

A *vector* is a quantity having a magnitude, direction, and sense. It is necessary that two vectors be combined using the parallelogram law. This law utilizes a particular form of construction which accounts for the combined magnitude, direction, and sense of the vector. Vector quantities which are encountered in the study of statics are the position, force, and moment vectors.

For analytical work, a vector is often represented by a letter with an arrow written over it, such as $\vec{A}$, and its magnitude is designated by $|\vec{A}|$ or simply A. In this book vectors will be designated in boldface type; for example **A** is used to designate the vector "A," while its magnitude will be indicated by A.

Graphically, a vector is represented by an arrow, used to define its magnitude and direction. The *magnitude* of the vector is indicated by the *length* of the arrow. The vector **A** shown in Fig. 2-1 has a magnitude of four units. The line of action has a *direction* of 20° above the horizontal with a *sense* indicated by the arrowhead. The point O is commonly

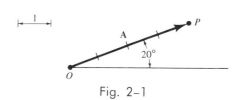

Fig. 2-1

13

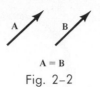

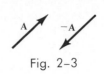

A = B

Fig. 2-2

Fig. 2-3

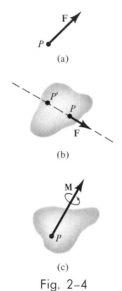

(a)

(b)

(c)

Fig. 2-4

referred to as the *initial point, origin,* or *tail* of the vector, and the point *P* is referred to as the *terminal point, terminus,* or *tip*.

The two vectors **A** and **B** shown in Fig. 2-2 are considered *equal* provided they have the same magnitude, direction, and sense. Although it is not necessary that they originate from the same point, it is required that a pair of equal vectors be of the same *type;* that is, the magnitude of the vectors must have the same units. For example, the magnitudes of two force vectors may both be expressed in units of pounds. Borrowing the equal sign from scalar algebra, we may write the equality of vectors **A** and **B** as

$$\mathbf{A} = \mathbf{B}$$

A *negative vector* has a direction opposite to its positive counterpart but has the same magnitude, as shown in Fig. 2-3.

There are three *kinds* of vectors which are important to us in our study of statics. They are the bounded or fixed vector, the sliding vector, and the free vector. A *fixed vector* is one that acts at a particular point in space. For example, a force vector **F** acting on the particle *P*, shown in Fig. 2-4a, must be a fixed vector, since a particle itself is a well-defined point of application. A *sliding vector* is a vector which may be applied anywhere along its line of action. A force applied to a rigid body may be thought of as a sliding vector when the effect of the force on the entire body is being considered (refer to the principle of transmissibility in Sec. 1-4). Provided this is the case, the force vector **F** shown in Fig. 2-4b may be applied at any point $P(P')$ lying along its line of action. *Free vectors* can act at any point in space; it is only necessary that they preserve their same magnitude, direction, and sense. In some instances the moment vector of a couple is treated as a free vector. This concept will be discussed later; however, if this is the case, the couple vector **M** acting on the rigid body shown in Fig. 2-4c may then be placed at *any point P* on the body.

2-2. Addition and Subtraction of Vectors

The law for addition of two vectors **A** and **B**, Fig. 2-5a, is defined using either the "triangle" or "parallelogram" rules. To form the sum $\mathbf{R} = \mathbf{A} + \mathbf{B}$ by means of the *triangle rule,* vector **B** is added to vector **A** by placing the initial point of **B** at the terminal point of **A** and then joining the initial point of **A** to the terminal point of **B** (see Fig. 2–5b). The vectors **A** and **B** are referred to as *component vectors,* and their sum yields the *resultant vector* **R.** In a similar manner, vector **R** can also be obtained by adding **A** to **B,** Fig. 2–5c. Both ways of addition form the basis for the *parallelogram law* of vector addition. According to this method, vectors **A** and **B** each form an adjacent side of a parallelogram. The resultant vector **R** is then determined by constructing an arrow from the initial point of **A** and **B** along the diagonal of the parallelogram to the opposite corner. The construction is shown in Fig. 2–5d. From this figure, or Figs. 2–5b and 2–5c, it can be seen that vector addition is commutative; i.e., **A** + **B** = **B** + **A.** It is important to note that when adding vectors, the addition must be carried out using either the "triangle" or "parallelogram" laws, as shown here. Furthermore, the vectors added must have magnitudes measured with a consistent set of units.

When adding two vectors *graphically,* the vector arrows must be drawn to scale to make the operation meaningful. The resultant vector's magnitude and its direction can then be measured directly from the graph. See Example 2–1.

In many cases the *resultant of two vectors* can be determined conveniently through analytical methods. Since the triangle rule forms the basis for vector addition, we can use trigonometry to find the resultant's magnitude and direction. In some problems the resultant vector may already be known, in which case the problem unknowns involve the magnitudes and/or the directions of the component vectors. (See Examples 2–3 and 2–4.) In any case, the law of sines and the law of cosines may be helpful in solving for the unknowns. These formulas are given in Fig. 2–6 for the triangle *ABC.*

When adding *three* or *more vectors* which are *coplanar,* i.e., lying in the same plane, the polygon rule, which is a simple extension of the triangle rule, may be used. This rule is illustrated in Fig. 2–7 for the addition of vectors **A, B,** and **C.** In forming the sum **R** = **A** + **B** + **C,** we arrange the vectors in a "tip-to-tail" fashion. The resultant **R** is thus

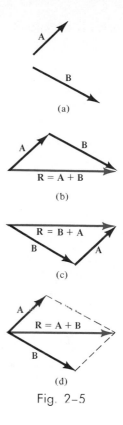

Fig. 2–5

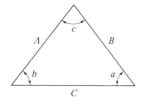

Sine law:
$$\frac{A}{\text{Sin } a} = \frac{B}{\text{Sin } b} = \frac{C}{\text{Sin } c}$$

Cosine law:
$$C = \sqrt{A^2 + B^2 - 2AB \text{ Cos } c}$$

Fig. 2–6

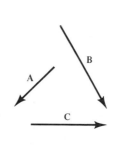

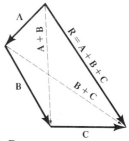

Fig. 2–7

formed by connecting the "tail" or origin of the first vector **A** with the "tip" of the last one **C.** This procedure is equivalent to applying the triangle rule twice; that is, adding **B** to **A,** we form the resultant $(\mathbf{A} + \mathbf{B})$, shown as a dashed arrow in Fig. 2–7. **C** is then added to this vector, which yields the resultant **R.**

Noting the dashed arrows in Fig. 2–7, we see that the addition of three vectors is associative; i.e.,

$$\mathbf{R} = (\mathbf{A} + \mathbf{B}) + \mathbf{C} = \mathbf{A} + (\mathbf{B} + \mathbf{C})$$

The associative rule can easily be extended to include more than three vectors. Since vector addition is commutative, the order of addition of the vectors according to the polygon rule is immaterial; that is, the vectors may be added together in any order.

In defining the (resultant) *difference* of two vectors **A** and **B,** one may write

$$\mathbf{R} = \mathbf{A} - \mathbf{B} = \mathbf{A} + (-\mathbf{B})$$

and then form the vector sum. It is seen that subtraction is defined as a special case of addition, and the rules that apply for vector addition will also apply for vector subtraction. A graphic example of vector subtraction is given in Fig. 2–8.

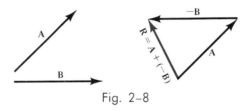

Fig. 2–8

If $\mathbf{A} = \mathbf{B}$ then the difference **R** is defined as a zero or *null vector,* written as

$$\mathbf{R} = \mathbf{A} - \mathbf{B} = 0$$

Null vectors have zero magnitude and arbitrary direction.

2–3. Multiplication of a Vector by a Scalar

The product of a vector **A** by a scalar m, yielding $m\mathbf{A}$, is defined as a vector having a magnitude $|m|\, A$. The sense of direction is the same as **A** provided m is positive, or opposite to **A** if m is negative. (If $m = 0$, then $m\mathbf{A}$ is a null vector.) The negative of a vector can thus be defined on the basis of multiplication of the vector by the scalar -1. By definition, the vector *magnitude* is always a *positive quantity. A minus sign in front of a vector simply means that its directional sense is reversed* (see Fig. 2–3).

Multiplication of a scalar by a vector can be shown to be associative; i.e.,

$$m(n\mathbf{A}) = (mn)\mathbf{A}$$

commutative; i.e.,

$$m\mathbf{A} = \mathbf{A}m$$

and distributive; i.e.,

$$(m + n)\mathbf{A} = m\mathbf{A} + n\mathbf{A}$$

and

$$m(\mathbf{A} + \mathbf{B}) = m\mathbf{A} + m\mathbf{B}$$

Note that these laws apply only when scalars are multiplied by vectors. The product of two vectors shall be defined in Chapter 4.

Division of a vector by a scalar can be defined by means of the laws of multiplication, since

$$\frac{\mathbf{A}}{m} = \frac{1}{m}\mathbf{A} \qquad m \neq 0$$

Graphic examples of multiplication and division of vectors by scalars are shown in Fig. 2–9.

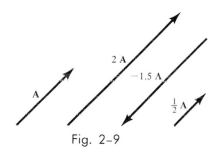

Fig. 2–9

2–4.   Force as a Vector Quantity

As mentioned in Chapter 1, *force* is considered as a push or pull that one body exerts on another. In other words, force might be regarded as a directed action which can be classified as a vector quantity. The *force magnitude* is commonly measured in terms of pounds (lb) or by using newtons (N). Large forces may be represented in units of kilopounds (kips) or tons (a *kip* and a *ton* are equivalent to 1,000 lb and 2,000 lb, respectively).

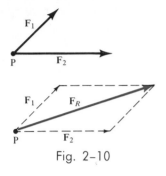

Fig. 2-10

To represent a force as a vector graphically, one would arbitrarily choose a scale of measuring units to represent the units of force. A line segment having a scaled length equivalent to the force *magnitude* would then be constructed in a *direction* acting along the line of action of the force. The *sense* of the force would be indicated by an arrowhead.

Since forces are vector quantities, they not only have a magnitude, direction, and sense, but they also must add according to the triangle or parallelogram laws of vector addition. The fact that forces do indeed obey these laws has been proven by *experimental observation*. If forces F_1 and F_2 act at the same point P, their effect on P is the same as if these forces are replaced by their vector resultant $F_R = F_1 + F_2$, Fig. 2–10.

When a system of two or more forces acts through the *same point,* the vectors are known as a system of *concurrent* forces. Furthermore, if all these forces act in the *same plane,* such as F_1 and F_2 in Fig. 2–10, the force system is both concurrent and *coplanar*. From this and the previous discussion of vectors, we will now give some examples involving con-current–coplanar force systems.

Example 2–1

The "eyebolt" in Fig. 2–11a is subjected to two forces F_1 and F_2. Determine the magnitude and direction of the resultant force acting on the "eyebolt."

Solution
Graphical Procedure. Choosing an arbitrary scale of 50 lb = $\frac{1}{2}$ in., the force parallelogram is constructed as shown in Fig. 2–11b. Using a scale

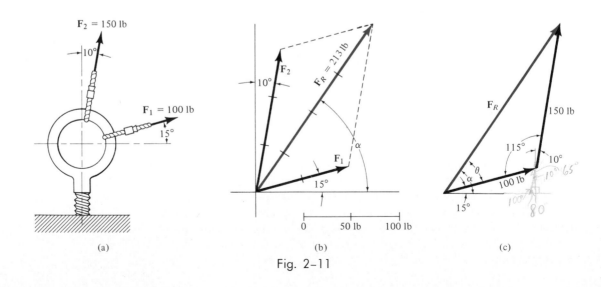

Fig. 2-11

and protractor, we can measure the force resultant $\mathbf{F}_R$ directly from this drawing. It is found that

$$F_R = 213 \text{ lb} \qquad\qquad Ans.$$
$$\alpha = 55° \qquad\qquad Ans.$$

Analytical Procedure. The two component force vectors may be added together in a "tip-to-tail" fashion according to the triangle law of vector addition, as shown in Fig. 2-11c. The magnitude of the resultant may be determined from the triangle by means of the law of cosines:

$$F_R = \sqrt{(100)^2 + (150)^2 - 2(100)(150)\cos 115°}$$
$$= \sqrt{10,000 + 22,500 - 30,000\,(-0.423)}$$
$$= 212.6 \text{ lb} \qquad\qquad Ans.$$

Applying the law of sines, using the computed value of F_R, we find the angle θ:

$$\frac{150}{\sin \theta} = \frac{212.6}{\sin 115°}$$
$$\sin \theta = \frac{150}{212.6}(0.906) = 0.639$$
$$\theta = 39.8$$

Thus,

$$\alpha = 39.8° + 15.0° = 54.8° \qquad\qquad Ans.$$

Example 2-2

The gusset plate in Fig. 2-12a is subjected to four forces which are concurrent at point O. Determine the resultant of these forces using the polygon method of vector addition.

Solution

Choosing an arbitrary scale of 50 lb $= \frac{1}{4}$ in. and starting with $\mathbf{F}_1$, we add all the vectors together in a "tip-to-tail" fashion, as shown in Fig. 2-12b. The resultant force $\mathbf{F}_R$ is then drawn from the initial point of $\mathbf{F}_1$ to the head of $\mathbf{F}_4$. Direct measurements from the figure give

$$F_R = 408 \text{ lb} \qquad\qquad Ans.$$
$$\theta = 26° \qquad\qquad Ans.$$

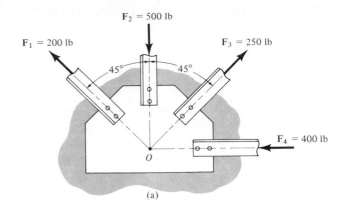

(a)

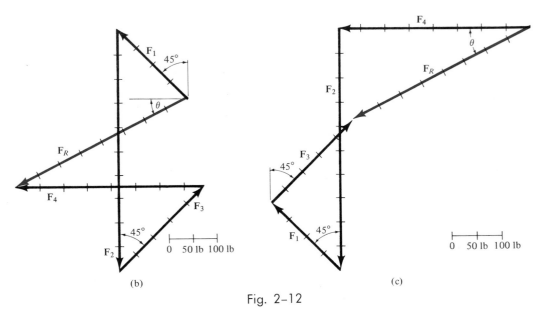

(b)

(c)

Fig. 2–12

Since vector addition is commutative, the same results are obtained from the construction shown in Fig. 2–12c. In this case $\mathbf{F}_R = \mathbf{F}_4 + \mathbf{F}_2 + \mathbf{F}_1 + \mathbf{F}_3$.

Example 2–3

Resolve the 200-lb force resultant shown acting on the pin, Fig. 2–13a, into components in (a) the x and y directions, (b) the x' and y' directions, and (c) the x' and y directions.

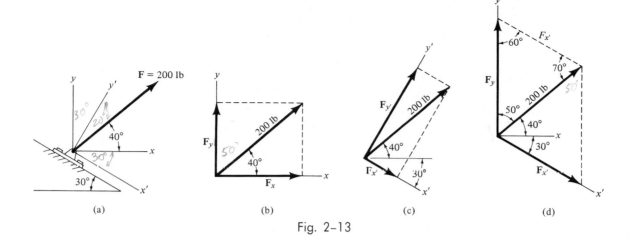

Fig. 2–13

Solution

Part (a). Using the parallelogram law, we resolve **F** into x and y components, Fig. 2–13b. From this figure,

$$F_x = 200 \cos 40° = 153.2 \text{ lb} \qquad \textit{Ans.}$$

$$F_y = 200 \sin 40° = 128.6 \text{ lb} \qquad \textit{Ans.}$$

Part (b). The x' and y' components of **F** are shown in Fig. 2–13c. The magnitudes of these components are

$$F_{x'} = 200 \cos 70° = 68.4 \text{ lb} \qquad \textit{Ans.}$$

$$F_{y'} = 200 \sin 70° = 187.9 \text{ lb} \qquad \textit{Ans.}$$

Part (c). The two components $\mathbf{F}_{x'}$ and $\mathbf{F}_y$ are shown in Fig. 2–13d. Note how the construction is based on the parallelogram law. Using the law of sines, to obtain the magnitude of each component,

$$\frac{F_y}{\sin 70°} = \frac{200 \text{ lb}}{\sin 60°}$$

$$F_y = 217.0 \text{ lb} \qquad \textit{Ans.}$$

$$\frac{F_{x'}}{\sin 50°} = \frac{200 \text{ lb}}{\sin 60°}$$

$$F_{x'} = 177.0 \text{ lb} \qquad \textit{Ans.}$$

Example 2–4

The ring shown in Fig. 2–14a is subjected to two forces $\mathbf{F}_1$ and $\mathbf{F}_2$. If it is required that the resultant of these two applied forces have a magni-

21

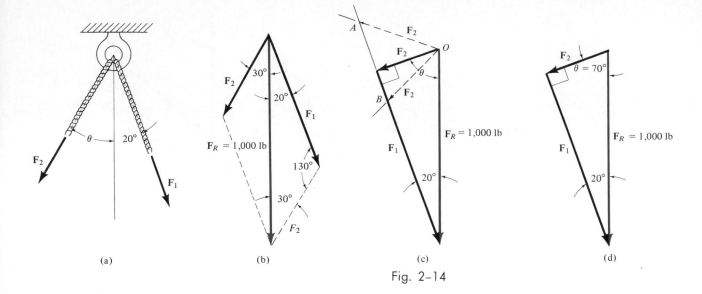

(a) (b) (c) (d)

Fig. 2–14

tude of 1,000 lb and be directed vertically downward, determine (a) the magnitude of $\mathbf{F}_1$ and $\mathbf{F}_2$ provided $\theta = 30°$, and (b) the magnitude of $\mathbf{F}_1$ and $\mathbf{F}_2$ when F_2 is a minimum.

Solution
Part (a). A sketch of the vector addition, using the parallelogram law, is given in Fig. 2–14b. The unknown magnitudes F_1 and F_2 can be found using the law of sines; namely,

$$\frac{F_1}{\sin 30°} = \frac{1{,}000 \text{ lb}}{\sin 130°}$$

$$F_1 = 652.7 \text{ lb} \qquad\qquad Ans.$$

$$\frac{F_2}{\sin 20°} = \frac{1{,}000 \text{ lb}}{\sin 130°}$$

$$F_2 = 446.5 \text{ lb} \qquad\qquad Ans.$$

Part (b). As shown in Fig. 2–14c, using the triangle law, vector $\mathbf{F}_2$ may be added to $\mathbf{F}_1$ in various ways to yield the net resultant $\mathbf{F}_R$. In particular, the *minimum* length or magnitude of $\mathbf{F}_2$ will occur when the line of action of $\mathbf{F}_2$ is perpendicular to $\mathbf{F}_1$. Any other direction, such as OA or OB, yields a larger value for the magnitude of $\mathbf{F}_2$. Hence, when $\theta = 90° - 20° = 70°$, the value of F_2 is minimum. From the triangle shown in Fig. 2–14d, it is seen that

$\cos 20°$

$$F_1 = 1{,}000 \sin 70° = 939.7 \text{ lb} \qquad\qquad Ans.$$

$$F_2 = 1{,}000 \sin 20° = 342.0 \text{ lb} \qquad\qquad Ans.$$

22

Problems

2-1. Find the resultant force acting on the pin.

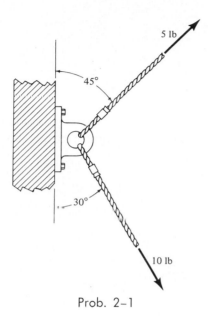

Prob. 2-1

2-2. Using the polygon law for vector addition, determine graphically the resultant vector of the four coplanar forces.

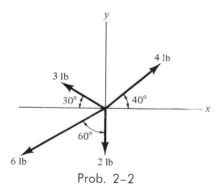

Prob. 2-2

2-3. The riveted bracket supports two forces. Determine the angle θ so that the line of action of the resultant force is horizontal. What is the magnitude of this resultant force?

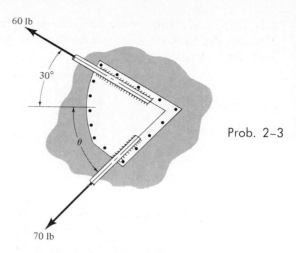

Prob. 2-3

2-4. Two forces are applied at the end of a "screw eye" in order to remove the post. Determine the angle θ so that the resultant force acting on the post is directed vertically upward and has a magnitude of 100 lb.

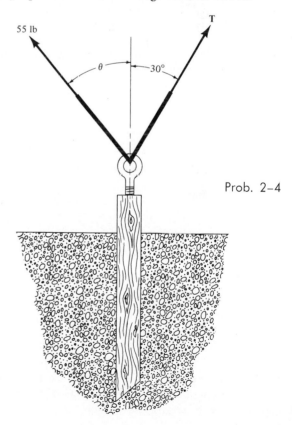

Prob. 2-4

23

2-5. Using a graphical procedure, determine the magnitude of the resultant force and its direction measured from the horizontal.

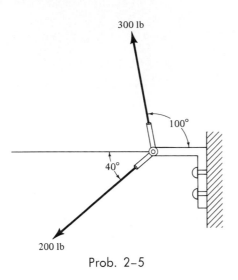

Prob. 2-5

2-6. Find the x and y components of the 500-lb force acting on the bracket.

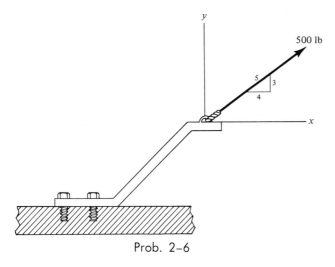

Prob. 2-6

2-7. Resolve the force **F** into components acting parallel and perpendicular to the aa axis of the boom. **F** is coplanar with aa and the vertical.

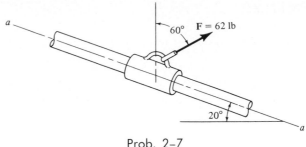

Prob. 2-7

2-8. Using the polygon law for vector addition, determine the resultant of the three forces acting at the end of the boom.

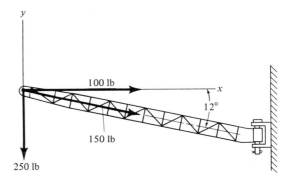

Prob. 2-8

2-9. Using trigonometry, determine (a) $\mathbf{F}_1 + \mathbf{F}_2$, and (b) $\mathbf{F}_1 - \mathbf{F}_2$.

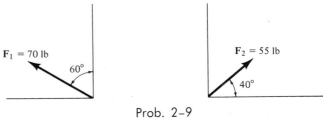

Prob. 2-9

2-10. The force **F** has a magnitude of 500 lb and is to be resolved into two components acting along the axes of booms AB and AC. Determine the angle θ so that the component of **F** directed along AC acts from A to C and has a magnitude of 200 lb.

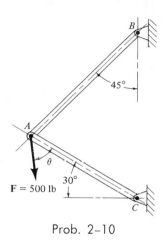

Prob. 2-10

(c) $2v_1 - 2v_2 - v_3$, where $v_1 = 0$, $v_2 = 1$ ft/sec, $v_3 = 5$ ft/sec.

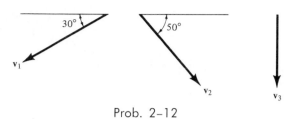

Prob. 2-12

2-11. The boom collar A resists the pull of the 1,000-lb applied loading. Resolve this force into components acting along the x and y axes.

2-13. Two forces act at the end of the boom. Determine the magnitude of force $\mathbf{F}$ and its direction θ such that (a) the resultant of the two forces, $\mathbf{F}_R$, has a magnitude of 20 lb and is directed along the negative x axis, (b) the resultant $\mathbf{F}_R$ is a null vector.

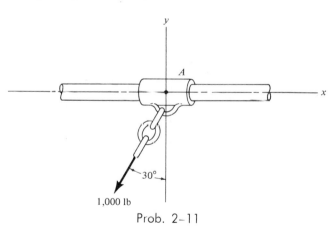

Prob. 2-11

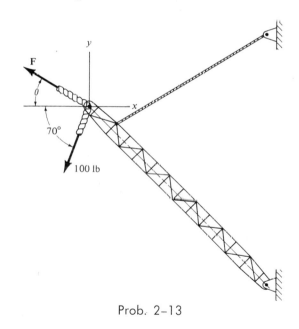

Prob. 2-13

2-12. Given the three velocity vectors $\mathbf{v}_1$, $\mathbf{v}_2$, and $\mathbf{v}_3$ having the directions shown, use the polygon rule to find the following sums:
(a) $\mathbf{v}_1 + \mathbf{v}_2 + \mathbf{v}_3$, where $v_1 = 7$ ft/sec, $v_2 = 8$ ft/sec, $v_3 = 12$ ft/sec.
(b) $\mathbf{v}_1 - \frac{1}{2}(\mathbf{v}_2 + \mathbf{v}_3)$, where $v_1 = 4$ ft/sec, $v_2 = 200$ ft/min, $v_3 = 24$ in./sec.

2-14. The jet aircraft is subjected to the towing forces developed in the cables AB and AC. If it is required that the resultant of these two forces have a magnitude of 500 lb and be directed along the axis of the fuselage of the aircraft, determine (a) the magnitude of the tow-

25

ing forces, provided $\theta = 15°$, and (b) the value of θ such that the force in cable AB is a minimum.

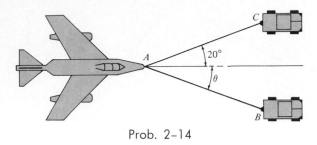

Prob. 2–14

2–15. Resolve the 175-lb force acting on the support into components acting in (a) the x' and y' directions, and (b) the x' and x directions.

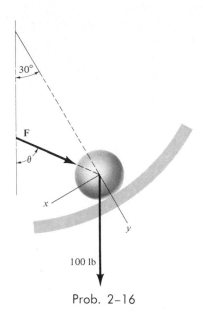

100 lb

Prob. 2–16

2–17. The 500-lb force acting on the frame is to be resolved into two components acting along the axes of the struts AB and AC. If the component of force along member AC is required to be 300 lb, directed from A to C, determine the magnitude of force acting along AB and the angle θ of the 500-lb force.

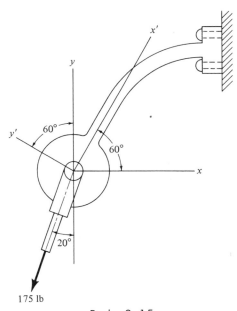

Prob. 2–15

2–16. Using trigonometry, determine the magnitude and direction θ of force **F**, which passes through the center of the 100-lb sphere so that the resultant of the two forces acting on the sphere has a magnitude of 210 lb and is directed along the positive y axis.

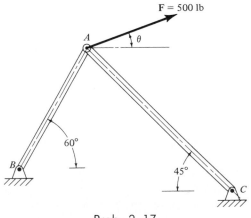

Prob. 2–17

26

2-18. A vertical force of 200 lb is applied to the end of the horizontal beam *AB*. If it is known that the component of this force acting along *CA* is 500 lb, directed from *C* to *A*, find the component of force acting along *AB*, and the angle θ.

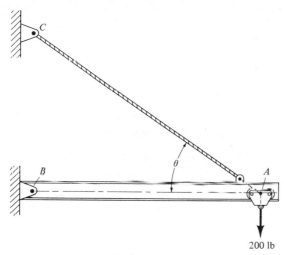

200 lb

Prob. 2-18

2-5. Unit Vectors

A *unit vector* is a vector having a magnitude of unity. If **A** is a vector having a magnitude $A \neq 0$, then a unit vector having the *same direction* as **A** is represented by

$$\mathbf{u}_A = \frac{\mathbf{A}}{A} \tag{2-1}$$

Rewriting this equation,

$$\mathbf{A} = A\mathbf{u}_A \tag{2-2}$$

Since vector **A** is of a certain kind, for example, a force vector, it is customary to assign to it the proper set of units used to describe it. The magnitude A also has this same set of units; hence, from Eq. 2-1, the *unit vector will be dimensionless.* Equation 2-2 indicates that vector **A** may therefore be expressed in terms of both its magnitude and direction *separately;* that is, A (a scalar) expresses the *magnitude* of **A**, and $\mathbf{u}_A$ (a dimensionless vector) expresses the *directional sense* of **A.**

2–6. Components of a Vector and Cartesian Unit Vectors

Any vector **A** may be represented by the sum of three component vectors acting along the x, y, and z axes of a rectangular coordinate system. The proof of this statement can be established with reference to Fig. 2–15.

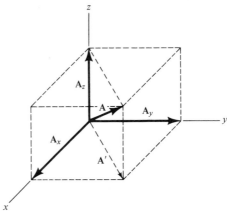

Fig. 2–15

Using the parallelogram law of vector addition, we have

$$\mathbf{A}' = \mathbf{A}_x + \mathbf{A}_y$$

and

$$\mathbf{A} = \mathbf{A}' + \mathbf{A}_z$$

Combining these equations,

$$\mathbf{A} = \mathbf{A}_x + \mathbf{A}_y + \mathbf{A}_z \tag{2-3}$$

In this book only right-hand Cartesian coordinate systems will be used. A coordinate system is said to be *right-handed* provided the thumb of the right hand points in the direction of the positive z axis, while the "curl" of the right-hand fingers is drawn from the positive x to the positive y axis, as shown in Fig. 2–16.

A set of unit vectors **i**, **j**, and **k** will be used to define the *positive direction* of the x, y, and z axes, respectively, as shown in Fig. 2–17. Using this set of unit vectors and our definition of a unit vector as expressed by Eq. 2–2, we may recast the vector components of Eq. 2–3 into a more convenient form:

$$\mathbf{A} = A_x\mathbf{i} + A_y\mathbf{j} + A_z\mathbf{k}$$

There is a distinct advantage to writing vectors in this manner, that is, in terms of their **i**, **j**, and **k** (or x, y, and z) components. In doing so,

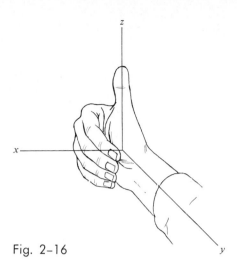

Fig. 2-16

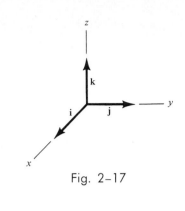

Fig. 2-17

the magnitude and direction of each component vector are *separated*, and as a result, this simplifies the operations of vector algebra. For example, to form the vector sum $\mathbf{R} = \mathbf{A} + \mathbf{B}$, we must add the corresponding vectors $\mathbf{A}$ and $\mathbf{B}$ according to the parallelogram law in the manner shown shaded in Fig. 2-18a. However, an easier method of vector addition consists of forming the resultant by adding together the magnitudes of each of the corresponding $\mathbf{i}$, $\mathbf{j}$, and $\mathbf{k}$ components of vectors $\mathbf{A}$ and $\mathbf{B}$. From Fig. 2-18a,

$$\mathbf{A} = A_x\mathbf{i} + A_y\mathbf{j} + A_z\mathbf{k}$$

and

$$\mathbf{B} = B_x\mathbf{i} + B_y\mathbf{j} + B_z\mathbf{k}$$

Thus,

$$\mathbf{R} = \mathbf{A} + \mathbf{B} = A_x\mathbf{i} + A_y\mathbf{j} + A_z\mathbf{k} + B_x\mathbf{i} + B_y\mathbf{j} + B_z\mathbf{k}$$

Since $A_x\mathbf{i}$ and $B_x\mathbf{i}$ are collinear vectors, their resultant is determined by the scalar addition of the components. Adding the $\mathbf{j}$ and $\mathbf{k}$ components in a similar manner, we obtain the necessary resultant

$$\mathbf{R} = (A_x + B_x)\mathbf{i} + (A_y + B_y)\mathbf{j} + (A_z + B_z)\mathbf{k}$$

This vector sum is illustrated graphically in Fig. 2-18b.

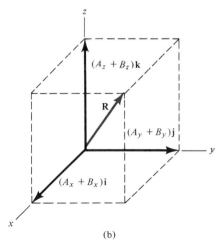

2-7. Magnitude and Direction of Cartesian Vectors

It is always possible to obtain the magnitude and direction of a vector when the vector is expressed in terms of its Cartesian components. If

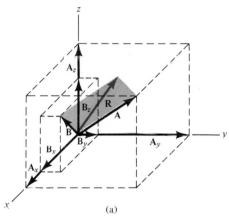

Fig. 2-18

29

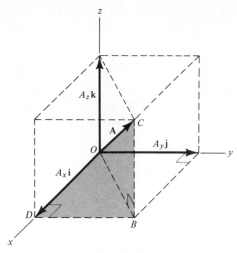

Fig. 2–19

$\mathbf{A} = A_x\mathbf{i} + A_y\mathbf{j} + A_z\mathbf{k}$, the *magnitude* of $\mathbf{A}$ can be found by applying the Pythagorean theorem. Consider the construction shown in Fig. 2–19. From the right triangle *ODB*, the magnitude of line segment *OB* may be represented as

$$OB = \sqrt{(OD)^2 + (DB)^2}$$

Similarly, from the right triangle *OBC*,

$$OC = \sqrt{(OB)^2 + (BC)^2}$$

Combining both equations,

$$OC = \sqrt{(OD)^2 + (DB)^2 + (BC)^2}$$

Recognizing that each of these line segments represents the magnitude of vector $\mathbf{A}$ and its components, we may express the magnitude of $\mathbf{A}$ as

$$A = \sqrt{(A_x)^2 + (A_y)^2 + (A_z)^2} \qquad (2\text{--}4)$$

Hence, *the magnitude of a vector is equal to the positive square root of the sum of the squares of the vector's Cartesian components.* The positive square root is chosen since the magnitude represents the measured *length* of the vector.

The *direction* of vector $\mathbf{A}$ is represented by *coordinate direction angles* α, β, and γ which the tail of vector $\mathbf{A}$ makes with the positive x, y, and z axes, as shown in Fig. 2–20. Note that α, β, or γ can never be greater than 180°. Referring to Fig. 2–20*a*, it is necessary that *ODB* be a right triangle, having a right angle at point *D*. Thus, provided the magnitude of $\mathbf{A}$ is calculated (see Eq. 2–4) the angle α can be determined from

$\cos \alpha = OD/OB = A_x/A$. In a similar manner, using right triangles OCB and OEB, shown in Figs. 2–20b and 2–20c, we obtain $\cos \beta = A_y/A$ and $\cos \gamma = A_z/A$. The numbers $\cos \alpha$, $\cos \beta$, and $\cos \gamma$ are known as the *direction cosines* of vector **A.** The angles α, β, and γ are therefore defined from the relations:

$$\alpha = \cos^{-1} \frac{A_x}{A}$$

$$\beta = \cos^{-1} \frac{A_y}{A} \qquad (2\text{–}5)$$

$$\gamma = \cos^{-1} \frac{A_z}{A}$$

Knowing the magnitude of **A,** it is possible to form the unit vector $\mathbf{u}_A$ which, by definition, has a magnitude of one (dimensionless unit) and acts in the direction of **A.** Using Eq. 2–1, this unit vector is

$$\mathbf{u}_A = \frac{\mathbf{A}}{A} = \frac{A_x}{A} \mathbf{i} + \frac{A_y}{A} \mathbf{j} + \frac{A_z}{A} \mathbf{k} \qquad (2\text{–}6)$$

From the definition of the direction cosines given above, it is seen that the **i, j,** and **k** *components, namely* A_x/A, A_y/A *and* A_z/A, *of the unit vector* $\mathbf{u}_A$ *represent the direction cosines of* **A.** Hence, we may also write,

$$\mathbf{u}_A = \cos \alpha \mathbf{i} + \cos \beta \mathbf{j} + \cos \gamma \mathbf{k} \qquad (2\text{–}7)$$

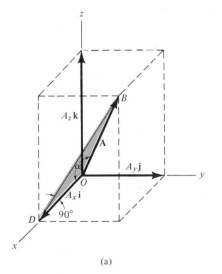

(a)

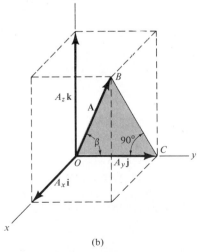

(b)

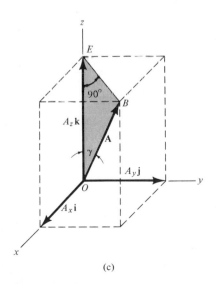

(c)

Fig. 2–20

Since the magnitude of a vector is equal to the square root of the sum of the squares of its Cartesian components, and $\mathbf{u}_A$ has a magnitude of unity, using Eq. 2–7, we obtain an important relation between the direction cosines:

$$\cos^2 \alpha + \cos^2 \beta + \cos^2 \gamma = 1 \qquad (2\text{–}8)$$

Hence, when two coordinate direction angles of a vector are known, the third direction angle is specified by using Eq. 2–8.

2–8. Position Vectors and Unit Vector Operations

In general, the coordinate axes are used as a space frame. Hence, the units along the three axes are measured in terms of length. By definition, a *position vector* is used to locate one point in space relative to another point. The position vector $\mathbf{r}_1$, Fig. 2–21, extending *from the origin to an arbitrary point* $P_1(x_1, y_1, z_1)$ in space is therefore

$$\mathbf{r}_1 = x_1\mathbf{i} + y_1\mathbf{j} + z_1\mathbf{k}$$

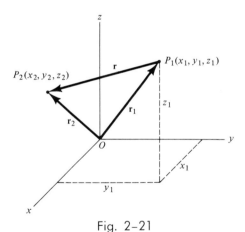

Fig. 2–21

A position vector may also be constructed between two arbitrary points in space. For example, consider finding the position vector $\mathbf{r}$ having an initial point $P_1(x_1, y_1, z_1)$ and terminal point $P_2(x_2, y_2, z_2)$, Fig. 2–21. Forming the position vectors $\mathbf{r}_1$ and $\mathbf{r}_2$ yields

$$\mathbf{r}_1 = x_1\mathbf{i} + y_1\mathbf{j} + z_1\mathbf{k}$$
$$\mathbf{r}_2 = x_2\mathbf{i} + y_2\mathbf{j} + z_2\mathbf{k}$$

Using the triangle rule for vector addition, Fig. 2–21, we require

$$\mathbf{r}_1 + \mathbf{r} = \mathbf{r}_2$$

Hence,

$$\mathbf{r} = \mathbf{r}_2 - \mathbf{r}_1 = (x_2\mathbf{i} + y_2\mathbf{j} + z_2\mathbf{k}) - (x_1\mathbf{i} + y_1\mathbf{j} + z_1\mathbf{k})$$

or

$$\mathbf{r} = (x_2 - x_1)\mathbf{i} + (y_2 - y_1)\mathbf{j} + (z_2 - z_1)\mathbf{k} \qquad (2\text{–}9)$$

Thus, *the components of a position vector acting between any two points in space may be formed by taking the coordinates of the terminus or head of the vector $P_2(x_2, y_2, z_2)$ and subtracting from them the corresponding coordinates $P_1(x_1, y_1, z_1)$ of its initial point or tail.*

Following the method used in Sec. 2–7, the *magnitude* of $\mathbf{r}$ is

$$r = \sqrt{(x_2 - x_1)^2 + (y_2 - y_1)^2 + (z_2 - z_1)^2} \qquad (2\text{–}10)$$

The *direction* of $\mathbf{r}$ can be determined by *first* constructing a unit vector $\mathbf{u}_r$ which is directed from point P_1 to point P_2. This vector is determined by using Eqs. 2–9 and 2–10, i.e.,

$$\mathbf{u}_r = \frac{\mathbf{r}}{r} = \frac{(x_2 - x_1)}{r}\mathbf{i} + \frac{(y_2 - y_1)}{r}\mathbf{j} + \frac{(z_2 - z_1)}{r}\mathbf{k}$$

See Fig. 2–22. On the basis of Eq. 2–7, the angles α, β, and γ which $\mathbf{r}$ makes with respect to the x, y, and z axes are found by using the *components* of this unit vector:

$$\alpha = \cos^{-1}\frac{(x_2 - x_1)}{r}$$

$$\beta = \cos^{-1}\frac{(y_2 - y_1)}{r}$$

$$\gamma = \cos^{-1}\frac{(z_2 - z_1)}{r}$$

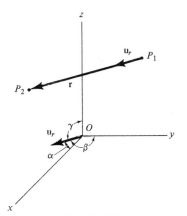

Fig. 2–22

The unit vector $\mathbf{u}_r$ can also be used to construct a vector of a *different kind* but having the same direction as $\mathbf{r}$. As an example, suppose that points P_1 and P_2 act as fixed end supports for a cord which has a tension of T lb, as shown in Fig. 2–23a. When the cord is removed, it exerts a force of $\mathbf{T}_{P_1 P_2}$, which acts on point P_1 toward point P_2; and, similarly, an equal and opposite force $\mathbf{T}_{P_2 P_1}$ acts on point P_2 toward point P_1, Fig. 2–23b. Both forces have a magnitude of T lb. The *direction* of force $\mathbf{T}_{P_1 P_2}$ may be specified by using the unit vector $\mathbf{u}_r$. Since $\mathbf{u}_r$ has a

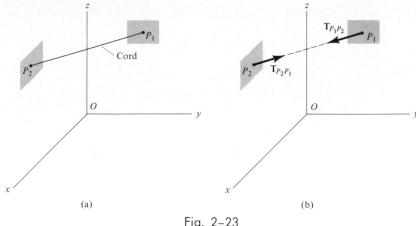

Fig. 2–23

magnitude of one (dimensionless) unit, we may form the force vector $\mathbf{T}_{P_1 P_2}$ by applying Eq. 2–2. Thus,

$$\mathbf{T}_{P_1 P_2} = (T \text{ lb})\mathbf{u}_r$$
$$= \left\{ T\frac{(x_2 - x_1)}{r}\,\mathbf{i} + T\frac{(y_2 - y_1)}{r}\,\mathbf{j} + T\frac{(z_2 - z_1)}{r}\,\mathbf{k} \right\} \text{lb}$$

Also,

$$\mathbf{T}_{P_2 P_1} = -\mathbf{T}_{P_1 P_2} = T \text{ lb}\,(-\mathbf{u}_r) = \{-T\mathbf{u}_r\}\ \text{lb}$$
$$= \left\{ -T\frac{(x_2 - x_1)}{r}\,\mathbf{i} - T\frac{(y_2 - y_1)}{r}\,\mathbf{j} - T\frac{(z_2 - z_1)}{r}\,\mathbf{k} \right\} \text{lb}$$

The following examples further illustrate the methods used to apply the above theory to the solution of problems.

Example 2–5

The rope in Fig. 2–24a is subjected to a tension force of 60 lb when used to pull the crate up the 20° incline. Express this force as a Cartesian vector having components parallel and perpendicular to the incline.

Solution I

As shown in Fig. 2–24b, the 60-lb force is resolved into its Cartesian components using the parallelogram law. From this figure,

$$F_x = 60 \cos 30° = 52.0 \text{ lb}$$
$$F_y = 60 \sin 30° = 30.0 \text{ lb}$$

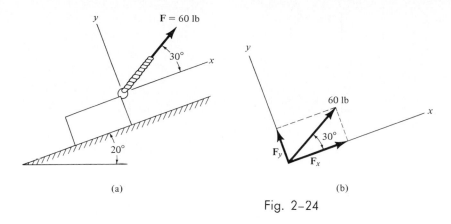

(a) (b) (c)

Fig. 2-24

Since the magnitude of the **i** and **j** components of **F** are now known, the force may be expressed as

$$\mathbf{F} = \{52.0\mathbf{i} + 30.0\mathbf{j}\}\ \text{lb} \qquad\qquad Ans.$$

Solution II

The result may be obtained by using a unit vector approach. As shown in Fig. 2-24c, the unit vector $\mathbf{u}_F$ acting in the direction of **F** has direction cosines along the x and y axes of $\cos\alpha = \cos 30°$ and $\cos\beta = \cos 60°$, respectively. Thus, from Eq. 2-7, or simply from the components,

$$\mathbf{u}_F = \cos\alpha\,\mathbf{i} + \cos\beta\,\mathbf{j} = \cos\alpha\,\mathbf{i} + \sin\alpha\,\mathbf{j} = \sin\beta\,\mathbf{i} + \cos\beta\,\mathbf{j}$$
$$= 0.866\mathbf{i} + 0.500\mathbf{j}$$

Since the force has a magnitude of 60 lb, from Eq. 2-2,

$$\mathbf{F} = (60\ \text{lb})\mathbf{u}_F = \{52.0\mathbf{i} + 30.0\mathbf{j}\}\ \text{lb} \qquad\qquad Ans.$$

Example 2-6

The gusset plate shown in Fig. 2-25a is subjected to four forces which are concurrent at point O. Using Cartesian vectors, determine the magnitude and direction of the resultant of these forces.

Solution

The resultant force is the vector sum of all the forces. Hence, it is first necessary to express each force in Cartesian vector form. This can be accomplished by first establishing a unit vector in the direction of each force, and then multiplying the components of the unit vector by the magnitude of the force in accordance with Eq. 2-2. Thus,

$$\mathbf{F}_1 = (400\ \text{lb})(-\mathbf{i}) = \{-400\mathbf{i}\}\ \text{lb}$$
$$\mathbf{F}_2 = (250\ \text{lb})(\sin 45°\mathbf{i} + \cos 45°\mathbf{j}) = \{176.8\mathbf{i} + 176.8\mathbf{j}\}\ \text{lb}$$

35

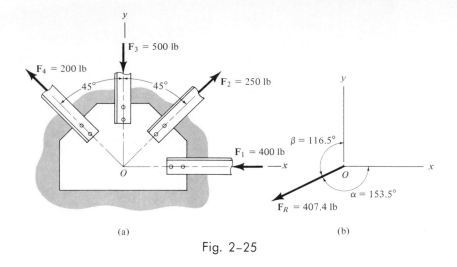

Fig. 2–25

$$\mathbf{F}_3 = (500 \text{ lb})(-\mathbf{j}) = \{-500\mathbf{j}\} \text{ lb}$$
$$\mathbf{F}_4 = (200 \text{ lb})(-\sin 45°\mathbf{i} + \cos 45°\mathbf{j}) = \{-141.4\mathbf{i} + 141.4\mathbf{j}\} \text{ lb}$$

The resultant force is therefore

$$\mathbf{F}_R = \mathbf{F}_1 + \mathbf{F}_2 + \mathbf{F}_3 + \mathbf{F}_4$$
$$= -400\mathbf{i} + (176.8\mathbf{i} + 176.8\mathbf{j}) + (-500\mathbf{j}) + (-141.4\mathbf{i} + 141.4\mathbf{j})$$
$$= \{-364.6\mathbf{i} - 181.8\mathbf{j}\} \text{ lb}$$

The magnitude of this vector is

$$F_R = \sqrt{(-364.6)^2 + (-181.8)^2} = 407.4 \text{ lb} \qquad Ans.$$

A unit vector acting in the direction of $\mathbf{F}_R$ is

$$\mathbf{u}_R = \frac{\mathbf{F}_R}{F_R} = -\frac{364.6}{407.4}\mathbf{i} - \frac{181.8}{407.4}\mathbf{j} = -0.895\mathbf{i} - 0.446\mathbf{j}$$

The direction cosines of $\mathbf{u}_R$ are therefore

$$\cos \alpha = -0.895, \qquad \text{so that } \alpha = 153.5° \qquad Ans.$$
$$\cos \beta = -0.446, \qquad \text{so that } \beta = 116.5° \qquad Ans.$$

The resultant $\mathbf{F}_R$ is illustrated graphically in Fig. 2–25b. Note, by definition, the direction angles α and β must be measured from the *positive* x and y axes to the tail of the force.

Example 2–7

Using the hoisting rig shown in Fig. 2–26a, a man lifts a 100-lb crate by pulling on the cable ABC. The pulley located at B is free to rotate,

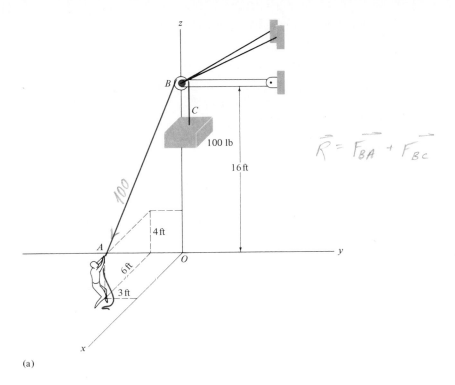

$$\vec{R} = \vec{F}_{BA} + \vec{F}_{BC}$$

(a)

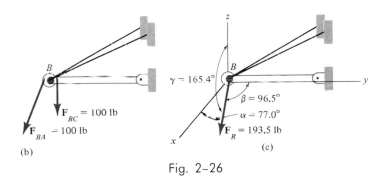

(b)

(c)

Fig. 2-26

and therefore the entire cable ABC is subjected to a tension of 100 lb. Determine the magnitude and direction of the resultant force which this cable exerts on the hoisting rig at point B.

Solution

As shown in Fig. 2-26b, there are two 100-lb forces acting on the hoisting rig which represent the effect of the cable after the cable is *removed*. It is the resultant of these two forces which is to be found. One of these forces is caused by the weight of the crate. Since this force acts in the $-\mathbf{k}$ direction and has a magnitude of 100 lb,

$$\mathbf{F}_{BC} = \{-100\mathbf{k}\} \text{ lb}$$

The second force $\mathbf{F}_{BA}$ is directed from point B (0 ft, 0 ft, 16 ft) to point A (6 ft, -3 ft, 4 ft). The direction of $\mathbf{F}_{BA}$ is computed using this fact. A position vector *from point B to point A* is calculated by Eq. 2–9.

$$\mathbf{r}_{BA} = (6 - 0)\mathbf{i} + (-3 - 0)\mathbf{j} + (4 - 16)\mathbf{k} = \{6\mathbf{i} - 3\mathbf{j} - 12\mathbf{k}\} \text{ ft}$$

The magnitude of this vector (which represents the distance from point B to point A) is

$$r_{BA} = \sqrt{(6)^2 + (-3)^2 + (-12)^2} = 13.75 \text{ ft}$$

Forming the unit vector $\mathbf{u}_{BA}$, which then specifies the *direction* of both $\mathbf{r}_{BA}$ and $\mathbf{F}_{BA}$,

$$\mathbf{u}_{BA} = \frac{\mathbf{r}_{BA}}{r_{BA}} = \frac{6}{13.75}\mathbf{i} - \frac{3}{13.75}\mathbf{j} - \frac{12}{13.75}\mathbf{k}$$

or

$$\mathbf{u}_{BA} = 0.436\mathbf{i} - 0.218\mathbf{j} - 0.873\mathbf{k}$$

Knowing the magnitude of $\mathbf{F}_{BA}$ is 100 lb, $\mathbf{F}_{BA}$ may therefore be expressed in Cartesian vector form as

$$\mathbf{F}_{BA} = (100 \text{ lb}) \mathbf{u}_{BA} = \{43.6\mathbf{i} - 21.8\mathbf{j} - 87.3\mathbf{k}\} \text{ lb}$$

The resultant force $\mathbf{F}_R$ acting at point B is then the vector sum:

$$\mathbf{F}_R = \mathbf{F}_{BA} + \mathbf{F}_{BC} = \{43.6\mathbf{i} - 21.8\mathbf{j} - 187.3\mathbf{k}\} \text{ lb}$$

The magnitude of this resultant is

$$F_R = \sqrt{(43.6)^2 + (-21.8)^2 + (-187.3)^2} = 193.5 \text{ lb} \qquad \textit{Ans.}$$

A unit vector acting in the direction of $\mathbf{F}_R$ is

$$\mathbf{u}_R = \frac{\mathbf{F}_R}{F_R} = \frac{43.6}{193.5}\mathbf{i} - \frac{21.8}{193.5}\mathbf{j} - \frac{187.3}{193.5}\mathbf{k}$$

or

$$\mathbf{u}_R = 0.225\mathbf{i} - 0.113\mathbf{j} - 0.968\mathbf{k}$$

The $\mathbf{i}$, $\mathbf{j}$, and $\mathbf{k}$ components of $\mathbf{u}_R$ represent the direction cosines of $\mathbf{F}_R$. Therefore,

$$\alpha = \cos^{-1}(0.225) = 77.0° \qquad \textit{Ans.}$$
$$\beta = \cos^{-1}(-0.113) = 96.5° \qquad \textit{Ans.}$$
$$\gamma = \cos^{-1}(-0.968) = 165.4° \qquad \textit{Ans.}$$

The resultant vector $\mathbf{F}_R$ is shown in Fig. 2–26c. Note that each of the direction angles is measured from the *positive* coordinate axis to the tail of the force.

Example 2–8

Three guy wires are attached to the top of a mast as shown in Fig. 2–27a. The tension in each of these wires is as follows: $T_{AB} = 200$ lb, $T_{AC} = 300$ lb, and $T_{AD} = 500$ lb. Determine the (x, y) coordinate position of point C so that the resultant of these three forces is directed downward along the axis of the mast, acting from point A to point O. What is the magnitude of the resultant force?

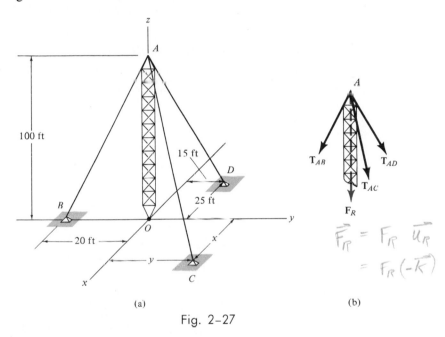

(a)   (b)

Fig. 2–27

Solution

When each cable is removed, the tension force in each cable is directed away from point A, as shown in Fig. 2–27b. Each of these three forces may be expressed in Cartesian vector form. This is done by *first* forming unit vectors along the cables. With reference to Fig. 2–27a,

$$\mathbf{r}_{AB} = \{-20\mathbf{j} - 100\mathbf{k}\} \text{ ft}; \quad r_{AB} = \sqrt{(-20)^2 + (-100)^2} = 102.0 \text{ ft}$$

so that,

$$\mathbf{u}_{AB} = \frac{\mathbf{r}_{AB}}{r_{AB}} = -0.196\mathbf{j} - 0.980\mathbf{k}$$

$$\mathbf{r}_{AC} = \{x\mathbf{i} + y\mathbf{j} - 100\mathbf{k}\} \text{ ft}; \quad r_{AC} = \sqrt{(x)^2 + (y)^2 + (-100)^2}$$

so that,

$$\mathbf{u}_{AC} = \frac{\mathbf{r}_{AC}}{r_{AC}} = \frac{x\mathbf{i} + y\mathbf{j} - 100\mathbf{k}}{\sqrt{x^2 + y^2 + (-100)^2}}$$

$$\mathbf{r}_{AD} = \{-25\mathbf{i} + 15\mathbf{j} - 100\mathbf{k}\} \text{ ft};$$
$$r_{AD} = \sqrt{(-25)^2 + (15)^2 + (-100)^2} = 104.2 \text{ ft}$$

so that,

$$\mathbf{u}_{AD} = \frac{\mathbf{r}_{AD}}{r_{AD}} = -0.240\mathbf{i} + 0.144\mathbf{j} - 0.960\mathbf{k}$$

In accordance with Eqs. 2–1 and 2–2, the force vectors acting along the cables are therefore

$$\mathbf{T}_{AB} = (200 \text{ lb})\mathbf{u}_{AB} = \{-39.2\mathbf{j} - 196.0\mathbf{k}\} \text{ lb}$$

$$\mathbf{T}_{AC} = (300 \text{ lb})\mathbf{u}_{AC} = \left\{\frac{300x\mathbf{i} + 300y\mathbf{j} - 30,000\mathbf{k}}{\sqrt{x^2 + y^2 + (-100)^2}}\right\} \text{ lb}$$

$$\mathbf{T}_{AD} = (500 \text{ lb})\mathbf{u}_{AD} = \{-120.0\mathbf{i} + 72.0\mathbf{j} - 480.0\mathbf{k}\} \text{ lb}$$

Since the *resultant force* $\mathbf{F}_R$ is to be directed downward along the mast axis, $\mathbf{F}_R$ acts in the $-\mathbf{k}$ direction (Fig. 2–27b). If the unknown magnitude of this force is represented as F_R, then

$$\mathbf{F}_R = -F_R\mathbf{k}$$

It is required that

$$\mathbf{F}_R = \mathbf{T}_{AB} + \mathbf{T}_{AC} + \mathbf{T}_{AD}$$

or

$$-F_R\mathbf{k} = (-39.2\mathbf{j} - 196.0\mathbf{k}) + \left(\frac{300x\mathbf{i} + 300y\mathbf{j} - 30,000\mathbf{k}}{\sqrt{x^2 + y^2 + (-100)^2}}\right)$$
$$+ (-120.0\mathbf{i} + 72.0\mathbf{j} - 480.0\mathbf{k})$$

To satisfy this vector equation, the corresponding magnitudes of each of the **i**, **j**, and **k** components of the vector on the left-hand side of the equation must be *equal* to the corresponding magnitudes of the **i**, **j**, and **k** components of the vectors on the right. Hence,

$$0 = \frac{300x}{\sqrt{x^2 + y^2 + (-100)^2}} - 120.0 \tag{1}$$

$$0 = -39.2 + \frac{300y}{\sqrt{x^2 + y^2 + (-100)^2}} + 72.0 \tag{2}$$

$$-F_R = -196.0 - \frac{30,000}{\sqrt{x^2 + y^2 + (-100)^2}} - 480.0 \tag{3}$$

After placing the constants in Eqs. (1) and (2) on the left-hand side of the equal sign, squaring and rearranging terms, we have

$$y^2 = 5.25x^2 - 10,000$$

and

$$x^2 = 82.7y^2 - 10,000$$

Substituting one equation into the other and solving yields $x = \pm 44.0$ ft and $y = \pm 12.0$ ft. The squaring of Eqs. (1) and (2) has introduced extraneous roots in the solution. By substitution, however, the only two of the four roots which satisfy Eqs. (1) and (2) are

$$x = 44.0 \text{ ft} \qquad Ans.$$
$$y = -12.0 \text{ ft} \qquad Ans.$$

Substituting these values into Eq. (3) yields

$$F_R = 949.0 \text{ lb} \qquad Ans.$$

Problems

2–19. For the bracket connection, express the forces **T** and **F** in Cartesian vector notation with respect to the x and y axes. Determine the magnitude of the resultant force and its direction with respect to the x axis.

2–21. Express each of the three forces acting on the bracket in Cartesian vector notation, and compute the magnitude and direction of the resultant force.

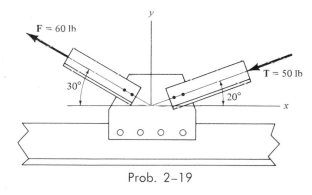

Prob. 2–19

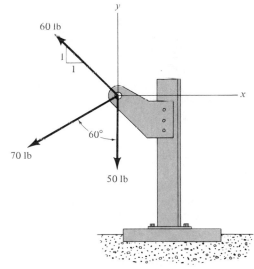

Prob. 2–21

2–20. Determine the magnitude and direction of (a) the force vector $\mathbf{F} = \{10\mathbf{i} + 25\mathbf{j} - 30\mathbf{k}\}$ lb, and (b) the position vector $\mathbf{r} = (-10 \text{ in.})\mathbf{i} + (2 \text{ ft})\mathbf{j}$.

2-22. Represent the position vector acting from points (3 ft, 5 ft, 6 ft) to (5 ft, −2 ft, 1 ft) in Cartesian vector notation. Give its direction cosines, and find the distance between these two points.

2-23. Find the magnitude and the direction of **h**, where **h** is the resultant of the Cartesian unit vectors; i.e.,

$$\mathbf{h} = \mathbf{i} + \mathbf{j} + \mathbf{k}$$

2-24. Given the three position vectors

$$\mathbf{r}_1 = \{4\mathbf{i} + 2\mathbf{j} + 5\mathbf{k}\} \text{ ft}$$
$$\mathbf{r}_2 = \{2\mathbf{i} + 1\mathbf{k}\} \text{ ft}$$
$$\mathbf{r}_3 = \{-24\mathbf{i} + 12\mathbf{j}\} \text{ in.}$$

find the magnitude and direction of (a) $\mathbf{r}_3$, and (b) $\mathbf{r}_1 - \mathbf{r}_2 + \frac{1}{2}\mathbf{r}_3$.

2-25. Determine the length of the sides *AB*, *BC*, and *AC* of the triangular plate.

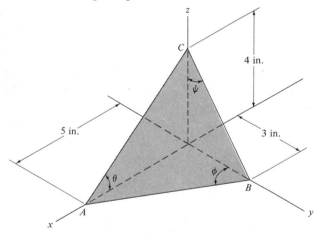

Prob. 2-25

2-26. Determine the angles θ, ϕ, and ψ which the edges of the triangular plate *ABC*, shown in Prob. 2-25, make with the *x*, *y*, and *z* axes.

2-27. If $\mathbf{r}_1 = \{3\mathbf{i} - 2\mathbf{j} + 3\mathbf{k}\}$ ft, $\mathbf{r}_2 = \{4\mathbf{i} - 3\mathbf{k}\}$ ft, $\mathbf{r}_3 = \{\mathbf{i} - 2\mathbf{j} + 10\mathbf{k}\}$ ft, determine the magnitude and direction of (a) $\mathbf{r}_1 - \mathbf{r}_2 + \mathbf{r}_3$, and (b) $-\mathbf{r}_1 + \mathbf{r}_2 - \mathbf{r}_3$.

2-28. Determine the magnitude and direction of the resultant of the three forces in Prob. 2-8 using Cartesian vector notation.

2-29. The cable *OA* exerts a force on point *O* of $\mathbf{F} = \{4\mathbf{i} + 3\mathbf{j} + 10\mathbf{k}\}$ lb, directed from *O* to *A*. If the length of the cable is 5 ft, what are the coordinates (x, y, z) of point *A*?

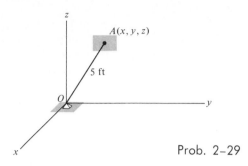

Prob. 2-29

2-30. A position vector is drawn from the origin to the point (4 ft, 3 ft, 10 ft). Determine the angles α, β, and γ which this vector makes with the *x*, *y*, and *z* axis, respectively.

2-31. The antenna cables *CA* and *CB* exert forces of 50 lb and 63 lb, respectively on point *C*. If these forces act away point *C* towards *A* and *B*, express the resultant of these two forces, acting on point *C*, as a vector. What is the magnitude and direction of the resultant?

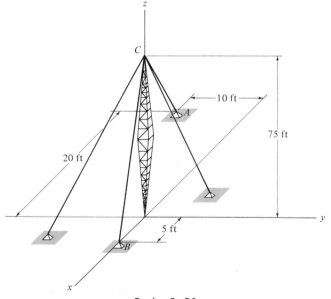

Prob. 2-31

42

2-32. The boom *OA* and the two guy wires support a 100-lb lamp. If the cables *AB* and *AC* exert forces of 50 and 70 lb, respectively on point *A,* determine the magnitude and direction of the resultant force of the weight of the lamp and the two cables acting on the boom at point *A.* The cable forces are directed from *A* to *B* and *A* to *C.*

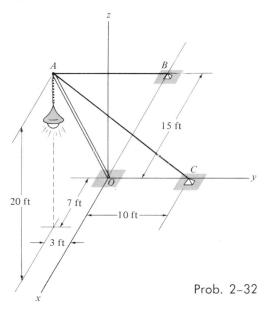

Prob. 2-32

2-33. The magnitude of the *y* and *z* components of the force **F** are known to be 30 and 10 lb, respectively, as shown. The angle α which **F** makes with the *x* axis is 45°. Determine the magnitude and direction cosines of **F.**

Prob. 2-33

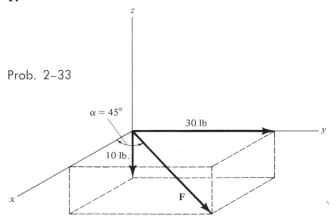

2-34. A position vector **r** has a magnitude of 10 ft and a direction defined by the angles $\alpha = 30°$, $\gamma = 75°$. If it is known that the *y* component of **r** is negative, determine the angle β and the components of **r.**

2-35. The guy line *OA* used to hold the umbrella tent up is 6 ft long and exerts a supporting force of $\mathbf{F} = \{4\mathbf{i} - 3\mathbf{j} - 12\mathbf{k}\}$ lb acting in a direction from point *A* to *O* on the tent. Determine the height *h* of point *A* relative to the ground.

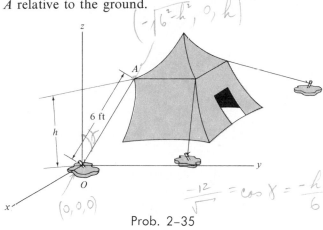

Prob. 2-35

2-36. A wire is bent into the shape shown. If it is known that a position vector acting from point *A* to point *B* is represented as $\mathbf{r}_{AB} = \{\mathbf{i} + 3\mathbf{j} - 5\mathbf{k}\}$ in., determine the length *OA* and its direction with respect to the *x*, *y*, and *z* axes.

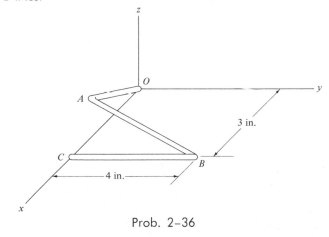

Prob. 2-36

43

2–37. The shaft S exerts three force components on the die D. Find the magnitude and direction of the resultant force.

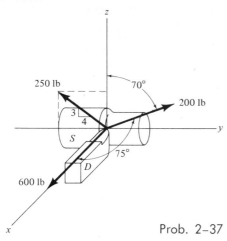

Prob. 2–37

2–38. The door is held open by means of two chains AB and CD. If the tension in AB and CD is 15 and 20 lb, respectively, express each of these forces in Cartesian vector notation. Consider the forces as acting on the door and directed from point D to C and point B to A.

2–39. The ring is subjected to the force of three springs, each spring having a tension of 50 lb. Express these forces as Cartesian vectors directed outward from point O, and find the resultant force acting on point O.

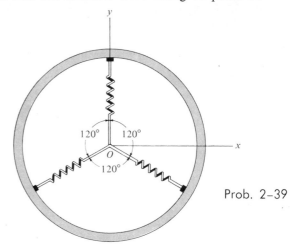

Prob. 2–39

2–40. Because of the action of the 200-lb weight, the boom AB exerts a 250-lb force on the pin at A directed from B to A. The cable AC exerts a force of 175 lb on A, acting from A to C. Determine the magnitude of force in the horizontal cord AD and the height h so that the resultant of the four forces is zero.

Prob. 2–40

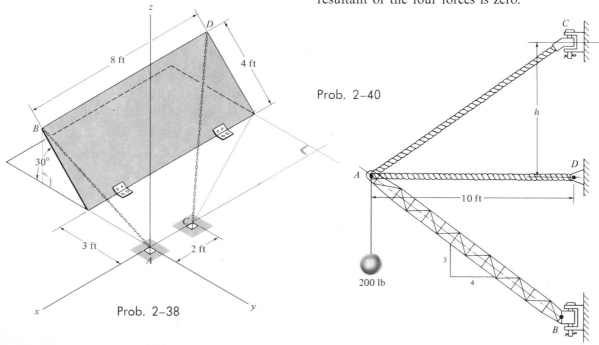

Prob. 2–38

Equilibrium of a Particle

3–1. Conditions for the Equilibrium of a Particle

In this section we will develop both the necessary and sufficient conditions required for the equilibrium of a particle. A *particle* may be defined as being a relatively small portion of matter such that its dimensions or size will be of no consequence in the analysis of the physical problem. (The concept of a particle used in mechanics is therefore analogous to the point used in geometry.) Thus, objects considered as particles can only be subjected to a system of *concurrent forces*. Since a body can be thought of as a combination of many particles, the study of the equilibrium of particles is a necessary prerequisite to the study of body equilibrium.

The conditions for *particle equilibrium* are based on a balance of forces. In particular, if a concurrent force system acts on a particle such that the resultant of the force system is zero, the particle will either remain motionless or continue to move in a straight line at constant speed, depending upon the initial condition of motion. In a physical sense, equilibrium means that there is as much force acting on the particle in one direction as in the opposite direction. This concept, which is both necessary and sufficient for equilibrium, is formally stated as Newton's first law of motion: If the *resultant force* acting on a particle is *zero,* the particle is in *equilibrium.*

As a consequence of equilibrium, motion of the particle is static, i.e., unchanging. Hence, as mentioned, equilibrium requires that the particle either be at rest, if originally at rest, or move in a straight line with constant speed, if originally in motion. Most often, however, the term "equilibrium" or more specifically, "static equilibrium," is used to describe an object at rest.

From a graphical point of view, equilibrium requires that the force polygon, constructed for the system of forces acting on the particle, form a *closed* polygon. Why? Thus, if the particle P, shown in Fig. 3–1a, is in equilibrium when subjected to the applied (coplanar) force system the forces, when added vectorially in a "head-to-tail" fashion, form a closed polygon. For example, starting with force $\mathbf{F}_1$ and adding the other forces, the head of vector $\mathbf{F}_4$ coincides with the starting point, O, and therefore the resultant of the applied force system is zero, Fig. 3–1b.

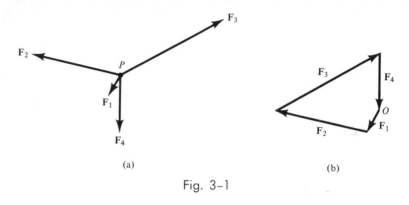

(a)   (b)

Fig. 3–1

The condition for particle equilibrium may be formulated mathematically as

$$\Sigma \mathbf{F} = 0 \tag{3–1}$$

where $\Sigma \mathbf{F}$ represents the *vector sum* of *all forces* acting on the particle. If each of the concurrent forces is resolved into its respective $\mathbf{i}$, $\mathbf{j}$, and $\mathbf{k}$ components, Eq. 3–1 may then be written in the form

$$\Sigma F_x \mathbf{i} + \Sigma F_y \mathbf{j} + \Sigma F_z \mathbf{k} = 0 \tag{3–2}$$

where ΣF_x, ΣF_y, and ΣF_z represent the *algebraic sum* of the vector components acting along the x, y, and z axis, respectively. Since the $\mathbf{i}$, $\mathbf{j}$, and $\mathbf{k}$ directions are mutually *orthogonal* or perpendicular to each other, vectors acting along any one of these directions cannot have components acting in any of the other two directions. Therefore, to satisfy Eq. 3–2, the force summations along each of the unit vector directions must be equal to zero, i.e.,

$$\begin{aligned} \Sigma F_x &= 0 \\ \Sigma F_y &= 0 \\ \Sigma F_z &= 0 \end{aligned} \tag{3–3}$$

Vector Eq. 3-1, or the scalar Eqs. 3-3, provide both necessary and sufficient conditions for the equilibrium of a particle.

3-2. Free-Body Diagrams

When solving equilibrium problems, it is strongly advised to draw a *free-body diagram* as the *first step* of the problem solution. Provided the free-body diagram is correctly drawn, the effect of all the forces acting on the particle is then taken into account when the equations of equilibrium are written. To construct a free-body diagram for a particle, the particle is isolated from its surroundings, an outlined shape of the particle is sketched, and *all* the forces acting *on the particle* are labeled on this sketch. All forces are either *active forces,* which tend to set the particle in motion, for example, weight, magnetic, and electrostatic interaction; or *reactive forces,* such as those caused by the supports, which tend to prevent motion. The forces on the free-body diagram which are known should be labeled with their proper magnitudes and directions. Letters are used to represent the magnitudes and directions of forces which are unknown.

Cables are often encountered in equilibrium problems. Except for Sec. 7-4, throughout this book all cables will be assumed to have negligible weight and to be inextensible, that is, they cannot be stretched. Such cables carry only tension forces, and these forces are always directed along the axes of the cables. In Chapter 5, it will be shown that the tension developed in a continuous cable, which passes over a frictionless pulley, must be *constant* to keep the cable in equilibrium.* For example, for *any* angle θ, a 5-lb force is needed to lift the 5-lb block shown in Fig. 3-2.

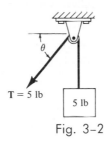

Fig. 3-2

If an *elastic spring* is attached to a cable, the length of the cable and spring will change in proportion to the tensile force developed in the cable. A characteristic which defines the elasticity of a spring is the

---

*If the pulley has an angular acceleration, this statement is no longer true. This case is discussed in *Engineering Mechanics: Dynamics.*

stiffness k. The magnitude of force, developed by an elastic spring which has a stiffness k and is deformed (compressed or elongated) a distance x, measured from its unloaded position, is $F = kx$. The spring shown in Fig. 3–3 has a stiffness of $k = 5$ lb/in. A 10-lb force is therefore needed to hold the spring at a distance of $x = \pm 2$ in. from its unstretched position. [$F = kx = (5$ lb/in.$)(2$ in.$) = 10$ lb]

$k = $ stiffness of spring

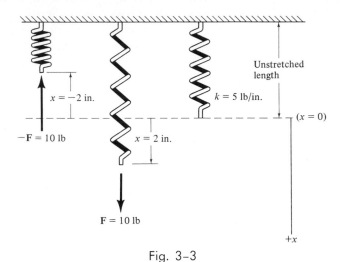

Fig. 3–3

A special case of equilibrium occurs when a *rigid body is subjected to a system of concurrent forces.* As an example, consider the 10-lb sphere shown in Fig. 3–4a, which is supported by the rope *AB* and the smooth plane. A free-body diagram of the sphere is shown in Fig. 3–4b. There

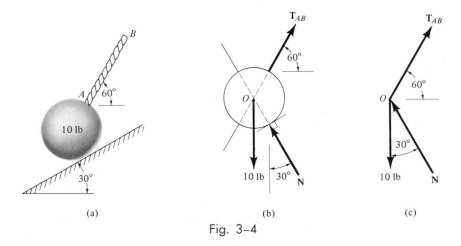

Fig. 3–4

are three forces acting *on* the sphere. The tensile force $\mathbf{T}_{AB}$ has an unknown magnitude of T_{AB} lb and acts in the direction of the rope. The reactive force of the plane has an unknown magnitude of N lb. Since the inclined surface is *smooth,* this force will act *normal to the tangent of the surface at the point of contact.*† Finally, there is the 10-lb weight of the sphere which represents the effect of gravity, and therefore acts downward toward the center of the earth. As you will recall from your study of physics, the weights for each particle of the sphere contribute to the total weight of the sphere. Provided the material of the sphere is homogeneous, the total weight acts through the geometric center O. (See Chapter 9 for further discussion.) As shown in Fig. 3–4*b*, the *lines of action* of these three forces intersect at the common point O. In Sec. 1–4, it was pointed out that a force acting on a rigid body may be considered as a sliding vector when analyzing the conditions of equilibrium for the rigid body (principle of transmissibility). Hence, for equilibrium of the sphere, the force system acting on the sphere may be considered *concurrent* at point O, as shown in Fig. 3–4*c*, and must therefore satisfy the same equilibrium condition as for a particle, i.e., Eq. 3–1.

Two other examples of free-body diagrams for a particle are given in Figs. 3–5 and 3–6. Besides its weight, the 5-lb ball in Fig. 3–5*a* is acted upon by the unknown force in the spring, $\mathbf{F}_s$, and the 6-lb vertical force. The free-body diagram, showing all these forces, is given in Fig. 3–5*b*. Point A located on the top of the mast in Fig. 3–6*a* is acted upon by four forces, namely, the tension forces $\mathbf{F}_{AB}$ and $\mathbf{F}_{AC}$ due to the cables AB and AC, the force of the banner, $\mathbf{F}_B$, and the reaction $\mathbf{F}_P$, which the pole AF exerts on A. The free-body diagram is shown in Fig. 3–6*b*. The force $\mathbf{F}_P$ acts at an angle with the vertical since the pole restrains *all* spatial movements of point A. Note that the force which the cable DE exerts on the pole is *not* shown on the free-body diagram of point A. This force acts on the pole at D, not at A.

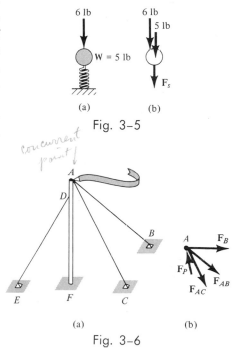

(a)   (b)

Fig. 3–5

Fig. 3–6

3–3. Two-Dimensional Force Systems Acting on a Particle

In some instances, the forces acting on a particle may all lie in the *same plane,* that is, the force system is *coplanar.* If this is the case, only *two* scalar equations must be satisfied for equilibrium. For an (x, y) Cartesian coordinate system,

$$\Sigma F_x = 0$$
$$\Sigma F_y = 0 \qquad (3\text{–}4)$$

---

†Rough surfaces of contact contribute frictional forces which act tangent to the surface at points of contact. This type of force is discussed in Chapter 8.

These two equations can be solved for, at most, two unknowns, generally represented as angles and/or magnitudes of forces shown on the free-body diagram of the particle.

When constructing a free-body diagram, the sense of direction of a force having an unknown magnitude can be assumed. The correctness of the assumed sense of direction will become apparent after solving the equilibrium equations for the unknown quantity. By definition, the *magnitude* of a force is *always positive,* hence, if the solution yields a positive magnitude, the sense of direction of the unknown force was assumed correctly; whereas, if the solution yields a negative magnitude, the minus sign indicates that the sense of direction is opposite to that which was assumed. As a simple example to illustrate this point again consider the free-body diagram of the 5-lb ball shown in Fig. 3–5b. The force $\mathbf{F}_s$ on this diagram represents the effect of the spring *on the ball.* The sense of direction of this force has been assumed downward as shown. Applying the equilibrium equation in the vertical direction to the force system, with the positive direction *assumed upward,**

$$+\uparrow \Sigma F_y = 0; \qquad -F_s - 6 \text{ lb} - 5 \text{ lb} = 0$$

Hence, $\qquad\qquad\qquad\qquad F_s = -11 \text{ lb}$

The negative sign indicates that the sense of direction of $\mathbf{F}_s$ is actually *upward* and not downward as shown on the free-body diagram in Fig. 3–5b.

Coplanar equilibrium problems may also be solved by using a graphical procedure. To satisfy vector Eq. 3–1, it is required that all forces acting on the particle form a closed polygon. Under the action of only three forces, the force polygon closes to form a triangle. When constructed, the unknowns may be found using either the *law of sines* and/or the *law of cosines* (see Example 3–2). In either case, a vector analysis (using Eq. 3–1), a scalar analysis (using Eqs. 3–4), or the force-polygon method leads to the same results.

Example 3–1

A 10-lb block is held in equilibrium by two cords of negligible weight, as shown in Fig. 3–7a. The cord ABC is continuous and passes over a frictionless pulley at B. Determine the tension in cord AD and the weight W needed to hold the 10-lb block in the equilibrium position.

Solution I   (Vector Analysis)

The first step in the solution is to draw a free-body diagram of point

---

*The downward direction can also be assumed positive when applying $\Sigma F_y = 0$. Check and see that you obtain the same result.

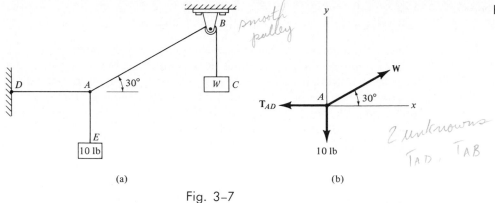

(a)   (b)

Fig. 3–7

A. Why? There are three concurrent forces acting *on* this point. Cable AE exerts a downward pull on A having a magnitude of 10 lb. The force in cable AD has an unknown magnitude T_{AD} and is directed from A to D. Since cable ABC is continuous, an unknown tension force having a magnitude of W lb acts on A and is directed from A to B. The free-body diagram for point A is shown in Fig. 3–7b.

Expressing each of the three forces in Cartesian vector form, we have

$$\mathbf{T}_{AD} = -T_{AD}\mathbf{i}$$
$$\mathbf{W} = W(\cos 30°\mathbf{i} + \sin 30°\mathbf{j}) = 0.866\,W\mathbf{i} + 0.500\,W\mathbf{j}$$
$$\mathbf{F} = \{-10\mathbf{j}\}\text{ lb}$$

Applying Eq. 3–1, in reference to the free-body diagram,

$$\Sigma\mathbf{F} = 0; \qquad\qquad \mathbf{T}_{AD} + \mathbf{W} + \mathbf{F} = 0$$
$$-T_{AD}\mathbf{i} + 0.866\,W\mathbf{i} + 0.500\,W\mathbf{j} - 10\mathbf{j} = 0$$

Equating the $\mathbf{i}$ and $\mathbf{j}$ components to zero, we have

$$\xrightarrow{+}\Sigma F_x = 0; \qquad\qquad -T_{AD} + 0.866\,W = 0$$
$$+\uparrow\Sigma F_y = 0; \qquad\qquad 0.500\,W - 10 = 0$$

Solving these two equations yields

$$W = 20.0\text{ lb} \qquad\qquad\qquad Ans.$$
$$T_{AD} = 17.3\text{ lb} \qquad\qquad\qquad Ans.$$

Solution II (Scalar Analysis)

After the free-body diagram for point A has been established, Eqs. 3–4 may be applied *directly* to the forces shown on this diagram, since vector components are easily obtained in two dimensions, Fig. 3–7b. Hence,

$$\overset{+}{\to}\Sigma F_x = 0; \qquad\qquad -T_{AD} + W\cos 30° = 0$$
$$+\uparrow\Sigma F_y = 0; \qquad\qquad W\sin 30° - 10 = 0$$

These equations are the same as those previously obtained.

If we compare the two solutions, it is clearly seen that expressing each force as a Cartesian vector (Solution I) prior to applying the equations of equilibrium has no added advantage when solving problems in two dimensions. Because of the extra labor involved, it is suggested that problems involving coplanar force systems be solved using a scalar analysis (Solution II). The real advantage of vector analysis will be realized when problems in three dimensions are considered.

Example 3-2

Two cables are used to support the 50-lb crate shown in Fig. 3–8a. Determine the tensile force developed in the cables.

Solution

The free-body diagram of point A is shown in Fig. 3–8b. There are

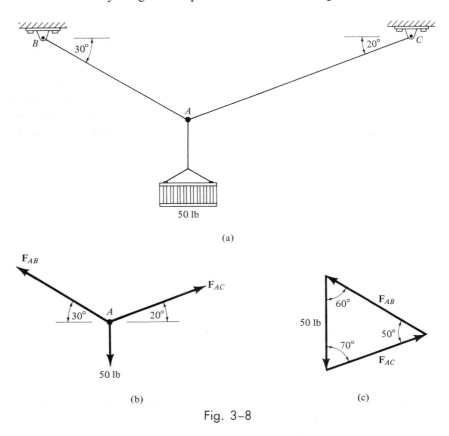

(a)

(b)

(c)

Fig. 3-8

three forces which act *on* this point—the cable forces $\mathbf{F}_{AB}$ and $\mathbf{F}_{AC}$, and the 50-lb weight. The two unknowns F_{AB} and F_{AC} can be obtained in the usual manner of applying the two equations of equilibrium. (See Example 3–1.) Here, however, we will illustrate the use of the force-polygon method for the solution.

Drawing the force polygon, the vectors on the free-body diagram are added in a "head-to-tail" fashion forming the *closed* triangle shown in Fig. 3–8c. Applying the law of sines to this triangle, we have

$$\frac{F_{AC}}{\sin 60°} = \frac{50}{\sin 50°}$$

$$F_{AC} = 50 \left(\frac{0.866}{0.766} \right) = 56.5 \text{ lb} \qquad \textit{Ans.}$$

$$\frac{F_{AB}}{\sin 70°} = \frac{50}{\sin 50°}$$

$$F_{AB} = 50 \left(\frac{0.940}{0.766} \right) = 61.3 \text{ lb} \qquad \textit{Ans.}$$

Example 3–3

The spring-loaded supporting rods AB and AC in Fig. 3–9a are used as shock absorbers for transporting fragile loads. Knowing that the elastic spring constants for the rods AB and AC are $k_{AB} = 30$ lb/in. and $k_{AC} = 50$ lb/in., respectively, determine how far point A moves vertically when the 1,000-lb load is removed. Neglect the weight of the rods.

Solution

If we know the forces $\mathbf{F}_{AB}$ and $\mathbf{F}_{AC}$ developed in rods AB and AC, we can then determine the *extension* of each rod when the rods support the 1,000-lb load. Using geometry, we may then arrive at the undeflected position of point A when the load is removed.

The free-body diagram of point A is shown in Fig. 3–9b. Applying the scalar equations of equilibrium, using the geometry to determine the sines and cosines of the angles, we have

$$\xrightarrow{+} \Sigma F_x = 0; \qquad \frac{4}{\sqrt{(4)^2 + (5)^2}} F_{AB} - \frac{6}{\sqrt{(6)^2 + (5)^2}} F_{AC} = 0$$

or
$$0.625 F_{AB} - 0.768 F_{AC} = 0 \qquad (1)$$

$$+\uparrow \Sigma F_y = 0;$$

$$\frac{5}{\sqrt{(4)^2 + (5)^2}} F_{AB} + \frac{5}{\sqrt{(6)^2 + (5)^2}} F_{AC} - 1{,}000 = 0$$

or
$$0.781 F_{AB} + 0.640 F_{AC} - 1{,}000 = 0 \qquad (2)$$

The tension forces in the rods can be determined by solving Eqs. (1) and (2) simultaneously. In particular, solving for F_{AB} in Eq. (1),

$$F_{AB} = 1.229 \, F_{AC} \qquad (3)$$

Substituting this into Eq. (2),

$$0.781(1.229 \, F_{AC}) + 0.640 \, F_{AC} - 1,000 = 0$$

or

$$1.600 \, F_{AC} = 1,000$$

Thus,

$$F_{AC} = 625 \text{ lb} \qquad \qquad \textit{Ans.}$$

Using Eq. (3),

$$F_{AB} = 1.229(625 \text{ lb})$$
$$F_{AB} = 768 \text{ lb} \qquad \qquad \textit{Ans.}$$

The forces shown on the free-body diagram of point A represent the effect of the rods and the weight *on* point A. According to Newton's third law of motion, point A must exert *equal, but opposite forces* on the rod and weight, as shown in Fig. 3–9c. (Note that the weight and rods are *not* represented as complete free-body diagrams in this figure.) The *extension* of each rod created by forces $\mathbf{F}_{AB}$ and $\mathbf{F}_{AC}$ is therefore

$$F_{AB} = k_{AB} \, \Delta x_{AB}; \ \Delta x_{AB} = \frac{768 \text{ lb}}{30 \text{ lb/in.}} = 25.6 \text{ in.} = 2.13 \text{ ft}$$

$$F_{AC} = k_{AC} \, \Delta x_{AC}; \ \Delta x_{AC} = \frac{625 \text{ lb}}{50 \text{ lb/in.}} = 12.5 \text{ in.} = 1.04 \text{ ft}$$

Using the Pythagorean theorem, we may determine the *extended length* of each rod when subjected to the 1,000-lb load. Referring to Fig. 3–9a, we have

$$l_{AB} = \sqrt{(4)^2 + (5)^2} = 6.40 \text{ ft}$$
$$l_{AC} = \sqrt{(6)^2 + (5)^2} = 7.81 \text{ ft}$$

Thus, the *unloaded length* of the rods becomes

$$l'_{AB} = l_{AB} - \Delta x_{AB} = 6.40 - 2.13 = 4.27 \text{ ft}$$
$$l'_{AC} = l_{AC} - \Delta x_{AC} = 7.81 - 1.04 = 6.77 \text{ ft}$$

With reference to Fig. 3–9d, when the weight is *removed*, point A moves to location (x, y). The distance y may be related to the distance x by the equations

$$y^2 + x^2 = (6.77)^2 \qquad (4)$$
$$y^2 + (10 - x)^2 = (4.27)^2 \qquad (5)$$

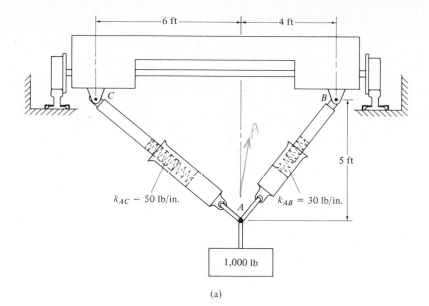

(a)

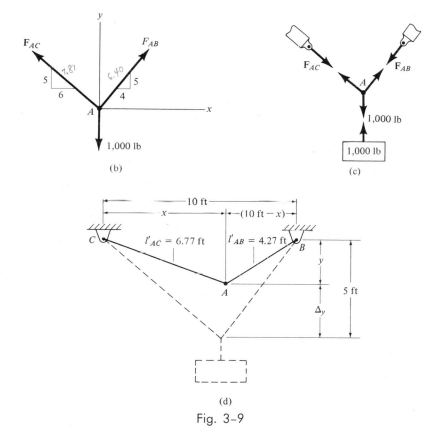

(b)

(c)

(d)

Fig. 3-9

Solving for y^2 in Eq. (4), and substituting into Eq. (5) yields

$$[(6.77)^2 - x^2] + (10 - x)^2 = (4.27)^2$$

or

$$20\,x - 127.6 = 0$$

Hence,

$$x = 6.38 \text{ ft}$$

From Eq. (4),

$$y^2 = (6.77)^2 - (6.38)^2 = 5.13$$

Choosing the positive square root for the solution of y, since it represents the physical situation,

$$y = 2.26 \text{ ft}$$

From Fig. 3–9d, point A therefore moves vertically a distance of

$$\Delta y = 5 \text{ ft} - y = 5 \text{ ft} - 2.26 \text{ ft}$$
$$\Delta y = 2.74 \text{ ft} \qquad\qquad Ans.$$

when the 1,000 lb load is removed.

Problems

3–1. Particle P is subjected to the concurrent force system shown. Determine the magnitude of F and its direction θ which is required to keep the particle in equilibrium.

3–2. The joint of a light metal truss is formed by riveting four angles to the gusset plate G. Knowing the force in members A and C, determine the necessary forces F_B and F_D acting on members B and D which are required for equilibrium. The force system is concurrent at point O.

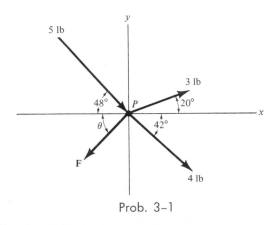

Prob. 3–1

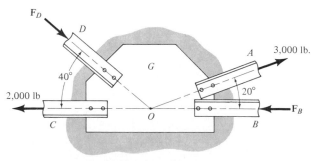

Prob. 3–2

3-3. The particle P is subjected to the action of four coplanar forces. Determine the magnitude of F and the angle θ for equilibrium.

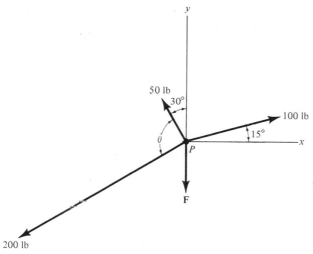

Prob. 3-3

3-4. Provided $\theta = 30°$, determine the forces F_A and F_B required to hold the 5-lb sphere in equilibrium. At what angle θ will the force F_B be a minimum? Assume that the line of action of each force is directed toward the center point O of the sphere.

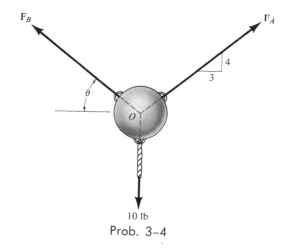

Prob. 3-4

3-5. Determine the length of string l so that $\theta = 20°$ and the spring AB remains horizontal. The unstretched length of AB is 1 ft.

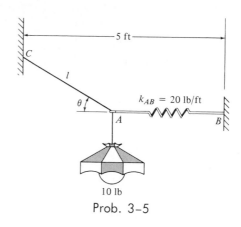

Prob. 3-5

3-6. The links AB, BC, and CD support the loading shown. Determine the tension in AB and the angle θ for equilibrium. The force in each link acts along the axis of the link.

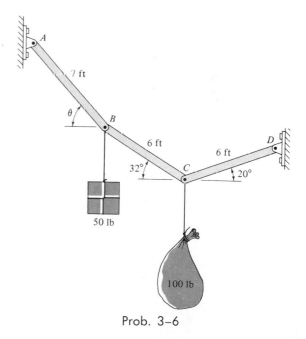

Prob. 3-6

3-7. The 25-lb pipe rests between the two smooth inclined planes. If plane A exerts a reaction of 8 lb on the pipe, determine the magnitude of the applied force $\mathbf{P}$ and the reaction that plane B exerts on the pipe.

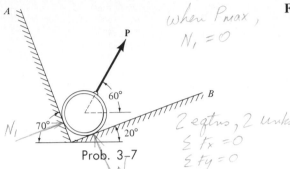

when P_{max},
$N_1 = 0$

2 eqtns, 2 unks.
$\Sigma f_x = 0$
$\Sigma f_y = 0$

Prob. 3-7

3-8. Determine the magnitude of the maximum force $\mathbf{P}$ required to hold the 25-lb pipe of Prob. 3-7 in equilibrium. Assume that $\mathbf{P}$ acts at 60°, as shown.

3-9. The 200-lb crate is suspended by means of a 6-ft long cable attached to the sides of the crate and which passes over the small pulley located at O. If the cable can be attached at either points A and B, or C and D, determine which attachment produces the least amount of tension in the cable. What is the cable tension in each case?

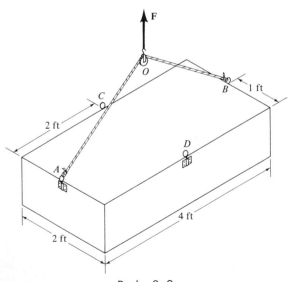

Prob. 3-9

3-10. The members of a truss are connected to the gusset plate. If the force acting in each member is directed along the axis of the member, as shown in the figure, then the force system acting on the plate is concurrent at point O. Determine the magnitude of forces $\mathbf{F}$ and $\mathbf{T}$ for equilibrium of the gusset plate.

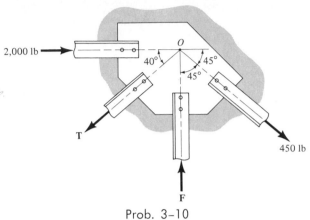

Prob. 3-10

3-11. Determine the magnitude of $\mathbf{R}$ and the angle θ required for equilibrium of particle P.

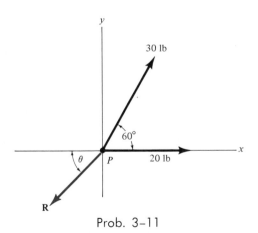

Prob. 3-11

3-12. Two small blocks A and B rest on the smooth inclines. The blocks are connected by a light inextensible cord which passes over a frictionless pulley. If block A weighs 15 lb, determine the weight W_B of block B for equilibrium.

58

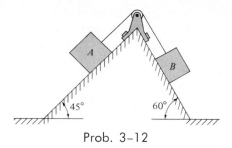

Prob. 3–12

3–13. The 10-lb roller mechanism is supported by two springs. If the springs are unstretched when the roller is at the equilibrium position A, determine the stiffness k so that the roller will be in equilibrium when the height $h = 1$ ft. Assume that the surfaces of contact are frictionless. Neglect the size of the roller.

3–14. Determine the distance s for the location of the horizontal strut AB so that a tension of 140 lb is developed in each of the links OA and OB. The force in each link acts along the axis of the link.

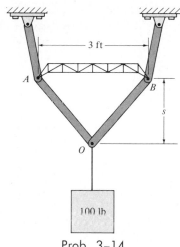

Prob. 3–14

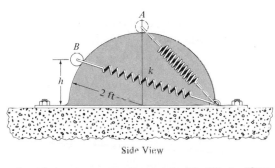

Side View

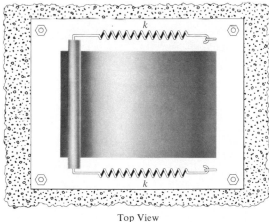

Top View
Prob. 3–13

3–15. The two spheres A and B have an equal weight and are electrostatically charged, such that the repulsive force acting between them has a magnitude of 0.6 lb and is directed along the dashed line. Determine the angle θ, the tension in the cables, and the weight W of each sphere.

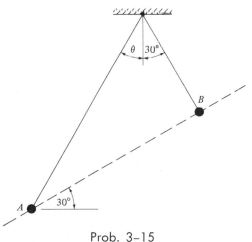

Prob. 3–15

3-16. The roller mechanism AB is at rest between the smooth inclines of the 30° wedge. If each of the rollers weighs 5 lb, and the undeformed length of each spring is 4 in., determine the distance h for equilibrium of the mechanism. Assume that both rollers remain in the same horizontal plane aa. The spring constant for each spring is $k = 1$ lb/in. Neglect the size of the roller.

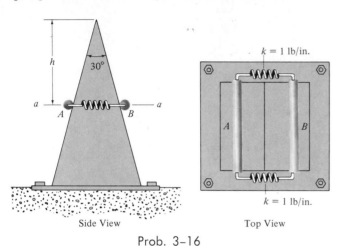

Side View   Top View

Prob. 3–16

3-17. The 50-lb sphere rests between two smooth inclined planes and is attached to a spring. If the unstretched length of the spring is 4 in., determine the normal reactions of the inclines acting on the sphere.

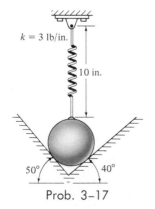

Prob. 3–17

3-18. Three weights are connected by the light inextensible cords shown. If the cords pass over small frictionless pulleys, determine the distance s for equilibrium.

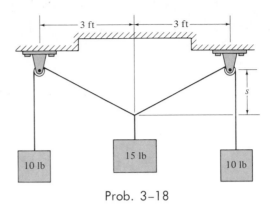

Prob. 3–18

3-19. A continuous cable of total length 40 in. is wrapped around the *small* frictionless pulleys at A, B, C, and D. If the spring constants are both $k = 3$ lb/in. and the springs are each stretched 6 in., determine the weight W of each block. Neglect the weight of the pulleys and cords. The springs are unstretched when $d = 20$ in.

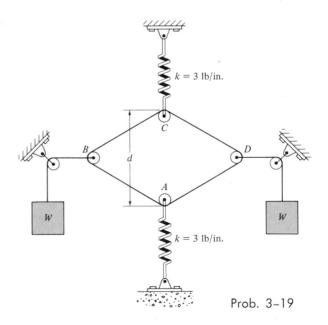

Prob. 3–19

60

3-20. A small 5-lb sphere is resting on the smooth parabolic surface. Determine the force it exerts on the surface and the weight W needed to hold it in the equilibrium position shown.

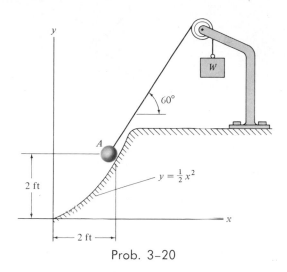

Prob. 3-20

3-4. Three-Dimensional Force Systems Acting on a Particle

The general force system acting on the particle is, of course, three-dimensional. *After* the free-body diagram for the particle is established, all the forces acting on the particle should be expressed in Cartesian vector form. Equation 3-1 may then be applied to solve for the unknown quantities. This vector equation actually represents the *three* scalar Eqs. 3-3. Thus, for a complete solution, there can be at most three unknown force magnitudes and/or directions on the free-body diagram. (In problems where two direction angles for a force are known, the third angle is specified by using Eq. 2-8, that is, $\cos^2 \alpha + \cos^2 \beta + \cos^2 \gamma = 1$.) The resulting equilibrium equations generally must be solved simultaneously to obtain a complete solution. If these equations form a set of linear algebraic equations, which is most often the case, it may be expedient to solve them by means of the computer program given in Appendix A.

Example 3-4

The small 50-lb block shown in Fig. 3-10a rests on a smooth inclined plane and is prevented from slipping down the plane by the two guy

61

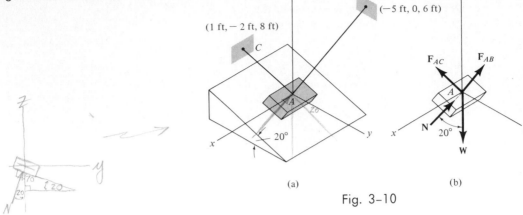

(a)   (b)

Fig. 3–10

wires AC and AB. Determine the tension developed in these wires and the reactive force at the contacting surface.

Solution

A free-body diagram of the block is shown in Fig. 3–10b. Why do we have to construct this diagram first? There are four forces acting *on* the block: the tensile forces $\mathbf{F}_{AC}$ and $\mathbf{F}_{AB}$ developed by the wires, the weight $\mathbf{W}$ of the block acting vertically downward, and the normal force $\mathbf{N}$ which the smooth plane exerts on the block. Having accounted for all the forces that act on the block, we may express each force as a vector.

$$\mathbf{F}_{AC} = F_{AC} \frac{\mathbf{r}_{AC}}{r_{AC}} = F_{AC} \left(\frac{\mathbf{i} - 2\mathbf{j} + 8\mathbf{k}}{\sqrt{69}} \right) = \frac{F_{AC}}{\sqrt{69}}\mathbf{i} - \frac{2F_{AC}}{\sqrt{69}}\mathbf{j} + \frac{8F_{AC}}{\sqrt{69}}\mathbf{k}$$

$$\mathbf{F}_{AB} = F_{AB} \frac{\mathbf{r}_{AB}}{r_{AB}} = F_{AB} \left(\frac{-5\mathbf{i} + 6\mathbf{k}}{\sqrt{61}} \right) = -\frac{5F_{AB}}{\sqrt{61}}\mathbf{i} + \frac{6F_{AB}}{\sqrt{61}}\mathbf{k}$$

$$\mathbf{N} = N(\sin 20°\mathbf{j} + \cos 20°\mathbf{k}) = (N\sin 20°)\mathbf{j} + (N\cos 20°)\mathbf{k}$$

$$\mathbf{W} = 50 \text{ lb}(-\mathbf{k}) = \{-50\mathbf{k}\} \text{ lb}$$

Applying Eq. 3–1 gives

$$\Sigma \mathbf{F} = 0; \qquad \mathbf{F}_{AC} + \mathbf{F}_{AB} + \mathbf{N} + \mathbf{W} = 0$$

or

$$\frac{F_{AC}}{\sqrt{69}}\mathbf{i} - \frac{2F_{AC}}{\sqrt{69}}\mathbf{j} + \frac{8F_{AC}}{\sqrt{69}}\mathbf{k} - \frac{5F_{AB}}{\sqrt{61}}\mathbf{i} + \frac{6F_{AB}}{\sqrt{61}}\mathbf{k}$$
$$+ (N\sin 20°)\mathbf{j} + (N\cos 20°)\mathbf{k} - 50\mathbf{k} = 0$$

Equating the components in the $\mathbf{i}$, $\mathbf{j}$, and $\mathbf{k}$ directions equal to zero, we obtain

$$\Sigma F_x = 0; \qquad \frac{1}{\sqrt{69}} F_{AC} - \frac{5}{\sqrt{61}} F_{AB} = 0 \qquad (1)$$

$$\Sigma F_y = 0; \qquad -\frac{2}{\sqrt{69}} F_{AC} + N \sin 20° = 0 \qquad (2)$$

$$\Sigma F_z = 0; \qquad \frac{8}{\sqrt{69}} F_{AC} + \frac{6}{\sqrt{61}} F_{AB} + N \cos 20° - 50 = 0 \qquad (3)$$

The three unknowns in the above equations may be obtained by simultaneous solution of the equations. For example, solve for F_{AB} in Eq. (1) and for N in Eq. (2)—both in terms of F_{AC}. Substitute these results in Eq. (3), thereby obtaining an equation in terms of the single unknown F_{AC}. After solving for F_{AC}, it is possible to obtain the values of F_{AB} and N by resubstituting into Eqs. (1) and (2) the value of F_{AC}. (Recognizing Eqs. (1–3) to be a set of three linear algebraic equations, the computer program in Appendix A may also be used for the solution.) The results are

$$F_{AC} = 28.3 \text{ lb} \qquad\qquad Ans.$$
$$F_{AB} = 5.31 \text{ lb} \qquad\qquad Ans.$$
$$N = 19.9 \text{ lb} \qquad\qquad Ans.$$

Example 3–5

A 1,000-lb crate is supported by three struts CF, CD, and CE and the cable arrangement shown in Fig. 3–11a. Determine the forces developed in the struts and the tension in the cables. Assume that the force developed in each strut passes along the axis of the strut. These forces may either be tensile or compressive.

Solution

It is first necessary to draw a free-body diagram of point C in order to expose the unknown forces in the struts and the cable BC. As shown in Fig. 3–11b, the four forces acting *on* this point are: the cable tension $\mathbf{F}_{CB}$, and the forces in the three struts $\mathbf{F}_{CD}$, $\mathbf{F}_{CE}$, and $\mathbf{F}_{CF}$. Due to geometry, the line of action (or direction) of each of the four forces is *known*. However, the sense of direction of the forces acting in the struts is not known, and it has been assumed that $\mathbf{F}_{CD}$ and $\mathbf{F}_{CE}$ are tensile forces; that is, struts CD and CE *pull* on point C. Similarly, the force $\mathbf{F}_{CF}$ is assumed to be compressive so that strut CF *pushes* on point C. Since only *three* scalar equilibrium equations can be applied to the force system acting on the free-body diagram at point C, it is necessary to solve for one of the four unknown force magnitudes with the aid of *another* free-body diagram. A free-body diagram of point B is shown in Fig. 3–11c. (Why is this a free-body diagram?) Since the force system at B is *coplanar*, the forces in the cables $\mathbf{F}_{BA}$ and $\mathbf{F}_{BC}$ may be determined using the *two* scalar equations of equilibrium, namely,

$$\xrightarrow{+}\Sigma F_y = 0; \qquad\qquad F_{BC}\cos 30° - F_{BA} = 0$$
$$+\uparrow\Sigma F_z = 0; \qquad\qquad F_{BC}\sin 30° - 1{,}000 = 0$$

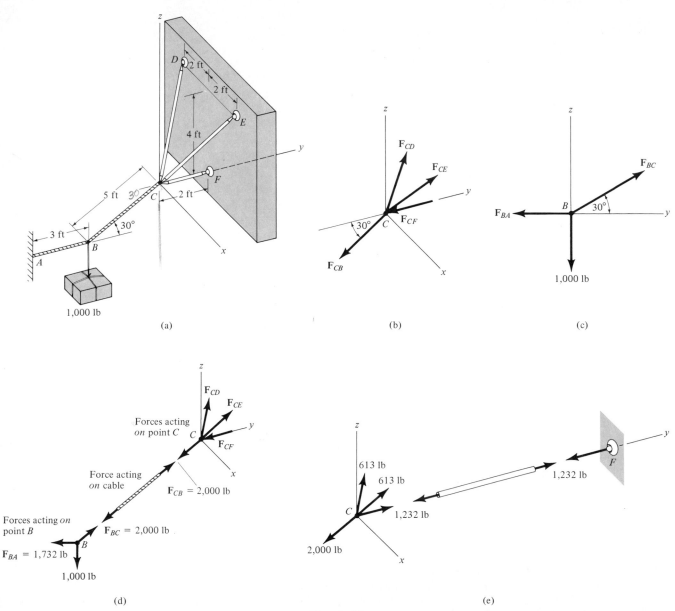

Fig. 3–11

Solving, we have

$$F_{BA} = 1{,}732 \text{ lb} \qquad\qquad Ans.$$
$$F_{BC} = 2{,}000 \text{ lb} \qquad\qquad Ans.$$

For every action there is an equal and opposite reaction. Therefore, force F_{BC} has a directional sense, as shown on each of the three free-body diagrams in Fig. 3–11d. (Notice how a *pull* on point B creates a *tension* in the rope.)

Since the magnitude of $\mathbf{F}_{BC}$ is known, the magnitudes of the other three forces acting at point C may now be computed. Expressing each of the forces acting on the free-body diagram of point C (Fig. 3–11b) as a vector, we have

$$\mathbf{F}_{CB} = (2{,}000 \text{ lb})\mathbf{u}_{CB} = 2{,}000 \text{ lb}(-\cos 30°\mathbf{j} - \sin 30°\mathbf{k})$$
$$= \{-1{,}732\mathbf{j} - 1{,}000\mathbf{k}\} \text{ lb}$$

$$\mathbf{F}_{CD} = F_{CD}\frac{\mathbf{r}_{CD}}{r_{CD}} = -\frac{2F_{CD}}{\sqrt{24}}\mathbf{i} + \frac{2F_{CD}}{\sqrt{24}}\mathbf{j} + \frac{4F_{CD}}{\sqrt{24}}\mathbf{k}$$

$$\mathbf{F}_{CE} = F_{CE}\frac{\mathbf{r}_{CE}}{r_{CE}} = \frac{2F_{CE}}{\sqrt{24}}\mathbf{i} + \frac{2F_{CE}}{\sqrt{24}}\mathbf{j} + \frac{4F_{CE}}{\sqrt{24}}\mathbf{k}$$

$$\mathbf{F}_{CF} = F_{CF}(-\mathbf{j}) = -F_{CF}\mathbf{j} \quad \text{(By inspection, Fig. 3–11b, note that } \mathbf{F}_{CF} \text{ acts}$$
$$\text{in the } -\mathbf{j} \text{ direction.)}$$

Applying Eq. 3–1 yields

$$\Sigma\mathbf{F} = 0; \qquad\qquad \mathbf{F}_{CB} + \mathbf{F}_{CD} + \mathbf{F}_{CE} + \mathbf{F}_{CF} = 0$$

or

$$-1{,}732\mathbf{j} - 1{,}000\mathbf{k} - \frac{2F_{CD}}{\sqrt{24}}\mathbf{i} + \frac{2F_{CD}}{\sqrt{24}}\mathbf{j} + \frac{4F_{CD}}{\sqrt{24}}\mathbf{k} + \frac{2F_{CE}}{\sqrt{24}}\mathbf{i} + \frac{2F_{CE}}{\sqrt{24}}\mathbf{j}$$
$$+ \frac{4F_{CE}}{\sqrt{24}}\mathbf{k} - F_{CF}\mathbf{j} = 0$$

Thus, equating the respective $\mathbf{i}$, $\mathbf{j}$, and $\mathbf{k}$ components equal to zero,

$$\Sigma F_x = 0; \qquad\qquad -\frac{2}{\sqrt{24}}F_{CD} + \frac{2}{\sqrt{24}}F_{CE} = 0$$

$$\Sigma F_y = 0; \qquad -1{,}732 + \frac{2}{\sqrt{24}}F_{CD} + \frac{2}{\sqrt{24}}F_{CE} - F_{CF} = 0$$

$$\Sigma F_z = 0; \qquad -1{,}000 + \frac{4}{\sqrt{24}}F_{CD} + \frac{4}{\sqrt{24}}F_{CE} = 0$$

The first and third of these equations may be solved simultaneously for F_{CD} and F_{CE}. Substituting these values into the second equation gives F_{CF}. The results are

$$F_{CD} = 612.4 \text{ lb} \qquad \textit{Ans.}$$
$$F_{CE} = 612.4 \text{ lb} \qquad \textit{Ans.}$$
$$F_{CF} = -1{,}232 \text{ lb} \qquad \textit{Ans.}$$

Since $\mathbf{F}_{CF}$ is calculated as a *negative* quantity, this force, as drawn on the free-body diagrams in Figs. 3–11*b* and 3–11*d*, acts in the opposite sense of direction. Strut *CF* must therefore exert a force of 1,232 lb on point *C*, acting as shown in Fig. 3–11*e*. With reference to this figure, given the equal but opposite reactions, strut *CF* is subjected to a tensile (elongation) force of 1,232 lb because of the weight of the crate. (Can you explain why the supporting bracket at *F* in Fig. 3–11*e* does not represent a complete free-body diagram?)

Problems

3-21. The small sphere having a weight of 10 lb is forced up against the corner of three smooth mutually perpendicular planes *A*, *B*, and *C*. The applied force **F** has a line of action which passes from point *P* (2 ft, 2 ft, 3 ft) through the center of the sphere. Determine the normal reactions of the three planes acting on the sphere.

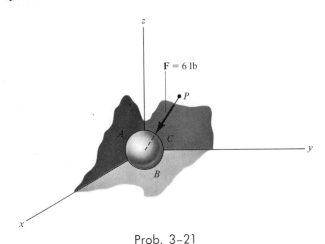

Prob. 3–21

3-22. A 1,500-lb homogeneous block is supported in the horizontal plane by means of four cables. Determine the magnitude of force developed in each of these cables if all the cables carry an equal force.

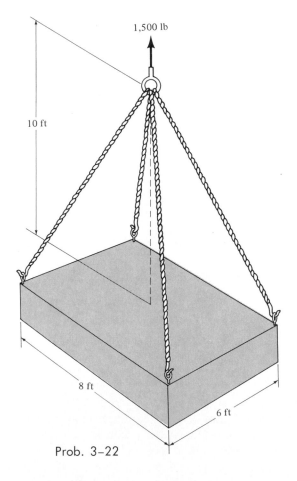

Prob. 3–22

3-23. The joint of a space frame is subjected to four forces. Strut OA lies in the xy plane and strut OB lies in the yz plane. Determine the forces acting in each of the struts required for equilibrium of the joint.

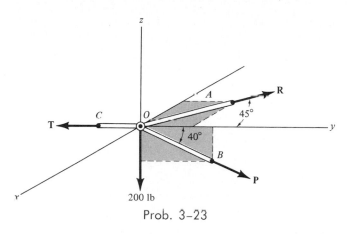

Prob. 3–23

3-24. Determine the magnitude and direction of the force **P** required to keep the concurrent force system in equilibrium.

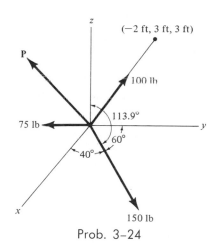

Prob. 3–24

3-25. Determine the force developed in each of the four cables and the strut OC used to support the 500-lb crate. The spring cable OA has an unstretched length of 2 ft and a stiffness $k_{OA} = 10$ lb/in. The force in the strut acts along the axis of the strut.

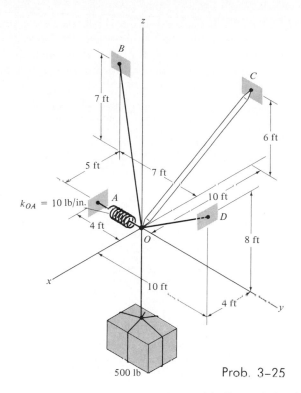

Prob. 3–25

3-26. Three electrostatically charged balls, each having a weight of 4.4×10^{-4} lb, are suspended from a common point. If the electrostatic repulsive force acting between any two balls is 1.0×10^{-3} lb and is directed along a line of action joining these two balls, determine the tension developed in each cord for equilibrium.

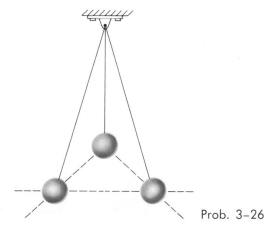

Prob. 3–26

3-27. Three 10-lb blocks and one 15-lb block are suspended from the pulley and cable system. If the pulleys are frictionless and the weights of the cables are negligible, determine the sag s for equilibrium of the system.

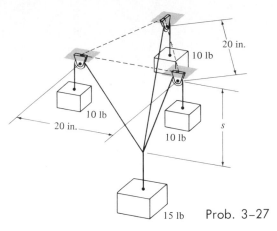

Prob. 3-27

3-28. Determine the tensile forces acting along the axis of struts DE and DF required to support the 500-lb load. The force acts along the axis of each strut.

3-29. A 5-lb sphere rests between the 45° grooves of a 30° incline and a vertical wall. If all the surfaces of contact are smooth, determine the reactions of the surfaces on the sphere.

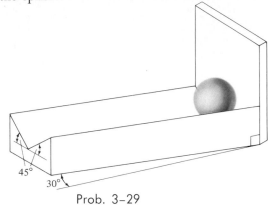

Prob. 3-29

3-30. A small peg P rests on a spring which is contained inside the smooth cylindrical pipe. When the spring is compressed so that $s = 12$ in, the spring exerts an upward force of 60 lb on the peg. Determine the point of attachment $(x, y, 0)$ of cable PA so that the tensions in cables PB and PC equal 20 and 30 lb, respectively.

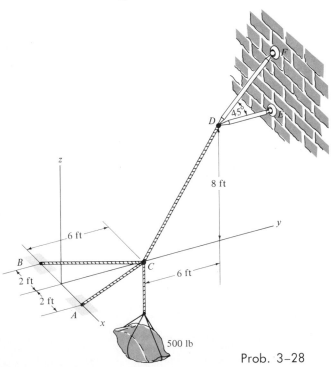

Prob. 3-28

Prob. 3-30

3-31. Determine the force acting along the axis of struts OA and OB and the tension developed in cables OC, OD, and DE.

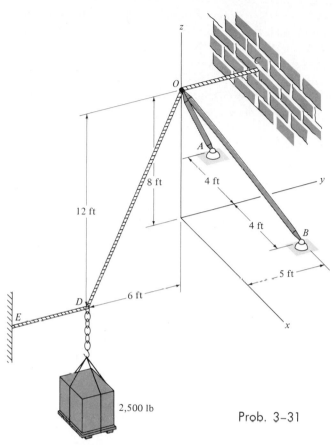

3-33. The boom OA is used to support a 1,500-lb crate. If the force of the boom acting on point A is directed from O to A, determine this force and the tension forces $\mathbf{F}_{AC}$ and $\mathbf{F}_{AB}$ acting in the cables.

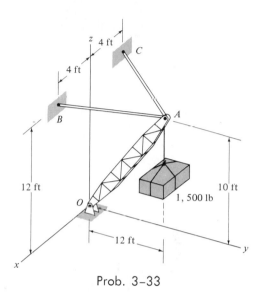

Prob. 3-33

2,500 lb

Prob. 3-31

3-32. If the tension acting in cable AD is 73 lb, determine the tension in BD and CD and the weight W of the bucket.

3-34. Determine the tension in cables AB and CB and the compression in strut OB for equilibrium of the automobile engine. Assume that the force in the strut acts along the axis of the strut.

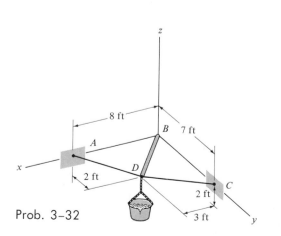

Prob. 3-32

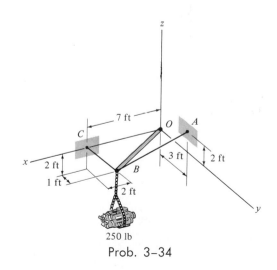

Prob. 3-34

69

3-35. The triangular frame *ABC* can be adjusted vertically between the three cords. Determine the distance *s* so that the tension in each of the slanted cords equals 40 lb. The frame remains in the horizontal plane.

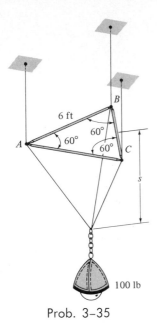

Prob. 3-35

3-36. Determine the magnitude of forces **P, R,** and **F** for equilibrium of the concurrent force system. The force **F** is located in the positive *x, y, z* octant.

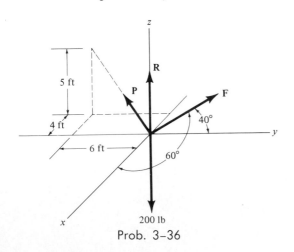

Prob. 3-36

3-37. For the tripod structure shown, determine the angle θ such that the tensile force developed in the legs *OB* and *OC* are equal. Neglect the weight of the tripod and assume that the force acting in each leg is directed along the axis of the leg. What is the force developed in each leg? Leg *OA* lies in the *zy* plane and force **F** lies in the *xy* plane.

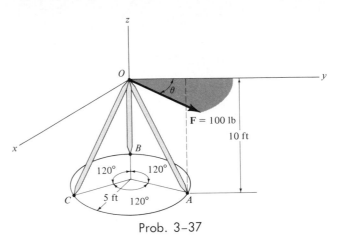

Prob. 3-37

3-38. Knowing that cord *OB* has been stretched 2 in., and fixed in place as shown, determine the tension developed in each of the other three cables in order to hold the 225-lb weight in equilibrium. Cable *OD* lies in the *xy* plane.

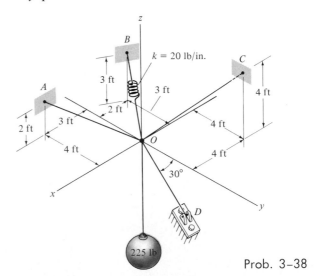

Prob. 3-38

3-39. Determine the tension developed in the three cables required to support the 60-lb traffic light.

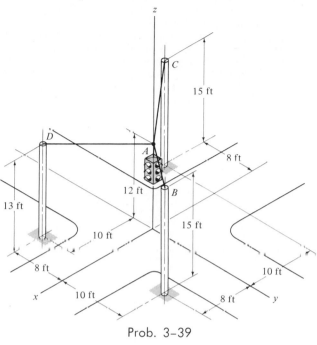

Prob. 3-39

3-41. A force of 100 lb holds the 400-lb crate in equilibrium. Determine the coordinates (O, y, z) of point A. The tension in cords AC and AB is 700 lb each.

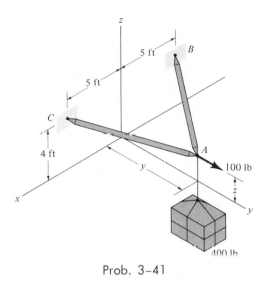

Prob. 3-41

3-40. Determine the magnitude of **P** and the direction of the 200-lb force required to keep the concurrent force system in equilibrium. Assume that the 200-lb force acts within the octant shown.

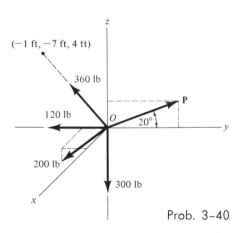

Prob. 3-40

71

4

Equivalent Force Systems

4-1. Force Systems Acting on a Rigid Body

In the last two chapters we have studied only the properties of a concurrent force system. This system of forces acts on a particle since geometrically a particle is represented as a point. As stated in Chapter 1, a *rigid body* can be considered as a combination of a large number of particles in which all the particles remain at a fixed distance from one another, both before and after applying a load. The size and shape of a rigid body often plays an important part in the force analysis since the applied force system will not necessarily be concurrent. Indeed, each force may act at *different points* on the rigid body. Clearly the two forces F_1 and F_2 acting on the block in Fig. 4-1 are not a system of concurrent forces; rather, the forces are noncollinear yet parallel to each other.

Vectors F_1 and F_2, shown in Fig. 4-1, represent *concentrated* forces applied at some point and along a unique line of action. This, of course, is an idealization. When any external loading is applied to the surface of a body it is actually *distributed* over a finite area. This distribution of force can be represented as a concentrated force only when the area over which the load is applied is rather small compared to the total surface area of the body. There are some cases, however, where this simplification cannot be made, and hence, a variation of the force distribution over the *surface area* must be taken into account. Such loadings may be caused by wind, hydrostatic pressure, or simply the weight of material supported by the body. Forces may also be distributed throughout the *volume* of the body. Weight and magnetic forces act in this manner.

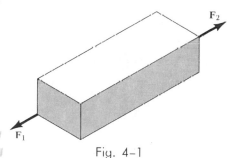

Fig. 4-1

In the last chapter it is shown that the condition for the equilibrium of a particle or a concurrent force system, simply requires that the resultant of the force system be equal to zero. In Chapter 5, it is shown that such a restriction is necessary but not sufficient for the equilibrium of rigid bodies. A further restriction must be made with regard to the nonconcurrency of the applied force system, giving rise to the concept of *moment*. In this chapter, we will develop a formal definition of a moment and discuss ways of finding the moments caused by concentrated forces and distributed loadings about points and axes. We will also develop methods of reducing nonconcurrent concentrated force systems and distributed loadings to equivalent, yet simpler, systems. Before doing any of this, however, we must first extend our knowledge of vector algebra.

4-2. Vector Cross Product

As shown in Sec. 2-3, there is only one way to multiply a vector by a scalar. In vector algebra, however, it is possible to *define* several ways of multiplying two vectors together. In this section we will discuss the *cross-product* method of vector multiplication. Since this operation yields a vector, it is often referred to as the *vector product*.

The vector cross product of two vectors **A** and **B** which yield the resultant vector **C** is written as

$$\mathbf{C} = \mathbf{A} \times \mathbf{B}$$

and read as "**C** equals **A** cross **B**." The *magnitude* of vector **C** is defined as the product of the magnitudes of the two vectors **A** and **B** and the sine of the angle θ made between them ($0° \leq \theta \leq 180°$). Thus, $C = AB \sin \theta$. Vector **C** has a *direction* which is perpendicular to the plane containing the two vectors **A** and **B** such that **A, B,** and **C** form a *right-handed system;* that is, the *sense* of the vector **C** is found by using the right-hand rule, curling the fingers of the right hand from vector **A** (cross) to vector **B.** The thumb then points in the direction of **C,** as shown in Fig. 4-2.

Knowing both the magnitude and direction of **C** it is possible to write this vector in vector notation as

$$\mathbf{C} = \mathbf{A} \times \mathbf{B} = (AB \sin \theta)\mathbf{u}_C \qquad (4-1)$$

Here $AB \sin \theta$ defines the *magnitude* of **C** and the unit vector $\mathbf{u}_C$ defines the *directional sense* of **C**, which is determined by the right-hand rule. The terms of Eq. 4-1 are illustrated graphically in Fig. 4-3.

If the resultant of the vector product $\mathbf{A} \times \mathbf{B}$ is zero (provided vectors **A** and **B** are not null vectors), then **A** must be *parallel* to **B**. This follows

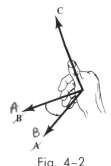

Fig. 4-2

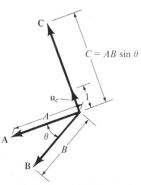

Fig. 4-3

from the definition of the cross product given by Eq. 4–1, i.e., $AB \sin \theta$ $\mathbf{u}_C = 0$. Thus, $\sin \theta = 0$, or $\theta = 0°$, $180°$, so that $\mathbf{A}$ is parallel to $\mathbf{B}$. In a similar manner

$$\mathbf{A} \times \mathbf{A} = 0 \qquad (4\text{--}2)$$

Three important relations valid for the cross product are as follows:

1. The cross product is *not* commutative, i.e.,

$$\mathbf{A} \times \mathbf{B} \neq \mathbf{B} \times \mathbf{A}$$

Rather,

$$\mathbf{A} \times \mathbf{B} = -\mathbf{B} \times \mathbf{A} \qquad (4\text{--}3)$$

This can be shown from Fig. 4–2 by using the right-hand rule. The cross product $\mathbf{B} \times \mathbf{A}$ yields a vector which acts in the opposite direction to $\mathbf{C}$, i.e., $\mathbf{B} \times \mathbf{A} = -\mathbf{C}$.

2. The distributive law:

$$\mathbf{A} \times (\mathbf{B} + \mathbf{D}) = (\mathbf{A} \times \mathbf{B}) + (\mathbf{A} \times \mathbf{D}) \qquad (4\text{--}4)$$

Given vectors $\mathbf{A}$, $\mathbf{B}$, and $\mathbf{D}$, the terms on the left and right-hand side of this equation are constructed as shown in Fig. 4–4. The proof is left as an exercise for the reader (see Prob. 4–4). It is important to note that proper order of the cross products in Eq. 4–4 must be maintained, since the cross product is not commutative. In accordance with Eq. 4–3, reversing the cross-product operation in any term requires a change in the sign of that term.

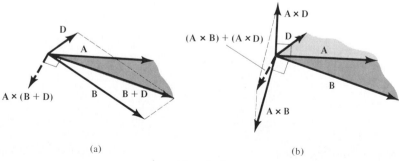

1. Add $\mathbf{B} + \mathbf{D}$

2. Form $\mathbf{A} \times (\mathbf{B} + \mathbf{D})$

1. Form $\mathbf{A} \times \mathbf{B}$

2. Form $\mathbf{A} \times \mathbf{D}$

3. Add $(\mathbf{A} \times \mathbf{B}) + (\mathbf{A} \times \mathbf{D})$

$$\mathbf{A} \times (\mathbf{B} + \mathbf{D}) = (\mathbf{A} \times \mathbf{B}) + (\mathbf{A} \times \mathbf{D})$$

(a)

(b)

Fig. 4–4

3. Multiplication by a scalar:

$$m(\mathbf{A} \times \mathbf{B}) = (m\mathbf{A}) \times \mathbf{B} = \mathbf{A} \times (m\mathbf{B}) = (\mathbf{A} \times \mathbf{B})m \qquad (4\text{--}5)$$

This property is easily shown, since the magnitude of the resultant vector $(|m|AB \sin \theta)$ and its direction are the same in each case.

In order to conveniently use the vector cross product, this operation will be formulated by using Cartesian component notation. To do this, we must first determine the cross products of each of the unit vectors **i**, **j**, and **k**. This can readily be done by using Eq. 4–1. For example, to find the cross product **i** × **j**, the magnitude of the resultant vector is $(i)(j)(\sin 90°) = (1)(1)(1) = 1$, and its direction is determined using the right-hand rule. As shown in Fig. 4–5, the resultant vector points in the $+\mathbf{k}$ direction. Thus,

$$\mathbf{i} \times \mathbf{j} = (1)\mathbf{k}$$

In a similar manner,

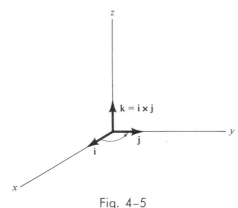

Fig. 4–5

$$
\begin{array}{lll}
\mathbf{i} \times \mathbf{j} = \mathbf{k} & \mathbf{i} \times \mathbf{k} = -\mathbf{j} & \mathbf{i} \times \mathbf{i} = 0 \\
\mathbf{j} \times \mathbf{k} = \mathbf{i} & \mathbf{j} \times \mathbf{i} = -\mathbf{k} & \mathbf{j} \times \mathbf{j} = 0 \\
\mathbf{k} \times \mathbf{i} = \mathbf{j} & \mathbf{k} \times \mathbf{j} = -\mathbf{i} & \mathbf{k} \times \mathbf{k} = 0
\end{array}
$$

These results should not be memorized; instead, you should comprehend how each "cross" product was derived, using Eq. 4–1.

In the general case $\mathbf{A} = A_x\mathbf{i} + A_y\mathbf{j} + A_z\mathbf{k}$ and $\mathbf{B} = B_x\mathbf{i} + B_y\mathbf{j} + B_z\mathbf{k}$, represent any two arbitrary vectors. We can form the cross product

$$\mathbf{A} \times \mathbf{B} = (A_x\mathbf{i} + A_y\mathbf{j} + A_z\mathbf{k}) \times (B_x\mathbf{i} + B_y\mathbf{j} + B_z\mathbf{k})$$

using the distributive law, Eq. 4–4, and the property of scalar multiplication, Eq. 4–5. Hence,

$$
\begin{aligned}
\mathbf{A} \times \mathbf{B} = {} & A_xB_x(\mathbf{i} \times \mathbf{i}) + A_xB_y(\mathbf{i} \times \mathbf{j}) + A_xB_z(\mathbf{i} \times \mathbf{k}) \\
& + A_yB_x(\mathbf{j} \times \mathbf{i}) + A_yB_y(\mathbf{j} \times \mathbf{j}) + A_yB_z(\mathbf{j} \times \mathbf{k}) \\
& + A_zB_x(\mathbf{k} \times \mathbf{i}) + A_zB_y(\mathbf{k} \times \mathbf{j}) + A_zB_z(\mathbf{k} \times \mathbf{k})
\end{aligned}
$$

Carrying out the cross-product operations and combining terms yields

$$\mathbf{A} \times \mathbf{B} = (A_yB_z - A_zB_y)\mathbf{i} - (A_xB_z - A_zB_x)\mathbf{j} + (A_xB_y - A_yB_x)\mathbf{k}$$

This equation may also be written in determinant form as

$$
\mathbf{A} \times \mathbf{B} = \begin{vmatrix} \mathbf{i} & \mathbf{j} & \mathbf{k} \\ A_x & A_y & A_z \\ B_x & B_y & B_z \end{vmatrix} \qquad (4\text{--}6)
$$

Thus, to find the cross product of any two Cartesian vectors **A** and **B**, we expand a determinant whose first row of elements are the unit vectors

i, j, and **k** and whose second and third rows represent the x, y, and z components of the two vectors **A** and **B,** respectively.* The order of arrangement is important because the commutative law for the cross product does not hold.

4-3. Principle of Transmissibility

The *principle of transmissibility* is an important concept often used in mechanics for studying the action of forces on rigid bodies. This principle states that the conditions of equilibrium or the motion of a rigid body remain *unchanged* when a force **F,** acting at a given point on the rigid body, is replaced to another point *lying on the line of action of the force.* As a simple example of this, consider the beam shown in Fig. 4–6. The force **F** acting at point P_1 represents the effect of some loading applied to the top of the beam. The beam is supported by a roller at A and a pin at B. Using the methods developed in the next chapter, we can calculate the forces at these supports. Clearly these reactions represent *external forces* acting on the beam. Rather than applying the force **F** at

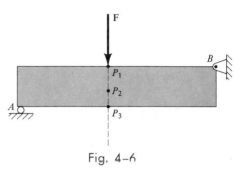

Fig. 4–6

---

*A determinant having three rows and three columns can be expanded using three minors, each of which is multiplied by one of the three terms in the first row. There are four elements in each minor, for example,

By *definition,* this notation represents the terms $(A_{11}A_{22}-A_{12}A_{21})$ which is simply the product of the two elements of the arrow slanting downwards to the right $(A_{11}A_{22})$ minus the product of the two elements intersected by the arrow slanting downwards to the left $(A_{12}A_{21})$. For a three-by-three determinant, such as Eq. 4–6, the three minors can be generated in accordance with the following scheme:

For element **i:**
$$\begin{vmatrix} \mathbf{i} & \mathbf{j} & \mathbf{k} \\ A_x & A_y & A_z \\ B_x & B_y & B_z \end{vmatrix} = \mathbf{i}(A_yB_z - A_zB_y)$$

For element **j:**
$$\begin{vmatrix} \mathbf{i} & \mathbf{j} & \mathbf{k} \\ A_x & A_y & A_z \\ B_x & B_y & B_z \end{vmatrix} = -\mathbf{j}(A_xB_z - A_zB_x)$$

For element **k:**
$$\begin{vmatrix} \mathbf{i} & \mathbf{j} & \mathbf{k} \\ A_x & A_y & A_z \\ B_x & B_y & B_z \end{vmatrix} = \mathbf{k}(A_xB_y - A_yB_x)$$

Adding the results, and noting that the **j** element must include the minus sign, yields the expanded form of **A × B** given above Eq. 4–6.

the beam's top surface, when computing the external forces we can hang the load from the bottom of the beam at point P_3, or drill a hole in the beam to point P_2 and apply the load at this point. In any case, since points P_1, P_2, and P_3 lie on the line of action of **F**, the principle of transmissibility states that **F** may be applied at *any* of these three points and the reactive forces developed at the supports A and B will remain the same. For our purposes, the principle of transmissibility is used for computing the *external reactions;* however, the *internal forces* developed in the beam will depend upon where **F** acts. Provided **F** acts at P_1, the internal forces in the beam have a high intensity around point P_1. When **F** acts at P_3, the effects of **F** will influence particles surrounding P_1 to a lesser degree than those particles surrounding point P_3.

When computing the *external effects* of forces acting on a rigid body, it follows from the principle of transmissibility that any force acting on the rigid body may be considered as a *sliding vector;* that is, *the force may act at any point along its line of action.* This is contrary to the notion of a force being a fixed vector, which applies to any force acting on a particle.

4–4. Moment of a Force About a Point

We can illustrate the concepts dealing with the moment of a force by using a simple example. Consider force **F** applied at the end of a pipe wrench, Fig. 4–7. The effect of this force tends to cause the pipe to twist about the *aa* axis. Experience teaches that to produce the greatest turning effect, the force should be applied at right angles to the handle, and the distance d should be made as large as possible. This twisting or rotational effect of a force about the *aa* axis is defined as the *moment of a force* or simply the *moment.* In all cases, the tendency for rotation will occur about an axis *perpendicular* to a plane containing both the force **F** and the distance line d, as shown in Fig. 4–7.

Consider now a force **F** and point O in space. The line of action of **F** and the point are contained within the shaded plane shown in Fig. 4–8a. We will define the moment of force **F** about point O as a *vector quantity.* This vector has a *magnitude* which is the product of the magnitude of the force vector **F** and the perpendicular distance d from the point to the line of action of the force, i.e., $M_O = Fd$. The units of moment magnitude are thus force times distance, e.g., lb-ft or Nm. The *direction* of the moment vector will be specified using the right-hand rule. The fingers are curled in the sense of rotation as caused by the force acting about the point; the *thumb* then *points* in the *directive sense* of the moment vector, which is *perpendicular* to the shaded plane containing **F** and d.

In three dimensions, the moment vector is illustrated by a regular vector with a curl on it to *distinguish* it from a force vector. See Figs. 4–7 and

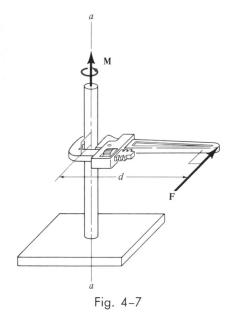

Fig. 4–7

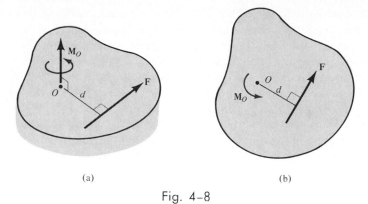

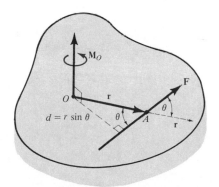

(a)　　　　　　　　　　　　　　(b)

Fig. 4–8

4–8a. Many problems in mechanics involve coplanar force systems. In such cases, these problems may be conveniently viewed in two dimensions. For example, a projected view of Fig. 4–8a is given in Fig. 4–8b. The moment M_O is simply represented here by the counterclockwise curl, which indicates the action of **F**. This curl is used to show the sense of rotation caused by the moment $\mathbf{M}_O$. Using the right-hand rule, realize that the *actual direction* of the moment vector in Fig. 4–8b points *out* of the page, since the fingers follow the curl.

The definition of moment of a force about point O may be expressed in terms of the vector cross product. With reference to Fig. 4–9, this expression is

$$\mathbf{M}_O = \mathbf{r} \times \mathbf{F} \tag{4-7}$$

As shown, **r** represents the vector drawn from point O to *any point A* lying on the line of action of the force **F**. We will now show that the moment vector determined by Eq. 4–7 is in accordance with the definition of a moment. From the definition of the vector cross product, Eq. 4–1, the *magnitude* of $\mathbf{M}_O$ is

$$M_O = rF \sin \theta = F(r \sin \theta) = Fd$$

Here θ defines the angle made between the *tails* of the two vectors **F** and **r** (see Fig. 4–3). This angle, shown in Fig. 4–9, is constructed by sliding vector **r** to point A. The *direction* of $\mathbf{M}_O$ is determined by means of the right-hand rule, based upon the definition of the cross product as given by Eq. 4–7. After extending **r** to the dotted position, we form the cross product $\mathbf{r} \times \mathbf{F}$ by curling the right-hand fingers from the direction of **r** toward the direction of **F** (vector **r** cross vector **F**). The thumb is then directed upward or perpendicular to the plane in the direction of $\mathbf{M}_O$, Fig. 4–9. Since the cross product is not commutative, it is important that the *proper order* of vector multiplication be maintained in Eq. 4–7.

Fig. 4–9

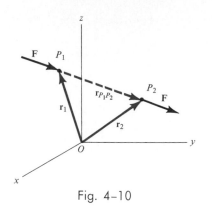

Fig. 4–10

If we reverse the order so that $\mathbf{M}_O = \mathbf{F} \times \mathbf{r}$, the sense of direction of $\mathbf{M}_O$ would be *opposite* to the *actual* sense of direction shown in Fig. 4–8a.

As stated before, $\mathbf{r}$ in Eq. 4–7 can be drawn from point O to *any point* lying on the line of action of $\mathbf{F}$. This definition for $\mathbf{r}$ is due to the transmissibility of $\mathbf{F}$, which was discussed qualitatively in Sec. 4–3. We will now show mathematically that $\mathbf{F}$ is transmissible; that is, $\mathbf{F}$ is a *sliding vector*. In Fig. 4–10, $\mathbf{F}$ is applied at two points, P_1 and P_2, lying along its line of action. These points lie at a distance $\mathbf{r}_1$ and $\mathbf{r}_2$, respectively, from the origin of coordinates O. For transmissibility, it is necessary that the moment of $\mathbf{F}$ about O be the *same* when $\mathbf{F}$ acts at either point P_1 or P_2, i.e.,

$$\mathbf{r}_1 \times \mathbf{F} = \mathbf{r}_2 \times \mathbf{F}$$

From the figure,

$$\mathbf{r}_2 = \mathbf{r}_1 + \mathbf{r}_{P_1 P_2}$$

Substituting gives

$$\mathbf{r}_1 \times \mathbf{F} = (\mathbf{r}_1 + \mathbf{r}_{P_1 P_2}) \times \mathbf{F}$$

Using the distributive law, Eq. 4–4, we obtain

$$\mathbf{r}_1 \times \mathbf{F} = \mathbf{r}_1 \times \mathbf{F} + \mathbf{r}_{P_1 P_2} \times \mathbf{F}$$

or

$$(\mathbf{r}_1 - \mathbf{r}_1) \times \mathbf{F} = \mathbf{r}_{P_1 P_2} \times \mathbf{F}$$
$$0 \equiv 0$$

The left-hand side of this equation is zero since $(\mathbf{r}_1 - \mathbf{r}_1)$ forms a null vector. The right-hand side is zero since $\mathbf{r}_{P_1 P_2}$ and $\mathbf{F}$ are parallel to one another; refer to Eq. 4–2. Thus, $\mathbf{F}$ is a sliding vector, and by definition $\mathbf{r}$ in Eq. 4–7 may be directed to *any point* lying on the line of action of $\mathbf{F}$.

To summarize the concepts covered in this section, consider the rigid body shown in Fig. 4–11.* Force $\mathbf{F}$ is applied at point $P_2(x_2, y_2, z_2)$. The moment of this force about point $P_1(x_1, y_1, z_1)$ may be computed on the basis of Eq. 4–7. The position vector $\mathbf{r}$ extends from point P_1 *to* point P_2 (or any other point lying on the line of action of the force). Hence,

$$\mathbf{r} = (x_2 - x_1)\mathbf{i} + (y_2 - y_1)\mathbf{j} + (z_2 - z_1)\mathbf{k}$$

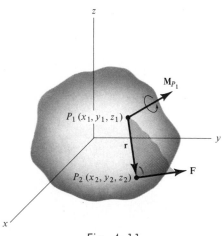

Fig. 4–11

*The shaded object shown in Fig. 4–11 represents a rigid body having an *arbitrary shape*. Similarly, the object shown in Fig. 4–17 represents the plane view of a rigid body. Such objects are simply *graphical representations* used to explain the theory. However, it should be kept in mind that the arbitrary shape of these objects may in reality represent an airplane, beam, bridge, stone, etc.

If **F** has Cartesian components having magnitudes F_x, F_y, and F_z, we may express **F** in vector notation as

$$\mathbf{F} = F_x\mathbf{i} + F_y\mathbf{j} + F_z\mathbf{k}$$

Thus,

$$\mathbf{M}_{P_1} = \mathbf{r} \times \mathbf{F} = \begin{vmatrix} \mathbf{i} & \mathbf{j} & \mathbf{k} \\ (x_2 - x_1) & (y_2 - y_1) & (z_2 - z_1) \\ F_x & F_y & F_z \end{vmatrix} \qquad (4\text{-}8)$$

As shown in Fig. 4–11, $\mathbf{M}_{P_1}$ is *perpendicular* to the shaded plane containing vectors **r** and **F**. Hence, the force **F** tends to rotate the body about an axis defined by the line of action of $\mathbf{M}_{P_1}$.

4–5. Varignon's Theorem

A theorem often used in mechanics is *Varignon's theorem*, which states that the sum of the moments of all the forces of a concurrent force system about a given point is equal to the same moment created by the resultant force of the concurrent force system about the point.

The proof of this theorem follows directly from the distributive property of the vector cross product, Eq. 4–4. For example, consider the system of three concurrent forces shown in Fig. 4–12. The resultant force is determined by the vector sum $\mathbf{F}_R = \mathbf{F}_1 + \mathbf{F}_2 + \mathbf{F}_3$. Hence, the total moment of the three forces about point O is

$$\mathbf{M}_R = \mathbf{r} \times \mathbf{F}_1 + \mathbf{r} \times \mathbf{F}_2 + \mathbf{r} \times \mathbf{F}_3 = \mathbf{r} \times (\mathbf{F}_1 + \mathbf{F}_2 + \mathbf{F}_3)$$

or

$$\mathbf{M}_R = \mathbf{r} \times \mathbf{F}_R$$

where **r** is the position vector drawn from O to P.

This property was originally developed by the French mathematician Varignon (1654–1722). It has important application to the solution of problems and proofs of theorems which follow, since it allows us to consider the moment of a force's two components rather than the force itself. Used in this way, Varignon's theorem states that the moment of a force about a point is equivalent to the moment of the force's two components about the point.

Example 4–1

A force **F** having a magnitude of 5 lb acts at the end of the block shown in Fig. 4–13a. Determine the x, y, and z components of the moment at point O created by this force.

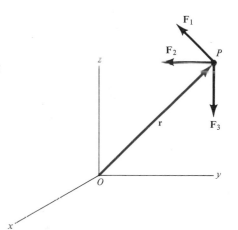

F_1, F_2, F_3 concurrent

Fig. 4–12

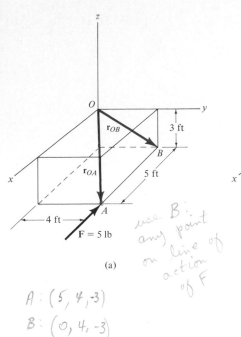

(a)

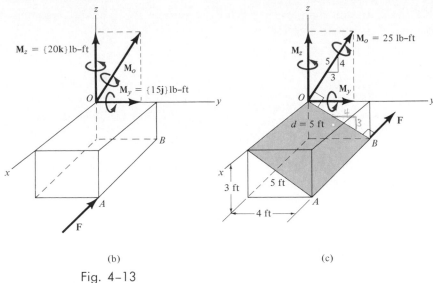

(b)   (c)

Fig. 4–13

[handwritten notes:]

use B: any point on line of action of F

$A: (5, 4, -3)$

$B: (0, 4, -3)$

$M_x = 0$

Solution I

We can compute the moment at point O using Cartesian unit vectors in accordance with Eq. 4–7, i.e., $\mathbf{M}_O = \mathbf{r} \times \mathbf{F}$. From Fig. 4–13a, $\mathbf{F} = \{-5\mathbf{i}\}$ lb. Either vector $\mathbf{r}_{OA} = \{5\mathbf{i} + 4\mathbf{j} - 3\mathbf{k}\}$ ft or $\mathbf{r}_{OB} = \{4\mathbf{j} - 3\mathbf{k}\}$ ft may be used in the cross product. Why? From Eq. 4–7,

$$\mathbf{M}_O = \mathbf{r}_{OA} \times \mathbf{F} = \begin{vmatrix} \mathbf{i} & \mathbf{j} & \mathbf{k} \\ 5 & 4 & -3 \\ -5 & 0 & 0 \end{vmatrix} = \mathbf{r}_{OB} \times \mathbf{F} = \begin{vmatrix} \mathbf{i} & \mathbf{j} & \mathbf{k} \\ 0 & 4 & -3 \\ -5 & 0 & 0 \end{vmatrix}$$

Expanding the determinants, yields the same result, namely,

$$\mathbf{M}_O = \{15\mathbf{j} + 20\mathbf{k}\} \text{ lb-ft} \qquad \qquad \textit{Ans.}$$

Hence, the moment has only two components $\mathbf{M}_y$ and $\mathbf{M}_z$, as shown in Fig. 4–13b. Each component represents the effect of $\mathbf{F}$ in tending to rotate the block about the y and z axis.

Solution II

According to the principle of transmissibility, the force $\mathbf{F}$ may be applied to the block at point B, as shown in Fig. 4–13c, without altering the moment of the force produced about point O. When applied at point B, the *perpendicular distance d* from the line of action of the force to point O is 5 ft. Hence, the magnitude of the moment $\mathbf{M}_O$ about point O is $M_O = F\,d = (5 \text{ lb})(5 \text{ ft}) = 25$ lb-ft. By the right-hand rule this vector acts *perpendicular* to the shaded diagonal plane containing d and $\mathbf{F}$, Fig. 4–13c. The magnitude of the two components of $\mathbf{M}_O$ are therefore

$$M_y = \tfrac{3}{5}(25) = 15 \text{ lb-ft}$$

and

$$M_z = \tfrac{4}{5}(25) = 20 \text{ lb-ft}$$

Thus, the moment at O can be expressed in Cartesian component form as

$$\mathbf{M}_O = \{15\ \mathbf{j} + 20\ \mathbf{k}\}\text{lb-ft} \qquad\qquad Ans.$$

Note that even though $\mathbf{F}$ acts at a perpendicular distance of 5 ft from the x axis (see Fig. 4–13c) this force does not create a tendency for rotation about the x axis since the force is *parallel* to the x axis.

Example 4–2

A 50-lb force acts on the handle of a lever, as shown in Fig. 4–14a. Determine the moment created by this force about point A.

Solution I

In Fig. 4–14b, the *perpendicular distance* from the line of action of the force to the moment point is computed using trigonometry. Since $\angle BCD$ is 120° then $\angle DBC$ is 15° so that

$$\frac{BC}{\sin 45°} = \frac{2 \text{ in.}}{\sin 15°}$$

$$BC = 2\left(\frac{0.707}{0.259}\right) = 5.46 \text{ in.}$$

$$AB = 10.00 - 5.46 = 4.54 \text{ in.}$$

Hence, from $\triangle ABE$,

$$d = 4.54 \sin 15° = 1.174 \text{ in.}$$

Therefore,

$$M_A = Fd = (50 \text{ lb})(1.174 \text{ in.}) = 58.7 \text{ lb-in.}$$

According to the right-hand rule, for the coordinate system shown counterclockwise rotation in the plane of the figure will be considered positive ($+\mathbf{k}$ direction). Since the 50-lb force tends to rotate the lever *clockwise* about point A, then

$$\mathbf{M}_A = \{-58.7\mathbf{k}\}\text{lb-in.} \qquad\qquad Ans.$$

Solution II

Following the principle of transmissibility, force **F** may be applied at point B. The force may then be resolved into components acting parallel and perpendicular to the lever, as shown in Fig. 4-14c. Only the component acting perpendicular to the lever produces a moment about point A. Why? Using the length of AB computed in Solution I, we have

$$M_A = F_\perp d_{AB} = (50 \sin 15°)4.54 = 58.7 \text{ lb-in.}$$

Since the moment is clockwise about point A,

$$\mathbf{M}_A = \{-58.7\mathbf{k}\} \text{ lb-in.} \qquad \qquad Ans.$$

The line of action of $\mathbf{F}_\parallel$ passes through point A and hence creates zero moment about this point.

Solution III

The 50-lb force is resolved into its x and y components, as shown in Fig. 4-14d. Applying Varignon's theorem, the total moment computed

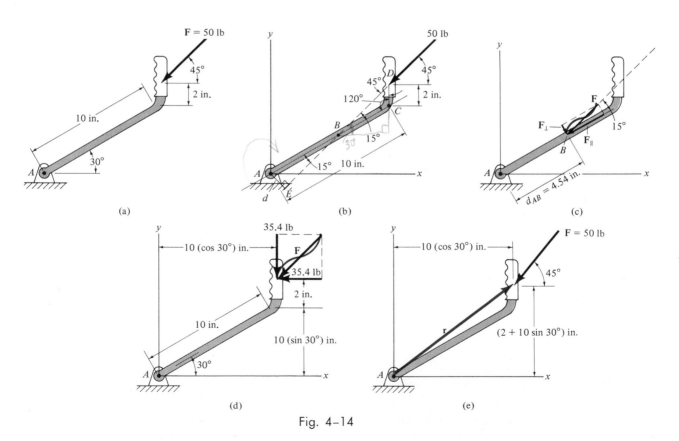

Fig. 4-14

about point A is equivalent to the sum of the moments produced by the two force components. Assuming counterclockwise rotation positive, i.e., $+\mathbf{k}$ direction,

$$\mathbf{M}_A = -35.4(10 \cos 30°)\mathbf{k} + 35.4(2 + 10 \sin 30°)\mathbf{k}$$

or

$$\mathbf{M}_A = \{-58.7\mathbf{k}\} \text{ lb-in.} \qquad Ans.$$

Solution IV

Using a vector approach, we can represent the required force and position vectors as shown in Fig. 4–14e. Expressing each of these vectors in Cartesian vector notation yields

$$\mathbf{r} = 10 \cos 30°\mathbf{i} + (2 + 10 \sin 30°)\mathbf{j} = \{8.66\mathbf{i} + 7.00\mathbf{j}\} \text{ in.}$$
$$\mathbf{F} = -50 \cos 45°\mathbf{i} - 50 \sin 45°\mathbf{j} = \{-35.4\mathbf{i} - 35.4\mathbf{j}\} \text{ lb}$$

Hence, the required moment becomes

$$\mathbf{M}_A = \mathbf{r} \times \mathbf{F} = \begin{vmatrix} \mathbf{i} & \mathbf{j} & \mathbf{k} \\ 8.66 & 7.00 & 0 \\ -35.4 & -35.4 & 0 \end{vmatrix} = \{-58.7\mathbf{k}\} \text{ lb-in.} \quad Ans.$$

From the analysis, it is seen that Solution III yields the most direct solution to this problem. This method, which involves dividing forces into their rectangular components *before* computing the moment, is generally recommended for solving problems involving coplanar force systems. Note, in particular, that the vector approach, Solution IV, becomes tedious when working problems represented in two dimensions. Its use is generally recommended for solving problems in three dimensions.

Example 4–3

Determine the point of application P and the direction for a 20-lb force, which lies in the plane of the square plate shown in Fig. 4–15a, so that this force creates the greatest counterclockwise moment about point O. What is this moment?

Solution

Since the maximum moment created by the force is required, the force must act on the plate at a distance *farthest* from point O. As shown in Fig. 4–15b, the point of application of $\mathbf{F}$ must therefore be at the diagonal corner. In order to produce counterclockwise rotation of the plate, the force $\mathbf{F}$ must act at an angle $45° < \theta < 225°$. The greatest moment is produced when the line of action of $\mathbf{F}$ is *perpendicular* to $\mathbf{r}_{OP}$, i.e., $\theta = 135°$, Fig. 4–15c. The maximum moment is therefore

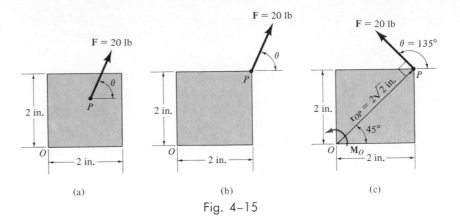

Fig. 4–15

$$M_O = F r_{OP} = (20\text{lb})(2\sqrt{2}\ \text{in.}) = 56.6\ \text{lb-in.} \quad \textit{Ans.}$$

By the right-hand rule, $\mathbf{M}_O$ has a sense of direction which is pointing out of the page.

Example 4–4

The cord BC shown in Fig. 4–16a exerts a force of 60 lb on pole AB. Determine the magnitude and the direction of the moment created by this force about point A.

Solution

Since this problem is expressed in three dimensions, it is recommended that a vector approach be used for the solution. For convenience, the

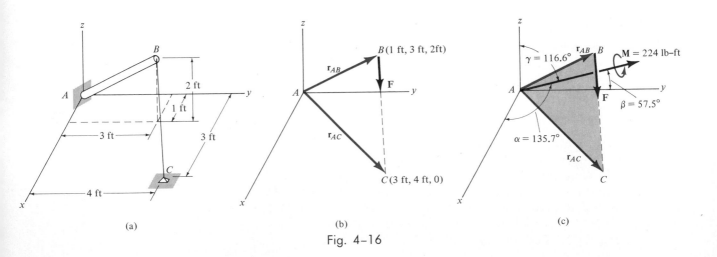

Fig. 4–16

origin of coordinates is established at point A, and the coordinates of points B and C are determined as shown in Fig. 4–16b.

The moment of force $\mathbf{F}$ about point A is $\mathbf{M}_A = \mathbf{r} \times \mathbf{F}$. $\mathbf{r}$ represents a position vector drawn from point A to *any point* on the line of action of the force. Two convenient position vectors which may be used are $\mathbf{r}_{AB}$ and $\mathbf{r}_{AC}$, as indicated in Fig. 4–16b. These vectors are represented as

$$\mathbf{r}_{AB} = \{\mathbf{i} + 3\mathbf{j} + 2\mathbf{k}\} \text{ ft} \qquad \text{and} \qquad \mathbf{r}_{AC} = \{3\mathbf{i} + 4\mathbf{j}\} \text{ ft}$$

The force $\mathbf{F}$, having a magnitude of 60 lb, may be expressed in Cartesian vector form as

$$\mathbf{F} = (60 \text{ lb}) \frac{\mathbf{r}_{BC}}{r_{BC}} = (60) \left(\frac{2\mathbf{i} + \mathbf{j} - 2\mathbf{k}}{\sqrt{(2)^2 + (1)^2 + (-2)^2}} \right) = \{40\mathbf{i} + 20\mathbf{j} - 40\mathbf{k}\} \text{ lb}$$

Therefore,

$$\mathbf{M}_A = \mathbf{r}_{AB} \times \mathbf{F} = \begin{vmatrix} \mathbf{i} & \mathbf{j} & \mathbf{k} \\ 1 & 3 & 2 \\ 40 & 20 & -40 \end{vmatrix} = \mathbf{r}_{AC} \times \mathbf{F} = \begin{vmatrix} \mathbf{i} & \mathbf{j} & \mathbf{k} \\ 3 & 4 & 0 \\ 40 & 20 & -40 \end{vmatrix}$$

or

$$\mathbf{M}_A = \{-160\mathbf{i} + 120\mathbf{j} - 100\mathbf{k}\} \text{ lb-ft}$$

The *magnitude* of $\mathbf{M}_A$ is therefore

$$M_A = \sqrt{(-160)^2 + (120)^2 + (-100)^2} = 224 \text{ lb-ft} \qquad Ans.$$

A unit vector acting in the direction of $\mathbf{M}_A$ is

$$\mathbf{u}_{M_A} = \frac{\mathbf{M}_A}{M_A} = -0.716\mathbf{i} + 0.537\mathbf{j} - 0.447\mathbf{k}$$

The components of $\mathbf{u}_{M_A}$ are the *direction cosines* of $\mathbf{M}_A$. Hence,

$$\alpha = \cos^{-1}(-0.716) = 135.7° \qquad\qquad Ans.$$
$$\beta = \cos^{-1}(0.537) = 57.5° \qquad\qquad Ans.$$
$$\gamma = \cos^{-1}(-0.444) = 116.6° \qquad\qquad Ans.$$

As shown in Fig. 4–16c, $\mathbf{M}_A$ acts perpendicular to the shaded plane containing vectors $\mathbf{F}$, $\mathbf{r}_{AB}$, and $\mathbf{r}_{AC}$. Why?

Problems

4-1. Find the resulting vector for each of the following:
(a) $(2\mathbf{i} - 2\mathbf{k}) \times 3\mathbf{j}$
(b) $5\mathbf{j} \times (3\mathbf{j} + 4\mathbf{k})$
(c) $(-10\mathbf{i} - 2\mathbf{k}) \times (3\mathbf{j} - \mathbf{k})$.

4-2. Given $\mathbf{A} = 3\mathbf{i} + 4\mathbf{j} + 2\mathbf{k}$, $\mathbf{B} = 3\mathbf{i} + 2\mathbf{k}$, and $\mathbf{C} = 2\mathbf{i} - 4\mathbf{j} + 3\mathbf{k}$, find (a) $(\mathbf{A} \times \mathbf{B}) \times \mathbf{C}$, and (b) $\mathbf{A} \times (\mathbf{B} \times \mathbf{C})$.

4-3. Determine a unit vector perpendicular to the plane containing the two vectors $A = 3i - 2j$ and $B = 2k$.

4-4. If A, B, and C are given vectors, prove the distributive law for the vector cross product, i.e., $A \times (B + C) = (A \times B) + (A \times C)$. *Suggestion:* Use Cartesian vectors.

4-5. Determine the cross product $r_1 \times r_2$ for the vectors shown in the figure.

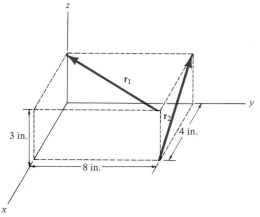

Prob. 4-5

4-6. A force of 30 lb is applied to the handle of the wrench. Determine the moment of this force about point O. Use both a scalar and vector approach to solve the problem.

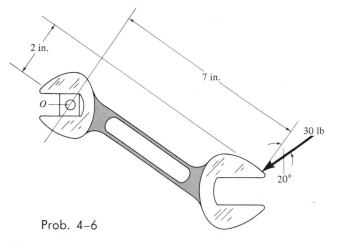

Prob. 4-6

4-7. Resolve the 100-lb force into its x and y components, and determine the moment of each of these components about point O. Solve the problem using both a scalar and a vector approach.

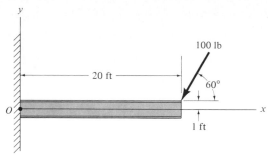

Prob. 4-7

4-8. If the tension in the cable BC is 30 lb, determine the moment created by this force acting on the flag pole at the base A.

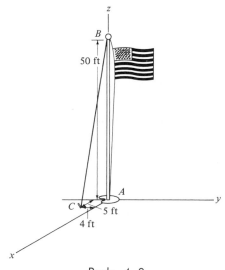

Prob. 4-8

4-9. Determine the angle α at which the 50-lb force must act so that the moment of this force about point B is equal to zero.

88

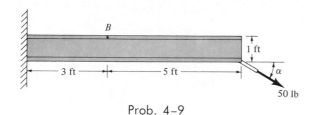

Prob. 4-9

4-10. A 20-lb force is applied 90° to the handle of the socket wrench. Determine the magnitude and direction of the moment created by this force about point O.

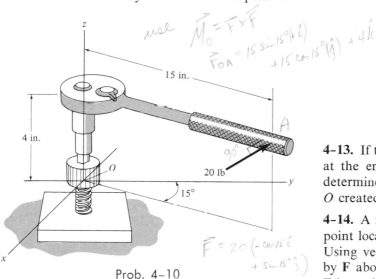

use $\vec{M}_O = \vec{r} \times \vec{F}$

$\vec{r}_{OA} = 15 \sin 15°(\hat{i})$
$\qquad + 15 \cos 15°(\hat{j}) + 4\hat{k}$

$\vec{F} = 20(-\cos 15° \hat{i} + \sin 15° \hat{j})$

Prob. 4-10

4-11. To prevent the bell crank from rotating about the pin connection at O, the total moment created by forces **T** and **R** about this point must be zero. If $R = 20$ lb, determine the magnitude of **T** to prevent rotation.

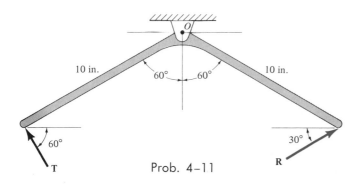

Prob. 4-11

4-12. Determine the magnitude of the force **F** which is applied at the end of the shift lever such that this force creates a clockwise moment of 20 lb-ft about point O when $\alpha = 30°$.

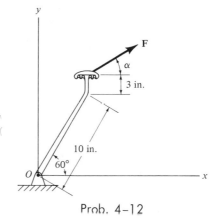

Prob. 4-12

4-13. If the maximum force **F** which can be developed at the end of the shift lever in Prob. 4-12 is 50 lb, determine the angle α so that the clockwise moment at O created by this force is 20 lb-ft.

4-14. A force **F** having a magnitude of 90 lb acts at a point located along the diagonal of the parallelepiped. Using vector notation, show that the moment created by **F** about point A is the same, regardless of whether **F** is applied at point B or point C.

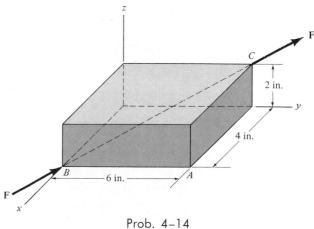

Prob. 4-14

89

4–15. To prevent rotation due to the 100-lb load W, a pawl at A exerts a horizontal force T on the ratchet of the winch. Determine the magnitude of this force so that the sum of the moments of T and W is zero about O.

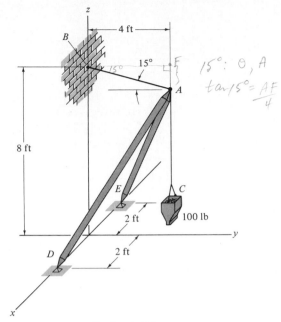

15°: 0, A

$\tan 15° = \dfrac{AF}{4}$

Prob. 4–16

4–17. Find the moment created by the 200-lb force acting at the end of the pipe assembly about each of the joints at A, B, and C.

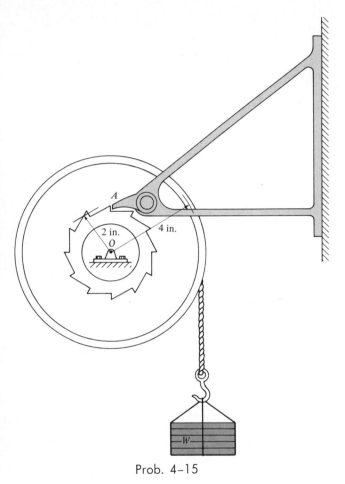

Prob. 4–15

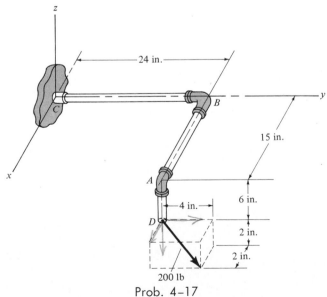

Prob. 4–17

4–16. The cable AB exerts a tension of 50 lb at A when the boom assembly is in the position shown. Calculate the total moment produced by this force and the 100-lb load about the support at D by (a) considering each force separately, and (b) determining the resultant of the two forces and then computing the moment of this resultant about D.

4-18. The three struts AB, AC, and AD hold the 10-lb lantern in equilibrium. Determine the force in each of these struts and show that the total moment of these three forces about point P is zero. Assume that the force in each strut acts along the axis of the strut. Is the total moment of these three forces also zero about point P'? Why or why not?

4-19. The moment created at point P by the applied force F acting on the block is $M = \{-i - 3j - 9k\}$ lb-in. Determine the dimensions b and c of the block if $a = 3$ in.

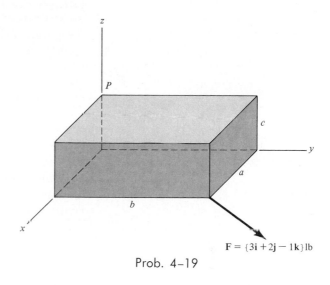

Prob. 4–19

4-20. Determine the direction of the force F applied at the end of the pipe section such that the moment created by F about point A is zero.

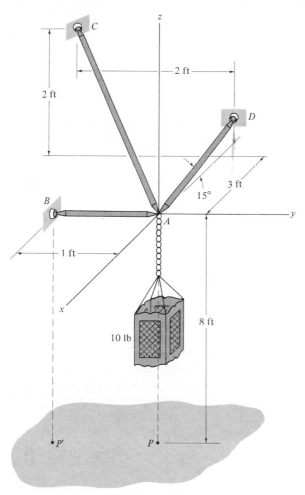

Prob. 4–18

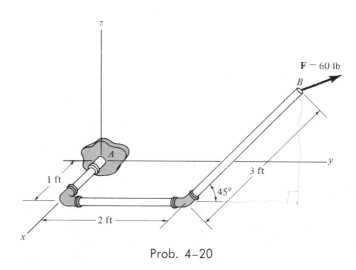

Prob. 4–20

91

4-6. Moment of a Couple

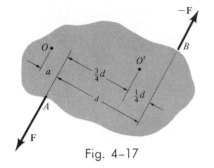

Fig. 4-17

A *couple* is defined as two parallel forces having the same magnitude, opposite direction, and acting at some perpendicular distance d apart. Since the resultant force of the two forces composing the couple is zero, the entire effect of a couple is to produce a pure *moment,* or tendency of rotation in a specified direction.

As shown in Fig. 4–17, the net effect of the two forces acting on the plate lying in the xy plane will produce a rotation of the plate about an axis *perpendicular* to the plate. By definition, these two forces constitute a couple. The moment produced by this couple, when computed about any point lying in the plane of the plate, can be calculated by using the definition of the moment of a force and the principle of transmissibility of a force. Hence, the moment about point O, Fig. 4–17, is equal to the moment of the force at A about point O plus the moment of the force at B about point O. Assuming positive moment counterclockwise, that is, directed out of the page,

$$M_O = -(a)F + (a + d)F = Fd \;\curvearrowleft$$

In a similar manner, the moment of the couple computed about the point O' is

$$M_{O'} = (\tfrac{3}{4}d)F + (\tfrac{1}{4}d)F = Fd \;\curvearrowleft$$

Since points O and O' were arbitrarily selected in the xy plane, these two calculations illustrate an important property regarding the moment of a couple: The magnitude of the moment and the direction of its rotation are the *same* when the couple moment is computed about *any point* lying in the plane of the couple. Hence, it may be concluded that the moment of a couple is a *free vector,* preserving its magnitude and direction but having no specific point of application. This free vector is obviously a moment vector. The *magnitude* of the couple moment is $M_C = Fd$, where F is the magnitude of one of the forces and d is the *perpendicular distance* between the two forces. The *direction* (and sense) of the couple moment is determined by the right-hand rule and acts perpendicular to the plane containing the two forces.

Since it was shown in Sec. 4–4 that a moment is represented in vector notation by the vector cross product, the moment of a couple can be defined by

$$\mathbf{M}_C = \mathbf{r} \times \mathbf{F} \qquad (4\text{–}9)$$

where $\mathbf{r}$ represents the position vector, drawn from *any point* on the line of action of one force to *any point* on the line of action of the other force. As shown in Figs. 4–18a and 4–18b, the force **F** in Eq. 4–9 represents that force to which the vector **r** is *directed*. The *magnitude* of the couple moment is

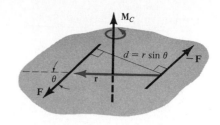

$$M_C = rF \sin \theta = F(r \sin \theta) = Fd$$

In accordance with the cross product, note how the angle θ is defined in Fig. 4–18. The *direction* of **M**$_C$ is defined by the right-hand rule. In both cases, the directional sense is upward, as shown in the figure. Recall that **M**$_C$ is a free vector, and can therefore act through *any point* in the plane, Fig. 4–18.

(a)

Two couples are said to be *equal* if they produce a moment vector having the same magnitude and direction. Since the moment produced by a couple is always perpendicular to the plane containing the couple forces, it is therefore necessary that the forces of equal couples lie either in the same plane or in corresponding planes that are *parallel* to one another. In this way, the line of action of each couple moment will be the same, that is, perpendicular to the parallel planes. For example, the two couples shown in Fig. 4–19a are equivalent. One couple is produced by forces of 10 lb acting at a distance of $d = 5$ ft, and the other is produced by forces of magnitude of 20 lb at a distance of 2.5 ft. Since the

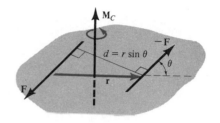

(b)

Fig. 4–18

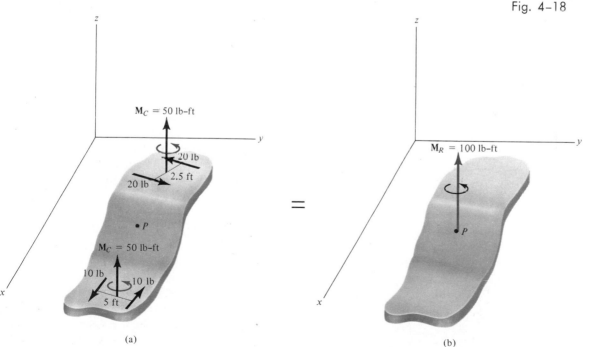

(a)

(b)

Fig. 4–19

planes in which the forces act are parallel, the moment produced by each of these couples may be expressed in vector form as

$$\mathbf{M}_C = \{50\mathbf{k}\}\text{lb-ft}$$

Since couple moments are free vectors, they may be applied at some *arbitrary point P*, and added vectorially. As shown in Fig. 4–19*b*, the resultant of both couple moments is therefore,

$$\mathbf{M}_R = 50\mathbf{k} + 50\mathbf{k} = \{100\mathbf{k}\}\text{lb-ft}$$

The moments of two couples acting on nonparallel planes are also added using the rules of vector addition. For example, the two couples acting on different planes of the rigid body in Fig. 4–20*a* may be replaced by their corresponding moment vectors $\mathbf{M}_{C_1}$ and $\mathbf{M}_{C_2}$, shown in Fig.

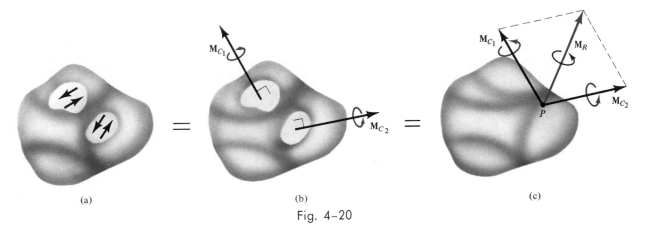

(a)   (b)   (c)

Fig. 4–20

4–20*b*. These free vectors may be moved to an *arbitrary point P* and added vectorially to obtain their resultant vector sum $\mathbf{M}_R = \mathbf{M}_{C_1} + \mathbf{M}_{C_2}$, shown in Fig. 4–20*c*. The effect of the two couples in Fig. 4–20*a* imparts a total twist or couple moment $\mathbf{M}_R$ to the body acting in the direction of $\mathbf{M}_R$.

4–7. Resolution of a Force into a Force and a Couple

Before the methods of rigid-body equilibrium can be developed, we must first study what effects are caused by moving a force from one point to another on a rigid body. For example, consider moving the force **F** acting at point *A* on the constrained rigid body in Fig. 4–21*a* to the arbitrary point *O* which does *not* lie along the line of action of **F**. Using the principle of transmissibility, **F** may first be applied at point *A′*, which lies at a perpendicular distance *d* from point *O* to the line of action of the force,

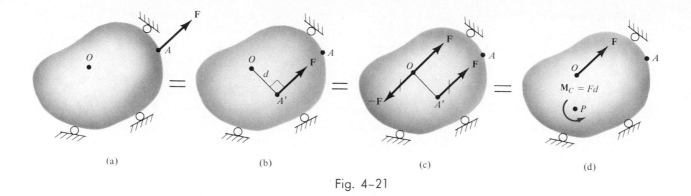

Fig. 4–21

as shown in Fig. 4–21b. Applying equal and opposite forces **F** *at point*
O, as shown in Fig. 4–21c, in no way alters the equilibrium state of the
body. Two of the three forces (indicated by a slash across them) in this
figure form a couple. The moment of this couple has a magnitude
$M_C = Fd$ and tends to rotate the body in a counterclockwise direction.
Since the couple moment is a free vector, it may be applied at *any point*
P on the rigid body, as shown in Fig. 4–21d, and still produce the *same*
external effects on the rigid body. In addition to this couple, force **F** now
acts at point *O*. Thus, when **F** acts at *A*, Fig. 4–21a, it will produce *the*
same reactions at the three roller supports as when **F** is applied at point
O and a couple moment **M**$_C$ is applied to the body, Fig. 4–21d. *The*
magnitude and direction of the couple moment is determined by taking
moments of **F** *about point O when the force is located at its original point*
A (or point A′). The line of action of **M**$_C$ *is thus perpendicular to the plane*
containing **F** *and d.*
  For the general case where the rigid body is viewed in three dimensions,
we can formulate the above procedure using vector notation. With refer-

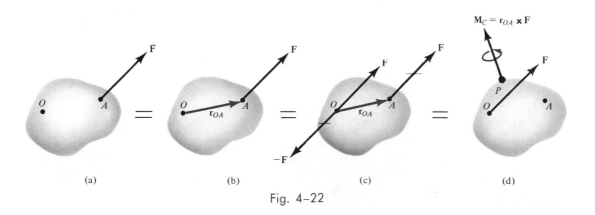

Fig. 4–22

ence to Fig. 4–22, force vector $\mathbf{F}$ is replaced from point A to point O, and a couple moment vector $\mathbf{M}_C$ is *added*, where

$$\mathbf{M}_C = \mathbf{r}_{OA} \times \mathbf{F}$$

The position vector $\mathbf{r}_{OA}$ *is drawn from point O to any point lying along the line of action of the force. According to the right-hand rule, the moment vector is perpendicular to the plane made by force* $\mathbf{F}$ *and position vector* $\mathbf{r}_{OA}$. (The constructions in Fig. 4–22 are equivalent to those used for the two-dimensional case shown in Fig. 4–21.) As before, since $\mathbf{M}_C$ is a free vector, it can act at *any point P* on the body.

note ————————→

Whenever one has a resulting force and a resulting couple moment which are *mutually perpendicular,* it is always possible to move the force from its original line of action to a unique parallel line of action, thereby eliminating the moment. To do this, simply reverse the procedure as just discussed. For example, the force $\mathbf{F}$ and moment $\mathbf{M}_C$, shown in Fig. 4–21*d*, are mutually perpendicular. (The direction of $\mathbf{M}_C$ is perpendicular to the page in accordance with the right-hand rule.) If $\mathbf{F}$ is moved so that its line of action passes through points AA', Fig. 4–21*b*, the moment $\mathbf{M}_C$ will be eliminated. In three dimensions, vectors should be used for this operation, Fig. 4–22. A further discussion of this is given in Sec. 4–10. See Example 4–6.

The concepts presented in this section regarding the movement of a force may be summarized by the following two statements:

1. If the force is to be moved to a *point located on its line of action,* by the principle of transmissibility, simply move the force to the point.
2. If the force is to be moved to a *point which is not located on its line of action,* move the force to the point and *add* a couple moment. The magnitude and direction of the couple moment are determined by the cross product of a *position vector,* directed from the point to any point lying on the line of action of the force, and the *force vector.*

Example 4–5

Replace the three couples acting on the block shown in Fig. 4–23*a* by a single resultant couple moment. Determine its magnitude and direction.

Solution

Each pair of equal and opposite forces may be replaced by its equivalent couple-moment vector, as shown in Fig. 4–23*b*. The sense of direction of these vectors is determined by using the right-hand rule. In particular, the inclined plane has a slope of $\frac{4}{3}$; hence, the unit vector $\mathbf{u}_n$ acting *perpendicular* to this plane, Fig. 4–23*b*, may be represented by

$$\mathbf{u}_n = \tfrac{4}{5}\mathbf{j} + \tfrac{3}{5}\mathbf{k}$$

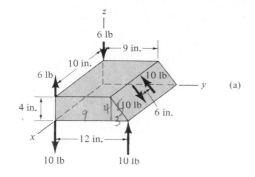

(a)

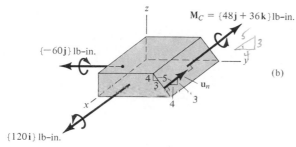

(b)

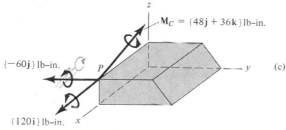

(c)

Fig. 4-23

The $(10 \text{ lb})(6 \text{ in.}) = 60$ lb-in. couple moment may therefore be written in Cartesian component notation as

$$\mathbf{M}_C = (60 \text{ lb-in.})\mathbf{u}_n = \{48\mathbf{j} + 36\mathbf{k}\} \text{ lb-in.}$$

Since couple moments are free vectors, they may be moved to some arbitrary point P on the block and added vectorially, Fig. 4-23c. The resultant moment becomes

$$\mathbf{M}_{C_R} = 120\mathbf{i} - 60\mathbf{j} + 48\mathbf{j} + 36\mathbf{k}$$
$$= \{120\mathbf{i} - 12\mathbf{j} + 36\mathbf{k}\} \text{ lb-in.} \qquad Ans.$$

The magnitude of this resultant is

$$M_{C_R} = \sqrt{(120)^2 + (-12)^2 + (36)^2} = 125.9 \text{ lb-in.} \qquad Ans.$$

The direction of M_{C_R} is determined from the unit vector

$$\mathbf{u}_C = \frac{\mathbf{M}_{C_R}}{M_{C_R}} = \frac{120}{125.9}\mathbf{i} - \frac{12}{125.9}\mathbf{j} + \frac{36}{125.9}\mathbf{k}$$

$$= 0.954\mathbf{i} - 0.095\mathbf{j} + 0.286\mathbf{k}$$

Thus,

$$\alpha = \cos^{-1}(0.954) = 17.4° \qquad\qquad Ans.$$
$$\beta = \cos^{-1}(-0.095) = 95.5° \qquad\qquad Ans.$$
$$\gamma = \cos^{-1}(0.286) = 73.4° \qquad\qquad Ans.$$

Example 4-6

Replace the force and couple acting on the beam shown in Fig. 4–24a by an equivalent force and couple-moment system acting at point A. Can this system be further reduced to a single force? If so, specify the location of the force.

Solution

Since this problem is represented in two dimensions, the solution is most easily obtained using a scalar approach. The couple moment formed by the two 10-lb forces acting at B and C has a magnitude of $M_1 = (3\text{ ft})(10\text{ lb}) = 30$ lb-ft and acts in the $+\mathbf{k}$ direction (counterclockwise). Because $\mathbf{M}_1$ is a *free vector*, it may be moved directly to point A, as shown in Fig. 4–24b. Since point A does *not* lie on the line of action of the 20-lb force, when this force is moved to point A a couple moment of magnitude $M_2 = (8\text{ ft})(20\text{ lb}) = 160$ lb-ft *must be added* to the beam, Fig. 4–24b. By the right-hand rule, this moment acts *clockwise*, i.e. in the $-\mathbf{k}$ direction. (The force, when acting at point D, tends to rotate the beam about point A clockwise.) Adding the two moments at point A, the total moment acting at A is thus

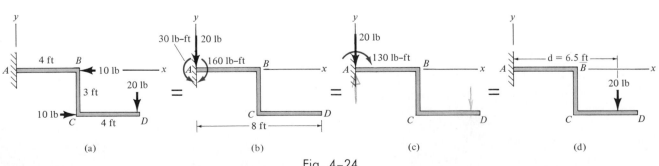

(a) (b) (c) (d)

Fig. 4–24

$$M = M_1 + M_2 = 30\,k - 160\,k = \{-130\,k\}\ \text{lb-ft}$$

The result is shown in Fig. 4–24c.

Since the resultant force and moment acting at A are mutually *perpendicular* to one another, this system may indeed be further reduced to a single resultant force. To do this the 20-lb force must be moved to the *right* a distance d to point A such that the couple moment created by the 20-lb force, when the force is moved, has a magnitude of 130 lb-ft. Hence,

$$130\ \text{lb-ft} = d(20\ \text{lb})$$

or

$$d = 6.5\ \text{ft} \qquad\qquad Ans.$$

The result is illustrated in Fig. 4–24d, where it is shown that when the 20-lb force acts to the *right* of point A, the force imparts the *required* 130 lb ft *clockwise* moment to the beam about point A.

Example 4–7

Replace the couple moment M and forces F_1 and F_2 acting on the rigid body shown in Fig. 4–25a by an equivalent force and couple-moment system acting at the origin of coordinates.

Solution

Expressing the forces and couple moment in Cartesian vector notation, we have

$$F_1 = (50\ \text{lb})\frac{r_{AB}}{r_{AB}} = 50\left(\frac{2i + j + 4k}{\sqrt{21}}\right) = \{21.8i + 10.9j + 43.6k\}\ \text{lb}$$

$$F_2 = (75\ \text{lb})\frac{r_{CO}}{r_{CO}} = 75\left(\frac{-3i - 9k}{\sqrt{90}}\right) = \{-23.7i - 71.2k\}\ \text{lb}$$

$$M = (200\ \text{lb-ft})\frac{r_{BC}}{r_{BC}} = 200\left(\frac{i - 3j + 5k}{\sqrt{35}}\right)$$

$$= \{33.8i - 101.4j + 169.0k\}\ \text{lb-ft}$$

Since M is a *free vector*, it may be moved directly to the origin O, as shown in Fig. 4–25b. Because force is a *sliding vector*, F_2 may be placed at the origin, since the origin is a point lying on the line of action of F_2. Force F_1 must be replaced at the origin using the method discussed in Sec. 4–7. This is accomplished by moving F_1 directly to the origin and *adding* a couple moment M_1, as shown in Fig. 4–25b. The moment is perpendicular to the shaded plane and defined by the cross product:

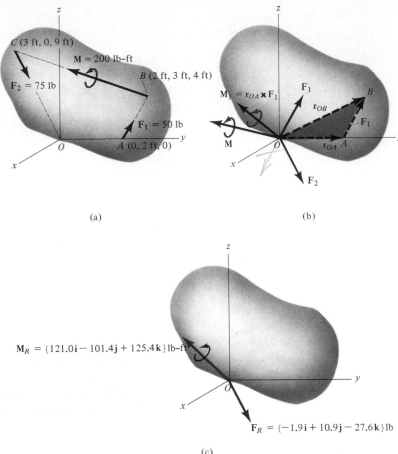

(a)

(b)

$$M_R = \{121.0i - 101.4j + 125.4k\}\,lb\text{-}ft$$

$$F_R = \{-1.9i + 10.9j - 27.6k\}\,lb$$

(c)

Fig. 4-25

$$M_1 = r_{OA} \times F_1 = 2j \times (21.8i + 10.9j + 43.6k)$$

or

$$M_1 = \{87.2i - 43.6k\}\ lb\text{-}ft$$

(From Fig. 4–25*a*, note also that $M_1 = r_{OB} \times F_1$ since point *B* is on the line of action of F_1.) The resultant force and moment system acting at the origin is thus

$$\begin{aligned}F_R = F_1 + F_2 &= (21.8 - 23.7)i + (10.9)j + (43.6 - 71.2)k\\ &= \{-1.9i + 10.9j - 27.6k\}\ lb \qquad\qquad\qquad Ans.\end{aligned}$$

$$\begin{aligned}M_R = M_1 + M &= (87.2 + 33.8)i + (-101.4)j + (-43.6 + 169.0)k\\ &= \{121.0i - 101.4j + 125.4k\}\ lb\text{-}ft \qquad\qquad Ans.\end{aligned}$$

These results are shown in Fig. 4–25*c*.

Problems

4-21. Determine the resultant couple moment at points *A* and *B* caused by the two couples acting on the block assembly.

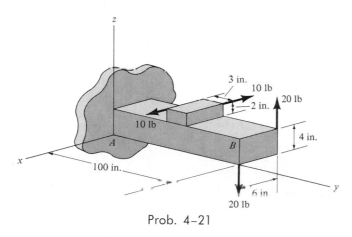

Prob. 4–21

4-22. The resultant moment created by the two couples acting on the disk is 10 kip-in. acting counterclockwise. Determine the magnitude of force **T**.

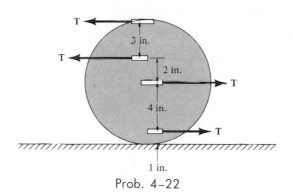

Prob. 4–22

4-23. When the engine of the plane is running, the vertical reaction which the ground exerts at *A* is measured as 1,100 lb. On the other hand, when the engine is turned off, the vertical reactions at *A* and *B* are 900 lb

each. The difference in readings at *A* is caused by the couple acting on the propeller when the engine is running. This couple tends to overturn the plane in the sense opposite to the counterclockwise rotation of the propeller. Determine the magnitude of the couple moment and the magnitude of the vertical force exerted at *B* when the engine is running.

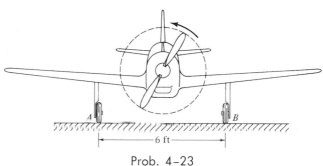

Prob. 4–23

4-24. Determine the magnitude and direction of the resultant couple of the three couples acting on the disk and bar assembly. At what point does this resultant couple act when you consider the effects of external forces acting on the assembly?

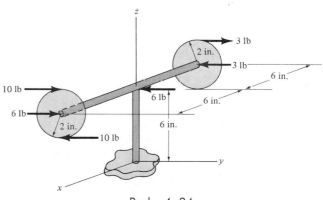

Prob. 4–24

101

4-25. Determine the magnitude and direction of the resultant couple moment acting on the pipe assembly. The 60-lb forces lie in the horizontal plane.

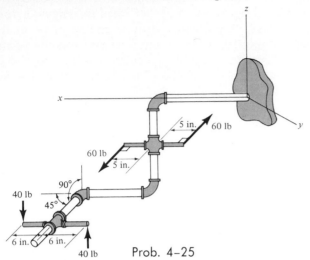

Prob. 4-25

4-26. If the resultant couple moment of the three couples acting on the triangular block is zero, determine the magnitude of forces **F** and **P**.

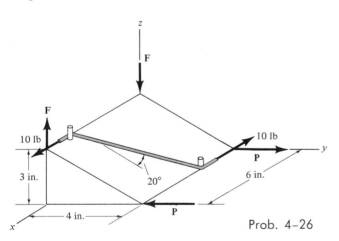

Prob. 4-26

4-27. The cord passing over the two small pegs A and B of the board is subjected to a tension of 10 lb. Determine the *minimum* tension **P** and the direction α of the cord passing over the pegs C and D, so that the resultant couple moment produced by the two cords is 20 lb-in., acting clockwise.

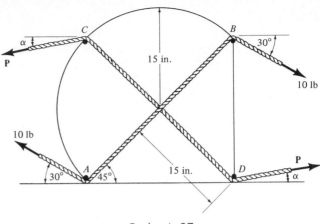

Prob. 4-27

4-28. If the resultant of the two couples acting on the fire hydrant is $\mathbf{M}_R = \{-32\mathbf{i} + 20\mathbf{j}\}$ lb-ft, determine the magnitude of the applied force **P**.

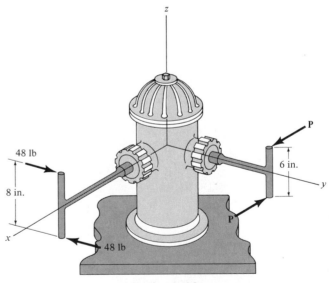

Prob. 4-28

4-29. A 40 lb-ft couple moment is developed by the electric motor. Determine the reactive forces caused by this couple at the supports A and B. Neglect the weight of the motor, and assume that the supports at A and B transmit only vertical forces.

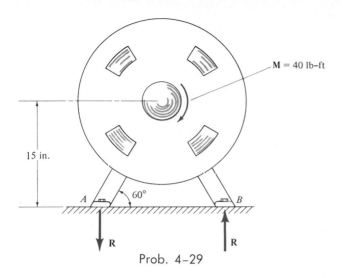

M = 40 lb-ft

15 in.

A   60°   B

R   R

Prob. 4–29

4-31. The wheel is subjected to a force of 10 lb and a couple moment of 6 lb-in. Determine an equivalent system of a force and a couple moment acting at point A; repeat for point B.

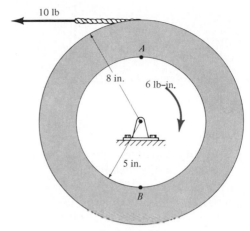

10 lb

A

8 in.   6 lb-in.

5 in.

B

Prob. 4–31

4-30. Replace the 100-lb vertical load acting on the bracket by a force and a couple moment at point P; then distribute the moment into a couple having a pair of horizontal forces acting along the axis of the rivets at A and B.

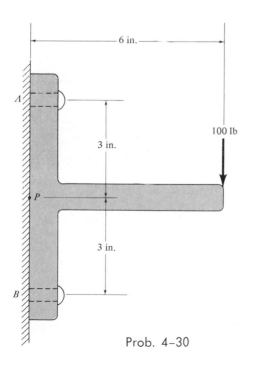

6 in.

A

3 in.

100 lb

P

3 in.

B

Prob. 4–30

4-32. Replace the force and couple-moment system acting on the rigid frame by an equivalent force and couple-moment system acting at point O.

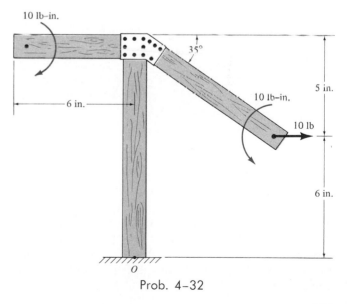

10 lb-in.

35°

6 in.

10 lb-in.

5 in.

10 lb

6 in.

O

Prob. 4–32

103

4-33. Replace the force and couple-moment system acting at the end of the beam by an equivalent system acting at point A.

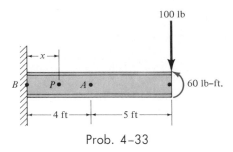

100 lb

B P A 60 lb-ft.

4 ft 5 ft

Prob. 4-33

4-34. Replace the force and couple-moment system acting at the end of the beam in Prob. 4-33 by an equivalent system at point B. Then replace this loading by a single resultant force. Determine the location, x, of point P where the line of action of the force intersects the axis of the beam.

4-35. Replace the couple moment and force acting on the welded pipe section by an equivalent force and couple-moment system acting at point O.

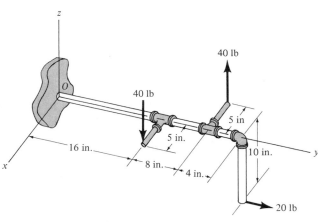

40 lb

40 lb

5 in

16 in.

5 in.

8 in.

4 in.

10 in.

y

x

z

O

20 lb

Prob. 4-35

4-36. A force of 100 lb acts at the end of the beam. Replace this force by an equivalent force and couple-moment system at (a) point A; (b) at point O. Determine the magnitude and direction of the resultant couple vector in each case.

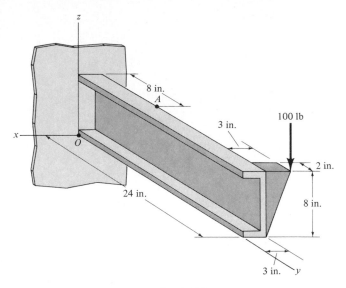

z

8 in.
A

3 in.

100 lb

2 in.

x

O

24 in.

8 in.

3 in. y

Prob. 4-36

4-37. Replace the 200-lb force acting at the end of the beam by an equivalent force and couple-moment system at point O.

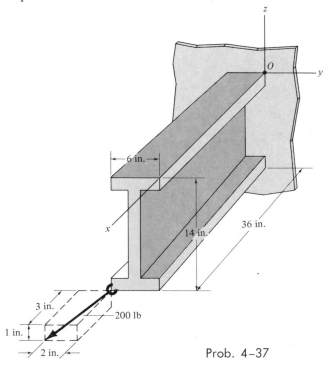

z

O y

6 in.

14 in.

36 in.

x

3 in.

1 in.

2 in.

200 lb

Prob. 4-37

104

4-38. Replace the two forces and couple moment by an equivalent force and couple-moment system acting at point O.

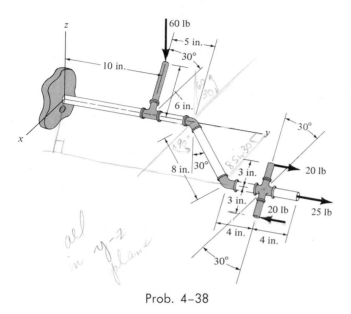

Prob. 4-38

4-39. Replace the loading acting on the cantilever shaft by an equivalent force and couple-moment system acting at point O.

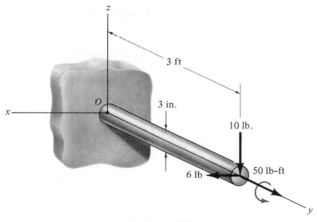

Prob. 4-39

4-40. Replace the system of three forces shown acting on the beam cross section by an equivalent force and couple-moment system acting at point A.

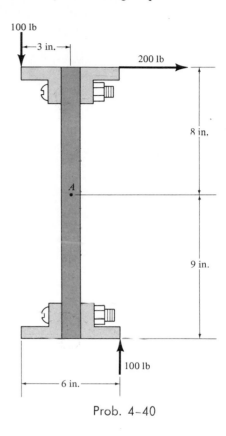

Prob. 4-40

105

4–8. Dot or Scalar Product

The *dot product* of two vectors **A** and **B**, written **A** · **B** (read **A** dot **B**), is defined as the product of the magnitude of vectors **A** and **B** and the cosine of the angle between them. Expressed in equation form,

$$\mathbf{A} \cdot \mathbf{B} = AB \cos \theta \qquad (4\text{--}10)$$

where $0° \leq \theta \leq 180°$. The dot product is often referred to as the *scalar product* of vectors since, unlike the cross product, the result is a *scalar* and not a vector. If the resultant of the dot product **A** · **B** is *zero* (provided vectors **A** and **B** are not null vectors), then **A** must be *perpendicular* to **B**. This follows from the definition of the dot product given by Eq. 4–10, i.e., $AB \cos \theta = 0$. Thus $\cos \theta = 0$, or $\theta = 90°$, so that **A** is perpendicular to **B**.

Three important laws of operation which are valid for the dot product are:

1. Commutative law:

$$\mathbf{A} \cdot \mathbf{B} = \mathbf{B} \cdot \mathbf{A} \qquad (4\text{--}11)$$

2. Multiplication by a scalar:

$$m(\mathbf{A} \cdot \mathbf{B}) = (m\mathbf{A}) \cdot \mathbf{B} = \mathbf{A} \cdot (m\mathbf{B}) = (\mathbf{A} \cdot \mathbf{B})m \qquad (4\text{--}12)$$

3. Distributive law:

$$\mathbf{A} \cdot (\mathbf{B} + \mathbf{D}) = (\mathbf{A} \cdot \mathbf{B}) + (\mathbf{A} \cdot \mathbf{D}) \qquad (4\text{--}13)$$

Equations 4–11 and 4–12 can be easily proven by using the definition of the dot product, Eq. 4–10. The proof of Eq. 4–13 is left as an exercise for the reader (see Prob. 4–42).

Equation 4–10 may be used to find the dot product of each of the Cartesian component unit vectors. For example,

$$\mathbf{i} \cdot \mathbf{i} = (1)(1) \cos 0° = 1$$

In a similar manner,

$$
\begin{array}{ccc}
\mathbf{i} \cdot \mathbf{i} = 1 & \mathbf{i} \cdot \mathbf{j} = 0 & \mathbf{i} \cdot \mathbf{k} = 0 \\
\mathbf{j} \cdot \mathbf{j} = 1 & \mathbf{j} \cdot \mathbf{k} = 0 & \mathbf{j} \cdot \mathbf{i} = 0 \\
\mathbf{k} \cdot \mathbf{k} = 1 & \mathbf{k} \cdot \mathbf{i} = 0 & \mathbf{k} \cdot \mathbf{j} = 0
\end{array}
\qquad (4\text{--}14)
$$

You should not memorize these results; rather, you should understand clearly how each is derived using Eq. 4–10.

The above results can be used to determine the dot product of two vectors **A** and **B** when these vectors are written in Cartesian component form. If

$$\mathbf{A} = A_x\mathbf{i} + A_y\mathbf{j} + A_z\mathbf{k}$$

and

$$\mathbf{B} = B_x\mathbf{i} + B_y\mathbf{j} + B_z\mathbf{k}$$

then

$$\mathbf{A} \cdot \mathbf{B} = (A_x\mathbf{i} + A_y\mathbf{j} + A_z\mathbf{k}) \cdot (B_x\mathbf{i} + B_y\mathbf{j} + B_z\mathbf{k})$$

Using the scalar and distributive laws of operation, Eqs. 4–12 and 4–13, we have

$$\mathbf{A} \cdot \mathbf{B} = A_xB_x(\mathbf{i} \cdot \mathbf{i}) + A_xB_y(\mathbf{i} \cdot \mathbf{j}) + A_xB_z(\mathbf{i} \cdot \mathbf{k})$$
$$+ A_yB_x(\mathbf{j} \cdot \mathbf{i}) + A_yB_y(\mathbf{j} \cdot \mathbf{j}) + A_yB_z(\mathbf{j} \cdot \mathbf{k})$$
$$+ A_zB_x(\mathbf{k} \cdot \mathbf{i}) + A_zB_y(\mathbf{k} \cdot \mathbf{j}) + A_zB_z(\mathbf{k} \cdot \mathbf{k})$$

In accordance with Eqs. 4–14, the final result becomes

$$\mathbf{A} \cdot \mathbf{B} = A_xB_x + A_yB_y + A_zB_z \tag{4–15}$$

Thus, to determine the dot product of two vectors, multiply the corresponding x, y, and z components together and sum their products.

The dot product may be applied to determine the *angle formed between two vectors*. This angle may be determined by solving for θ in Eq. 4–10,

$$\theta = \cos^{-1}\frac{\mathbf{A} \cdot \mathbf{B}}{AB}, \ 0 \le \theta \le \pi$$

The dot product may also be used to find the *projected magnitude of a vector in a given direction*. For example, the magnitude of the projection of vector $\mathbf{A}$ in the direction of $\mathbf{B}$, as shown in Fig. 4–26 is defined by $A \cos \theta$, where θ is the angle formed between vectors $\mathbf{A}$ and $\mathbf{B}$. Using Eq. 4–10, this magnitude may be expressed as

$$A \cos \theta = \frac{1}{B}(\mathbf{A} \cdot \mathbf{B})$$

or

$$A \cos \theta = \mathbf{A} \cdot \frac{\mathbf{B}}{B} = \mathbf{A} \cdot \mathbf{u}_B$$

Here $\mathbf{u}_B$ is a unit vector acting in the direction of $\mathbf{B}$, Fig. 4–26.

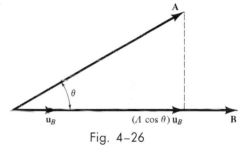

Fig. 4–26

4–9. Moment of a Force About a Specified Axis

A useful application of the dot product, in statics, consists of finding the projection of a moment vector along a given axis. As an example, let us consider what effect the force $\mathbf{F}$, acting at the end of the socket

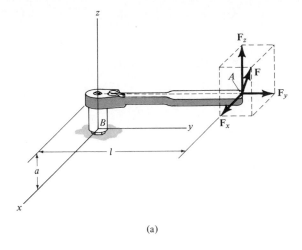

(a)

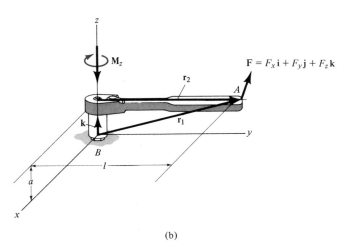

(b)

Fig. 4–27

wrench shown in Fig. 4–27*a*, has on turning the bolt *B*. The effective action of **F** in this regard depends upon the *moment* which **F** creates about the *z* axis (since a rotation about this axis will cause the bolt to turn). Separating **F** into its rectangular components $\mathbf{F}_x$, $\mathbf{F}_y$, and $\mathbf{F}_z$, as shown in Fig. 4–27*a*, it is seen that *only* component $\mathbf{F}_x$ causes a rotation of the wrench about the *z* axis. (Since the line of action of $\mathbf{F}_y$ passes through a point lying on the *z* axis and the line of action of $\mathbf{F}_z$ is parallel to the *z* axis both of these forces create zero moment about the *z* axis.) The moment created by the force component $\mathbf{F}_x$ has a magnitude $M_z = F_x l$ and a direction defined by the right-hand rule, that is, in the $-\mathbf{k}$ direction. Thus, $\mathbf{M}_z = -F_x l\mathbf{k}.$

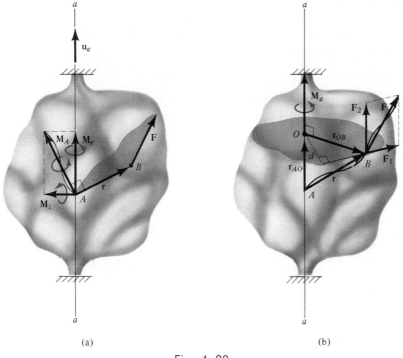

(a)   (b)

Fig. 4-28

The problem of determining the moment component of a force along a given axis may be greatly simplified by using vector analysis. Consider the rigid body, shown in Fig. 4–28a, which is subjected to a force **F**. This force imparts a tendency for rotation of the body about the fixed *aa* axis (provided, of course, the line of action of **F** does not intersect *aa*). If **r** represents a vector which is directed from the arbitrary point *A lying on the axis* to *any point B*, lying on the line of action of force **F**, then the moment produced by **F** about point *A* is

$$\mathbf{M}_A = \mathbf{r} \times \mathbf{F}$$

In accordance with the definition of the cross product, the direction of $\mathbf{M}_A$ is perpendicular to the shaded plane containing vectors **r** and **F**, as shown in Fig. 4–28a.

The vector $\mathbf{M}_A$ can be separated into two rectangular *components,* $\mathbf{M}_a$ and $\mathbf{M}_\perp$, acting parallel and perpendicular to the *aa* axis, as shown in Fig. 4–28a. In particular, the magnitude of $\mathbf{M}_a$ represents the *projection* of $\mathbf{M}_A$ onto the *aa* axis and can be found using the dot product, as discussed in Sec. 4–8. Hence,

dot product is commutative

$$M_a = \mathbf{u}_a \cdot \mathbf{M}_A = \bar{M}_A \cdot \bar{u}_a$$

where $\mathbf{u}_a$ is a unit vector defining the *direction* of the *aa* axis. Combining the last two equations yields

$$M_a = \mathbf{u}_a \cdot (\mathbf{r} \times \mathbf{F}) \qquad (4\text{--}16)$$

In vector algebra, this combination of dot and cross products, yielding the scalar M_a, is termed the *mixed triple product*. Knowing the Cartesian components of each of the vectors, the mixed triple product may be written in determinant form as

$$M_a = (u_{a_x}\mathbf{i} + u_{a_y}\mathbf{j} + u_{a_z}\mathbf{k}) \cdot \begin{vmatrix} \mathbf{i} & \mathbf{j} & \mathbf{k} \\ r_x & r_y & r_z \\ F_x & F_y & F_z \end{vmatrix}$$

or simply

$$M_a = \mathbf{u}_a \cdot (\mathbf{r} \times \mathbf{F}) = \begin{vmatrix} u_{a_x} & u_{a_y} & u_{a_z} \\ r_x & r_y & r_z \\ F_x & F_y & F_z \end{vmatrix} \qquad (4\text{--}17)$$

Here u_{a_x}, u_{a_y}, and u_{a_z} represent the Cartesian components of the unit vector defining the direction of the *aa* axis; r_x, r_y, and r_z represent the Cartesian components of the position vector drawn from *any point* on the *aa* axis to *any point* on the line of action of the force; and F_x, F_y, and F_z represent the Cartesian components of the force vector.

The fact that $\mathbf{M}_a$ represents the tendency created by force $\mathbf{F}$ for rotating the body about the *aa* axis can be shown with reference to Fig. 4–28*b*. The shaded plane is perpendicular to the *aa* axis and intersects this axis at point *O*. Both the position vector $\mathbf{r}$ and the force $\mathbf{F}$ are resolved into two components which lie in and perpendicular to this plane. The perpendicular component of force, $\mathbf{F}_2$, does not contribute a moment about the *aa* axis, since this force is parallel to the axis. $\mathbf{M}_a$ results only from the action of $\mathbf{F}_1$, which lies at a perpendicular distance *d* from the axis. Thus, the magnitude of $\mathbf{M}_a$ is $M_a = F_1 d = |\mathbf{r}_{OB} \times \mathbf{F}_1| = \mathbf{u}_a \cdot (\mathbf{r} \times \mathbf{F})$.

The socket-wrench problem discussed earlier may be solved using Eq. 4–17. As shown in Fig. 4–27*b*, the axis of rotation is defined by the unit vector $\mathbf{u}_a = \mathbf{k}$. Both vectors $\mathbf{r}_1 = l\mathbf{j} + a\mathbf{k}$ and $\mathbf{r}_2 = l\mathbf{j}$ satisfy the requirements for $\mathbf{r}$, defined in Eq. 4–17. Why? Hence,

$$M_z = \mathbf{u}_a \cdot (\mathbf{r}_1 \times \mathbf{F}) = \begin{vmatrix} 0 & 0 & 1 \\ 0 & l & a \\ F_x & F_y & F_z \end{vmatrix} = -lF_x$$

or

$$M_z = \mathbf{u}_a \cdot (\mathbf{r}_2 \times \mathbf{F}) = \begin{vmatrix} 0 & 0 & 1 \\ 0 & l & 0 \\ F_x & F_y & F_z \end{vmatrix} = -lF_x$$

Since both the magnitude and direction of $\mathbf{M}_z$ are known, $\mathbf{M}_z$ may be written in vector form as

$$\mathbf{M}_z = M_z(-\mathbf{k}) = -F_x l\mathbf{k}$$

4–10. Reduction of a Force and Couple System

For purposes of simplification, it is possible to reduce a system of forces and couple-moment vectors acting on a rigid body to a *single* resultant force acting at an arbitrary point and a *single* resultant moment. Consider, for example, the rigid body subjected to the system of force and couple moment vectors shown in Fig. 4–29a. To simplify this loading system, each vector is transferred to some *arbitrary point O* on the body. The couple moments $\mathbf{M}$ and $\mathbf{M}'$ are free vectors; hence they may be applied

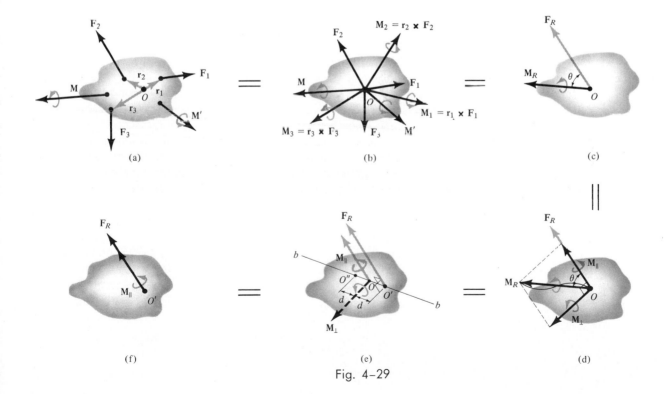

Fig. 4–29

directly at point O, as shown in Fig. 4–29*b*. The forces $\mathbf{F}_1$, $\mathbf{F}_2$, and $\mathbf{F}_3$ are sliding vectors, and since point O does *not* lie along the line of action of any of these forces, each force must be replaced at point O in accordance with the procedure outlined in Sec. 4–7. For example, when vector $\mathbf{F}_1$ is applied to point O, a corresponding couple-moment vector $\mathbf{M}_1 = \mathbf{r}_1 \times \mathbf{F}_1$ must be *applied* to the body. The *equivalent* system of force and moment vectors applied at point O is shown in Fig. 4–29*b*. Using the laws of vector addition, we may sum this concurrent system of vectors to a single resultant force and resultant moment.

$$\mathbf{F}_R = \Sigma\mathbf{F} = \mathbf{F}_1 + \mathbf{F}_2 + \mathbf{F}_3$$
$$\mathbf{M}_R = \Sigma\mathbf{M}_o = \mathbf{M} + \mathbf{M}' + (\mathbf{r}_1 \times \mathbf{F}_1) + (\mathbf{r}_2 \times \mathbf{F}_2) + (\mathbf{r}_3 \times \mathbf{F}_3)$$

The results are shown in Fig. 4–29*c*. Note that if the force and couple-moment system in Fig. 4–29*a* was replaced at some other reference point, other than O, one would obtain the *same* force resultant $\mathbf{F}_R$ but a *different* resultant moment $\mathbf{M}_R$. The force resultant is simply the sum of all the force vectors of the system, whereas the moment resultant depends upon the location of the reference point.

It was discussed in Sec. 4–7 that if $\mathbf{F}_R$ is *perpendicular* to $\mathbf{M}_R$, the system of a force and a moment may be reduced to a *single force* acting through some unique point. Provided $\mathbf{F}_R$ and $\mathbf{M}_R$ are not null vectors, perpendicularity is guaranteed if

$$\mathbf{F}_R \cdot \mathbf{M}_R = 0 \qquad\qquad (4\text{–}18)$$

A procedure for eliminating the moment vector in this case follows the steps outlined in Fig. 4–21, going from Fig. 4–21*d* to Fig. 4–21*a*; or in Fig. 4–22, going from Fig. 4–22*d* to Fig. 4–22*a*. In particular, if a force system is *coplanar* or all the forces act *parallel* to one another, the system of forces can always be resolved into a single resultant force. In *both* these cases, if the force systems are reduced to a single resultant force and moment acting at some *arbitrary point* on the body, the moment vector will *always* be perpendicular to the force and, therefore, one can always locate the force at some unique point in order to eliminate the moment vector. These two specific cases involving coplanar and parallel force systems are discussed further in Examples 4–10 and 4–11.

For the general case, the resultant force $\mathbf{F}_R$ will not be perpendicular to the moment $\mathbf{M}_R$, Fig. 4–29*c*. As shown in Fig. 4–29*d*, however, $\mathbf{M}_R$ may be resolved into two components; one perpendicular, $\mathbf{M}_\perp$, and the other parallel, $\mathbf{M}_\parallel$, to the line of action of the force resultant $\mathbf{F}_R$. The magnitude of component $\mathbf{M}_\parallel$ may be found using the dot product:

$$M_\parallel = M_R \cos\theta = \frac{\mathbf{F}_R}{F_R} \cdot \mathbf{M}_R = \mathbf{u}_R \cdot \mathbf{M}_R$$

Here $\mathbf{u}_R$ denotes a unit vector in the direction of $\mathbf{F}_R$. In vector notation,

$$\mathbf{M}_\parallel = M_\parallel \mathbf{u}_R$$

Since the component $\mathbf{M}_\perp$ is *perpendicular* to $\mathbf{F}_R$, $\mathbf{M}_\perp$ may be *eliminated* by *moving* $\mathbf{F}_R$ to point O', as shown in Fig. 4–29e. Why? The point O' lies along the line segment bb at a distance d from point O. Because bb is perpendicular to both $\mathbf{M}_\perp$ and $\mathbf{F}_R$, then

$$M_\perp = F_R d$$

or

$$d = \frac{M_\perp}{F_R}$$

It should be clearly understood that $\mathbf{F}_R$ must be located at point O' and *not* O'', as shown in Fig. 4–29e. If $\mathbf{F}_R$ is applied at point O', the moment of $\mathbf{F}_R$ tending to cause rotation of the body *about* point O is in the *same* direction as $\mathbf{M}_\perp$ (shown dashed in the figure).

The resulting force $\mathbf{F}_R$ and *collinear* moment $\mathbf{M}_\parallel$, Fig. 4–29f, is called a *wrench*. The *axis of the wrench* has the same line of action as the force. The wrench tends to cause both a translation along and a rotation about this axis. Comparing Fig. 4–29a with Fig. 4–29f, it is therefore possible to simplify a general system of force and couple-moment vectors, acting on a rigid body, to a wrench. The axis of the wrench and a point through which this axis passes is unique and can always be determined.

Example 4-8

Given the two position vectors

$$\mathbf{r}_1 = \{3\mathbf{i} + 2\mathbf{j} - 4\mathbf{k}\} \text{ ft and } \mathbf{r}_2 = \{-1\mathbf{i} + 3\mathbf{j} + 5\mathbf{k}\} \text{ ft.}$$

Determine (a) the angle θ formed between the two vectors $\mathbf{r}_1$ and $\mathbf{r} = \mathbf{r}_2 - \mathbf{r}_1$, and (b) the angle β which $\mathbf{r}_2$ makes with the y axis.

Solution
Part (a). Vectors $\mathbf{r}_1$ and $\mathbf{r}_2$ are represented graphically in Fig. 4–30a. (Note that $\mathbf{r}_1 + \mathbf{r} = \mathbf{r}_2$, so that $\mathbf{r} = \mathbf{r}_2 - \mathbf{r}_1$.) θ is defined as the angle formed between the *tails* of vectors $\mathbf{r}_1$ and $\mathbf{r}$ ($0° < \theta < 180°$). This angle can be determined using the dot product of vectors $\mathbf{r}_1$ and $\mathbf{r}$. Computing the required quantities,

$$\mathbf{r} = \mathbf{r}_2 - \mathbf{r}_1 = \{-4\mathbf{i} + 1\mathbf{j} + 9\mathbf{k}\} \text{ ft}$$
$$r = \sqrt{(-4)^2 + (1)^2 + (9)^2} = 9.90 \text{ ft}$$
$$r_1 = \sqrt{(3)^2 + (2)^2 + (-4)^2} = 5.39 \text{ ft}$$

Using Eq. 4–15, we write

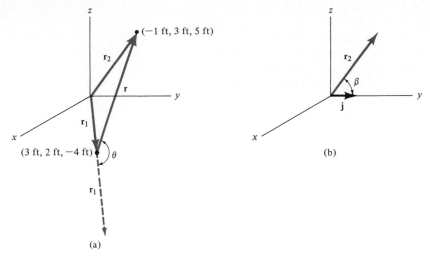

Fig. 4–30

$$\mathbf{r} \cdot \mathbf{r}_1 = (-4\mathbf{i} + 1\mathbf{j} + 9\mathbf{k}) \cdot (3\mathbf{i} + 2\mathbf{j} - 4\mathbf{k})$$
$$= -4(3) + 1(2) + 9(-4) = -46 \text{ ft}^2$$

Thus, by definition of the dot product

$$\mathbf{r} \cdot \mathbf{r}_1 = rr_1 \cos \theta$$

or

$$\theta = \cos^{-1}\frac{\mathbf{r} \cdot \mathbf{r}_1}{rr_1} = \cos^{-1}\frac{-46}{9.90(5.39)}$$
$$= \cos^{-1}(-0.862) = 149.6° \qquad \qquad Ans.$$

Part (b).   The required angle β is shown in Fig. 4–30*b*. The direction of the *y* axis is represented by the **j** unit vector. Since,

$$\mathbf{r}_2 = \{-1\mathbf{i} + 3\mathbf{j} + 5\mathbf{k}\} \text{ ft}, \; r_2 = \sqrt{(-1)^2 + (3)^2 + (5)^2} = 5.92 \text{ ft}$$
$$\mathbf{r}_2 \cdot \mathbf{j} = (-1\mathbf{i} + 3\mathbf{j} + 5\mathbf{k}) \cdot (\mathbf{j}) = -1(0) + 3(1) + 5(0) = 3 \text{ ft}$$

Then,

$$\mathbf{r}_2 \cdot \mathbf{j} = r_2 j \cos \beta$$

or

$$\beta = \cos^{-1}\frac{\mathbf{r}_2 \cdot \mathbf{j}}{(r_2)(j)} = \cos^{-1}\frac{3 \text{ ft}}{(5.92 \text{ ft})(1)}$$
$$= \cos^{-1}(0.507) = 59.5° \qquad \qquad Ans.$$

We can obtain this same result by determining the *direction cosine* of $\mathbf{r}_2$ using the unit vector $\mathbf{u}_2$ acting in the direction of $\mathbf{r}_2$.

$$\mathbf{u}_2 = \frac{\mathbf{r}_2}{r_2} = -\frac{1}{\sqrt{35}}\mathbf{i} + \frac{3}{\sqrt{35}}\mathbf{j} + \frac{5}{\sqrt{35}}\mathbf{k} = -0.169\mathbf{i} + 0.507\mathbf{j} + 0.845\mathbf{k}$$

Hence, from the $\mathbf{j}$ component of this vector,

$$\cos \beta = 0.507$$
$$\beta = \cos^{-1}(0.507) = 59.5° \qquad\qquad Ans.$$

Example 4-9

Find the projections of the force vector $\mathbf{F} = \{40\mathbf{i} + 30\mathbf{j}\}$ lb in the direction of the position vectors $\mathbf{r}_1 = \{2\mathbf{j} + 4\mathbf{k}\}$ ft and $\mathbf{r}_2 = \{1\mathbf{i} + 5\mathbf{j} + 2\mathbf{k}\}$ ft, shown in Fig. 4–31a.

Solution

The projection of a vector in a given direction can be determined using the dot product. The unit vectors in Fig. 4–31a, which define the directions of $\mathbf{r}_1$ and $\mathbf{r}_2$, are

$$\mathbf{u}_1 = \frac{\mathbf{r}_1}{r_1} = \frac{2\mathbf{j} + 4\mathbf{k}}{\sqrt{20}} = 0.447\mathbf{j} + 0.894\mathbf{k}$$

$$\mathbf{u}_2 = \frac{\mathbf{r}_2}{r_2} = \frac{1\mathbf{i} + 5\mathbf{j} + 2\mathbf{k}}{\sqrt{30}} = 0.183\mathbf{i} + 0.913\mathbf{j} + 0.365\mathbf{k}$$

These unit vectors, along with the force vector $\mathbf{F}$, are shown in Figs. 4–31b and 4–31c. It is assumed that $\mathbf{F}$ makes an angle of ψ with $\mathbf{u}_1$ and ϕ with $\mathbf{u}_2$. If we consider the x', y', and z' axes to be measured in units of pounds, the *magnitude* of each projected vector becomes

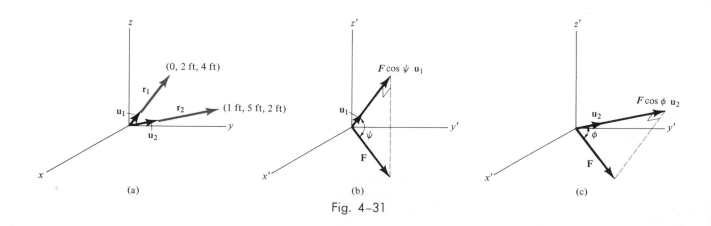

Fig. 4–31

$$\overset{\smile}{\qquad}(\overline{F} \cdot \overline{u}_1)\,\overline{u}_1$$

$$F \cos \psi = \mathbf{F} \cdot \mathbf{u}_1 = (40\mathbf{i} + 30\mathbf{j}) \cdot (0.447\mathbf{j} + 0.894\mathbf{k})$$
$$= 40(0) + 30(.447) + 0(.894) = 13.41 \text{ lb}$$

$$F \cos \phi = \mathbf{F} \cdot \mathbf{u}_2 = (40\mathbf{i} + 30\mathbf{j}) \cdot (0.183\mathbf{i} + 0.913\mathbf{j} + 0.365\mathbf{k})$$
$$= 40(0.183) + 30(0.913) + 0(0.365) = 34.71 \text{ lb}$$

Hence, the projected *vectors* are

$$\mathbf{F} \cos \psi = (F \cos \psi)\mathbf{u}_1 = (13.41 \text{ lb})(0.447\mathbf{j} + 0.894\mathbf{k})$$
$$= \{6.00\mathbf{j} + 12.00\mathbf{k}\} \text{ lb} \qquad\qquad Ans.$$

$$\mathbf{F} \cos \phi = (F \cos \phi)\mathbf{u}_2 = (34.7 \text{ lb})(0.183\mathbf{i} + 0.913\mathbf{j} + 0.365\mathbf{k})$$
$$= \{6.35\mathbf{i} + 31.70\mathbf{j} + 12.67\mathbf{k}\} \text{ lb} \qquad\qquad Ans.$$

The results are shown in Figs. 4–31*b* and 4–31*c*.

Example 4–10

The beam *AE* in Fig. 4–32*a* is subjected to a series of concentrated loads acting along its length. Determine the magnitude, the direction, and the location of a single resultant force which is equivalent to the given system of forces.

Solution I

The force system can be reduced to a single resultant force and couple moment acting at point *E* (or any other arbitrary point along the axis of the beam). Position vectors, shown in Fig. 4–32*b*, are drawn *from* point *E* to *any point* lying on the line of action of each of the forces. Each force **F** is then moved to point *E*, and a moment $\mathbf{M}_E = \Sigma \mathbf{r} \times \mathbf{F}$ must be *added* to the beam. Why? The resultant force and resultant moment acting at point *E* is therefore

$$\mathbf{F}_R = \mathbf{F}_1 + \mathbf{F}_2 + \mathbf{F}_3$$
$$= (50 \cos 60°\mathbf{i} - 50 \sin 60°\mathbf{j}) + 20\mathbf{j} + 10\mathbf{i}$$

or

$$\mathbf{F}_R = \{35.0\mathbf{i} - 23.3\mathbf{j}\} \text{ lb}$$

and

$$i \times j = \uparrow k$$

$$\mathbf{M}_E = (\mathbf{r}_{EB} \times \mathbf{F}_1) + (\mathbf{r}_{EC} \times \mathbf{F}_2) + (\mathbf{r}_{ED} \times \mathbf{F}_3)$$
$$= -8\mathbf{i} \times (50 \cos 60°\mathbf{i} - 50 \sin 60°\mathbf{j}) + (-5\mathbf{i}) \times 20\mathbf{j}$$
$$\qquad\qquad\qquad\qquad + (-3\mathbf{i} + \mathbf{j}) \times 10\mathbf{i}$$

$$0$$

or

$$j \times i = -k$$

$$\mathbf{M}_E = \{236.4\mathbf{k}\} \text{ lb-ft}$$

These results are shown in Fig. 4–32*c*.

Since the force system, Fig. 4–32*a*, is *coplanar*, $\mathbf{F}_R$ is *perpendicular to* $\mathbf{M}_E$, i.e., $\mathbf{M}_E \cdot \mathbf{F}_R = 0$. Thus, the resultant force $\mathbf{F}_R$ can be located at a

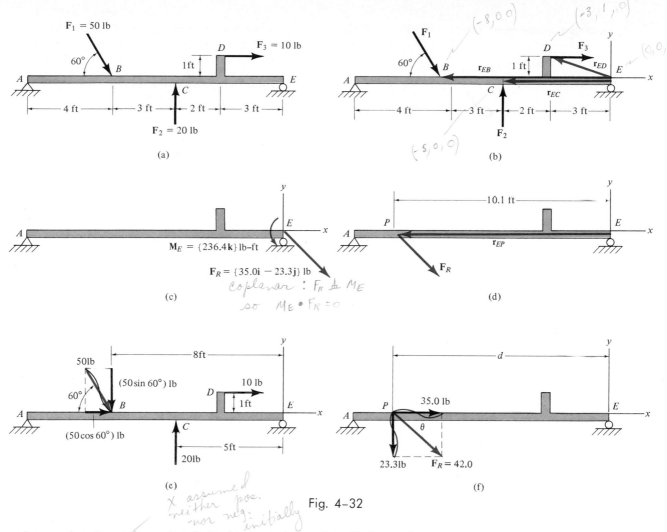

(a)

(b)

(c)

(d)

(e)

(f)

Fig. 4-32

unique point P on the axis of the beam and thereby eliminate the moment. If $\mathbf{r}_{EP} = x\mathbf{i}$ denotes a position vector drawn *from* point E *to* point P, it is necessary that

$$\mathbf{M}_E = \mathbf{r}_{EP} \times \mathbf{F}_R$$
$$236.4\mathbf{k} = x\mathbf{i} \times (35.0\mathbf{i} - 23.3\mathbf{j}) \qquad (1)$$

or

$$236.4 = -23.3x$$

Hence,

$$x = -\frac{236.4}{23.3} = -10.1 \text{ ft} \qquad \textit{Ans.}$$

The negative sign indicates that $\mathbf{F}_R$ must be placed 10.1 ft to the *left* of

117

point E, as shown in Fig. 4–32d. The required (counterclockwise) moment $\mathbf{M}_E$ will then be produced when $\mathbf{F}_R$ is moved from point P to point E.*
  The magnitude of $\mathbf{F}_R$ is

$$F_R = \sqrt{(35.0)^2 + (-23.3)^2} = 42.0 \text{ lb} \qquad \textit{Ans.}$$

Measuring θ from *below* the x axis, we have

$$\theta = \tan^{-1}\frac{23.3}{35.0} = 33.6° \qquad \text{\textit{FR}} \qquad \textit{Ans.}$$

Solution II

Since the problem involves a coplanar force system, the solution is facilitated using a semi-scalar approach. For convenience, the 50-lb force acting at B is separated into its two rectangular components as shown in Fig. 4–32e. The resultant force, acting on the beam, is the vector sum of all the forces acting on the beam. Thus,

$$\mathbf{F}_R = 50 \cos 60°\mathbf{i} - 50 \sin 60°\mathbf{j} + 20\mathbf{j} - 10\mathbf{i}$$

or

$$\mathbf{F}_R = \{35.0\mathbf{i} - 23.3\mathbf{j}\} \text{ lb}$$

So that

$$F_R = \sqrt{(35.0)^2 + (-23.3)^2} = 42.0 \text{ lb}$$

and

$$\theta = \tan^{-1}\frac{23.3}{35.0} = 33.6° \qquad \text{\textit{FR}}$$

The resultant force $\mathbf{F}_R$ is shown acting on the beam in Fig. 4–32f.
  The location of the force along the axis of the beam, P, can be determined by realizing that the moment of the *force resultant* $\mathbf{F}_R$ about point E, $(\mathbf{M}_R)_E$, must be equivalent to the moment of *all the forces* shown in Fig. 4–32e about point $E(\Sigma\mathbf{M}_E)$. (The 35-lb component of $\mathbf{F}_R$ does not create a moment about point E. Why?) Hence, assuming moments are positive counterclockwise, i.e., $+\mathbf{k}$ direction, we have

$$\zeta+ \qquad\qquad (\mathbf{M}_R)_E = \Sigma\mathbf{M}_E$$

$$d(23.3 \text{ lb}) + 0(35.0 \text{ lb}) = (8 \text{ ft})(50 \sin 60° \text{ lb}) - (5 \text{ ft})(20 \text{ lb}) - (1 \text{ ft})(10 \text{ lb})$$
Thus,

$$d = 10.1 \text{ ft} \qquad \textit{Ans.}$$

---

*Except for purposes of explanation, as stated here, it is not strictly necessary to replace all the forces at point E. Essentially what is required is to realize that the *moment of all the forces* in Fig. 4–32b must be *equivalent* to the *moment produced by the force resultant* $\mathbf{F}_R$ acting at P, Fig. 4–32d. In this way Eq. (1) can be written *directly* without the intermediate step which involves Fig. 4–32c. See Solution II.

Since d is a positive quantity, $\mathbf{F}_R$ acts 10.1 ft to the *left* of E as shown in Fig. 4–32*f*.

Example 4–11

The slab in Fig. 4–33*a* is subjected to a series of five parallel forces. Determine the magnitude and direction of a single resultant force equivalent to the given force system, and locate its point of application on the slab.

Solution

Since the force system is represented in three dimensions, a vector approach will be used for the solution. The resultant of the force system is the sum of all the forces, that is,

$$\mathbf{F}_R = \Sigma\mathbf{F} = -600\mathbf{k} + 100\mathbf{k} - 300\mathbf{k} - 400\mathbf{k} - 500\mathbf{k}$$

or

$$\mathbf{F}_R = \{-1{,}700\mathbf{k}\}\ \text{lb}$$

The moment $\mathbf{M}_O$ created by the force system about the origin O can be obtained by means of the position vectors shown in Fig. 4–33*b*. Each position vector is drawn from O to a point on the line of action of each force. Thus,

$$\mathbf{M}_O = \Sigma\mathbf{r}\times\mathbf{F} = [\mathbf{r}_{OA}\times(-600\mathbf{k})] + [\mathbf{r}_{OB}\times 100\mathbf{k}] + [\mathbf{r}_{OC}\times(-300\mathbf{k})]$$
$$+ [\mathbf{r}_{OD}\times(-400\mathbf{k})]$$

or

$$\mathbf{M}_O = [8\mathbf{i}\times(-600\mathbf{k})] + [(6\mathbf{i}+5\mathbf{j})\times 100\mathbf{k}] + [(2\mathbf{i}+5\mathbf{j})\times(-300\mathbf{k})]$$
$$+ [10\mathbf{j}\times(-400\mathbf{k})]$$
$$= \{-5{,}000\mathbf{i} + 4{,}800\mathbf{j}\}\ \text{lb-ft} \tag{1}$$

$A = (8, 0, 0)$

$B = (6, 5, 0)$

$C = (2, 5, 0)$

$D = (0, 10, 0)$

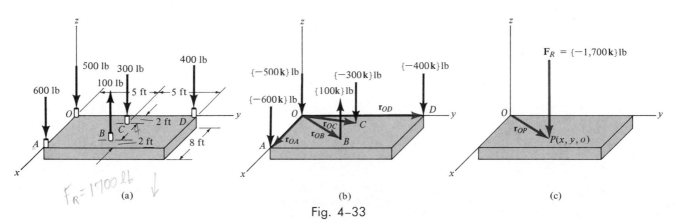

$F_R = 1700\ lb$

(a)   (b)   (c)

Fig. 4–33

Since all the force vectors are *parallel* to one another, $\mathbf{F}_R$ is perpendicular to $\mathbf{M}_O$, i.e., $\mathbf{F}_R \cdot \mathbf{M}_O = 0$. Therefore, the resultant force $\mathbf{F}_R$ can be placed at a unique point $P(x, y, 0)$ on the slab and produce the equivalent moment $\mathbf{M}_O$. If $\mathbf{r}_{OP} = x\mathbf{i} + y\mathbf{j}$ denotes a position vector acting from the origin to point P on the surface of the slab, Fig. 4–33c, then

$$\mathbf{M}_O = \mathbf{r}_{OP} \times \mathbf{F}_R = \begin{vmatrix} \mathbf{i} & \mathbf{j} & \mathbf{k} \\ x & y & 0 \\ 0 & 0 & -1{,}700 \end{vmatrix} = \{-1{,}700y\mathbf{i} + 1{,}700x\mathbf{j}\} \text{ lb-ft} \quad (2)$$

Hence, equating Eqs. (1) and (2)*

$$-5{,}000\mathbf{i} + 4{,}800\mathbf{j} = -1{,}700y\mathbf{i} + 1{,}700x\mathbf{j}$$

The $\mathbf{i}$ and $\mathbf{j}$ components on the left and right-hand sides of the equation must be equal. Thus,

$$-5{,}000 = -1{,}700y; \qquad y = 2.94 \text{ ft} \qquad\qquad Ans.$$
$$4{,}800 = 1{,}700x; \qquad x = 2.82 \text{ ft} \qquad\qquad Ans.$$

The single resultant force of 1,700 lb acting on the slab at point P (2.82 ft, 2.94 ft, 0) is therefore equivalent to the system of parallel forces in Fig. 4–33a.

Example 4–12

The rectangular block, shown in Fig. 4–34a, is subjected to a system of force and couple-moment vectors. Determine (a) an equivalent force-moment system acting at point A; and (b) the projection of moment of this system acting along the diagonal AB.

Solution
Part (a). By the principle of transmissibility, the force $\mathbf{F}_1$ may be moved directly to point A, since A lies on the line of action of $\mathbf{F}_1$. The couple-moment vectors may be moved directly to point A because they are free vectors. Moving the force $\mathbf{F}_2$ to point A requires adding an additional moment $\mathbf{M}_{AB} = \mathbf{r}_{AB} \times \mathbf{F}_2$. Hence, the force and moment resultants are

$$\mathbf{F}_R = \Sigma\mathbf{F} = \mathbf{F}_1 + \mathbf{F}_2 = (-10\mathbf{k}) + (-3\mathbf{i} + 2\mathbf{j} + 5\mathbf{k})$$
$$= \{-3\mathbf{i} + 2\mathbf{j} - 5\mathbf{k}\} \text{ lb} \qquad\qquad Ans.$$

---

*This can be done directly. In words, the moment due to the *force system* about point O, Fig. 4–33b, is *equivalent* to the moment due to the *resultant force* about point O, Fig. 4–33c. (This principle applies, as well, to any arbitrary point lying in the plane of the slab.)

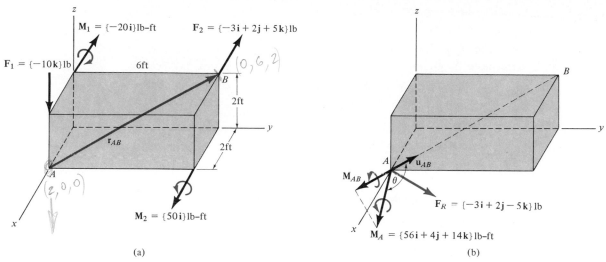

Fig. 4-34

$$\mathbf{M}_A = \mathbf{M}_1 + \mathbf{M}_2 + (\mathbf{r}_{AB} \times \mathbf{F}_2)$$
$$= [-20\mathbf{i}] + [50\mathbf{i}] + [(-2\mathbf{i} + 6\mathbf{j} + 2\mathbf{k}) \times (-3\mathbf{i} + 2\mathbf{j} + 5\mathbf{k})]$$
$$= \{56\mathbf{i} + 4\mathbf{j} + 14\mathbf{k}\} \text{ lb-ft} \qquad\qquad Ans.$$

The results are shown in Fig. 4–34b.

Part (b). As shown in Fig. 4–34b, a unit vector which defines an axis directed from A to B is

$$\mathbf{u}_{AB} = \frac{\mathbf{r}_{AB}}{r_{AB}} = \frac{-2\mathbf{i} + 6\mathbf{j} + 2\mathbf{k}}{\sqrt{(-2)^2 + (6)^2 + (2)^2}} = -0.302\mathbf{i} + 0.905\mathbf{j} + 0.302\mathbf{k}$$

The projection of $\mathbf{M}_A$ acting along the diagonal is thus

$$M_{AB} = M_A \cos\theta = \mathbf{M}_A \cdot \mathbf{u}_{AB}$$
$$= (56\mathbf{i} + 4\mathbf{j} + 14\mathbf{k}) \cdot (-0.302\mathbf{i} + 0.905\mathbf{j} + 0.302\mathbf{k})$$
$$= (56)(-0.302) + (4)(0.905) + (14)(0.302)$$
$$= -9.06 \text{ lb-ft}$$

The negative sign indicates that the moment projection acts in the *opposite direction* to $\mathbf{u}_{AB}$. Expressed as a vector, this projection is

$$\mathbf{M}_{AB} = M_{AB}\mathbf{u}_{AB} = (-9.06 \text{ lb-ft})(-0.302\mathbf{i} + 0.905\mathbf{j} + 0.302\mathbf{k})$$

or

$$\mathbf{M}_{AB} = \{2.74\mathbf{i} - 8.20\mathbf{j} - 2.74\mathbf{k}\} \text{ lb-ft} \qquad\qquad Ans.$$

Problems

4-41. If $A = (3\text{ ft})i + (24\text{ in.})j$ and $B = (1\text{ ft})i + (2\text{ ft})j + (30\text{ in.})k$, determine $A \cdot B$.

4-42. Given the three vectors **A**, **B**, and **C**, show that $A \cdot (B + C) = A \cdot B + A \cdot C$. *Suggestion:* Express as Cartesian vectors and expand.

4-43. Given the three nonzero vectors **A**, **B**, and **C**, show that if $A \cdot (B \times C) = 0$, the three vectors *must* then lie in the same plane.

4-44. Find the equation of a plane which contains the three points $(2, 4, -1)$, $(3, 1, 1)$, and $(2, -2, 4)$. (*Hint:* Construct position vectors to each of these points and some arbitrary point (x, y, z) lying in the plane, and use the result of Prob. 4–43.)

4-45. Determine the angle made between the two forces F_1 and F_2 shown acting on the plate. What is the moment of these two forces about the z axis?

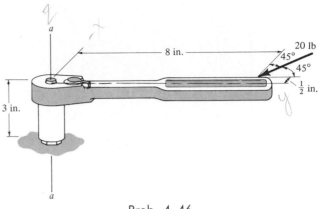

Prob. 4–46

4-47. Determine the angle which the force **F** makes with the diagonal AB of the crate. The force **F** lies in the plane $DBEC$ and makes an angle of $10°$ with the extended line DB as shown.

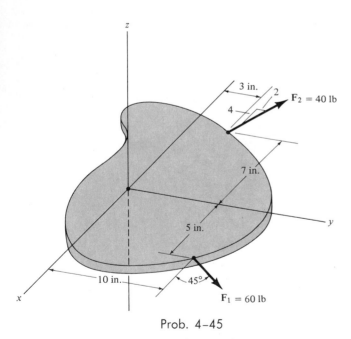

Prob. 4–45

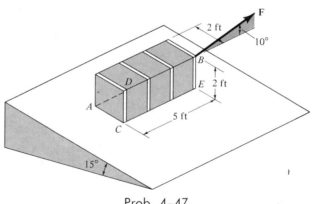

Prob. 4–47

4-48. For the crate in Prob. 4–47, determine the angle which **F** makes with the vertical.

4-46. Determine the projection of the moment created by the 20-lb force which acts along the *aa* axis of the socket wrench. The force lies in the horizontal plane.

4-49. The ropes AB and CD exert a tension force of 20 lb each on the plane. Determine the resultant force and moment created by these forces at the midsection point O of the plane wing.

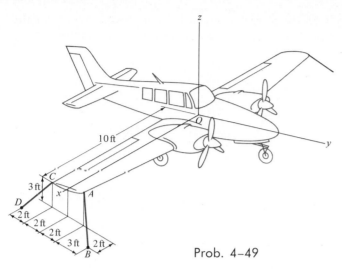

Prob. 4–49

4-50. The door is held open by two chains AB and AC. These chains exert a force of 20 and 40 lb, respectively, on the door. Determine the moment created by these two forces about point O and the direction of the axis about which this moment acts. What is the projection of this moment about axis OD?

4-51. A 70-lb force acts vertically on the "Z" bracket. Determine the moment of this force about the bolt axis (z axis).

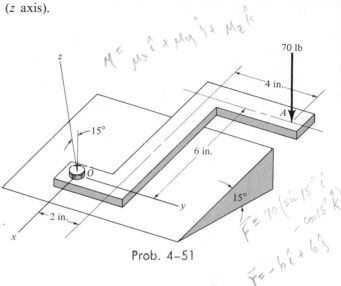

Prob. 4–51

4-52. The chain AB exerts a force of 20 lb on the door at B. Determine the projection of the moment of this force acting along the hinged axis x of the door.

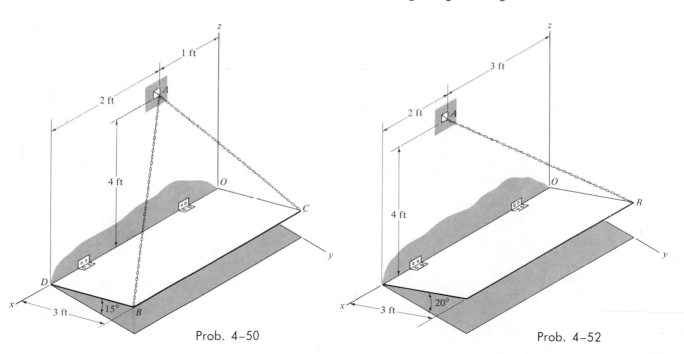

Prob. 4–50

Prob. 4–52

123

4-53. Determine the total moment created by forces **P** and **W** about the *AB* axis of the hoist.

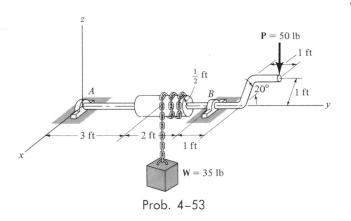

Prob. 4–53

4-54. Force **F**, having a magnitude of 50 lb and a direction specified by $\mathbf{u} = 0.200\mathbf{i} + 0.959\mathbf{j} + 0.200\mathbf{k}$, acts at point *G* of the block. (a) Determine the *x*, *y*, and *z* components of **F** when this force is moved to point *B*. (b) Using the scalar product, show that the projections of **F** along the *x*, *y*, and *z* axes equal the respective *x*, *y*, and *z* components of **F**. Explain why this is so.

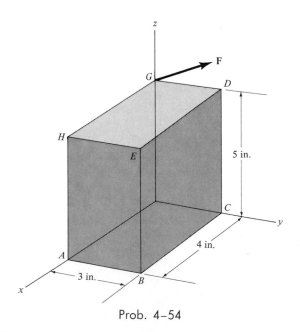

Prob. 4–54

4-55. Replace the given loading system acting on the beam by an equivalent force and couple moment acting at *O*.

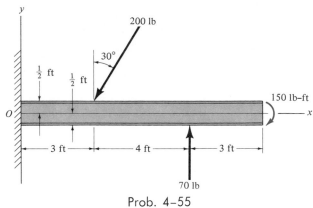

Prob. 4–55

4-56. Replace the force system acting on the plate by an equivalent single resultant force. Specify the location of this force.

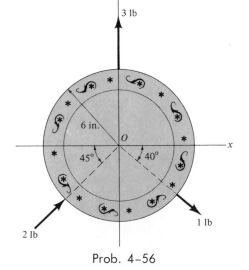

Prob. 4–56

124

4–57. Three forces act at the end of the cantilever beam. Determine the moment created by each of these forces about the x axis. Solve the problem using both a vector and a scalar approach.

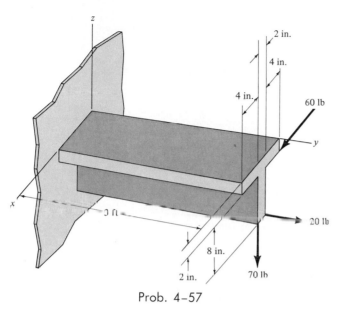

Prob. 4–57

4–59. Two forces $\mathbf{F}_1$ and $\mathbf{F}_2$ are applied at the end of the pipe assembly. If $\mathbf{F}_1$ acts in the direction shown and has a magnitude of 90 lb, and $\mathbf{F}_2$ has a magnitude of 50 lb, determine the appropriate direction angles β and γ for $\mathbf{F}_2$ so that the resultant moment of both forces about point O is $\mathbf{M}_R = \{-400\mathbf{i} + 240\mathbf{k}\}$ lb-in. Require $\alpha = 90°$ for $\mathbf{F}_2$.

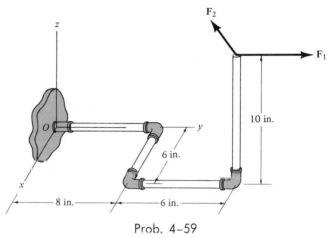

Prob. 4–59

4–58. Replace the two wrenches and the 100-lb force acting on the pipe assembly by an equivalent force and couple-moment system acting at point O.

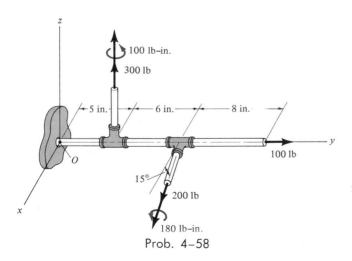

Prob. 4–58

4–60. Replace the two forces shown acting on the rectangular block by an equivalent force and couple-moment system acting at point A.

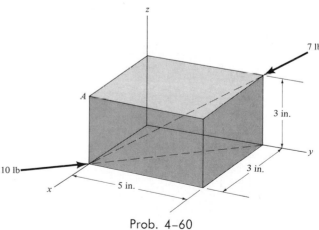

Prob. 4–60

125

4-61. Determine the moment of force **F** about the centerline of the shaft. In what direction does the moment tend to twist the shaft? The centerline of the shaft lies in the *zy* plane.

4-62. Specify the location $(x, y, 0)$ for the resultant of the three parallel column forces acting on the circular slab.

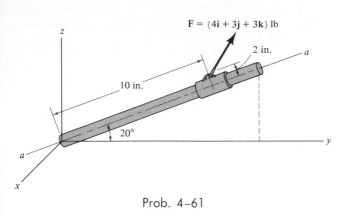

Prob. 4-61

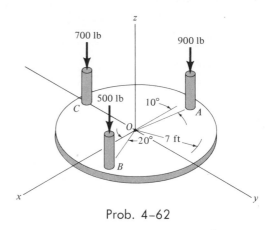

Prob. 4-62

4-11. Reduction of a Distributed Loading

In the previous sections of this chapter, we have considered ways of simplifying a system of *concentrated forces* which act on a body. In many practical situations, however, the surface of a body may be subjected to *distributed loadings*. Such loadings are caused by wind, hydrostatic pressure, or simply the weight of material supported by the body. The distribution of such surface loadings is described by a *loading function*. In general, at any point on the surface of the body, this loading function defines the intensity of load measured as a *force per unit area* or *pressure* acting on the surface. The direction of the intensity of distributed loading is indicated by arrows acting on the load intensity diagram. For example, the loading distribution or pressure acting on the plate shown in Fig. 4-35 is described by the loading function $p = p(x,y)$ lb/ft². Knowing this function, it is possible to determine the magnitude of *force* $d\mathbf{F}$ acting on an elemental surface area dA ft² of the plate located at the arbitrary point (x, y). This force magnitude is $dF = (p(x, y) \text{ lb/ft}^2)(dA \text{ ft}^2) = dV$ lb, where dV represents the small *differential volume element* shown shaded in Fig. 4-35. We can obtain the magnitude of the *total resultant force* by *integrating* the loading function over the entire surface area A of the plate, i.e.,

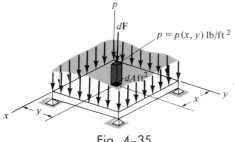

Fig. 4-35

$$F_R = \int_A p(x,y)\, dA = \int_V dV = V$$

126

Hence, the *magnitude of the resultant force is equal to the volume under the distributed loading diagram.* Using the methods of Chapter 9, it will be shown that *the line of action of the force resultant,* $\mathbf{F}_R$, *passes through the geometric-center or centroid of this volume.*

A simple example which illustrates these principles is shown in Fig. 4–36a. The plate is subjected to a uniform load of 10 lb/ft². Hence, the *resultant force* of this distributed loading is equal to the *volume* of the rectangular block,

$$F_R = V = (10 \text{ lb/ft}^2)(2 \text{ ft})(4 \text{ ft}) = 80 \text{ lb}$$

The line of action of this force acts through the centroid or geometric center of the block and therefore is located on the plate at point

$$x = 1 \text{ ft, and } y = 2 \text{ ft}$$

If the loading function is *symmetric* about any axis, it can be *simplified geometrically* and thereby represented as an *area* rather than a *volume.* The loading intensity is then measured as a *force per unit length,* rather than a force per unit area. Consider again the uniformally loaded plate, Fig. 4–36a. The loading function has two axes of symmetry. If the distributed loading is multiplied by the width of the plate, the loading function is rectangular and represents the distribution of load *along the length* of the plate. Hence,

$$w_l = (10 \text{ lb/ft}^2)(2 \text{ ft}) = 20 \text{ lb/ft}$$

This distributed loading is uniform and is shown in Fig. 4–36b. In a

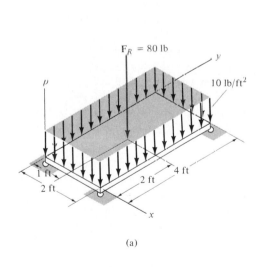

(a)

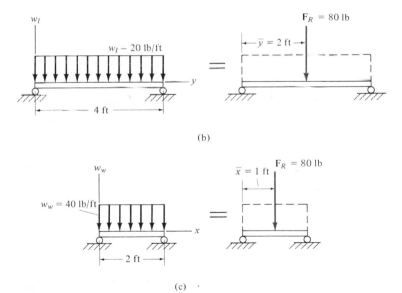

(b)

(c)

Fig. 4–36

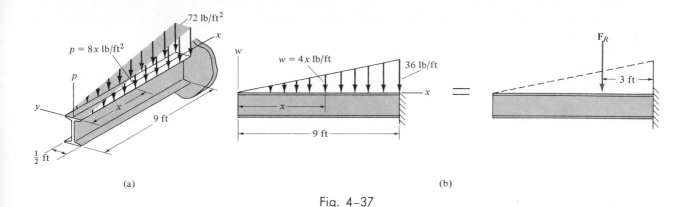

Fig. 4–37

similar manner, the loading *along the width* of the plate, Fig. 4–36c, is

$$w_w = (10 \text{ lb/ft}^2)(4 \text{ ft}) = 40 \text{ lb/ft}$$

As a second example, consider the beam shown in Fig. 4–37a which is subjected to the distributed loading $p = 8x$ lb/ft². In particular, where $x = 9$ ft, the pressure intensity is $p = 8(9) = 72$ lb/ft², as shown. Note that the beam has a constant width of $\frac{1}{2}$ ft and the load is *symmetric* with respect to the *width*. The loading diagram can therefore be viewed in two dimensions along the *length* of the beam, provided

$$w = (8x \text{ lb/ft}^2)(\tfrac{1}{2} \text{ ft}) = 4x \text{ lb/ft}$$

This loading is shown in Fig. 4–37b where at $x = 9$ ft, $w = 4(9) = 36$ lb/ft. Throughout the rest of this section, we will consider only loading functions which are represented as an area, i.e., $w = w(x)$ lb/ft. Methods for simplifying the more general loading function, $p = p(x,y)$ lb/ft², are discussed further in Sec. 9–5.

The magnitude and location of the resultant force of the distributed loading $w = w(x)$ lb/ft can be determined using the methods of Sec. 4–10. Specifically, the method used is the *same* as that used for finding the magnitude and location of the resultant force of a system of coplanar parallel forces. For example, consider the beam shown in Fig. 4–38a which is subjected to the arbitrary distributed loading $w = w(x)$ lb/ft. An element of the beam, dx, located at a distance x from the left support, is subjected to a force having a magnitude of $dF = (w(x) \text{ lb/ft})$ $(dx \text{ ft}) = dA$ lb. This force represents the shaded differential area segment dA under the loading curve. By integration, the magnitude of the total resultant force $\mathbf{F}_R$, supported by the beam, is determined by integration, i.e.,

$$F_R = \int_0^L w(x)\, dx = \int_A dA = A \tag{4–19}$$

Hence, it is seen that *the magnitude of the total resultant force is equal to the area under the loading diagram.*

In order to replace the distributed loading system $w(x)$ by $\mathbf{F}_R$, it is necessary to determine *where* on the beam $\mathbf{F}_R$ must act. To obtain this location, first move the incremental force $d\mathbf{F}$, shown in Fig. 4–38a, to the origin O. When this is done, a clockwise couple moment having a magnitude of $dM_O = x\, dF = x(w(x)\, dx)$ must be added to the beam. Provided *all* the differential forces dF acting from $x = 0$ to $x = L$ are replaced at point O, the resultant moment acting at the origin will be

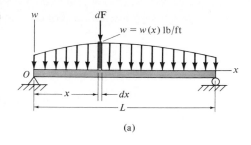

(a)

$$M_O = \int_0^L x\, w(x)\, dx$$

From this derivation, the resultant force $\mathbf{F}_R$ and moment $\mathbf{M}_O$ shown in Fig. 4–38b are therefore *equivalent* to the distributed loading $w(x)$ shown in Fig. 4–38a. Since $\mathbf{M}_O$ is *perpendicular* to $\mathbf{F}_R$, the force-moment system may be reduced to the single resultant force $\mathbf{F}_R$ acting at a distance $\bar{x}$ from point O, where

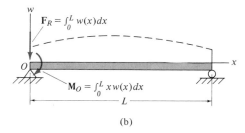

(b)

$$M_O = \bar{x} F_R \quad \checkmark$$

or

point of action of force from origin →

$$\bar{x} = \frac{M_O}{F_R} = \frac{\displaystyle\int_0^L x\, w(x)\, dx}{\displaystyle\int_0^L w(x)\, dx} = \frac{\displaystyle\int_A x\, dA}{\displaystyle\int_A dA} \tag{4-20}$$

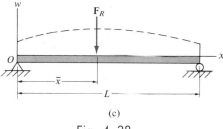

(c)

Fig. 4–38

See Fig. 4–38c. *The distance $\bar{x}$, computed from Eq. 4–20, may be interpreted as the coordinate distance from the origin O to the geometric center or centroid of the area under the loading curve.*

A detailed treatment for locating the centroid of an area is given in Chapter 9. Essentially the centroid is located using integration formulas similar to Eq. 4–20, provided the boundaries of the area can be described by mathematical functions. The centroids of common area shapes such as triangles, trapezoids, etc. have been computed using the techniques of Sec. 9–2 and are tabulated in Appendix B. If the area shape of the loading diagram is contained in Appendix B, the centroidal distance can be obtained *directly* from this table without the need for integration.

To illustrate the techniques used to reduce a distributed area loading to single resultance force, consider again the uniform loading shown in Fig. 4–36b. The loading diagram is represented geometrically as a rectangle. The *area of this rectangle* is equal to the *magnitude of the resultant force,* i.e.,

$$F_R = (20\ \text{lb/ft})(4\ \text{ft}) = 80\ \text{lb}$$

The *line of action* of this force acts through the *centroid* of the rectangle, i.e., $\bar{y} = 2$ ft. In a similar manner, F_R in Fig. 4–36c is

$$F_R = (40 \text{ lb/ft})(2 \text{ ft}) = 80 \text{ lb}$$

and $\bar{x} = 1$ ft as shown. Notice that the above results are equivalent to those obtained previously for F_R in Fig. 4–36a.

As a second example to illustrate these techniques, consider the triangular load distribution shown in Fig. 4–37b. The *area of the triangle* represents the *magnitude of the resultant force*, i.e.,

$$F_R = \tfrac{1}{2}(9 \text{ ft})(36 \text{ lb/ft}) = 162 \text{ lb}$$

The line of action of this force passes through the centroid of the triangle. Thus, using Appendix B, the centroid is $\tfrac{1}{3}(9 \text{ ft}) = 3$ ft from the fixed support (see Fig. 4–37b).

Besides being distributed over a surface area, forces can also be distributed throughout the *volume* of a body. These forces are termed *body forces*. Their loading intensity is given in units of *force per unit volume*. The most common body force encountered in statics is that due to the earth's gravitational field. In the case of a *particle*, the magnitude of this force of attraction is termed the *weight* of the particle. The weight can be found using Newton's universal law of gravitation, Eq. 1–1. This force acts along a line directed from the particle to the center of the earth. Thus, *the resultant weight of a body is the resultant of the weights of all the particles that compose it*. Provided we deal with bodies that are small compared to the size of the earth, it is reasonable to assume that all the particles of the body contribute weight forces which are parallel to one another. It is shown in Chapter 9 that the resultant weight of a body can be represented as a *concentrated force* which acts through a unique point in the body, commonly referred to as the *center of gravity*. Provided the body is composed of *homogeneous matter,* the center of gravity *coincides* with the geometric center or centroid of the volume of the body. The techniques for integration used for finding the center of gravity and centroids of volume shapes are given in Sec. 9–3. The volume centroids for geometrically simple shapes, however, are *tabulated* in Appendix B. These data provide a useful means for locating the line of action of the resultant weight of homogeneous bodies encountered in some of the problems given in the following chapters.

Example 4–13

Determine the magnitude and location of the resultant of the distributed load acting on the beam shown in Fig. 4–39a.

Solution

As shown in Fig. 4–39b, the loading may be divided into three segments: the parabolic loading ($0 \leq x < 4$ ft), the triangular loading (4 ft $< x < 7$ ft), and the trapezoidal loading (7 ft $< x \leq 13$ ft). The *area* under each of the three distributed loading curves equals the *resultant force* for that loading curve.

Parabolic loading. Using Eq. 4–19 in conjunction with the differential element shown in Fig. 4–39a, the area is found by integration.

$$F_P = \int_0^4 w(x)\,dx = \int_0^4 12x^2\,dx = \frac{12}{3}x^3 \Big]_0^4 = 4(4^4 - 0^4) = 256 \text{ lb}$$

Triangular loading. The area of the triangle is

$$F_T = \tfrac{1}{2}(3 \text{ ft})(200 \text{ lb/ft}) = 300 \text{ lb}$$

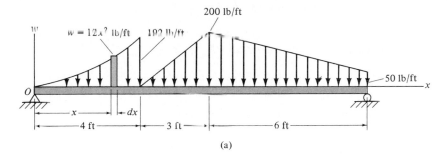

(a)

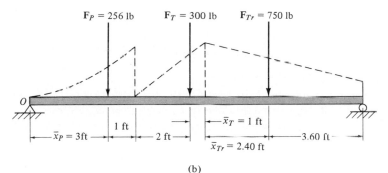

(b)

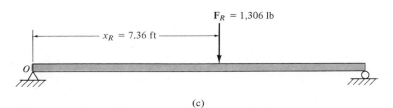

(c)

Fig. 4–39

Trapezoidal loading. The area of the trapezoid can be found by using the formula in Appendix B:

$$F_{Tr} = \tfrac{1}{2}h(a + b) = \tfrac{1}{2}(6 \text{ ft})(50 \text{ lb/ft} + 200 \text{ lb/ft}) = 750 \text{ lb}$$

Each of these resultant forces *acts* through the *centroid* of its respective loading curve area.

Parabolic loading. Referring to the differential element shown in Fig. 4–39a, and using Eq. 4–20, we have

$$\bar{x}_P = \frac{\displaystyle\int_0^L x\,w(x)\,dx}{\displaystyle\int_0^L w(x)\,dx} = \frac{\displaystyle\int_0^4 x(12x^2)\,dx}{\displaystyle\int_0^4 12x^2\,dx} = \frac{\dfrac{12}{4}x^4\Big]_0^4}{\dfrac{12}{3}x^3\Big]_0^4} = \frac{3(4^4 - 0^4)}{4(4^3 - 0^3)} = 3 \text{ ft}$$

measured from the left support.

Triangular loading. Using Appendix B, we have

$$\bar{x}_T = \frac{h}{3} = \frac{3}{3} = 1 \text{ ft}$$

measured from the right side of the triangle.

Trapezoidal loading. Using Appendix B, we have

$$\bar{x}_{Tr} = \frac{1}{3}\left(\frac{2a + b}{a + b}\right)h = \frac{1}{3}\left(\frac{2(50 \text{ lb/ft}) + 200 \text{ lb/ft}}{50 \text{ lb/ft} + 200 \text{ lb/ft}}\right)(6 \text{ ft}) = 2.40 \text{ ft}$$

measured from the left side of the trapezoid.

These results are all shown in Fig. 4–39b. By means of the method discussed in Sec. 4–10, this system of three *coplanar parallel forces* may be replaced by a *single concentrated force* acting at a unique point on the beam. Why? As shown in Fig. 4–39c, the resultant concentrated load for these three forces is

$$F_R = \Sigma F = 256 + 300 + 750 = 1{,}306 \text{ lb} \qquad\qquad Ans.$$

Assuming that this force acts at a distance x_R from point O, we require

$$F_R\, x_R = \Sigma M_O$$
$$1{,}306\, x_R = 256(3) + 300(6) + 750(9.40)$$

Thus,

$$x_R = 7.36 \text{ ft} \qquad\qquad Ans.$$

Problems

4-63. Determine the magnitude and location of the resultant force acting on the beam.

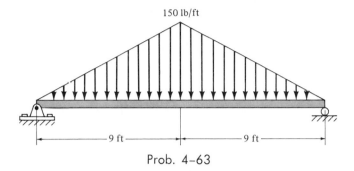

Prob. 4-63

4-64. Determine the equivalent force and couple-moment system acting at point O on the beam.

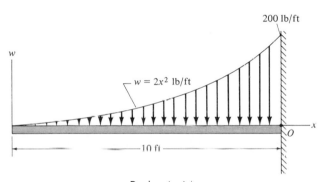

Prob. 4-64

4-65. The beam supports forty sandbags, each weighing 90 lb. Approximate the magnitude and the location of the resultant force due to the loading.

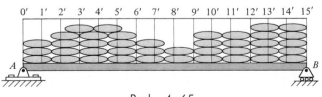

Prob. 4-65

4-66. Replace the loading system shown acting on the beam by a single resultant force. Where is this force located on the beam?

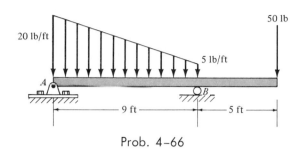

Prob. 4-66

4-67. Determine the resultant force acting on the beam.

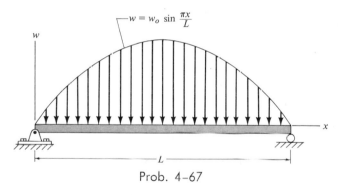

Prob. 4-67

4-68. Determine the magnitude and location of the resultant force of the distributed loading shown acting on the beam.

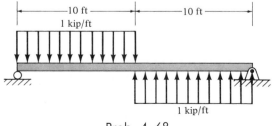

Prob. 4-68

133

4-69. Determine the magnitude and location of the resultant force acting on the beam.

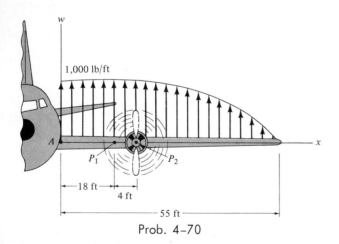

Prob. 4-69

4-70. The lifting force acting across the span of a wing on an airplane has a parabolic distribution (symmetrical about the w axis). The wing weighs 15,654 lb with a center of gravity at point P_1. The engine weighs 13,000 lb with a center of gravity at point P_2. Replace the force system by an equivalent force and couple-moment system at point A.

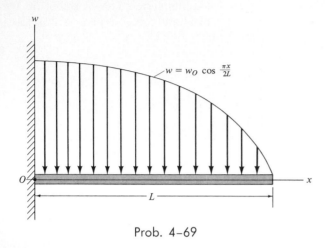

Prob. 4-70

4-71. The beam is subjected to an upward triangular load and a downward uniform load as shown in the figure. Determine the length b of uniform load and its position a on the beam such that the total resultant force and couple-moment acting on the beam is zero.

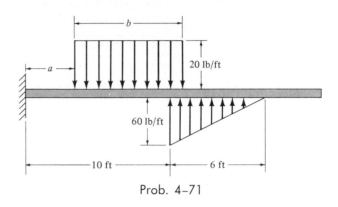

Prob. 4-71

4-72. The curved beam is subjected to a uniform load of 2 kip/ft. Determine an equivalent force and couple-moment system acting at point A.

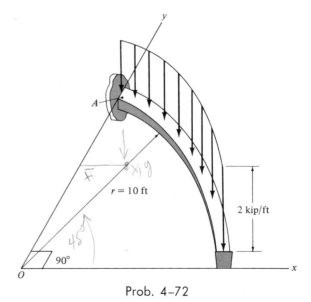

Prob. 4-72

134

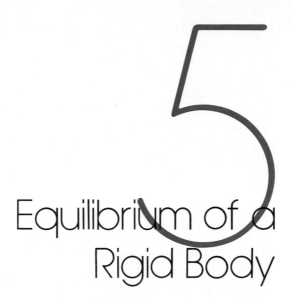

Equilibrium of a Rigid Body

In this chapter we will discuss the fundamental concepts which underlie the equilibrium of a rigid body. In particular, it was pointed out in Chapter 3 that the methods of particle equilibrium pertain as well to the equilibrium of a rigid body subjected to a system of *concurrent forces*. (Recall that according to the principle of transmissibility, a system of concurrent forces may be represented as acting on a specific particle of the body.) In the first part of this chapter, we will consider the equilibrium of a body subjected to a *coplanar force system*. By this we assume that the body and the forces which are applied to it can be projected onto a single plane. Consequently, the reactions needed to maintain equilibrium of the body may also be represented in this same plane. The more general discussion of a *three-dimensional force system* acting on a rigid body will be given in the second part of this chapter.

Two-Dimensional Force Systems Acting on a Rigid Body

5-1. Free-Body Diagrams and Support Reactions

The free-body diagram concept, which was first introduced in Chapter 3 in connection with problems involving the equilibrium of a particle, plays an important role in the solution of equilibrium problems for a rigid body. Provided the free-body diagram is correctly drawn, the effects of all the applied forces and couples acting on the rigid body can be accounted for when the equations of equilibrium are written. Any force or couple moment omitted from the diagram will obviously lead to errors in the solution. *For this reason, a comprehensive understanding in drawing correct free-body diagrams is of primary importance for solving problems in mechanics.* It is the preliminary step before the equations of equilibrium can be applied.

Important

To construct a free-body diagram for a rigid body, the body (or group of bodies, considered as a single system) is *isolated* from all its supports and adjacent contacting bodies. An outlined shape of the body is drawn, and all the forces and couple moments acting *on the body* are labeled on this sketch. Included also are dimensions of the body necessary for computing the moments of forces. All *known* quantities should be drawn and labeled with their proper magnitude and direction. Letters are used to represent the magnitudes and directions of forces and couple moments which are *unknown*. The vector sense (represented by the arrowhead) of a force or couple moment having an unknown magnitude but known direction can be assumed. The correctness of the assumed sense will become apparent after solving the equilibrium equations for the unknown quantity. A positive sign indicates that the assumed sense was correct; a minus sign indicates that the sense is opposite to that which was assumed.

Forces and couple moments generally encountered are those due to (1) applied external loadings, (2) reactions occurring at the supports or at points of contact between bodies, and (3) the weight of the isolated body. (Forces which are *internal* to the body, such as the forces occuring between any two particles of the body, are *not shown* on the free-body diagram of the body since these forces always occur in equal and opposite collinear pairs. The net effect of these forces on the body will then be zero.)

Before we are able to draw a free-body diagram for a rigid body, it is necessary to first consider the various types of *reactions* that occur at supports and points of contact between rigid bodies. For two-dimensional problems, that is, bodies subjected to coplanar force systems, the types of support reactions commonly encountered are given in Table 5–1. You should *carefully study* the symbols used to represent these reactions, and you should clearly *understand* how the forces and/or couple moments are developed at all the supports. In particular, a *force* is developed on a connecting member by the support if the support *prevents translation* of the connecting member, and a couple moment is developed by the support if it *prevents rotation* of the connecting member. For example, a body in contact with the smooth surface (6) is prevented from translating *only* in a direction (downward) *normal* to the surface. Hence the surface exerts only a *normal force* on the body at the point of contact. The magnitude of this force represents *one unknown*. Since the body is free to rotate on the surface, no couple moment is developed by the surface on the body at its point of contact. The pin or hinge support (8) prevents translation of the connecting member at its point of connection. Unlike

Table 5-1   Support Reactions for Rigid Bodies Subjected to Two-Dimensional Force Systems

Types of connection	*Reaction*	*Number of unknowns*
(1) light cable	*or T (must be tension, not compression)*	One unknown: magnitude of force **F**; this force acts in the direction of the cable so that the cable remains in tension
(2) weightless link	*tension or compression*	One unknown: magnitude of force **F**; this force acts in the direction of the link
(3) roller	*not moving*	One unknown: magnitude of force **F**; this force acts normal to the supporting surface
(4) roller or pin in confined smooth slot	*supported by one surface at a time, not both*	One unknown: magnitude of force **F**; this force acts in either direction normal to the confined slot
(5) rocker		One unknown: magnitude of force **F**; this force acts normal to the inclined surface
(6) smooth contacting surface	*no friction*	One unknown: magnitude of force **F**; this force acts perpendicular to the tangent at the point of contact
(7) collar on smooth rod		One unknown: magnitude of force **F**; this force acts normal to the axis of the supporting rod

137

Table 5–1 (Contd.)

Types of connection	Reaction	Number of unknowns
(8) 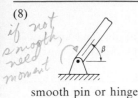 smooth pin or hinge *no resistance*	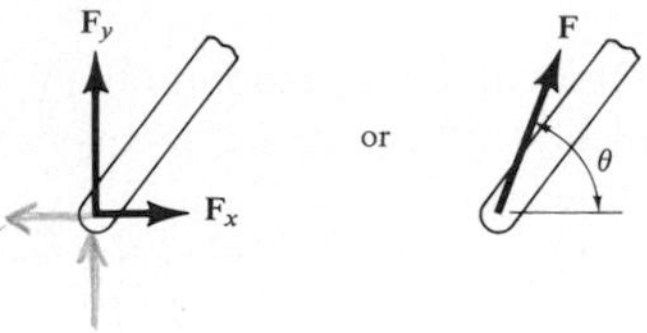 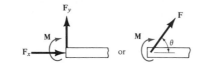 or	Two unknowns: the magnitudes of the two force components F_x and F_y, or the magnitude of the force F and its direction θ; note that β and θ are not necessarily equal [usually not, unless the rod shown is a link as in (2)]
(9) 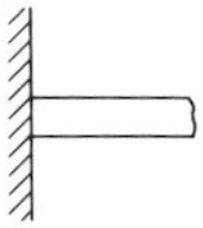 fixed support	$\quad$ or $\quad$	Three unknowns: the magnitudes of the couple M and two force components F_x and F_y, or the magnitudes of the couple M and force F and the direction of the force, θ

[handwritten annotation:] if not smooth, need moment

the smooth surface, the translation is prevented in all directions. Hence, an unknown force **F** must be developed at the support. This force has *two unknowns,* namely, its magnitude F and direction θ, or the magnitudes of its two components $\mathbf{F}_x$ and $\mathbf{F}_y$. Since the connecting member is allowed to rotate freely in the plane about the support at its point of contact, a pin connection does not resist a couple moment acting perpendicular to this plane. On the other hand, the fixed support (9) prevents *both* planar translation and rotation of the connecting member at the point of connection. Therefore, this type of support exerts both a force and a couple moment on the member. Note that the couple moment acts *perpendicular* to the plane of the page since rotation is prevented in the plane. Hence, there are *three unknowns* at a fixed support.*

In reality, all supports actually exert only *distributed surface loads* on their contacting members. The concentrated force and/or couple-moment vectors shown in Table 5–1 represent the *resultants* of this load distribution. This representation is, of course, an idealization. However, it can be used here since the surface area over which the distributed load acts on the support is considerably *smaller* than the *total* surface area of the connecting member.

Before proceeding further, carefully review this section. Then attempt to draw the free-body diagrams for the following example problems before "looking" at the solution. Further practice in drawing free-body diagrams may be gained by solving the problems given at the end of this section.

---

*A free body diagram for a body having a fixed support is shown in Fig. 5–1*b*.

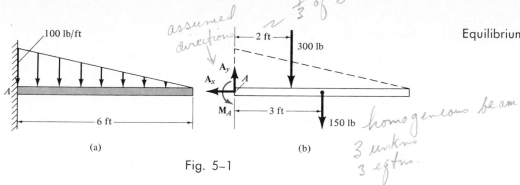

(handwritten annotations on figure: "assumed direction", "⅓ of 6", "homogeneous beam", "3 unkns 3 eqtns.")

(a)   (b)

Fig. 5-1

Example 5-1

Draw the free-body diagram for the uniform beam shown in Fig. 5-1a. The beam weighs 150 lb.

Solution

The free-body diagram for the beam is shown in Fig. 5-1b. Since the support is a fixed wall, there are three reactions acting *on the beam* at A, denoted as A_x, A_y, and M_A. The magnitudes of these vectors are *unknown* and their sense of direction have all been *assumed*. (How does one realize the *correct sense* of direction for these unknown magnitudes?)

For convenience in computing the reactions at A, the distributed loading is reduced to a concentrated force acting on the beam. Using the methods of Sec. 4-11, the resultant of the distributed loading is equal to the area under the triangular loading diagram, i.e., $\frac{1}{2}(6\text{ ft})(100\text{ lb/ft}) = 300$ lb. This force acts through the centroid of the triangle, i.e., 2 ft from A. The 150-lb weight of the beam acts 3 ft from A since the beam has a uniform weight.

(handwritten margin note: "ANS. go ahead and construct the structure with the assumed directions and apply the loads. If the structure collapses, your assumption was incorrect. JB")

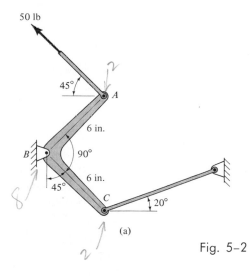

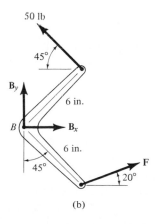

(a)   (b)

Fig. 5-2

Example 5–2

Draw the free-body diagram for the bell crank *ABC* shown in Fig. 5–2a, and determine the number of unknown force components.

Solution

The free-body diagram is shown in Fig. 5–2b. The pin support at *B* exerts forces $\mathbf{B}_x$ and $\mathbf{B}_y$ on the crank, each component having a known line of direction, but unknown magnitude. The link at *C* exerts an unknown magnitude of force $\mathbf{F}$ acting in the direction of the link. The dimensions of the crank are also labeled on the free-body diagram since this information will be useful in computing the moments of the forces. As usual, the sense of direction of the three unknown forces have been assumed. The correct sense of direction will become apparent after solving the equilibrium equations.

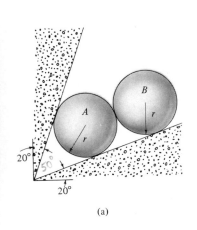

(a)

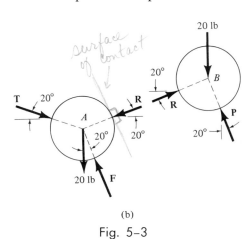

(b)

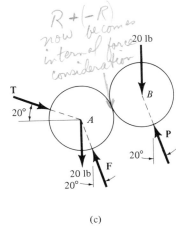

(c)

Fig. 5–3

Example 5–3

Two smooth balls *A* and *B*, each weighing 20 lb, rest between the smooth inclined planes shown in Fig. 5–3a. Draw the free-body diagrams for (a) ball *A* and ball *B* individually, and (b) balls *A* and *B* combined.

Solution

Part (a).   The free-body diagrams for balls *A* and *B* individually are shown in Fig. 5–3b. Since all the contacting surfaces are *smooth,* the reactive forces **P, T, R,** and **F** act in a direction *normal* to the tangent at their surface of contact. In particular, the reactive force **R** acting *on ball A* represents the effect which ball *B exerts on ball A.* Using Newton's third law, the free-body diagram of ball *B* must include an *equal but opposite force* **R** which ball *A exerts on ball B.*

Part (b). The free-body diagram for both balls *A* and *B* combined is shown in Fig. 5–3c. The reactions at the surfaces of contact with the inclined planes must be the *same* as those listed on the separate free-body diagrams given in Part (a). These unknowns represent the magnitudes of the forces which the planes exert *on* the balls. Since the contact force **R**, which acts between balls *A* and *B*, occurs as an equal and opposite collinear pair of forces, it is considered here as an *internal force* and hence is not shown on the free-body diagram in Fig. 5–3c.

Problems

Draw the free-body diagram in each of the following problems and determine the total number of unknown force and couple magnitudes and/or directions. Neglect the weight of the members unless otherwise stated.

5–1. The 10-lb sphere resting between the smooth inclined planes.

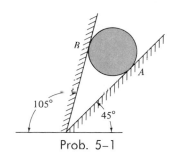

Prob. 5–1

5–2. The uniform 8-ft long beam pinned at *A* and supported by a cord at *B*; the total weight of the beam is 40 lb.

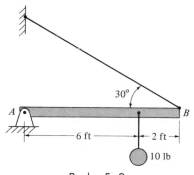

Prob. 5–2

5–3. The "spanner wrench" subjected to the 20-lb force; the support at *A* is pinned and the surface of contact at *B* is smooth.

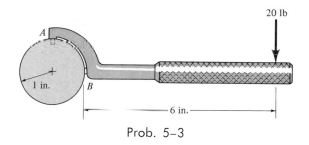

Prob. 5–3

5–4. The "*C*" bracket supported at *A*, *B*, and *C* by rollers.

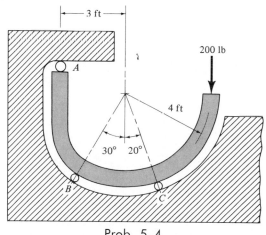

Prob. 5–4

5-5. The beam supported at A by a smooth roller and at B by a fixed foundation.

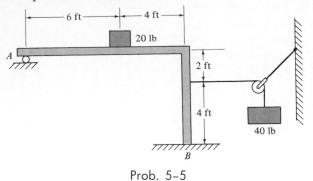

Prob. 5-5

5-6. The homogeneous triangular plate supported by cables at A and B and having a weight of 60 lb.

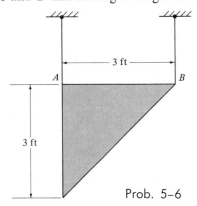

Prob. 5-6

5-7. The uniform beam supported at A by a pin, at B by a spring, and at C by a cord; the beam weighs 150 lb.

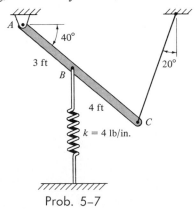

Prob. 5-7

5-8. The bell-crank supported at A by a pin and subjected to cable forces at points B and C.

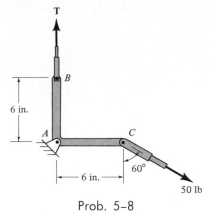

Prob. 5-8

5-9. The bent beam supported at A by a fixed support and at B by a roller, and subjected to the weight of the 100-lb load.

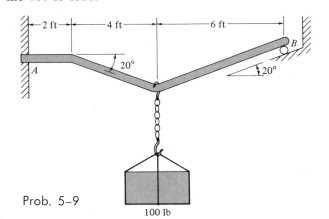

Prob. 5-9

5-10. The beam supported at A by a smooth roller and at B by a pin.

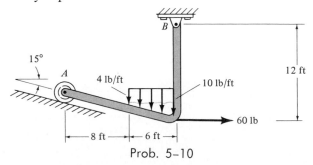

Prob. 5-10

142

5-11. The homogeneous concrete slab weighing 3,000 lb and supported on its platform by the cables at A and B.

5-12. The uniform rod supported by a pin at A and a short link BC.

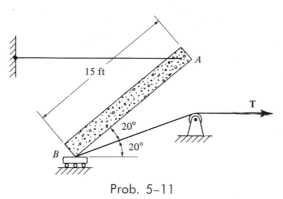

Prob. 5-11

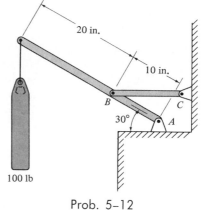

Prob. 5-12

5-2. Equations of Coplanar Equilibrium

In Sec. 4-10 it was shown that a system of *coplanar forces* acting on a rigid body may be simplified to a single resultant force $\mathbf{F}_R = \Sigma \mathbf{F}$, acting through some arbitrary point O on the body, and a single resultant couple moment $\mathbf{M}_R = \Sigma \mathbf{M}_O$. The resultant force is equal to the vector sum of all the forces of the system and will therefore have the *same* magnitude and direction regardless of the location of point O. The magnitude and sense of direction of the couple moment, however, *depends* upon the location of point O. For a coplanar force system, $\mathbf{M}_R$ will always be directed *perpendicular* to the plane containing the system of forces.

In particular, if the *resultant force and moment* of the external forces acting on a body is *zero*, at any arbitrary point O, the body is said to be in *static equilibrium*. Physically, this means that equilibrium maintains a balance of force and moment. Equations which express these two conditions of equilibrium are

$$\Sigma \mathbf{F} = 0$$
$$\Sigma \mathbf{M}_O = 0 \qquad (5\text{-}1)$$

$\Sigma \mathbf{F}$ represents the vector sum of all the forces acting on the body. If the free-body diagram is drawn in the xy plane, the applied system of forces may be expressed in terms of their respective $\mathbf{i}$ and $\mathbf{j}$ force *components*, i.e., $\Sigma \mathbf{F} = \Sigma F_x \mathbf{i} + \Sigma F_y \mathbf{j}$. The resultant moment vector acts in either the plus or minus $\mathbf{k}$ direction and has a magnitude ΣM_O. Thus, $\Sigma \mathbf{M}_O = \Sigma M_O \mathbf{k}$. Since the $\mathbf{i, j,}$ and $\mathbf{k}$ directions are mutually perpendicular, Eqs. 5-1 may be expressed in the form of *three independent scalar equations:*

$$\Sigma F_x = 0$$
$$\Sigma F_y = 0$$
$$\Sigma M_O = 0 \qquad (5\text{–}2)$$

In these equations, ΣF_x and ΣF_y represent the summation of the *components* of all the forces shown on the free-body diagram in the x and y directions, respectively. ΣM_O represents the sum of the applied couple moments acting on the body and the moments of all the forces about the arbitrary point O.

Although Eqs. 5–2 are *most often* used for solving statics problems involving coplanar force systems, certain alternate sets of three equilibrium equations may be used instead. One such set is

$$\Sigma F_y = 0$$
$$\Sigma M_A = 0$$
$$\Sigma M_B = 0 \qquad (5\text{–}3)$$

In using these equations, it is required that the moment points A and B do *not* lie on a line *perpendicular* to the y axis. To show that Eqs. 5–3 form a necessary set of three equilibrium conditions, consider the body shown in Fig. 5–4. $\mathbf{F}_R$ represents the *resultant* of *all* the external forces acting on the body.* For $\mathbf{F}_R$ to satisfy the equation $\Sigma F_y = 0$, $\mathbf{F}_R$ must be perpendicular to the y axis, as shown. Also, the equation $\Sigma M_A = 0$ is satisfied provided point A is chosen so that it lies along the line of action of $\mathbf{F}_R$. If point B is chosen such that line AB does not coincide with the line of action of $\mathbf{F}_R$ (which is perpendicular to the y axis), then $\Sigma M_B = 0$ is satisfied only if $\mathbf{F}_R$ is equal to zero.

In a similar manner, it can be shown that

$$\Sigma F_x = 0$$
$$\Sigma M_A = 0$$
$$\Sigma M_B = 0 \qquad (5\text{–}4)$$

form a complete set of three necessary equilibrium equations provided A and B do *not* lie on a line *perpendicular* to the x axis.

A third alternate set of equilibrium equations is

$$\Sigma M_A = 0$$
$$\Sigma M_B = 0$$
$$\Sigma M_C = 0 \qquad (5\text{–}5)$$

Here it is required that points A, B, and C do not lie along the *same*

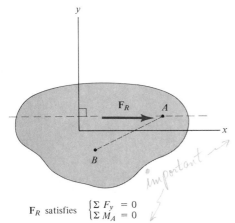

$\mathbf{F}_R$ satisfies $\begin{cases} \Sigma F_y = 0 \\ \Sigma M_A = 0 \end{cases}$

Require $\mathbf{F}_R = 0$ to satisfy $\Sigma M_B = 0$

Fig. 5–4

---

*It was shown in Sec. 4–10 that a system of forces can always be replaced by a resultant force $\mathbf{F}_R$ and resultant moment $\mathbf{M}_R$. For a *coplanar force system*, however, $\mathbf{F}_R$ will *always* be perpendicular to $\mathbf{M}_R$, hence, the force-moment system may be further reduced to the *single resultant force* $\mathbf{F}_R$ acting through some unique point.

line. If both $\Sigma M_A = 0$ and $\Sigma M_B = 0$, then the resultant force $\mathbf{F}_R$, if it exists, must pass through the line connecting points A and B as shown in Fig. 5–5. Provided point C is not collinear with A and B, $\mathbf{F}_R$ must equal zero in order to satisfy $\Sigma M_C = 0$. Thus, Eqs. 5–5 form a necessary set of complete equilibrium equations.

If one *violates* the stated restriction for using the sets of equilibrium Eqs. 5–3, 5–4, or 5–5, one obtains equations which *are not linearly independent,* that is, one equation will differ from another by a constant multiple. It will then be necessary to choose other points or axes about which to sum moments or forces, until three independent equations are finally written.

An essential point to keep in mind is that one can write only *three independent scalar equations for the equilibrium of a rigid body subjected to a coplanar force system.* In solving equilibrium problems in two dimensions, it is best to *orient* the x and y axes in a direction which will facilitate *reduction* of all the forces into their x and y components. Similarly, moments should be summed about points which lie along the line of action of as *many unknown forces* as possible. Doing this reduces the number of unknowns in the moment equations and will generally eliminate the need for solving a set of simultaneous equations.

It is *not* recommended that equilibrium problems involving coplanar force systems be solved by direct application of vector Eqs. 5–1 (see Example 5–4). It is true that a vector approach to the solution is mathematically more sophisticated than a scalar approach; however, a vector solution really becomes advantageous when the geometry of the problem becomes complicated, as in the case of three dimensions. A scalar solution is more direct and lends greater insight into the physical effects caused by each of the applied forces and couple moments.

The three independent scalar equations of equilibrium provide the *necessary conditions* of equilibrium for a coplanar force system acting on a rigid body. If the body is properly supported so that all the forces acting on the body are determined solely from the equilibrium equations, then these equations are also *sufficient conditions* for equilibrium. Those types of problems for which the equilibrium equations do not provide sufficient conditions for equilibrium will be discussed in Sec. 5–5.

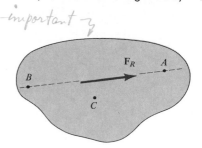

$\mathbf{F}_R$ satisfies $\quad \begin{cases} \Sigma M_A = 0 \\ \Sigma M_B = 0 \end{cases}$

Require $\mathbf{F}_R = 0$ to satisfy $\Sigma M_C = 0$

Fig. 5–5

Example 5–4

Determine the support reactions for the loaded beam shown in Fig. 5–6a. Neglect the weight of the beam in the calculations.

Solution I

The *first step* is to draw a free-body diagram of the beam. Why? This diagram, shown in Fig. 5–6b, accounts for all the forces that act *on the beam*. The reaction at A is "vertical," since there is a smooth *roller* at

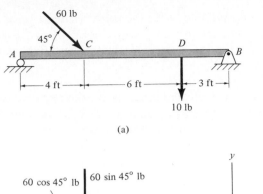

(a)

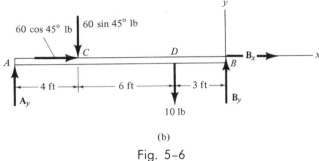

(b)

Fig. 5–6

this support. The *pin support* at B exerts an unknown force, represented by the two components $\mathbf{B}_x$ and $\mathbf{B}_y$. The directional sense of the three vectors $\mathbf{A}_y$, $\mathbf{B}_x$, and $\mathbf{B}_y$ have been assumed. The correct sense of these vectors will become apparent after solving the equations of equilibrium. For simplicity in applying the equilibrium equations, the 60-lb force is represented by its two orthogonal components as shown.

Applying the equilibrium equation $\Sigma F_x = 0$ to the force system acting on the free-body diagram in Fig. 5–6b yields

$$\xrightarrow{+} \Sigma F_x = 0;$$

$$60 \cos 45° \text{ lb} + B_x = 0, \qquad B_x = -42.4 \text{ lb}$$

Since the result is a negative quantity, $\mathbf{B}_x$ has a sense of direction *opposite* to that shown (assumed) in Fig. 5–6b.

Equating to zero the sum of moments about point B of *all* the forces shown on the free-body diagram we can directly calculate the unknown A_y. Why? As stated in Sec. 4–4, the moment of a force is determined by multiplying the magnitude of the force by its *perpendicular distance* from the line of action of the force to point B. Considering counterclockwise rotation about point B to be positive, ($+\mathbf{k}$ direction) we have

$$\zeta + \Sigma M_B = 0;$$

$$10 \text{ lb (3 ft)} + (60 \sin 45° \text{ lb})(9 \text{ ft}) - A_y(13 \text{ ft}) = 0, \quad A_y = 31.7 \text{ lb} \quad Ans.$$

(Show that this same result would be obtained if moments had been assumed positive clockwise.) It should be apparent that the moments of forces 60 cos 45° lb, $\mathbf{B}_x$ and $\mathbf{B}_y$ do not appear in the moment equation, since the line of action of these force vectors passes through point B.

Summing forces in the y direction, using the result $A_y = 31.7$ lb obtained above, yields

$$+\uparrow\Sigma F_y = 0;$$

$$31.7 \text{ lb} - 60 \sin 45° \text{ lb} - 10 \text{ lb} + B_y = 0, \qquad B_y = 20.7 \text{ lb}$$

The magnitude of force $\mathbf{B}_y$ may also be obtained by summing moments about point A, i.e.,

$$\zeta + \Sigma M_A = 0;$$

$$-(60 \sin 45° \text{ lb})(4 \text{ ft}) - 10 \text{ lb} (10 \text{ ft}) + B_y(13 \text{ ft}) = 0, \qquad B_y = 20.7 \text{ lb}$$

The first solution for B_y is the least complicated; however, the second solution is desirable, since, for accuracy, it does not depend upon prior knowledge of the magnitude of $\mathbf{A}_y$.

The resultant force at B may be computed by adding vectorially the components $\mathbf{B}_x$ and $\mathbf{B}_y$, i.e.,

$$F_B = \sqrt{(B_x)^2 + (B_y)^2} = \sqrt{(42.4)^2 + (20.7)^2} = 47.2 \text{ lb} \qquad Ans.$$

Realizing that $\mathbf{B}_x$ acts in the opposite sense to that shown in Fig. 5–6b,

$$\theta = \tan^{-1}\frac{B_y}{B_x} = \tan^{-1}\frac{20.7}{42.4} = 26.0° \qquad {}_\theta\diagdown F_B \qquad Ans.$$

Solution II

After the free-body diagram for the beam is drawn, using the methods of vector algebra, we may apply Eqs. 5–1 directly to obtain the solution. With reference to the x and y axes shown in Fig. 5–6b, each of the forces acting on the free-body diagram must be expressed in Cartesian vector form.

$$\mathbf{F}_A = A_y\mathbf{j}$$
$$\mathbf{F}_1 = \{60 \cos 45° \, \mathbf{i} - 60 \sin 45° \, \mathbf{j}\} \text{ lb}$$
$$\mathbf{F}_2 = \{-10\mathbf{j}\} \text{ lb}$$
$$\mathbf{F}_B = B_x\mathbf{i} + B_y\mathbf{j}$$

Thus,

$$\Sigma \mathbf{F} = 0;$$

$$A_y\mathbf{j} + 60 \cos 45° \, \mathbf{i} - 60 \sin 45° \, \mathbf{j} - 10\mathbf{j} + B_x\mathbf{i} + B_y\mathbf{j} = 0$$

To satisfy this vector equation, the scalar components in the $\mathbf{i}$ and $\mathbf{j}$ directions must be equated to zero. Hence,

$$\xrightarrow{+}\Sigma F_x = 0; \qquad\qquad 60\cos 45° + B_x = 0 \qquad\qquad (1)$$

$$+\uparrow\Sigma F_y = 0; \qquad A_y - 60\sin 45° - 10 + B_y = 0 \qquad (2)$$

Summing moments about point B yields

$$\Sigma M_B = 0; \qquad (\mathbf{r}_{BD} \times \mathbf{F}_2) + (\mathbf{r}_{BC} \times \mathbf{F}_1) + (\mathbf{r}_{BA} \times \mathbf{F}_A) = 0$$
$$(-3\mathbf{i}) \times (-10\mathbf{j}) + (-9\mathbf{i}) \times (60\cos 45°\,\mathbf{i} - 60\sin 45°\,\mathbf{j})$$
$$+ (-13\mathbf{i}) \times (A_y\mathbf{j}) = 0$$

In this equation, each vector cross product yields a moment vector acting in the positive or negative $\mathbf{k}$ direction. After computing the cross products, the above equation reduces to

$$\zeta+\Sigma M_B = 0; \qquad 10(3) + 60\sin 45°\,(9) - A_y(13) = 0 \qquad (3)$$

By comparison, note that Eqs. (1) through (3) are identical to those obtained in Solution I.

Although the vector approach is mathematically more elegant than the scalar approach, the extra labor needed to obtain the above results generally does not justify the use of Cartesian vectors for the solution of equilibrium problems involving *coplanar force systems*. For this reason, the remaining example problems will be solved using a scalar analysis.

Example 5-5

Determine the reactions at the fixed support A for the loaded frame shown in Fig. 5-7a.

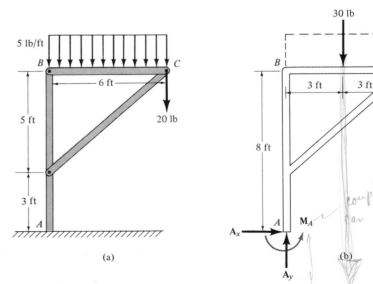

(a)

(b)

Fig. 5-7

M_A: resistance to turn

Solution

The free-body diagram for the frame is shown in Fig. 5–7b. There are three unknowns at the fixed support, represented by the magnitudes of A_x, A_y, and M_A. The distributed load is simplified using the methods of Sec. 4–11. Specifically, the resultant force of this loading is equal to the area under the loading curve, that is (6 ft)(5 lb/ft) = 30 lb. This force acts through the centroid, or geometric center of the loading curve, 3 ft from B or C.

Applying the equilibrium equations to the system of forces yields,

$$\xrightarrow{+}\Sigma F_x = 0; \qquad\qquad A_x = 0 \qquad\qquad Ans.$$
$$+\uparrow\Sigma F_y = 0; \quad A_y - 30\text{ lb} - 20\text{ lb} = 0, \qquad A_y = 50\text{ lb} \qquad Ans.$$
$$\zeta+\Sigma M_A = 0; \quad M_A - 30\text{ lb (3 ft)} - 20\text{ lb (6 ft)} = 0,$$
$$M_A = 210\text{ lb-ft} \qquad\qquad Ans.$$

Rather than summing moments about point A, any other point (*on or off* the free-body diagram) might have been used. However, point A was chosen since the lines of action of forces A_x and A_y pass through point A, and therefore these forces were not included in the moment summation about this point. Note in particular that the couple-moment M_A must be *included* in the moment summation. (Actually M_A is a free vector and can therefore be placed at any point on the free-body diagram.)

Although only *three* independent equilibrium equations can be written for a rigid body, it is a good practice to check all calculations using a fourth equilibrium equation. This later equation may be obtained from one of the other sets of equilibrium Eqs. 5–3, 5–4, or 5–5. For example, the above computations may be verified by summing moments about point C:

$$\zeta+\Sigma M_C = 0; \quad 30\text{ lb (3 ft)} - 50\text{ lb (6 ft)} + 210\text{ lb-ft} \equiv 0$$
$$90\text{ lb-ft} - 300\text{ lb-ft} + 210\text{ lb-ft} \equiv 0$$

Example 5–6

The uniform beam shown in Fig. 5–8a weighs 50 lb and is subjected to a concentrated force and couple moment. If the beam is supported at A by a smooth wall and at B and C by rollers, determine the reactions at the supports.

Solution

The free-body diagram for the beam is shown in Fig. 5–8b. All the support reactions act normal to the surface of contact since the contacting surfaces are smooth. The reactions at B and C are shown acting in the positive y' direction. This assumes that only the rollers located on the bottom of the beam are used for support. Since the beam is uniform, its 50-lb weight acts at the midpoint. The 800-lb-ft couple moment is a

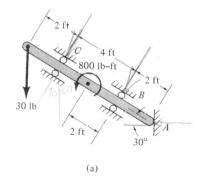

(a)

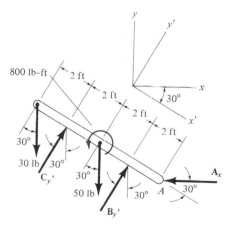

(b)

Fig. 5–8

free vector, and it can therefore be shown acting at *any point* on the free-body diagram without affecting the computed results.

Using the xy coordinate system in Fig. 5-8b and applying the equations of equilibrium, we have

$$\overset{+}{\rightarrow} \Sigma F_x = 0; \qquad C_{y'} \sin 30° + B_{y'} \sin 30° - A_x = 0 \qquad\qquad (1)$$

$$+\uparrow\Sigma F_y = 0; \quad -30 \text{ lb} + C_{y'} \cos 30° - 50 \text{ lb} + B_{y'} \cos 30° = 0 \qquad (2)$$

$$\zeta +\Sigma M_A = 0; \; -B_{y'}(2 \text{ ft}) + (50 \cos 30° \text{ lb})(4 \text{ ft}) + 800 \text{ lb-ft}$$
$$-C_{y'}(6 \text{ ft}) + (30 \cos 30° \text{ lb})(8 \text{ ft}) = 0 \quad (3)$$

In writing the moment equation, it should be noticed that the lines of action of the force components $30 \sin 30°$ lb and $50 \sin 30°$ lb pass through point A, and therefore these forces are not included in the moment equation.

If we solve Eqs. (2) and (3) simultaneously,

$$B_{y'} = -52.8 \text{ lb} \qquad\qquad\qquad Ans.$$
$$C_{y'} = 145.2 \text{ lb} \qquad\qquad\qquad Ans.$$

Since $B_{y'}$ is a negative quantity, its sense of direction is opposite to that shown on the free-body diagram in Fig. 5-8b. Therefore, the top roller at B serves as the support rather than the bottom roller.

When the values of $B_{y'}$ and $C_{y'}$ are substituted into Eq. (1) we obtain

$$145.2 \sin 30° \text{ lb} - 52.8 \sin 30° \text{ lb} - A_x = 0, \qquad A_x = 46.2 \text{ lb} \quad Ans.$$

Note that the negative sign of $B_{y'}$ must be *retained* when substituting into this equation, since the equations of equilibrium were *originally* written with the assumption that the sense of direction of all the forces acting on the free-body diagram was correct.

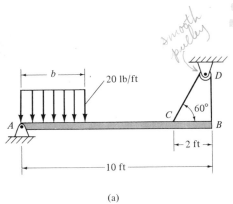

(a)

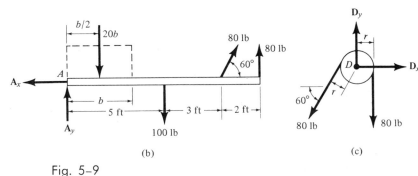

(b)   (c)

Fig. 5-9

Example 5-7

The uniform beam AB shown in Fig. 5-9a weighs 100 lb and is supported at A by a pin and at B and C by a continuous cable which wraps around a frictionless pulley located at D. If a maximum tension force of 80 lb can be developed in the cable before it breaks, determine the greatest length b of a uniform 20-lb/ft distributed load which can be placed on the beam. The uniform load begins at the left-hand support. What is the reaction at A just before the cable breaks?

Solution

A free-body diagram of the beam is shown in Fig. 5–9b. Two unknown force components act at A since the beam is supported there by a pin. As stated in the problem, the maximum tensile force which can be developed in the cable is 80 lb. Since the cable is continuous and passes over a frictionless pulley, the entire cable is subjected to this force. Hence, the cable exerts an 80-lb force at points C and B *on the beam* in the direction of the cable.

The fact that the cable maintains a *constant tensile force* of 80 lb throughout its length when passing over the pulley at D can be easily proved by considering rotational equilibrium of the pulley about the axis of the pin. Assuming that the radius of the pulley is r and using the free-body diagram of the pulley shown in Fig. 5–9c, we see that

$$\zeta + \Sigma M_D = 0; \qquad r(80 \text{ lb}) - r(80 \text{ lb}) \equiv 0$$

Notice that this result is *independent* of the *direction* of the ends of the cable. It indicates that the cable must always sustain the same force of 80 lb at its end points. (If needed, the magnitude of the force components $\mathbf{D}_x$ and $\mathbf{D}_y$ can be found using the force equilibrium equations.)

The uniformly distributed load is reduced to a concentrated force in accordance with the methods of Sec. 4–11. The magnitude of this force is equivalent to the area under the diagram, that is $20b$ lb. The force acts through the centroid of the area, a distance of $b/2$ from point A. Summing moments of the force system about point A (Fig. 5–9b) we can obtain a direct solution for the dimension b. Why?

$$\zeta + M_A = 0; \quad -(20b \text{ lb})\left(\frac{b}{2} \text{ ft}\right) - 100 \text{ lb (5 ft)} + (80 \sin 60° \text{ lb})(8 \text{ ft}) +$$

$$80 \text{ lb (10 ft)} = 0, \qquad b = 9.24 \text{ ft} \quad Ans.$$

Using this result and summing forces in the x and y direction, we have

$$\overset{+}{\rightarrow} \Sigma F_x = 0; \qquad -A_x + 80 \cos 60° \text{ lb} = 0, \qquad A_x = 40 \text{ lb}$$

$$+\uparrow \Sigma F_y = 0; \quad A_y - 20 \text{ lb/ft (9.24 ft)} - 100 \text{ lb} + 80 \sin 60° \text{ lb}$$

$$+ 80 \text{ lb} = 0, \qquad A_y = 135.5 \text{ lb}$$

By vector addition of the two force components at A, the total reaction at A becomes

$$F_A = \sqrt{(A_x)^2 + (A_y)^2} = \sqrt{(40)^2 + (135.5)^2} = 141.4 \text{ lb} \qquad Ans.$$

$$\theta = \tan^{-1}\frac{A_y}{A_x} = \tan^{-1}\frac{135.5}{40} = 73.6° \qquad \theta\!\!\searrow^{F_A} \qquad Ans.$$

Problems

Neglect the weight of the members in the following problems unless specified.

5-13. Determine the reactive force components **T, R,** and **F** acting on ball *A* shown in Fig. 5–3*b*, p. 140.

5-14. Determine the tensile force acting in the vertical cables which supports the 60-lb triangular plate in Prob. 5–6.

5-15. Determine the horizontal and vertical components of force developed by the pin at *A*, and the force in link *BC*, of the rod in Prob. 5–12.

5-16. Three smooth rollers, each having a weight of 50 lb, rest on the 20° inclined plane. Determine the reaction of this plane on each of the rollers.

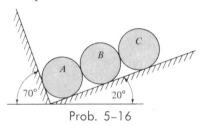

Prob. 5–16

5-17. Determine the horizontal and vertical components of reaction acting at the pin *A* and the reaction at roller *B* for the loaded beam.

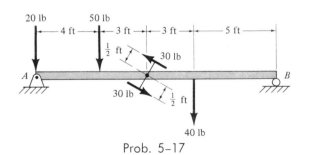

Prob. 5–17

5-18. The bent beam is supported by a pin at *A* and by a smooth surface at *B*. Determine the horizontal and vertical components of reaction at *A* and the reaction at *B*. The spring is stretched three inches.

152

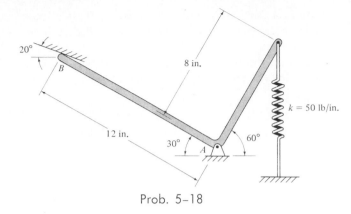

Prob. 5–18

5-19. Determine the reactions at the wall, *A*, for the beam loaded as shown.

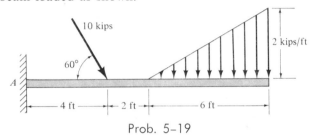

Prob. 5–19

5-20. A 150-lb man stands uniformly on a smooth ladder rung at *A*. Assuming the man's leg bone is only subjected to a compressive force **F**$_B$, determine this force and the muscle force **T**. Discuss the validity of the solution. The man stands with both feet on the ladder.

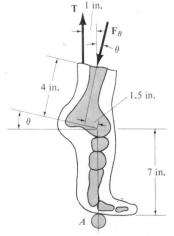

Prob. 5–20

5-21. Determine the bone force F_B and muscle force T necessary to hold the 10-lb ball in equilibrium.

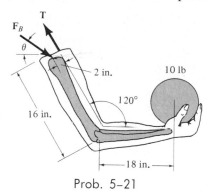

Prob. 5-21

5-22. Determine the tension in the cable and the horizontal and vertical components of reaction of the pin A. The pulley at D is frictionless.

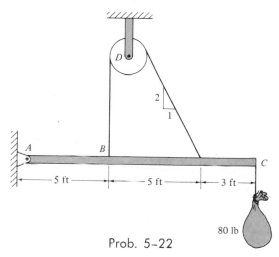

Prob. 5-22

5-23. Determine the components of reaction at pin A and roller B for the beam loaded as shown.

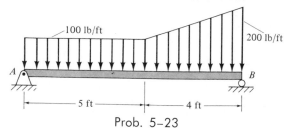

Prob. 5-23

5-24. Determine the reactions at A and B for the beam loaded as shown.

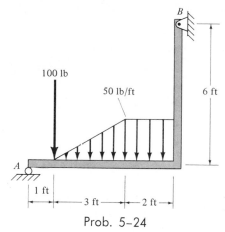

Prob. 5-24

5-25. Determine the horizontal and vertical components of reaction at the pin support A and the reaction at the roller B for the loaded frame.

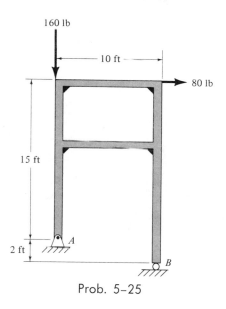

Prob. 5-25

5-26. Determine the horizontal and vertical components of reaction at the pin support A and the reaction of the smooth wall at B for the beam loaded as shown.

153

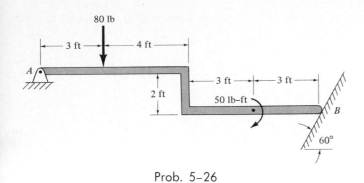

Prob. 5-26

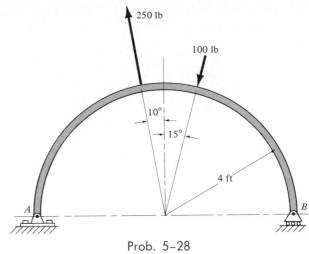

Prob. 5-28

5-27. Determine the horizontal and vertical components of reaction at the pin A and the tension in the cable BC for the boom. Two of these booms are used to support the 1,000-lb lifeboat. *Hint:* the pulley at D exerts a total downward reaction of 500 lb on the boom.)

5-29. Calculate the components of reaction at the fixed wall A for the loaded beam. The cable is fixed at B and passes over a smooth peg at C.

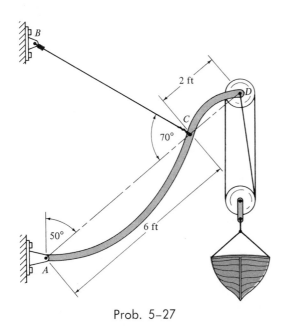

Prob. 5-27

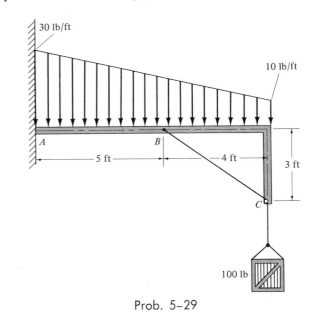

Prob. 5-29

5-28. Determine the horizontal and vertical components of reaction at the pin and the reaction at the roller support for the loaded semicircular arch.

5-30. Two spheres, each weighing 20 lb, are suspended from the same point by equal length cords. Determine

154

the tension in each cord and the reactive force acting between the spheres.

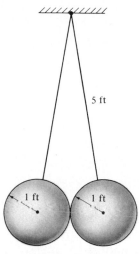

Prob. 5-30

5-31. The forces acting on the jet aircraft, which is flying level at constant velocity, must be in equilibrium. If the aircraft weighs 18,000 lb, and the jet provides a thrust **T** of 1,200 lb, determine the lift provided by both the wings, **L**$_w$, and tail **L**$_t$, and the drag **D.** The center of gravity of the aircraft is at *B* as shown.

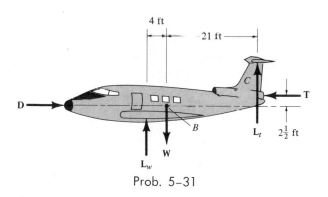

Prob. 5-31

5-32. Determine the reactions at *A* and *B* for the loaded truss.

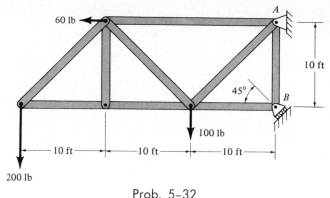

Prob. 5-32

5-33. Determine the horizontal and vertical components of reaction at the pin support *A* and the force in the link *CE* for the loaded frame.

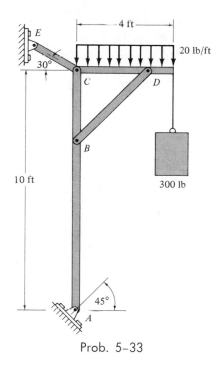

Prob. 5-33

5-34. A uniform rod *AB* having a weight of 70 lb supports a 50-lb block. Determine the angles α and β of the supporting cables, and the necessary weight *W*

155

which is required to hold the rod in the horizontal position. The pulleys are frictionless.

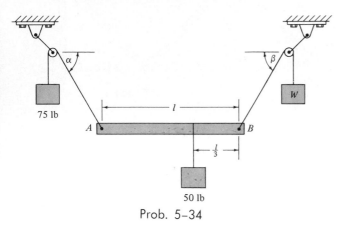

75 lb

50 lb

Prob. 5–34

around a fixed drum at B and passes over a frictionless pulley located at C.

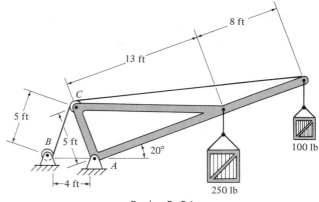

8 ft

13 ft

5 ft

20°

4 ft

100 lb

250 lb

Prob. 5–36

5–35. Determine the horizontal and vertical components of reaction at the pin A and the tension in the cable BCD required to support the 250-lb beam. The cord is attached to a fixed drum at B and passes over a smooth peg at C. The center of gravity for the beam and drum is located at G.

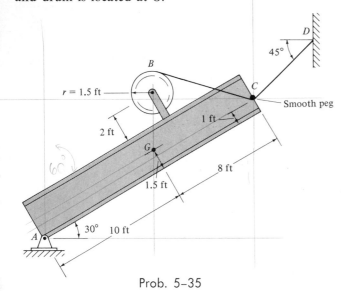

D

45°

B

$r = 1.5$ ft

C

Smooth peg

2 ft

1 ft

G

8 ft

1.5 ft

30° 10 ft

A

Prob. 5–35

5–36. Calculate the tension in the cable at B required to hold the boom in the position shown. The cable wraps

5–37. Two smooth tubes A and B, each having the same weight W, are suspended from a common point by means of equal length cords. A third tube, C, is placed between A and B. Determine the greatest weight of C without upsetting equilibrium.

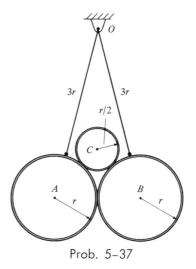

O

$3r$ $3r$

$r/2$

C

A r B r

Prob. 5–37

5–38. A uniform beam having a weight W and length l rests horizontally on the surface of two smooth inclined planes. If α is known, show that $\theta = \alpha$ is required for equilibrium. Also, compute the reactions at the ends of the beam.

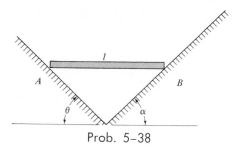

Prob. 5–38

5-39. Determine the tension in the supporting cables *BC* and *DEF*, and the reaction at the smooth incline *A* of the loaded beam.

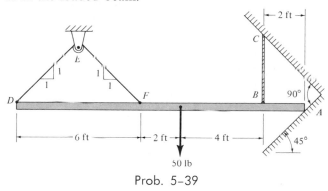

Prob. 5–39

5-40. Determine the least force **F** and the angle θ required to move the 250-lb roller over the 3-in. block.

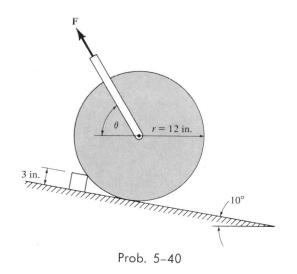

Prob. 5–40

5-41. The bracket is used to support a smooth cylindrical tube having a weight of 40 lb. If the bracket is pinned at *D*, determine the angle θ such that the normal reaction at *A* is 10 lb. What are the normal reactions at points *B* and *C*?

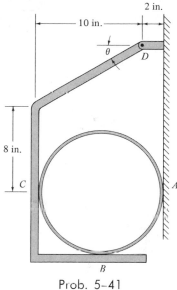

Prob. 5–41

5-42. Determine the maximum load *W* which can be supported by the crane. For the calculation, assume that the cable *BC* is attached at both ends. The tractor portion weighs 20,000 lb and has a center of gravity at *G*. Neglect the weight of the boom *AB*.

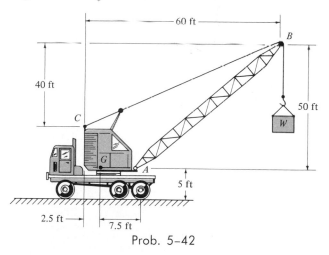

Prob. 5–42

157

Three-Dimensional Force Systems Acting on a Rigid Body

5-3. Free-Body Diagrams and Support Reactions

The *first step* in solving equilibrium problems involving three-dimensional force systems, as in the case of two dimensions, is to draw a free-body diagram of the body (or group of bodies considered as a system). Why would you want to do this? The procedure for constructing the free-body diagram is identical with that given for two dimensional problems. In drawing a free-body diagram, it is important to include *all* forces and couple moments which act *on* the body or group of bodies in question. These interactions are commonly caused by the external applied loadings, contact forces exerted by adjacent bodies on the body, support reactions, and the weight of the body. Once the free-body diagram is drawn, the equations of equilibrium can then readily be applied.

The reactive forces and moments acting at various types of supports and connections, when the members are viewed in three dimensions, are listed in Table 5-2. It is important both to recognize the symbols used to represent each of the supports and to clearly understand how the forces and/or couple moments are developed by each support. In particular, a *force* is developed by a support which restricts the *translation* of the connecting member in a given direction. A *couple moment* is developed when *rotation* of the connecting member is prevented. For example, in Table 5-2, the ball-and-socket joint (4) prevents any translation of the connecting member; therefore, a force must act on the member at the point of connection. This force has three force components acting in orthogonal directions and having unknown magnitudes, F_x, F_y, F_z. Provided these three components are known, one can obtain the magnitude of the force, $F = \sqrt{F_x^2 + F_y^2 + F_z^2}$, and its direction, defined by $\alpha = \cos^{-1} F_x/F$, $\beta = \cos^{-1} F_y/F$, and $\gamma = \cos^{-1} F_z/F$.* Since the connecting member is allowed to rotate freely about *any* axis, no moment is resisted at this support.† The smooth bearing (5) allows both translation and rotation of its connecting shaft only along the y axis. However, motion is restricted in the xz plane. As a result, force and couple-moment components act on the shaft along the x and z axes.

In some cases, not all the reactive forces existing at a support can be developed because of other physical constraints acting on the rigid body. For example, the single hinge (7) may develop a total of five unknowns (three force components and two moment components) when it acts as

---

*The three unknowns may also be represented as an unknown force magnitude F, and two unknown direction cosines for the force. The third direction cosine is obtained using the identity $\cos^2 \alpha + \cos^2 \beta + \cos^2 \gamma = 1$ (Eq. 2-8).

†A free-body diagram for a body having a ball-and-socket joint is shown in Fig. 5-15*b*.

Table 5-2

Types of connection	Reaction	Number of unknowns
(1) light cable	F	One unknown: magnitude of **F**; this force acts in the direction of the cable
(2) smooth surface support	F	One unknown: magnitude of **F**; this force acts normal to the surface at the point of contact
(3) roller on a smooth surface	F	One unknown: magnitude of **F**; this force acts normal to the surface at the point of contact
(4) ball and socket	F_z, F_y, F_x	Three unknowns: magnitudes of three force components F_x, F_y, and F_z
(5) smooth bearing	M_z, F_z, M_x, F_x	Four unknowns: magnitudes of two force components F_x, F_z and the two couples M_x, M_z
(6) smooth pin	M_z, F_z, F_x, F_y, M_y	Five unknowns: magnitudes of three force components F_x, F_y, F_z and two couples M_y, M_z

Table 5–2 (Contd.)

Types of connection	Reaction	Number of unknowns
(7) single hinge	*no moment p o b*	Five unknowns: magnitudes of three force components $\mathbf{F}_x$, $\mathbf{F}_y$, $\mathbf{F}_z$ and two couples $\mathbf{M}_x$, $\mathbf{M}_z$
(8) fixed support		Six unknowns: magnitudes of three force components $\mathbf{F}_x$, $\mathbf{F}_y$, $\mathbf{F}_z$ and three couples $\mathbf{M}_x$, $\mathbf{M}_y$, $\mathbf{M}_z$

a *primary single means of support*. However, when two hinges are present and aligned properly along the *same axis,* only three unknown components of force may be developed. Moment reactions cannot occur in this case, since rotation about the axis of one hinge is prevented by constraining forces developed at the other hinge. (See Examples 5–8 and 5–11.)

All reactions which *can exist* at a support must be included on the free-body diagram. Those unknowns which are zero will automatically be accounted for when the equations of equilibrium are applied. As usual, when an unknown is represented as the magnitude of a force or couple moment, the sense of direction for the vector may be *assumed*. If the solution yields a negative answer for the unknown, the vector sense of direction is then opposite to the assumed direction.

5–4. Equations of Equilibrium

A necessary condition for the equilibrium of a rigid body subjected to a three-dimensional force system requires that the total *resultant* force and *resultant* couple moment acting on the body be equal to *zero*. By reducing the system of forces acting on a rigid body to a single resultant force $\Sigma\mathbf{F}$ acting through a specified point O and a resultant moment $\Sigma\mathbf{M}_O$, these necessary conditions for equilibrium may be postulated in vector component form as

$$\Sigma\mathbf{F} = \Sigma F_x\mathbf{i} + \Sigma F_y\mathbf{j} + \Sigma F_z\mathbf{k} = 0 \qquad (5\text{–}6a)$$

$$\Sigma\mathbf{M}_O = \Sigma M_x\mathbf{i} + \Sigma M_y\mathbf{j} + \Sigma M_z\mathbf{k} = 0 \qquad (5\text{–}6b)$$

Since the components in the **i, j,** and **k** directions are independent of one another, the necessary conditions for the equilibrium of a rigid body may be expressed in the form of *six independent scalar equations:*

$$\Sigma F_x = 0$$
$$\Sigma F_y = 0 \qquad\qquad (5\text{--}7a)$$
$$\Sigma F_z = 0$$

and

$$\Sigma M_x = 0$$
$$\Sigma M_y = 0 \qquad\qquad (5\text{--}7b)$$
$$\Sigma M_z = 0$$

These six equations may be used to solve for at most six unknowns shown on the free-body diagram.

Equations 5–7a express the fact that the sum of the force components acting in the x, y, and z directions, respectively, must be zero. The coordinate axes x, y, and z should be oriented in a direction which will enable one to easily calculate the force components to be used in Eqs. 5–7a. Equations 5–7b require the sum of the moment components directed along the x, y, and z *axes,* respectively, to be zero. It is *not necessary* that the set of axes chosen for moment summation *coincide* with the set of axes chosen for force summation. It is recommended that one *choose the direction of one of the moment axes such that it intersects the line of action of as many unknown forces as possible.* The moment of forces passing through points on this axis or parallel to the axis will then be zero.

It will be stated without proof that *any three nonorthogonal axes* may be chosen for either force or moment summations. These axes must, however, *not be parallel* to one another or else linearly dependent equations may result. By the proper choice of axes, it may be possible to solve directly for an unknown quantity, or at least reduce the need for solving a large number of simultaneous equations for the unknowns. In some cases, however, after applying the equations of equilibrium, one may unavoidably obtain a complicated system of linear algebraic equations which must then be solved simultaneously, e.g., six equations with six unknowns. In such cases the equations may be solved using the computer program listed in Appendix A.

Often, the three-dimensional geometry of a problem may be complicated. In such circumstances, it is recommended that the (two) vector equations of equilibrium (Eqs. 5–6) *first* be used to obtain the necessary (six) scalar equations. A vector approach to the solution is very methodical and eliminates the need for having to visualize the direction of moments created by the force components.

5–5. Sufficient Conditions for Equilibrium

Equations 5–2 and 5–7 provide the necessary conditions for equilibrium of a rigid body subjected to two- and three-dimensional force systems, respectively. In all problems presented thus far, these equations are also sufficient conditions for equilibrium. Such problems are termed *statically determinate*. There are, however, certain types of problems in which the equilibrium equations are not sufficient for determining all the forces acting on a rigid body. These types of problems are called *statically indeterminate*.

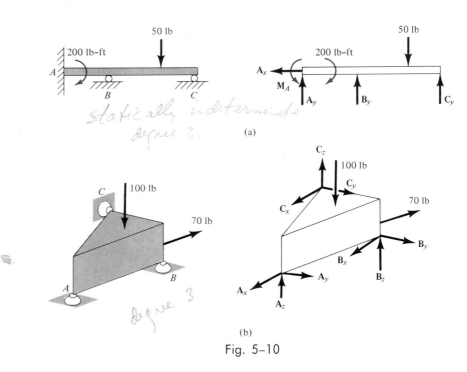

(a)

(b)

Fig. 5–10

Statical indeterminacy can arise if a body has more supports than are necessary (redundant) to maintain the equilibrium configuration. For example, the two-dimensional problem, Fig. 5–10*a*, and the three-dimensional problem, Fig. 5–10*b*, shown together with their free-body diagrams, are both statically indeterminate because of redundancy in the number of support reactions. In the two-dimensional case, there are five unknowns, that is, A_x, A_y, B_y, C_y, and M_A, for which only three equilibrium equations can be written (Eqs. 5–2). Two more equations are needed for a complete solution to the problem. This problem is termed indeterminate to the second degree (five unknowns minus three equations). The three-dimensional problem has nine unknowns, for which only six equilibrium equations can be written (Eqs. 5–7). It is indeterminate to the third degree. The additional equations needed to solve indeterminate problems of the type shown in Fig. 5–10 are obtained from the conditions of deformation which occur between the loads and the internal movements within the body. These relations involve the physical properties of the body which are studied in subjects relating to mechanics of deformation, such as strength of materials.

In some cases, there may be an equal number of unknown forces as there are equations of equilibrium; however, *instability* can develop because of *improper constraining* action by the supports. This may occur in two ways. In the case of three-dimensional problems, the body is improperly constrained if the support reactions all intersect a common axis. In two-dimensional problems, the axis is *perpendicular* to the figure, and appears as a point. When the reactive forces are concurrent at this point, the body is improperly constrained. Examples of both cases are given in Fig. 5–11. From the free-body diagram of each body it is seen that the summation of moments about axis AB, Fig. 5–11a, or point O, Fig. 5–11b, will *not* be equal to zero; thus rotation about axis AB or point O will take place.* It becomes impossible to solve completely for all the unknowns, since one can write a moment equation which does not involve any of the unknown support reactions. (This limits by one the number of available equilibrium equations.)

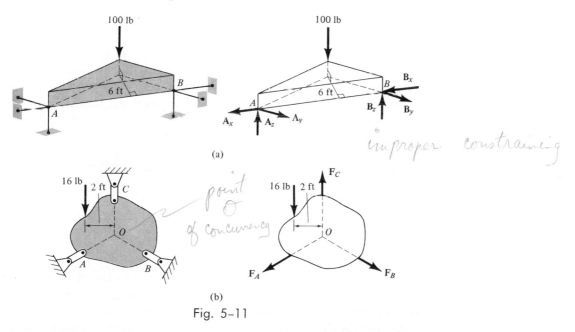

(a)

(b)

Fig. 5–11

*For the three dimensional problem $\Sigma M_{AB} = (100 \text{ lb})(6 \text{ ft}) \neq 0$, and for the two dimensional problem $\Sigma M_O = (16 \text{ lb})(2 \text{ ft}) \neq 0$.

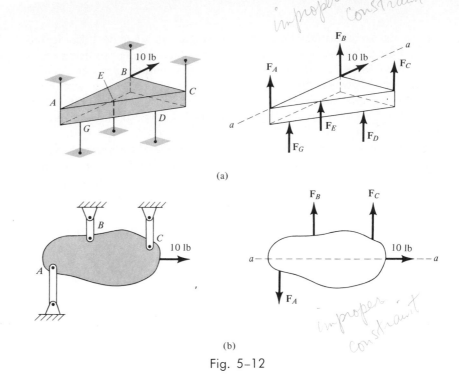

(a)

(b)

Fig. 5–12

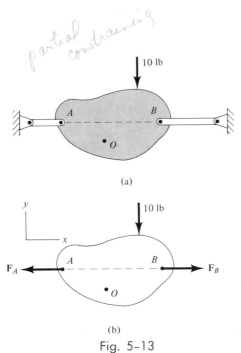

(a)

(b)

Fig. 5–13

Another way in which partial constraining leads to instability occurs when the *reactive forces* are all parallel. Three- and two-dimensional examples of this are shown in Figs. 5–12*a* and *b*. In both cases the summation of forces along the horizontal *aa* axis will *not* be equal to zero. The problem is unstable since a force equilibrium equation in this direction *will not* involve any unknown *reactive* forces.

In some cases, a body may have *fewer* reactive forces than equations of equilibrium which must be satisfied. Under these conditions, the body is only *partially constrained*. Consider the body shown in Fig. 5–13*a* with its corresponding free-body diagram in Fig. 5–13*b*. Although the equations $\Sigma F_x = 0$ and $\Sigma M_O = 0$ (O lies at some point not on the line of action AB) will be satisfied by proper choice of the reactions $\mathbf{F}_A$ and $\mathbf{F}_B$, the equation $\Sigma F_y = 0$ will not be satisfied under the loading conditions and therefore equilibrium will not be maintained.

To ensure equilibrium of a rigid body, it is therefore necessary to properly constrain the body. This can be accomplished provided: (1) there are at least as many reactive forces as equations of equilibrium, (2) the lines of action of the reactive forces do not intersect points on a common axis, and (3) the reactive forces are not parallel to one another. When the number of reactive forces needed to properly constrain the body in question

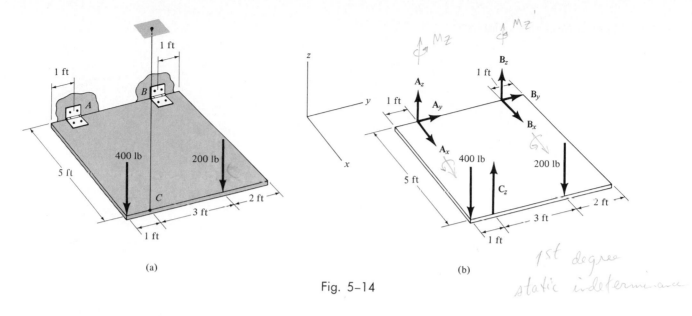

1 ft

1 ft

A

B

400 lb

200 lb

5 ft

C

3 ft

2 ft

1 ft

(a)

z

y

x

M_z

M_z'

B_z

1 ft

A_z

B_y

A_y

1 ft

B_x

A_x

400 lb

200 lb

5 ft

C_z

3 ft

2 ft

1 ft

1st degree
static indeterminance

(b)

Fig. 5–14

is a minimum, the equations of equilibrium are *both* necessary and sufficient conditions for determining all the forces acting on the body.

Example 5-8

The platform shown in Fig. 5–14*a* has negligible weight and is subjected
to two concentrated forces. It is supported at *A* and *B* by hinges and at *C*
by a vertical cable. Draw a free-body diagram of the platform.

Solution

The free-body diagram of the platform is shown in Fig. 5–14*b*. This
diagram includes the dimensions of the body which will be necessary for
computing the moments of the forces. Provided the hinges are *properly
aligned*, three components of force act at each hinge. Because of the
constraints caused by *both* hinges, rotation about the *x* or *z* axis of a
single hinge is prevented; hence, unknown moment components of the
hinges do not act on the body and are therefore excluded from the
free-body diagram (see (7) in Table 5–2). For example, any rotation of
the hinge at *A* about the *z* axis is prevented by the moment of force B_x
developed at *B*, that is, $(B_x)(3 \text{ ft})$, *not* by a moment component $(\mathbf{M}_A)_z$. On
the free-body diagram there is a total of *seven* unknown magnitudes of
force: A_x, A_y, A_z, B_x, B_y, B_z, and C_z. Only *six* scalar equilibrium equations
can be written to relate these unknowns and therefore only a partial solu-
tion to the problem can be obtained (see Prob. 5–43). Since there is one
more unknown than equations of equilibrium, this problem is statically
indeterminate to the first degree.

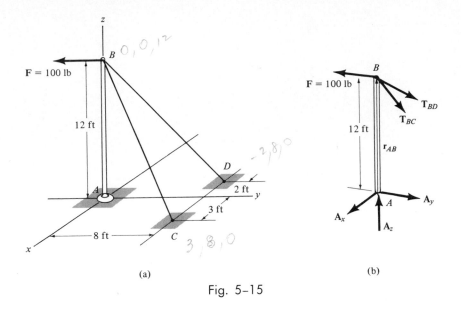

Fig. 5–15

Example 5–9

Determine the tensions in the cables BC and BD, and the reaction at the support A for the vertical mast shown in Fig. 5–15a. Neglect the weight of the mast.

Solution

The first step is to draw the free-body diagram of the mast, Fig. 5–15b. Why? Since the support at A is a ball-and-socket joint, three unknown force components act at this point. The cable tension forces $\mathbf{T}_{BC}$ and $\mathbf{T}_{BD}$ have a known direction and unknown magnitude. There are, therefore, five unknown force magnitudes shown on the free-body diagram.

Expressing each force acting on the free-body diagram in Cartesian vector notation,

$$\mathbf{F} = \{-100\mathbf{j}\} \text{ lb}$$

$$\mathbf{F}_A = A_x\mathbf{i} + A_y\mathbf{j} + A_z\mathbf{k}$$

$$\mathbf{T}_{BC} = T_{BC}\left(\frac{\mathbf{r}_{BC}}{r_{BC}}\right) = \frac{3T_{BC}}{\sqrt{217}}\mathbf{i} + \frac{8T_{BC}}{\sqrt{217}}\mathbf{j} - \frac{12T_{BC}}{\sqrt{217}}\mathbf{k}$$

$$= 0.204T_{BC}\mathbf{i} + 0.543T_{BC}\mathbf{j} - 0.815T_{BC}\mathbf{k}$$

$$\mathbf{T}_{BD} = T_{BD}\left(\frac{\mathbf{r}_{BD}}{r_{BD}}\right) = \frac{-2T_{BD}}{\sqrt{212}}\mathbf{i} + \frac{8T_{BD}}{\sqrt{212}}\mathbf{j} - \frac{12T_{BD}}{\sqrt{212}}\mathbf{k}$$

$$= -0.137T_{BD}\mathbf{i} + 0.549T_{BD}\mathbf{j} - 0.824T_{BD}\mathbf{k}$$

Applying the two vector equations of equilibrium gives

$\Sigma \mathbf{F} = 0;$ $\qquad \mathbf{F} + \mathbf{F}_A + \mathbf{T}_{BC} + \mathbf{T}_{BD} = 0$

$$-100\mathbf{j} + A_x\mathbf{i} + A_y\mathbf{j} + A_z\mathbf{k} + 0.204T_{BC}\mathbf{i} + 0.543T_{BC}\mathbf{j} - 0.815T_{BC}\mathbf{k}$$
$$-0.137T_{BD}\mathbf{i} + 0.549T_{BD}\mathbf{j} - 0.824T_{BD}\mathbf{k} = 0$$

or

$$(A_x + 0.204T_{BC} - 0.137T_{BD})\mathbf{i} + (-100 + A_y + 0.543T_{BC}$$
$$+ 0.549T_{BD})\mathbf{j} + (A_z - 0.815T_{BC} - 0.824T_{BD})\mathbf{k} = 0$$

Equating to zero the **i, j,** and **k** components we obtain the three scalar equilibrium equations:

$\Sigma F_x = 0;$ $\qquad A_x + 0.204T_{BC} - 0.137T_{BD} = 0$ $\qquad\qquad (1)$

$\Sigma F_y = 0;$ $\qquad A_y + 0.543T_{BC} + 0.549T_{BD} - 100 = 0$ $\qquad (2)$

$\Sigma F_z = 0;$ $\qquad A_z - 0.815T_{BC} - 0.824T_{BD} = 0$ $\qquad\qquad (3)$

Summing moments about axes passing through point A to eliminate the three unknown force components passing through this point,

$\Sigma \mathbf{M}_A = 0;$ $\qquad (\mathbf{r}_{AB} \times \mathbf{F}) + (\mathbf{r}_{AB} \times \mathbf{T}_{BC}) + (\mathbf{r}_{AB} \times \mathbf{T}_{BD}) = 0$

The position vector $\mathbf{r}_{AB}$ in this equation extends from point A to point B. Since this vector is a common term in the cross product, by the distributive law, it may be factored out, yielding,

$$\mathbf{r}_{AB} \times (\mathbf{F} + \mathbf{T}_{BC} + \mathbf{T}_{BD}) = 0$$

Substituting, we have

$$12\mathbf{k} \times (-100\mathbf{j} + 0.204T_{BC}\mathbf{i} + 0.543T_{BC}\mathbf{j} - 0.815T_{BC}\mathbf{k}$$
$$-0.137T_{BD}\mathbf{i} + 0.549T_{BD}\mathbf{j} - 0.824T_{BD}\mathbf{k}) = 0$$

or

$$-12(0.543T_{BC} + 0.549T_{BD} - 100)\mathbf{i} + 12(0.204T_{BC} - 0.137T_{BD})\mathbf{j} = 0$$

Setting the **i** and **j** components equal to zero yields

$\Sigma M_x = 0;$ $\qquad 0.543T_{BC} + 0.549T_{BD} - 100 = 0$ $\qquad (4)$

$\Sigma M_y = 0;$ $\qquad 0.204T_{BC} - 0.137T_{BD} = 0$ $\qquad\qquad (5)$

(The equilibrium equation about the z axis, $\Sigma M_z = 0$, is automatically satisfied for the given loading system since the lines of action of all the forces acting on the body pass through the z axis.)

Solving Eqs. (4) and (5) for T_{BC} and T_{BD} and substituting these values into Eqs. (1) through (3) yield

$$A_x = 0.0 \text{ lb} \qquad\qquad Ans.$$
$$A_y = 0.0 \text{ lb} \qquad\qquad Ans.$$
$$A_z = 150.0 \text{ lb} \qquad\qquad Ans.$$
$$T_{BC} = 73.5 \text{ lb} \qquad\qquad Ans.$$
$$T_{BD} = 109.4 \text{ lb} \qquad\qquad Ans.$$

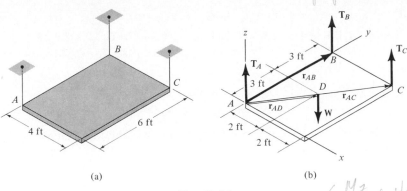

without T_B →
improper constraint

Fig. 5-16

no Σ M_z
because all the
forces are parallel
to z-axis

Example 5-10

The homogeneous plate shown in Fig. 5-16a weighs 100 lb/ft². The plate is suspended in the horizontal plane by means of three parallel cords. Determine the tension in each of these cords.

Solution

A free-body diagram of the plate is shown in Fig. 5-16b. The weight acts at the center of gravity of the plate (which coincides with the centroid). The magnitude of this force is the product of 100 lb/ft² times the area of the plate. Hence $W = (100 \text{ lb/ft}^2)(4 \text{ ft})(6 \text{ ft}) = 2{,}400$ lb. Therefore $\mathbf{W} = \{-2{,}400\mathbf{k}\}$ lb.

Orientating the x, y, and z axes as shown in the figure, we can write the vector force equilibrium equation as

$$\Sigma \mathbf{F} = 0; \qquad T_A\mathbf{k} + T_B\mathbf{k} + T_C\mathbf{k} - 2{,}400\mathbf{k} = 0$$

or

$$\Sigma F_z = 0; \qquad T_A + T_B + T_C - 2{,}400 = 0 \qquad (1)$$

Summing moments of all the forces about the origin yields

$$\Sigma \mathbf{M}_A = 0; \quad (\mathbf{r}_{AB} \times T_B\mathbf{k}) + (\mathbf{r}_{AC} \times T_C\mathbf{k}) + (\mathbf{r}_{AD} \times \mathbf{W}) = 0$$

The position vectors can be determined from the geometry of the plate. Hence,

$$[6\mathbf{j} \times T_B\mathbf{k}] + [(4\mathbf{i} + 6\mathbf{j}) \times T_C\mathbf{k}] + [(2\mathbf{i} + 3\mathbf{j}) \times (-2{,}400\mathbf{k})] = 0$$

or

$$(6T_B + 6T_C - 7{,}200)\mathbf{i} + (-4T_C + 4{,}800)\mathbf{j} = 0$$

Equating to zero the corresponding $\mathbf{i}$ and $\mathbf{j}$ components gives

$$\Sigma M_x = 0; \qquad 6T_B + 6T_C - 7{,}200 = 0 \qquad (2)$$
$$\Sigma M_y = 0; \qquad -4T_C + 4{,}800 = 0 \qquad (3)$$

These two scalar equations represent the moment summation of forces about the x and y axes, respectively. The moment of a force about an axis is equal to the product of the force magnitude and the perpendicular distance from the line of action of the force to the axis. Hence, for example, taking moments of the forces $\mathbf{T}_C$ and $\mathbf{W}$ about the y axis shown in Fig. 5–16b yields the scalar Eq. (3).

Solving Eqs. (1) through (3), we obtain

$$T_A = 1{,}200 \text{ lb} \qquad\qquad Ans.$$
$$T_B = 0 \qquad\qquad Ans.$$
$$T_C = 1{,}200 \text{ lb} \qquad\qquad Ans.$$

Note that these reactions provide the necessary *vertical support* for the loading. If a force acting in the xy plane is applied to the plate, other supports would be required to maintain equilibrium. For this reason, the plate is only partially constrained.

Example 5–11

Determine the magnitude of the vertical force $\mathbf{P}$, which must be applied to the handle of the windlass shown in Fig. 5–17a, to maintain equilibrium of the 150-lb weight. Also calculate the reactions at the smooth bearings A and B.

Solution

The free-body diagram of the windlass is shown in Fig. 5–17b. Provided the bearings at A and B are aligned correctly, *only* force reactions occur at these supports. (Moment reactions are not developed at these supports since rotation about the axis of one bearing is prevented by a *reactive force* occurring at the other bearing. For example, there is no moment

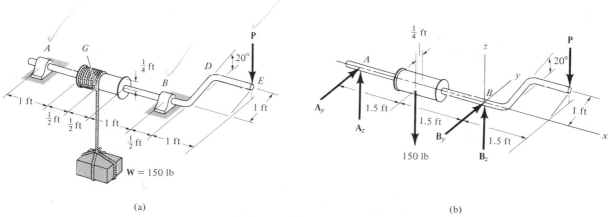

(a)   (b)

Fig. 5–17

component $(\mathbf{M}_A)_z$ developed at A since rotation about A is prevented by the reactive force $\mathbf{B}_y$ acting at B.)

For this particular problem, each of the five unknown force magnitudes shown on the free-body diagram can easily be obtained by direct application of the scalar equations of equilibrium. Summing moments about the x axis, we can obtain a direct solution for P. Why? For the scalar moment summation, we must compute the moment of each force as the product of the *perpendicular distance* from the x axis to the line of action of the force. Assuming positive moments act in the $+\mathbf{i}$ direction,

$$\Sigma(M_B)_x = 0; \quad 150 \text{ lb } (\tfrac{1}{4} \text{ ft}) - P(1 \cos 20° \text{ ft}) = 0, \quad P = 39.9 \text{ lb} \quad Ans.$$

Using this result for P and summing moments in a similar manner about the y and z axes passing through point B we have,

$$\Sigma(M_B)_y = 0;$$

$$-150 \text{ lb } (1.5 \text{ ft}) + A_z(3 \text{ ft}) + (39.9 \text{ lb})(1.5 \text{ ft}) = 0, \quad A_z = 55.0 \text{ lb} \quad Ans.$$

and

$$\Sigma(M_B)_z = 0; \quad -A_y(3 \text{ ft}) = 0, \quad A_y = 0 \quad Ans.$$

(Note that summation of moments was taken about axes which pass through the bearing support at B in order to eliminate the two unknown force components $\mathbf{B}_y$ and $\mathbf{B}_z$ from the moment equation.)

The reactions at B are obtained by a force summation, using the results computed above,

$$\Sigma F_y = 0; \quad 0 + B_y = 0, \quad B_y = 0 \quad Ans.$$

$$\Sigma F_z = 0; \quad 55.0 - 150 + B_z - 39.9 = 0, \quad B_z = 134.9 \text{ lb} \quad Ans.$$

As shown on the free-body diagram, the supports do not provide resistance against movement of the windlass in the x direction. Hence, the windlass is only partially constrained.

Example 5–12

The bent rod shown in Fig. 5–18a is supported at A by a smooth collar, at E by a ball-and-socket joint, and at B by means of cable BC. (a) Determine the forces developed at these supports when the rod is subjected to the 100-lb weight shown; and (b) using only *one equilibrium equation*, obtain a direct solution for the tension in cable BC. The smooth collar attachment at A is capable of exerting force components only in the z and y directions, since it is aligned properly on the shaft axis.

Solution

Part (a). The free-body diagram for the rod is shown in Fig. 5–18b. There are six unknowns in this problem. These include the three unknown force

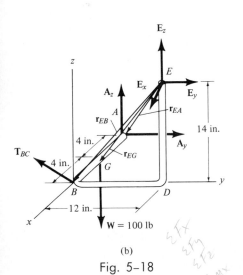

(a)

(b)

Fig. 5–18

components at the ball-and-socket joint, two at the smooth collar bearing, and an unknown tension force in the cable. Expressing each force on the free-body diagram in vector component notation, we have

$$\mathbf{W} = \{-100\mathbf{k}\}\ \text{lb}$$
$$\mathbf{F}_A = A_y\mathbf{j} + A_z\mathbf{k}$$
$$\mathbf{F}_E = E_x\mathbf{i} + E_y\mathbf{j} + E_z\mathbf{k}$$
$$\mathbf{T}_{BC} = T_{BC}\left(\frac{\mathbf{r}_{BC}}{r_{BC}}\right) = \frac{3T_{BC}}{\sqrt{98}}\mathbf{i} - \frac{5T_{BC}}{\sqrt{98}}\mathbf{j} + \frac{8T_{BC}}{\sqrt{98}}\mathbf{k}$$
$$= 0.303T_{BC}\mathbf{i} - 0.505T_{BC}\mathbf{j} + 0.808T_{BC}\mathbf{k}$$

Force equilibrium requires

$$\Sigma\mathbf{F} = 0; \qquad \mathbf{W} + \mathbf{F}_A + \mathbf{F}_E + \mathbf{T}_{BC} = 0$$
$$-100\mathbf{k} + (A_y\mathbf{j} + A_z\mathbf{k}) + (E_x\mathbf{i} + E_y\mathbf{j} + E_z\mathbf{k}) + (0.303T_{BC}\mathbf{i}$$
$$-0.505T_{BC}\mathbf{j} + 0.808T_{BC}\mathbf{k}) = 0$$

or

$$(E_x + 0.303T_{BC})\mathbf{i} + (A_y + E_y - 0.505T_{BC})\mathbf{j}$$
$$+ (A_z + E_z + 0.808T_{BC} - 100)\mathbf{k} = 0$$

Thus, equating the **i** and **j** components equal to zero,

$$\Sigma F_x = 0; \qquad\qquad E_x + 0.303T_{BC} = 0 \qquad\qquad (1)$$
$$\Sigma F_y = 0; \qquad\qquad A_y + E_y - 0.505T_{BC} = 0 \qquad\qquad (2)$$
$$\Sigma F_z = 0; \qquad\qquad A_z + E_z + 0.808T_{BC} - 100 = 0 \qquad\qquad (3)$$

Summing moments about point E, to eliminate the three components of force acting there,

$$\Sigma\mathbf{M}_E = 0; \qquad (\mathbf{r}_{EB} \times \mathbf{T}_{BC}) + (\mathbf{r}_{EG} \times \mathbf{W}) + (\mathbf{r}_{EA} \times \mathbf{F}_A) = 0$$

Expressing each of the cross products in determinant form,

$$\begin{vmatrix} \mathbf{i} & \mathbf{j} & \mathbf{k} \\ 0 & -12 & -14 \\ 0.303T_{BC} & -0.505T_{BC} & 0.808T_{BC} \end{vmatrix} + \begin{vmatrix} \mathbf{i} & \mathbf{j} & \mathbf{k} \\ -4 & -12 & -14 \\ 0 & 0 & -100 \end{vmatrix}$$

$$+ \begin{vmatrix} \mathbf{i} & \mathbf{j} & \mathbf{k} \\ -8 & -12 & -14 \\ 0 & A_y & A_z \end{vmatrix} = 0$$

Expanding and rearranging terms,

$$(-16.77T_{BC} - 12A_z + 14A_y + 1{,}200)\mathbf{i} + (-4.24T_{BC} + 8A_z - 400)\mathbf{j}$$
$$+ (3.64T_{BC} - 8A_y)\mathbf{k} = 0$$

Equating the $\mathbf{i}$, $\mathbf{j}$, and $\mathbf{k}$ components equal to zero yields

$$\Sigma M_x = 0; \qquad -16.77T_{BC} - 12A_z + 14A_y + 1{,}200 = 0 \qquad (4)$$

$$\Sigma M_y = 0; \qquad -4.24T_{BC} + 8A_z - 400 = 0 \qquad (5)$$

$$\Sigma M_z = 0; \qquad 3.64T_{BC} - 8A_y = 0 \qquad (6)$$

The simultaneous solution of Eqs. (1) through (6) may be rather tedious. Consequently, the computer program listed in Appendix A may be used to solve these equations. The final solution is

$$A_y = 16.3 \text{ lb} \qquad \qquad Ans.$$

$$A_z = 69.0 \text{ lb} \qquad \qquad Ans.$$

$$E_x = -10.84 \text{ lb} \qquad \qquad Ans.$$

$$E_y = 1.79 \text{ lb} \qquad \qquad Ans.$$

$$E_z = 2.09 \text{ lb} \qquad \qquad Ans.$$

$$T_{BC} = 35.8 \text{ lb} \qquad \qquad Ans.$$

Part (b). Without knowing the other reactions, the cable tension $\mathbf{T}_{BC}$ may be obtained *directly* by summing moments about an axis passing through points A and E, Fig. 5–18b. (Note that the line of action of the other five unknown force components passes through this axis and hence, these forces are eliminated from the moment summation.) The unit vector $\mathbf{u}_{AE}$ shown in Fig. 5–18a which defines the position of this axis is

$$\mathbf{u}_{AE} = \frac{\mathbf{r}_{AE}}{r_{AE}} = \frac{8}{\sqrt{404}}\mathbf{i} + \frac{12}{\sqrt{404}}\mathbf{j} + \frac{14}{\sqrt{404}}\mathbf{k}$$

$$= 0.398\mathbf{i} + 0.597\mathbf{j} + 0.696\mathbf{k}$$

Hence, the sum of moments about this axis is zero provided

$$\Sigma M_{AE} = \mathbf{u}_{AE} \cdot \Sigma(\mathbf{r} \times \mathbf{F}) = 0$$

In this equation $\mathbf{r}$ represents a position vector drawn from *any point* on the axis to *any point* on the line of action of the force, $\mathbf{F}$. (See Eq. 4–17, p. 110.) Thus, with reference to Fig. 5–18b, we have

$$\mathbf{u}_{AE} \cdot [(\mathbf{r}_{AB} \times \mathbf{T}_{BC}) + (\mathbf{r}_{AG} \times \mathbf{W})] = 0$$

$$(0.398\mathbf{i} + 0.597\mathbf{j} + 0.696\mathbf{k}) \cdot [(8\mathbf{i}) \times (0.303T_{BC}\mathbf{i}$$
$$-0.505T_{BC}\mathbf{j} + 0.808T_{BC}\mathbf{k}) + (4\mathbf{i}) \times (-100\mathbf{k})] = 0$$

or

$$-6.67T_{BC} + 238.8 = 0, \qquad T_{BC} = 35.8 \text{ lb} \qquad Ans.$$

Since the cable tension is known, Eqs. (1) through (6) may be readily solved for the remaining unknown reactions.

Problems

Neglect the weight of the members in the following problems except when specified.

5-43. Using a single equilibrium equation, solve for the tension in the cable located at C, for the platform in Example 5–8.

5-44. Calculate the magnitude and direction of the resultant force and moment acting at the fixed wall of the cantilevered beam.

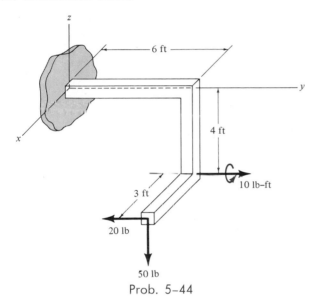

Prob. 5–44

5-45. Determine the tension developed in the three supporting cables. The plate is held in the horizontal xy plane by the three cables.

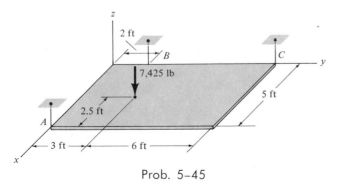

Prob. 5–45

5-46. The windlass is subjected to a load of 150 lb. Determine the horizontal force **P** needed to hold the handle in the position shown, and the components of reaction at the ball-and-socket joint A and the smooth bearing B. The bearing at B is in proper alignment and exerts only a force reaction on the windlass.

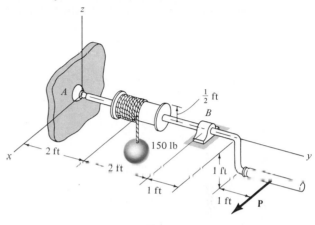

Prob. 5–46

5-47. The homogeneous block weighs 1,000 lb and is supported at A by a ball-and-socket and at B by a smooth roller. Determine the tensions in the cables CD and EF and the reactions at A and B. The cable CD lies in a plane which is parallel to the yz plane.

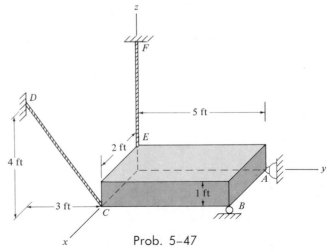

Prob. 5–47

173

5-48. The wing of the jet aircraft is subjected to the following force system: the weight of the 1,500-lb engine having a center of gravity point G_C, the weight of the wing and internal gas supply of 2,500 lb having a center of gravity G_W, and the vertical upward reaction of 3,000 lb exerted by the ground on *each* tire, T. For this loading system, calculate the magnitude and direction of the resultant force and moment exerted by the fuselage on the wing at the fixed point of attachment, A.

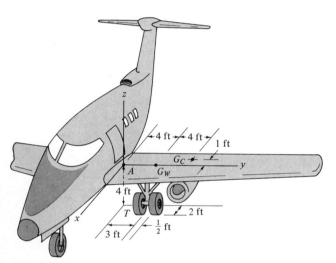

Prob. 5-48

5-49. A smooth 20-lb sphere rests along the surface of the arc support. Determine the force per unit length along the ring of contact which is exerted on the sphere.

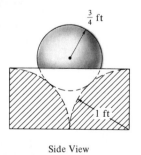

Side View

Top View

Prob. 5-49

5-50. The composite rods are supported at points A and B by a smooth surface and at E by a ball-and-socket joint. Determine the reaction components if each rod weighs 2 lb/ft.

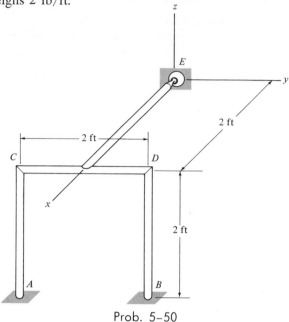

Prob. 5-50

5-51. Determine the reaction components at the two ball supports A and B and the ball-and-socket joint at C for the triangular plate.

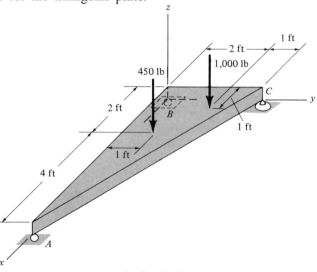

Prob. 5-51

174

5-52. Determine the components of reaction at the smooth bearing supports A and B for the shaft. Both pulleys are firmly fixed to the shaft and lie in planes parallel to the xz plane. Is the shaft in complete equilibrium under the given loading system? The bearing supports are in proper alignment and exert only force reactions on the shaft.

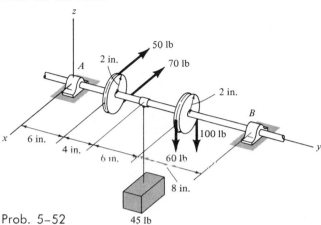

Prob. 5–52

5-53. The uniform lid on a chest is propped open by means of the light rod CD. If the hinge at A prevents sliding of the lid along the axis AB while the hinge at B does not offer resistance in this direction, calculate the compressive force in the rod CD and the components of reaction at the hinges A and B. The lid weighs 25 lb. The hinges are in proper alignment and exert only force reactions on the lid.

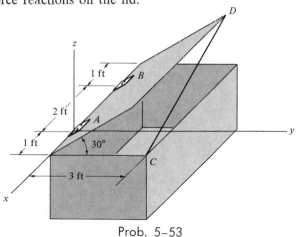

Prob. 5–53

5-54. Determine the compressive force in the strut AB and the reactive components at the hinge C of the 3-ft-diameter hatch door. The door weighs 60 lb and has a center of gravity at its midpoint.

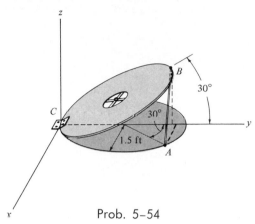

Prob. 5–54

5-55. The boom AC is subjected to a load of 400 lb and is supported at A by a ball-and-socket joint and by two cables BDC and CE. The cable BDC is continuous and passes around a frictionless pulley at D. Calculate the tension in the cables and the components of reaction at A.

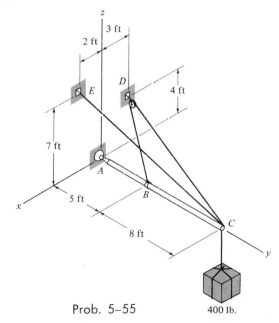

Prob. 5–55

5-56. The triangular plate is supported by a single hinge at A and a vertical cable BC. If the cable can support a maximum tension of 300 lb, determine the maximum force $\mathbf{F}$ which may be applied to the plate. Compute the reactive components at A for this loading.

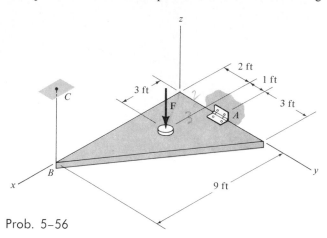

Prob. 5–56

5-57. Determine the forces acting in the cables AB and AC and the components of reaction at the ball-and-socket joint D for the boom.

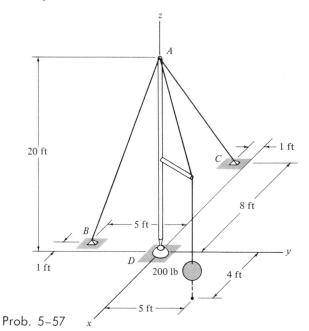

Prob. 5–57

5-58. The semicircular metal plate supports a 150-lb load. Determine the tensions in cables BD and CD and the components of reaction at the ball-and-socket joint at A.

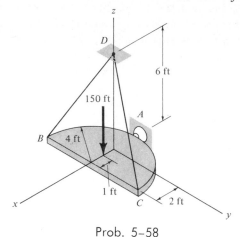

Prob. 5–58

5-59. The bent rod is supported at A, B, and C by smooth bearings. Compute the reaction components at the bearings if the rod is subjected to a 200-lb vertical force and a 30-lb-ft couple as shown. The bearings are in proper alignment and exert only force reactions on the rod.

Prob. 5–59

5-60. Determine the components of reaction at the ball supports B and C and the ball-and-socket A for the uniformly loaded plate.

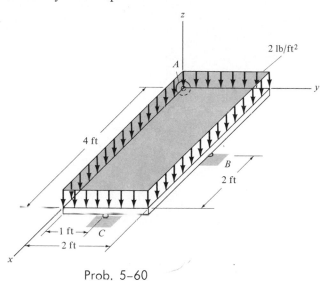

Prob. 5-60

5-61. The uniform rod AB weighs 30 lb and is supported at A by a ball-and-socket joint and leans against the smooth vertical wall at B. A cable is attached at B to help support the rod. Determine the unknown force components acting on the rod.

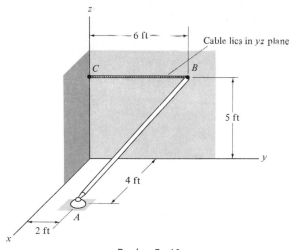

Prob. 5-61

5-62. The uniform door weighs 40 lb and is supported at A and B by hinges. The hinge at A supports only forces in the horizontal plane, while B supports both horizontal and vertical components of force. If the spring CE is fixed at the top of the door as shown in the figure, determine the magnitude of horizontal force **P** required to keep the door open at the position shown. What are the components of reaction at hinges A and B? The spring is unstretched when the door is closed.

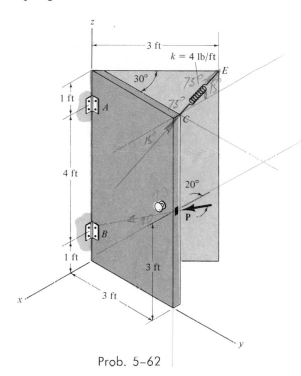

Prob. 5-62

6
Structural Analysis

6-1. Two-Force Member

When forces are applied at only two points on a member, the member is commonly referred to as a *two-force member*. For *equilibrium,* the force acting at one point on the member must be of *equal magnitude, opposite direction, and collinear* with the force acting at the other point. To prove this statement, consider the two-force member shown in Fig. 6-1*a* which

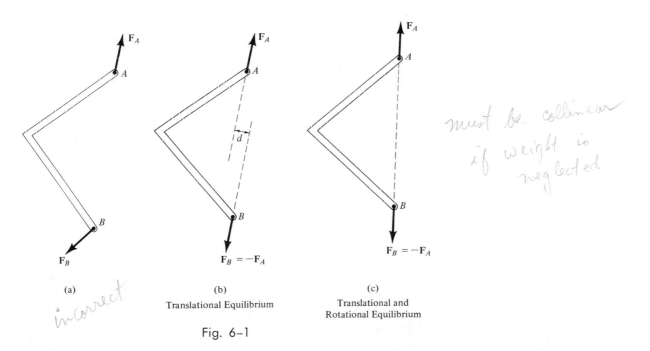

(a)	(b)	(c)
	Translational Equilibrium	Translational and Rotational Equilibrium

incorrect

must be collinear if weight is neglected

Fig. 6-1

179

is subjected to the *resultant forces* $\mathbf{F}_A$ and $\mathbf{F}_B$. (If more than one force acts at any of these two points the resultant force at that point is found by vector addition.) Translational equilibrium is satisfied provided $\Sigma F_x = 0$ and $\Sigma F_y = 0$ regardless of how the x and y axes are orientated. Hence, it is necessary that $\mathbf{F}_A = -\mathbf{F}_B$. As shown in Fig. 6–1*b*, if the line of action of these two forces is separated by a perpendicular distance d, a couple having a magnitude of $M = F_A d$ is produced which tends to rotate the member. Rotational equilibrium, however, is satisfied (e.g., $\Sigma M_A = 0$) provided $d = 0$. Therefore $\mathbf{F}_A$ and $\mathbf{F}_B$ must not only be of equal magnitude and opposite direction but also collinear as shown in Fig. 6–1*c*.

6–2. Simple Trusses

A *truss* is a structure composed of slender members joined together at their end points. The members commonly used in construction consist of wood struts, metal bars, angles, or channels. The joint connections are usually formed by bolting or welding the ends of the members to a common plate (called a *gusset plate*), as shown in Fig. 6–2, or by simply

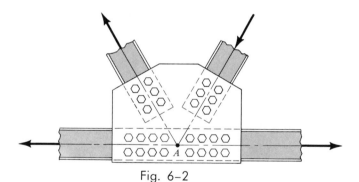

Fig. 6–2

passing large bolts or pins through each of the members. Most *planar* trusses are used for roof and bridge construction. The *Pratt truss, ABCDE,* shown in Fig. 6–3*a*, is an example of a typical roof-supporting truss. In this figure, the roof load is transmitted to the truss *at the joints* by means of a series of "purlins" such as beam *DD'*. Since the imposed loading acts in the same plane as the truss, Fig. 6–3*b*, the analysis of the forces developed in the truss members may be considered two dimensional.

To design both the members and the connections of a truss, it is *first necessary* to determine the *forces* developed in each of the members when the truss is subjected to a given loading. In this regard two important assumptions will be made in determining the forces acting in the members of a truss:

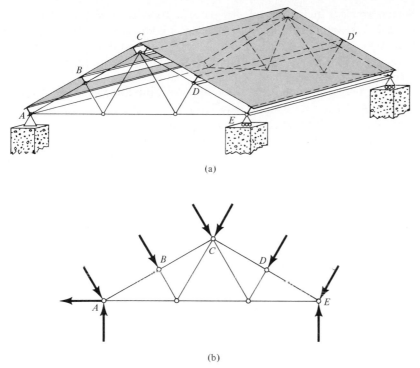

(a)

(b)

Fig. 6-3

1. The members are joined together by smooth pins. In cases where bolted or welded joint connections are used, this assumption is satisfactory provided the center lines of the joining members are concurrent at a point, as in the case of point A in Fig. 6-2.
2. All the loadings are applied at the joints. In most situations, such as for bridge and roof trusses, this assumption is true. The deck or floor of a bridge is usually supported by crossbeams which are connected to the side trusses at the joints. The loads acting on a roof are transmitted to the joints of the roof-supporting trusses by a series of purlins. Frequently in the force analysis the weight of the members is neglected, since the force supported by the members is large in comparison with their weight. If the weight of each of the members is to be included in the analysis, it is satisfactory to apply half the weight of each member as a vertical force acting at the end of each member.

In accordance with these assumptions *each truss member acts as a two-force member,* and therefore, the forces acting on a member must act axially along the member. If this force tends to *elongate* the member, it is a *tensile* force. When the force tends to *shorten* the member, the force is *compressive.* In the actual design of a truss it is important to state whether the nature of the force is tensile or compressive. Most often, the compression members must be made thicker than the tension members, because of the buckling or column effect which occurs in compression members.

In this book we will be concerned only with the force analysis of simple trusses. To form a rigid stable unit lying in a single plane and consisting of pin-connected members, we must arrange the members as a series of connecting *triangular* elements. If we form polygons having more than three sides, the frame will collapse. For example, consider the four-sided frame shown in Fig. 6-4. When the load **P** is applied to this frame it will collapse unless a diagonal member *AB* is added to make the frame stable. When a truss is constructed entirely of triangular elements, it is known as a *simple truss.*

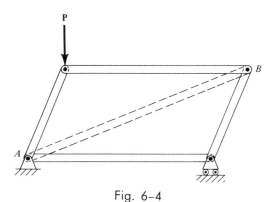

Fig. 6-4

The forces developed in simple truss members can be determined by means of the method of joints or the method of sections. Once the force analysis of the truss has been completed, the size of both the members and connections can then be determined using the theory of strength of materials.

6-3. Method of Joints

If a truss is in equilibrium, each of its joints must be in equilibrium. The *method of joints* consists of satisfying equilibrium for all the forces exerted *on the pin* at each joint. Since truss members are all straight two-force members, the force developed in each member is *directed along the axis of the member.* Hence, for planar trusses *the force system acting on the pin at each joint will be both coplanar and concurrent.* Equilibrium conditions for each joint therefore require $\Sigma F_x = 0$ and $\Sigma F_y = 0$.* Because

---

*Rotational or moment equilibrium is automatically satisfied since the force system is concurrent.

there are only two equations of equilibrium for each joint, the force analysis should generally begin at joints having at most two unknown forces. In this way one obtains two equations which have a unique solution. After having determined the forces at some joints, the forces at the other joints may be analyzed in turn. The following two examples illustrate the procedure.

Example 6–1

A plane truss is acted upon by the force system shown in Fig. 6–5a. Determine the force in each member of the truss. Indicate whether the members are in tension or compression. The truss is supported at A by means of rollers and at B by means of a pin.

Solution

If initially a free-body diagram of each joint were drawn, it would be found that no joint is subjected to *only* two unknown forces; therefore, it is first necessary to determine the external reactions at joints A and B. A free-body diagram of the truss is given in Fig. 6–5b. Applying the equations of equilibrium, we have

$$\xrightarrow{+}\Sigma F_x = 0; \qquad 500 \text{ lb} - B_x = 0, \qquad B_x = 500 \text{ lb}$$

$$(+\Sigma M_B = 0; \quad -A_y(20 \text{ ft}) + 500 \text{ lb} (10 \text{ ft}) = 0, \qquad A_y = 250 \text{ lb}$$

$$+\uparrow\Sigma F_y = 0; \quad 250 \text{ lb} - 500 \text{ lb} - 1{,}000 \text{ lb} + B_y = 0, \qquad B_y = 1{,}250 \text{ lb}$$

Knowing these reaction forces, we can now begin the analysis by starting either at joints A or B, since there are two unknown member forces acting at each of these joints.

Joint A, Fig. 6–5c. As shown on the free-body diagram, there are three forces which act at joint A. In particular, force $\mathbf{F}_{AD}$ has been assumed to be directed *away* from the joint. Because for every action there is an equal but opposite reaction, this *"pulling on the pin"* causes a *tension* in member AD*. If, in the calculations, the numerical value of F_{AD} is positive, the assumed direction is correct; however, if it is negative, the force direction is reversed and the member is in compression.

In some cases it is possible to tell *by inspection* whether or not the sense of direction of an unknown member force is tensile or compressive. For example, the force in member AE must be compressive, Fig. 6–5c, since the vertical component of this force must act downward to balance the upward 250-lb force ($\Sigma F_y = 0$). The horizontal component of force $\mathbf{F}_{AE}$ then acts to the left, which requires member AD to be in tension ($\Sigma F_x = 0$). *In all cases,* the correct sense of an unknown force should be verified by drawing the free-body diagrams of each joint and then applying and solving the equations of equilibrium.

*To see this clearly, refer to Fig. 6–5h. Here it is likewise seen that a force which is *pushing on a pin* causes a corresponding *pushing* on the member and hence a *compression* in the member.

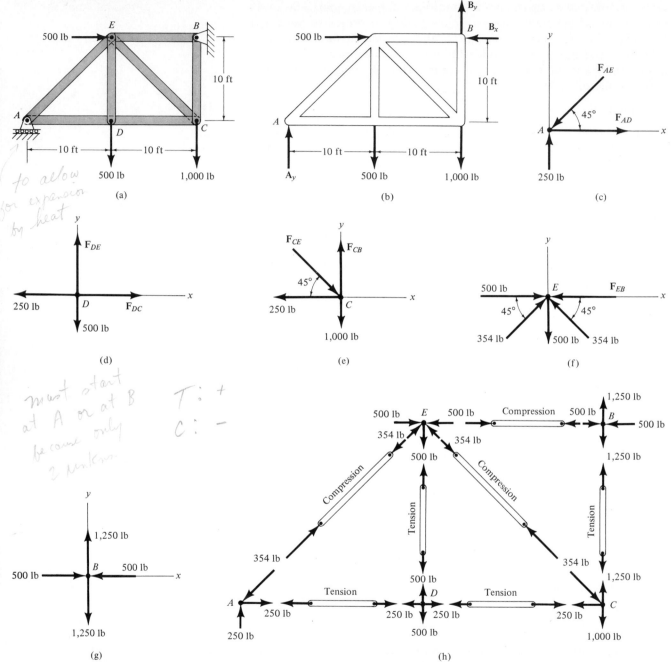

Handwritten annotations:

one pin, one roller
to make statically determinate

to allow
for expansion
by heat

must start
at A or at B
because only
2 unknown

T: +
C: −

(a)

(b)

(c)

(d)

(e)

(f)

(g)

(h)

Fig. 6-5

The equations of equilibrium when applied to joint A yield

$$\xrightarrow{+}\Sigma F_x = 0; \qquad\qquad F_{AD} - F_{AE}\cos 45° = 0$$
$$+\uparrow\Sigma F_y = 0; \qquad\qquad 250\text{ lb} - F_{AE}\sin 45° = 0$$

Solving, we have

$$F_{AE} = 354\text{ lb} \quad\text{(compression)} \qquad\qquad Ans.$$
$$F_{AD} = 250\text{ lb} \quad\text{(tension)} \qquad\qquad Ans.$$

Joint D, Fig. 6-5d.   Having found the force in member AD, we may next analyze joint D, since there are only two unknown forces acting at this joint. The force $F_{AD} = 250$ lb is a *tensile* force and therefore acts *away* from joint D. This force is transferred from joint A to joint D via member AD, as shown by means of equal and opposite reactions in Fig. 6-5h. Applying the equations of equilibrium yields

$$\xrightarrow{+}\Sigma F_x = 0; \quad F_{DC} - 250\text{ lb} = 0, \qquad F_{DC} = 250\text{ lb} \quad\text{(tension)} \qquad Ans.$$
$$+\uparrow\Sigma F_y = 0; \, F_{DE} - 500\text{ lb} = 0, \qquad F_{DE} = 500\text{ lb} \quad\text{(tension)} \qquad Ans.$$

Continuing in the same manner, we may analyze joints C and E next.

Joint C, Fig. 6-5e.

$$\xrightarrow{+}\Sigma F_x = 0; \qquad\qquad -250\text{ lb} + F_{CE}\cos 45° = 0$$
$$+\uparrow\Sigma F_y = 0; \qquad F_{CB} - F_{CE}\sin 45° - 1{,}000\text{ lb} = 0$$

Hence,

$$F_{CE} = 354\text{ lb} \quad\text{(compression)} \qquad\qquad Ans.$$
$$F_{CB} = 1{,}250\text{ lb} \quad\text{(tension)} \qquad\qquad Ans.$$

Joint E, Fig. 6-5f.

$$\xrightarrow{+}\Sigma F_x = 0; \quad -F_{EB} - 354\cos 45°\text{ lb} + 354\cos 45°\text{ lb} + 500\text{ lb} = 0$$
$$F_{EB} = 500\text{ lb} \quad\text{(compression)} \qquad\qquad Ans.$$
$$+\uparrow\Sigma F_y = 0; \quad 2[354\sin 45°\text{ lb}] - 500\text{ lb} \equiv 0 \quad\text{(check)}$$

All the forces in the members have been found; however, it is always prudent to analyze the last joint (joint B) in order to check the accuracy of the solution.

Joint B, Fig. 6-5g.

$$\xrightarrow{+}\Sigma F_x = 0; \qquad\qquad 500\text{ lb} - 500\text{ lb} \equiv 0 \quad\text{(check)}$$
$$+\uparrow\Sigma F_y = 0; \qquad\qquad 1{,}250\text{ lb} - 1{,}250\text{ lb} \equiv 0 \quad\text{(check)}$$

The results of this force analysis are summarized in Fig. 6–5*h*, which shows the complete free-body diagrams for each joint. Applying the principle of action and reaction, the forces acting in the members are equal and opposite to those acting at the joints, as shown in the figure. The truss members are labeled as being in either tension or compression.

Example 6–2

Using the method of joints, show that members *QP*, *PG*, *HJ*, *JG*, and *GK* of the *Fink truss,* shown in Fig. 6–6*a*, are subjected to zero force when the truss is loaded as shown.

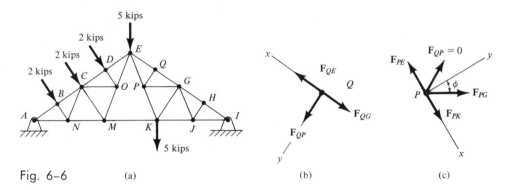

Fig. 6–6   (a)   (b)   (c)

Solution

At each joint the equations $\Sigma F_x = 0$ and $\Sigma F_y = 0$ must be satisfied. The orientation of the *x* and *y* axes is arbitrary for the application of these equations. Hence, if we consider a free-body diagram of joint *Q* so that the *y* axis is directed along member *QP*, as shown in Fig. 6–6*b*, the line of action of forces $\mathbf{F}_{QE}$ and $\mathbf{F}_{QG}$ are both along the *x* axis. Therefore the equation $\Sigma F_y = 0$ is satisfied provided $\mathbf{F}_{PQ} = 0$, i.e., *QP* is a zero-force member.

A free-body diagram of joint *P* is shown in Fig. 6–6*c*. By appropriate orientation of the *x* axis, equilibrium in the *y* direction is satisfied provided $\Sigma F_y = F_{PG} \cos \phi = 0$. Hence $F_{PG} = 0$. In a similar manner, by considering, in turn, free-body diagrams of joints *H*, *J*, and *G*, complete this example and show that the force in the respective members *HJ*, *JG*, and *GK* is zero.

Although the zero-force members are not necessary for supporting the loading shown in Fig. 6–6*a*, their use is important in the construction of the truss. Understand that zero-force members are actually determined on the basis of assuming the truss to be *rigid*. In reality, however, the truss may deform when it is loaded thereby transmitting, slightly, the applied loads to the zero-force members. Furthermore, these members add to the stability of the truss during construction and provide support if the applied loading is changed.

Problems

6-1. Determine the force in each member of the truss. Indicate whether the members are in tension or compression.

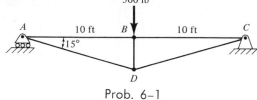

Prob. 6–1

6-2. Determine the force in each member of the truss. Indicate whether the members are in tension or compression.

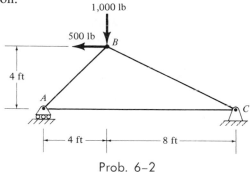

Prob. 6–2

6-3. Compute the force in each member of the truss. Indicate whether the members are in tension or compression.

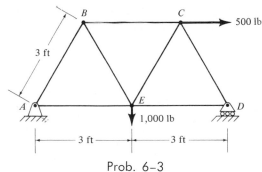

Prob. 6–3

6-4. Determine the force in each member of the truss. Indicate whether the members are in tension or compression.

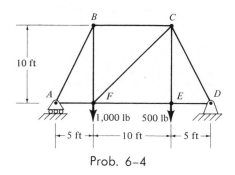

Prob. 6–4

6-5. Determine the force in each member of the truss. Indicate whether the members are in tension or compression.

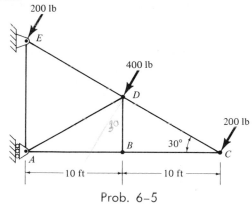

Prob. 6–5

6-6. The *Howe roof truss* supports the vertical loading shown. Determine the force in members *CL*, *MC*, and *CD*. Indicate whether these forces are tensile or compressive.

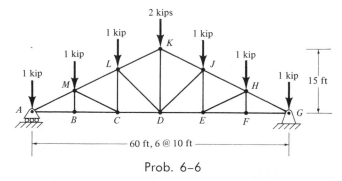

Prob. 6–6

187

6-7. The *Pratt bridge truss* is subjected to the loading shown. Determine the force in members *MD* and *BC*. Indicate whether the members are in tension or compression.

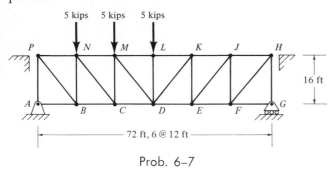

Prob. 6-7

6-8. Determine the forces developed in members *AG*, *GF*, and *BC* of the bridge truss. Indicate whether the members are in tension or compression.

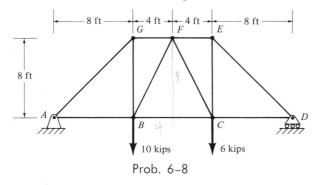

Prob. 6-8

6-9. Determine the force in members *AJ*, *DI*, and *CJ*, and indicate all the zero-force members of the *Howe bridge truss*. State whether members *AJ*, *DI*, and *CJ* are in tension or compression.

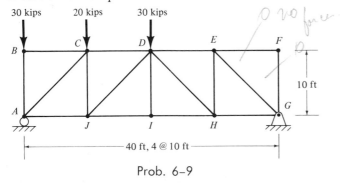

Prob. 6-9

6-10. Determine the forces in members *CD*, *AG*, and *BF* of the truss shown. Indicate whether the members are in tension or compression.

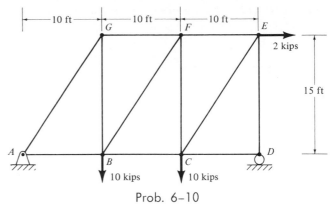

Prob. 6-10

6-11. Determine the forces in all the members of the truss. Indicate whether the members are in tension or compression.

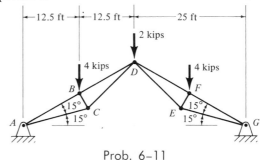

Prob. 6-11

6-12. Determine the forces in all the members of the supporting truss. State whether the members are in tension or compression. The pulley at *C* is frictionless.

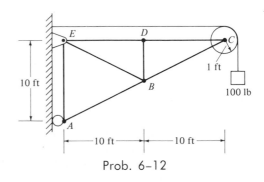

Prob. 6-12

188

6-13. Determine the force in members *CF*, *BH*, and *AH* of the *Warren roof truss*. Indicate whether the members are in tension or compression.

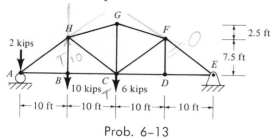

Prob. 6–13

6-14. Determine the force in each member of the truss in terms of the applied force **P**. Indicate whether the members are in tension or compression.

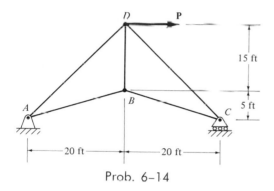

Prob. 6–14

6-15. Determine the forces in members *DC* and *HK* of the crane truss. Indicate whether the members are in tension or compression.

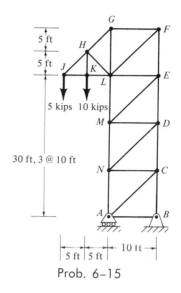

Prob. 6–15

6–4. Method of Sections

A second method for finding the forces in the members of a truss, the *method of sections,* consists of passing a section through the truss, thus cutting it into two parts. If the entire truss is in equilibrium, then each of the two parts must also be in equilibrium. Hence, after the truss has been sectioned, either part may be used to form a free-body diagram. Since only three equilibrium equations are available, the forces in all the members at the cut section may be determined provided the cutting section passes through not more than three members in which the forces are unknown. By choosing the proper points about which to sum moments, or directions for summation of forces, each of the three unknown forces may generally be solved for from a *single equation* rather than from a series of simultaneous equations.

When the forces in only a *few members* of a truss are to be found, the method of sections combined with the method of joints generally provides the most direct means of obtaining these forces.

Example 6–3

Determine the force in members *GE*, *GC*, and *BC* of the bridge truss shown in Fig. 6–7*a*. Indicate whether the members are in tension or compression.

Solution

To solve this problem by the method of sections, it is *first* necessary to determine the external reactions at points *A* and *D*. A free-body diagram of the entire truss is shown in Fig. 6–7*b*. Applying the equations of equilibrium, we have

$$\xrightarrow{+}\Sigma F_x = 0; \qquad 400 \text{ lb} - A_x = 0, \qquad A_x = 400 \text{ lb}$$

$$\zeta + \Sigma M_A = 0; \qquad -1{,}000 \text{ lb} (20 \text{ ft}) - 400 \text{ lb} (10 \text{ ft}) + D_y (30 \text{ ft}) = 0,$$

$$D_y = 800 \text{ lb}$$

$$+\uparrow \Sigma F_y = 0; \quad A_y - 1{,}000 \text{ lb} + 800 \text{ lb} = 0, \qquad A_y = 200 \text{ lb}$$

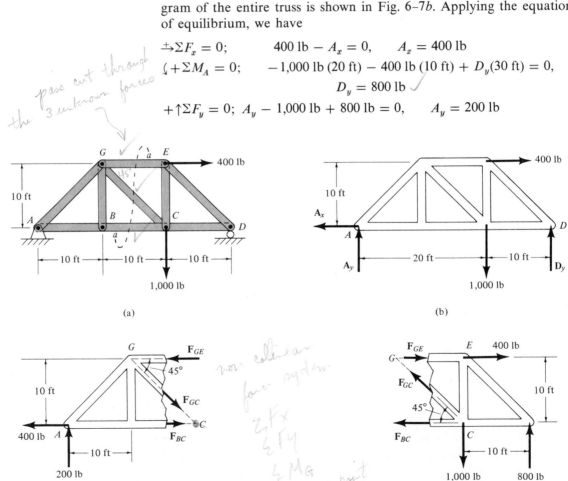

Fig. 6–7

Knowing these reactions, the truss can now be sectioned along the dotted line *aa*, cutting the three members in Fig. 6-7a. Either the right- or the left-hand side may be used to draw a free-body diagram of the cut section as shown in Figs. 6-7c and 6-7d. In constructing the two diagrams, note that the three unknown member forces acting on one side of the truss must be equal but opposite to those acting on the other side (Newton's third law of motion). Also, the line of action of each member force is specified from the *geometry of the truss* since the force in a member passes along the axis of the member.

In many cases the sense of direction of an unknown force may be determined by inspection *before* the equilibrium equations are applied. For example, the force in member GE, that is, F_{GE}, must be compressive, as shown in Fig. 6-7c.* Summing moments about point C, this force will then provide a necessary counterclockwise moment which will balance the clockwise moment created by the 200-lb force—note that the line of action of F_{GC}, F_{BC} and 400 lb passes through point C. Similarly, when moments are summed about point G, one comes to the conclusion that force F_{BC} must be tensile. To satisfy $\Sigma F_y = 0$, the force F_{GC} must be tensile so that its vertical component acts downward to balance the 200-lb reactive force acting upward at A. *In all cases,* the correct sense of an unknown member force will be verified after solving the equations of equilibrium. If the sense of direction of an unknown force was chosen *correctly,* the answer will be *positive* when the equations are solved for the force magnitude. A negative answer indicates that the force acts in the opposite direction to that shown on the free-body diagram.

By judicious application of the equations of equilibrium, we can solve directly for each of the three unknown forces at a cut section, rather than solving three equations simultaneously. Using the free-body diagram in Fig. 6-7c and summing moments about point G, as just discussed, eliminates the two unknown forces F_{GE} and F_{GC}. Hence,

$$\zeta + \Sigma M_G = 0; \qquad -400 \text{ lb (10 ft)} - 200 \text{ lb (10 ft)} + F_{BC}(10 \text{ ft}) = 0,$$
$$F_{BC} = 600 \text{ lb} \quad \text{(tension)} \qquad\qquad Ans.$$

In the same manner, by summing moments about point C we obtain a direct solution for the force in GE.

$$\zeta + \Sigma M_C = 0; \qquad -200 \text{ lb (20 ft)} + F_{GE}(10 \text{ ft}) = 0,$$
$$F_{GE} = 400 \text{ lb} \quad \text{(compression)} \qquad\qquad Ans.$$

Since F_{BC} and F_{GE} have no vertical components of force, summing forces in the y direction yields F_{GC}, i.e.,

---

*By definition, a free-body diagram of the cut section of a truss must show *all* the forces acting *directly on the members located at the cut section.* Hence, the force acting on member GE in Figs. 6-7c or 6-7d is *compressive* since it tends to *push* on the member, likewise, the forces in members GC and BC are *tensile* since they tend to *pull* on the member.

$$+\uparrow\Sigma F_y = 0; \qquad\qquad 200\text{ lb} - F_{GC}\sin 45° = 0,$$

$$F_{GC} = 282.9\text{ lb}\quad\text{(tension)}\qquad\qquad Ans.$$

The same results can also be obtained by applying the equations of equilibrium to the free-body diagram shown in Fig. 6–7d. With this diagram how would you obtain each unknown force using a *single equation* of equilibrium for each calculation?

Example 6–4

Determine the force in member *GC* of the truss shown in Fig. 6–8a. Indicate whether the member is in tension or compression.

Solution

A free-body diagram of the entire truss is shown in Fig. 6–8b. We must first solve for the external reactions. Why?

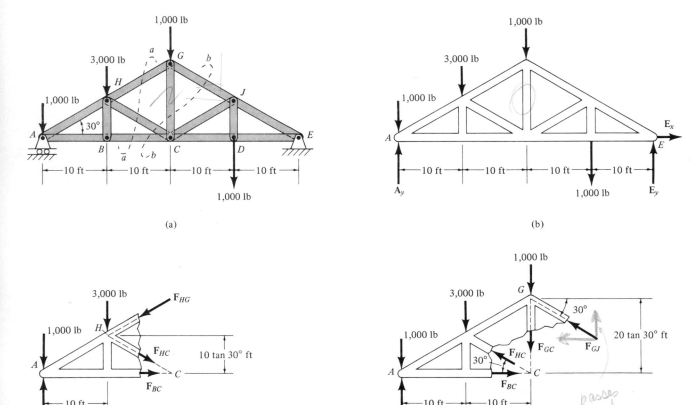

(a)

(b)

(c)

(d)

Fig. 6–8

$\zeta + \Sigma M_A = 0;$

$-3,000 \text{ lb } (10 \text{ ft}) - 1,000 \text{ lb } (20 \text{ ft}) - 1,000 \text{ lb } (30 \text{ ft}) + E_y(40 \text{ ft}) = 0,$

$$E_y = 2,000 \text{ lb}$$

$\Rightarrow \Sigma F_x = 0; \qquad\qquad E_x = 0$

Using the computed value of E_y,

$+\uparrow \Sigma F_y = 0;$

$A_y - 1,000 \text{ lb} - 3,000 \text{ lb} - 1,000 \text{ lb} - 1,000 \text{ lb} + 2,000 \text{ lb} = 0,$

$$A_y = 4,000 \text{ lb}$$

According to the method of sections, any imaginary section which cuts through member GC will also have to cut through three other members whose forces are unknown. For example, the section bb shown in Fig. 6–8a cuts through members GJ, GC, HC, and BC. If we consider a free-body diagram of the left-hand portion of this section, (Fig. 6–8d) it is possible to determine the force in member GJ (F_{GJ}) by summing moments about point C to eliminate the other three unknowns; however, the force in GC cannot be determined from the remaining two equilibrium equations. It is therefore necessary to determine the force in either HC or BC before using section bb. We may, for example, determine the force in member BC by considering the adjacent section aa, Fig. 6–8a. A free-body diagram of the truss on the left-hand side of section aa is given in Fig. 6–8c. Summing moments about point H, we may obtain the force in BC directly from one equation:

$\zeta + \Sigma M_H = 0; -4,000 \text{ lb } (10 \text{ ft}) + 1,000 \text{ lb } (10 \text{ ft}) + F_{BC}(10 \tan 30° \text{ ft}) = 0,$

$$F_{BC} = 5,200 \text{ lb} \quad \text{(tension)}$$

Knowing the magnitude and direction of this force we can now use a free-body diagram of the truss to the left of section bb, Fig. 6–8d. Applying the three equations of equilibrium, we have

$\zeta + \Sigma M_C = 0; \quad -4,000 \text{ lb } (20 \text{ ft}) + 1,000 \text{ lb } (20 \text{ ft}) + 3,000 \text{ lb } (10 \text{ ft})$
$$+ (F_{GJ} \cos 30°)(20 \tan 30° \text{ ft}) = 0,$$

$$F_{GJ} = 3,000 \text{ lb} \quad \text{(compression)}$$

(Note that the component ($F_{GJ} \sin 30°$) is not included in the moment equation since the line of action of this force at G passes through point C.)   *= important*

$\zeta + \Sigma M_G = 0;$

$-4,000 \text{ lb } (20 \text{ ft}) + 1,000 \text{ lb } (20 \text{ ft}) + 3,000 \text{ lb } (10 \text{ ft}) + F_{BC}(20 \tan 30° \text{ ft})$
$$- (F_{HC} \cos 30°)(20 \tan 30° \text{ ft}) = 0$$

Substituting for F_{BC} and solving,

$$F_{HC} = 3,000 \text{ lb} \quad \text{(compression)}$$

(Note that F_{HC} might also be obtained by taking moments about point A, Fig. 6–8c.)

$$+\uparrow\Sigma F_y = 0; \qquad 4{,}000\text{ lb} - 1{,}000\text{ lb} - 3{,}000\text{ lb} - 1{,}000\text{ lb} - F_{GC}$$
$$+ (F_{GJ}\sin 30°) + (F_{HC}\sin 30°) = 0$$

Substituting for F_{GJ} and F_{HC} and solving,

$$F_{GC} = 2{,}000\text{ lb}\quad(\text{tension}) \qquad\qquad Ans.$$

Problems

6-16. Determine the forces in members EB and ED of the truss. Indicate whether the members are in tension or compression.

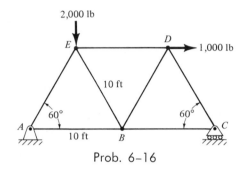

Prob. 6–16

6-17. Determine the forces in members EH and IH of the airplane supporting frame. Indicate whether the members are in tension or compression.

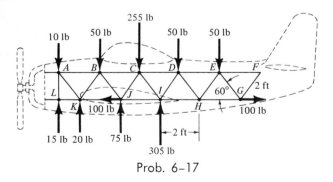

Prob. 6–17

6-18. Determine the forces in the members GF and BC of the truss. Indicate whether the members are in tension or compression.

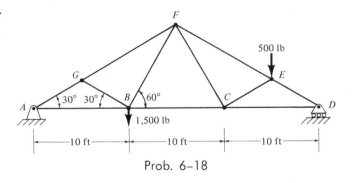

Prob. 6–18

6-19. Determine the forces in members BG and BF of the truss. Indicate whether the members are in tension or compression.

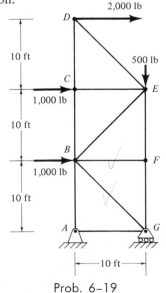

Prob. 6–19

6-20. Determine the force in members *GF*, *FC*, and *BC* for the truss in Prob. 6–10. Solve for each force directly using a single equilibrium equation. Indicate whether the members are in tension or compression.

6-21. Compute the force in members *EF* and *CB* for the truss in Prob. 6–8.

6-22. Determine the force in members *FE*, *FB*, and *BC* of the truss. Solve for each force directly using a single equilibrium equation. Indicate whether the members are in tension or compression.

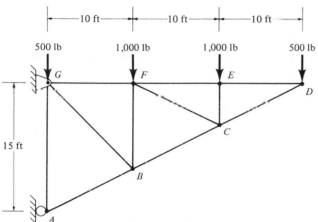

Prob. 6–22

6-23. Determine the force in members *GF* and *CF* of the truss. Indicate whether the members are in tension or compression.

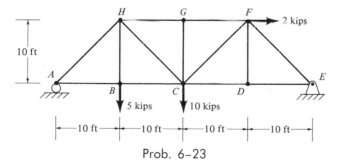

Prob. 6–23

6-24. Determine the force in members *FC*, *FB*, and *GA* of the crane truss. The pulley at *D* is frictionless. Indicate whether the members are in tension or compression.

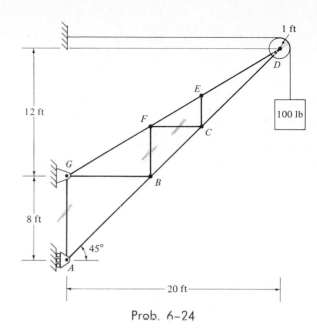

Prob. 6–24

6-25. The crane truss supports a load of 1,000 lb. A 2,500-lb counterweight, having a center of gravity at *G*, is used to stabilize the truss from tipping. Determine the force in member *CE* for this loading. Indicate whether the members are in tension or compression.

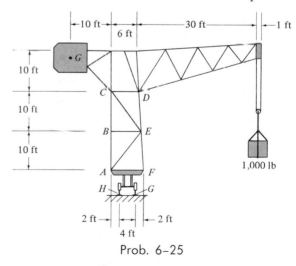

Prob. 6–25

6-26. Compute the force in members *BG* and *HG* of the truss. Indicate whether the members are in tension or compression.

195

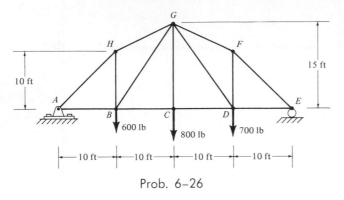

Prob. 6-26

6-29. Determine the forces in members *LM* and *MK* of the *K truss*. Indicate whether the members are in tension or compression.

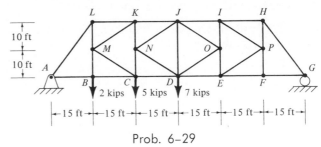

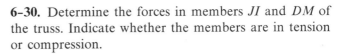

Prob. 6-29

6-27. Determine the force in members *CD* and *GC* of the truss. Indicate whether the members are in tension or compression.

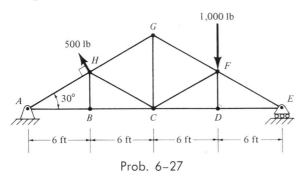

Prob. 6-27

6-30. Determine the forces in members *JI* and *DM* of the truss. Indicate whether the members are in tension or compression.

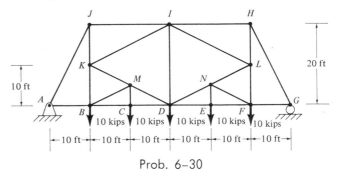

Prob. 6-30

6-28. Determine the force in members *DE* and *LE* of the *Baltimore truss*. Indicate whether the members are in tension or compression.

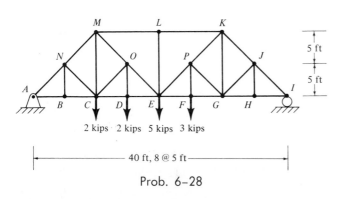

Prob. 6-28

6-31. Determine the forces in members *SG*, *EF*, *ME*, and *SF* of the truss. Indicate whether the members are in tension or compression.

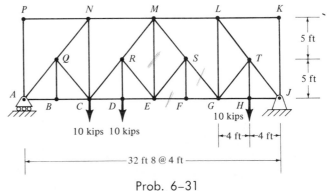

Prob. 6-31

*6–5. Space Trusses

A *space truss* consists of members joined together at their ends to form a stable three-dimensional structure. In Sec. 6–2 it was shown that the simplest form of a stable two-dimensional truss consists of the members arranged in the form of a triangle. We then built up the simple plane truss from this basic triangular element by adding two members at a time to form further triangular elements. In a similar manner, the simplest element of a stable space truss is a *tetrahedron*, formed by connecting six members together, as shown in Fig. 6–9. Any additional members added to this basic element would be redundant in supporting the force **P**. A simple space truss can be built from this basic tetrahedron element by adding three additional members, forming multiconnected tetrahedrons.

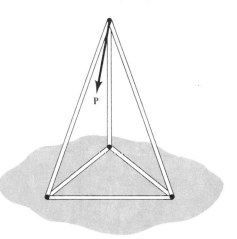

Fig. 6–9

Because truss members are slender, the external loading is assumed to act only at the joints. Assuming that each joint consists of a ball-and-socket connection, each member of a space truss may be treated as a two-force member. This assumption is justified provided the center lines of the joined members intersect at a common point and the weight of the member can be neglected. If the weight of each member is to be included in the analysis, it is generally satisfactory to apply half the weight of each member as a vertical force acting at the end of each member.

We may use either the method of joints or the method of sections to determine the forces developed in the members of a space truss. In using the method of joints, the three scalar equilibrium equations $\Sigma F_x = 0, \Sigma F_y = 0$, and $\Sigma F_z = 0$ must be satisfied at each joint. Rotational equilibrium is satisfied since the force system is concurrent. The force analysis must start at a joint where not more than three unknown forces exist. In using the method of sections, we can have no more than *six* unknown forces, shown on the free-body diagram of the isolated section, if all the forces at the cut sections are to be determined. If a section of the truss is isolated, the force system must satisfy the six scalar equilibrium equations $\Sigma F_x = 0, \Sigma F_y = 0, \Sigma F_z = 0, \Sigma M_x = 0, \Sigma M_y = 0$, and $\Sigma M_z = 0$. Because of the difficulty often encountered with three-dimensional geometry, it is recommended that you express the equilibrium equations in *vector form* when applying the method of joints or the method of sections in the force analysis of space trusses.

Since it is relatively easy to draw the free-body diagrams and apply the equations of equilibrium at each joint, the method of joints is very consistent in its application. However, as is often the case, one is left with a set of simultaneous equations to solve for the unknown forces.* When the method of sections is applied, however, many of the unknown forces may be computed *directly,* using a single equilibrium equation. The following example illustrates the use of both methods of solution.

*The computer program listed in Appendix A may be helpful for this type of analysis.

Example 6–5

Determine the forces acting in each of the members of the space frame shown in Fig. 6–10a. Indicate whether the members are in tension or compression.

Solution I (Method of Joints)

Since there is one known force and three unknown forces acting at joint A, we may begin the force analysis of this truss by applying the method of joints to joint A.

Joint A, Fig. 6–10b. Expressing each of the forces that acts on the free-body diagram of joint A in vector notation yields

$$\mathbf{P} = \{-4\mathbf{j}\} \text{ kips}$$

$$\mathbf{F}_{AB} = F_{AB}\mathbf{j}$$

$$\mathbf{F}_{AC} = -F_{AC}\mathbf{k}$$

$$\mathbf{F}_{AE} = F_{AE}\left(\frac{\mathbf{r}_{AE}}{r_{AE}}\right) = F_{AE}\frac{(\mathbf{i} + \mathbf{j} - \mathbf{k})}{\sqrt{3}}$$

For equilibrium,

$$\Sigma\mathbf{F} = 0; \qquad \mathbf{P} + \mathbf{F}_{AB} + \mathbf{F}_{AC} + \mathbf{F}_{AE} = 0$$

$$-4\mathbf{j} + F_{AB}\mathbf{j} - F_{AC}\mathbf{k} + \frac{1}{\sqrt{3}}F_{AE}\mathbf{i} + \frac{1}{\sqrt{3}}F_{AE}\mathbf{j} - \frac{1}{\sqrt{3}}F_{AE}\mathbf{k} = 0$$

$$\frac{1}{\sqrt{3}}F_{AE}\mathbf{i} + \left(-4 + F_{AB} + \frac{1}{\sqrt{3}}F_{AE}\right)\mathbf{j} + \left(-F_{AC} - \frac{1}{\sqrt{3}}F_{AE}\right)\mathbf{k} = 0$$

Equating the **i**, **j**, and **k** components to zero gives

$$\Sigma F_x = 0; \qquad \frac{1}{\sqrt{3}}F_{AE} = 0$$

$$\Sigma F_y = 0; \qquad -4 + F_{AB} + \frac{1}{\sqrt{3}}F_{AE} = 0$$

$$\Sigma F_z = 0; \qquad -F_{AC} - \frac{1}{\sqrt{3}}F_{AE} = 0$$

Solving these equations, we have

$$F_{AC} = F_{AE} = 0 \qquad\qquad\qquad\qquad Ans.$$

$$F_{AB} = 4 \text{ kips} \quad \text{(tension)} \qquad\qquad\qquad Ans.$$

Knowing the force $\mathbf{F}_{AB}$, we may proceed to joint B.

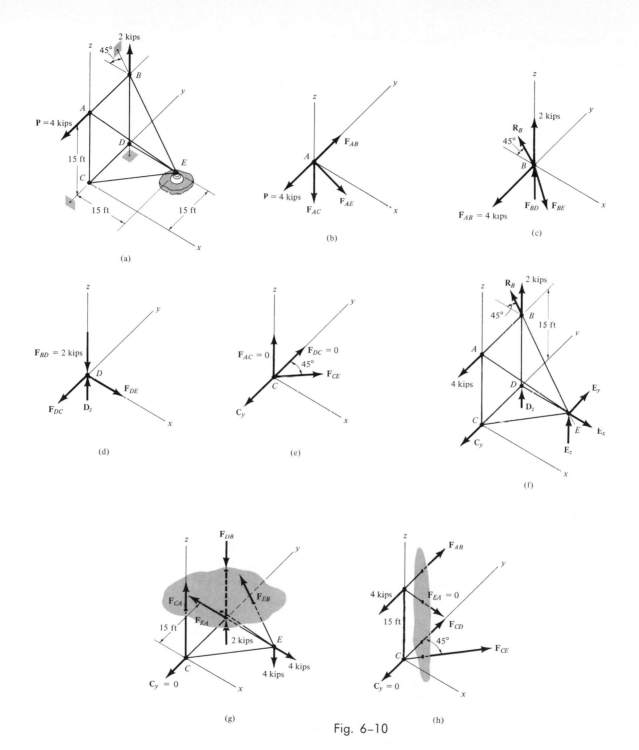

Fig. 6-10

Joint B, Fig. 6-10c.

$$\Sigma \mathbf{F} = 0; \qquad 2\mathbf{k} + \mathbf{F}_{AB} + \mathbf{R}_B + \mathbf{F}_{BD} + \mathbf{F}_{BE} = 0$$

$$2\mathbf{k} - 4\mathbf{j} - \frac{1}{\sqrt{2}} R_B \mathbf{i} + \frac{1}{\sqrt{2}} R_B \mathbf{j} + F_{BD}\mathbf{k} + \frac{1}{\sqrt{2}} F_{BE}\mathbf{i} - \frac{1}{\sqrt{2}} F_{BE}\mathbf{k} = 0$$

$$\left(-\frac{1}{\sqrt{2}} R_B + \frac{1}{\sqrt{2}} F_{BE} \right)\mathbf{i} + \left(-4 + \frac{1}{\sqrt{2}} R_B \right)\mathbf{j} +$$

$$\left(2 + F_{BD} - \frac{1}{\sqrt{2}} F_{BE} \right)\mathbf{k} = 0$$

Thus,

$$\Sigma F_x = 0; \qquad -\frac{1}{\sqrt{2}} R_B + \frac{1}{\sqrt{2}} F_{BE} = 0$$

$$\Sigma F_y = 0; \qquad -4 + \frac{1}{\sqrt{2}} R_B = 0$$

$$\Sigma F_z = 0; \qquad 2 + F_{BD} - \frac{1}{\sqrt{2}} F_{BE} = 0$$

Solving these equations yields

$$R_B = F_{BE} = 5.66 \text{ kips} \quad \text{(tension)} \qquad\qquad Ans.$$
$$F_{BD} = 2 \text{ kips} \quad \text{(compression)} \qquad\qquad Ans.$$

In a similar manner, applying the equations of equilibrium to the force system acting on the free-body diagrams of joints *D* and *C*, respectively, yields the following results.

Joint D, Fig. 6-10d.

$$\Sigma F_x = 0; \qquad\qquad F_{DE} = 0 \qquad\qquad\qquad Ans.$$
$$\Sigma F_y = 0; \qquad\qquad F_{DC} = 0 \qquad\qquad\qquad Ans.$$
$$\Sigma F_z = 0; \qquad\qquad D_z - 2 = 0; \quad D_z = 2 \text{ kips}$$

Joint C, Fig. 6-10e.

$$\Sigma F_x = 0; \qquad\qquad F_{CE} \sin 45° = 0; \quad F_{CE} = 0 \qquad Ans.$$
$$\Sigma F_y = 0; \qquad\qquad C_y = 0$$

Solution II (Method of Sections)

When applying the method of sections, it is first necessary to calculate the external reactions acting at the supports. Why? A free-body diagram of the entire truss is shown in Fig. 6–10*f*. If moments are summed about an axis passing through *EB*, it is possible to solve for $\mathbf{C}_y$ directly from one equation. Since the lines of action of all the forces except $\mathbf{C}_y$ pass

through points lying on this axis, it is therefore necessary that $C_y = 0$
to insure $\Sigma M_{EB} = 0$. Summing moments about axis DE, we may obtain R_B. Using the theory in Sec. 4–9, this requires

$$\Sigma M_{DE} = 0; \quad \mathbf{i} \cdot [(15\mathbf{k}) \times (-4\mathbf{j}) + (15\mathbf{k}) \times R_B(-0.707\mathbf{i} + 0.707\mathbf{j})]$$

$$\mathbf{i} \cdot [60\mathbf{i} - 10.61\,R_B\mathbf{j} - 10.61\,R_B\mathbf{i}]$$

Thus

$$R_B = 5.66 \text{ kips}$$

so that

$$\mathbf{R}_B = \{-4\mathbf{i} + 4\mathbf{j}\} \text{ kips}$$

In a similar manner, the force $\mathbf{D}_z$ can be found using $\mathbf{R}_B$ and summing moments about an axis passing through CE. The result is

$$\mathbf{D}_z = \{2\mathbf{k}\} \text{ kips}$$

Finally, using the computed results, the force at E, $\mathbf{F}_E$, can be found by summing all the forces on the free-body diagram.

$$\Sigma \mathbf{F} = 0; \quad -4\mathbf{j} + 2\mathbf{k} + (-4\mathbf{i} + 4\mathbf{j}) + (2\mathbf{k}) + \mathbf{F}_E = 0$$

$$\mathbf{F}_E = \{4\mathbf{i} - 4\mathbf{k}\} \text{ kips}$$

so that

$$E_x = 4 \text{ kips}, E_y = 0, E_z = -4 \text{ kips}$$

Having obtained these reactions, consider now the isolated section of the truss shown in Fig. 6–10g. Summing moments about axis CE eliminates the three unknown forces $\mathbf{F}_{EA}$, $\mathbf{F}_{EB}$ and $\mathbf{F}_{CA}$ and allows us to solve directly for $\mathbf{F}_{DB}$:

$$\Sigma M_{CE} = 0; \quad \mathbf{u}_{CE} \cdot [15\mathbf{j} \times (2 \quad F_{DB})\mathbf{k}] = 0$$

$$\mathbf{u}_{CE} \cdot [15(2 - F_{DB})\mathbf{i}] = 0$$

$$15(2 - F_{DB})(\mathbf{u}_{CE} \cdot \mathbf{i}) = 0$$

Since

$$\mathbf{u}_{CE} \cdot \mathbf{i} \neq 0$$

then

$$15(2 - F_{DB}) = 0$$

Hence,

$$F_{DB} = 2 \text{ kips} \quad \text{(compression)} \qquad \textit{Ans.}$$

or

$$\mathbf{F}_{DB} = \{-2\mathbf{k}\} \text{ kips}$$

Summing forces on the free-body diagram, we have

$$\Sigma \mathbf{F} = 0; \qquad 2\mathbf{k} + 4\mathbf{i} - 4\mathbf{k} + \mathbf{F}_{DB} + \mathbf{F}_{EB} + \mathbf{F}_{EA} + \mathbf{F}_{CA} = 0$$

Using the result for $\mathbf{F}_{DB}$,

$$2\mathbf{k} + 4\mathbf{i} - 4\mathbf{k} - 2\mathbf{k} - \frac{1}{\sqrt{2}} F_{EB}\mathbf{i} + \frac{1}{\sqrt{2}} F_{EB}\mathbf{k} - \frac{1}{\sqrt{3}} F_{EA}\mathbf{i} - \frac{1}{\sqrt{3}} F_{EA}\mathbf{j}$$
$$+ \frac{1}{\sqrt{3}} F_{EA}\mathbf{k} + F_{CA}\mathbf{k} = 0$$

or

$$\left(4 - \frac{1}{\sqrt{2}} F_{EB} - \frac{1}{\sqrt{3}} F_{EA}\right)\mathbf{i} + \left(-\frac{1}{\sqrt{3}} F_{EA}\right)\mathbf{j}$$
$$+ \left(2 - 4 - 2 + \frac{1}{\sqrt{2}} F_{EB} + \frac{1}{\sqrt{3}} F_{EA} + F_{CA}\right)\mathbf{k} = 0$$

Hence,

$$\Sigma F_x = 0; \qquad 4 - \frac{1}{\sqrt{2}} F_{EB} - \frac{1}{\sqrt{3}} F_{EA} = 0$$

$$\Sigma F_y = 0; \qquad -\frac{1}{\sqrt{3}} F_{EA} = 0$$

$$\Sigma F_z = 0; \qquad 2 - 4 - 2 + \frac{1}{\sqrt{2}} F_{EB} + \frac{1}{\sqrt{3}} F_{EA} + F_{CA} = 0$$

Solving these equations,

$$F_{EB} = 5.66 \text{ kips} \quad \text{(tension)} \qquad\qquad Ans.$$
$$F_{EA} = F_{CA} = 0 \qquad\qquad Ans.$$

To obtain the forces in the remaining members, consider the isolated section shown in Fig. 6–10h. Using the result that $F_{EA} = 0$ and summing moments about the x axis yields

$$\Sigma M_x = 0; \qquad\qquad \mathbf{i} \cdot [(15\mathbf{k}) \times (F_{AB} - 4)\mathbf{j}]$$
$$-15(F_{AB} - 4) = 0$$

Thus,

$$F_{AB} = 4 \text{ kips} \quad \text{(tension)} \qquad\qquad Ans.$$

Forces $\mathbf{F}_{CE}$ and $\mathbf{F}_{CD}$ may be obtained by the force equilibrium equations.

$$\Sigma F_x = 0; \qquad\qquad F_{CE} \sin 45° = 0; \quad F_{CE} = 0 \qquad\qquad Ans.$$
$$\Sigma F_y = 0; \qquad\qquad F_{CD} - 4 + 4 = 0; \quad F_{CD} = 0 \qquad\qquad Ans.$$

Problems

6-32. Determine the forces in members *AB*, *CB*, and *DB* of the space truss. Members *BD* and *BC* have the same length. Indicate whether the members are in tension or compression.

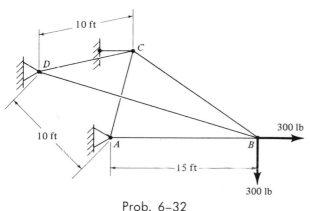

Prob. 6-32

6-33. A space truss in the form of a cube is subjected to two loads. Determine the forces acting in members *IC* and *EC*. Indicate whether the members are in tension or compression. Is this space truss stable enough to resist any type of loading?

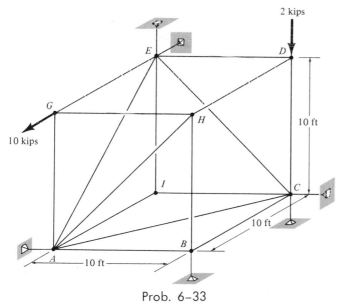

Prob. 6-33

6-34. Determine the forces developed in all the members of the space truss. Indicate whether the members are in tension or compression.

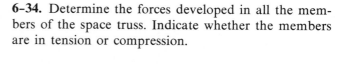

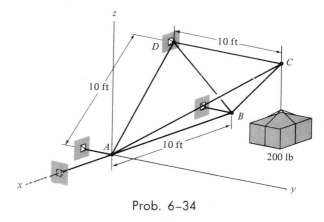

Prob. 6-34

6-35. Determine the forces developed in all the members of the space truss. Indicate whether the members are in tension or compression.

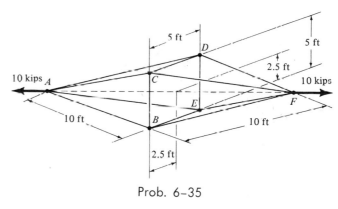

Prob. 6-35

6-36. The triangular space frame is subjected to both a horizontal and vertical load at its apex *G*. Determine

the force in member *AG*. Indicate whether the member
is in tension or compression.

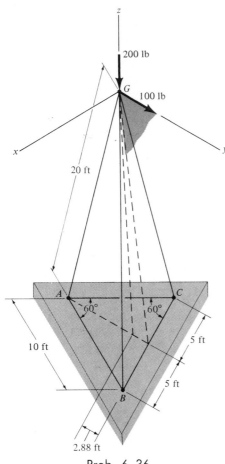

Prob. 6–36

6–6. Multiforce Members, Frames, and Machines

Since two-force members are subjected to loads only at the supporting
joints, the two forces have equal magnitudes, are collinear, and opposite
in direction. However, if a member is subjected to a loading *between* its
supporting joints, the forces acting *at* the joints will, in general, *not* be
directed along a line connecting the joints. These types of members are
often called *multiforce members*. Consider for example the beam shown
in Fig. 6–11*a* with its corresponding free-body diagram shown in Fig.
6–11*b*. The end reactions at *A* and *B* can be found by applying the three
equations of equilibrium, i.e.,

$$(+\Sigma M_A = 0; \qquad -10\sin 60° \text{ lb } (2\text{ ft}) + 5\text{ lb }(7\text{ ft}) - B_y(10\text{ ft}) = 0,$$
$$B_y = 1.77 \text{ lb}$$

$$\Rightarrow \Sigma F_x = 0; \qquad A_x - 10\cos 60° \text{ lb} = 0, \qquad A_x = 5.00 \text{ lb}$$

$$+\uparrow\Sigma F_y = 0; \qquad A_y - 10\sin 60° \text{ lb} + 5\text{ lb} - 1.77\text{ lb} = 0,$$
$$A_y = 5.43 \text{ lb}$$

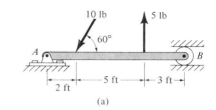

(a)

Hence,

$$F_A = \sqrt{(A_x)^2 + (A_y)^2} = \sqrt{(5.00\text{ lb})^2 + (5.43\text{ lb})^2} = 7.38 \text{ lb}$$

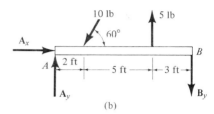

(b)

$$\theta = \tan^{-1}\frac{A_y}{A_x} = \tan^{-1}\frac{5.43\text{ lb}}{5.00\text{ lb}} = 47.5° \qquad \measuredangle_\theta \mathbf{F}_A$$

Obviously, the forces $\mathbf{F}_A$ and $\mathbf{B}_y$ acting at the two joints are *not* directed along the axis of the beam. As a consequence, if the beam has elastic properties, the loading will actually *bend* the beam into a shape similar to that shown in Fig. 6–11c.*

Frames and machines are two common types of structures which are often composed of pin-connected, multiforce members. *Frames* are generally stationary and are used to support loads; whereas, *machines* contain moving parts and are designed to transmit and alter the effect of forces. Both types of structures cannot be analyzed using the method of joints or the method of sections since the applied loading generally tends to bend the members as stated above. A partial analysis of the structure may be made, however, by removing the pin connections at the joints, and considering each member as a *separate* rigid body. The forces acting at the joints may then be determined by applying the equations of equilibrium to the free-body diagram of each member. Provided the structure is properly constrained and contains no more supports or members than are necessary to prevent collapse, the force analysis will be statically determinate. Hence, the equations of equilibrium for each member will provide both necessary and sufficient conditions for equilibrium. When the structure is subjected to a coplanar system of forces, *it is possible to write three independent equilibrium equations for the forces shown on the free-body diagram of each member.* By proper application of the equilibrium equations some of the unknowns may be solved for directly from a single equation rather than from a series of simultaneous equations.

A step-by-step procedure which may be useful in analyzing the *joint reactions* for frames and machines composed of multiforce members is as follows:

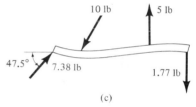

(c)

Fig. 6–11

---

*Using the theory developed in Chapter 7, it will be shown that in order to hold any section of the beam in equilibrium it is necessary that both an internal force and bending moment be developed at the cut section.

1. Draw a free-body diagram of the entire structure, apply the three equations of equilibrium, and solve for as many of the unknown *external reactions* as possible. (It may not be possible to solve for all the external reactions on the free-body diagram since the whole structure is generally composed of many rigid bodies, consisting of struts, beams, pulleys, etc. See Examples 6–6 and 6–11.)

2. Separate the members of the structure and draw a free-body diagram for each member. Forces common to two members act with equal magnitude but opposite direction on the respective free-body diagrams of the members. Recall that all *two-force members* have only one unknown, that is, the magnitude of force which acts along a line joining the end points of the member. The unknown forces acting at the joints of multiforce members should be represented by their rectangular components. In many cases it is possible to tell "by inspection" or experience in which direction these unknown forces act. If this is impossible, a direction is assumed.

3. Apply the three equations of equilibrium to the force system shown on each of the free-body diagrams and solve for the unknown forces. If an unknown force magnitude is found to be a positive quantity, its assumed direction, as shown on the free-body diagram, is correct; if it is negative, the direction of the force is reversed. In particular, if a force is "negative", the negative sign must be *retained* with the force magnitude if the force magnitude is used in the solution of any other equations of equilibrium. The retention of the negative sign is necessary since the equilibrium equations were all written so as to account for the direction of the forces *originally* shown on the free-body diagrams.

The examples which follow should be *thoroughly understood* before proceeding to solve the problems. Specifically, each example illustrates the step-by-step procedure just discussed for obtaining the force which acts at the joints and connections of frames and machines. When these forces are obtained, it is possible to properly design the connections and supports using the theory of strength of materials. In particular, the design of a member follows from a force analysis of the member. This force analysis will be discussed in Chapter 7. It should be noted, however, that a force analysis of the member *first* requires a force analysis of the joints as discussed in this section.

Example 6–6

Determine the tension in the cables and also the force **P** required to support the 600-lb block, utilizing the frictionless pulley system shown in (a) Fig. 6–12a, and (b) Fig. 6–13a.

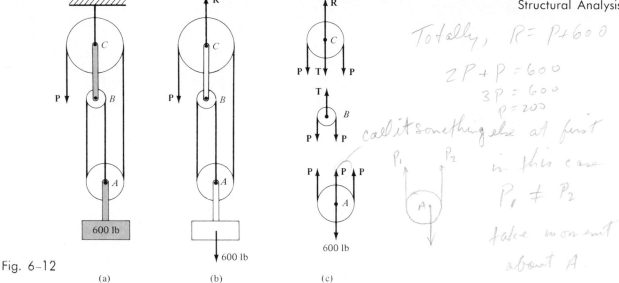

Totally, $R = P + 600$

$2P + P = 600$
$3P = 600$
$P = 200$

call it something else at first

P_1 P_2 in this case

$P_1 \neq P_2$

take moment about A

Fig. 6–12

(a)   (b)   (c)

Solution

Part (a). *Step 1:* A free-body diagram of the entire pulley system is shown in Fig. 6–12*b*. Applying the translational equilibrium equation in the vertical direction gives

$$+\uparrow\Sigma F_y = 0; \quad R - P - 600 \text{ lb} = 0, \qquad R = 600 \text{ lb} + P \qquad (1)$$

Step 2: A free-body diagram of each pulley is given in Fig. 6–12*c*. Since the cable is *continuous* and the pulleys are frictionless, the cable has a *constant tension* of P lb acting throughout its length. (See Example 5–7.) The link connection between pulleys B and C is a two-force member and it therefore has an unknown tension of T lb acting in it. Notice that the *principle of action and reaction* must be carefully observed for forces **P** and **T** when drawing the *separate* free-body diagrams, as shown in Fig. 6–12*c*.

Step 3: If we apply the equilibrium equation $\Sigma F_y = 0$ to each pulley, we have for pulley A,

$$+\uparrow\Sigma F_y = 0; \qquad 3P - 600 \text{ lb} = 0, \qquad P = 200 \text{ lb} \qquad \qquad Ans.$$

for pulley B,

$$+\uparrow\Sigma F_y = 0; \quad T - 2P = T - 400 \text{ lb} = 0, \qquad T = 400 \text{ lb}$$

and for pulley C,

$$+\uparrow\Sigma F_y = 0; \quad R - 2P - T = R - 2(200 \text{ lb}) - 400 \text{ lb} = 0, \quad R = 800 \text{ lb}$$

This same result for R may also be obtained by using Eq. (1).

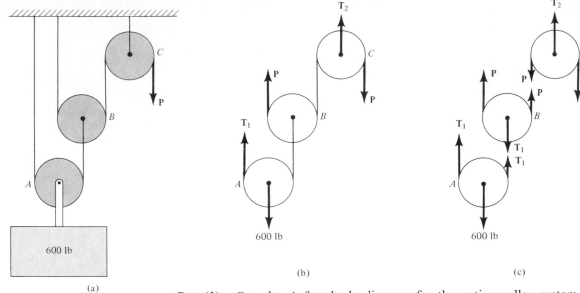

Fig. 6-13

(a)

(b)

(c)

Part (b). *Step 1:* A free-body diagram for the entire pulley system is shown in Fig. 6–13*b*. Since the cable passing over pulleys *B* and *C* is continuous, the tension in this cable is *P* lb. The other cables have tensions T_1 lb and T_2 lb acting in them. Applying the equation of equilibrium yields

$$+\!\uparrow\Sigma F_y = 0; \quad T_1 - 600 \text{ lb} + P + T_2 - P = 0, \quad T_1 + T_2 = 600 \text{ lb} \quad (2)$$

Step 2: A free-body diagram of each pulley is shown in Fig. 6–13*c*. Observe how the principle of action and reaction is applied to forces T_1 and **P** on the separate free-body diagrams.

Step 3: If we apply the equilibrium equation $\Sigma F_y = 0$ to each pulley, we have for pulley *A*,

$$+\!\uparrow\Sigma F_y = 0; \qquad 2T_1 - 600 \text{ lb} = 0, \qquad T_1 = 300 \text{ lb} \qquad \qquad \textit{Ans.}$$

for pulley *B*,

$$+\!\uparrow\Sigma F_y = 0; \quad 2P - T_1 = 2P - 300 \text{ lb} = 0, \qquad P = 150 \text{ lb} \qquad \textit{Ans.}$$

and for pulley *C*,

$$+\!\uparrow\Sigma F_y = 0; \quad T_2 - 2P = T_2 - 300 \text{ lb} = 0, \qquad T_2 = 300 \text{ lb} \qquad \textit{Ans.}$$

The solution can be easily checked by using Eq. (2).

Example 6-7

Determine the forces which the pins at points *B* and *C* exert on member *ABCD* of the loaded frame shown in Fig. 6–14*a*.

208

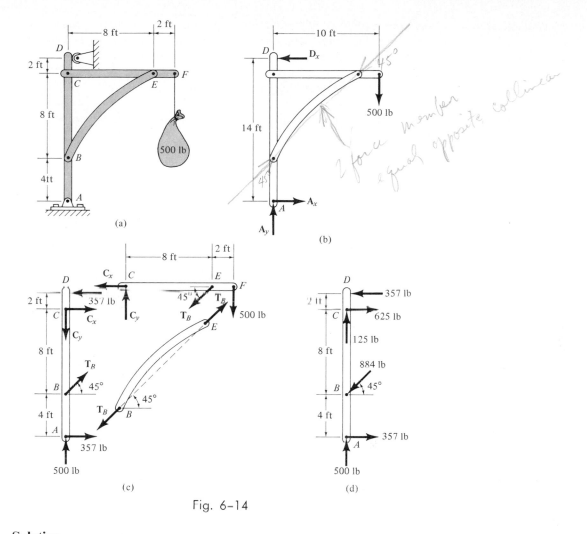

Fig. 6-14

Solution

Step 1: A free-body diagram of the entire structure is shown in Fig. 6–14*b*. Applying the three equations of equilibrium yields

$$\zeta + \Sigma M_A = 0; \qquad -500 \text{ lb } (10 \text{ ft}) + D_x(14 \text{ ft}) = 0, \qquad D_x = 357 \text{ lb}$$
$$\overset{+}{\rightarrow} \Sigma F_x = 0; \qquad A_x - 357 \text{ lb} = 0, \qquad A_x = 357 \text{ lb}$$
$$+ \uparrow \Sigma F_y = 0; \qquad A_y - 500 \text{ lb} = 0, \qquad A_y = 500 \text{ lb}$$

Since all the unknown forces are numerically positive, their assumed directions, indicated on the free-body diagram in Fig. 6–14*b*, are correct.

Step 2: A free-body diagram of each member of the frame is shown in Fig. 6–14*c*. Notice that member *BE* is a two-force member, and hence

209

only the magnitude of force acting at its two end points is *unknown* (see Sec. 6–1). The force acting at pin C has two unknowns represented by the two rectangular components $\mathbf{C}_x$ and $\mathbf{C}_y$.* As shown, the principle of action and reaction of forces must be applied at joints B, C, and E when the separate free-body diagrams are drawn.

Step 3: If we apply the three equations of equilibrium to member *CEF*, we have

$$\zeta + \Sigma M_C = 0; \quad -500 \text{ lb } (10 \text{ ft}) - (T_B \sin 45°)8 \text{ ft} = 0,$$
$$T_B = -884 \text{ lb} \quad {}^{45°}\!\!\nearrow\!\!_{\mathbf{T}_B} \quad Ans.$$

$$\xrightarrow{+}\Sigma F_x = 0; \quad -C_x - (-884 \cos 45° \text{ lb}) = 0, \quad C_x = 625 \text{ lb}$$
$$+\uparrow\Sigma F_y = 0; \quad C_y - (-884 \sin 45° \text{ lb}) - 500 \text{ lb} = 0, \quad C_y = -125 \text{ lb}$$

Since the magnitudes of forces $\mathbf{T}_B$ and $\mathbf{C}_y$ were calculated as negative quantities, they were assumed to be acting with the wrong sense of direction on the free-body diagrams shown in Fig. 6–14c. The correct directional sense of these forces might have been determined "by inspection" *before* applying and solving the equations of equilibrium for member *CEF*. As shown in Fig. 6–14c, moment equilibrium about point E on member *CEF* indicates that $\mathbf{C}_y$ must actually act *downward* to counteract the moment created by the 500-lb force about point E. Similarly, summing moments about point C, we can see that the vertical component of force $\mathbf{T}_B$ must actually act *upward*.

A free-body diagram of member *ABCD*, showing the magnitude and *correct sense of direction* of all the computed forces acting on it, is given in Fig. 6–14d. To check the previous calculations we may apply the three equations of equilibrium to this member:

$$\xrightarrow{+}\Sigma F_x = 0; \quad -357 \text{ lb} + 625 \text{ lb} - 884 \cos 45° \text{ lb} + 357 \text{ lb} \equiv 0$$
$$+\uparrow\Sigma F_y = 0; \quad 125 \text{ lb} - 884 \sin 45° \text{ lb} + 500 \text{ lb} \equiv 0$$
$$\zeta + \Sigma M_B = 0; \quad 357 \text{ lb } (10 \text{ ft}) - 625 \text{ lb } (8 \text{ ft}) + 357 \text{ lb } (4 \text{ ft}) \equiv 0$$

The total magnitude of force which the pin C exerts on member *ABCD* is therefore

$$F_C = \sqrt{(C_x)^2 + (C_y)^2} = \sqrt{(625 \text{ lb})^2 + (125 \text{ lb})^2} = 637 \text{ lb} \quad Ans.$$

The direction of this force is

$$\theta = \tan^{-1}\frac{C_y}{C_x} = \tan^{-1}\frac{125 \text{ lb}}{625 \text{ lb}} = 11.3° \quad \angle^{\theta}\mathbf{F}_C \quad Ans.$$

---

*The two rectangular components of an unknown force are considered here instead of the magnitude and direction of the force. It is generally easier to determine these two components using the equations of equilibrium.

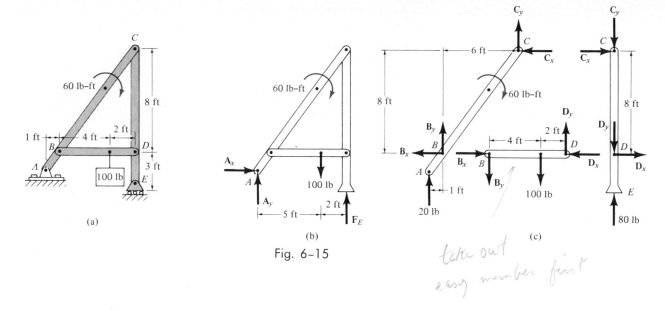

Fig. 6-15

(handwritten note: take out easy member first)

Example 6-8

The frame shown in Fig. 6–15a supports a load of 100 lb. If joints A, B, C, and D are all pin-connected, determine the horizontal and vertical components of force acting at each of these joints.

Solution

Step 1: A free-body diagram of the entire frame is shown in Fig. 6–15b. Applying the three equations of equilibrium gives

$\zeta + \Sigma M_A = 0;$ $\quad -100$ lb $(5$ ft$) - 60$ lb-ft $+ F_E(7$ ft$) = 0,$ $\quad F_E = 80$ lb

$\xrightarrow{+} \Sigma F_x = 0;$ $\quad A_x = 0$ *Ans.*

$+\uparrow \Sigma F_y = 0;$ $\quad A_y \quad 100$ lb $+ 80$ lb $= 0,$ $\quad A_y = 20$ lb *Ans.*

(handwritten note: moment is a free vector; it acts anywhere)

Step 2: Using these values for the reactions at A and E a free-body diagram of each member of the frame is shown in Fig. 6–15c. Since all the members are multiforce members, there are two unknown components of force acting at each of the joints B, C, and D. In accordance with the principle of action and reaction, these force components act with equal magnitude and opposite direction on adjacent free-body diagrams, as shown. (Each of the free-body diagrams should be carefully studied.)

The 60-lb-ft couple, being a "free vector," can act at any point on the free-body diagram of member ABC. This couple cannot, however, act on the adjacent members CDE or BD, since these members have been *separated* from member ABC, that is, ABC is a *separate* rigid body from the other members.

Step 3:   Applying the three equations of equilibrium, we have for member *ABC*,

$$(\Sigma M_B = 0; \quad -20 \text{ lb (1 ft)} - 60 \text{ lb-ft} + C_x(8 \text{ ft}) + C_y(6 \text{ ft}) = 0 \tag{1}$$

$$\xrightarrow{+}\Sigma F_x = 0; \qquad\qquad -B_x - C_x = 0 \tag{2}$$

$$+\uparrow\Sigma F_y = 0; \qquad\qquad 20 \text{ lb} + B_y + C_y = 0 \tag{3}$$

and for member *BD*,

$$(+\Sigma M_B = 0; \qquad -100 \text{ lb (4 ft)} + D_y(6 \text{ ft}) = 0 \tag{4}$$

$$\xrightarrow{+}\Sigma F_x = 0; \qquad\qquad B_x - D_x = 0 \tag{5}$$

$$+\uparrow\Sigma F_y = 0; \qquad\qquad D_y - 100 \text{ lb} - B_y = 0 \tag{6}$$

Six *independent equations* have been written which contain six unknowns: B_x, B_y, C_x, C_y, D_x, and D_y. Due to the nature of these equations the solution is rather direct. For example, solve for D_y in Eq. (4) then proceed to obtain the remaining unknowns using Eqs. (6), (3), (1), (2), and (5), in that order. The final results are

$$B_x = 0.0 \qquad\qquad\qquad Ans.$$
$$B_y = -33.3 \text{ lb} \qquad\qquad Ans.$$
$$C_x = 0.0 \qquad\qquad\qquad Ans.$$
$$C_y = 13.3 \text{ lb} \qquad\qquad Ans.$$
$$D_x = 0.0 \qquad\qquad\qquad Ans.$$
$$D_y = 66.7 \text{ lb} \qquad\qquad Ans.$$

Since the magnitude of force $\mathbf{B}_y$ has been computed as a negative quantity, it was assumed acting in the wrong direction on the free-body diagrams in Fig. 6–15c. Hence, its direction is opposite to that shown on these diagrams. The above calculations may be checked in part by applying the equations of equilibrium to member *EDC*.

Example 6–9

Determine the horizontal and vertical force components acting at the pin connections *B* and *C* of the loaded frame shown in Fig. 6–16a.

Solution

Step 1:   The free-body diagram of the entire frame is shown in Fig. 6–16b. Applying the three equations of equilibrium yields

$$(+\Sigma M_A = 0; \quad M_A - 100 \text{ lb (4 ft)} = 0, \qquad M_A = 400 \text{ lb-ft}$$

$$\xrightarrow{+}\Sigma F_x = 0; \quad A_x = 0$$

$$+\uparrow\Sigma F_y = 0; \qquad A_y - 100 \text{ lb} = 0, \qquad A_y = 100 \text{ lb}$$

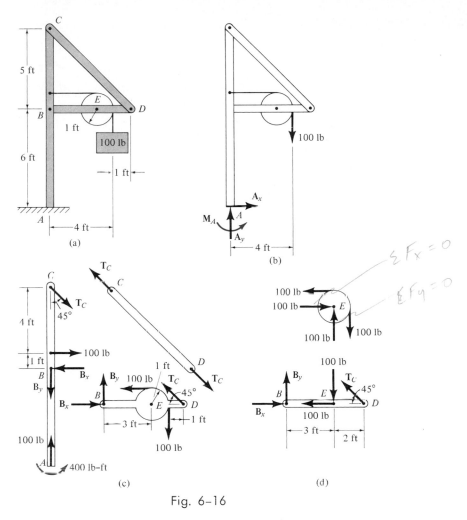

Fig. 6–16

Step 2: Using these values for the reactions, the free-body diagram for each of the members is shown in Fig. 6–16c. Notice that member *CD* is a two-force member. Member *BED* and the pulley are considered to be one system that is, acting together as a single body. The cable, being continuous, is subjected to a tensile force of 100 lb throughout its entire length. Hence, when the cable is *removed,* a force of 100 lb pulls horizontally on member *ABC*, and both horizontally and vertically on the pulley.

Step 3: Applying the three equations of equilibrium to member *BED* yields

$$\zeta+\Sigma M_B = 0; \quad -100 \text{ lb } (4 \text{ ft}) + 100 \text{ lb } (1 \text{ ft}) + T_C \sin 45° (5 \text{ ft}) = 0,$$
$$T_C = 84.9 \text{ lb} \qquad\qquad\qquad \textit{Ans.}$$

Using this result for T_C,

$$\stackrel{+}{\rightarrow}\Sigma F_x = 0; \quad B_x - 100 \text{ lb} - 84.9 \cos 45° \text{ lb} = 0, \qquad B_x = 160 \text{ lb} \quad Ans.$$
$$+\uparrow\Sigma F_y = 0; \quad 84.9 \sin 45° \text{ lb} - 100 \text{ lb} + B_y = 0, \qquad B_y = 40 \text{ lb} \quad Ans.$$

It is suggested that the above calculations be checked by applying the three equations of equilibrium to member ABC.

An alternative approach may be used to solve for the forces acting on member BED. If the pulley is *removed*, it must be held in equilibrium by 100-lb force components exerted *on* it by the pin at point E, Fig. 6–16d. By inspection, both translational and rotational equilibrium of the pulley are satisfied. According to the principle of action and reaction, the force components exerted by the pulley on member BED are equal but opposite to those exerted by the member on the pulley. Hence, the free-body diagram of member BED shown in Fig. 6–16d may be used to obtain the reactions $\mathbf{B}_x$, $\mathbf{B}_y$, and $\mathbf{T}_C$. The results will be identical to those obtained previously. Can you show this?

Example 6–10

The frame shown in Fig. 6–17a is supported at A by a pin and at E by a smooth inclined plane. Determine the horizontal and vertical components of force that the pin connections exert on the frame. The pulley at C is frictionless.

Solution

Step 1: A free-body diagram of the entire frame is shown in Fig. 6–17b. Writing the three equations of equilibrium, we have

$$\zeta+\Sigma M_A = 0; \quad -200 \text{ lb (13 ft)} + F_E \cos 45°(12 \tan 30° \text{ ft}) = 0,$$
$$F_E = 531 \text{ lb}$$

(Note that the component $F_E \sin 45°$ is not included in the moment equation since the line of action of this force passes through point A.) Using the computed value of F_E,

$$\stackrel{+}{\rightarrow}\Sigma F_x = 0; \quad 531 \cos 45° \text{ lb} - A_x = 0, \qquad A_x = 375 \text{ lb} \qquad Ans.$$
$$+\uparrow\Sigma F_y = 0; \quad -A_y + 531 \sin 45° \text{ lb} - 200 \text{ lb} = 0, \qquad A_y = 175 \text{ lb} \quad Ans.$$

Step 2: A free-body diagram of each member, including the pins at D and C, and the pulley is shown in Fig. 6–17c. The force $\mathbf{F}_E$ is shown on the free-body diagram of member EDC as two components having magnitudes of $(531 \text{ lb})(0.707) = 375 \text{ lb}$. In all cases, equal but opposite reactions are shown between two connected members, when the members are separated. You are strongly urged to study each of the free-body diagrams carefully. In particular, note that *three force interactions* occur

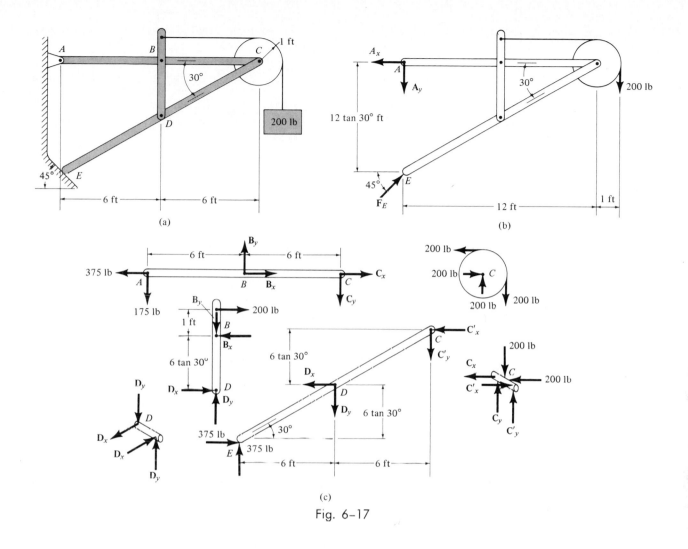

(a)

(b)

(c)

Fig. 6–17

on the pin located at C, namely, the force components $\mathbf{C}_x$ and $\mathbf{C}_y$ representing the force exerted by member ABC, the force components $\mathbf{C}'_x$ and $\mathbf{C}'_y$ representing the force exerted by member EDC, and finally the two 200-lb force components exerted by the pulley. Writing the equilibrium equations $\Sigma F_x = 0$ and $\Sigma F_y = 0$ for the pin at C will enable us to obtain two equations which relate the unknown forces magnitudes C_x, C'_x, and C_y, C'_y (Equations (4) and (5) in Step 3). When only *two force interactions* occur at a pin connection (such as pin D in Fig. 6–17c), to satisfy $\Sigma F_x = 0$ and $\Sigma F_y = 0$ the force components acting must be equal in magnitude but opposite in direction. For this reason the free-body diagrams for *pins* which connect *only two members* together were *not considered* in the force analysis of the previous examples. In all cases, the length of the pin is

215

considered *short* so that the moment created by the force interactions on the pin can be neglected.

Step 3: Applying the three equations of equilibrium, we have for member *ABC*,

$$\xrightarrow{+}\Sigma F_x = 0; \qquad -375 \text{ lb} + B_x + C_x = 0 \qquad\qquad (1)$$

$$+\uparrow\Sigma F_y = 0; \qquad -175 \text{ lb} + B_y - C_y = 0 \qquad\qquad (2)$$

$$\zeta+\Sigma M_B = 0; \qquad 175 \text{ lb } (6 \text{ ft}) - C_y(6 \text{ ft}) = 0 \qquad\qquad (3)$$

for pin *C*,

$$\xrightarrow{+}\Sigma F_x = 0; \qquad -C_x + C_x' - 200 \text{ lb} = 0 \qquad\qquad (4)$$

$$+\uparrow\Sigma F_y = 0; \qquad C_y + C_y' - 200 \text{ lb} = 0 \qquad\qquad (5)$$

and for member *EDC*,

$$\xrightarrow{+}\Sigma F_x = 0; \qquad 375 \text{ lb} - D_x - C_x' = 0 \qquad\qquad (6)$$

$$+\uparrow\Sigma F_y = 0; \qquad 375 \text{ lb} - D_y - C_y' = 0 \qquad\qquad (7)$$

$$\zeta+\Sigma M_D = 0; \qquad -375 \text{ lb } (6 \text{ ft}) + 375 \text{ lb } (6 \tan 30° \text{ ft}) - C_y'(6 \text{ ft})$$
$$+ C_x'(6 \tan 30° \text{ ft}) = 0 \quad (8)$$

Eight independent linear equations have been written which may be solved for the eight unknowns: B_x, B_y, C_x, C_y, C_x', C_y', D_x, and D_y.

Due to the nature of these equations, however, each equation may be solved directly for each unknown. This is done by first solving Eq. (3) for C_y then proceeding to obtain the remaining unknowns using Eqs. (2), (5), (8), (4), (6), (7), and (1), in that order. The final results are

$$B_x = 257 \text{ lb} \qquad\qquad\qquad Ans.$$

$$B_y = 350 \text{ lb} \qquad\qquad\qquad Ans.$$

$$C_x = 118 \text{ lb} \qquad\qquad\qquad Ans.$$

$$C_y = 175 \text{ lb} \qquad\qquad\qquad Ans.$$

$$C_x' = 318 \text{ lb} \qquad\qquad\qquad Ans.$$

$$C_y' = 25 \text{ lb} \qquad\qquad\qquad Ans.$$

$$D_x = 57 \text{ lb} \qquad\qquad\qquad Ans.$$

$$D_y = 350 \text{ lb} \qquad\qquad\qquad Ans.$$

It is suggested that the above calculations be checked by applying the equations of equilibrium to member *BD*.

Example 6–11

The piston and link mechanism shown in Fig. 6–18*a* is used for purposes of compacting material contained within the cylinder *C*. If a force

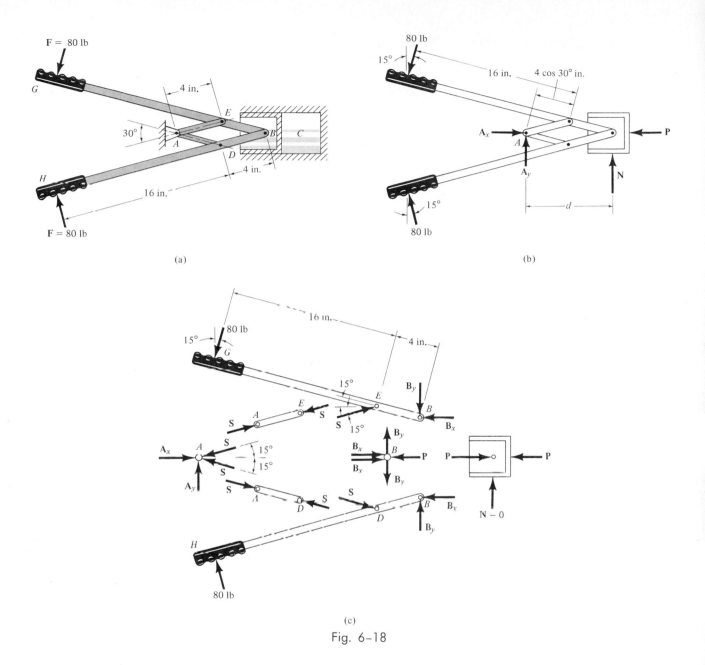

Fig. 6–18

of 80 lb is applied at a right angle to each handle of the mechanism, determine the compaction force exerted by the piston and the horizontal and vertical components of force at pins *A* and *B*. Assume that the surface of contact between the piston and the cylinder wall is smooth.

Solution

Step 1: A free-body diagram of the piston and link mechanism is shown in Fig. 6–18*b*. In particular, **N** represents the *resultant force* exerted by the walls of the cylinder on the piston and *d* is the horizontal distance at which this force acts from the pin at *A*. Applying the three equations of equilibrium yields

$$\xrightarrow{+} \Sigma F_x = 0; \qquad A_x - P - 2(80 \sin 15° \text{ lb}) = 0$$

$$P = A_x - 41 \text{ lb} \tag{1}$$

$$\zeta + \Sigma M_A = 0; -80 \text{ lb } (16 \text{ in.} - 4 \cos 30° \text{ in.}) +$$

$$80 \text{ lb } (16 \text{ in.} - 4 \cos 30° \text{ in.}) - Nd = 0$$

$$N = 0 \quad (\text{since } d \neq 0)$$

$$+\uparrow \Sigma F_y = 0; \quad -80 \cos 15° \text{ lb} + 80 \cos 15° \text{ lb} + A_y + 0 = 0,$$

$$A_y = 0$$

Note that we *cannot* obtain a direct solution for the compaction force **P** using the single free-body diagram, Fig. 6–18*b*. It is therefore necessary to separate the mechanism into its component parts and write equations of equilibrium for each rigid body.

Step 2: A free-body diagram of each member *including* pins *A* and *B* of the mechanism is shown in Fig. 6–18*c*. The pins at *A* and *B* are shown since *three connections* are made at each of these pins. Since both the loading and mechanism are symmetrical, forces having equal magnitudes occur in the corresponding (two-force) members *AE* and *AD*, and in members *GEB* and *HDB*. You should study each of the separate free-body diagrams carefully and note that the principle of action and reaction of forces must be observed when drawing the separate free-body diagrams.

Step 3: Applying the equations of equilibrium to member *GEB* and pin *A*; for member *GEB*,

$$\zeta + \Sigma M_B = 0; \quad -S \sin 30°(4 \text{ in.}) + 80 \text{ lb } (20 \text{ in.}) = 0, \qquad S = 800 \text{ lb}$$

Using the computed value of *S*,

$$\xrightarrow{+} \Sigma F_x = 0; \qquad -80 \sin 15° \text{ lb} + 800 \cos 15° \text{ lb} - B_x = 0,$$

$$B_x = 752 \text{ lb} \qquad\qquad\qquad Ans.$$

$$+\uparrow \Sigma F_y = 0; \qquad -80 \cos 15° \text{ lb} + 800 \sin 15° \text{ lb} - B_y = 0,$$

$$B_y = 130 \text{ lb} \qquad\qquad\qquad Ans.$$

and for pin *A*, using the computed value of *S*,

$$\xrightarrow{+} \Sigma F_x = 0; \quad A_x - 2(800 \cos 15° \text{ lb}) = 0, \qquad A_x = 1{,}545 \text{ lb} \qquad Ans.$$

$$+\uparrow \Sigma F_y = 0; \quad A_y - 800 \sin 15° \text{ lb} + 800 \sin 15° \text{ lb} = 0, \quad A_y = 0 \quad Ans.$$

The magnitude of the compaction force **P** can be obtained from Eq. (1), using the value of A_x.

$$P = 1,545 \text{ lb} - 41 \text{ lb} \qquad P = 1,504 \text{ lb} \qquad \textit{Ans.}$$

This value can be checked by considering the equilibrium of the pin at B, namely,

$$\xrightarrow{+} \Sigma F_x = 0; \qquad 2B_x - P = 0,$$
$$2(752 \text{ lb}) - 1,504 \text{ lb} \equiv 0$$

Problems

Neglect the weight of the members unless stated otherwise.

6-37. Determine the horizontal and vertical components of force acting at A, B, and C of the frame.

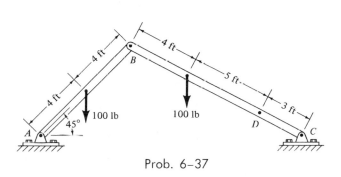

Prob. 6-37

6-38. Determine the reactions at pins A and C for the two-member frame.

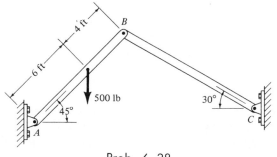

Prob. 6-38

6-39. Determine the horizontal and vertical components of the forces developed at pin connections A, B, and C for the two-member frame.

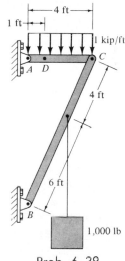

Prob. 6-39

6-40. Determine the horizontal and vertical components of force at pins A and C of the mechanism.

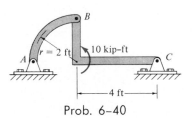

Prob. 6-40

6-41. Determine the angle α which the pulley-supporting link makes with the vertical. Neglect the weight of the pulleys.

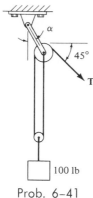

Prob. 6-41

6-42. Determine the tension in member BC of the frame and the horizontal and vertical components of force acting on the pin at D.

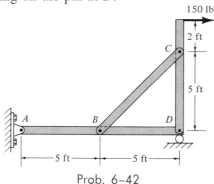

Prob. 6-42

6-43. If a force of 40 lb is applied to the handles of the pliers, determine the force applied to the bolt B.

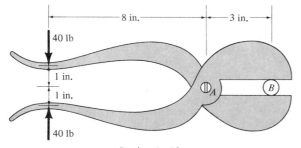

Prob. 6-43

6-44. Determine the horizontal and vertical components of force at pins A and C of the mechanism. The pulley at D is frictionless. The mechanism is pin connected at B.

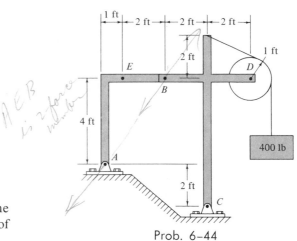

Prob. 6-44

6-45. The jack shown supports a 800-lb automobile engine. Determine the compression in the hydraulic cylinder C and the reaction at the pin B.

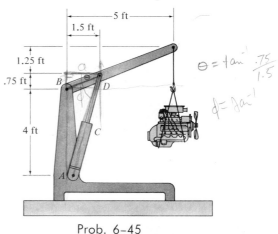

Prob. 6-45

6-46. The 5,600-lb car, having a center of gravity at G, is supported by a hydraulic jack AD. Determine the compression in the cylinder C when the car is in the position shown.

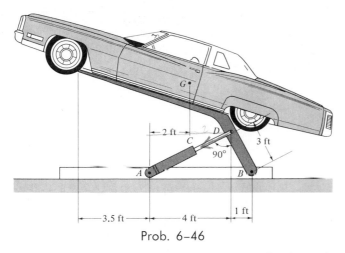

Prob. 6–46

6-47. Determine the force **P** required to maintain equilibrium of the pulley mechanisms.

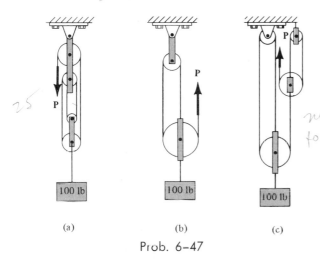

(a)   (b)   (c)

Prob. 6–47

6-48. Compute the reactions at supports *A*, *B*, *C*, and *D* of the compound beam.

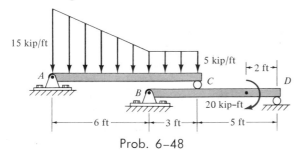

Prob. 6–48

6-49. Determine the clamping force exerted on the pipe at *B* if a force of 50 lb is applied to each of the handles of the wrench.

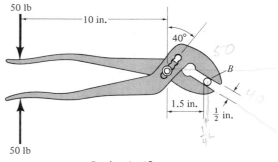

Prob. 6–49

6-50. Determine the compressive force developed in member *BC* and the horizontal and vertical components of the force which the pin at *A* exerts on member *AB* of the frame.

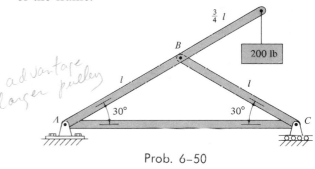

Prob. 6–50

6-51. Determine the horizontal and vertical components of force acting at *A*, *B*, and *C* in the two-member arch.

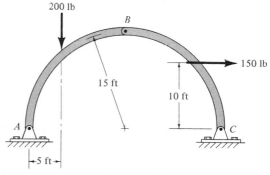

Prob. 6–51

221

6–52. The tongs are used to lift the 100-lb crate. Determine the force developed at pins B and C. Due to friction, the shoes at E and F prevent the crate from slipping.

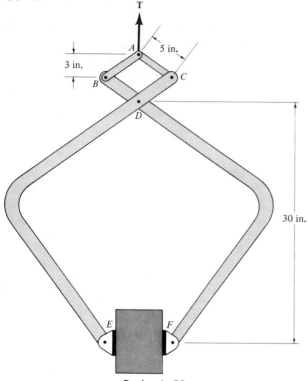

Prob. 6–52

6–53. The tractor shovel shown carries a 1,000-lb load of gravel, having a center of gravity at G. Compute the forces developed in the hydraulic cylinders BC and IJ due to this loading.

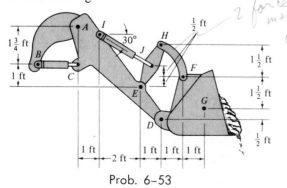

Prob. 6–53

6–54. Two blocks A and B are suspended from a ceiling by means of two cables. If block A weighs 50 lb and block B weighs 30 lb, determine the tension in the cables and the reactive force which block B exerts on block A.

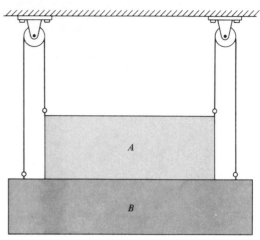

Prob. 6–54

6–55. Determine the reactions at pins A and B of the frame. The large pulley is pinned at C and has a radius of $\frac{1}{2}$ ft. The small pulley at D has a radius of $\frac{1}{4}$ ft.

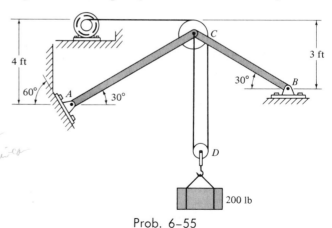

Prob. 6–55

6–56. The semicircular arch AB weighs 20 lb/ft, and the smooth cylinder D weighs 50 lb. Neglecting the weight of the brace BCD, determine the horizontal and vertical reactions at the pin B and the reaction of the roller C.

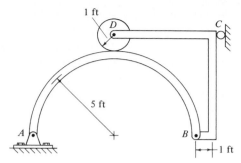

Prob. 6-56

6-57. The extension ladder rests against a smooth wall at *A* and is held from slipping at *B* by means of a friction shoe. If a 150-lb man climbs up the ladder to the position shown, determine the reactions at the (pin) connection *C* and the smooth contact *D*. Each section of the ladder weighs 25 lb and has a center of gravity at its midlength. Neglect the distance "*s*" in the calculations. Assume that the only force which the man exerts on the ladder is his total weight, acting as a vertical reaction at *E*. Horizontal and vertical components of force act at *B*.

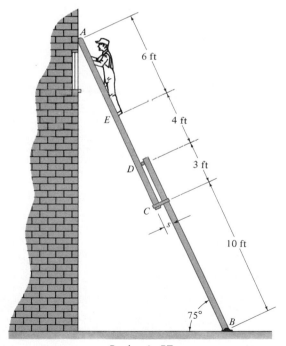

Prob. 6-57

6-58. The mechanism is subjected to a horizontal force of 80 lb. Determine the magnitude of the vertical force **P** which must be applied to the smooth block at *B*, required to maintain equilibrium.

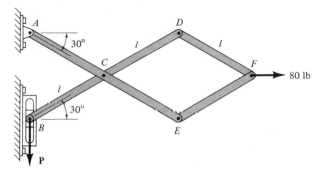

Prob. 6-58

6-59. If a vertical force of $P = 60$ lb is applied to the handle of the punch, determine the force exerted on the plate at *A*.

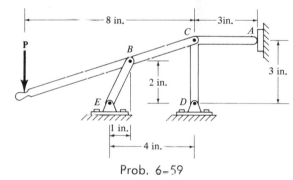

Prob. 6-59

6-60. Determine the horizontal and vertical components of the forces acting at pins *A*, *B*, and *C* of the frame.

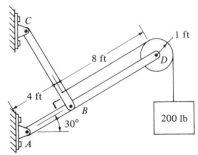

Prob. 6-60

223

6-61. The drafting table is supported at B by a pin and a spring at A. If the table weighs 20 lb and has a center of gravity at G, determine the stiffness k of the spring so that the table remains in equilibrium for $\theta = 30°$. The spring is unstretched when $\theta = 90°$.

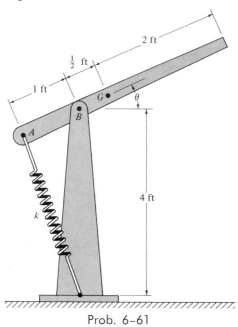

Prob. 6-61

6-62. Determine the horizontal and vertical components of force developed at pins A, B, and D of the "A" frame.

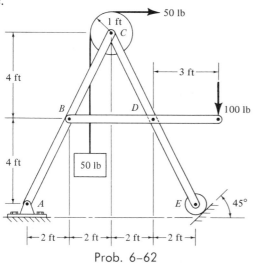

Prob. 6-62

6-63. The hoisting frame is supported at A by a pin and at C by a short link. The cable is attached to a drum at B and passes over frictionless pulleys at D and E. Determine the magnitude of force which the pins exert on members CD and AD and the force $\mathbf{P}$ needed for equilibrium. The pinion gear rotates about a fixed axle passing through its center.

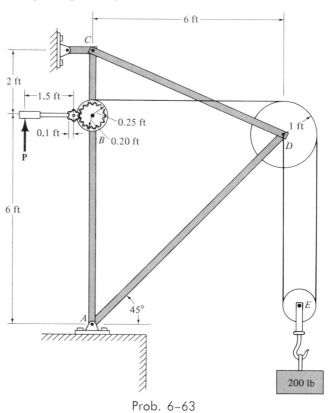

Prob. 6-63

6-64. Determine the horizontal and vertical components of reaction at the pin supports A and D of the compound beam.

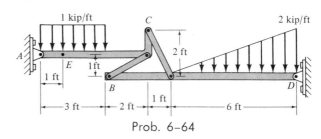

Prob. 6-64

6-65. Determine the tension in chain CD and the force which the pin at B exerts on member CB of the frame.

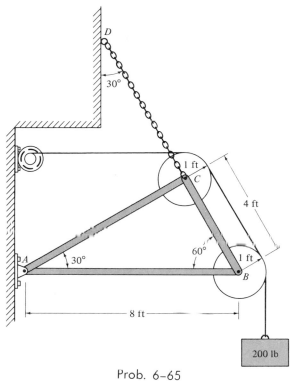

Prob. 6-65

6-66. Determine the horizontal and vertical components of the forces acting on the pins A and C of the frame. The pulley at D is frictionless. Neglect the weight of the motor.

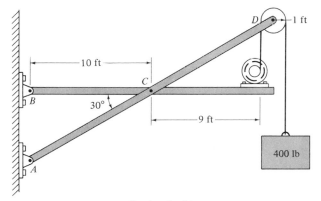

Prob. 6-66

6-67. Determine the horizontal force **P** which must be applied to the lever of the mechanism in order to hold the 250-lb gate open. There is a smooth roller at F.

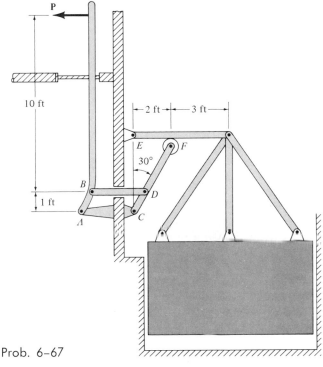

Prob. 6-67

6-68. The mechanism for a tractor is shown in the figure. Determine the force created in the hydraulic cylinder AD and pin H to hold the shovel in equilibrium. The load weighs 1,500 lb and has its center of gravity at G. All joints are pin connected.

also EF

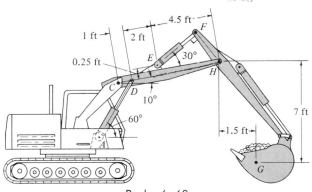

Prob. 6-68

Internal Forces

*7-1. Internal Forces Developed in Structural Members

In Secs. 6–3 and 6–6, we discussed methods for computing the equilibrium forces acting at supports and joint connections of rigid structural members. Given these forces, we may use the theory developed in strength of materials to design all the supports and connections required to hold the structure together. In a similar manner, before we can properly design a structural *member,* it is first necessary to know the *internal forces* acting within the member, when the member is subjected to a given system of loads.

The internal forces acting at any cross section along a member may be determined by using the *method of sections.** This method is generally applied after all the external forces acting on the member are computed. For example, consider the simply-supported beam loaded as shown in Fig. 7–1a. We can solve for the support reactions A_x, A_y, and B_y by applying the three equations of equilibrium to the force system on the free-body diagram shown in Fig. 7–1b. To determine the internal forces acting at location C along the axis of the beam (or any other location), the beam is sectioned perpendicular to its axis into two segments at that location, and the free-body diagrams shown in Fig. 7–1c are obtained. Since the two segments were prevented from both translating and rotating with respect to one another *before* the beam was sectioned, equilibrium is maintained when a *resultant* internal force, having rectangular components A_C and V_C and a *resultant* internal bending moment M_C, are developed at the cut section. In structural mechanics, the force components A_C (acting normal to the section) and V_C (acting tangent to the section) are termed the *axial force* and *shear force,* respectively. In accor-

---

*We discussed the method of sections briefly in Sec. 6–4, where it was used in connection with obtaining the internal force in truss (two-force) members.

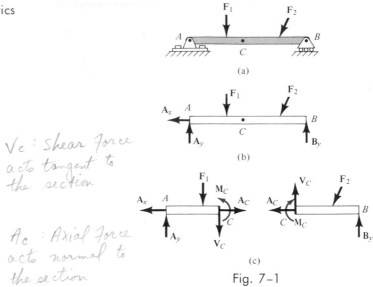

V_C : shear force acts tangent to the section

A_C : Axial force acts normal to the section

Fig. 7-1

dance with Newton's third law of motion, these internal forces and bending moment acting on an adjacent segment must be equal in magnitude and opposite in direction, as shown in Fig. 7-1c. The magnitudes of the internal forces and bending moment may be obtained by applying the three equations of equilibrium to *either* segment AC or CB.

The following examples further illustrate the application of the method of sections for obtaining the axial force, shear force, and bending moment at arbitrary points lying along the axis of a structural member.

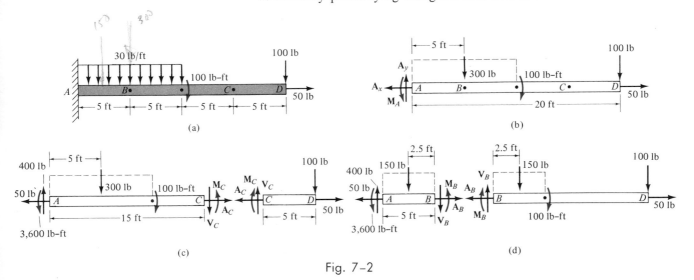

Fig. 7-2

Example 7-1

Determine the axial force, shear force, and bending moment acting at points B and C of the cantilevered beam loaded as shown in Fig. 7–2a. The 50-lb axial load is applied along the central axis of the beam.

Solution

A free-body diagram of the entire beam is shown in Fig. 7–2b. Since the wall prevents both rotation and translation of the beam, an unknown moment and two unknown force components must act at this support. The distributed load has been replaced by its resultant force in accordance with the principles outlined in Sec. 4–11. Applying the three equations of equilibrium yields

$\xrightarrow{+} \Sigma F_x = 0;$ $-A_x + 50 \text{ lb} = 0,$ $A_x = 50 \text{ lb}$

$+\uparrow \Sigma F_y = 0;$ $A_y - 300 \text{ lb} - 100 \text{ lb} = 0,$ $A_y = 400 \text{ lb}$

$\zeta + \Sigma M_A = 0;$ $-300 \text{ lb} (5 \text{ ft}) - 100 \text{ lb-ft} - 100 \text{ lb} (20 \text{ ft}) + M_A = 0,$

$$M_A = 3,600 \text{ lb-ft}$$

These forces and end moment keep the *entire beam* in equilibrium.

Passing an imaginary cutting section, perpendicular to the axis of the beam, through point C, we obtain the free-body diagrams of the beam segments AC and CD shown in Fig. 7–2c. The magnitudes of the internal forces $\mathbf{A}_C$ and $\mathbf{V}_C$ and the internal moment $\mathbf{M}_C$ are obtained by applying the equations of equilibrium to either segment AC or CD. For segment CD we have

$\xrightarrow{+} \Sigma F_x = 0;$ $50 \text{ lb} - A_C = 0,$ $A_C = 50 \text{ lb}$ *Ans.*

$+\uparrow \Sigma F_y = 0;$ $V_C - 100 \text{ lb} = 0,$ $V_C = 100 \text{ lb}$ *Ans.*

$\zeta + \Sigma M_C = 0;$ $-M_C - 100 \text{ lb} (5 \text{ ft}) = 0,$ $M_C = -500 \text{ lb-ft}$ *Ans.*

or for segment AC we have

$\xrightarrow{+} \Sigma F_x = 0;$ $A_C - 50 \text{ lb} = 0,$ $A_C = 50 \text{ lb}$ *Ans.*

$+\uparrow \Sigma F_y = 0;$ $400 \text{ lb} - 300 \text{ lb} - V_C = 0,$ $V_C = 100 \text{ lb}$ *Ans.*

$\zeta + \Sigma M_C = 0;$

$M_C - 100 \text{ lb-ft} + 300 \text{ lb} (10 \text{ ft}) - 400 \text{ lb} (15 \text{ ft}) + 3,600 \text{ lb-ft} = 0,$

$$M_C = -500 \text{ lb-ft} \checkmark \qquad \textit{Ans.}$$

As shown, segment CD provides the *simplest* solution for the internal forces since there are *fewer loads* on the free-body diagram of this segment. Also, the results were obtained without having to first obtain the external reactions at A. Because the magnitude of $\mathbf{M}_C$ has been computed as a *negative* quantity, the sense of direction of $\mathbf{M}_C$ is *opposite* to that assumed on the free-body diagrams in Fig. 7–1c. Therefore, the correct direction of $\mathbf{M}_C$ is clockwise on segment AC and counterclockwise on segment CD.

Before the beam is sectioned, it is important that each load act at its exact point of application on the beam; otherwise erroneous free-body diagrams will result. For example, using the principle of transmissibility discussed in Sec. 4–3, the 50-lb horizontal load at D may be moved to point A *before* calculating the external reactions. However, if this is done *prior* to sectioning the beam at C, segment CD will *not* be subjected to the 50-lb load as it should be.

Passing a section through point B, we obtain the free-body diagrams of the two beam segments AB and BD shown in Fig. 7–2d. *After sectioning the beam,* the portion of the distributed load acting on each segment is replaced by its resultant force. Do you see why we must section the beam *first* before simplifying the distributed load? Applying the three equations of equilibrium to segment AB yields

$$\xrightarrow{+} \Sigma F_x = 0; \qquad A_B - 50 \text{ lb} = 0, \qquad A_B = 50 \text{ lb} \qquad\qquad Ans.$$

$$+\uparrow \Sigma F_y = 0; \quad 400 \text{ lb} - 150 \text{ lb} - V_B = 0, \qquad V_B = 250 \text{ lb} \qquad\qquad Ans.$$

$$\zeta + \Sigma M_B = 0; \quad M_B + 150 \text{ lb} (2.5 \text{ ft}) - 400 \text{ lb} (5 \text{ ft}) + 3{,}600 \text{ lb-ft} = 0,$$

$$M_B = -1{,}975 \text{ lb-ft} \qquad\qquad Ans.$$

Since the magnitude of $\mathbf{M}_C$ is a negative quantity, the sense of direction of $\mathbf{M}_C$ shown on the free-body diagrams in Fig. 7–2d must be reversed.

Example 7–2

Determine the axial force, shear force, and bending moment acting at points E, H, and D of the frame shown in Fig. 7–3a. Neglect the weights of the members.

Solution

The free-body diagram of the entire frame is shown in Fig. 7–3b. Applying the three equations of equilibrium yields

$$+\uparrow \Sigma F_y = 0; \qquad A_y - 200 \text{ lb} = 0, \qquad A_y = 200 \text{ lb}$$

$$\zeta + \Sigma M_A = 0; \qquad -200 \text{ lb} (4 \text{ ft}) + B_x(8 \text{ ft}) = 0, \qquad B_x = 100 \text{ lb}$$

$$\xrightarrow{+} \Sigma F_x = 0; \qquad 100 \text{ lb} - A_x = 0, \qquad A_x = 100 \text{ lb}$$

A free-body diagram of each member of the frame, including the pins at A and C, is shown in Fig. 7–3c. Since the weights of the members are neglected, GC and CA are both two-force members, and thus the forces acting at their respective endpoints must be equal, opposite, and collinear. (Are you able to understand why these end forces must be equal, opposite, and collinear? Refer to Sec. 6–1.) The 200- and 100-lb forces shown on the free-body diagram of the pin at A represent the effect of the *pin support* at A acting *on* the pin. (These are the same forces shown on the free-body diagram in Fig. 7–3b. There they represent the effect of the pin support on the entire frame.)

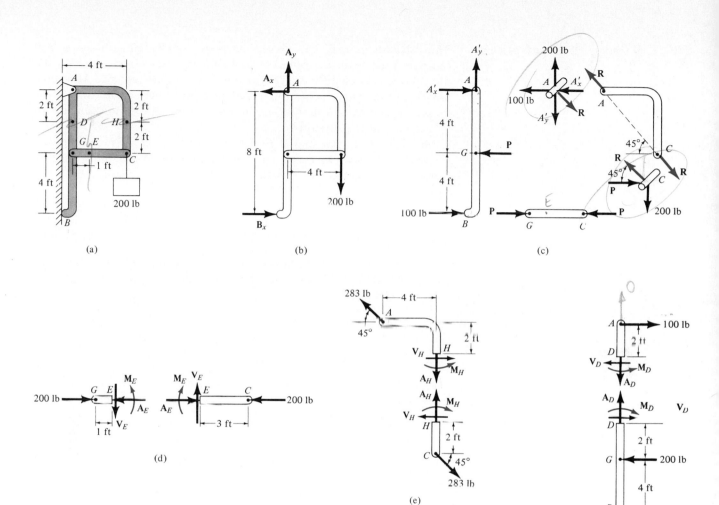

Fig. 7–3

Applying the equations of equilibrium to the pin at C gives

$+\uparrow\Sigma F_y = 0;$ $R \sin 45° - 200 \text{ lb} = 0,$ $R = 283 \text{ lb}$

$\stackrel{+}{\rightarrow}\Sigma F_x = 0;$ $P - 283 \cos 45° \text{ lb} = 0,$ $P = 200 \text{ lb}$

Knowing the magnitude of **P**, we may calculate A'_x and A'_y by applying the equations of equilibrium to member AGB:

$+\uparrow\Sigma F_y = 0;$ $A'_y = 0$

$\stackrel{+}{\rightarrow}\Sigma F_x = 0;$ $100 \text{ lb} - 200 \text{ lb} + A'_x = 0,$ $A'_x = 100 \text{ lb}$

$\zeta+\Sigma M_G = 0;$ $100 \text{ lb} (4 \text{ ft}) - 100 \text{ lb} (4 \text{ ft}) \equiv 0$ (check)

The calculations may be *checked* by applying the magnitudes of the computed forces on the pin at A and showing that these forces satisfy the equations of equilibrium for the pin. (Note that a separate free-body diagram of the pins has been included here since there are *three* connections at each pin. For example, at pin A the forces are caused by members AC, AGB and the support.)

Member GC is sectioned at E and the free-body diagrams of the two segments are shown in Fig. 7–3d. Applying the three equations of equilibrium to either segment reveals that

$$\xrightarrow{+}\Sigma F_x = 0; \qquad\qquad A_E = 200 \text{ lb} \qquad\qquad\qquad Ans.$$

$$+\uparrow\Sigma F_y = 0; \qquad\qquad V_E = 0 \qquad\qquad\qquad\qquad Ans.$$

$$(+\Sigma M_E = 0; \qquad\qquad M_E = 0 \qquad\qquad\qquad\qquad Ans.$$

The free-body diagrams shown in Fig. 7–3e are obtained when member AC is sectioned at H. Applying the three equations of equilibrium to section CH yields

$$\xrightarrow{+}\Sigma F_x = 0; \quad 283\cos 45°\text{lb} - V_H = 0, \quad V_H = 200 \text{ lb} \qquad Ans.$$

$$+\uparrow\Sigma F_y = 0; \quad -283\sin 45°\text{lb} + A_H = 0, \quad A_H = 200 \text{ lb} \qquad Ans.$$

$$(+\Sigma M_H = 0; \quad 283\cos 45°\text{lb (2 ft)} - M_H, \quad M_H = 400 \text{ lb-ft} \qquad Ans.$$

The free-body diagrams of sections AD and DGB are shown in Fig. 7–3f. Applying the equations of equilibrium to segment AD gives

$$+\uparrow\Sigma F_y = 0; \qquad\qquad A_D = 0 \qquad\qquad\qquad\qquad Ans.$$

$$\xrightarrow{+}\Sigma F_x = 0; \quad 100\text{ lb} - V_D = 0, \quad V_D = 100 \text{ lb} \qquad Ans.$$

$$(+\Sigma M_D = 0; \quad -100\text{ lb (2 ft)} + M_D = 0, \quad M_D = 200 \text{ lb-ft} \qquad Ans.$$

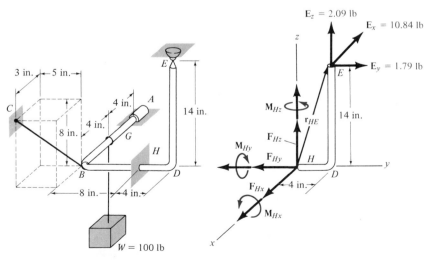

Fig. 7–4   (a)   (b)

Example 7-3

Determine the components of axial force, shear force, and bending moment at section H of the bent pipe shown in Fig. 7–4a.

Solution

The external reactions at A, B, and E have been solved for in Example 5–12. If the pipe is cut at section H and the segment HDE is isolated, the resulting free-body diagram is shown in Fig. 7–4b. Since the loading is three-dimensional, there are three unknown force components, and three unknown moment components acting at H. Using Cartesian vector notation, the vectors on this free-body diagram may be represented as

$$\mathbf{F}_H = F_{Hx}\mathbf{i} - F_{Hy}\mathbf{j} + F_{Hz}\mathbf{k}$$
$$\mathbf{M}_H = M_{Hx}\mathbf{i} - M_{Hy}\mathbf{j} + M_{Hz}\mathbf{k}$$
$$\mathbf{F}_E = \{\ 10.84\mathbf{i} + 1.79\mathbf{j} + 2.09\mathbf{k}\}\ \text{lb}$$

Applying the two vector equations of equilibrium yields

$$\Sigma\mathbf{F} = 0; \quad \mathbf{F}_H + \mathbf{F}_E = 0$$
$$F_{Hx}\mathbf{i} - F_{Hy}\mathbf{j} + F_{Hz}\mathbf{k} - 10.84\mathbf{i} + 1.79\mathbf{j} + 2.09\mathbf{k} = 0 \qquad (1)$$

$$\Sigma\mathbf{M}_H = 0; \qquad\qquad \mathbf{M}_H + (\mathbf{r}_{HE} \times \mathbf{F}_E) = 0$$
$$M_{Hx}\mathbf{i} - M_{Hy}\mathbf{j} + M_{Hz}\mathbf{k} + (4\mathbf{j} + 14\mathbf{k}) \times (-10.84\mathbf{i} + 1.79\mathbf{j} + 2.09\mathbf{k}) = 0$$

or

$$M_{Hx}\mathbf{i} - M_{Hy}\mathbf{j} + M_{Hz}\mathbf{k} - 16.7\mathbf{i} - 151.8\mathbf{j} + 43.4\mathbf{k} = 0 \qquad (2)$$

Thus, equating the $\mathbf{i}$, $\mathbf{j}$, and $\mathbf{k}$ components of Eqs. (1) and (2) equal to zero, gives,

$\Sigma F_x = 0;$	$F_{Hx} - 10.84 = 0,$	$F_{Hx} = 10.84\ \text{lb}$	*Ans.*
$\Sigma F_y = 0;$	$-F_{Hy} + 1.79 = 0,$	$F_{Hy} = 1.79\ \text{lb}$	*Ans.*
$\Sigma F_z = 0;$	$F_{Hz} + 2.09 = 0,$	$F_{Hz} = -2.09\ \text{lb}$	*Ans.*
$\Sigma M_x = 0;$	$M_{Hx} - 16.7 = 0,$	$M_{Hx} = 16.7\ \text{lb-in.}$	*Ans.*
$\Sigma M_y = 0;$	$M_{Hy} - 151.8 = 0,$	$M_{Hy} = 151.8\ \text{lb-in.}$	*Ans.*
$\Sigma M_z = 0;$	$M_{Hz} + 43.4 = 0,$	$M_{Hz} = -43.4\ \text{lb-in.}$	*Ans.*

Are you able to recognize the significance of the negative signs of F_{Hz} and M_{Hz}?

Problems

7-1. Determine the internal axial force, shear force, and moment at point D for the frame in Prob. 6–37.

7-2. Determine the internal axial force, shear force, and moment developed at point D of the two-member frame in Prob. 6–39.

7-3. Determine the internal axial force, shear force, and moment developed at point E of the frame in Prob. 6–44.

7-4. Determine the internal axial force, shear force, and moment at points F and E of the compound beam.

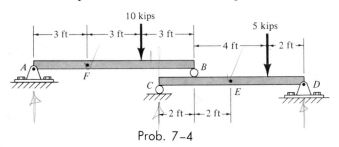

Prob. 7–4

7-5. Determine the internal axial force, shear force, and moment at points C, D, and E of the frame. Specifically, points D and E are located just to the left and just to the right of the concentrated force of 10 kips.

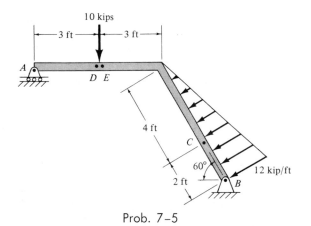

Prob. 7–5

7-6. Determine the internal axial force, shear force, and moment at points D and E of the beam.

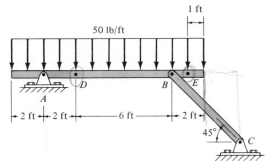

Prob. 7–6

7-7. Determine the internal axial force, shear force, and moment at points D and E of the frame.

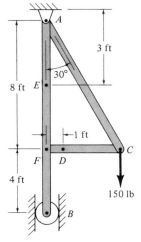

Prob. 7–7

7-8. Determine the internal axial force, shear force, and moment of points D and E of the frame.

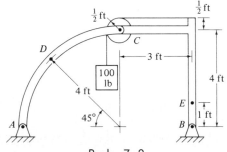

Prob. 7–8

7-9. Determine the internal axial force, shear force, and moment at points C and D of the beam.

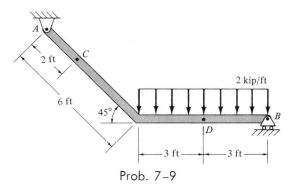

Prob. 7-9

7-10. Determine the components of internal axial force, shear force, and moment at point B of the cantilever rod.

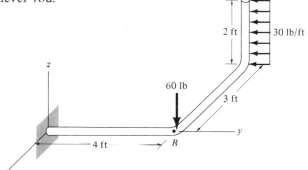

Prob. 7-10

7-11. Determine the internal force and moment developed at point D in the frame.

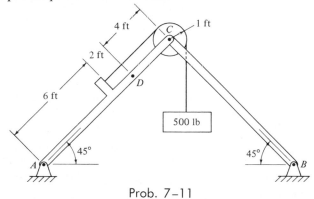

Prob. 7-11

7-12. Determine the internal axial force, shear force, and moment developed at point E of the compound beam in Prob. 6-64.

7-13. Determine the internal axial force, shear force, and moment at points D and E of the frame.

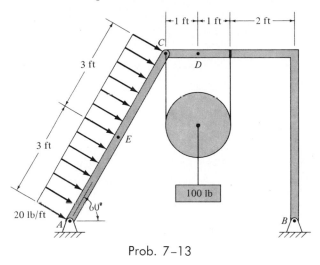

Prob. 7-13

7-14. The bent rod is subjected to two concentrated forces acting at its end. Determine the components of internal axial force, shear force, and moment acting at point B.

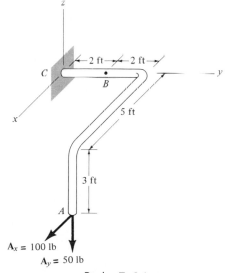

Prob. 7-14

235

7-15. Determine the internal axial force, shear force, and moment at the points E and F of the frame.

7-16. Determine the components of internal axial force, shear force, and moment at point A of the pipe. The pipe weighs 8 lb/ft.

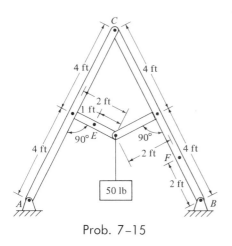

Prob. 7-15

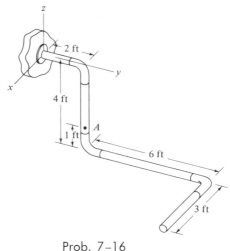

Prob. 7-16

*7-2. Shear and Bending-Moment Diagrams for a Beam

Beams are structural members which are designed to support transverse loadings, that is, loadings applied perpendicular to the axis of the member. In general, beams are long and straight bars, having a constant cross section. The design of such members requires a detailed knowledge of the internal shear forces and internal bending moment acting at *all points* along the longitudinal axis of the beam. When this force and bending moment analysis is complete, one can then use the theory of strength of materials to design the proper cross-sectional area of the beam.

In Example 7-1 we discussed a method for finding the internal axial force A, shear force V, and bending moment M at *specific points* along a beam axis. In that example it was shown that these internal forces and moment *vary* from one point to another, which is generally the case. In this section, we will discuss a general method for obtaining a variation of the internal shear force and bending moment in a beam as a function at any point, x along the beam axis. Graphs which show a variation of V and M as a function of x are termed the *shear diagram* and *bending-moment diagram*, respectively. We will not consider the internal axial force in the discussion for two reasons. In most cases, the loads applied to a beam act perpendicular to the axis of the beam and hence produce only internal shear and bending moment. For design purposes, the beam's resistance to shear, and particularly to bending, is more crucial than its ability to resist axial force.

Before presenting a method for determining the shear and bending moment as functions of x and later plotting these functions (shear and bending-moment diagrams), we must first establish a *sign convention* so as to define "positive" and "negative" shear force and bending moment acting in the beam. [This is analogous to assigning coordinate directions x positive to the right and y positive upward, for plotting a function $y = f(x)$.] The sign convention to be adopted here is illustrated in Fig. 7–5a. On the *right-hand face* (R.H.F.) of a beam segment, the internal shear force V acts upward and the internal moment M acts clockwise. In accordance with Newton's third law, an equal and opposite shear force and bending moment must act on the *left-hand face* (L.H.F.) of a segment. An easy way to remember this sign convention is to isolate a small beam segment and note that *positive shear tends to rotate the segment clockwise* (Fig. 7–5b) and a *positive bending moment tends to bend the segment, if it were elastic, concave upward* (Fig. 7–5c).

In determining the shear force and bending-moment functions, it is *first* necessary to compute all the external forces acting on the beam. The beam is then sectioned perpendicular to the axis of the beam at an arbitrary distance x measured from the *left end*. The unknown internal shear force and bending moment are indicated on the free-body diagram of the beam segment at the cut section. These internal loads are *always assumed to act in the positive direction* in accordance with the sign convention given in Fig. 7–5. Applying the two equations of equilibrium $\Sigma F_y = 0$ and $\Sigma M = 0$ to either of the two segmented portions of the beam, one obtains V and M, respectively, as functions of x. In general, the internal shear and bending moment functions will either be discontinuous or their slope will be discontinuous at points where a distributed load changes, and at points where concentrated loads or couples are applied. Because of this, the shear and bending-moment functions must be determined for *each segment* of the beam located between any two discontinuities of loading. As noted earlier, a graphical representation of the shear function (V versus x) is called the *shear diagram*. The *moment diagram* is a plot of M versus x. In plotting these functions, if computed values are positive, the magnitudes are plotted above the x axis, whereas negative values are plotted below the axis.

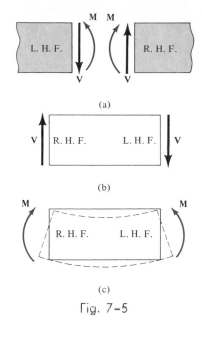

Fig. 7–5

Example 7–4

Draw the shear and bending-moment diagrams for the beam shown in Fig. 7–6a.

Solution

Using the equations of equilibrium, we can easily show that the support reactions are $A_y = C_y = 25$ kips, acting upward, and $A_x = 0$, Fig. 7–6d. If the beam is sectioned an arbitrary distance x from point A, extending within the region AB, the free-body diagram of the left-hand segment

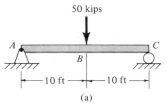

50 kips

(a)

$0 \leqslant x < 10$ ft

(b)

50 kips

10 ft

25 kips

10 ft $< x \leqslant 20$ ft

(c)

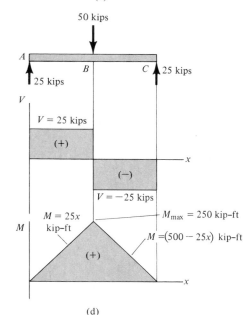

(d)

Fig. 7–6

is shown in Fig. 7–6b. The unknowns **V** and **M** are indicated acting in the *positive direction* on the right-hand face of the element according to the established sign convention. Why? Summing forces in the vertical direction, we have

$$+\uparrow \Sigma F_y = 0; \qquad\qquad 25 - V = 0$$

or

$$V = 25 \text{ kips}, \qquad 0 \leq x < 10 \text{ ft} \qquad (1)$$

Summing moments about point S yields

$$\zeta + \Sigma M_S = 0; \qquad\qquad M - 25(x) = 0$$

or

$$M = 25x \text{ kip-ft}, \qquad 0 \leq x \leq 10 \text{ ft} \qquad (2)$$

A free-body diagram for a left-hand segment of the beam extended to a distance x within the region BC is shown in Fig. 7–6c. As always, **V** and **M** are shown acting in the positive sense. Summing forces, we have

$$+\uparrow \Sigma F_y = 0; \qquad\qquad 25 - 50 - V = 0$$

or

$$V = -25 \text{ kips}, \qquad 10 \text{ ft} < x \leq 20 \text{ ft} \qquad (3)$$

Summing moments about point S, we obtain

$$\zeta + \Sigma M_S = 0; \qquad M + 50(x - 10) - 25(x) = 0$$

or

$$M = (500 - 25x) \text{ kip-ft}, \qquad 10 \text{ ft} \leq x \leq 20 \text{ ft} \qquad (4)$$

Comparing the results, do you see why it was necessary to separate the beam into the two regions AB and BC?

When the above shear-force and bending-moment Eqs. (1) through (4) are plotted within the regions in which they are valid, we obtain the shear-force and bending-moment diagrams shown in Fig. 7–6d. The shear-force diagram indicates that the internal shear force is always 25 kips (positive) along the beam segment AB. Just to the right of point B, the shear force changes sign and remains at a constant value of -25 kips for segment BC. The moment diagram starts at zero, increases linearly to point C ($x = 10$ ft), where $M_{max} = 25$ kips (10 ft) = 250 kip-ft, and thereafter decreases back to zero.

It is seen in Fig. 7–6d that the graph of the shear and moment diagrams are discontinuous at points of concentrated force, that is, points A, B, and C. For this reason, as stated earlier, it is necessary to express the shear and bending-moment functions separately for regions between concentrated loads. It should be realized, however, that all loading discontinuities are mathematical, arising from the *idealization* of a *concentrated force* and *couple*. Physically, all loads are applied over a finite area, and if this load variation could be accounted for, all shear and bending-moment diagrams would actually be continuous over the entire length of the beam.

Example 7–5

Draw the shear and bending-moment diagrams for the beam shown in Fig. 7–7a.

Solution

A free-body diagram of the entire beam is shown in Fig. 7–7b. To compute the external reactions, the distributed load has been temporarily reduced to two concentrated forces. Applying the three equations of equilibrium, we have

$$\xrightarrow{+}\Sigma F_x = 0; \qquad\qquad A_x = 0$$

$$\zeta + \Sigma M_A = 0; \quad -6 \text{ kips } (4 \text{ ft}) - 16 \text{ kips } (10 \text{ ft}) + C_y(14 \text{ ft}) = 0,$$
$$C_y = 13.14 \text{ kips}$$

$$+\uparrow\Sigma F_y = 0; \quad A_y - 6 \text{ kips} - 16 \text{ kips} + 13.14 \text{ kips} = 0, \quad A_y = 8.86 \text{ kips}$$

A free-body diagram for a segment of the beam extending within region *AB* is shown in Fig. 7–7c. The distributed loading acting on this segment has been replaced by a concentrated force *after* the segment is isolated as a free-body diagram. Since the distributed load now has a length *x*, the *magnitude* of the *concentrated force* is equal to the *area* under the distributed loading, i.e., $\frac{1}{2}(x)(\frac{1}{3}x) = x^2/6$. This force *acts* through the *centroid* of the distributed loading area, a distance $x/3$ from the right end (Appendix B). Applying the two equations of equilibrium yields

$$+\uparrow\Sigma F_y = 0; \qquad\qquad 8.86 - \frac{x^2}{6} - V = 0$$

$$V = \left(8.86 - \frac{x^2}{6}\right) \text{kips}, \qquad 0 \le x \le 6 \text{ ft} \qquad (1)$$

$$\zeta + \Sigma M_S = 0; \qquad M + \frac{x^2}{6}\left(\frac{x}{3}\right) - 8.86x = 0$$

$$M = \left(8.86x - \frac{x^3}{18}\right) \text{kip-ft}, \qquad 0 \le x \le 6 \text{ ft} \qquad (2)$$

Since the distributed loading diagram *changes slope* at point *B,* another section of the beam must be chosen within region *BC.* The free-body diagram for the *left-hand segment* which extends within this region is shown in Fig. 7–7d. Notice how the distributed loading has been simplified on this diagram. Applying the equilibrium equations gives

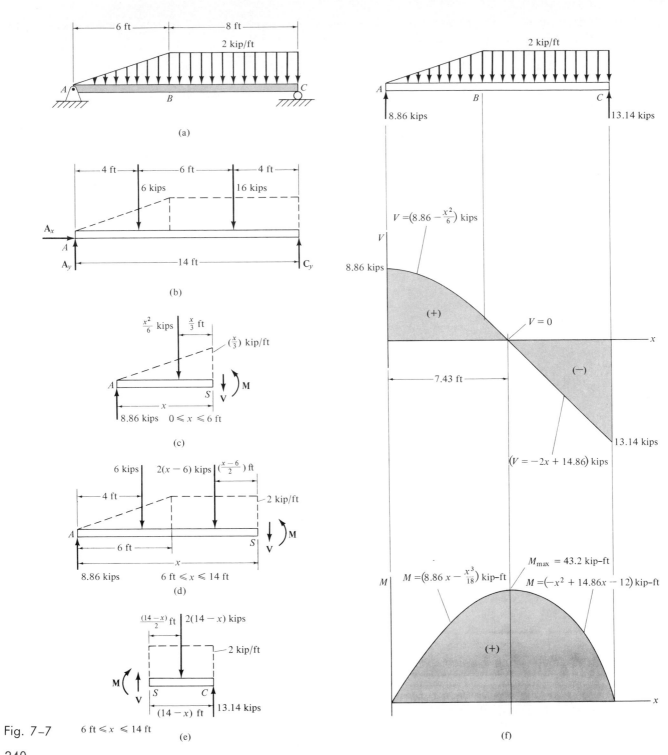

Fig. 7–7

$+\uparrow \Sigma F_y = 0; \qquad 8.86 - 6 - 2(x - 6) - V = 0$

$$V = (-2x + 14.86) \text{ kips}, \qquad 6 \text{ ft} \le x \le 14 \text{ ft} \qquad (3)$$

$\zeta + \Sigma M_S = 0; \quad M + 2(x - 6)\left(\dfrac{x - 6}{2}\right) + 6(x - 4) - 8.86x = 0$

$$M = (-x^2 + 14.86x - 12) \text{ kip-ft}, \qquad 6 \text{ ft} \le x \le 14 \text{ ft} \qquad (4)$$

A second method for obtaining these *same* shear and bending-moment equations for segment BC consists of isolating the *right-hand segment* of the beam. Since the origin of the x axis has been established at point A, the length of this segment is $(14 - x)$ ft. The free-body diagram is shown in Fig. 7–7e. According to the established sign convention, note that the internal shear and bending moment acting at the cut section are indicated in the positive direction. For equilibrium, we again obtain

$+\uparrow \Sigma F_y = 0; \qquad V - 2(14 - x) + 13.14 = 0$

$$V = (-2x + 14.86) \text{ kips}, \qquad 6 \text{ ft} \le x \le 14 \text{ ft} \qquad (3)$$

$\zeta + \Sigma M_S = 0; \quad M - 2(14 - x)\left(\dfrac{14 - x}{2}\right) + 13.14(14 - x) = 0$

$$M = (-x^2 + 14.86x - 12) \text{ kip-ft} \qquad 6 \text{ ft} \le x \le 14 \text{ ft} \qquad (4)$$

The shear and bending-moment diagrams shown in Fig. 7–7f are obtained by plotting Eqs. (1) through (4) within the regions in which they are valid.

The point of *zero shear* can be found using Eq. (3):

$$V = -2x + 14.86 = 0$$
$$x = 7.43 \text{ ft}$$

This value of x represents the point on the beam where the *maximum moment* occurs (see Sec. 7–3). Using Eq. (4), we have

$$M_{\text{max}} = (-(7.43)^2 + 14.86(7.43) - 12) \text{ kip-ft}$$
$$= 43.2 \text{ kip-ft}$$

Problems

7-17. Draw the shear and bending-moment diagrams for the beam.

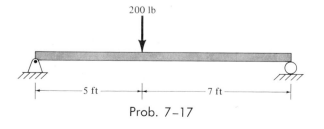

Prob. 7–17

7-18. Draw the shear and bending-moment diagrams for the beam.

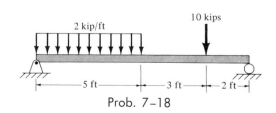

Prob. 7–18

7–19. Draw the shear and bending-moment diagrams for the cantilever beam.

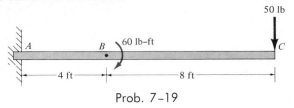

Prob. 7–19

7–20. Draw the shear and bending-moment diagrams for the beam.

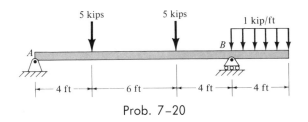

Prob. 7–20

7–21. Draw the shear and bending-moment diagrams for the beam.

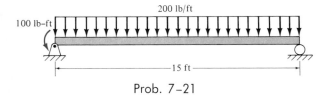

Prob. 7–21

7–22. Draw the shear and bending-moment diagrams for the cantilever beam.

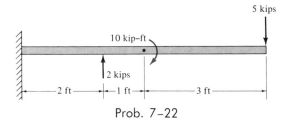

Prob. 7–22

7–23. Draw the shear and bending-moment diagrams for the beam.

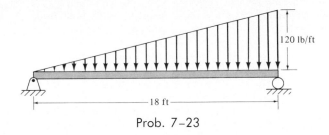

Prob. 7–23

7–24. Draw the shear and bending-moment diagrams for each of the two segments of the compound beam.

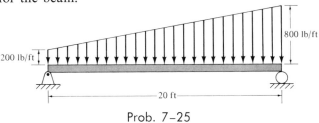

Prob. 7–24

7–25. Draw the shear and bending-moment diagrams for the beam.

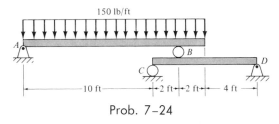

Prob. 7–25

7–26. Draw the shear and bending-moment diagrams for the axle *AB* of the train wheels. The load transferred to the axle is 10 kips, distributed as shown.

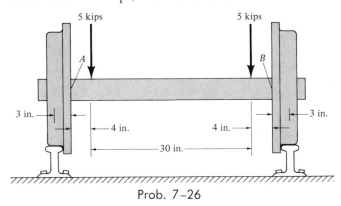

Prob. 7–26

7-27. Draw the shear and bending-moment diagrams for the beam.

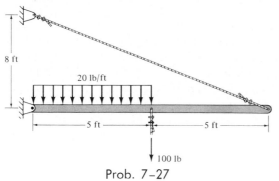

Prob. 7-27

7-28. Draw the shear and bending-moment diagrams for the beam.

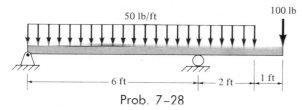

Prob. 7-28

7-29. Draw the shear and bending-moment diagrams for the beam.

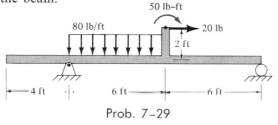

Prob. 7-29

7-30. Draw the shear and bending-moment diagrams for the beam.

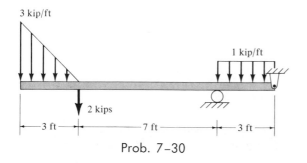

Prob. 7-30

7-31. Draw the shear and bending-moment diagrams for the beam *ABCD*. Neglect the weight of the beam and pulley arrangement.

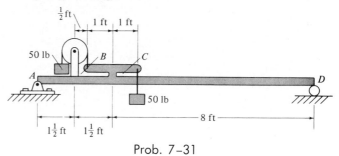

Prob. 7-31

7-32. Draw the shear and bending-moment diagrams for the beam *ABCDE*. All pulleys have a radius of 1 ft. Neglect the weight of the beam and pulley arrangement.

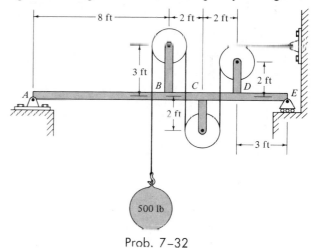

Prob. 7-32

7-33. Determine the internal shear, axial load, and bending moment as a function of θ for the cantilevered semicircular arch. The total weight of the arch is 500 lb.

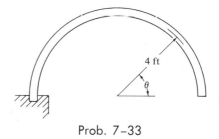

Prob. 7-33

*7–3. Relations Between Distributed Load, Shear, and Bending Moment

In cases where a beam is subjected to a series of several concentrated forces, couples, and distributed loads, the method of constructing the shear and bending-moment diagrams discussed in Sec. 7–2 may become quite tedious. In this section, we will discuss a simpler method for constructing these diagrams—a method based upon differential relations which exist between the load, shear, and bending moment.

Consider the beam AD shown in Fig. 7–8a, which is subjected to an arbitrary distributed loading $w = w(x)$ and a series of concentrated forces and moments. In the following discussion, *the distributed load will be considered positive when the loading acts upward,* as shown. The free-body diagram for a small segment of the beam having a length Δx is shown in Fig. 7–8b. This segment has been chosen at a point, x along the beam, which is *not* subjected to a concentrated force or couple. For this reason, any results obtained will not apply at points of concentrated loading. The internal shear force and bending moment, shown on the free-body diagram, are assumed to act in the *positive direction* according to the established sign convention. The shear force and moment acting on the right-hand face must be increased by a small finite amount in order to keep the segment in equilibrium. The distributed loading has been replaced by a force $w(x) \Delta x$, which acts at a fractional distance $\epsilon(\Delta x)$ from the right end, where $0 < \epsilon < 1$. Applying the equations of equilibrium,

$$+\uparrow\Sigma F_y = 0; \qquad V + w(x)\,\Delta x - (V + \Delta V) = 0$$
$$\Delta V = w(x)\,\Delta x$$

and

$$\zeta + \Sigma M_O = 0; \qquad -V\,\Delta x - M - w(x)\,\Delta x\,\epsilon(\Delta x) + (M + \Delta M) = 0$$

$$\Delta M = V\,\Delta x + w(x)\epsilon(\Delta x)^2$$

Dividing by Δx and taking the limit as $\Delta x \to 0$ these two equations become

$$\frac{dV}{dx} = w(x) \qquad (7\text{–}1)$$

and

$$\frac{dM}{dx} = V \qquad (7\text{–}2)$$

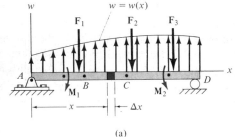

(a)

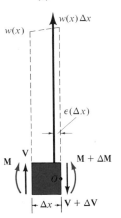

(b)

Fig. 7–8

The above equations provide a very useful means for plotting the shear-force and bending-moment diagrams of a loaded beam. For a specific point on the beam, Eq. 7–1 states that the *slope* of the *shear diagram* is equal to the intensity of *loading* at the point, while Eq. 7–2 states that the *slope* of the *moment diagram* is equal to the corresponding intensity of *shear force* at the point. In particular, if the shear is equal to zero, $dM/dx = 0$, and therefore, points of zero shear correspond to points of maximum (or possibly minimum) moment.

Equations 7–1 and 7–2 may be integrated between points B and C of the beam, in which case

$$\Delta V_{BC} = \int_{x_B}^{x_C} w(x)\,dx \tag{7–3}$$

and

$$\Delta M_{BC} = \int_{x_B}^{x_C} V\,dx \tag{7–4}$$

Equation 7–3 states that the *change in shear* between points B and C is equal to the *area* under the *loading curve* between these points. Similarly, from Eq. 7–4, the *change in moment* between points B and C is equal to the *area* under the *shear diagram* from B to C.

From the given derivation and the discussion in Sec. 7–2, it should be noted that Eqs. 7–1 and 7–3 are invalid at points where a concentrated force acts, since these equations do not account for the sudden change in shear at these points. Likewise, because of a discontinuity of moment, Eqs. 7–2 and 7–4 are invalid at points where a couple is applied.

The following two examples illustrate the method used to apply these equations for the construction of the shear and bending-moment diagrams. After working through these examples, it is recommended that you solve Examples 7–4 and 7–5 using this method.

Example 7–6

Sketch the shear and bending-moment diagrams for the cantilever beam shown in Fig. 7–9a.

Solution

The reactions at A are first calculated by using the equations of equilibrium and are indicated on the free-body diagram shown in Fig. 7–9b. It is convenient to plot both the shear and bending-moment diagrams directly below the free-body diagram of the beam, as shown in the figure.

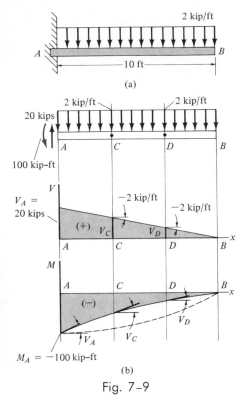

(a)

(b)

Fig. 7–9

Shear Diagram.   When constructing the shear diagram, the shear force at points A and B are plotted first, since their value can be taken directly from the free-body diagram of the beam. The shear force at A is $V_A = +20$ kips and at B, $V_B = 0$ (refer to Fig. 7–5). At an intermediate point C, the intensity of load acting on the beam is -2 kips/ft (a negative value since the load acts downward). In accordance with Eq. 7–1, the slope of the shear diagram at this point is $\dfrac{dV}{dx}\Big|_C = -2$ kips/ft. In a similar manner, the slope at point D is also $\dfrac{dV}{dx}\Big|_D = -2$ kips/ft. Since the distributed load is uniform, for other points along the beam we also obtain this same slope. Thus, the shear diagram has a *constant* negative slope of -2 kips/ft which extends from end A to end B.

Moment Diagram.   From the free-body diagram, the moment diagram must start at a value of $M_A = -100$ kip-ft and terminate at a value of $M_B = 0$. Do you see why M_A is negative? Refer to Fig. 7–5. Using Eq. 7–2, we find that the slope of the moment diagram at point A, as shown in Fig. 7–9b, is $\dfrac{dM}{dx}\Big|_A = V_A = +20$ kip-ft/ft. The *slope* of the moment diagram will always be positive along the entire axis of the beam since the *shear* is always positive; however, the *slope* will *decrease* as the distance x increases because the *shear decreases*. The resulting moment function is thus a parabola, as shown in Fig. 7–9b. You may ask why this curve is not concave upward as shown by the dashed lines. This cannot be the case since the slope of the moment diagram at A is required to be greater than the slope at C; i.e., $V_A > V_C$ as shown in the shear diagram. Similarly, $V_C > V_D$ and more specifically, the slope at B must be zero.

From these diagrams, it is seen that when the distributed loading is constant, the shear diagram will vary linearly with x and the moment diagram will be proportional to x^2. The actual equations of these curves can be obtained using the methods discussed in Sec. 7–2. In a similar manner, if the distributed loading is triangular, that is, varies linearly with x, the shear diagram will be proportional to x^2 and the bending-moment diagram will be a function of x^3. This increase in the exponential power of x in going from the loading to the shear diagram to the bending-moment diagram is due to the integration expressed by Eqs. 7–3 and 7–4.

Example 7–7

Sketch the shear and bending-moment diagrams for the beam shown in Fig. 7–10a. Give values at the points where the slopes of the shear and bending-moment diagrams change.

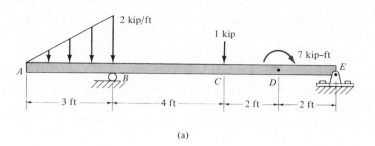

(a)

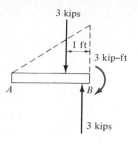

(c)

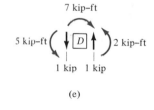

(d)

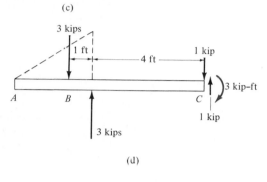

(e)

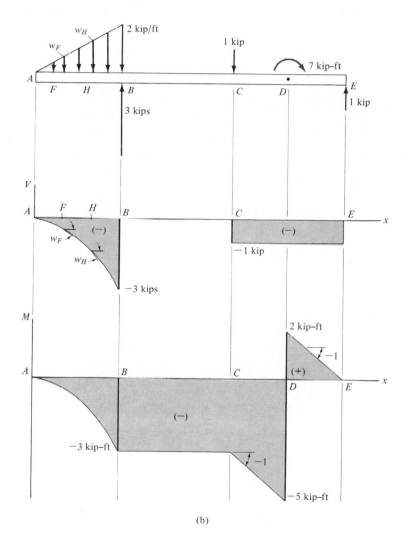

(b)

Fig. 7–10

Solution

The free-body diagram of the beam is shown in Fig. 7–10b. For equilibrium, the vertical reactions at B and E are 3 kips and 1 kip, respectively. Why is it necessary to compute these external reactions?

Shear Diagram. Since the shear force at point A is zero, the shear diagram starts at zero. The triangular *load* acts *downward* and *increases* in magnitude from points A to B; hence, from Eq. 7–1, the *slope* of the *shear diagram* is *negatively increasing* from points A to B. For example, the slope at points F and H are $\dfrac{dV}{dx}\bigg|_F = -w_F$ and $\dfrac{dV}{dx}\bigg|_H = -w_H$, respectively, where $|w_H| > |w_F|$. Since the distributed loading within region AB is triangular (varies with x), the shear diagram within this region is parabolic (varies with x^2). The total resultant force of the distributed loading is $\frac{1}{2}$ (3 ft)(2 kips/ft) = 3 kips; hence, the internal shear force just to the *left* of point B is -3 kips. This follows from Eq. 7–3; that is, the change in shear ($V_B - 0$) is equal to the area under the loading diagram between points A and B. A free-body diagram of segment AB of the beam extending just to the *right* of point B, Fig. 7–10c, reveals that the shear force just to the *right* of support B must be zero for equilibrium. Since no load acts between points B and C, $dV/dx = 0$, and therefore, the shear force remains constant within this region, Fig. 7–10b. A free-body diagram for a segment of the beam extending just to the right of point C, Fig. 7–10d, indicates a jump in the shear load to $-$ 1 kip. (Why is it negative?) Within region CDE of the beam the shear force again remains constant, since no concentrated force or distributed loads act within this region, Fig. 7–10b.

Moment Diagram. The moment acting at point A on the free-body diagram of the beam is zero, and therefore the moment diagram begins at zero. From Eq. 7–2, the *slope* of the moment diagram between points A and B becomes increasingly *negative*, since the *shear* within region AB is increasing *negative*. The curve within this region varies with x^3. As shown on the free-body diagram in Fig. 7–10c, the required internal moment acting at point B is $M_B = -3$ kip-ft, for equilibrium. Since the shear jumps from a value of -3 kips to zero at point B, the slope of the moment diagram makes a corresponding change. The slope within region BC remains at a constant value of $\dfrac{dM}{dx}\bigg|_{BC} = 0$. Why? We can verify the moment at point C by isolating segment ABC of the beam and determining the internal moment at point C, using the equations of equilibrium (see Fig. 7–10d). However, another method for determining this internal moment consists of using Eq. 7–4. The change in moment between points B and C is $\Delta M_{BC} = $ (4 ft)(0 kips) = 0 (the area under the shear diagrams within region BC). The moment acting at point C is therefore $M_C = M_B + \Delta M_{BC} = -3$ kip-ft $+ 0 = -3$ kip-ft. The jump made in the shear diagram at point C causes the moment diagram to change slope from 0 to -1.0 (kip-ft)/ft. This slope like the shear remains constant to point D, as shown on the moment diagram. The internal moment acting at the left of point D is $M_D = M_C + \Delta M_{CD} = -3$ kip-ft $+ (-1$ kip$)(2$ ft$) = -5$ kip-ft. Using this value, a free-body diagram for a segment of the beam about point D, Fig. 7–10e, indicates that the internal moment acting to the right of the concentrated 7-kip-ft couple must be 2 kip-ft for equilibrium. Therefore, there is a jump in the moment diagram at this point, Fig. 7–10b. The moment diagram has a constant slope of -1 kip-ft/ft within region DE and closes to zero at point E. The moment must be zero at E, since the pin cannot support any moment.

Problems

7-34. Sketch the shear and bending-moment diagrams for Prob. 7–18.

7-35. Sketch the shear and bending-moment diagrams for Prob. 7–20.

7-36. Sketch the shear and bending-moment diagrams for Prob. 7–21.

7-37. Sketch the shear and bending-moment diagrams for Prob. 7–27.

7-38. Sketch the shear and bending-moment diagrams for Prob. 7–31.

7-39. Sketch the shear and bending-moment diagrams for Prob. 7–32.

7-40. Sketch the shear and bending-moment diagrams for the beam.

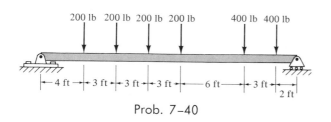

Prob. 7–40

7-41. Sketch the shear and bending-moment diagrams for the beam.

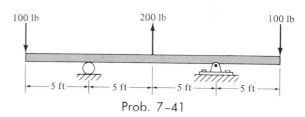

Prob. 7–41

7-42. Sketch the shear and bending-moment diagrams for the beam.

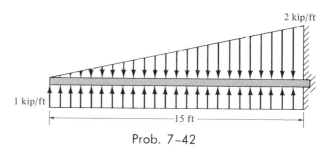

Prob. 7–42

7-43. Sketch the shear and bending-moment diagrams for the beam.

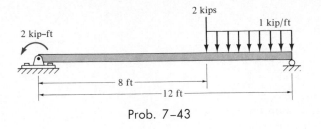

Prob. 7–43

7-45. Sketch the shear and bending-moment diagrams for the beam.

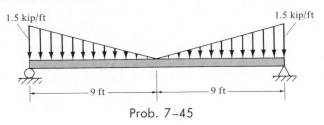

Prob. 7–45

7-44. Sketch the shear and bending-moment diagrams for the beam.

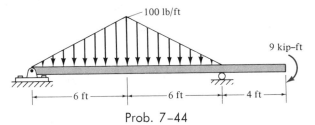

Prob. 7–44

7-46. Sketch the shear and bending-moment diagrams for the beam.

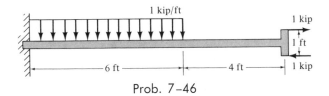

Prob. 7–46

*7–4. Cables

Flexible cables and chains are often used in engineering structures for support and to transport loads from one member to another. When used for supporting suspension bridges and trolley wheels, cables form the main load-carrying element of the structure. In the force analysis of such systems, the weight of the cable itself may frequently be neglected. However, when cables are used for transmission lines and guys for radio antennas and derricks, the cable weight may become important and must be included in the structural analysis. Regardless of which loading conditions are present, provided this loading is coplanar with the cable, the requirements for equilibrium are formulated in an identical manner. We will consider two cases in the analysis which follows: (1) a cable subjected to an external distributed load, and (2) a cable subjected to its own weight.

In deriving the necessary relations between the tensile force, sag, length, and span of a cable, we will make the assumption that the cable is *perfectly flexible* and *inextensible*. Because of the flexibility assumption, the cable offers no resistance to bending, and therefore, the tensile force acting in the cable is always tangent to the cable at points along the cable. Being inextensible, the cable has a constant length both before and after the load is applied. The derivations which follow are based on knowing the *final configuration* of the cable; that is, the geometry of the cable *after* the loading is applied. With the geometry known, a cable segment is then treated the same as a rigid body.

Case I: Cable Subjected to an External Distributed Load. Consider the weightless cable shown in Fig. 7–11a, which is subjected to a loading function $w(x)$ pounds per unit length, *as measured in the x direction*. The free-body diagram of a small segment of the cable having a length Δs is shown in Fig. 7–11b. The tensile force in the cable changes continuously in both magnitude and direction along the length of the cable. Consequently, on the free-body diagram of the cable segment this change in cable tension is denoted by $\Delta \mathbf{T}$. The resultant of the distributed load is simply $w(x)(\Delta x)$. This force acts at a fractional distance $\epsilon \Delta x$ from point O, where $0 < \epsilon < 1$. Applying the equations of equilibrium to the element yields

$$\xrightarrow{+}\Sigma F_x = 0; \quad -T\cos\theta + (T + \Delta T)\cos(\theta + \Delta\theta) = 0$$

$$+\uparrow\Sigma F_y = 0; \quad -T\sin\theta - w(x)(\Delta x) + (T + \Delta T)\sin(\theta + \Delta\theta) = 0$$

$$\zeta + \Sigma M_O = 0; \quad w(x)(\Delta x)\,\epsilon\,(\Delta x) - T\cos\theta\,\Delta y + T\sin\theta\,\Delta x = 0$$

If we divide each of the above equations by Δx and take the limit as $\Delta x \to 0$, and hence $\Delta y \to 0$ and $\Delta T \to 0$, we obtain

$$\frac{d(T\cos\theta)}{dx} = 0 \tag{7-5}$$

$$\frac{d(T\sin\theta)}{dx} - w(x) = 0 \tag{7-6}$$

and

$$\frac{dy}{dx} = \tan\theta \tag{7-7}$$

Integrating Eq. 7–5, we have

$$T\cos\theta = \text{const} = F_H \tag{7-8}$$

where F_H represents a horizontal component of tensile force at any point along the cable.

Integrating Eq. 7–6 gives

$$T\sin\theta = \int w(x)\,dx \tag{7-9}$$

Dividing Eq. 7–9 by Eq. 7–8 eliminates T. Then, using Eq. 7–7 we obtain

$$\tan\theta = \frac{dy}{dx} = \frac{1}{F_H}\int w(x)\,dx$$

Performing a second integration gives

$$y = \frac{1}{F_H}\int\left(\int w(x)\,dx\right)dx \tag{7-10}$$

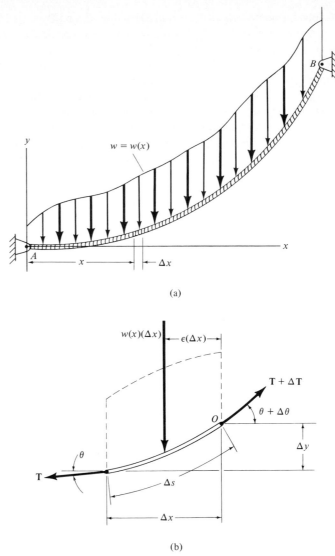

(a)

(b)

Fig. 7-11

This equation is used to determine the deflection curve for the cable. The two constants, say C_1 and C_2, resulting from the integration of Eq. 7–10 are determined by applying the boundary conditions for the cable. See Example 7–8.

Case II: Cable Subjected to its Own Weight. When the weight of the cable becomes important in the force analysis, for example, transmission lines, the loading function along the cable becomes a function of the arc

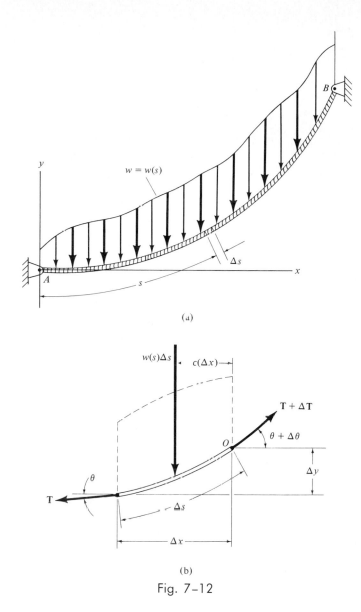

(a)

(b)

Fig. 7–12

length s, rather than the projected length x. A generalized loading function $w = w(s)$ acting on the cable is shown in Fig. 7–12a. The free-body diagram for a segment of the cable is shown in Fig. 7–12b. Applying the equilibrium equations to the force system on this diagram, we obtain identical relationships as those given by Eqs. 7–5, 7–6, and 7–7, except with ds replacing dx. Therefore, it may be shown that

$$T \cos \theta = F_H$$

$$T \sin \theta = \int w(s) \, ds$$

$$\frac{dy}{dx} = \frac{1}{F_H} \left(\int w(s) \, ds \right) \tag{7-11}$$

To perform a direct integration of Eq. 7–11, we must first substitute dy/dx with ds/dx. Since

$$\frac{dy}{dx} = \sqrt{\left(\frac{ds}{dx} \right)^2 - 1}$$

We get

$$\frac{ds}{dx} = \left\{ 1 + \frac{1}{F_H^2} \left[\int w(s) \, ds \right]^2 \right\}^{1/2}$$

Separating the variables and integrating, we obtain

$$x = \int \frac{ds}{\left\{ 1 + \dfrac{1}{F_H^2} \left[\int w(s) \, ds \right]^2 \right\}^{1/2}} \tag{7-12}$$

The two constants of integration, say C_1 and C_2, are found using the boundary conditions for the cable.

The following examples illustrate the method for solving cable problems using these derived equations.

Example 7–8

The cable of a suspension bridge is used to support the uniform road surface between the two columns at A and B, as shown in Fig. 7–13a. If the road surface weighs w_o lb/ft, determine the maximum force developed in the cable and the length of the complete cable. The span length L and sag h are known.

Solution

For reasons of symmetry, the origin of coordinates has been placed at the center of the cable. The equation for the deflection curve of the cable can be found by using Eq. 7–10. Noting that $w(x) = w_o$,

$$y = \frac{1}{F_H} \int \left(\int w_o \, dx \right) dx$$

Integrating this equation twice,

$$y = \frac{1}{F_H} \left(\frac{w_o x^2}{2} + C_1 x + C_2 \right) \tag{1}$$

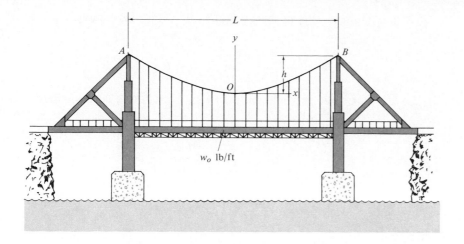

(a)

(b)

Fig. 7–13

The constants of integration may be determined by using the boundary conditions $y = 0$ at $x = 0$, and $dy/dx = 0$ at $x = 0$. Substituting these conditions into Eq. (1) yields $C_1 = C_2 = 0$. The deflection curve then becomes

$$y = \frac{w_o}{2F_H} x^2 \tag{2}$$

This is the equation of a *parabola*. The constant F_H may be obtained by using the boundary condition $y = h$ at $x = L/2$. Thus,

$$F_H = \frac{w_o L^2}{8h} \tag{3}$$

Therefore, the deflection curve, Eq. (2), becomes

$$y = 4\frac{hx^2}{L^2} \tag{4}$$

The maximum tension in the cable may be determined using Eq. 7–8. Since

$$T = \frac{F_H}{\cos \theta}, \qquad \text{for} \qquad 0 \le \theta \le \pi$$

T_{max} will occur when θ is maximum. From Eq. (2) this occurs when

$$\left. \frac{dy}{dx} \right|_{max} = \tan \theta_{max} = \left. \frac{w_o}{F_H} x \right|_{x = L/2}$$

or

$$\theta_{max} = \tan^{-1} \frac{w_o L}{2F_H}$$

Therefore,

$$T_{max} = \frac{F_H}{\cos \theta_{max}} \qquad (5)$$

Using the triangular relationship shown in Fig. 7–13b, we may write Eq. (5) as

$$T_{max} = \frac{\sqrt{4F_H^2 + w_o^2 L^2}}{2}$$

Substituting Eq. (3) into the above equation yields

$$T_{max} = \frac{w_o L}{2} \sqrt{1 + \left(\frac{L}{4h}\right)^2} \qquad \textit{Ans.}$$

For a differential segment of cable length,

$$ds = \sqrt{(dx)^2 + (dy)^2} = \sqrt{1 + \left(\frac{dy}{dx}\right)^2} \, dx$$

Since $dy/dx = w_o x / F_H$, the total length of the cable $\mathcal{L}$ can be determined from

$$\mathcal{L} = 2 \int_0^{L/2} \sqrt{1 + \left(\frac{w_o x}{F_H}\right)^2} \, dx \qquad (6)$$

Integrating and substituting the limits yields

$$\mathcal{L} = \frac{L}{2} \sqrt{1 + \left(\frac{w_o L}{2F_H}\right)^2} + \frac{F_H}{w_o} \sinh^{-1}\left(\frac{w_o L}{2F_H}\right)$$

Using Eq. (3) and rearranging terms, we have

$$\mathcal{L} = \frac{L}{2}\left[\sqrt{1 + \left(\frac{4h}{L}\right)^2} + \frac{L}{4h} \sinh^{-1}\left(\frac{4h}{L}\right)\right] \qquad \textit{Ans.}$$

Example 7-9

Determine the deflection curve, the length of cable, and the maximum tension in the uniform cable shown in Fig. 7–14. The cable weighs $w_o = 5$ lb/ft.

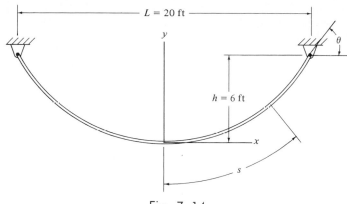

Fig. 7–14

Solution

For reasons of symmetry, the origin of coordinates is located at the center of the cable. Applying Eq. 7–12 where $w(s) = w_o$ yields

$$x = \int \frac{ds}{\left[1 + \frac{1}{F_H{}^2}\left(\int w_o\, ds\right)^2\right]^{1/2}}$$

Integrating the term under the integral sign in the denominator we have

$$x = \int \frac{ds}{\left[1 + \frac{1}{F_H{}^2}\left(w_o s + C_1\right)^2\right]^{1/2}}$$

Substituting $u = 1/F_H\,(w_o s + C_1)$ so that $du = (w_o/F_H)\, ds$, a second integration yields

$$x = \frac{F_H}{w_o}\left[\sinh^{-1} u + C_2\right]$$

or

$$x = \frac{F_H}{w_o}\left\{\sinh^{-1}\left[\frac{1}{F_H}(w_o s + C_1)\right] + C_2\right\} \tag{1}$$

From Eq. 7–11,

$$\frac{dy}{dx} = \frac{1}{F_H}\left(\int w_o\, ds\right)$$

or

$$\frac{dy}{dx} = \frac{1}{F_H}(w_o s + C_1)$$

Since $dy/dx = 0$ at $s = 0$, $C_1 = 0$ and

$$\frac{dy}{dx} = \tan \theta = \frac{w_o s}{F_H} \qquad (2)$$

where θ is the angle of the cable. The constant C_2 may be evaluated by using the condition $s = 0$ at $x = 0$ in Eq. (1), in which case $C_2 = 0$. Solving for s in Eq. (1) yields

$$s = \frac{F_H}{w_o} \sinh\left(\frac{w_o}{F_H}x\right) \qquad (3)$$

Substituting Eq. (3) into Eq. (2), we have

$$\frac{dy}{dx} = \sinh\left(\frac{w_o}{F_H}x\right)$$

Thus,

$$y = \frac{F_H}{w_o} \cosh\left(\frac{w_o}{F_H}x\right) + C_4 \qquad (4)$$

If we use the boundary condition $y = 0$ at $x = 0$, the constant $C_4 = -F_H/w_o$, and therefore the deflection curve becomes

$$y = \frac{F_H}{w_o}\left[\cosh\left(\frac{w_o}{F_H}x\right) - 1\right] \qquad Ans.$$

This equation is often referred to as a *catenary curve*. The constant F_H is obtained by using the boundary condition that $y = h$ at $x = L/2$, in which case

$$h = \frac{F_H}{w_o}\left[\cosh\left(\frac{w_o L}{2F_H}\right) - 1\right] \qquad (5)$$

Since $w_o = 5$ lb/ft, $h = 6$ ft, and $L = 20$ ft, Eqs. (4) and (5) become

$$y = \frac{F_H}{5 \text{ lb/ft}}\left[\cosh\left(\frac{5 \text{ lb/ft}}{F_H}x\right) - 1\right] \qquad (6)$$

$$6 \text{ ft} = \frac{F_H}{5 \text{ lb/ft}}\left[\cosh\left(\frac{50 \text{ lb}}{F_H}\right) - 1\right] \qquad (7)$$

Equation (7) can be solved for F_H by using a trial and error procedure. The result is

$$F_H = 45.8 \text{ lb}$$

and therefore Eq. (6) becomes

$$y = 9.16[\cosh(0.109x) - 1] \text{ ft} \qquad Ans.$$

Using Eq. (3), we see that the half-length of the cable is ($x = 10$ ft)

$$\frac{\mathcal{L}}{2} = \frac{45.8 \text{ lb}}{5 \text{ lb/ft}}\sinh\left[\frac{5 \text{ lb/ft}}{45.8 \text{ lb}}(10 \text{ ft})\right] = 12.1 \text{ ft}$$

Hence,

$$\mathcal{L} = 24.2 \text{ ft} \qquad Ans.$$

Since $T = F_H/\cos\theta$, the maximum tension occurs when θ is maximum, i.e., at $s = \mathcal{L}/2 = 12.1$ ft. Using Eq. (2) yields

$$\frac{dy}{dx}\bigg|_{max} = \tan\theta_{max} = \frac{5 \text{ lb/ft}(12.1 \text{ ft})}{45.8 \text{ lb}} = 1.32$$

$$\theta_{max} = 52.8°$$

Thus,

$$T_{max} = \frac{45.8 \text{ lb}}{\cos 52.8°} = \frac{45.8 \text{ lb}}{0.604} = 75.8 \text{ lb} \qquad Ans.$$

Problems

7-47. The cable will break when the maximum tension reaches 2,000 lb. Determine the minimum length of cable and the sag h if the cable carries a uniform distributed load of 30 lb/ft of horizontal projection.

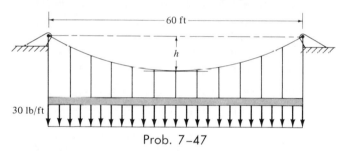

Prob. 7-47

7-48. The platform has a total weight of 5,000 lb and is supported between walls at points A and B by means of two cables. Determine the maximum force developed in the cables.

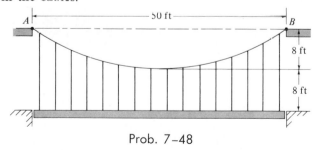

Prob. 7-48

7-49. The cord is capable of sustaining a maximum tension force of 800 lb before it will snap. Determine the maximum loading w_o lb/ft which the cable can support.

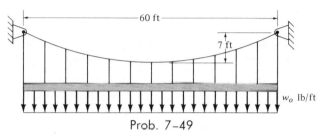

Prob. 7-49

7-50. The weightless cable is subjected to the triangular loading. If the slope of the cable at point A is zero, determine the deflection curve of the cable and the maximum tension developed in the cable. L, h and w_o are known.

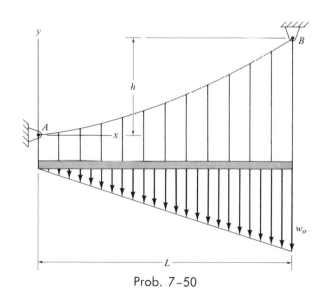

Prob. 7-50

7-51. The cable is subjected to a uniform load of 60 lb/ft. Determine the maximum tension developed in the cable.

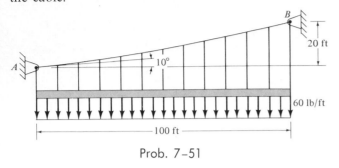

Prob. 7–51

7-52. The cable weighs 6 lb/ft and is 150 ft in length. Determine the sag h so that the cable spans 100 ft. Compute the minimum tension in the cable.

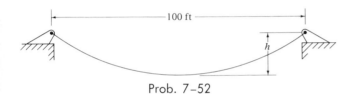

Prob. 7–52

7-53. The telephone cable weighs 0.1 lb per foot of length. At a temperature of 100° F, the cable sags 180 in. Determine the maximum tension in the cable and the length of the cable at this temperature.

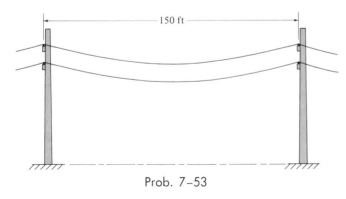

Prob. 7–53

7-54. The cable weighs 5 lb/ft. Determine the maxi-

mum and minimum tension in the cable and the length of the cable.

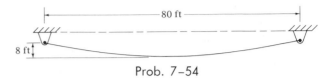

Prob. 7–54

7-55. A 100-lb wire is attached between two points at a distance of 50 ft apart, having equal elevations. If the maximum tension developed in the cable is 75 lb, determine the length of wire and the sag.

7-56. A 100-ft chain has a total weight of 150 lb and is suspended between two points 25 ft apart, at the same elevation. Determine the maximum tension and the sag in the chain.

7-57. A 50-ft cable is suspended between two points a distance 15 ft apart and at the same elevation. If the minimum tension in the cable is 200 lb, determine the total weight of the cable and the maximum tension developed in the cable.

7-58. The yacht is anchored with a 400-ft chain which weighs 8 lb/ft and makes a 60° angle with the horizontal. The tension in the chain at point A is 1,500 lb. Determine the length of the chain, l_d, which is lying at the bottom of the sea, and the depth d. Assume that the buoyancy effects of the water on the chain are negligible. (*Hint:* Establish the coordinate system at B as shown.)

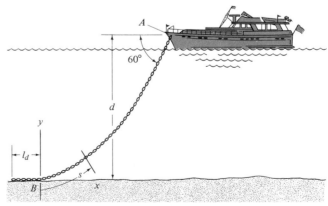

Prob. 7–58

260

7-59. Show that the deflection curve of a cable discussed in Example 8–9 reduces to Eq. (4) in Example 8–8 when the *hyperbolic cosine function* is expanded in terms of a series, and only the first two terms are retained. (The answer indicates that the *catenary* may be replaced by a *parabola* in the analysis of problems in which the cable tension is very taut, that is, a small sag. In this case the cable weight is assumed uniformly distributed along the horizontal.

7-60. A uniform cord is suspended between two points having the same elevation. Determine the sag-to-span ratio so that the maximum tension in the cable equals the total weight of the cable.

7-61. The buoyant (or vertical) force acting on the weather balloon is 80 lb. If cable *OB* is 200 ft in length and the cable weighs 0.25 lb/ft, determine the height *h* of the balloon.

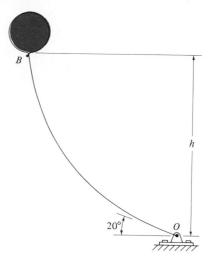

Prob. 7–61

Friction

8–1. Characteristics of Dry Friction

In the previous chapters we have considered the surface of contact between one body and another to be perfectly *smooth*. Because of this, the force of interaction between the bodies always acts *normal* to the surface at points of contact. In reality, however, all surfaces are *rough,* and depending upon the nature of the problem, the ability of a body to support a *tangential* as well as a *normal* force at its contacting surface must be taken into consideration. The tangential force developed at a surface of contact is caused by friction. Specifically, *friction* may be defined as a force of resistance acting between two contacting bodies which prevents or inhibits any possible slipping motion between the two bodies. This force always acts *tangent* to the surface at points of contact and is directed so as to oppose the possible or existing motion of the body at that point.

The effects of friction are both advantageous and detrimental. Without friction we would be unable to walk, or make use of any sort of transportation vehicle such as an automobile or boat. Furthermore, many engineering devices, such as belt drives and brakes, require frictional forces in order to function. The adverse effects of friction caused by the rubbing and wearing away of surfaces are reduced when bearings, rollers, and lubricants are used in machines.

In general, there are two types of friction which can occur between surfaces. *Fluid friction* exists when the contacting surfaces are separated by a thin film of fluid such as oil. When relative motion between the bodies occurs, frictional forces are developed between layers of fluid elements. This force depends upon the relative velocity of the fluid layers and viscosity or shearing resistance of the fluid. For this reason problems involving fluid friction are generally studied in fluid mechanics. In this book we will study only the effects of *dry friction*. This type of friction is often called *Coulomb friction,* since its characteristics were extensively studied by C. A. Coulomb in 1781. Dry friction occurs between the contacting surfaces of rigid bodies in the absence of a lubricating fluid.

The theory of dry friction can best be explained by considering what effect a horizontal force **P** has on moving a block of weight **W** which is resting on a horizontal floor. The free-body diagram of the block is shown in Fig. 8–1a. Regardless of the magnitude of the applied force **P,** *vertical equilibrium* is always maintained provided the *resultant* normal force **N** is equal and opposite to **W.** * Consider now the variation of the applied force **P** with the *resultant* frictional force **F** developed at the floor. This variation is shown in Fig. 8–1b. Provided the magnitude of **P** is small enough, $\mathbf{F} = -\mathbf{P}$, and the block remains in *equilibrium*. Under these circumstances, the force **F** is called the *static-friction force,* and its value is obtained directly from the *equation of equilibrium* $\Sigma F_x = 0$, Fig. 8–2a.

not collinear

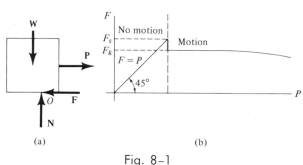

(a)

(b)

Fig. 8–1

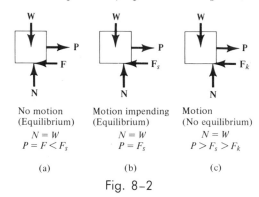

No motion
(Equilibrium)
$N = W$
$P = F < F_s$

Motion impending
(Equilibrium)
$N = W$
$P = F_s$

Motion
(No equilibrium)
$N = W$
$P > F_s > F_k$

(a)

(b)

(c)

Fig. 8–2

As the magnitude of force **P** is slowly increased, the magnitude of the friction force **F** attains a certain *maximum value* F_s, called the *limiting static-friction force* for which *motion impends*, Fig. 8–1b. This point causes a condition of *unstable equilibrium;* that is, a slight increase in P will cause sliding of the block, Fig. 8–2b. If P is increased slightly, F drops to a smaller value of F_k, Fig. 8–1b. F_k is now a function of velocity and is called the *kinetic-friction force.* As shown on the graph it remains essentially constant for a time, and then as P increases, due to aerodynamic effects, F_k decreases somewhat. This situation of loading on the block is shown in Fig. 8–2c. In summary then, the frictional force **F** is categorized in three different ways, namely, **F** is a static-frictional force if equilibrium is maintained, **F** is a limiting static-frictional force $\mathbf{F}_s$ when its magnitude reaches its maximum value needed to maintain equilibrium, and finally, **F** is termed a kinetic-frictional force $\mathbf{F}_k$ when sliding at the contacting surface occurs.

*Physically, note that the line of action of **N** must be to the *right* of the line of action of **W** so that moments about point O are balanced.

A close examination of the contacting surfaces between the floor and block, Fig. 8–3, reveals the nature of how frictional forces are developed. It can be seen that many microscopic irregularities exist between the two surfaces (those that are not theoretically smooth), and as a result, reactive forces $\Delta\mathbf{R}_n$ are developed at the protuberances. These forces act at points of contact, and must be directed both upward and in a direction opposed to the motion or tendency of motion of the block. In this way, each reactive force contributes both a frictional component of force $\Delta\mathbf{F}_n$ which tends to prevent or retard motion of the block, and a normal component $\Delta\mathbf{N}_n$. The drop made in the frictional force from F_s (static) to F_k (kinetic), Fig. 8–1b, occurs because the applied load $\mathbf{P}$ shears off some of the humps and the block "rides" on top of the humps. The contact forces $\Delta\mathbf{R}_n$ are then aligned slightly more in the vertical direction than before and hence contribute a smaller frictional component $\Delta\mathbf{F}_n$ as when the irregularities are meshed. For very large magnitudes of $\mathbf{P}$, Fig. 8–1b, the magnitude

Important

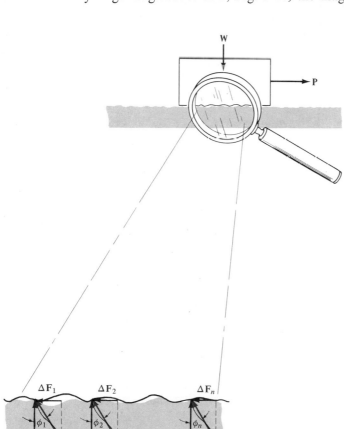

Fig. 8–3

of **F** becomes smaller. Such effects cause an even greater vertical alignment of $\Delta \mathbf{R}_n$ and consequently a smaller magnitude of $\Delta \mathbf{F}_n$.

As a result of *experiments* that pertain to this discussion, we may state the following rules which apply to bodies subjected to dry friction:

1. The frictional force acts *tangent* to the contacting surfaces in a direction *opposed* to the *relative motion,* (or tendency for motion) of one surface against another.
2. The limiting static-frictional force F_s which can be developed is independent of the area of contact, provided the normal pressure is not great enough to alter the contacting surface of the bodies.
3. The limiting static-frictional force F_s is generally greater than the kinetic frictional force F_k for any two surfaces of contact. At *extremely low* relative velocities, however, F_k becomes large, and hence, approximately equal to the limiting static-frictional force.
4. The limiting frictional force F_s is (approximately) proportional to the normal force N at the point of contact. This may be expressed in mathematical form as

$$\mu_s = \frac{F_s}{N}$$

(8-1)

where μ_s is called the *coefficient of static friction.*

5. The kinetic-frictional force F_k is (approximately) proportional to the normal force N at the point of contact. This may be expressed in mathematical form as

$$\mu_k = \frac{F_k}{N}$$

(8-2)

where μ_k is called the *coefficient of kinetic friction.*

Table 8-1 lists some typical values of the coefficients of static friction found in most engineering handbooks and journals. It should be noted that the last value gives a coefficient of static friction greater than 1. For surfaces consisting of soft metals, this is often the case. Corresponding

Table 8-1

Contact Materials	Coefficient of Static Friction (μ_s)
metal on ice	0.03–0.05
wood on wood	0.30–0.70
leather on wood	0.20–0.50
leather on metal	0.30–0.60
aluminum on aluminum	1.10–1.70

values of the coefficient of kinetic friction would be approximately 25 per cent smaller than those listed in the table. In general, it is seen that a wide range of values is given for each of the coefficients of friction. This is due to the variable conditions of normal pressure, roughness, and cleanliness of the contacting surfaces with which the investigators worked. It is therefore important that both caution and judgment be exercised when selecting a coefficient of friction for a given set of conditions. When a more exact determination of the frictional forces acting between two surfaces is required, the coefficient of friction should be determined directly by an experiment which involves the two materials to be used.

It should be observed that Eqs. 8–1 and 8–2 have a specific, yet limited, use in the solution of friction problems. In particular, the frictional force acting at a contacting surface is determined from Eq. 8–2 *only* if relative *motion* is occurring between the two surfaces. Furthermore, if two bodies are *stationary*, the magnitude of frictional force, F, acting at the contacting surfaces, is *not necessarily* equal to $\mu_s N$ (Eq. 8–1). F must, however, satisfy the inequality $F \leq \mu_s N$. Only when impending motion occurs does F reach its upper limit, $F = F_s = \mu_s N$. To better understand the inequality, however, consider the block shown in Fig. 8–4a. In this case, the applied load has a magnitude of $P_s = F_s$. By equilibrium, this force and the weight of the block create a resultant reactive force $\mathbf{R}_s$ at the contacting surface having components $\mathbf{F}_s$ and $\mathbf{N}$. The block is thus *on the verge of sliding* (impending motion). The angle ϕ_s, which $\mathbf{R}_s$ makes with $\mathbf{N}$, is called the angle of static friction or the *angle of repose*. From the figure

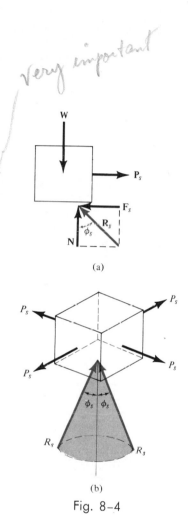

(a)

(b)

Fig. 8–4

$$\phi_s = \tan^{-1}\frac{F_s}{N} = \tan^{-1}\frac{\mu_s N}{N} = \tan^{-1}\mu_s$$

If the limiting force $\mathbf{F}_s$ is applied from *any direction* along the sides of the block, ϕ_s may be used to describe the locus of possible directions for the reaction $\mathbf{R}_s$. This locus will be a right circular cone, known as the *cone of static friction*, having a vertex angle $2\phi_s$, Fig. 8–4b. Provided the block is not in motion, any horizontal force $P < P_s = F_s$ causes a reactive force $\mathbf{R}$ having a line of action which lies *within* the cone of friction. Thus, it is necessary that the frictional force $F \leq F_s$ if the block is not in motion.

8–2. Problems Involving Dry Friction

If a rigid body is in equilibrium under a system of forces which includes the effect of friction, the force system must not only satisfy the equations of equilibrium but *also* the laws which govern the frictional forces. In general, there are three types of mechanics problems involving dry friction. In the *first type,* it is known that either the *motion* of the body is *impending* along all its contacting surfaces, in which case $F = \mu_s N$, or the body is *sliding* with some velocity, so that $F = \mu_k N$. With the aid of the frictional equations, the equilibrium equations are applied in the usual manner to solve for any unknowns shown on the free-body diagram of the body (see Examples 8–1, 8–2, 8–5, and 8–6). In the *second type* of problem, the applied loads acting on the rigid body are *known,* and one has to determine whether or not the frictional forces developed at surfaces of contact are large enough to *hold the body in equilibrium.* At each rough point of contact there is a normal force **N** and associated frictional force **F.** One method for solving this type of problem is to use the equations of equilibrium and solve for both forces F and N, which are required to *hold the body in equilibrium.* Knowing the equilibrium normal force N at each contacting surface, the corresponding *maximum friction force* can be easily calculated using Eq. 8–1 ($F_s = \mu_s N$). By comparing this value of F_s with the friction force F needed for equilibrium it is possible to determine whether or not the body remains in equilibrium. Hence, if $F \leq F_s$, the body is in equilibrium; however, if $F > F_s$, slipping occurs at the contact point. (See Example 8–3.) The *third type* of problem is similar to the second type, that is, for a given loading one has to determine if the body or system of bodies remains in equilibrium. In this case, however, there may be several different ways in which the body or system of bodies may move out of equilibrium. For example, a block resting on a rough horizontal surface may either remain stationary, slide, or tip if it is subjected to a horizontal force. The solution follows the procedure of the second type of problem, except one must perform an analysis for each of the possible cases which may cause motion. (See Example 8–4.)

In Chapters 3 and 5, it was shown that one can *assume the sense of direction* of a force having an *unknown magnitude.* The correct sense of direction of the force is made known after the equations of equilibrium are applied and the magnitude of the force is determined. If the magnitude is positive, the sense of direction of the force was assumed correctly. However, if the magnitude is negative, the sense of direction of the force is the reverse of that which was assumed. This convenience of *assuming* the sense of direction prior to applying the equations of equilibrium is possible, since the equilibrium equations are *vector* equations. That is, the scalar equilibrium equations equate to zero the *components of vectors* acting in the *same direction.* For example, $\Sigma F_x = 0$ equates to zero the components of all force vectors acting in the x direction. The frictional equation $F_s = \mu_s N$, (or $F_k = \mu_k N$) however, relates the magnitudes of vectors acting in *perpendicular directions.* (**F**$_s$ is always perpendicular to **N.**) For this reason, when the frictional equation is applied and used *in conjunction with* the equilibrium equations to solve for any unknowns, it is necessary that the frictional forces acting on the free-body diagram be shown acting in their *correct sense of direction*. The sense of direction of frictional forces acting on a body will always be such as to either *oppose the motion or impend the motion of the body*.

In most problems, the force system acting on the body is coplanar, in which case the scalar equations of equilibrium provide the most direct solution to the problem. When three-dimensional force systems are encountered, a vector approach is generally most convenient.

Example 8–1

The block shown in Fig. 8–5a weighs 200 lb and is subjected to a 100-lb force. Determine the angle θ such that the block is on the verge of moving (a) up the plane, and (b) down the plane. The coefficient of static friction is $\mu_s = 0.3$.

Solution

Part (a). The free-body diagram for the block is shown in Fig. 8–5b. Since motion is *impending* up the plane, the frictional force *must* act in the opposite direction to oppose the tendency for motion. The applied force system must satisfy *both* the equilibrium equations and the law of dry friction. *Impending motion* requires that $F = \mu_s N = 0.3N$. Why? Applying two of the equations of equilibrium, we write

$$+ \nearrow \Sigma F_x = 0; \qquad 100 \text{ lb} - 0.3N - 200 \sin\theta \text{ lb} = 0 \qquad (1)$$
$$+ \nwarrow \Sigma F_y = 0; \qquad N - 200 \cos\theta \text{ lb} = 0 \qquad (2)$$

Solving for N in terms of θ in Eq. (2), substituting into Eq. (1), and simplifying yields,

$$100 \text{ lb} - 60 \cos\theta \text{ lb} - 200 \sin\theta \text{ lb} = 0$$

The angle θ can be obtained by trial and error. The magnitude of the normal force N is then readily obtained from Eq. (2). The final results are

$$N = 195.7 \text{ lb}$$
$$\theta = 12.0° \qquad\qquad Ans.$$

Knowing the height of the block, the distance d in Fig. 8–5b may be obtained by summing moments about point O, i.e.,

$$\zeta + \Sigma M_O = 0; \qquad N(d) - 0.3N(3 \text{ in.}) = 0$$

N cancels from the equation so that $d = 0.9$ in. Note in particular, that the line of action of N lies to the *right* of point O because of the nature of the moment balance.

Part (b). The free-body diagram for the block having *impending motion*

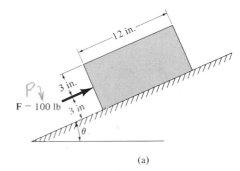

(a)

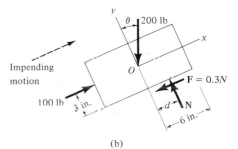

(b)

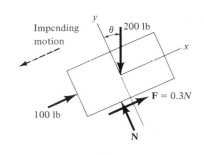

(c)

Fig. 8–5

down the plane is shown in Fig. 8–5c. Again, $F = 0.3N$. The equations of equilibrium become

$$+ \nearrow \Sigma F_x = 0; \qquad 100 \text{ lb} + 0.3N - 200 \sin \theta \text{ lb} = 0$$
$$+ \nwarrow \Sigma F_y = 0; \qquad N - 200 \cos \theta \text{ lb} = 0$$

in which case

$$N = 140.6 \text{ lb}, \qquad \theta = 45.3° \qquad \qquad Ans.$$

Example 8–2

The uniform 60-lb plank shown in Fig. 8–6a rests against a floor and wall for which the coefficients of static friction are $(\mu_s)_f = 0.30$ and $(\mu_s)_w = 0.20$, respectively. Determine the distance s to which a 150-lb man can climb without causing the plank to slip.

Solution

The free-body diagram for the plank is shown in Fig. 8–6b. The frictional forces $\mathbf{F}_A$ and $\mathbf{F}_B$ oppose the motion of the plank. Since motion is impending at both surfaces,

$$F_A = (\mu_s)_f N_A = 0.30 N_A$$
$$F_B = (\mu_s)_w N_B = 0.20 N_B$$

Using these relations and applying the three equations of equilibrium, we obtain

$$\xrightarrow{+} \Sigma F_x = 0; \qquad 0.30 N_A - N_B = 0$$
$$+ \uparrow \Sigma F_y = 0; \qquad N_A - 150 \text{ lb} - 60 \text{ lb} + 0.20 N_B = 0$$
$$\zeta + \Sigma M_A = 0; \quad -150 \text{ lb}(s \cos 40°) - 60 \text{ lb}(15 \cos 40° \text{ ft})$$
$$+ 0.2 N_B (30 \cos 40° \text{ ft}) + N_B (30 \sin 40° \text{ ft}) = 0$$

Solving for the three unknowns yields

$$N_A = 198.1 \text{ lb}$$
$$N_B = 59.4 \text{ lb}$$
$$s = 6.34 \text{ ft} \qquad \qquad Ans.$$

Example 8–3

The brake shown in Fig. 8–7a bears against the outer surface of a 30-lb drum for which $\mu_s = 0.45$ and $\mu_k = 0.40$. Determine the magnitude of the force acting at pin O.

Solution

It is not known initially if the 20-lb force, applied to the brake, is

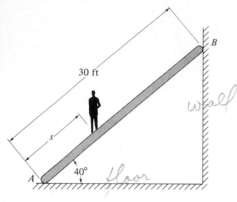

30 ft

B

s

40°

(a)

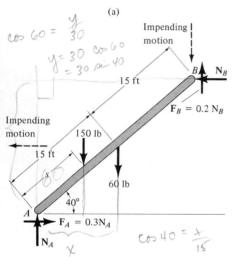

$\cos 60 = \dfrac{y}{30}$

$y = 30 \cos 60$
$= 30 \sin 40$

Impending motion

15 ft

B N_B

$F_B = 0.2 N_B$

Impending motion

150 lb

15 ft

s

60 lb

40°

A

$F_A = 0.3 N_A$

N_A

x

$\cos 40 = \dfrac{x}{15}$

(b) $x = 15 \cos 40$

Fig. 8–6

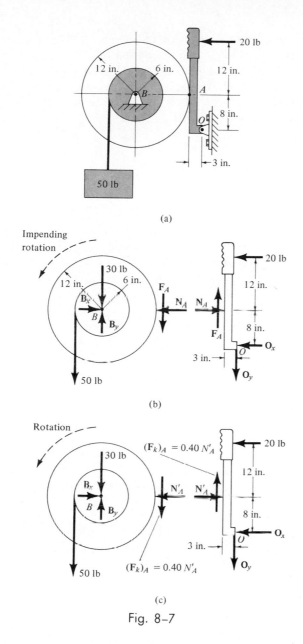

Fig. 8–7

adequate to prevent the wheel from rotating. This is important since the actual force developed at point O will depend upon whether or not the wheel is at rest or is rotating. In each of these two cases the frictional forces developed at A will be different.

Case I: Wheel Is Assumed at Rest. The free-body diagrams for both the wheel and brake are shown in Fig. 8–7b. Due to the brake, the frictional force $\mathbf{F}_A$ tends to *prevent motion of the wheel* and so acts *downward on the wheel*. This force is assumed as an *equilibrium force* and is *not necessarily equal* to the *maximum frictional force* developed by the brake. Summing moments about point B on the wheel yields a direct solution for the magnitude of $\mathbf{F}_A$.

$$\zeta + \Sigma M_B = 0; \qquad 50 \text{ lb } (6 \text{ in.}) - F_A(12 \text{ in.}) = 0; \qquad F_A = 25 \text{ lb}$$

Summing moments about point O on the brake to obtain N_A gives

$$\zeta + \Sigma M_O = 0; \qquad 20 \text{ lb } (20 \text{ in.}) - 25 \text{ lb } (3 \text{ in.}) - N_A \text{ } (8 \text{ in.}) = 0,$$
$$N_A = 40.6 \text{ lb}$$

The forces $\mathbf{F}_A$ and $\mathbf{N}_A$ as calculated here must be developed at point A to *hold the wheel in equilibrium*. It is *also* necessary that $\mathbf{F}_A$ satisfy the law of static friction at point A. Since $\mu_s = 0.45$, the *maximum* value of frictional force which can be developed at point A, where $N_A = 40.6 \text{ lb}$, is

$$(F_s)_A = \mu_s N_A = 0.45(40.6 \text{ lb}) = 18.3 \text{ lb}$$

By comparison, it is seen that the force required for equilibrium, F_A, is greater than the maximum frictional force $(F_s)_A$ developed at the brake. Hence, the wheel is *rotating* so that our initial assumption was wrong.

Case II: Wheel Is Rotating.   Since *motion* is occurring, the frictional force developed by the brake is related to the normal force by Eq. 8–2, i.e.,

$$(F_k)_A = \mu_k N'_A = 0.40 N'_A$$

The free-body diagrams of the wheel and brake are shown in Fig. 8–7c. Applying the three equations of equilibrium to the brake, since the brake does not move,

$$\xrightarrow{+} \Sigma F_x = 0; \qquad -O_x + N'_A - 20 \text{ lb} = 0$$
$$+\uparrow \Sigma F_y = 0; \qquad -O_y + 0.40 N'_A = 0$$
$$\zeta + \Sigma M_O = 0; \qquad -N'_A \text{ } (8 \text{ in.}) - 0.40 N'_A \text{ } (3 \text{ in.}) + 20 \text{ lb } (20 \text{ in.}) = 0$$

Hence,

$$N'_A = 43.5 \text{ lb}$$
$$O_x = 23.5 \text{ lb}$$
$$O_y = 17.4 \text{ lb}$$

The total force at pin O is therefore

$$F_O = \sqrt{O_x{}^2 + O_y{}^2} = \sqrt{(23.5 \text{ lb})^2 + (17.4 \text{ lb})^2} = 29.2 \text{ lb} \qquad Ans.$$

$$\theta = \tan^{-1}\frac{O_y}{O_x} = \tan^{-1}\frac{17.4 \text{ lb}}{23.5 \text{ lb}} = 36.6° \quad {}^\theta\!\swarrow\!\mathbf{F}_O \qquad Ans.$$

Example 8-4

The homogeneous blocks A and B shown in Fig. 8-8a weigh 100 and 60 lb, respectively. Determine the greatest magnitude for the applied force P without causing the blocks to move. The static coefficients of friction between the contacting surfaces are given in the figure.

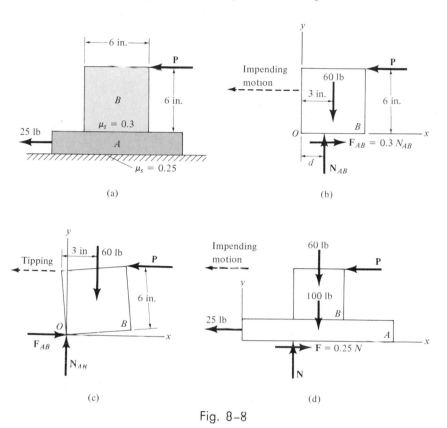

Fig. 8-8

Solution

There are three possible ways in which the blocks may begin to move: (1) impending motion of B on A with no motion of A; (2) tipping of B on A with no motion of A; and (3) no impending motion of B while motion of A is impending on the horizontal plane. (Since block A is relatively flat and long, tipping of this block is of no consequence in the analysis of the problem.) The magnitude of P needed to cause each of these motions will be computed. The least value of P is the required answer. Why?

Case I: Impending Motion of B; A Remains Stationary. The free-body diagram of block B is shown in Fig. 8–8b. Impending motion of B implies that $F_{AB} = 0.3 N_{AB}$. There are two unknown force magnitudes on the free-body diagram, N_{AB} and P.

Applying the equations of equilibrium* gives

$$\xrightarrow{+} \Sigma F_x = 0; \qquad\qquad 0.3 N_{AB} - P = 0$$
$$+\uparrow \Sigma F_y = 0; \qquad\qquad N_{AB} - 60 \text{ lb} = 0$$

Solving these equations, we obtain

$$N_{AB} = 60 \text{ lb}$$
$$P = 18 \text{ lb}$$

Case II: B tips; A Remains Stationary. When block B is on the verge of tipping, the normal reaction $\mathbf{N}_{AB}$ acts at point O. This situation is shown in Fig. 8–8c. Applying the equations of equilibrium, we have

$$\xrightarrow{+} \Sigma F_x = 0; \qquad\qquad F_{AB} - P = 0$$
$$+\uparrow \Sigma F_y = 0; \qquad\qquad N_{AB} - 60 \text{ lb} = 0$$
$$\zeta + \Sigma M_O = 0; \qquad\qquad P(6 \text{ in.}) - 60 \text{ lb} (3 \text{ in.}) = 0$$

Hence,

$$N_{AB} = 60 \text{ lb}$$
$$F_{AB} = 30 \text{ lb}$$
$$P = 30 \text{ lb}$$

Case III: A Has Impending Motion on the Horizontal Plane; B Remains Stationary on A. The free-body diagram of both blocks as one system is shown in Fig. 8–8d. Since block A is on the verge of moving, $F = 0.25 \, N$. Applying the equations of equilibrium yields

$$\xrightarrow{+} \Sigma F_x = 0; \qquad\qquad -25 \text{ lb} + 0.25N - P = 0$$
$$+\uparrow \Sigma F_y = 0; \qquad\qquad N - 100 \text{ lb} - 60 \text{ lb} = 0$$

Hence,

$$N = 160 \text{ lb}$$
$$P = 15 \text{ lb} \qquad\qquad\qquad\qquad Ans.$$

The smallest magnitude of force $\mathbf{P}$ is developed under the conditions

---

*A third unknown d specifies the line of action of $\mathbf{N}_{AB}$. Since tipping is assumed not to occur, $0 < d \leq 3$ in. The magnitude of d may be computed by summing moments about point O, which yields

$$\zeta + \Sigma M_O = 0; \quad 60 \text{ lb} (3 \text{ in.}) - P(6 \text{ in.}) - N_{AB} (d) = 0$$

Using the values of N_{AB} and P calculated above we obtain a value of $d = 1.50$ in.

of Case III. Therefore, motion will first occur when $P > 15$ lb, and as a result both blocks will initially slide together.

as P increases, Case II & Case III

Example 8-5

The 30-lb block shown in Fig. 8–9a rests on an inclined plane for which $\mu_s = 0.35$. Determine the magnitude of minimum force **P** required to move the block and the direction of impending motion. The force **P** acts along the surface of the inclined plane.

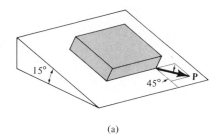

(a)

Solution

A free-body diagram of the block is shown in Fig. 8–9b. Since the problem is three-dimensional, a vector approach to the solution will be considered. For simplicity, the x, y, and z axes are shown such that the x and y axes are located on the surface of the plane. Expressing each force in vector notation, we have

$$\mathbf{N} = N\mathbf{k}$$
$$\mathbf{P} = -P\sin 45°\mathbf{i} + P\cos 45°\mathbf{j} = -0.707P\mathbf{i} + 0.707P\mathbf{j}$$
$$\mathbf{W} = 30\sin 15°\,\mathbf{j} - 30\cos 15°\,\mathbf{k} = \{7.76\mathbf{j} - 29.0\mathbf{k}\}\text{ lb}$$
$$\mathbf{F} = F\sin\theta\mathbf{i} - F\cos\theta\mathbf{j}$$

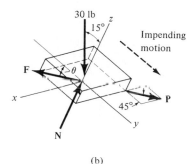

(b)

Fig. 8–9

Using the vector force equation for equilibrium, we obtain

$$\Sigma\mathbf{F} = 0; \qquad \mathbf{N} + \mathbf{P} + \mathbf{W} + \mathbf{F} = 0$$

or

$$N\mathbf{k} - 0.707P\mathbf{i} + 0.707P\mathbf{j} + 7.76\mathbf{j} - 29.0\mathbf{k} + F\sin\theta\mathbf{i} - F\cos\theta\mathbf{j} = 0$$

Equating to zero each of the respective **i**, **j**, and **k** components gives

$$\Sigma F_x = 0; \qquad -0.707P + F\sin\theta = 0 \qquad (1)$$
$$\Sigma F_y = 0; \qquad 0.707P + 7.76\text{ lb} - F\cos\theta = 0 \qquad (2)$$
$$\Sigma F_z = 0; \qquad N - 29.0\text{ lb} = 0 \qquad (3)$$

Since the block is subjected to impending motion,

$$F = 0.35N \qquad (4)$$

Equation (3) may be solved for N and the value substituted into Eq. (4) to obtain F. When Eqs. (1) and (2) are added, P is eliminated and a solution for θ is obtained by trial and error. The value of P is then obtained using the computed value of θ in either Eq. (1) or (2). The final results are

$$N = 29.0\text{ lb}$$
$$F = 10.14\text{ lb}$$
$$P = 3.03\text{ lb} \qquad\qquad Ans.$$
$$\theta = 12.2° \qquad\qquad Ans.$$

Since the frictional force acts in the opposite direction of impending motion, the block will move down the plane at an angle $\theta = 12.2°$ with the y axis when $P > 3.03$ lb.

Example 8–6

The 150-lb block A is used to lift the 200-lb block B by applying a horizontal force P, as shown in Fig. 8–10a. If the static coefficient of friction for all contacting surfaces is $\mu_s = 0.25$, determine the greatest magnitude of force P needed to cause impending motion of the blocks.

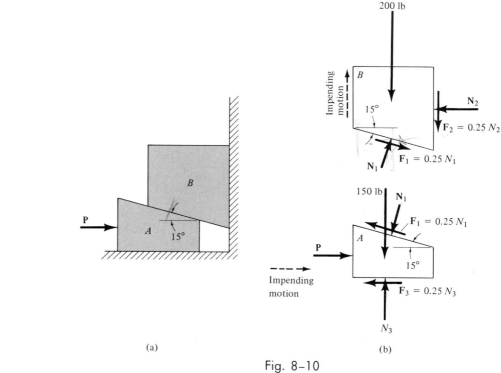

(a)   (b)

Fig. 8–10

Solution

The free-body diagram for each block is shown in Fig. 8–10b. Since motion is impending, Eq. 8–1 is used to relate the normal and frictional force at each contacting surface. As shown on block A, the friction forces F_1 and F_3 at each contacting surface act in the opposite direction to impending motion at their contacting surface. Equal but opposite reactions of N_1 and F_1 must act on block B as shown. Since this block is forced upward, F_2 acts downward. Applying the two force equations of equilibrium to block B, we have

$\xrightarrow{+}\Sigma F_x = 0;$ $N_1 \sin 15° + 0.25N_1(\cos 15°) - N_2 = 0$

$+\uparrow\Sigma F_y = 0;$ $N_1 \cos 15° - 0.25 N_1(\sin 15°) - 0.25 N_2 - 200\,\text{lb} = 0$

Solving these equations simultaneously yields

$$N_1 = 258\,\text{lb}$$
$$N_2 = 129\,\text{lb}$$

Using the value of $N_1 = 258$ lb and applying the two force equations of equilibrium to block A we can write

$\xrightarrow{+}\Sigma F_x = 0;$ $P - 0.25 N_3 - 0.25(258 \cos 15°\,\text{lb}) - 258 \sin 15°\,\text{lb} = 0$

$+\uparrow\Sigma F_y = 0;$ $N_3 - 258 \cos 15°\,\text{lb} + 0.25(258 \sin 15°\,\text{lb}) - 150\,\text{lb} = 0$

Solving these equations simultaneously, we obtain

$$N_3 = 383\,\text{lb}$$
$$P = 225\,\text{lb} \qquad\qquad\qquad Ans.$$

Problems

Assume that $\mu = \mu_s = \mu_k$ in the following problems where specified.

8-1. The footing of a ladder rests on a concrete surface for which $\mu = 0.8$ for the two materials. If the magnitude of a force, directed along the axis of the ladder, is 600 lb, determine the friction force acting at the bottom of the ladder. What is the minimum coefficient of friction which will prevent the ladder from slipping?

8-2. An ax is driven into the block of wood. If the coefficient of friction between the ax and the wood is $\mu = 0.2$, determine the smallest angle α of the blade which will cause the ax to be "self-locking." Neglect the weight of the ax.

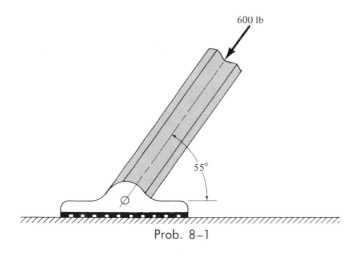

600 lb

55°

∅

Prob. 8-1

α

Prob. 8-2

8-3. Determine the force **P** which must be applied to the wedge to lift the 1,000-lb block. The coefficient of friction for all contacting surfaces is $\mu = 0.3$. Neglect the weight of the wedge.

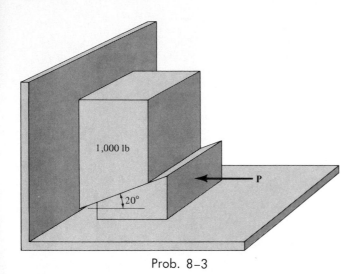

Prob. 8-3

8-4. The block weighs 60 lb and is subjected to a force **P** acting at an angle $\alpha = 20°$ with the horizontal. If $\mu_s = 0.5$, determine the magnitude of force **P** to just start the block moving down the plane.

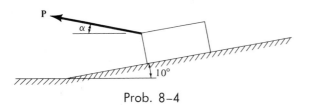

Prob. 8-4

8-5. If the coefficient of kinetic friction between the inclined surface and the block in Prob. 8-4 is $\mu_k = 0.3$, determine the angle α of the force $P = 20$ lb which will allow the block to move down the plane with constant velocity.

8-6. The 100-lb block rests on the horizontal plane for which $\mu_s = 0.5$. If a force having a magnitude of 20 lb is applied to the block, determine the friction force developed between the block and the plane. Does the block slip?

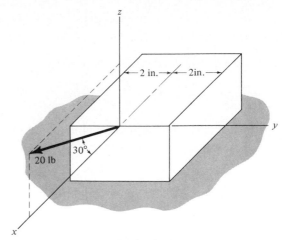

Prob. 8-6

8-7. The mine car has a uniform weight of 6,000 lb. If the coefficient of friction between the wheels and the tracks is $\mu_s = 0.4$ when the wheels are locked, find the normal force acting on each of the two wheels at points A and B when (a) the brakes at A are locked, and (b) the brakes at both A and B are locked. Does the car move when only the brakes at A are locked?

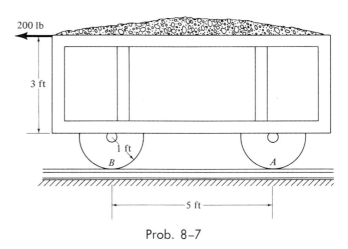

Prob. 8-7

8-8. The rectangular tank is filled with water having a density of 62.4 lb/ft^3. If the tank weighs 20 lb empty, determine the height of water h which may be placed in the tank so that the tank is on the verge of tipping when the horizontal force $P = 200$ lb.

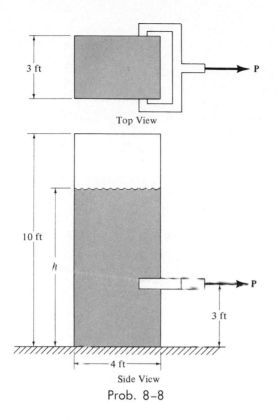

3 ft

Top View

10 ft

h

3 ft

├── 4 ft ──┤

Side View

Prob. 8-8

8-9. If block B is placed upon block A, determine the maximum angle α so that block A does not slip. Each block weighs 1,000 lb, and all surfaces of contact have a coefficient of friction $\mu = 0.2$.

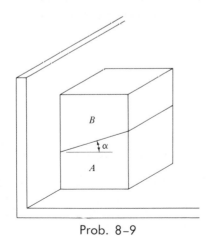

B

α

A

Prob. 8-9

8-10. The 50-lb block is subjected to a horizontal force of 20 lb. Determine the smallest width w so that the block does not slide or tip.

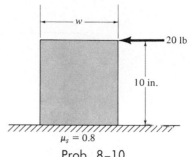

w

20 lb

10 in.

$\mu_s = 0.8$

Prob. 8-10

8-11. Two blocks A and B each weighing 50 lb are joined by a light 3-ft rod having a pin at each end. Determine the maximum height h for which block B may be placed up the inclined plane without causing the assembly to slip down the plane. Neglect the size of the blocks in the calculations. $\mu = 0.15$ at the contacting surfaces.

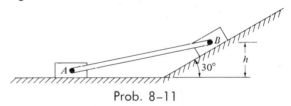

B

A

30°

h

Prob. 8-11

8-12. Two blocks A and B, each weighing 50 lb, are connected by the linkage shown. If the coefficient of friction at the contacting surfaces is $\mu_s = 0.5$, determine the maximum vertical force **P** which may be applied to the linkage without causing the blocks to move.

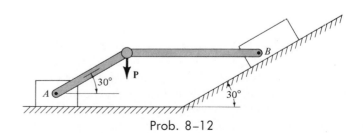

A

30°

P

B

30°

Prob. 8-12

8-13. The hub of the 150-lb wheel bears against the vertical wall. If the coefficient of friction between all contacting surfaces is $\mu = 0.6$, determine the horizontal force **P** needed to rotate the wheel.

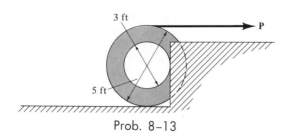

Prob. 8-13

8-14. Determine the minimum applied force **P** required to push wedge B in place. The spring is compressed a distance of 6 in. Neglect the weight of the wedges and block C. The coefficient of friction for all contacting surfaces is $\mu = 0.35$. Neglect friction at the rollers.

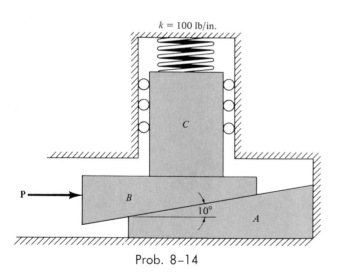

Prob. 8-14

8-15. If the vertical load **P** acting on the bracket is 500 lb, determine the horizontal force **F** required to move the wedge to the left. Neglect the weight of the wedge and the bracket. The bracket is pinned at A. The coefficient of friction between all the contacting surfaces of the wedge is $\mu = 0.2$.

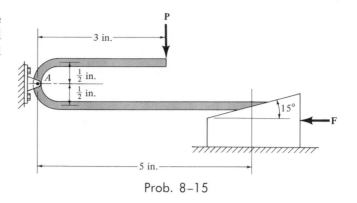

Prob. 8-15

8-16. A 100-lb weight rests on a 15° inclined plane. Determine the minimum force P which will cause impending motion of the weight up the plane; $\mu_s = 0.3$.

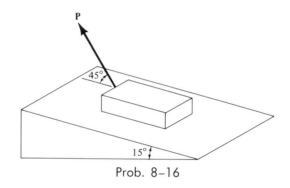

Prob. 8-16

8-17. A 100-lb disk rests on an inclined surface for which $\mu_s = 0.2$. Determine the maximum vertical load **P** which may be applied to the link AB without causing the disk to slip.

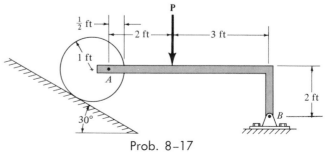

Prob. 8-17

8–18. Blocks A and B weigh 50 and 100 lb, respectively. If the coefficient of friction for all surfaces of contact is $\mu_s = 0.3$, calculate the magnitude of force P needed to cause impending motion of B to the right. What is the tension in the cord?

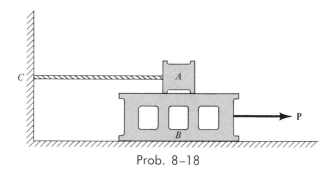

Prob. 8–18

8–19. Solve Prob. 8–18 assuming that the cord slopes upward to the left at an angle of $20°$.

8–20. A 50-lb beam rests on two surfaces at points A and B. Determine the maximum distance x to which a girl can walk up the beam before the beam begins to slip. Assume that the girl weighs 120 lb and moves up the beam with a constant velocity.

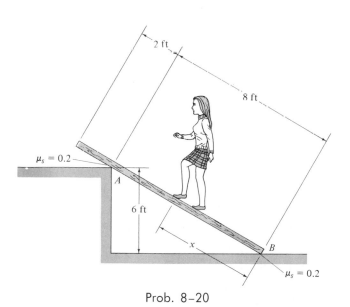

Prob. 8–20

8–21. A 150-lb man squats 4 ft from the top of the ladder. If the ladder weighs 50 lb, with center of gravity at point G, and the coefficients of friction at points A and B are $(\mu_s)_A = 0.3$ and $(\mu_s)_B = 0.2$, respectively, determine the range of horizontal force which the man may exert on the ladder at point C without causing the ladder to move. Assume that the man squatting on the ladder exerts only a vertical force on the ladder at point D.

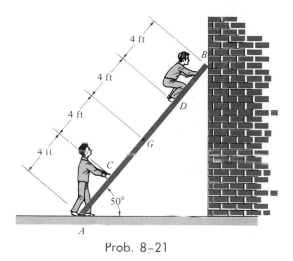

Prob. 8–21

8–22. Solve Prob. 8–21 given that the wall surface at point B is smooth.

8–23. Determine the minimum force F needed to push the two 150-lb cylinders up the plane. The coefficient of friction between all surfaces of contact is $\mu = 0.3$.

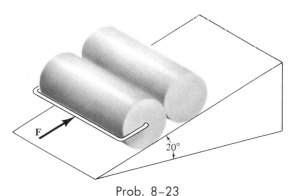

Prob. 8–23

8-24. A single force **P** is applied to the handle of the drawer. If friction is neglected at the bottom of the drawer, and the coefficient of friction along the sides is μ_s, determine the spacing s between the handles so that the drawer does not bind at the corner when the force **P** is applied.

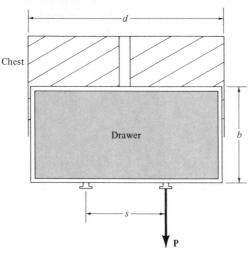

Chest

Drawer

Prob. 8-24

8-25. If the coefficient of friction for the drum and brake mechanism is $\mu_s = 0.6$, determine the reaction at the pin O. Does the 60-lb vertical force prevent the drum from rotating? Neglect the weight of the brake.

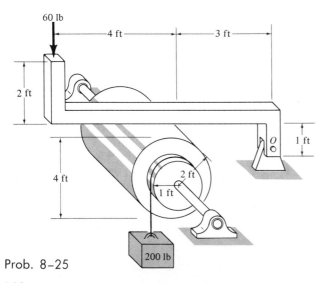

Prob. 8-25

282

8-26. The compound beam is adjusted into the horizontal position by means of a wedge located at its right support. If the coefficient of friction between the wedge and the surfaces of contact is $\mu = 0.25$, determine the horizontal force **P** required to remove the wedge.

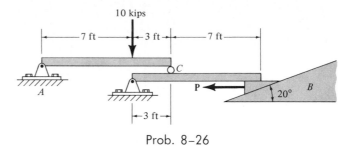

Prob. 8-26

8-27. The 100-lb sphere rests between the two supports at A and B. Determine the minimum value of P and the coefficient of friction μ_s needed to roll the sphere off the edge B without causing the sphere to slip.

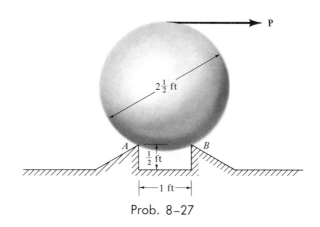

Prob. 8-27

8-28. If $\mu_s = 0.15$ for the contacting surfaces at A and B in Prob. 8-27, determine the magnitude of force **P** for impending motion of the sphere. What are the normal reactions at points A and B?

8-29. Two blocks A and B rest on the inclined planes. If the weight of block A is 60 lb, determine the weight of block B so that (a) block B is on the verge of sliding up the plane, and (b) block B moves at constant velocity down the plane. $\mu_s = 0.5$ and $\mu_k = 0.25$ for all surfaces.

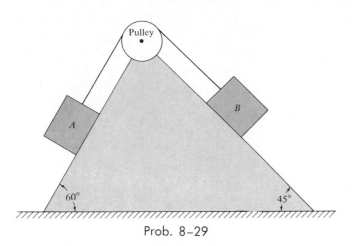

Prob. 8-29

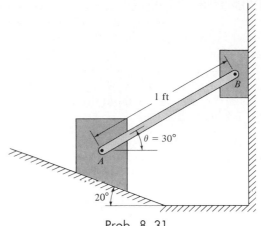

Prob. 8-31

8-30. A 50-lb block is attached to a light rod AB which pivots at pin A. If the coefficient of friction between the plane and the block is $\mu_s = 0.4$, determine the minimum angle θ at which the block may be placed without slipping on the plane.

8-32. The 100-lb crate C rests on a 10-lb dolly D. If the front casters of the dolly at A are locked to prevent them from rolling, determine the maximum force **P** which may be applied without causing motion of the crate. The coefficient of friction between the casters and the floor is $\mu_s = 0.4$, and between the dolly and the crate, $\mu_s = 0.3$.

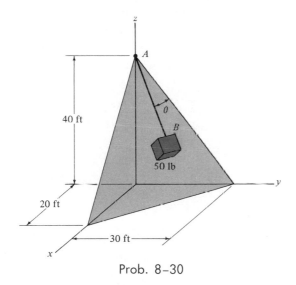

Prob. 8-30

8-31. Two blocks are connected by a uniform 2-lb link making an angle of $\theta = 30°$ with the horizontal. If the coefficient of friction is $\mu_s = 0.35$ for the inclined plane and $\mu_s = 0.2$ for the vertical wall, determine the maximum weight of block B without upsetting the equilibrium position for the two blocks. Block A weighs 50 lb.

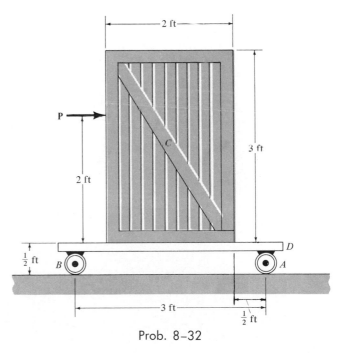

Prob. 8-32

8-33. The 10-ft-long slender beam weighs 100 lb and is connected at A by means of a ball-and-socket joint. If the beam rests against a vertical wall at B, determine the maximum angle θ_{max} at which the beam may be placed so that it does not rotate about the z axis. The coefficient of friction at the wall is $\mu_s = 0.3$. Is rotation of the beam also prevented about the x and y axes when $\theta = \theta_{max}$? Why is this so?

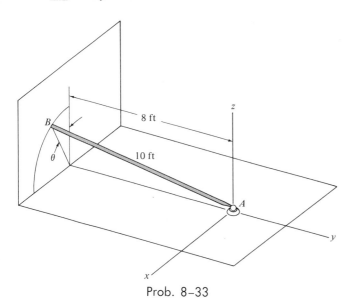

Prob. 8-33

8-34. If the coefficient of friction for all surfaces is $\mu_s = 0.5$, determine the maximum angle θ for which the uniform 100-lb beam AB may be placed against the wall and still not slip.

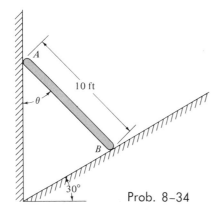

Prob. 8-34

8-35. The wheel C is subjected to the braking action caused by both wheel B and the brake arm A. If the coefficient of friction at all points of contact is $\mu_s = 0.3$, determine the least amount of force $\mathbf{P}$ which must be applied to the brake handle to prevent wheel C from slipping. Neglect friction at pins O and D. Wheel B weighs 100 lb.

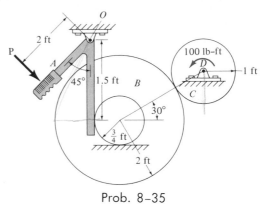

Prob. 8-35

8-36. The 600-lb force applied to the wedge creates a compressive force at A. If friction at B is neglected, determine the compression at A if the coefficient of friction for the wedge is (a) $\mu = 0.3$, and (b) $\mu = 0$.

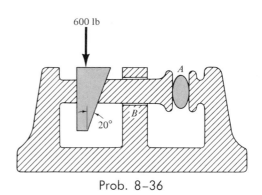

Prob. 8-36

8-37. A 100-lb cylinder rests against a wall and on the surface of a 20° wedge. Assuming that the cylinder, wedge, wall, and horizontal plane A all have the same surface characteristics, determine the coefficient of friction μ which will make the wedge "self-locking;" i.e., $\mathbf{P} = 0$.

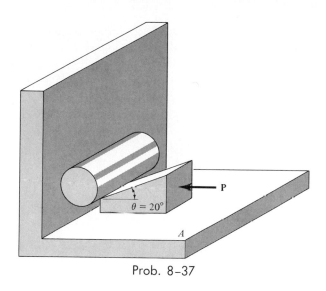

Prob. 8-37

8-39. A 50-lb wedge is placed in the grooved slot of an inclined plane. Determine the maximum angle θ for the inclined plane without causing the wedge to slip. The coefficient of friction for the wedge and surface is $\mu = 0.2$.

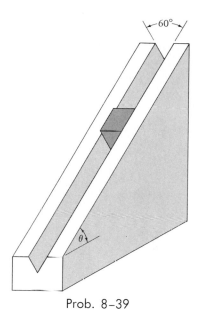

Prob. 8-39

8-38. The friction grip is used to lift steel plates. This is done by inserting a plate p between the loose fitting cylinder C having negligible weight and applying the lifting force **P** to the grip. If the coefficient of friction between the grip and the plate is μ, determine the angle α which will allow any size plate to be lifted.

8-40. The two rods each have a weight W and are pinned together at point B. If the coefficient of friction at C is $\mu_s = 0.5$, determine the maximum angle θ for equilibrium.

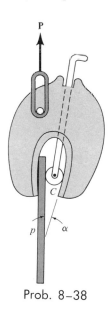

Prob. 8-38

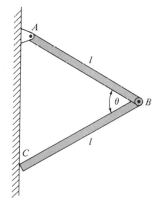

Prob. 8-40

285

8-41. The 100-lb cylindrical boiler rests between the two inclined planes. When $P = 15$ lb, the boiler is on the verge of impending motion. Determine the coefficient of friction μ between the surfaces of contact and the boiler.

8-42. The wedge used in the cotter joint has a coefficient of friction $\mu = 0.3$ with all contacting surfaces. Determine the angle α so that the wedge is self-locking, that is, that the wedge does not slip for any magnitude of **P**.

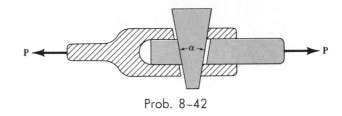

Prob. 8-42

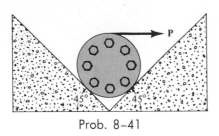

Prob. 8-41

*8-3. Frictional Forces in Screws

A *screw* may be thought of simply as an inclined plane wrapped around a cylinder. A nut initially at position A on the screw shown in Fig. 8-11 will move to B when rotated 360° around the screw. This rotation is equivalent to translating the nut up an inclined plane of height p and length $l = 2\pi r$, where r is the mean radius of the thread. The rise p is often referred to as the *pitch* of the screw. The *pitch angle* is given by $\theta_p = \tan^{-1}(p/2\pi r)$.

In most cases screws are used as fasteners. In many types of machines screws are incorporated to transmit power or motion from one part of the machine to another. A *square-threaded screw* is most commonly used for this latter purpose, especially when large forces are applied along the

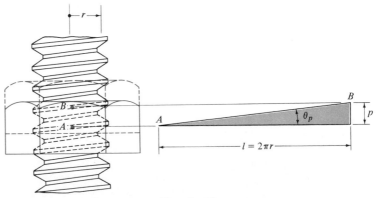

Fig. 8-11

axis of the screw. When subjected to large axial loads, the frictional forces developed at the thread of the screw become important in the analysis to determine the force needed to turn the screw. Consider, for example, the square-threaded jack screw shown in Fig. 8–12 which is subjected to an axial load **W** and a horizontal force **P,** acting at a right angle on the end of the lever of length L. Summing moments about the axis of the screw indicates that a horizontal force of magnitude $S = PL/r$, acting at the mean radius r of the thread, creates the same moment about the axis of the screw as the force **P.**

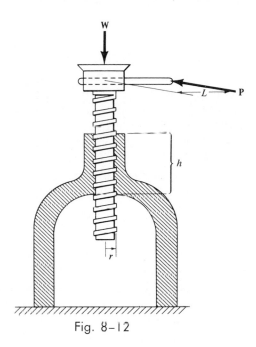

Fig. 8–12

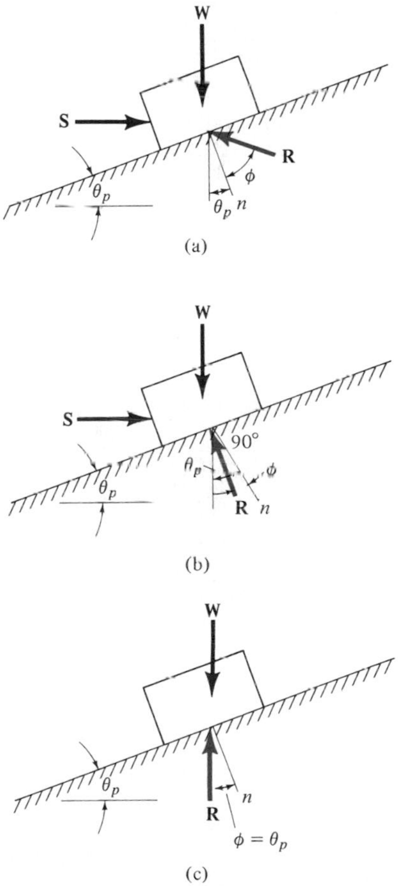

The reactive forces of the jack to loads S and W are distributed over the circumference of the screw thread in contact with the screw hole in the jack, that is, within region h shown in Fig. 8–12. For simplicity, we will consider this portion of thread as a simple block resting on an inclined plane having a pitch angle of θ_p, as shown in Fig. 8–13a. The inclined plane represents the inside *supporting thread* of the jack base. The block is subjected to the total axial load **W** acting on the jack, the horizontal force **S** (which is related to the magnitude of force **P**), and the *resultant force* **R,** which the plane exerts on the block. Although not shown, force **R** has components acting normal, **N,** and tangent, **F,** to the contacting surface. Provided force **P** is great enough, the thread (and hence the block) is either on the verge of impending motion, or motion is occurring. Under these conditions, **R** acts at an angle $(\phi + \theta_p)$ from

Fig. 8–13

the vertical as shown in the figure, where $\phi = \tan^{-1} F/N = \tan^{-1} \mu N/N = \tan^{-1} \mu$. ($\mu_s$ is used here if impending motion occurs; otherwise μ_k is used in the case of motion.) Applying the two force equations of equilibrium to the block, we obtain

$$\xrightarrow{+} \Sigma F_x = 0; \qquad\qquad S - R \sin(\phi + \theta_p) = 0$$
$$+\uparrow \Sigma F_y = 0; \qquad\qquad R \cos(\phi + \theta_p) - W = 0$$

Eliminating R and solving for S, then substituting this value into the equation $P = Sr/L$, yields the force needed to *raise* the block.

$$P = \frac{Wr}{L} \tan(\phi + \theta_p) \qquad\qquad (8\text{-}3)$$

This equation gives the required value P necessary to cause upward impending motion of the screw when $\phi = \phi_s = \tan^{-1} \mu_s$ (the angle of static friction). If ϕ is replaced by $\phi_k = \tan^{-1} \mu_k$ (the angle of kinetic friction), Eq. 8-3 would give a smaller value P necessary to maintain uniform upward motion of the screw.

When the load **W** is to be *lowered,* the direction of **P** is reversed, in which case the angle ϕ (ϕ_s or ϕ_k) lies on the opposite side of the normal n to the plane supporting the block. This case is shown in Fig. 8-13b for $\phi < \theta_p$. Thus, Eq. 8-3 becomes

$$P = \frac{Wr}{L} \tan(\phi - \theta_p) \qquad\qquad (8\text{-}4)$$

If the load **P** is *removed,* the screw will remain self-locking; that is, it will support the weight **W** by friction forces alone, provided $\phi > \theta_p$. However, if $\phi = \phi_s = \theta_p$, Fig. 8-13c, the screw will be on the verge of rotating downward. When $\theta_p > \phi_s$, a restraining load is needed to prevent the screw from moving downward.

*8–4. Frictional Forces in Bearings and Disks

Rotational shafts or axles are generally supported by means of *bearings.* This type of support provides resistance to axial and lateral loads acting on the shaft without restricting the rotation of the shaft about its longitudinal axis. Well-lubricated bearings are subjected to the laws of fluid mechanics, in which the viscosity of the lubricant, the speed of shaft rotation, and the amount of clearance between the shaft and bearing are needed to determine the frictional resistance of the bearing. When the bearing is not lubricated, or only partially lubricated, a reasonable analysis of the frictional resistance may be based on the laws of dry friction.

Pivot or *collar* bearings are commonly used to support the *axial or normal loads* of a rotating shaft. These two types of support are shown in Fig. 8-14. If it is assumed that the normal pressure acting at the bearing

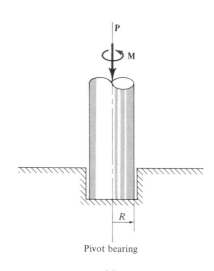

Pivot bearing

(a)

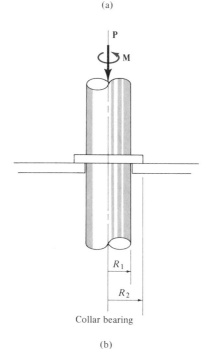

Collar bearing

(b)

Fig. 8–14

surface is *uniformly distributed* over the contact area, an analysis of the frictional forces developed by these supports can easily be performed. Consider, for example, the end of a collar-bearing shaft shown in Fig. 8–15, which is subjected to an axial thrust **P**. The total bearing or contact area is $\pi(R_2^2 - R_1^2)$. Since $\Sigma F_z = 0$, the uniform normal *pressure* or force per unit area acting at the bearing surface is

$$p = \frac{P}{\pi(R_2^2 - R_1^2)}$$

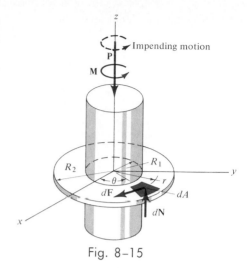

Fig. 8–15

An applied moment **M,** needed to cause impending rotation of the shaft, can be determined by considering the frictional forces developed at the bearing surface. A small area element $dA = (r\, d\theta)(dr)$, shown in Fig. 8–15, is subjected to a normal force

$$dN = p\, dA = \frac{P}{\pi(R_2^2 - R_1^2)}\, dA$$

and a frictional force

$$dF = \mu_s dN = \frac{\mu_s P}{\pi(R_2^2 - R_1^2)}\, dA$$

The normal force dN does not create a moment about the z axis of the shaft; however, the frictional force does, namely, $dM = r\, dF$. Integration is needed to compute the total moment created by all the frictional forces acting on differential areas dA. Therefore, for impending rotational motion,

$$\Sigma M_z = 0; \qquad\qquad M - \int_A r\, dF = 0$$

Integrating over the entire area $dA = (r\, d\theta)(dr)$, we have

$$M = \int_{R_1}^{R_2}\int_0^{2\pi} r\left(\frac{\mu_s P}{\pi(R_2^2 - R_1^2)}\right)(r\, d\theta\, dr) = \frac{\mu_s P}{\pi(R_2^2 - R_1^2)}\int_{R_1}^{R_2} r^2 dr \int_0^{2\pi} d\theta$$

or

$$M = \frac{2}{3}\mu_s P\left(\frac{R_2^3 - R_1^3}{R_2^2 - R_1^2}\right) \qquad\qquad (8\text{–}5)$$

Equation 8–5 gives the magnitude of moment **M** required for the impending motion of a shaft supported by a collar bearing. The frictional moment developed at the end of the shaft when the shaft is *rotating* at constant speed can be found by substituting μ_k for μ_s in Eq. 8–5. This equation may also be used for determining the moment transmitted between the surfaces of *disk-type brakes* or *clutches,* having a contact area described by an inner radius R_1 and an outer radius R_2. When $R_2 = R_0$

and $R_1 = 0$, as in the case of the pivot bearing, shown in Fig. 8–14a, Eq. 8–5 reduces to

$$M = \frac{2}{3}\mu_s PR_0$$

When a shaft or axle is subjected to *lateral loads*, a *journal bearing* is commonly used for support. A typical journal-bearing support is shown in Fig. 8–16. As the shaft rotates in the direction shown in the figure, it rolls up against the wall of the bearing to some point A where slippage occurs. If the lateral load acting at the end of the shaft is **W**, it is necessary that the bearing reactive force **R** acting at A be equal and opposite to **W**. The moment **M** needed to maintain the rotation of the shaft can be found by summing moments about the z axis of the shaft; that is,

$$\Sigma M_z = 0; \qquad -M + R(r \sin \phi_k) = 0$$

or

$$M = Rr \sin \phi_k$$

where ϕ_k is the angle of kinetic friction defined by $\tan \phi_k = \dfrac{F}{N} = \dfrac{\mu_k N}{N} = \mu_k$. If the bearing is partially lubricated, μ_k is small, and therefore

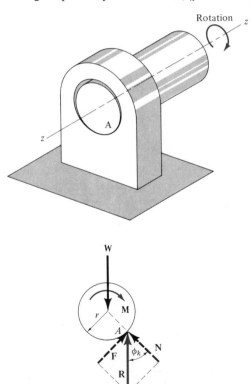

Fig. 8–16

$\mu_k = \tan \phi_k \approx \sin \phi_k \approx \phi_k$. Under these conditions, a reasonable approximation to the moment needed to overcome the frictional resistance becomes

$$M \approx Rr\mu_k$$

Example 8–9 illustrates a common application of this equation.

Example 8–7

The turnbuckle shown in Fig. 8–17 has a square thread with a mean radius of 0.3 in. and a pitch of 0.12 in. If the coefficient of friction between the screw and the turnbuckle is $\mu = 0.25$, determine the moment **M** which must be applied to the turnbuckle to draw the end screws closer together. Is the turnbuckle "self-locking"?

Solution

The moment M applied to the turnbuckle may be obtained by using Eq. 8 3. Since friction at two screws must be overcome, this requires

$$M = 2PL = 2Wr\tan(\phi + \theta_p) \qquad (1)$$

In this equation, the load $W = 200$ lb, $r = 0.3$ in., $\phi = \tan^{-1}\mu = \tan^{-1}(0.25) = 14.04°$, and $\theta_p = \tan^{-1}(p/2\pi r) = \tan^{-1}\{0.12 \text{ in.}/[2\pi(0.3 \text{ in.})]\} = 3.64°$. Substituting these values into Eq. (1) and solving gives

$$M = 2(200 \text{ lb})(0.3 \text{ in.})[\tan(14.04° + 3.64°)]$$

$$M = 38.3 \text{ lb-in.} \qquad\qquad Ans.$$

When the moment M is *removed,* the turnbuckle will be self-locking since $\phi > \theta_p$.

Example 8–8

The uniform bar shown in Fig. 8–18a has a total weight of W lb. If it is assumed that the normal pressure acting at the contacting surface is uniformly distributed, determine the couple moment **M** required to rotate the bar. Assume that the width s is negligible in comparison to the length l. The coefficient of friction is equal to μ.

Solution

A free-body diagram of the bar is shown in Fig. 8–18b. Since the bar has a total weight of W lb, the weight per unit length along the x axis of the bar is $w = W/l$. The magnitude of force dN acting on a segment of area having a length dx is

$$dN = w \, dx = \frac{W}{l} \, dx$$

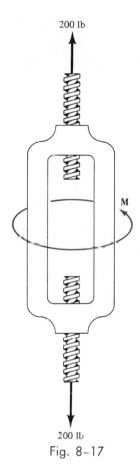

200 lb

M

200 lb

Fig. 8–17

and therefore the frictional force acting on this same element of area is

$$dF = \mu \, dN = \frac{\mu W}{l} \, dx$$

The moment created by this frictional force about the z axis becomes

$$dM = x \, dF = \frac{\mu W}{l} x \, dx$$

Summing moments about the z axis of the bar gives

$$M = \int_{-l/2}^{l/2} \frac{\mu W}{l} x \, dx$$

or

$$M = \frac{\mu W l}{4} \qquad\qquad Ans.$$

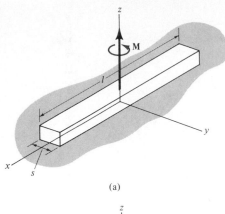

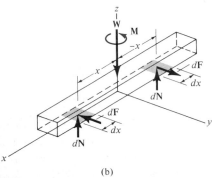

(a)

(b)

Fig. 8–18

Example 8–9

The 5-in.-diameter pulley shown in Fig. 8–19a fits loosely on a 1-in.-diameter shaft for which the coefficients of static and kinetic friction are $\mu = 0.26$. Determine the minimum tension $\mathbf{T}$ in the belt to (a) raise the 100-lb weight at constant velocity, and (b) lower the weight at constant velocity. Assume no slipping between the belt and pulley and neglect the weight of the pulley.

Solution

Part (a). A free-body diagram of the pulley is shown in Fig. 8–19b. When the pulley is subjected to cable tensions of 100 lb each, the pulley makes contact with the shaft at point P_1. As the tension $\mathbf{T}$ is increased, the pulley will roll around the shaft to point P_2 before motion impends. From the

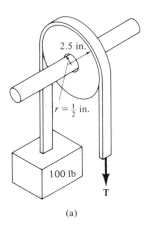

(a)

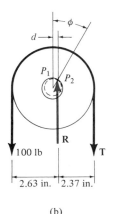

(b)

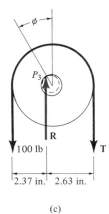

(c)

Fig. 8–19

figure, $d = r \sin \phi$. As stated in the text, $\sin \phi \approx \mu$. Hence, $d \approx r\mu = (\frac{1}{2}$ in.$)0.26 = 0.13$ in., so that summing moments about point P_2 gives

$\zeta + \Sigma M_{P_2} = 0$;

$$100 \text{ lb } (2.63 \text{ in.}) - T(2.37 \text{ in.}) = 0, \qquad T = 111.0 \text{ lb} \qquad Ans.$$

Part (b).   When the weight is lowered, the resultant force **R** acting on the shaft passes through point P_3, as shown in Fig. 8–19c. Summing moments about this point yields

$\zeta + \Sigma M_{P_3} = 0$;

$$100 \text{ lb } (2.37 \text{ in.}) - T(2.63 \text{ in.}) = 0, \qquad T = 90.1 \text{ lb} \qquad Ans.$$

Problems

8-43. The threads of the jack screw shown in Fig. 8–12 have a mean radius of 1 in. and a pitch of $\frac{1}{4}$ in. If the static coefficient of friction is $\mu_s = 0.2$ and the lever arm has a length of 2 ft, determine the force **P** which must be initially applied to lift a weight $W = 5,000$ lb. What initial force **P** is required to lower the weight?

8-44. Prove that the pitch p must be less than $2\pi r\mu$ for the jack screw, shown in Fig. 8–12, to be "self-locking."

8-45. The square-threaded bolt is used to join two plates together. If the bolt has a mean diameter of $\frac{3}{4}$ in. and a pitch of $\frac{3}{16}$ in., determine the torque required to loosen the bolt if the tension in the bolt is 35,000 lb. The coefficient of friction between the threads and the bolt is $\mu_s = 0.15$.

8-46. The square-threaded screw of the vise clamps has a mean diameter of $\frac{1}{2}$ in. and a pitch of $\frac{1}{7}$ in. If $\mu_s = 0.25$ for the threads, and the load **P**, applied normal to the handle, is 50 lb, determine the compressive force in the block.

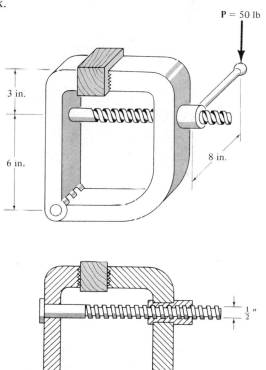

Prob. 8–46

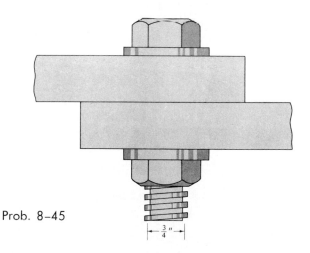

Prob. 8–45

8-47. The *universal testing machine* is used to measure the strength of a specimen *S* when the specimen is subjected to large tensile or compressive loads. These forces are applied by raising or lowering the movable head *H* of the machine. The head weighs 500 lb, and rests on two square threaded screws, each with a mean diameter of 3 in. and a pitch of $\frac{3}{8}$ in. The coefficient of static friction for the threads is $\mu_s = 0.2$. If the specimen is compressed in the machine such that the dial reads 3,000 lb, determine the torque *T* (lb-ft) which must be applied to each of the screws, by the motors of the machine, to increase the load. Neglect friction acting on the four guide posts *G*.

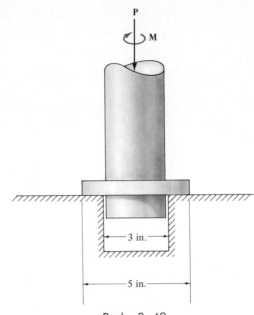

Prob. 8–49

8-50. The *double-collar bearing* is subjected to an axial load $P = 1,000$ lb. Assuming that collar *A* supports $\frac{3}{4}P$ and collar *B* supports $\frac{1}{4}P$, both with a uniform distribution of pressure, determine the maximum frictional moment **M** which may be resisted by the bearing. $\mu_s = 0.2$ for both collars.

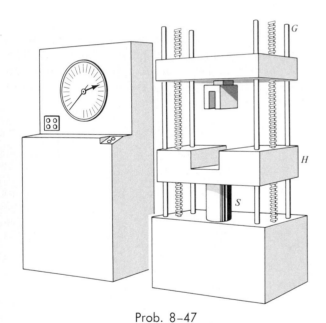

Prob. 8–47

8-48. If a tensile specimen is placed in the testing machine of Prob. 8–47, determine the torque which must be applied to each of the screws by the machine to create a tensile force in the specimen of 6,000 lb.

8-49. The collar bearing supports an axial load of 1,500 lb. If a moment of 160 lb-ft is required to overcome the friction developed by the bearing, determine the coefficient of friction μ acting at the bearing surface.

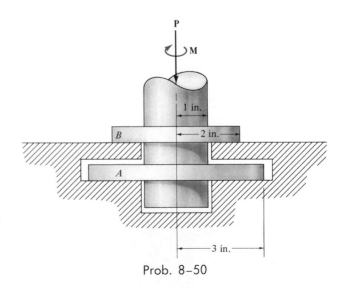

Prob. 8–50

8-51. Determine the moment **M** which must be applied to the collar bearing in Prob. 8–50 to cause impending motion of the collar. Assume that the load $P = 1,000$ lb is distributed equally to each collar. The coefficient of friction for collar A is $\mu_s = 0.2$, and for collar B, $\mu_s = 0.3$.

8-52. The automobile jack is subjected to a vertical load of 6,000 lb. If the square-threaded screw has a pitch of $\frac{1}{4}$ in. and a mean diameter of $\frac{1}{2}$ in., determine the force which must be applied to the handle to (a) raise the load, and (b) lower the load; $\mu_s = 0.25$. The supporting plate exerts only vertical forces at A and B, and each cross-link has a length of 4 in.

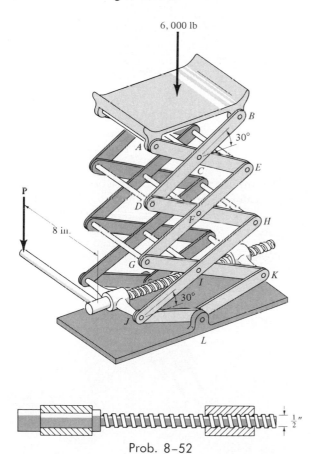

Prob. 8–52

8-53. The pivot bearing has been bored out at its end. If the coefficient of friction at the bearing surface is $\mu_s = 0.35$, and a moment $M = 10$ lb-ft is required to rotate the shaft, determine the applied axial load P.

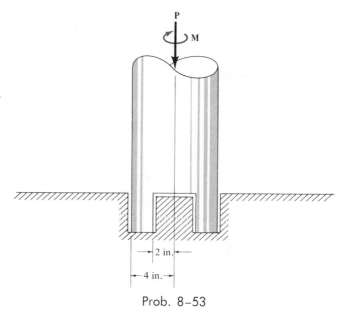

Prob. 8–53

8-54. The *disk clutch* is used in standard transmissions of automobiles. If four springs are used to force the two plates A and B together, determine the force in each spring required to transmit a moment of $M = 600$ lb-ft across the plates. The coefficient of friction is $\mu_s = 0.3$.

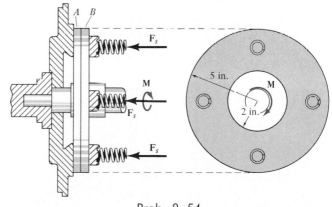

Prob. 8–54

8-55. The plate A is engaged to plate B using three springs. Each spring exerts a normal force of 500 lb on plate B. If $\mu_s = 0.35$ for the contacting surfaces, determine the maximum moment M which may be transmitted across the plates.

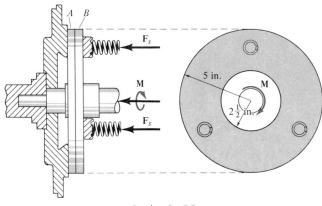

Prob. 8–55

8-56. Because of wearing at the edges, the pivot bearing is subjected to a conical-pressure distribution at its surface of contact. Determine the moment M required to turn the shaft which supports an axial load P. The coefficient of friction is μ.

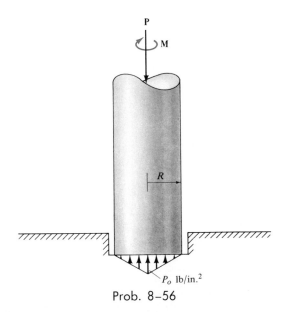

Prob. 8–56

8-57. Determine the moment M required to rotate the "conical" pivot bearing when the bearing is subjected to an axial load P. The coefficient of friction for the contacting surfaces is μ. Assume that the pressure acting between the conical surface of contact is uniform.

Prob. 8–57

8-58. Determine the normal and frictional components of force developed on the collar bushing. The coefficient of friction is $\mu = 0.21$. Assume that the belt moves in the direction of force $\mathbf{T}$.

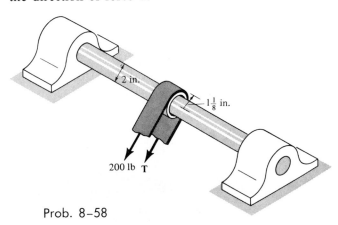

Prob. 8–58

8-59. If a tension force $T = 215$ lb is required to pull the 200-lb force around the collar bushing in Prob. 8–58, determine the coefficient of friction at the contacting surface.

8-60. A 4-in.-diameter post is driven 12 ft into mud for which $\mu = 0.15$. If the normal pressure acting around the post varies linearly with depth as shown, determine the frictional moment **M** which must be overcome to rotate the post.

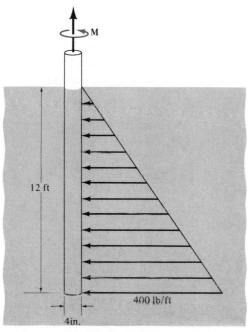

Prob. 8–60

8-61. Because of drying, the coefficient of friction of the mud acting on the post in Prob. 8–60 varies linearly from $\mu = 0.3$ at the top of the post to $\mu = 0.1$ at its base. Determine the frictional moment **M** needed to rotate the post. Use the data in Prob. 8–60.

8-62. A 12-in.-diameter disk fits loosely over a 3-in.-diameter shaft in which the coefficient of friction is $\mu = 0.15$. If the disk weighs 100 lb, determine the vertical tangential force which must be applied to the disk to cause it to slip over the shaft.

8-63. The 4-in.-diameter pulley fits loosely on a $\frac{1}{2}$-in.-diameter axle. If $\mu = 0.30$, determine the minimum tension **T** required to raise the 250-lb load. Neglect the weight of the pulley.

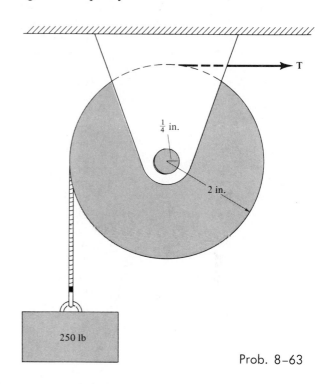

Prob. 8–63

8-64. The collar fits loosely around a 2-in.-diameter shaft. If the coefficient of friction between the shaft and the collar is $\mu = 0.29$, determine the maximum belt tension **T** needed to lower the 150-lb load.

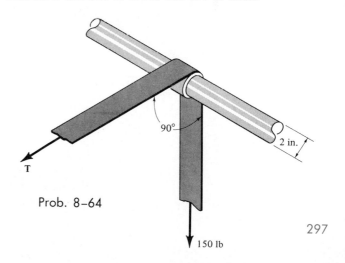

Prob. 8–64

297

8-5. Frictional Forces in Flat Belts

In the design of belt drives or band brakes it is necessary to determine the frictional forces developed between a belt and its contacting surface. Consider the flat belt acting over a fixed drum of radius r, as shown in Fig. 8–20a. The *total angle of belt contact* is β, and the coefficient of friction between the two surfaces is μ. If it is known that the tension acting in the belt on the right of the drum is T_1, let it be required to find the tension T_2 needed to pull the belt counterclockwise over the surface of the drum. *Obviously, T_2 must be greater than T_1, since the belt must overcome the resistance of friction at the surface of contact.* A free-body diagram of the *entire belt* is shown in Fig. 8–20b. Because of the frictional effects acting over the curved surface, it is seen that the normal force N and the frictional force **F**, acting at various points along the contacting surface of the belt, will vary both in magnitude and direction. Due to this unknown force distribution, the analysis of the problem will proceed on the basis of initially studying the forces acting on a differential element of the belt.

A free-body diagram of an element of the belt having a length $r\,d\theta$ is shown in Fig. 8–20c. Assuming either impending motion, or motion of the belt, the magnitude of frictional force $dF = \mu\,dN$. This force opposes the sliding motion of the belt and thereby increases the magnitude of tensile force acting in the belt. Applying the two force equations of equilibrium, we have

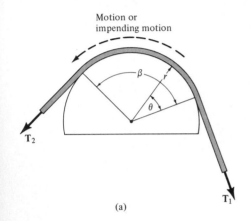

(a)

$$\xrightarrow{+}\Sigma F_x = 0; \qquad T \cos\frac{d\theta}{2} + \mu\,dN - (T + dT)\cos\frac{d\theta}{2} = 0$$

$$+\uparrow\Sigma F_y = 0; \qquad dN - (T + dT)\sin\frac{d\theta}{2} - T\sin\frac{d\theta}{2} = 0$$

For an angle of infinitesimal size, $\sin d\theta/2$ and $\cos d\theta/2$ may be replaced by $d\theta/2$ and 1, respectively. Also, the *product* of two infinitesimals dT and $d\theta/2$ may be neglected when compared to infinitesimals of the first order. The above two equations therefore reduce to

$$\mu\,dN = dT$$

and

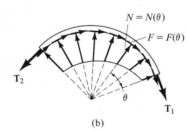

(b)

$$dN = T\,d\theta$$

Eliminating dN between these two relations yields

$$\frac{dT}{T} = \mu\,d\theta$$

We may integrate this equation between all the points of contact which the belt makes with the drum. Since $T = T_1$ at $\theta = 0$, and $T = T_2$ at $\theta = \beta$, then

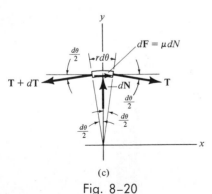

(c)

Fig. 8–20

$$\int_{T_1}^{T_2} \frac{dT}{T} = \mu \int_0^\beta d\theta$$

or

$$\ln \frac{T_2}{T_1} = \mu\beta$$

Solving for T_2, we obtain

$$T_2 = T_1 e^{\mu\beta} \qquad (8\text{-}6)$$

This equation is valid for flat belts placed on *any shape* of contacting surface. In summary, the terms in this equation are defined as follows:

  μ = coefficient of static or kinetic friction between the belt and the surface of contact

  β = angle of belt and surface contact, measured in radians

T_2, T_1 = belt tensions; T_1 opposes the direction of motion (or impending motion) of the belt, while T_2 acts in the direction of belt motion (or impending motion); because of friction, $T_2 > T_1$.

  e = 2.718, base of natural logarithm.

An application of Eq. 8–6 is given in Example 8–10.

*8–6. Rolling Resistance

If a *rigid* cylinder of weight W rolls at constant velocity along a *rigid* surface, the normal force exerted by the surface on the cylinder acts at the tangent point of contact, as shown in Fig. 8–21a. Under these condi-

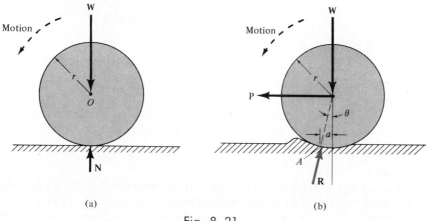

(a)

(b)

Fig. 8–21

tions, provided the cylinder does not encounter frictional resistance from the air, motion of the cylinder would continue indefinitely. Actually, however, no two materials are perfectly rigid. Hence, a normal reaction of the surface on the cylinder consists of a *distribution* of normal forces. Assuming that the cylinder is much harder than the surface, a small ridge is formed in front of the rolling cylinder caused by the indentation of the cylinder into the surface, Fig. 8–21*b*. Since the cylinder can never really "climb" over this "hill," the total reactive force R at the surface acts at some angle θ from the vertical. To keep the cylinder in equilibrium, that is, moving at constant velocity, it is necessary that R be *concurrent* with the driving force P and the weight W. Taking moments about point A gives $Wa = P(r \cos \theta)$. Since the deformations of the cylinder are generally small in relation to the radius, $\cos \theta \approx 1$; hence,

$$Wa \approx Pr$$

or

$$P \approx \frac{Wa}{r}$$

The distance "*a*" is termed the *coefficient of rolling resistance,* which has the dimension of length. Experimentally, this factor is difficult to measure, since it depends upon such parameters as the rate of rotation of the cylinder, the elastic properties of the contacting surfaces, and the frictional effects of the surfaces. For this reason, little reliance is placed on the data for determining a. The analysis presented here does, however, indicate why a heavy load offers greater resistance to motion than a light load under the same conditions.

The driving force P needed to roll a cylinder over a surface, however, is much less than that needed to slide the cylinder across the surface. For this reason roller or ball bearings are often used to minimize the frictional resistance between moving parts.

Example 8–10

The maximum tension which can be developed in the belt, shown in Fig. 8–22*a*, is 500 lb. If the pulley at A is free to rotate and the coefficient of friction at the fixed drums B and C is $\mu = 0.25$, determine the largest load W which can be lifted by the belt. Assume that the force T applied at the end of the belt is directed vertically downward, as shown.

Solution

Lifting the weight W causes the belt to move counterclockwise over the drums at B and C; hence, the maximum tension T_2 in the belt occurs at D. Thus, $T_2 = 500$ lb. A section of the belt passing over the drum at

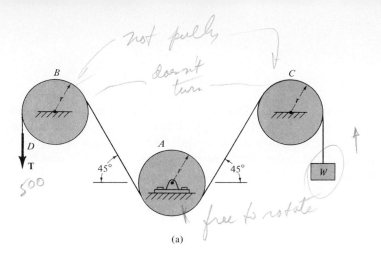

not pulley
does not turn

(a)

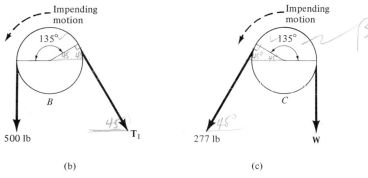

(b)   (c)

Fig. 8–22

B is shown in Fig. 8 22*b*. The angle of contact between the drum and the belt is $\beta = (135°/180°)\pi = 3\pi/4$ rad. Using Eq. 8–6, we have

$$T_2 = T_1 e^{\mu\beta}$$
$$500 \text{ lb} = T_1 e^{0.25[(3/4)\pi]}$$

Hence,

$$T_1 = \frac{500 \text{ lb}}{e^{0.25[(3/4)\pi]}} = 277 \text{ lb}$$

Since the pulley at *A* is free to rotate, equilibrium requires that the tension in the belt remains the *same* on both sides of the pulley. Can you show this?

The section of the belt passing over the drum at *C* is shown in Fig. 8–22*c*. The load $W < 277$ lb. Why? Applying Eq. 8–6, we obtain

$$277 \text{ lb} = W e^{0.25[(3/4)\pi]}$$
$$W = 153 \text{ lb} \qquad\qquad Ans.$$

Problems

8-65. A "hawser" is wrapped around a fixed "capstan" to secure a ship for docking. If the tension in the rope, caused by the ship, is 1,500 lb, determine the least number of complete turns the rope must be wrapped around the capstan in order to prevent slipping of the rope. The greatest horizontal force that a longshoreman can exert on the rope is 50 lb. The coefficient of friction is $\mu_s = 1/\pi$.

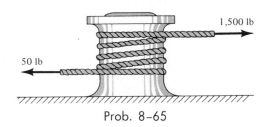

Prob. 8-65

8-66. A flat belt is wrapped over the elliptical drum. If a weight of 10 lb is suspended from one end of the belt, determine the tension **T** in the belt needed to (a) raise the weight, and (b) lower the weight, at constant velocity. The coefficient of friction is $\mu = 1/\pi$.

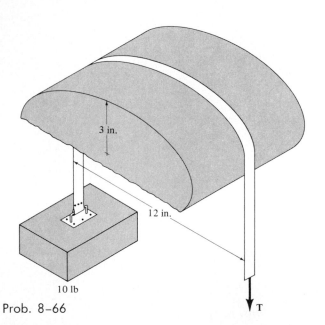

Prob. 8-66

8-67. Determine the maximum and minimum values of weight W which may be applied without causing the 50-lb block to slip. The coefficient of friction between the block and the plane is $\mu_s = 0.2$, and between the rope and the drum $D, \mu_s = 0.3$.

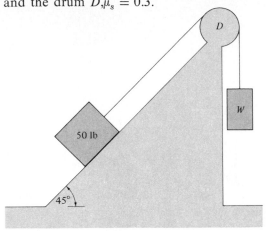

Prob. 8-67

8-68. If the applied moment **M** acting on the wheel is 200 lb-ft, determine the vertical force **P** which must be applied to the band brake to stop the wheel. The coefficient of friction for the brake is $\mu_k = 0.4$. 101.8 lb

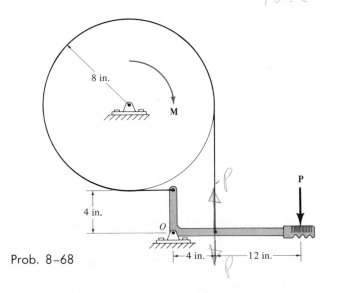

Prob. 8-68

302

8-69. The band brake is used to stop the wheel. If slipping of the belt occurs when a vertical load of 50 lb is applied to the lever, determine the reaction at the pin O. The coefficient of friction for the brake is $\mu_k = 0.25$.

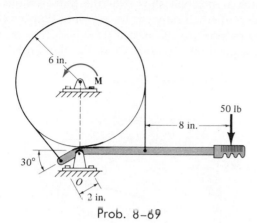

Prob. 8–69

8-70. The blocks A and B weigh 100 and 50 lb respectively. The coefficient of friction at each contacting surface is indicated in the figure. Determine the maximum weight W which may be applied without causing motion of block B.

16.79 lb

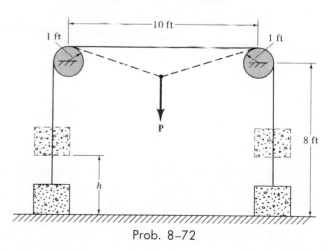

Prob. 8–70

8-71. The 14-ft uniform beam AB weighs 20 lb, and is supported by a rope which passes over a pulley at C and a fixed wheel at D. If the coefficient of friction at D is $\mu_s = 0.3$, determine the distance x from the end of the beam at which a 5-lb weight may be placed and not cause the beam to tip.

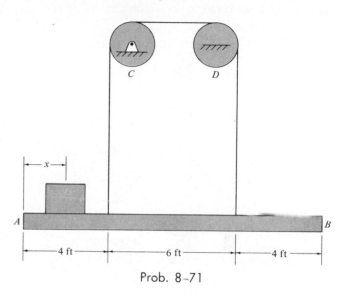

Prob. 8–71

8-72. Two 50-lb blocks are attached to a cable which passes over two drums. If $\mu = 0.3$ for the drums, determine the height h the blocks raise if a vertical load $P = 200$ lb is applied to the cable as shown. When $h = 0$ the tension in the cable is zero.

Prob. 8–72

8-73. A small motor is attached to the floor of the platform. If the total weight of the platform and its contents is 500 lb, determine the torque T which must be supplied by the motor to (a) raise the platform at constant velocity, and (b) lower the platform at constant velocity. In both cases, assume the pulley at A is suddenly fixed from rotating, in which case $\mu_k = 1/\pi$.

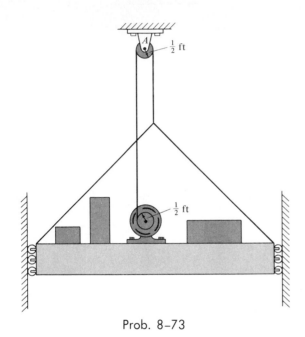

Prob. 8–73

8-74. Show that the frictional relation between the belt tensions, the coefficient of friction μ, and the angular contacts α and β for the V-belt is $T_2 = T_1 e^{[\mu\beta/\sin(\alpha/2)]}$.

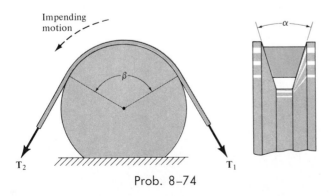

Prob. 8–74

8-75. A 60° V-fan belt of the automobile engine passes around the hub H of a generator G and over the housing F to a fan. If the generator locks, causing the hub to become fixed, determine the moment resisted by the generator as the belt slips over the hub. Assume that slipping of the belt only occurs at H and that the coefficient of friction for the hub is $\mu_s = 0.30$. The belt can sustain a maximum tension of 50 lb. (See Prob. 8–74.)

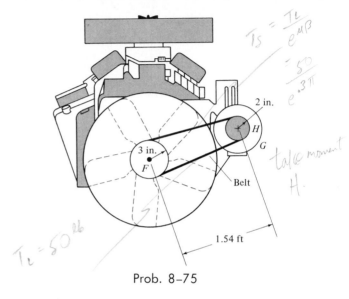

Prob. 8–75

8-76. Experimentally it is found that a 3-in.-diameter cylinder rolls at constant velocity down an inclined plane having a slope of $\frac{1}{16}$ in./ft. Determine the coefficient of rolling resistance for the cylinder.

8-77. The eight wheels on a tank car are each 30 in. in diameter. If the coefficient of rolling resistance is 0.002 in. with the tracks and the car weighs 30 tons, determine the amount of horizontal force **P** required to overcome the rolling resistance of the wheels.

8-78. The lawn roller weighs 300 lb. If the rod BA is held at an angle of 30° from the horizontal and the coefficient of rolling resistance for the roller is 2 in., determine the horizontal component of force, $\mathbf{F}_x$, needed to push the roller at constant speed. Neglect the friction developed at the axle and assume that the resultant force acting on the handle is applied along BA.

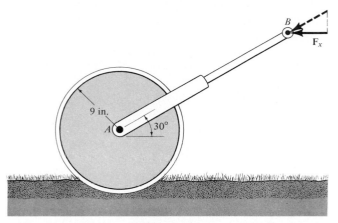

Prob. 8-78

8-79. The roller is subjected to the load of W lb. If the coefficient of rolling resistance for the top surface of the roller is a_1 and at the bottom surface is a_2, show that a force of $P = [W(a_1 + a_2)]/2r$ is required to move the load and the roller forward. Neglect the weight of the roller.

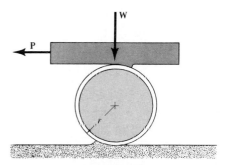

Prob. 8-79

8-80. The 3,000-lb steel beam is moved over a level surface by using a series of 3-in.-diameter rollers for which the coefficient of rolling resistance is $\frac{1}{8}$ in. at the ground and $\frac{1}{16}$ in. at the surface of the beam. Determine the horizontal force **P** needed to move the beam at constant speed. (*Hint:* See Prob. 8-79.)

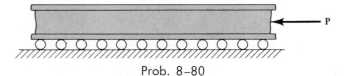

Prob. 8-80

Center of Gravity and Centroids

9-1. Introduction

In Sec. 4-11, it was pointed out that distributed loads can act either on the surface of a body or throughout its volume. Since these types of loads often vary in some complex fashion, it becomes necessary to develop a general method for reducing distributed loads to a single resultant force having a specified location. Occasionally this general method is also used for finding the *centroid* or geometric center of a body. For example, it was stated in Sec. 4-11 that the center of gravity of a *homogeneous body* coincides with the volume centroid of the body. Recall that the weight of the body can then be replaced by a single resultant force acting through this point. In a similar manner, the resultant force of a distributed surface loading acts through the centroid of the distributed loading diagram. In the theory of strength of materials, the centroid of the cross-sectional *area* of a beam or column must be located in order to properly design these members.

In this chapter we will discuss a general method for determining the center of gravity of a body and the centroid of various geometric shapes. Before discussing this method as applied to continuous systems, however, it is instructive to first apply this same method to finding the center of gravity of a system of discrete particles.

9-2. Center of Gravity of a System of Particles

Consider the system of three particles shown in Fig. 9-1*a*. Each particle has a different weight, and the particles are distributed across the top surface of an imaginary weightless beam in a manner shown in the figure. Using the methods developed in Sec. 4–10, this parallel system of forces may be reduced to an equivalent force-moment system acting at an arbitrary point O on the beam, as shown in Fig. 9–1*b*. From this figure,

$$W = W_1 + W_2 + W_3$$

and

$$\zeta + M_O = \tilde{x}_1 W_1 + \tilde{x}_2 W_2 + \tilde{x}_3 W_3$$

$\tilde{x}_1$, $\tilde{x}_2$, and $\tilde{x}_3$ represent the *algebraic distances* from the particles to the origin O. Since $\mathbf{M}_O$ is *perpendicular* to $\mathbf{W}$, the force-moment system may be further resolved to a single force resultant $\mathbf{W}$. To do this, $\mathbf{W}$ must be moved a distance $\bar{x}$ to the right of point O in order to create an equivalent moment $\mathbf{M}_O$ at point O, i.e., $M_O = \bar{x}W$. The distance $\bar{x}$ becomes

$$\bar{x} = \frac{M_O}{W} = \frac{\tilde{x}_1 W_1 + \tilde{x}_2 W_2 + \tilde{x}_3 W_3}{W_1 + W_2 + W_3}$$

We may conclude from this result that the effect caused by a single particle having a weight W (equal to the total weight of all the particles) and placed at point G located a distance $\bar{x}$ to the right of point O, as shown in Fig. 9–1*c*, is *equivalent* to the effect caused by the weights of all three particles shown in Fig. 9–1*a*. The point G is termed the *center of gravity* of the system of particles. (For this special case G may be considered as a "balance point" for the unsupported weightless beam; that is, if a fulcrum were placed under the beam at point G as shown in Figs. 9–1*a*, 9–1*b*, or 9–1*c*, the beam would remain balanced in the horizontal position.)

The equation for $\bar{x}$ may be generalized to include n particles acting on the beam. For this case,

$$\bar{x} = \frac{\displaystyle\sum_{i=1}^{n} \tilde{x}_i W_i}{\displaystyle\sum_{i=1}^{n} W_i} \tag{9–1}$$

where W_i is the weight of the *i*th particle and $\tilde{x}_i$ is the *algebraic distance* from the origin to the *i*th particle.

If n particles, having weights $W_1, W_2, \ldots, W_n$, are all contained in the xy plane, the location of the *i*th particle may be specified using coordinates $(\tilde{x}_i, \tilde{y}_i)$. Summing moments of the weights of these particles about the x and y axes, respectively, in the same manner as above, one obtains the relations

$$\bar{x} = \frac{\displaystyle\sum_{i=1}^{n} \tilde{x}_i W_i}{\displaystyle\sum_{i=1}^{n} W_i}, \qquad \bar{y} = \frac{\displaystyle\sum_{i=1}^{n} \tilde{y}_i W_i}{\displaystyle\sum_{i=1}^{n} W_i} \tag{9–2}$$

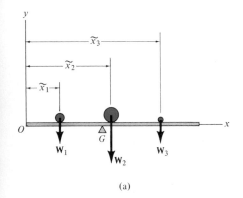

(a)

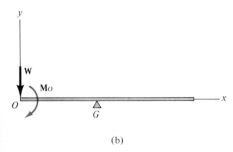

(b)

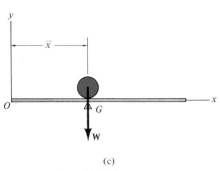

(c)

Fig. 9–1

These equations locate the position $(\bar{x}, \bar{y})$ of the center of gravity for the system of particles.

In the most general case, the ith particle is located at a point $(\tilde{x}_i, \tilde{y}_i, \tilde{z}_i)$ in space. If the system of n particles is rotated with respect to any of the three axes, the weights of the various particles will not remain in the same relative positions; therefore, the resultant weight will be in a different position relative to the n particles. The line of action of the resultant weight, however, does act through the center of gravity $(\bar{x}, \bar{y}, \bar{z})$ regardless of how the system of particles is rotated. The location of this point can be determined by using the moment principle just described. The results are

$$\bar{x} = \frac{\sum\limits_{i=1}^{n} \tilde{x}_i W_i}{\sum\limits_{i=1}^{n} W_i}, \qquad \bar{y} = \frac{\sum\limits_{i=1}^{n} \tilde{y}_i W_i}{\sum\limits_{i=1}^{n} W_i}, \qquad \bar{z} = \frac{\sum\limits_{i=1}^{n} \tilde{z}_i W_i}{\sum\limits_{i=1}^{n} W_i} \qquad (9\text{-}3)$$

important.

for a system of particles

In order to study problems concerning the motion of *matter* under the influence of forces, that is, dynamics, it is necessary to locate the *center of mass*. In finding the location of this point for a system of particles one must consider the weighted average of the *mass* of each particle. In this way, equations analogous to Eq. 9-3 are used to locate the center of mass, only with m_i substituted for W_i in these expressions. Since particles have weight only when under the influence of a gravitational attraction, the center of gravity depends upon the existence of a gravitational field for its definition. The center of mass is independent of gravitational forces. For example, it would be meaningless to define the center of gravity of particles representing the planets of our solar system, whereas the center of mass of this system is important.

If all the particles are approximately the *same distance* from the center of the earth, the acceleration of gravity g for the particles may be considered a *constant*. Newton's second law of motion (see Chapter 1) then becomes $W_i = m_i g$ for all i. Substituting this expression into Eqs. 9-3, the constant g will cancel from both numerator and denominator; hence, for this case the points defining the center of mass and center of gravity for the system of particles will coincide.

Example 9-1

Determine the location of the center of gravity G for the system of four particles shown in Fig. 9-2a with respect to the particle at B.

Solution

Locating the origin of coordinates at (the arbitrary) point B, as shown in Fig. 9-2a, the distance $\bar{x}$ from B to the center of gravity can be found using Eq. 9-1.

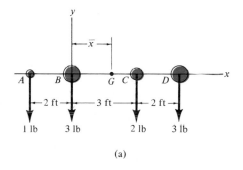

(a)

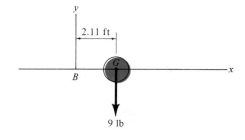

(b)

Fig. 9-2

$$\bar{x} = \frac{\Sigma \tilde{x}_i W_i}{\Sigma W_i} = \frac{-2 \text{ ft}(1 \text{ lb}) + 0 \text{ ft}(3 \text{ lb}) + 3 \text{ ft}(2 \text{ lb}) + 5 \text{ ft}(3 \text{ lb})}{1 \text{ lb} + 3 \text{ lb} + 2 \text{ lb} + 3 \text{ lb}}$$

$$= \frac{19 \text{ lb-ft}}{9 \text{ lb}} = 2.11 \text{ ft} \qquad \textit{Ans.}$$

The four particles shown in Fig. 9–2a may, therefore, be replaced by a 9-lb particle acting at G, 2.11 ft to the right of B. See Fig. 9–2b.

Example 9–2

Locate the center of gravity G of the three particles shown in Fig. 9–3a.

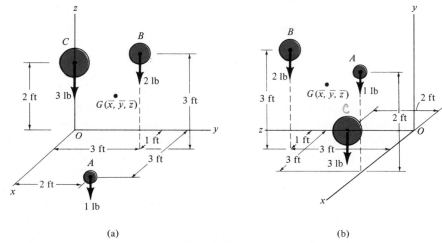

(a)   (b)

Fig. 9–3

Solution

Since the particle weights all act parallel to the z axis, Fig. 9–3a, they create no moment about this axis; hence, the calculations for the position $\bar{x}$ and $\bar{y}$ of the center of gravity for the system of particles can be visualized when the coordinate axis is oriented as shown. Using Eq. 9–3, we obtain

$$\bar{x} = \frac{\Sigma \tilde{x}_i W_i}{\Sigma W_i} = \frac{3 \text{ ft}(1 \text{ lb}) + 1 \text{ ft}(2 \text{ lb}) + 0 \text{ ft}(3 \text{ lb})}{1 \text{ lb} + 2 \text{ lb} + 3 \text{ lb}} = 0.833 \text{ ft} \quad \textit{Ans.}$$

$$\bar{y} = \frac{\Sigma \tilde{y}_i W_i}{\Sigma W_i} = \frac{2 \text{ ft}(1 \text{ lb}) + 3 \text{ ft}(2 \text{ lb}) + 0 \text{ ft}(3 \text{ lb})}{1 \text{ lb} + 2 \text{ lb} + 3 \text{ lb}} = 1.33 \text{ ft} \quad \textit{Ans.}$$

To determine the location $\bar{z}$ it may be helpful to imagine the coordinate axis as being rotated 90° about the x axis as shown in Fig. 9–3b. (Although it is not necessary, this is done here to "visualize" how the moments of forces are developed.) For this orientation of the axes, it is possible to see how both $\bar{x}$ and $\bar{z}$ are determined. In particular,

$$\bar{z} = \frac{\Sigma \tilde{z}_i W_i}{\Sigma W_i} = \frac{0 \text{ ft}(1 \text{ lb}) + 3 \text{ ft}(2 \text{ lb}) + 2 \text{ ft}(3 \text{ lb})}{1 \text{ lb} + 2 \text{ lb} + 3 \text{ lb}} = 2.00 \text{ ft} \quad \textit{Ans.}$$

Problems

9-1. Locate the center of gravity G of the five particles with respect to the origin O.

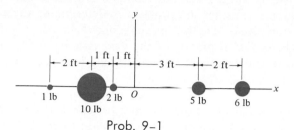

Prob. 9-1

9-2. Locate the center of gravity $(\bar{x}, \bar{y}, \bar{z})$ of the three particles.

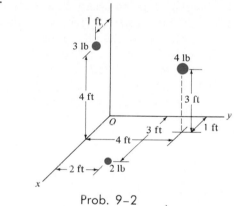

Prob. 9-2

9-3. Locate the center of gravity $(\bar{x}, \bar{y}, \bar{z})$ of the four particles.

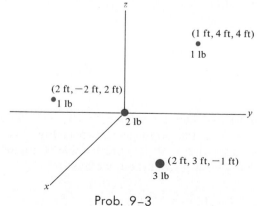

Prob. 9-3

9-4. Determine the location (x, y) of a 7-lb particle so that the three particles have a center of gravity located at the origin of coordinates.

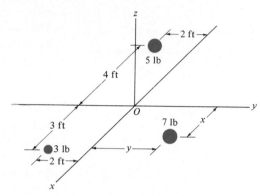

Prob. 9-4

9-5. If the four particles can be replaced by a single 10-lb particle acting at a distance 2 ft to the left of the origin, determine the position $\tilde{x}_p$ and the weight W_p of particle P.

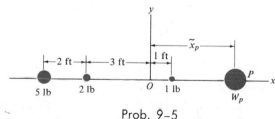

Prob. 9-5

9-6. Locate the coordinates $(\bar{x}, \bar{y})$ of the center of gravity for the system of four particles lying on the xy plane.

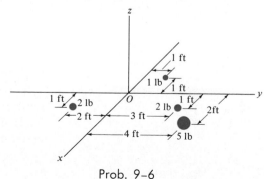

Prob. 9-6

9-3. Center of Gravity and Centroid of a Body

The principles used to determine the center of gravity for a system of discrete particles may also be used to determine the center of gravity for continuous systems which essentially contain an infinite number of particles. For example, consider the problem of determining the center of gravity G of a thin wire of length L placed along the x axis, Fig. 9–4a. The location of the center of gravity of the wire may be *approximated* by dividing the wire into segments and considering each segment to be a separate particle. For example, the ith particle, shown in the figure, has a length Δx_i and weight ΔW_i. Provided the cross-sectional area of the wire is constant, the density of the wire may be represented as a *linear density* ρ_L which has units of weight per unit length. In general, ρ_L will vary along the length of the wire, i.e., $\rho_L = \rho_L(x)$. The weight of the ith segment of wire therefore becomes $\Delta W_i = \rho_L \Delta x_i$.

When the weight ΔW_i is replaced at the origin O, it is also necessary to include a moment $\Delta M_i = \tilde{x}_i \, \Delta W_i$, where $\tilde{x}_i$ represents the *algebraic distance* from the origin of coordinates to the ith segment of wire. When the weight of all the n segments of wire are transferred to the origin, Fig. 9–4b, the total force becomes $W = \Sigma_{i=1}^{n} \Delta W_i = \Sigma_{i=1}^{n} \rho_L \Delta x_i$, and the resultant moment becomes $M_O = \Sigma_{i=1}^{n} \tilde{x}_i \, \Delta W_i = \Sigma_{i=1}^{n} \tilde{x}_i \rho_L \Delta x_i$. Since $\mathbf{M}_O$ is perpendicular to the total weight $\mathbf{W}$, the weight may be transferred to a point, $\bar{x}$, which locates the center of gravity of the wire. This requires

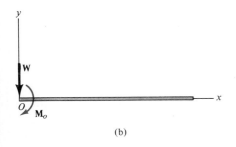

$$\bar{x} = \frac{M_O}{W} = \frac{\displaystyle\sum_{i=1}^{n} \tilde{x}_i \rho_L \, \Delta x_i}{\displaystyle\sum_{i=1}^{n} \rho_L \, \Delta x_i}$$

Taking smaller and smaller Δx_i segments until $\Delta x_i \to 0$, and hence $n \to \infty$, we obtain an integral relation which defines the exact position of the center of gravity, i.e.,

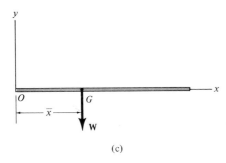

$$\bar{x} = \frac{\displaystyle\lim_{\Delta x_i \to 0} \sum_{i=1}^{n} \tilde{x}_i \rho_L \, \Delta x_i}{\displaystyle\lim_{\Delta x_i \to 0} \sum_{i=1}^{n} \rho_L \, \Delta x_i} = \frac{\displaystyle\int_0^L \tilde{x} \rho_L \, dx}{\displaystyle\int_0^L \rho_L \, dx}$$

See Fig. 9–4c.

In particular, a differential element of length dx, is located at an arbitrary distance $\tilde{x} = x$ from the origin as shown in Fig. 9–4d. If the linear density ρ_L is constant—that is, if the wire is made of homogeneous material, then, using the above formulation, we have

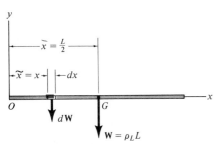

Fig. 9–4

$$\bar{x} = \frac{\rho_L \displaystyle\int_0^L x \, dx}{\rho_L \displaystyle\int_0^L dx} = \frac{\rho_L \dfrac{L^2}{2}}{\rho_L L} = \frac{L}{2}$$

for homogeneous wire with constant density.

The total weight of the wire $W = \rho_L L$ may therefore be represented as a concentrated force acting at the midpoint of the wire, Fig. 9–4d.

In general, the geometry for a slender rod or wire may be described in three directions by a *curve* such as shown in Fig. 9–5. If the wire has a total length L and linear density ρ_L, the center of gravity G is determined using the formulas

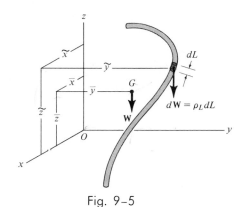

Fig. 9–5

$$\bar{x} = \frac{\int_L \tilde{x} \rho_L \, dL}{\int_L \rho_L \, dL}, \qquad \bar{y} = \frac{\int_L \tilde{y} \rho_L \, dL}{\int_L \rho_L \, dL}, \qquad \bar{z} = \frac{\int_L \tilde{z} \rho_L \, dL}{\int_L \rho_L \, dL} \qquad (9\text{–}4)$$

The derivation of these formulas is based upon the moment principle used for finding the center of gravity of the straight wire just described. As in the case of a system of particles, the center of gravity G may lie at a point in space, not located on the body, Fig. 9–5.

When a continuous body assumes the shape of a flat or curved surface having an area A and constant thickness, such as a plate or shell, the center of gravity may be found by dividing the surface into a number of area elements. The differential element shown in Fig. 9–6 has an area

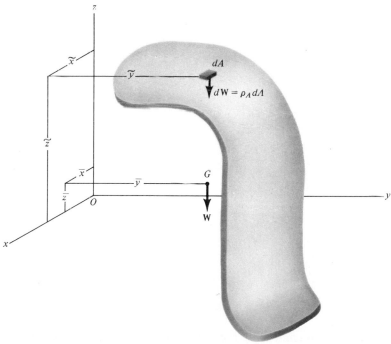

Fig. 9–6

dA and corresponding weight $dW = \rho_A\, dA$, where ρ_A represents a *surface density* or weight per unit area of the material composing the surface. In general, ρ_A may vary across the surface. In a manner similar to using the moment principle just described for linear elements, it may be shown that the center of gravity G for a surface has coordinates

$$\bar{x} = \frac{\displaystyle\int_A \tilde{x}\rho_A\, dA}{\displaystyle\int_A \rho_A\, dA}, \qquad \bar{y} = \frac{\displaystyle\int_A \tilde{y}\rho_A\, dA}{\displaystyle\int_A \rho_A\, dA}, \qquad \bar{z} = \frac{\displaystyle\int_A \tilde{z}\rho_A\, dA}{\displaystyle\int_A \rho_A\, dA} \qquad (9\text{–}5)$$

A body of volume V, having a *density* or weight per unit volume ρ_V, may be divided into volume segments, having volume dV and weight $dW = \rho_V\, dV$, Fig. 9–7. It may then be shown that the center of gravity G for the body has coordinates

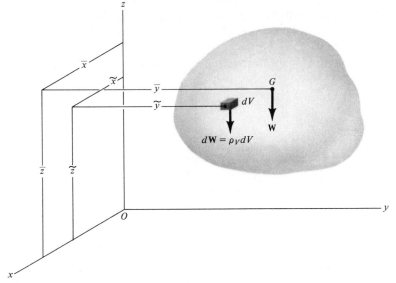

Fig. 9–7

$$\bar{x} = \frac{\displaystyle\int_V \tilde{x}\rho_V\, dV}{\displaystyle\int_V \rho_V\, dV}, \qquad \bar{y} = \frac{\displaystyle\int_V \tilde{y}\rho_V\, dV}{\displaystyle\int_V \rho_V\, dV}, \qquad \bar{z} = \frac{\displaystyle\int_V \tilde{z}\rho_V\, dV}{\displaystyle\int_V \rho_V\, dV} \qquad (9\text{–}6)$$

If the material composing the body is *homogeneous,* the density ρ will be *constant* throughout, and therefore, this term will factor out of the integrals and hence *cancel* from both the numerator and denominator in Eqs. 9–4, 9–5, and 9–6. The resulting formulas will then *depend* purely on the *size* and *shape* of the body. As mentioned earlier, when the calculations depend entirely upon the geometrical properties of the solid, the point $(\bar{x}, \bar{y}, \bar{z})$ is called the *centroid* of the body.*

For uniform rods or wires having a *constant linear density* ρ_L,

$$\bar{x} = \frac{\int_L \tilde{x}\, dL}{\int_L dL}, \qquad \bar{y} = \frac{\int_L \tilde{y}\, dL}{\int_L dL}, \qquad \bar{z} = \frac{\int_L \tilde{z}\, dL}{\int_L dL} \qquad (9\text{–}7)$$

For thin homogeneous plates and shells having a uniform thickness and *constant surface density* ρ_A,

$$\bar{x} = \frac{\int_A \tilde{x}\, dA}{\int_A dA}, \qquad \bar{y} = \frac{\int_A \tilde{y}\, dA}{\int_A dA}, \qquad \bar{z} = \frac{\int_A \tilde{z}\, dA}{\int_A dA} \qquad (9\text{–}8)$$

For volume shapes of constant density ρ_V,

$$\bar{x} = \frac{\int_V \tilde{x}\, dV}{\int_V dV}, \qquad \bar{y} = \frac{\int_V \tilde{y}\, dV}{\int_V dV}, \qquad \bar{z} = \frac{\int_V \tilde{z}\, dV}{\int_V dV} \qquad (9\text{–}9)$$

The *centroids* of some shapes may be partially or completely specified by using *symmetry conditions*. In cases where the shape has an axis of symmetry, the centroid of the shape will lie along that axis. For example, the centroid C for the homogeneous wire shown in Fig. 9–8 must lie along the y axis, since for every elemental length dL at a distance $+x$ to the right of the y axis, there is an identical element at a distance $-x$ to the left of the y axis. The total moment for all of the elements about the axis of symmetry will therefore cancel, that is, $\int_L \tilde{x}\, dL = 0$ so that $\bar{x} = 0$. In cases where a shape has two or three axes of symmetry, it follows that the centroid lies at the intersection of these axes. See Fig. 9–9.

---

*Of course, a nonhomogeneous body also has a centroid. In this case, however, the centroid and center of gravity will *not* coincide.

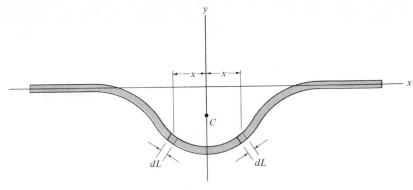

Fig. 9–8

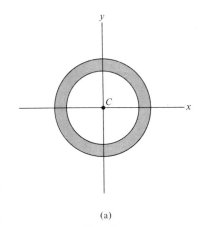

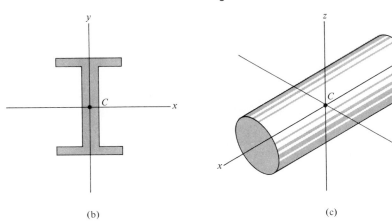

(a)   (b)   (c)

Fig. 9–9

In general, when integrating Eqs. 9–4 through 9–9 it is best to choose a coordinate system which simplifies the equations of the boundary as much as possible. For example, polar coordinates are generally appropriate in solving problems having circular boundaries. The differential element should be chosen so that only one integration is required to cover the entire region. This can be done provided the element is of differential size or thickness in one direction only. Such an element is called a *first-order element*. If it is not possible to use first-order elements, a second-order element (having a differential size in two directions) should be chosen in preference to a third-order element. For second-order elements two integrations are required.

The example problems given at the end of this section illustrate the techniques for computing the center of gravity and centroids for lines, surfaces, and volumes using first-order elements. It is important that you study these examples carefully in order to obtain a clear understanding of how to apply the necessary formulas. In general, the following step-by-step procedure may be applied for computing the center of gravity or centroid of a solid using a first-order element for integration.

1. Specify the coordinate axes, and choose a differential element for the solid. For lines (wires, rods) this element is represented as a differential line segment; for areas (plates, shells) the element is generally a rectangle, having a finite height and differential width; and for volumes (bodies) the element is either a circular disk, having a finite radius and differential thickness, or a shell having a finite length and radius, and differential thickness.
2. Construct the element so that it intersects the surface boundary of the line, area, or volume at *some arbitrary point*. This fixes the dimensions of the element.
3. Express the length, area, or volume of the element in terms of the coordinates used to define the boundary of the solid.
4. Determine the perpendicular distance from the coordinate axes to the *centroid or center of gravity of the element*. For an x, y, z coordinate system, these dimensions are expressed as $\tilde{x}$, $\tilde{y}$, and $\tilde{z}$.
5. Substitute the data computed in steps 3 and 4 into the appropriate equations (Eqs. 9–4 through 9–9) and perform the integration. (For computing the center of gravity of nonhomogeneous solids, using Eqs. 9–4, 9–5, or 9–6, the material density must be expressed in terms of the coordinates of the boundary.) In particular, integration using a first-order element is accomplished when the function in the integrand is expressed in terms of the *same variable as the differential thickness of the element*. The limits of the integral are then defined from the two extreme locations of the element's differential thickness, so that when the elements are summed (or the integration performed), the entire region is covered.

This step-by-step procedure is used in solving the following examples.

Example 9–3

Locate the centroid of the circular wire segment shown in Fig. 9–10.

Solution
Step 1: Polar coordinates will be used to solve this problem since the arc is circular. The differential element is shown in Fig. 9–10.
Step 2: The element intersects the curve at (R, θ).
Step 3: The element length is $dL = R\, d\theta$.
Step 4: The element centroid is located at $\tilde{x} = R \cos \theta$, $\tilde{y} = R \sin \theta$.
Step 5: Using Eqs. 9–7, and integrating with respect to θ, we obtain

$$\bar{x} = \frac{\int_L \tilde{x}\, dL}{\int_L dL} = \frac{\int_0^{\pi/2} (R \cos \theta) R\, d\theta}{\int_0^{\pi/2} R\, d\theta} = \frac{R^2 \int_0^{\pi/2} \cos \theta\, d\theta}{R \int_0^{\pi/2} d\theta} = \frac{2R}{\pi} \quad Ans.$$

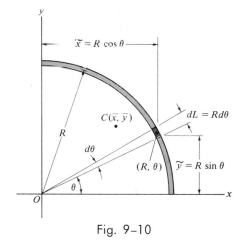

Fig. 9–10

$$\bar{y} = \frac{\int_L \tilde{y}\, dL}{\int_L dL} = \frac{\int_0^{\pi/2} (R \sin \theta) R\, d\theta}{\int_0^{\pi/2} R\, d\theta} = \frac{R^2 \int_0^{\pi/2} \sin \theta\, d\theta}{R \int_0^{\pi/2} d\theta} = \frac{2R}{\pi} \qquad Ans.$$

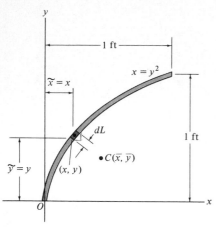

Fig. 9–11

Example 9-4

Locate the centroid of the wire bent into the shape of a parabolic arc, as shown in Fig. 9–11.

Solution
Step 1: The differential element is shown in Fig. 9–11.
Step 2: The element intersects the curve at (x, y).
Step 3: The element length is determined using the Pythagorean Theorem.

$$dL = \sqrt{(dx)^2 + (dy)^2} = \sqrt{\left(\frac{dx}{dy}\right)^2 + 1}\, dy$$

Since $x = y^2$, then $dx/dy = 2y$. Therefore

$$dL = \sqrt{(2y)^2 + 1}\, dy$$

Step 4: The centroid of the element is located at $\tilde{x} = x$, $\tilde{y} = y$.

Step 5: Using Eqs. 9–7 and integrating with respect to y, we obtain

$$\bar{x} = \frac{\int_L \tilde{x}\, dL}{\int_L dL} = \frac{\int_0^1 x\sqrt{4y^2 + 1}\, dy}{\int_0^1 \sqrt{4y^2 + 1}\, dy} = \frac{\int_0^1 y^2 \sqrt{4y^2 + 1}\, dy}{\int_0^1 \sqrt{4y^2 + 1}\, dy}$$

$$= \frac{0.739}{1.412} = 0.412 \text{ ft} \qquad Ans.$$

$$\bar{y} = \frac{\int_L \tilde{y}\, dL}{\int_L dL} = \frac{\int_0^1 y\sqrt{4y^2 + 1}\, dy}{\int_0^1 \sqrt{4y^2 + 1}\, dy} = \frac{0.848}{1.470} = 0.577 \text{ ft} \qquad Ans.$$

Example 9-5

Locate the centroid of the shaded area shown in Fig. 9–12a.

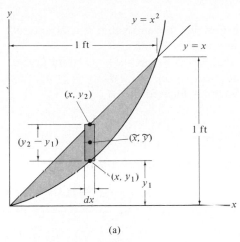

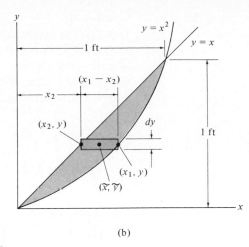

(a)   (b)

Fig. 9–12

Solution I

Step 1: The differential element is shown in Fig. 9–12a.

Step 2: The element intersects the curves at points (x, y_1) and (x, y_2).

Step 3: The element area is $dA = (y_2 - y_1)\, dx$.

Step 4: The centroid of the element is located at $\tilde{x} = x$,

$$\tilde{y} = y_1 + \left(\frac{y_2 - y_1}{2}\right) = \frac{y_1 + y_2}{2}.$$

Step 5: Using Eqs. 9–8, and integrating with respect to x, we obtain

$$\bar{x} = \frac{\int_A \tilde{x}\, dA}{\int_A dA} = \frac{\int_0^1 x(y_2 - y_1)\, dx}{\int_0^1 (y_2 - y_1)\, dx} = \frac{\int_0^1 x(x - x^2)\, dx}{\int_0^1 (x - x^2)\, dx}$$

$$= \frac{\int_0^1 (x^2 - x^3)\, dx}{\int_0^1 (x - x^2)\, dx} = \frac{1/12}{1/6} = 0.5 \text{ ft} \qquad\qquad Ans.$$

$$\bar{y} = \frac{\int_A \tilde{y}\, dA}{\int_A dA} = \frac{\int_0^1 \left(\frac{y_1 + y_2}{2}\right)(y_2 - y_1)\, dx}{\int_0^1 (y_2 - y_1)\, dx} = \frac{\int_0^1 \left(\frac{x^2 + x}{2}\right)(x - x^2)\, dx}{\int_0^1 (x - x^2)\, dx}$$

$$= \frac{\frac{1}{2}\int_0^1 (x^2 - x^4)\, dx}{\int_0^1 (x - x^2)\, dx} = \frac{1/15}{1/6} = 0.4 \text{ ft} \qquad\qquad Ans.$$

Solution II

Step 1: The rectangular element may be chosen so that it is orientated horizontally. This element is shown in Fig. 9–12*b*.

Step 2: The element intersects the curves at points (x_2, y) and (x_1, y).

Step 3: The area of the element is $dA = (x_1 - x_2)\, dy$.

Step 4: The centroid of the element is located at

$$\tilde{x} = x_2 + \left(\frac{x_1 - x_2}{2}\right) = \frac{x_1 + x_2}{2}, \quad \tilde{y} = y.$$

Step 5: Using Eqs. 9–8, and integrating with respect to y, we obtain

$$\bar{x} = \frac{\int_A \tilde{x}\, dA}{\int_A dA} = \frac{\int_0^1 \left(\frac{x_1 + x_2}{2}\right)(x_1 - x_2)\, dy}{\int_0^1 (x_1 - x_2)\, dy} = \frac{\int_0^1 \left(\frac{\sqrt{y} + y}{2}\right)(\sqrt{y} - y)\, dy}{\int_0^1 (\sqrt{y} - y)\, dy}$$

$$= \frac{\frac{1}{2}\int_0^1 (y - y^2)\, dy}{\int_0^1 (\sqrt{y} - y)\, dy} = \frac{1/12}{1/6} = 0.5 \text{ ft} \qquad\qquad Ans.$$

$$\bar{y} = \frac{\int_A \tilde{y}\, dA}{\int_A dA} = \frac{\int_0^1 y(x_1 - x_2)\, dy}{\int_0^1 (x_1 - x_2)\, dy} = \frac{\int_0^1 y(\sqrt{y} - y)\, dy}{\int_0^1 (\sqrt{y} - y)\, dy}$$

$$= \frac{\int_0^1 (y^{3/2} - y^2)\, dy}{\int_0^1 (\sqrt{y} - y)\, dy} = \frac{1/15}{1/6} = 0.4 \text{ ft} \qquad\qquad Ans.$$

Example 9–6

Determine the distance $\bar{y}$ to the centroid of the area of the triangle shown in Fig. 9–13.

Solution

Step 1: Consider a rectangular element having thickness dy and *variable length* x', Fig. 9–13. By similar triangles, $b/h = x'/(h - y)$ or $x' = \frac{b}{h}(h - y)$.

Step 2: The element intersects the sides of the triangle at a height y above the x axis.

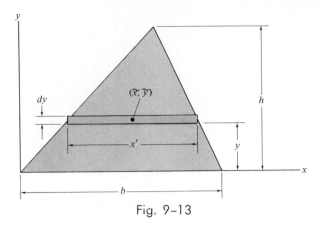

Fig. 9–13

Step 3: The area of the element is $dA = x' \, dy = \dfrac{b}{h}(h - y) \, dy.$

Step 4: The centroid of the element is located a distance $\tilde{y} = y$ from the x axis.

Step 5: Using the second of Eqs. 9–8, and integrating with respect to y, we obtain

$$\bar{y} = \frac{\displaystyle\int_A \tilde{y} \, dA}{\displaystyle\int_A dA} = \frac{\displaystyle\int_0^h y \frac{b}{h}(h - y) \, dy}{\displaystyle\int_0^h \frac{b}{h}(h - y) \, dy}$$

$$= \frac{\dfrac{b}{h} \displaystyle\int_0^h (hy - y^2) \, dy}{\dfrac{b}{h} \displaystyle\int_0^h (h - y) \, dy} = \frac{h}{3} \qquad\qquad Ans.$$

Example 9–7

Locate the centroid for the area of a quarter circle shown in Fig. 9–14a.

Solution I

Step 1: Using polar coordinates, we choose the element in the shape of a triangle, Fig. 9–14a. (Actually the shape is a circular sector; however, neglecting higher-order differentials, the element becomes triangular.)

Step 2: The element intersects the curve at point (R, θ).

Step 3: The area of the element is $dA = \frac{1}{2}(R)(R \, d\theta) = \dfrac{R^2}{2} \, d\theta.$

Step 4: Using the results in Example 9–6, the centroid of the (triangular) element is located at $\tilde{x} = \frac{2}{3}R \cos\theta,$ $\tilde{y} = \frac{2}{3}R \sin\theta.$

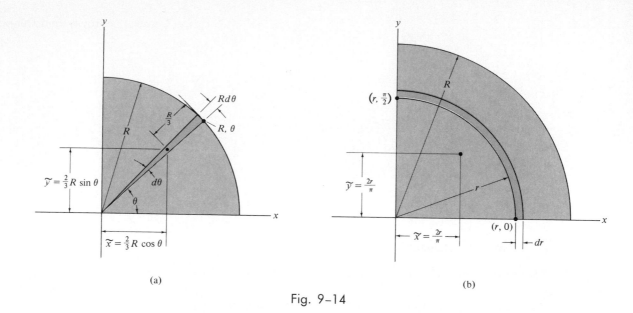

(a)

(b)

Fig. 9–14

Step 5: Using Eqs. 9–8, and integrating with respect to θ, we obtain

$$\bar{x} = \frac{\displaystyle\int_A \tilde{x}\, dA}{\displaystyle\int_A dA} = \frac{\displaystyle\int_0^{\pi/2} \left(\frac{2}{3}R\cos\theta\right)\frac{R^2}{2}\, d\theta}{\displaystyle\int_0^{\pi/2} \frac{R^2}{2}\, d\theta}$$

$$= \frac{\dfrac{R^3}{3}\displaystyle\int_0^{\pi/2}\cos\theta\, d\theta}{\dfrac{R^2}{2}\displaystyle\int_0^{\pi/2} d\theta} = \frac{4}{3}\frac{R}{\pi} \qquad \text{Ans.}$$

$$\bar{y} = \frac{\displaystyle\int_A \tilde{y}\, dA}{\displaystyle\int_A dA} = \frac{\displaystyle\int_0^{\pi/2} \left(\frac{2}{3}R\sin\theta\right)\frac{R^2}{2}\, d\theta}{\displaystyle\int_0^{\pi/2} \frac{R^2}{2}\, d\theta}$$

$$= \frac{\dfrac{R^3}{3}\displaystyle\int_0^{\pi/2}\sin\theta\, d\theta}{\dfrac{R^2}{2}\displaystyle\int_0^{\pi/2} d\theta} = \frac{4}{3}\frac{R}{\pi} \qquad \text{Ans.}$$

Solution II
Step 1: The differential element may be chosen in the form of a circular arc having a thickness dr as shown in Fig. 9–14b.

Step 2:   The element intersects the axes at points $(r, 0)$ and $\left(r, \dfrac{\pi}{2}\right)$.

Step 3:   The area of the element is $dA = \dfrac{2\pi r}{4}\, dr$.

Step 4:   Since the centroid of a 90° circular arc was determined in Example 9–3, then for the element $\tilde{x} = \dfrac{2r}{\pi}, \tilde{y} = \dfrac{2r}{\pi}$.

Step 5:   Using Eqs. 9–8, and integrating with respect to r, we obtain

$$\bar{x} = \frac{\int_A \tilde{x}\, dA}{\int_A dA} = \frac{\int_0^R \dfrac{2r}{\pi}\left(\dfrac{2\pi r}{4}\right) dr}{\int_0^R \dfrac{2\pi r}{4}\, dr} = \frac{\int_0^R r^2\, dr}{\dfrac{\pi}{2}\int_0^R r\, dr} = \frac{4}{3}\frac{R}{\pi} \qquad Ans.$$

$$\bar{y} = \frac{\int_A \tilde{y}\, dA}{\int_A dA} = \frac{\int_0^R \dfrac{2r}{\pi}\left(\dfrac{2\pi r}{4}\right) dr}{\int_0^R \dfrac{2\pi r}{4}\, dr} = \frac{\int_0^R r^2\, dr}{\dfrac{\pi}{2}\int_0^R r\, dr} = \frac{4}{3}\frac{R}{\pi} \qquad Ans.$$

Example 9–8

Locate the centroid for the paraboloid of revolution, which is generated by revolving the shaded area shown in Fig. 9–15a about the y axis.

Solution I

Since the volume is *symmetric* with respect to the y axis,

$$\bar{x} = \bar{z} = 0 \qquad Ans.$$

Step 1:   To simplify the integration process, a first-order element having the shape of a *thin disk* is chosen. As shown in Fig. 9–15a, this element has a radius of $r = z$ and a thickness of dy.

Step 2:   The element intersects the generating curve at point $(0, y, z)$.

Step 3:   The volume of the element is $dV = (\pi z^2)\, dy$.

Step 4:   The centroid of the element is located at $\tilde{y} = y$.

Step 5:   Using the second of Eqs. 9–9, and integrating with respect to y, we have

$$\bar{y} = \frac{\int_V \tilde{y}\, dV}{\int_V dV} = \frac{\int_0^1 y(\pi z^2)\, dy}{\int_0^1 (\pi z^2)\, dy} = \frac{\int_0^1 \pi y^2\, dy}{\int_0^1 \pi y\, dy} = 0.667 \text{ ft} \qquad Ans.$$

Solution II

Step 1: As shown in Fig. 9–15b, the volume element can be chosen in the form of a *thin cylindrical shell*, where the shell radius is $r = z$ and the thickness is dz.

Step 2: The element intersects the generating curve at point $(0, y, z)$.

Step 3: The volume of the element is $dV = 2\pi r\, dA = 2\pi z(1 - y)\, dz$.

Step 4: The centroid of the element is located at

$$\tilde{y} = y + \frac{1 - y}{2} = \frac{1 + y}{2}$$

Step 5: Using the second of Eqs. 9–9, and integrating with respect to z, we obtain

$$\bar{y} = \frac{\int_V \tilde{y}\, dV}{\int_V dV} = \frac{\int_0^1 \left(\frac{1 + y}{2}\right) 2\pi z(1 - y)\, dz}{\int_0^1 2\pi z(1 - y)\, dz}$$

$$= \frac{\pi \int_0^1 z(1 - z^4)\, dz}{2\pi \int_0^1 z(1 - z^2)\, dz} = 0.667 \text{ ft} \qquad\qquad Ans.$$

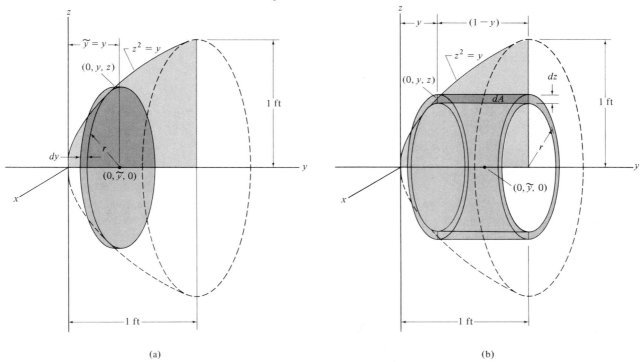

(a)   (b)

Fig. 9–15

Example 9-9   Center of Gravity and Centroids   325

Locate the center of gravity of the right circular cylinder shown in Fig. 9-16a if the density of the cylinder varies directly with its distance from the base, such that $\rho_V = 2z$ lb/ft³.

Solution

For reasons of material symmetry

$$\bar{x} = \bar{y} = 0 \qquad\qquad \textit{Ans.}$$

Step 1: A disk element is chosen for integration, Fig. 9-16a, since the *density of this entire element is constant* for a given value of z. This element has a constant radius of $\frac{1}{2}$ ft and a thickness of dz.

Step 2: The element is located along the z axis at point $(0, 0, z)$.

Step 3: The volume of the element is $dV = \pi\left(\dfrac{1}{2}\right)^2 dz$.

Step 4. The centroid of the element is located at $\tilde{z} = z$.

Step 5: Using the third of Eqs. 9-6, and integrating with respect to z, noting that $\rho_V = 2z$, we obtain

$$\bar{z} = \frac{\displaystyle\int_V \rho_V \tilde{z}\, dV}{\displaystyle\int_V \rho_V\, dV} = \frac{\displaystyle\int_0^1 (2z)(z)\pi\left(\frac{1}{2}\right)^2 dz}{\displaystyle\int_0^1 (2z)\pi\left(\frac{1}{2}\right)^2 dz}$$

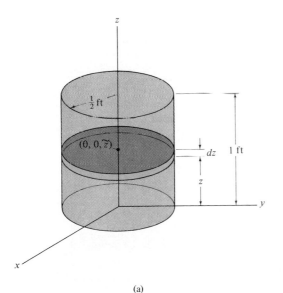

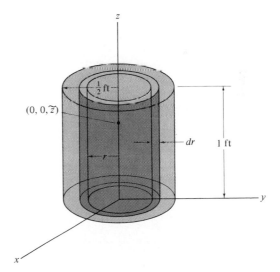

(a)   (b)

Fig. 9-16

$$\bar{z} = \frac{\dfrac{\pi}{2}\displaystyle\int_0^1 z^2\,dz}{\dfrac{\pi}{2}\displaystyle\int_0^1 z\,dz} = 0.667 \text{ ft} \qquad\qquad Ans.$$

If a shell element were chosen for integration, as shown in Fig. 9–16b, the density of the material composing the shell would *vary* along the height of the shell; hence the location of $\bar{z}$ for the element is not easily determined. It would, therefore, be necessary to further subdivide the shell into second- or third-order differential elements to locate $\tilde{z}$. Doing this simply complicates the integration process, since use of second- and third-order differential elements requires two and three integrations, respectively, to obtain the location of the center of gravity.

Problems

9–7. Locate the centroid of the thin wire bent in the form of the parabola.

9–8. Locate the centroid of the shaded area.

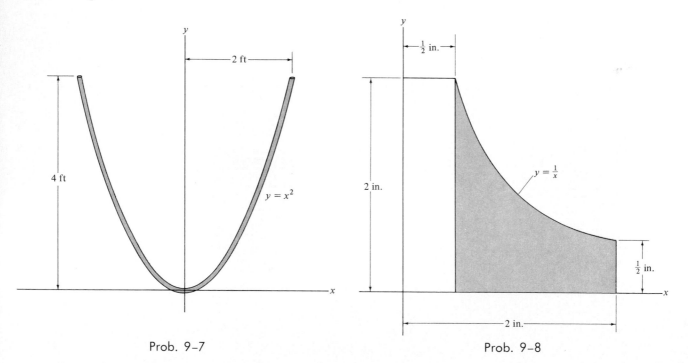

Prob. 9–7   Prob. 9–8

9-9. Locate the centroid of the wire bent into the shape of the circular arc.

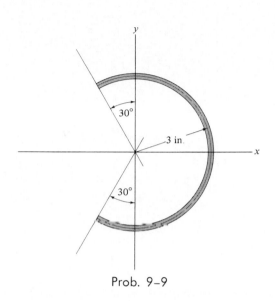

Prob. 9–9

9-10. Locate the centroid of the shaded area.

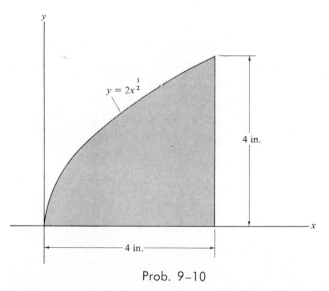

Prob. 9–10

9-11. Locate the centroid of the area under the curve $y = 3 \sin 2x$ from $x = 0$ to $x = \pi/2$.

9-12. Locate the centroid of the shaded area.

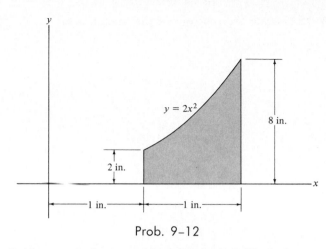

Prob. 9–12

9-13. Locate the centroid of the shaded elliptical sector.

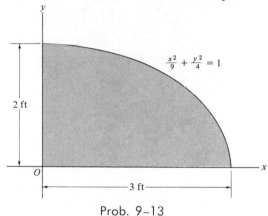

Prob. 9–13

9-14. Locate the centroid of the wire bent into the shape shown.

Prob. 9–14

9–15. Locate the centroid of the shaded area.

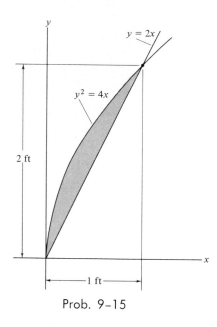

$y = 2x$

$y^2 = 4x$

2 ft

1 ft

Prob. 9–15

9–16. Locate the centroid of the shaded area.

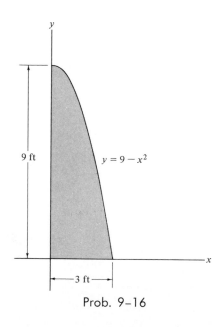

9 ft

$y = 9 - x^2$

3 ft

Prob. 9–16

9–17. Locate the centroid of the thin cylindrical shell.

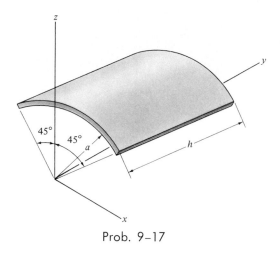

45°

45°

a

h

Prob. 9–17

9–18. Locate the centroid of the "bell-shaped" volume formed by revolving the shaded area shown about the y axis.

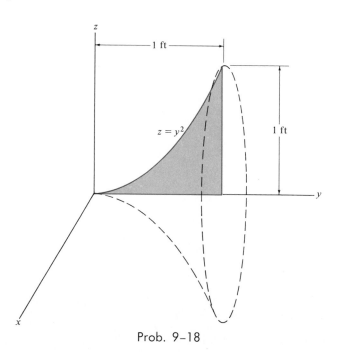

1 ft

1 ft

$z = y^2$

Prob. 9–18

9-19. Locate the centroid of the volume generated by revolving the shaded area shown about the z axis.

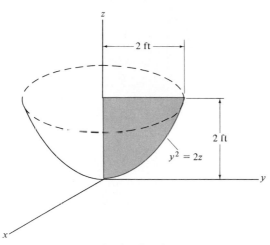

Prob. 9-19

9-20. Locate the center of gravity of the hemisphere. The density of the material varies linearly from zero at the origin O to ρ_0 at the surface. (*Hint:* Establish a differential element using the results of Prob. 9-23.)

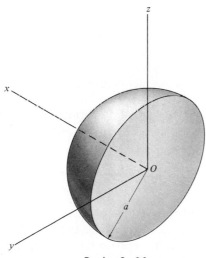

Prob. 9-20

9-21. Locate the centroid of the cone formed by rotating the shaded area about the y axis.

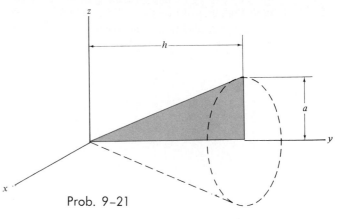

Prob. 9-21

9-22. Locate the centroid of the volume generated by revolving the shaded area shown about the y axis.

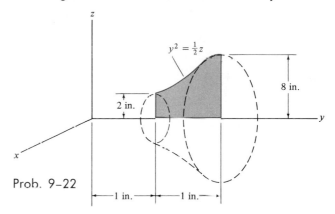

Prob. 9-22

9-23. Show that the centroid of the thin hemispherical shell is located at $(a/2, 0, 0)$.

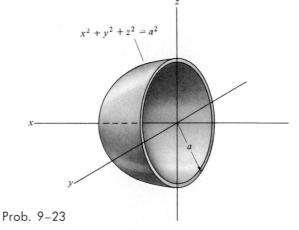

Prob. 9-23

9-24. Locate the centroid of the solid formed by rotating the shaded area about the *aa* axis.

9-25. Locate the centroid for the half cone.

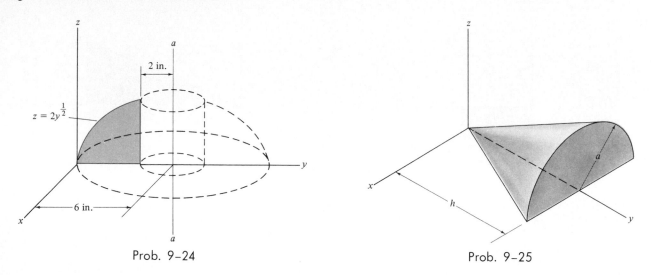

Prob. 9-24

Prob. 9-25

9-4. Composite Bodies

In many cases, a body or figure can be sectioned or divided into several parts having simpler shapes. Provided the weights and location of the center of gravity of each of these composite parts are known, one can eliminate the need for using integration in determining the center of gravity for the entire body. For example, consider a body having several parts which weigh W_1, W_2, . . ., and whose center of gravity coordinates $\tilde{x}$ are $\tilde{x}_1$, $\tilde{x}_2$, ... The principle of moments applied to the body yields $\bar{x}(W_1 + W_2 + . . .) = \tilde{x}_1 W_1 + \tilde{x}_2 W_2 + . . .$, where $\bar{x}$ is the center of gravity of the entire body. Thus, the necessary formulas for finding the center of gravity for a three-dimensional body become

$$\bar{x} = \frac{\Sigma \tilde{x} W}{\Sigma W}, \qquad \bar{y} = \frac{\Sigma \tilde{y} W}{\Sigma W}, \qquad \bar{z} = \frac{\Sigma \tilde{z} W}{\Sigma W} \qquad (9\text{--}10)$$

where ΣW represents the sum of the weights of each of the component parts of the body, or simply the *total weight* of the entire body. If a *hole*, or geometric region having no material, represents one of the component parts, the "weight" of the hole is considered a *negative* quantity. See Example 9–11. $\tilde{x}$, $\tilde{y}$, and $\tilde{z}$ in Eq. 9–10 represent the *algebraic distances* from the center of gravity of each component part to the origin of the coordinates.

When the entire body has a *constant density,* the center of gravity coincides with the geometric center or centroid of the body. The centroid for composite lines, areas, and volumes can be found using relations analogous to Eq. 9–10; however, the W's are replaced by L's, A's, and V's, respectively. Centroids for common shapes of lines, areas, shells, and volumes are given in Appendix B.

Computation errors for composite shapes can be kept to a minimum by labeling each component part on a sketch of the body and arranging the calculations in a tabular form. This procedure is used in the following two examples.

Example 9–10

Locate the centroid of the composite wire shown in Fig. 9–17a.

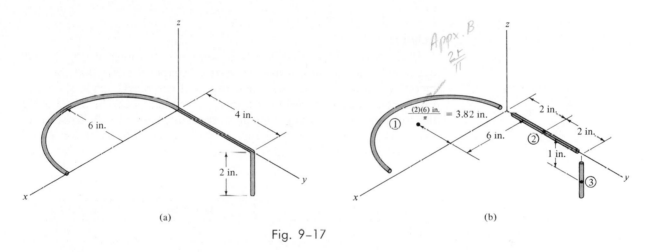

Fig. 9–17

Solution

The wire is divided into three segments, as shown in Fig. 9–17b. The centroid of segment 1 is determined either by integration or using the formula in Appendix B. The calculations are listed in the following table:

Segment	L (in.)	$\tilde{x}$ (in.)	$\tilde{y}$ (in.)	$\tilde{z}$ (in.)	$\tilde{x}L$ (in.²)	$\tilde{y}L$ (in.²)	$\tilde{z}L$ (in.²)
1	$\pi(6) = 18.85$	6	-3.82	0	113.1	-72.0	0
2	4	0	2	0	0	8	0
3	2	0	0	-1	0	8	-2
	$\Sigma L = 24.85$				$\Sigma \tilde{x}L = 113.1$	$\Sigma \tilde{y}L = -56.0$	$\Sigma \tilde{z}L = -2.0$

Thus,

$$\bar{x} = \frac{\Sigma \tilde{x} L}{\Sigma L} = \frac{113.1}{24.85} = 4.55 \text{ in.} \qquad Ans.$$

$$\bar{y} = \frac{\Sigma \tilde{y} L}{\Sigma L} = \frac{-56.0}{24.85} = -2.26 \text{ in.} \qquad Ans.$$

$$\bar{z} = \frac{\Sigma \tilde{z} L}{\Sigma L} = \frac{-2.0}{24.85} = -0.08 \text{ in.} \qquad Ans.$$

Example 9–11

Locate the center of gravity of the composite shape shown in Fig. 9–18a. The surface density of the vertical and horizontal plates are 6 lb/ft² and 4 lb/ft², respectively. The 2-ft-diameter cylinder has a density of 160 lb/ft³.

Solution

The assembly is divided into four segments, as shown in Fig. 9–18b. Segment 4 must be taken as a "negative" shape in order that the four pieces, when added together, yield the total composite shape shown in Fig. 9–18a. The location of the centroid for segment 4 can be found using the formula for a semi-circular area given in Appendix B. Because of *symmetry* of the composite shape, $\bar{y} = 0$. The computations for $\bar{x}$ and $\bar{z}$ are given in the following table:

Segment	W (lb)	$\tilde{x}$ (ft)	$\tilde{z}$ (ft)	$\tilde{x}W$ (ft-lb)	$\tilde{z}W$ (ft-lb)
1	4(4)4 = 64.0	2	0	128.0	0
2	$\pi(1)^2(2)160 = 1,005.3$	2	1	2,010.6	1,005.3
3	5(4)6 = 120.0	0	2.5	0	300.0
4	$-\frac{1}{2}\pi(2)^2 6 = -37.7$	0	5 − 0.85 = 4.15	0	−156.5
	$\Sigma W = 1,151.6$			$\Sigma \tilde{x}W = 2,138.6$	$\Sigma \tilde{z}W = 1,148.8$

measured from origin

Applying Eqs. 9–10 yields

$$\bar{x} = \frac{\Sigma \tilde{x} W}{\Sigma W} = \frac{2,138.6}{1,151.6} = 1.857 \text{ ft} \qquad Ans.$$

$$\bar{y} = 0 \qquad Ans.$$

$$\bar{z} = \frac{\Sigma \tilde{z} W}{\Sigma W} = \frac{1,148.8}{1,151.6} = 0.998 \text{ ft} \qquad Ans.$$

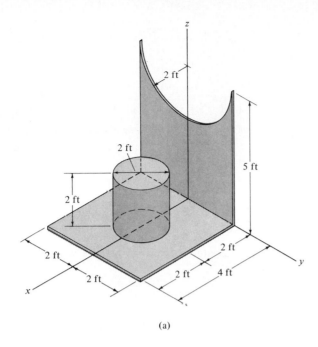

(a)

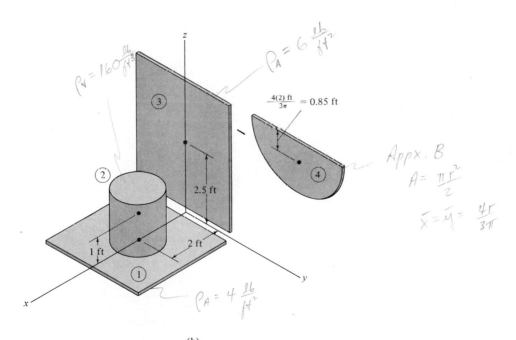

(b)

Fig. 9–18

Problems

9-26. Locate the centroid of the wire.

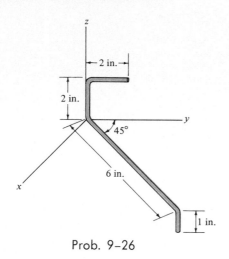

Prob. 9-26

9-27. Locate the center of gravity of the homogeneous rod.

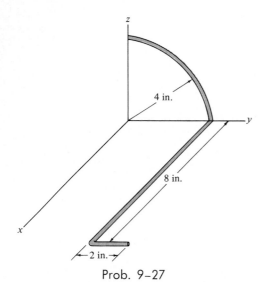

Prob. 9-27

9-28. Determine the length of the wire segment AB such that the centroid for the entire composite is located at point C.

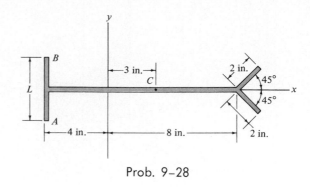

Prob. 9-28

9-29. Locate the centroid of the wire.

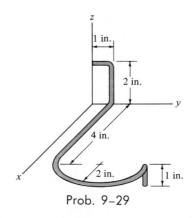

Prob. 9-29

9-30. Locate the centroid of the wire.

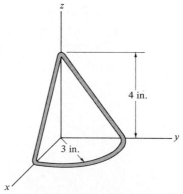

Prob. 9-30

9–31. Locate the centroid for the cross-sectional area of the beam.

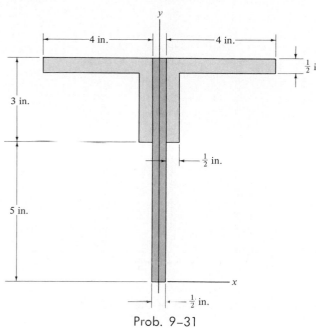

Prob. 9–31

9–32. Locate the centroid of the shaded area.

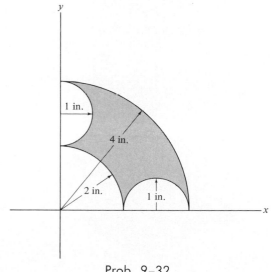

Prob. 9–32

9–33. Locate the centroid of the shaded area.

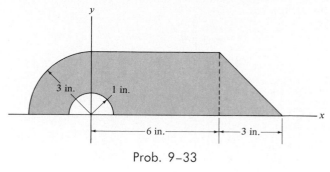

Prob. 9–33

9–34. Locate the centroid of the shaded area.

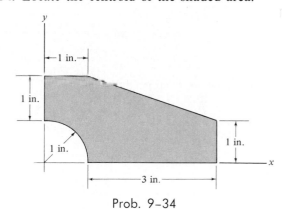

Prob. 9–34

9–35. Locate the centroid of the shaded area.

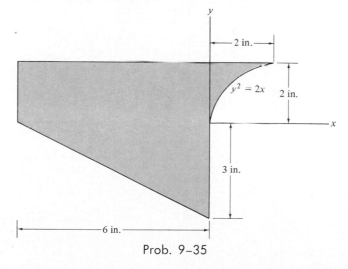

Prob. 9–35

9-36. Locate the centroid for the cross-sectional area of the beam.

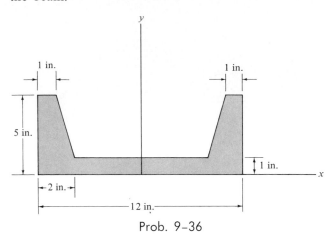

Prob. 9–36

9-37. Locate the centroid of the solid.

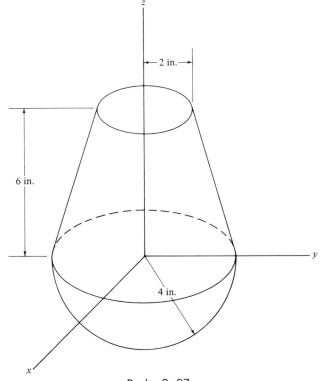

Prob. 9–37

9-38. Locate the centroid for the area of the built-up structural section.

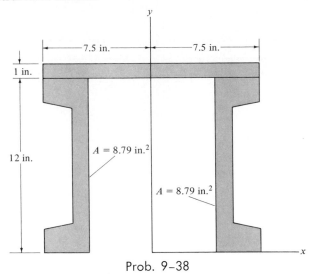

Prob. 9–38

9-39. Locate the centroid of the solid.

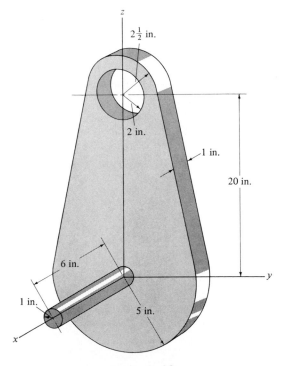

Prob. 9–39

9-40. Locate the centroid of the thin plate.

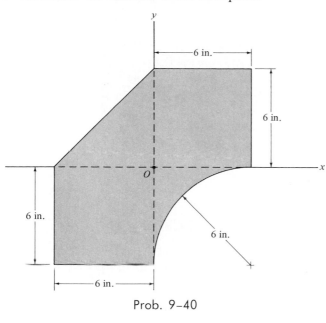

Prob. 9–40

9-41. Locate the center of gravity of the composite part. The density of materials A and B are 150 lb/ft³ and 400 lb/ft³, respectively.

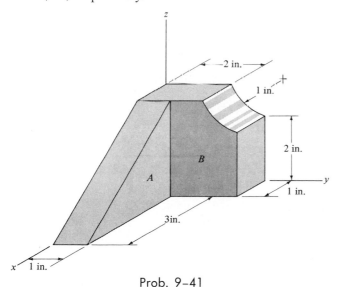

Prob. 9–41

9-42. The frustum has a hole drilled through its center. Locate the centroid for this piece.

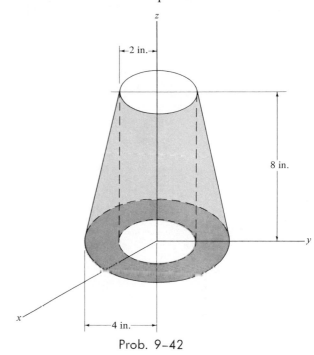

Prob. 9–42

9-43. Determine the center of gravity of the airplane. The weights of the various items are shown in the table.

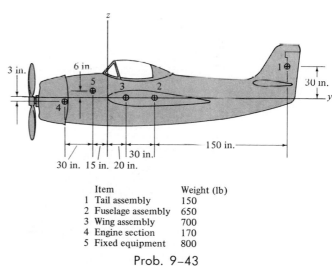

Item	Weight (lb)
1 Tail assembly	150
2 Fuselage assembly	650
3 Wing assembly	700
4 Engine section	170
5 Fixed equipment	800

Prob. 9–43

9–44. Locate the center of gravity of the assembly. The density for the materials is as follows: rod R, $\rho_L = 0.6$ lb/ft; thin plate B, $\rho_A = 5$ lb/ft²; and block C, $\rho_V = 450$ lb/ft³.

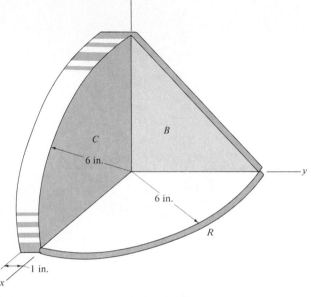

Prob. 9–44

9–45. By approximation, locate the centroid of the plate.

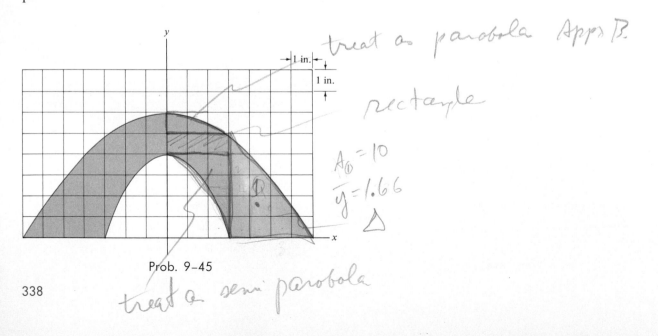

Prob. 9–45

9–46. Locate the centroid of the sheet-metal bracket.

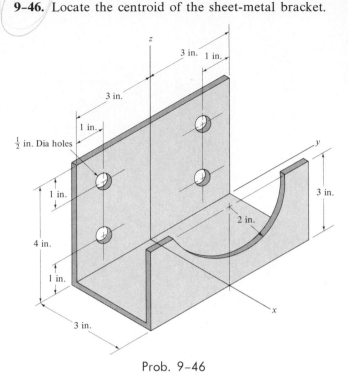

Prob. 9–46

treat as parabola Appx B.

rectangle

$A_① = 10$

$\bar{y} = 1.66$

treat a semi parabola

The *theorems of Pappus and Guldinus,* which were first developed by Pappus of Alexandria during the third century A.D. and somewhat later by the Swiss mathematician Paul Guldin or Guldinus (1577–1643), are used to find the surface area or volume of any solid of revolution.

A *surface area of revolution* is generated by revolving a *curve* about a fixed axis. For example, the surface area of a cone is generated by rotating the line segment *AB*, shown in Fig. 9–19, about the *x* axis. In

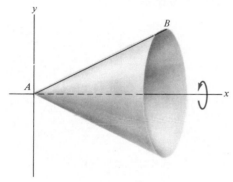

Fig. 9–19

a similar manner, a *volume of revolution* is generated by revolving an *area* about a fixed axis. Thus, the volume of a cone is formed by rotating the triangular area *ABC*, shown in Fig. 9–20, about the *x* axis.

The statements and proofs of the theorems of Pappus and Guldinus follow. The proofs require that the generating curves and areas do *not* cross the axis about which they are generated, although they may touch it.

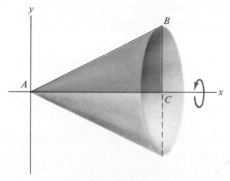

Fig. 9–20

Theorem I. *The area of a surface of revolution equals the product of the length of the generating curve and the distance traveled by the centroid of the curve in generating the surface area.*

Proof. When a differential length dL of a curve is revolved about the y axis, as shown in Fig. 9–21, it generates a ring having a surface area $dA = 2\pi x \, dL$. The entire surface area generated by revolving L about the y axis is therefore $A = 2\pi \int_L x \, dL$. Since $\int_L x \, dL = \bar{x}L$, where $\bar{x}$ locates the centroid C of the generating curve L, the area becomes $A = 2\pi\bar{x}L$. If the surface area is formed by revolving the line L through an angle θ (measured in radians) which is less than 2π, then $A = \theta\bar{x}L$.

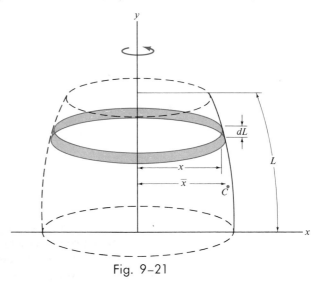

Fig. 9–21

Theorem II. *The volume of a surface of revolution equals the product of the generating area and the distance traveled by the centroid of the area in generating the volume.*

Proof. When the differential area dA, shown in Fig. 9–22, is revolved about the y axis, it generates a ring having volume $dV = 2\pi x \, dA$. The entire volume generated by revolving A about the y axis is therefore $V = 2\pi \int_A x \, dA$. Since $\int_A x \, dA = \bar{x}A$, where $\bar{x}$ locates the centroid C of the generating area A, the volume becomes $V = 2\pi\bar{x} A$. If the volume is formed by revolving the area A through an angle θ (measured in radians), which is less than 2π, then $V = \theta\bar{x} A$.

In these proofs, it should be noted that the generating curve or area is restricted from crossing the axis of revolution; otherwise two sections on either side of the axis would generate areas or volumes having opposite signs and hence would cancel each other.

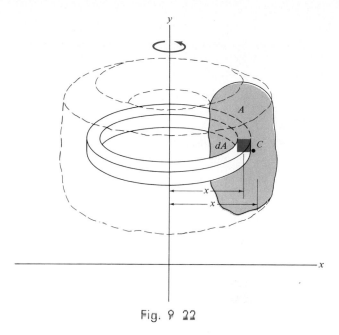

Fig. 9 22

Using Theorem I of Pappus-Guldinus, prove that the surface area of a sphere is $4\pi R^2$.

Solution

From Theorem I of Pappus-Guldinus, we know that the surface area generated by a curve equals the product of the curve length and the distance "traveled" by the centroid of the curve. A sphere is generated by rotating the semicircular arc shown in Fig. 9-23 about the x axis. Using

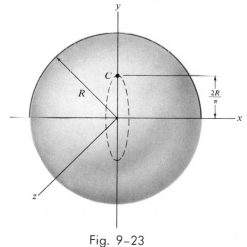

Fig. 9-23

Appendix B, it is seen that the centroid of this arc is located at a distance of $2R/\pi$ from the axis of rotation. The centroid moves through a distance of $2\pi(2R/\pi) = 4R$ in generating the sphere shown in Fig. 9–23. Hence, the surface area of the sphere becomes

$$A = 4R(\pi R) = 4\pi R^2 \qquad \textit{Ans.}$$

Example 9–13

Determine the weight of concrete needed to construct the arched beam shown in Fig. 9–24. The density of concrete is $\rho_c = 150$ lb/ft^3.

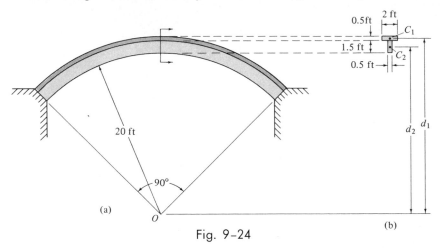

Fig. 9–24

Solution

The weight of the arch may be determined by using the density ρ_c provided we know the volume of concrete. The cross-sectional area of the beam is a "T-section" composed of two rectangles having centroids at points C_1 and C_2, as shown in Fig. 9–24b. Using Theorem II of Pappus-Guldinus, we know that the volume generated by each of these areas is equal to the product of the given cross-sectional area and the distance traveled by its centroid. In generating the arch, the centroid passes through an angle of $\theta = \pi(90°/180°) = 1.57$ radians. Point C_1 acts at a distance of $d_1 = 20 + (1.5 + 0.25) = 21.75$ ft from the center of rotation, point O. C_2 acts at $d_2 = 20 + 0.75 = 20.75$ ft from O. The total volume is thus

$$V_T = \Sigma \theta \bar{x} A$$
$$= (1.57 \text{ rad})(21.75 \text{ ft})(2 \text{ ft})(0.5 \text{ ft}) + (1.57 \text{ rad})(20.75 \text{ ft})(1.5 \text{ ft})(0.5 \text{ ft})$$
$$= 58.6 \text{ ft}^3$$

The required weight of concrete is the product of the density and the volume.

$$W = \rho_c(V_T) = (150 \text{ lb/ft}^3)(58.6 \text{ ft}^3) = 8{,}790 \text{ lb} \qquad \textit{Ans.}$$

Problems

9-47. Using the theorem of Pappus-Guldinus, determine the surface area of a cone, using an inclined line segment to generate the cone. See Fig. 9–19.

9-48. Determine the surface area and volume of the torus.

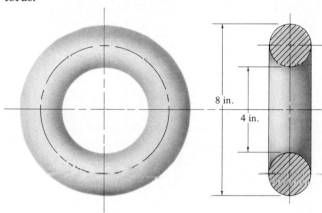

Prob. 9–48

9-50. Determine the weight of the wedge which is generated by rotating a right triangle of base 6 in. and height 3 in. through an angle of 30°. The density of the material is $\rho_V = 0.22$ lb/in^3.

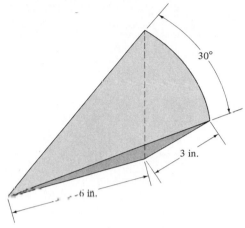

Prob. 9–50

9-49. A steel wheel has a sectional view shown. Determine the total weight of the wheel if $\rho_V = 0.25$ lb/in^3.

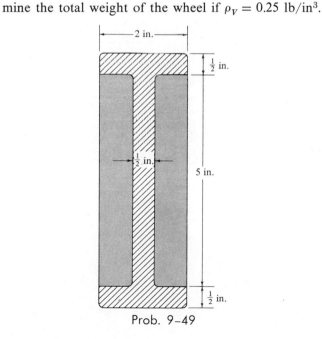

Prob. 9–49

9-51. A V-belt has an inner radius of 6 in., and a cross-sectional area as shown. Determine the volume of material used in making the V-belt.

Prob. 9–51

343

9–52. Using integration, determine the area and the centroidal distance $\bar{y}$ of the shaded area. Then, using Theorem II of Pappus-Guldinus, determine the volume of a paraboloid formed by revolving the area about the x axis.

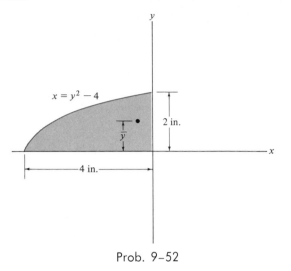

Prob. 9–52

9–53. Compute both the area A and the centroidal distance $\bar{x}$ for the shaded region. Using Theorem II of Pappus-Guldinus, compute the volume of the solid generated by revolving the shaded area about the aa axis.

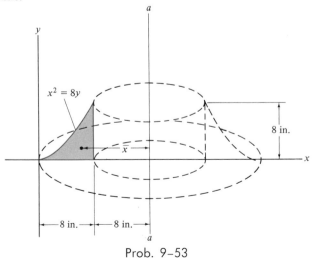

Prob. 9–53

9–54. Determine both the surface area and the volume of material for the casting shown.

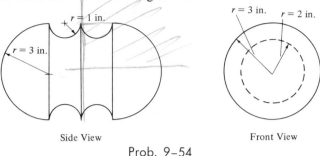

Side View   Front View

Prob. 9–54

9–55. The surface of the water tank is to be painted with two coats of noncorrosive paint. If a gallon of paint covers 300 ft², determine by approximate means (a) the volume of water which may be contained in the tank, and (b) the number of gallons of paint required to paint the surface of the tank.

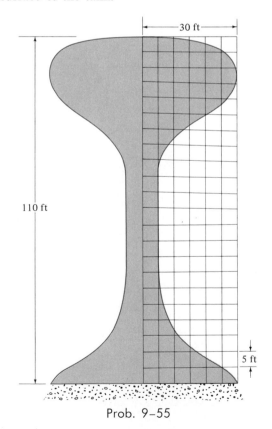

Prob. 9–55

9-56. A circular sea wall is made of concrete. Determine the total weight of the wall if the concrete has a density of 150 lb/ft³.

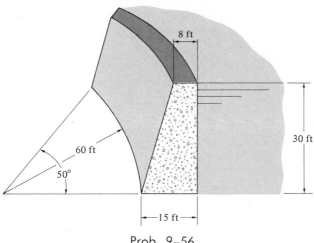

Prob. 9–56

*9–6. Pressure Loadings on Submerged Surfaces

An important application of force distributed over a surface area is that caused by the action of pressure acting on a surface submerged in a fluid. Provided the fluid is at rest, the pressure force will always act *normal* to the submerged surface.

According to Pascal's law, the pressure p, measured as a force per unit area and acting at any point in a fluid is the same in all directions. If ρ represents the density (weight/volume) of a fluid, the magnitude of pressure p, acting at a point located a depth z from the surface of the fluid is

$$p = \rho z \quad \text{(force/area)} \qquad (9\text{-}11)$$

This equation is valid only for fluids which are incompressible, as is the case of most liquids. Gases on the other hand are compressible fluids, and since their density changes significantly with both vertical height and temperature, Eq. 9–11 cannot be used. All matter lying on the earth's surface is subjected to an atmospheric pressure of approximately 14.7 lb/in.² at sea level. Hence, Eq. 9–11 is actually a measure of the gauge pressure exerted by the liquid at some point. The *gauge pressure* is that pressure greater than the atmospheric pressure. In studying the action of pressures acting on a surface, we will not be concerned with atmospheric pressure, since it acts over the total surface and yields a zero force resultant.

Let us now consider what effect a liquid having a density ρ_l has at points A, B, and C, located on the top of a submerged plate, shown in Fig. 9–25. Since both points A and B are at the same depth z_2 from the surface of the liquid, the *pressure* at these points (and all other points along the line containing A and B) has a magnitude of $p_2 = \rho_l z_2$. Point C acts at a depth z_1 from the liquid surface; hence, $p_1 = \rho_l z_1$. In all cases, the pressure acts *normal* to the submerged plate. The *force* acting on an element of surface area dA, located at points A and B, has a magnitude of $dF_2 = p_2\, dA = \rho_l z_2\, dA$. Similarly, $dF_1 = \rho_l z_1\, dA$ for point C. (See Fig. 9–25.)

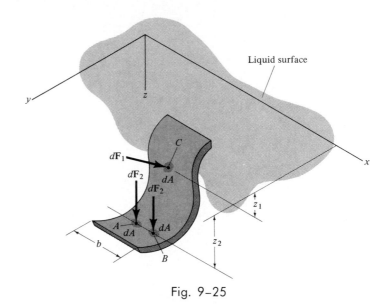

Fig. 9–25

To find the entire pressure force distribution acting across the top of a submerged plate, consider the *flat plate of variable width x,* shown in Fig. 9–26. The plane of this plate makes an angle θ with the horizontal. A strip of area $dA = x\, dy'$, located a distance z below the surface of liquid, has a pressure distribution $p = \rho_l z$ (force/area) acting on it. The magnitude of the differential force $d\mathbf{F}$, acting on the area dA located at the top surface of the plate, is equal to the *volume* of the shaded element. Hence, $dF = dV = p\, dA = \rho_l z(x\, dy')$. The magnitude of the resultant force acting over the plate is found by integration, and is therefore,

$$F = \int_V dV = V$$

This total volume is described by the plate area as its base and linear varying pressure distribution as its altitude, Fig. 9–26. To account for any

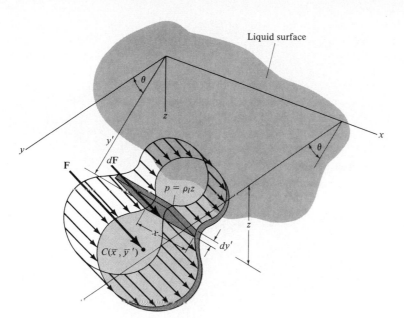

Fig. 9-26

moments created by the pressure loading, the resultant force **F** produces an equivalent moment, provided it acts through the *centroid of the volume V*; that is, **F** must act through coordinate point $C(\bar{x}, \bar{y}')$ located on the surface of the plate defined by

$$\bar{x} = \frac{\int_V \tilde{x}\, dV}{\int_V dV}, \qquad \bar{y}' = \frac{\int_V \tilde{y}'\, dV}{\int_V dV}$$

This point should *not* be mistaken for the centroid of the plate area.

Consider now the submerged *rectangular flat plate having a constant width b*, shown in Fig. 9-27a. In this case a strip of area $dA = b\, dy'$, located a distance z below the surface of the liquid, is subjected to a pressure distribution $p = \rho_l z$ (force/area). The magnitude of the differential force acting across this strip of area is therefore $dF = \rho_l z\, dA = \rho_l z(b\, dy')$. As stated previously, in the case of the plate having a *variable width*, the resultant pressure force is equal to the volume under the loading diagram and the force acts through the centroid of this volume. For this rectangular plate, however, the pressure distribution along the *width* of the entire plate is uniform. Hence, the loading function can easily be projected as an area, shown in two dimensions, rather than using the loading function represented geometrically as a volume (see

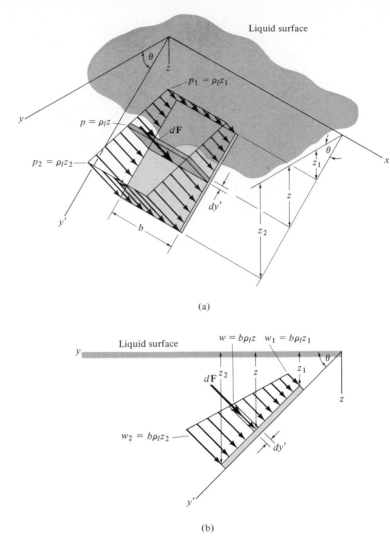

(a)

(b)

Fig. 9–27

Sec. 4–11). On this diagram, Fig. 9–27b, the loading function $w = bp = b\rho_l z$ (force/length) represents a trapezoidal area. The intensity of loading varies linearly from $w_1 = b\rho_l z_1$ to $w_2 = b\rho_l z_2$ across the surface. From the theory of Sec. 4–11, the *magnitude of the resultant force* **F**, created by this distributed load, is equal to the *area* under this trapezoid. The *line of action* of this force passes through the *centroid* of the trapezoidal area.

In the case of a submerged *curved surface,* the resultant force of a distributed pressure loading involves considerably more calculation than for a flat plate, because the pressure acting normal to the plate continually changes direction. For example, if the rectangular plate in Fig. 9–27 is curved, Fig. 9–28a, the pressure distribution acting along the length of the plate is as shown in Fig. 9–28b. The y and z components of force $\mathbf{F}$ acting on the surface can be found by integration, noting from the figure that $p/dL = p_y/dy = p_z/dz$. Hence,

$$F_y = \int_L w\,dy = \int_L bp\,dy = b \int_0^L p_y\,dL \qquad (9\text{–}12)$$

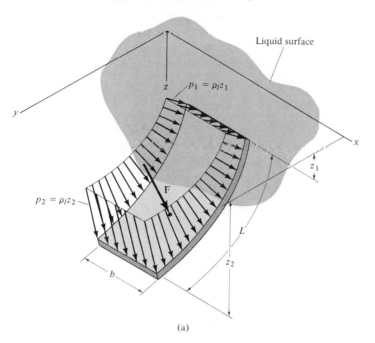

(a)

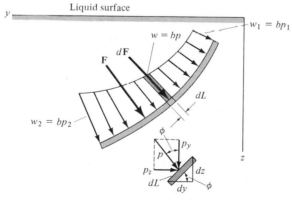

(b)

Fig. 9–28

$$F_z = \int_L w\, dz = \int_L bp\, dz = b \int_0^L p_z\, dL \qquad (9\text{--}13)$$

The magnitude of **F** then becomes $F = \sqrt{(F_y)^2 + (F_z)^2}$. This magnitude represents the *area* under the loading diagram in Fig. 9–28b, or the *volume* under the loading diagram in Fig. 9–28a. **F** acts through the centroid of this loading diagram normal to the surface of the plate.

Carrying out the integration needed to find both the magnitude of **F** and its location on a plate having a curved surface is, in many cases, not easy since the direction of the pressure forces changes. For this reason, a simpler method will now be discussed for finding this resultant force. This method is applicable *only* to *flat and curved plates having a constant width*. To illustrate the method, consider again the curved plate shown in Fig. 9–28a. Because the width of the plate is constant, the pressure loadings acting on the top surface of the plate can be graphed in two dimensions. Using the methods previously discussed, we can calculate the forces acting along the separate *horizontal and vertical projections* of the plate, Fig. 9–29. The force $\mathbf{F}_{AD}$ acting on the vertical projection AD has a magnitude which equals the area under the trapezoidal pressure diagram, and acts through the centroid C_{AD} of this area. (The magnitude of this force is equivalent to F_y defined by Eq. 9–12.) The pressure distribution along the horizontal plane AB is constant, since all points lying in this plane are at equal distances from the surface of the liquid. The magnitude of force $\mathbf{F}_{AB}$ is then simply the area under the rectangle. This force acts through the centroid C_{AB} (or midpoint) of AB. This would be the only vertical force acting if the surface shape were BAD. However, the curved surface BD must support the *weight of fluid* $\mathbf{W}_f$ contained within the area BAD in addition to the forces $\mathbf{F}_{AD}$ and $\mathbf{F}_{AB}$. The magnitude

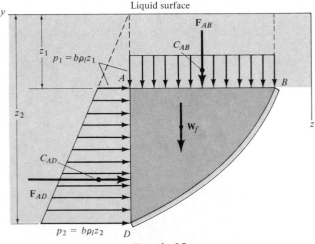

Fig. 9–29

of $\mathbf{W}_f$ is $W_f = \rho_t(b)(\text{area } BAD)$. This force acts through the centroid of the area BAD. Why? The magnitude of the resultant of $\mathbf{F}_{AB}$ and $\mathbf{W}_f$ is then equivalent to F_z defined by Eq. 9–13. Summing the three coplanar forces shown in Fig. 9–29, one obtains the single force resultant $\mathbf{F}$ acting normal to the plate and passing through the centroid of the loading diagram, Fig. 9–28a.

Example 9–14

The rectangular plate $ABCD$ shown in Fig. 9–30a serves as an access opening to a water tank. Determine the magnitude and location P of the resultant force of the hydrostatic load acting on the plate. The density of water is $\rho_w = 62.4 \text{ lb/ft}^3$.

Solution I
A three-dimensional view of the pressure loading acting on the plate is shown in Fig. 9–30b. The pressure acting along AB is

$$p_{AB} = \rho_w z_{AB} = 62.4 \text{ lb/ft}^3(14 \sin 45° \text{ ft}) = 617.6 \text{ lb/ft}^2$$

and the pressure acting along CD is

$$p_{CD} = \rho_w z_{CD} = 62.4 \text{ lb/ft}^3(12 \sin 45° \text{ ft}) = 529.4 \text{ lb/ft}^2$$

The resultant force acting on the plate equals the volume under this pressure diagram. This force acts through the centroid of the volume. Because of the symmetry of the volume shape, the centroid must lie along the y' axis shown in Fig. 9–30b. Hence,

$$\bar{x} = 0 \qquad\qquad Ans.$$

Since the plate has a *constant width* of 3 ft, the pressure loading may be projected in two dimensions, as shown in Fig. 9–30c. The loading per unit length along AB becomes

$$w_{AB} = bp_{AB} = (3 \text{ ft})(617.6 \text{ lb/ft}^2) = 1{,}853 \text{ lb/ft}$$

Similarly, the loading per unit length along CD is

$$w_{CD} = bp_{CD} = (3 \text{ ft})(529.4 \text{ lb/ft}^2) = 1{,}588 \text{ lb/ft}$$

Since the loading varies linearly with depth, the distributed loading along the length of the plate is trapezoidal, as shown. The resultant force $\mathbf{F}_R$ of the trapezoidal loading, and its location, may be obtained using the data listed in Appendix B.

$$F = (\text{area of trapezoid})$$
$$= \tfrac{1}{2}(2 \text{ ft})(1{,}853 \text{ lb/ft} + 1{,}588 \text{ lb/ft}) = 3{,}441 \text{ lb} \qquad Ans.$$

The force acts through the centroid P, where

$$d = \frac{1}{3}\left(\frac{2(1{,}588 \text{ lb/ft}) + 1{,}853 \text{ lb/ft}}{1{,}588 \text{ lb/ft} + 1{,}853 \text{ lb/ft}}\right) 2 \text{ ft} = 0.97 \text{ ft} \qquad Ans.$$

measured to the right of *AB*, Fig. 9–30*d*.

Solution II

Since the plate has a *constant width,* the projection method may be used to solve this problem. As shown in Fig. 9–30*e*, the *vertical projection* of the plate, *EA*, is subjected to a distributed trapezoidal loading. The loading at *E* is

$$w_E = b\rho_w z_E = 62.4 \text{ lb/ft}^3 (3 \text{ ft})(12 \sin 45^\circ \text{ ft}) = 1{,}588 \text{ lb/ft}$$

and the loading at *A* is

$$w_A = b\rho_w z_A = 62.4 \text{ lb/ft}^3 (3 \text{ ft})(14 \sin 45^\circ \text{ ft}) = 1{,}853 \text{ lb/ft}$$

Using Appendix B, the magnitude of the resultant force $\mathbf{F}_T$ created by this distribution is

$$F_T = (\text{area of trapezoid})$$
$$= \tfrac{1}{2}(2 \sin 45^\circ \text{ ft})(1{,}853 \text{ lb/ft} + 1{,}588 \text{ lb/ft}) = 2{,}433 \text{ lb}$$

This resultant acts through the centroid of the area,

$$t = \frac{1}{3}\left(\frac{2(1{,}588 \text{ lb/ft}) + 1{,}853 \text{ lb/ft}}{1{,}588 \text{ lb/ft} + 1{,}853 \text{ lb/ft}}\right)(2 \sin 45^\circ \text{ ft}) = 0.69 \text{ ft}$$

measured upward from point *A*. See Fig. 9–30*f*.

In a similar manner, the magnitude of the resultant force $\mathbf{F}_R$ acting on the *horizontal projection EC* in Fig. 9–30*e*, is

$$F_R = (\text{area of rectangle})$$
$$= (2 \cos 45^\circ \text{ ft})1{,}588 \text{ lb/ft} = 2{,}246 \text{ lb}$$

This force passes through the centroid of the rectangular area located at

$$r = \tfrac{1}{2}(2 \cos 45^\circ \text{ ft}) = 0.71 \text{ ft}$$

from either end *A* or *C*. See Fig. 9–30*f*.

The force **W** equals the weight of water contained within the triangular shaped block *AEC*. Hence,

$$W = 62.4 \text{ lb/ft}^3 [\tfrac{1}{2}(2 \sin 45^\circ \text{ ft})(2 \cos 45^\circ \text{ ft})3 \text{ ft}]$$
$$= 187 \text{ lb}$$

The centroid for this loading is

$$s = \tfrac{1}{3}(2 \sin 45^\circ \text{ ft}) = 0.47 \text{ ft}$$

measured to the right of *A*.

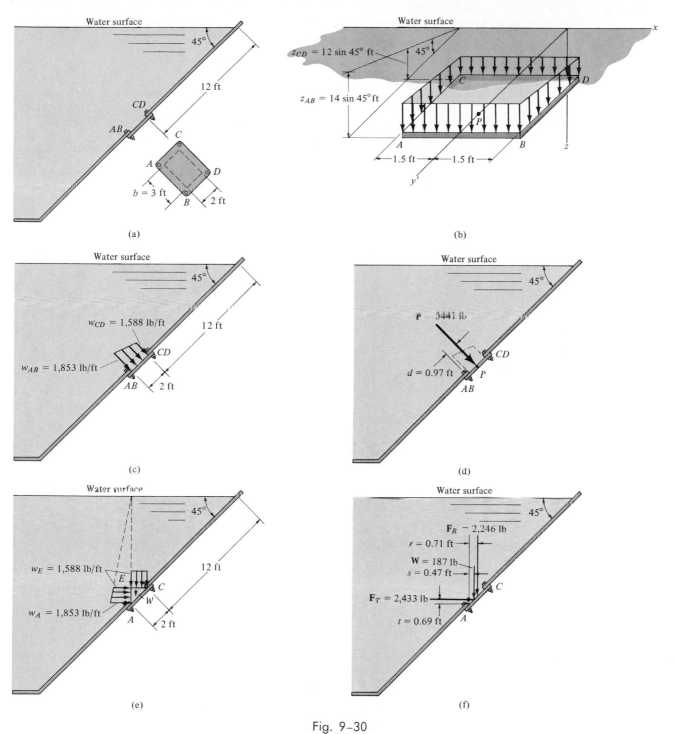

(a)

(b)

(c)

(d)

(e)

(f)

Fig. 9-30

353

The three forces $\mathbf{F}_T$, $\mathbf{F}_R$, and $\mathbf{W}$ are shown acting on the plate in Fig. 9–30f. The resultant force is therefore the vector sum, i.e.,

$$F = \sqrt{(2{,}246 \text{ lb} + 187 \text{ lb})^2 + (2{,}433 \text{ lb})^2} = 3{,}441 \text{ lb} \qquad Ans.$$

where

$$\theta = \tan^{-1} \frac{2{,}246 \text{ lb} + 187 \text{ lb}}{2{,}433 \text{ lb}} = 45° \qquad \text{⟍}^{\theta}_{\mathbf{F}} \qquad Ans.$$

Since θ is measured from the horizontal, the resultant force acts *perpendicular* to the plate. (This result is expected since the entire distributed load acts perpendicular to the plate, Fig. 9–30b.)

The location, d, of the resultant force, Fig. 9–30d, can be determined from a balance of moments about point A. It is required that the moment produced by $\mathbf{F}$ about point A (Fig. 9–30d) be equivalent to the moment of each of the three forces $\mathbf{F}_T$, $\mathbf{F}_R$, and $\mathbf{W}$ about this point, Fig. 9–30f. Hence, choosing clockwise moments positive,

$\zeta M_A = (3{,}441 \text{ lb})d = (2{,}433 \text{ lb})0.69 \text{ ft} + (187 \text{ lb})0.47 \text{ ft}$

$$+ (2{,}246 \text{ lb})0.71 \text{ ft}$$

or

$$(3{,}441 \text{ lb})d = 3{,}340 \text{ lb-ft}$$

so that,

$$d = \frac{3{,}340 \text{ lb-ft}}{3{,}441 \text{ lb}} = 0.97 \text{ ft} \qquad Ans.$$

Example 9–15

Determine the magnitude and location of the resultant force acting on the triangular end plates of the water trough shown in Fig. 9–31a. The density of water is $\rho_w = 62.4 \text{ lb/ft}^3$.

Solution

The pressure loading acting on the end plate E is shown in Fig. 9–31b. The magnitude of the resultant force $\mathbf{F}$ is equal to the volume of this diagram. Choosing the differential volume element shown in the figure yields

$$dF = dV = p \, dA = \rho_w z (2x \, dz) = 2(62.4 \text{ lb/ft}^3)zx \, dz$$

The equation of line AB is

$$x = \frac{2 - z}{2}$$

Hence, substituting and integrating with respect to z from 0 to 2 ft yields,

$$F = V = \int_V dV = \int_0^2 (124.8)z \left(\frac{2 - z}{2} \right) dz$$

$$= 62.4 \int_0^2 (2z - z^2)dz = 83.2 \text{ lb} \qquad Ans.$$

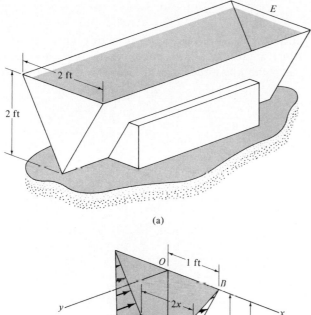

(a)

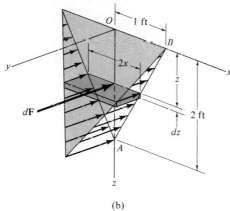

(b)

Fig. 9–31

This resultant passes through the *centroid of the volume*. Because of symmetry,

$$\bar{x} = 0 \qquad Ans.$$

Since $\bar{z} = z$ for the volume element, then

$$\bar{z} = \frac{\int_V \bar{z}\, dV}{\int_V dV} = \frac{\int_0^2 z\, 124.8z\left(\frac{2-z}{2}\right) dz}{83.2 \text{ lb}} = \frac{62.4 \int_0^2 (2z^2 - z^3)\, dz}{83.2 \text{ lb}}$$

or

$$\bar{z} = 1.0 \text{ ft} \qquad Ans.$$

Problems

9-57. Determine the magnitude and location of the resultant hydrostatic force acting on the dam. The width of the dam is 20 ft. The density of water is $\rho_w = 62.4$ lb/ft³.

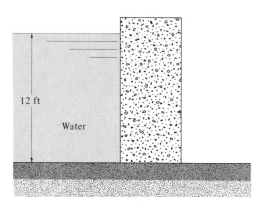

12 ft

Water

Prob. 9-57

9-58. The wind pressure acting on a triangular sign is approximately uniform. Determine the resultant force and couple moment due to this loading at point O.

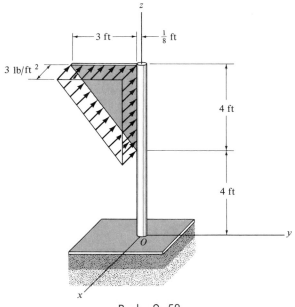

3 ft $\frac{1}{8}$ ft

3 lb/ft²

4 ft

4 ft

O

y

x

Prob. 9-58

9-59. The wind loading acting on a square plate has a pressure distribution which is parabolic. Determine the magnitude and location of the resultant force.

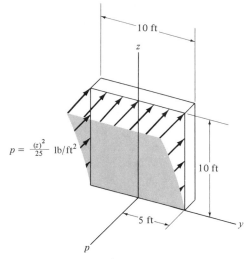

10 ft

z

$p = \frac{(z)^2}{25}$ lb/ft²

10 ft

5 ft

y

p

Prob. 9-59

9-60. Wind blowing across a roof creates a suction pressure on the leeward side perpendicular to the roof. Determine the magnitude and direction of the resultant force of this pressure distribution.

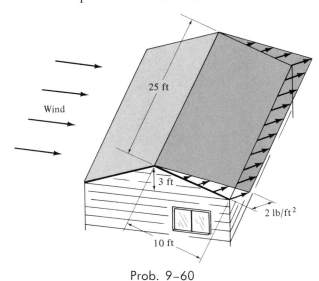

25 ft

Wind

3 ft

10 ft

2 lb/ft²

Prob. 9-60

9-61. Determine the resultant hydrostatic force acting per unit width on the sea wall; $\rho_w = 62.4$ lb/ft³.

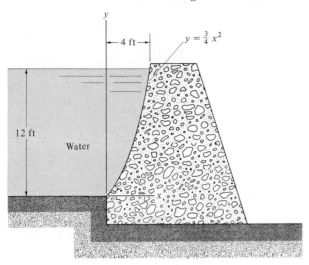

Prob. 9-61

9-62. The rectangular plate is subjected to a distributed load over the surface of the plate given by the expression $p = p_o \sin(\pi x/a) \sin(\pi y/b)$, where p_o represents the intensity of the load acting at the center of the plate. Determine the magnitude and location of the resultant force acting on the plate.

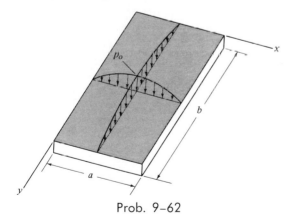

Prob. 9-62

9-63. The storage tank contains oil having a density of $\rho_o = 40$ lb/ft³. If the tank is 6 ft wide, calculate the resultant force acting on the inclined side AB of the tank caused by the oil pressure.

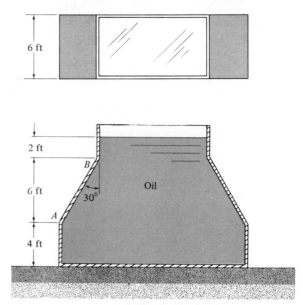

Prob. 9-63

9-64. The form is used to cast columns. Determine the resultant force acting on the plates A and B when the form is filled with a liquid having a density of $\rho_c = 150$ lb/ft³.

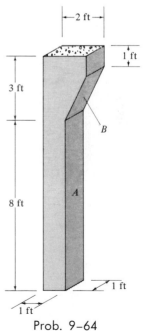

Prob. 9-64

357

9-65. A 4-ft-square tank, 10 ft high, is filled to a depth of 3 ft with water and 7 ft with oil. Determine the magnitude and location of the resultant force created by these two fluids along the side of the tank; $\rho_o = 50$ lb/ft³, and $\rho_w = 62.4$ lb/ft³.

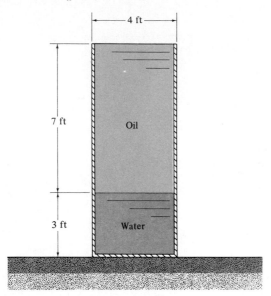

Prob. 9–65

9-66. Determine the magnitude and direction of the resultant force acting on each of the cover plates A and B. The density of liquid is $\rho_l = 50$ lb/ft³.

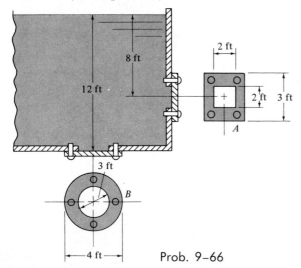

Prob. 9–66

9-67. Determine the magnitude of the resultant force acting on the gate ABC due to hydrostatic pressure. The gate is 4 ft wide; $\rho_w = 62.4$ lb/ft³.

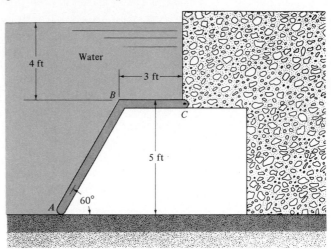

Prob. 9–67

Moments of Inertia for an Area

10–1. Definition of Moments of Inertia for Areas

In Chapter 4 it was shown that a distributed load acting along a beam may be replaced by a single concentrated force equal in magnitude to the area of the loading diagram and having a line of action which passes through the *centroid* of this area. You will recall that the *centroid of an area* is determined by considering the *first moment of the area* about an axis; that is, it is necessary to evaluate integrals of the form $M = \int_A x \, dA$.

There are many important topics in mechanics which require evaluation of an integral of the *second moment of an area* about an axis. These integrals are of the form $\int_A x^2 \, dA$, where x is the shortest distance from the element to an axis which is either perpendicular to, or lying in the plane of, the area. Often in engineering practice such integrals are referred to as the *moment of inertia for the area*. This phrase is actually a misnomer; however, it has been adopted because of the similarity with integrals of the same form related to mass.*

The moment of inertia of an area originates when one computes the *moment* of a linearly varying distributed force system about a given axis. A common example of this type of loading occurs in the study of fluid mechanics. It was pointed out in Sec. 9–6 that the pressure p, or

*The moment of inertia for mass is discussed in *Engineering Mechanics: Dynamics*.

force per unit area, exerted at a point located a distance z below the surface of a liquid is $p = \rho z$, where ρ is the density of the liquid. Thus, the magnitude of force exerted by a liquid on the area dA of the submerged plate shown in Fig. 10-1a is $dF = p \, dA = \rho z \, dA$. The moment of this force about the x axis of the plate is $dM = dF\, z = \rho z^2 \, dA$ and, therefore, the moment created by the entire distributed (pressure) loading is

$$M = \rho \int_A z^2 \, dA.$$

The area moment of inertia also appears when one relates the *normal stress,* or force per unit area, acting on a transverse cross section of an elastic beam to the applied external moment **M,** which causes bending of the beam. From the theory of strength of materials, it can be shown that the normal stress σ within the beam varies linearly with its distance from an axis passing through the centroid C of the beam's cross-sectional area; that is, $\sigma = kz$, Fig. 10-1b. The magnitude of force $d\mathbf{F}$ acting on the area element dA, shown in the figure, is therefore $dF = \sigma \, dA = kz \, dA$. Since this force is located a distance z from the y axis, the moment of $d\mathbf{F}$ about the y axis is $dM = dF\, z = kz^2 \, dA$. The resulting moment of the entire stress distribution is caused by the applied moment **M.** Therefore, for equilibrium it is necessary that $M = k \int_A z^2 \, dA$.

As a third example to illustrate the formulation of area moments of inertia, consider the elastic twisting of a circular shift about its longitudinal axis, as shown in Fig. 10-1c. The applied external torsional moment **T** causes a *shearing stress* distribution at a transverse cross-section which varies linearly along any radial line segment; i.e., $\sigma = kr$. The magnitude of the applied torque **T** may be related to the internal stress distribution by summing moments about the x axis of the shaft, which results in

$$T = \int_A r \, dF = k \int_A r\sigma \, dA = k \int_A r^2 \, dA.$$

Since the moments of inertia for areas frequently appear in design formulas used in fluid mechanics, strength of materials, and structural mechanics, it is important that the student become familiar with the methods used to compute these quantities.

In general, the moment of inertia for an element of area dA, about an axis either lying in the plane of this area or normal to it and lying at a perpendicular distance s away from the area element, is defined by the expression

$$dI = s^2 \, dA \qquad (10\text{-}1)$$

If dA represents a segment of the area A, the moment of inertia for the entire area A is found by integrating over the entire area; hence,

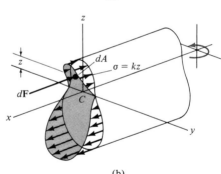

Liquid surface

$p = \rho z$

(a)

$\sigma = kz$

(b)

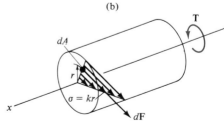

$\sigma = kr$

(c)

Fig. 10-1

moment of inertia $\longrightarrow I = \int_A s^2 \, dA$

Since both dA and s^2 are always positive quantities, the moment of inertia for an area element is always a *positive* quantity. Furthermore, the moment of inertia of the finite area, represented as the sum or integral of these differential moments, is also positive.

From Eq. 10–1, it is seen that the dimensions for the moment of inertia of an area are in terms of length raised to the fourth power, e.g., in.^{4}, ft^4, or m^4.

Consider the area A shown in Fig. 10–2 which lies in the xy plane. In accordance with Eq. 10–1, the moment of inertia of the differential planar area, $dA = dx\,dy$, about the x, y, and z axes, respectively, is defined as

$$dI_x = y^2\,dA$$
$$dI_y = x^2\,dA$$
$$dJ_O = r^2\,dA$$

For the entire planar area A, the moments of inertia become

$$I_x = \int_A y^2\,dA \tag{10-2a}$$

$$I_y = \int_A x^2\,dA \tag{10-2b}$$

$$J_O = \int_A r^2\,dA = I_x + I_y \tag{10-2c}$$

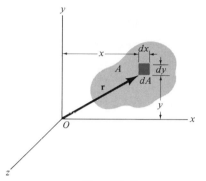

Fig. 10–2

The terms I_x and I_y are called the *rectangular moments of inertia* for the area, and J_O is referred to as the *polar moment of inertia*. From Fig. 10–2, it is seen that $r^2 = x^2 + y^2$, so that the polar moment of inertia represents the *sum* of the rectangular moments of inertia for any two perpendicular axes which intersect the polar (or z) axis, Eq. 10–2c. In particular, the rectangular moments of inertia are required for the fluid pressure and bending problems mentioned earlier, whereas the torsional computation requires use of the polar moment of inertia. The techniques for the integration of Eqs. 10–2 are given in Sec. 10–4.

10–2. Parallel-Axis Theorem for an Area

If the moment of inertia for an area is given about an axis, it is sometimes desirable to calculate this quantity about a parallel axis. The *parallel-axis theorem* may be used for this calculation, provided the perpendicular distances from the centroid of the area to both axes are known. (This theorem relates the moment of inertia about an axis to the moment of inertia about a parallel axis passing through the centroid of the area.)

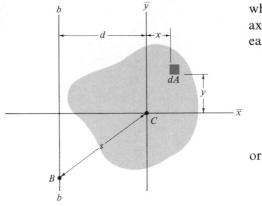

Fig. 10–3

To derive this theorem, let us consider finding the moment of inertia of the shaded area shown in Fig. 10–3 about the *bb* axis. Using Eq. 10–1, we have

$$dI = (x + d)^2\, dA$$

where *d* represents the perpendicular distance between the centroidal $\bar{y}$ axis and the parallel *bb* axis. Expanding this expression and integrating each term to obtain the moment of inertia for the entire area yields

$$I = \int_A (x + d)^2\, dA$$

$$= \int_A x^2\, dA + 2d \int_A x\, dA + d^2 \int_A dA$$

or

$$I = \bar{I} + 2d \int_A x\, dA + Ad^2 \tag{10-3}$$

The second term on the right-hand side of Eq. 10–3 represents the first moment of the area about the $\bar{y}$ axis. Since this axis passes through the *centroid C* of the area, this term is zero, in which case Eq. 10–3 becomes

$$I = \bar{I} + Ad^2 \tag{10-4}$$

In words, the moment of inertia *I* about an axis is equal to the moment of inertia $\bar{I}$ of the area about a parallel axis passing through the centroid plus the product of the area *A* and the square of the perpendicular distance *d* between the axes.

In a similar manner, it can be shown that the parallel-axis theorem for determining the polar moment of inertia J_B about an axis perpendicular to the $\bar{x}\bar{y}$ plane and passing through point *B* is

$$J_B = \bar{J} + As^2 \tag{10-5}$$

Here $\bar{J}$ represents the polar moment of inertia of the area *A* about the $\bar{z}$ axis which passes through the centroid *C* and is perpendicular to the $\bar{x}\bar{y}$ plane, and *s* is the distance between points *B* and *C*, that is, the perpendicular distance between the parallel axes, Fig. 10–3.

10–3. Radius of Gyration of an Area

The *radius of gyration* of an area is a useful term in structural mechanics that serves to determine the strength of columns. For an area *A* having a moment of inertia I_x about the *x* axis, we define the radius of gyration

k_x, having units of length, using a formula similar to Eq. 10-1, namely,

$$I_x = k_x^2 A$$

w.r.t. 'x' axis

or

$$k_x = \sqrt{\frac{I_x}{A}} \qquad (10\text{-}6a)$$

In a similar manner, the radii of gyration k_y and k_O may be defined as

$$k_y = \sqrt{\frac{I_y}{A}} \qquad (10\text{-}6b)$$

$$k_O = \sqrt{\frac{J_O}{A}} \qquad (10\text{-}6c)$$

Substituting Eqs. 10-6 into Eq. 10-2c, we see that

$$k_O^2 = k_x^2 + k_y^2$$

Hence, the square of the radius of gyration of a planar area about the polar (or z) axis is equal to the sum of the squares of its radii of gyration about the x and y axes.

10-4 Moments of Inertia for a Planar Area by Integration

When all the boundaries for a planar area can be expressed by mathematical functions, Eqs. 10-2 may be used to determine the moments of inertia for the area. The integration is simplified, provided the coordinate system chosen is compatible with the boundaries. For example, it is generally convenient to use polar coordinates for areas having circular boundaries.

When a planar area element is chosen which has a differential size in two directions (second-order element) as in Fig. 10-2, a double integration must be performed to evaluate the moment of inertia. Provided the limits of integration can be determined, it is often easier, and hence more convenient, to choose a first-order element, that is an element having a differential size in only one direction, since it simplifies the integration process. In accordance with Eq. 10-1, *the entire differential element must lie at the same distance from the moment axis*. This will always be the case when a second-order element $dA = dx\,dy$ is chosen for integration (see Fig. 10-2). If a first-order element is chosen, however, this condition is satisfied only when the element is *properly oriented* with respect to the axis. For example, the rectangular element $dA = y\,dx$, shown in Fig. 10–4, satisfies this requirement when computing the moment of inertia of the shaded area about the y axis, since all parts of the element lie at the *same distance x* from the y axis. (The element is infinitesimally "thin" in the x direction.) However, when the moment of inertia for the area is required about the x axis, one cannot directly apply Eq. 10–1 using the same element shown in the figure. The element is not infinitesimally thin in the y direction, and thus parts of its entirety lie at different distances from the x axis. It is possible, however, to use this same element to calculate I_x for the area. To do this, it is *first necessary to obtain the moment of inertia for the (rectangular) element about its centroidal axis, and then determine the moment of inertia for this element about the x axis using the parallel-axis theorem.* This technique is further explained in Examples 10–2 and 10–3.

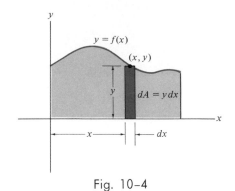

Fig. 10–4

Example 10–1

Determine the radius of gyration for the rectangular area shown in Fig. 10–5a with respect to (a) the centroidal $\bar{x}$ axis, (b) an axis perpendicular to the $\bar{x}\bar{y}$ plane and passing through the centroid O, and (c) an axis parallel to the $\bar{x}$ axis and passing through the base of the rectangle.

Solution

Part (a). The radius of gyration $k_{\bar{x}}$ may be found after first obtaining the moment of inertia $\bar{I}_{\bar{x}}$. The second-order differential element shown in Fig. 10–5a is chosen for integration. The element is located at the point (x, y). Note that the entire element is located at a distance y from the x axis. The entire region is covered if we integrate from $x = -b/2$ to $x = b/2$, and from $y = -h/2$ to $y = h/2$. Hence,

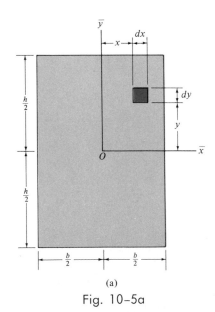

(a)

Fig. 10–5a

$$\bar{I}_{\bar{x}} = \int_A y^2\,dA = \int_{-h/2}^{h/2}\int_{-b/2}^{b/2} y^2\,dx\,dy = b\int_{-h/2}^{h/2} y^2\,dy = \tfrac{1}{12}bh^3 \quad (1)$$

Applying Eq. 10–6a, we obtain

$$k_{\bar{x}} = \sqrt{\frac{\bar{I}_{\bar{x}}}{A}} = \sqrt{\frac{\tfrac{1}{12}bh^3}{bh}} = \frac{h}{\sqrt{12}} \qquad Ans.$$

Part (b). The rectangular moment of inertia $\bar{I}_{\bar{y}}$ may be found by interchanging the dimensions b and h in Eq. (1), in which case

$$\bar{I}_{\bar{y}} = \tfrac{1}{12}hb^3$$

Using Eq. 10–2c, we obtain

$$\bar{J}_O = \bar{I}_{\bar{x}} + \bar{I}_{\bar{y}} = \tfrac{1}{12}bh(h^2 + b^2)$$

From Eq. 10-6c,

$$k_O = \sqrt{\frac{J_O}{A}} = \sqrt{\frac{\frac{1}{12}bh(h^2 + b^2)}{bh}} = \sqrt{\frac{h^2 + b^2}{12}} \qquad Ans.$$

Part (c). We can obtain the moment of inertia I_{x_b}, computed with respect to an axis passing through the base of the rectangle by applying Eq. 10-2a, using a first-order element. As shown in Fig. 10-5b, a rectangular element having a width b, and thickness dy has been chosen for integration. We have selected this element because all points on the element act at the *same distance* y from the x_b axis. Hence,

$$I_{x_b} = \int_A y^2 \, dA = \int_0^h y^2 b \, dy = \tfrac{1}{3}bh^3$$

This same result can be obtained by applying the parallel-axis theorem, Eq. 10-4 in conjunction with Eq. (1) in Part (a):

$$I_{x_b} = I_{\bar{x}} + Ad^2$$

$$= \tfrac{1}{12}bh^3 + bh\left(\frac{h}{2}\right)^2 = \tfrac{1}{3}bh^3$$

The radius of gyration is therefore

$$k_{x_b} = \sqrt{\frac{I_{x_b}}{A}} = \sqrt{\frac{\tfrac{1}{3}bh^3}{bh}} = \frac{h}{\sqrt{3}} \qquad Ans.$$

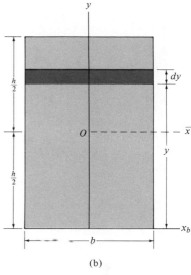

(b)

Fig. 10-5b

Example 10-2

Compute the polar moment of inertia for the shaded area shown in Fig. 10-6a with respect to a polar axis passing through the origin O of the coordinate system.

Solution

The polar moment of inertia J_O can easily be computed provided I_x and I_y are known. The moment of inertia I_x can be computed by choosing elements of area *parallel* to the x axis. When this is done, *all parts of the element* lie at an *equal distance* y from the axis. An element intersecting the arbitrary point (x, y) on the curve is shown in Fig. 10-6a. Hence, integrating with respect to y from $y = 0$ to $y = 2$ in. yields

$$I_x = \int_A y^2 \, dA = \int_A y^2(4 - x) \, dy$$

$$= \int_0^2 y^2\left[4 - \left(\frac{y^2}{2} + 2\right)\right] dy = 2.13 \text{ in.}^4$$

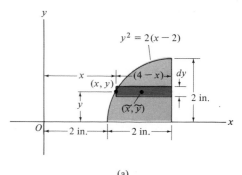

(a)

Fig. 10-6a

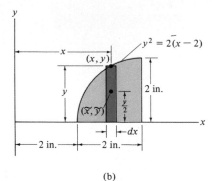

(b)

Fig. 10–6b

This same result can be obtained by using elements parallel to the y axis, such as shown in Fig. 10–6b. In this case, however, the entire element does *not* lie at a fixed distance from the x axis, and therefore the parallel-axis theorem must be used to determine the *moment of inertia of the element* with respect to the axis. For a rectangle having a base b and height h, the moment of inertia about its centroidal $\bar{x}$ axis has been computed in Example 10–1. There it was found that $\bar{I}_{\bar{x}} = \frac{1}{12}bh^3$. For the differential element shown in Fig. 10–6b, $b = dx$ and $h = y$, and thus $d\bar{I}_{\bar{x}} = \frac{1}{12}dx\, y^3$. The centroid of the element is located at coordinates $(\tilde{x}, \tilde{y})$, where

$$\tilde{x} = x, \qquad \tilde{y} = \frac{y}{2}$$

Hence, the moment of inertia of the element about the x axis is

$$dI_x = d\bar{I}_{\bar{x}} + dA\,(\tilde{y})^2$$
$$= \frac{1}{12}\,dx\, y^3 + y\, dx \left(\frac{y}{2}\right)^2 = \frac{1}{3}y^3\, dx$$

Therefore, integrating this result with respect to x from $x = 2$ in. to $x = 4$ in. yields the same result as before,

$$I_x = \int_A dI_x = \int_A \frac{1}{3}y^3\, dx = \int_2^4 \frac{1}{3}[2(x-2)]^{3/2}\, dx = 2.13 \text{ in.}^4$$

When I_y is obtained using the rectangular element shown in Fig. 10–6b, the *entire element* lies at a distance x from the y axis; therefore, the moment of inertia is*

$$I_y = \int_A x^2\, dA = \int_A x^2 y\, dx = \int_2^4 x^2[2(x-2)]^{1/2}\, dx = 28.04 \text{ in.}^4$$

If rectangular elements orientated as shown in Fig. 10–6a are used for computing I_y, the parallel-axis theorem must be used to compute the moment of inertia of the element about the y axis. Why? From Fig. 10–6a, the centroid for the element is located at $(\tilde{x}, \tilde{y})$, where

$$\tilde{x} = x + \left(\frac{4-x}{2}\right) = \frac{4+x}{2}, \qquad \tilde{y} = y$$

Hence, in this case,

---

*If the parallel-axis theorem were used to determine this result, the moment of inertia of the element chosen about its centroidal axis becomes $d\bar{I}_{\bar{y}} = \frac{1}{12}y(dx)^3$. Thus $dI_y = \frac{1}{12}y(dx)^3 + x^2\, dA$. The first term on the right goes to zero, since it is a third-order differential, whereas dA is of the second order. The resulting integration is thus $I_y = \int_A x^2\, dA$, which is the same as that used above.

$$dI_y = d\bar{I}_{\bar{y}} + dA\, d^2$$

$$= \frac{1}{12} dy\,(4-x)^3 + (4-x)\,dy \left(\frac{4+x}{2}\right)^2$$

or

$$dI_y = \frac{1}{3}(64 - x^3)\,dy$$

Integrating with respect to y from $y = 0$ to $y = 2$ in. yields the same result as before,

$$I_y = \int_A dI_y = \frac{1}{3}\int_0^2 (64 - x^3)\,dy$$

$$= \frac{1}{3}\int_0^2 \left[64 - \left(\frac{y^2+4}{2}\right)^3\right] dy = 28.04 \text{ in.}^4$$

The polar moment of inertia is therefore

$$J_O = I_x + I_y = 2.13 \text{ in.}^4 + 28.04 \text{ in.}^4$$
$$= 30.17 \text{ in.}^4 \qquad\qquad Ans.$$

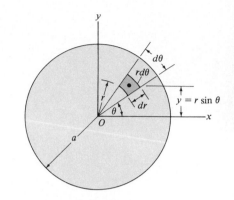

(a)

Example 10-3

For the circular area shown in Fig. 10-7a, determine the moment of inertia with respect to the x axis.

Solution I

This problem is most conveniently solved by using double integration and polar coordinates. For an arbitrary element having an area $dA = (r\,d\theta)\,dr$ and located at point (r, θ), as shown in Fig. 10-7a, the moment of inertia about the x axis is

$$I_x = \int_A y^2\,dA = \int_0^a \int_0^{2\pi} (r\sin\theta)^2\, r\,d\theta\,dr = \int_0^a r^3\,dr \int_0^{2\pi} \sin^2\theta\,d\theta$$

$$= \frac{r^4}{4}\Big|_0^a \left(\frac{\theta}{2} - \frac{\sin 2\theta}{r}\right)\Big|_0^{2\pi} = \frac{\pi a^4}{4} \qquad Ans.$$

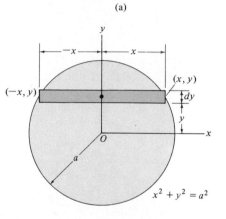

(b)

Solution II

The result may be obtained by using a rectangular element and single integration. For the element chosen as shown in Fig. 10-7b,

$$I_x = \int_A y^2\,dA = \int_A y^2(2x)\,dy$$

Integrating with respect to y,

$$I_x = \int_{-a}^a y^2(2\sqrt{a^2 - y^2})\,dy = \frac{\pi a^4}{4} \qquad Ans.$$

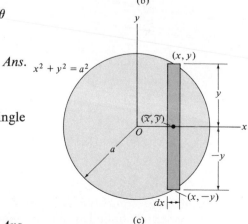

(c)

Fig. 10-7

Solution III

When rectangular elements are chosen as shown in Fig. 10–7c, the parallel-axis theorem must be used. Why? The centroid for the element has coordinates $\tilde{x} = x$, and $\tilde{y} = 0$. Hence, applying Eq. 10–4, we have

$$dI_x = dI_{\tilde{x}} + dA\,(d)^2$$

$$= \frac{1}{12}\,dx\,(2y)^3 + 2y\,dx\,(0)$$

or

$$dI_x = \frac{2}{3}(y)^3\,dx$$

Therefore, integrating with respect to x,

$$I_x = \int_{-a}^{a} \frac{2}{3}(a^2 - x^2)^{3/2}\,dx = \frac{\pi a^4}{4} \qquad\qquad Ans.$$

Problems

10–1. The irregular area has a moment of inertia about the AA axis of 500 in.^{4} If the total area is 12 in.^{2}, determine the moment of inertia of the area about the BB axis. The CC axis passes through the centroid of the area.

10–3. Determine the moments of inertia of the shaded elliptical area about the x and about the y axis, and the polar moment of inertia about the origin O and about the point P (1 in., 0).

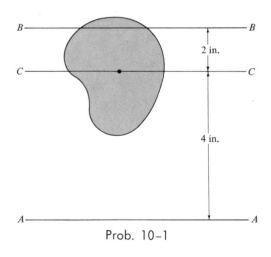

Prob. 10–1

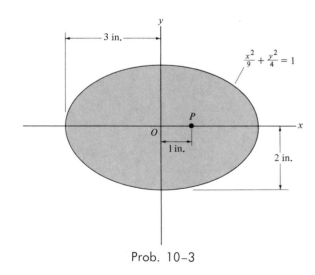

Prob. 10–3

10–2. Determine the moment of inertia about the x axis of an area which is bounded by the lines $x = 0$, $y = 1$ in., and the parabola $y = 3x^2$.

10–4. Determine the moments of inertia of an area, bounded by the curve $y^2 = 2x$, and the lines $x = 2$ in. and $y = 0$, about the x and about the y axis.

10-5. Determine the moment of inertia of the shaded area about the y axis. Solve this problem two ways, using rectangular differential elements having a thickness of dx and dy, respectively.

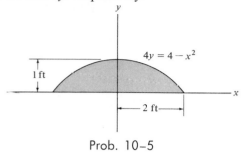

$$4y = 4 - x^2$$

1 ft

2 ft

Prob. 10-5

10-6. Determine the moment of inertia I_x and I_y of the shaded portion of the cosine curve about the x and about the y axis.

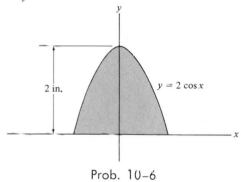

2 in.

$$y = 2 \cos x$$

Prob. 10-6

10-7. The polar moment of inertia of the irregular area is $J_C = 900$ in.^{4} at the centroid point C. If the moment of inertia about the y axis is 600 in.^{4}, and the moment of inertia about the x' axis is 800 in.^{4}, determine the area A.

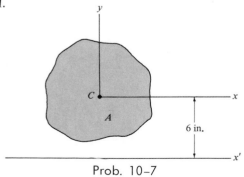

C

A

6 in.

Prob. 10-7

10-8. Determine the polar moment of inertia of the shaded area (a) with respect to an axis perpendicular to the xy plane and passing through the origin of coordinates O, and (b) with respect to an axis perpendicular to the xy plane and passing through the point P (2 in., 0).

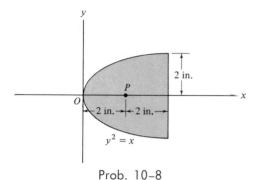

2 in.

O

2 in. 2 in.

$$y^2 = x$$

Prob. 10-8

10-9. Determine the moment of inertia of the shaded area about the x axis.

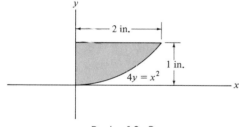

2 in.

1 in.

$$4y = x^2$$

Prob. 10-9

10-10. Determine the moment of inertia of the area of the circular sector about the x axis.

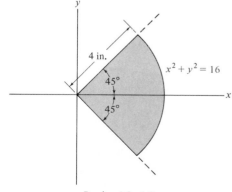

4 in.

$$x^2 + y^2 = 16$$

$45°$

$45°$

Prob. 10-10

369

10-11. For the shaded area, determine (a) the radius of gyration k_y about the y axis, and (b) the radius of gyration k_O about an axis perpendicular to the xy plane and passing through the origin O.

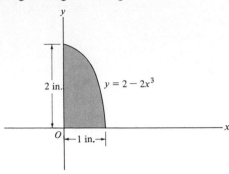

$y = 2 - 2x^3$

2 in.

1 in.

Prob. 10-11

10-12. Compute the moment of inertia of the triangular area about (a) an axis passing through the base of the triangle, and (b) the x axis (the centroidal axis of the triangle).

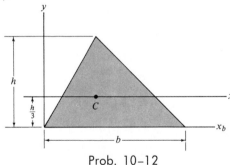

Prob. 10-12

10-13. Determine the moment of inertia for the quarter circle about the $\bar{x}$ axis passing through the centroid C.

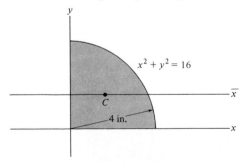

$x^2 + y^2 = 16$

4 in.

Prob. 10-13

10-14. Determine the moment of inertia of the shaded area about the x and about the y axis.

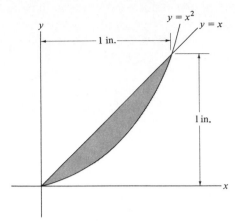

$y = x^2$

$y = x$

1 in.

1 in.

Prob. 10-14

10-15. Determine the radius of gyration k_x of the shaded area with respect to the x axis.

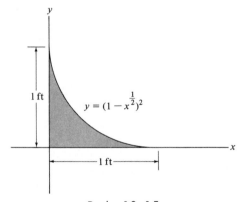

1 ft

$y = (1 - x^{\frac{1}{2}})^2$

1 ft

Prob. 10-15

A composite area generally consists of a series of connected "simpler" area shapes, such as semicircles, rectangles, and triangles. The moments of inertia for each of these simpler shapes can be determined by using the methods of integration discussed in Sec. 10-4. Since the integral used to compute the moment of inertia for a composite area may be subdivided into integrals computed over the simpler parts, the total moment of inertia for the composite area with respect to a given axis is obtained by "adding together" the moments of inertia of the composite parts about the same axis. The parallel-axis theorem should be used to transfer the moment of inertia of each composite area to the desired axis. When the region of an area has a hole, the moment of inertia for the region is found by "subtracting" the moment of inertia for the hole from the moment of inertia for the entire area, including the hole.

The moments of inertia for some common area shapes are given in Table 10-1. Furthermore, in many cases beams and columns are composed of two or more structural elements, such as angles and channels, which are welded together. The moment of inertia or radius of gyration for such a composite cross-sectional area is frequently required when using structural design formulas. The moments of inertia for standard

Table 10-1   Moments of Inertia for Common Geometric Area Shapes

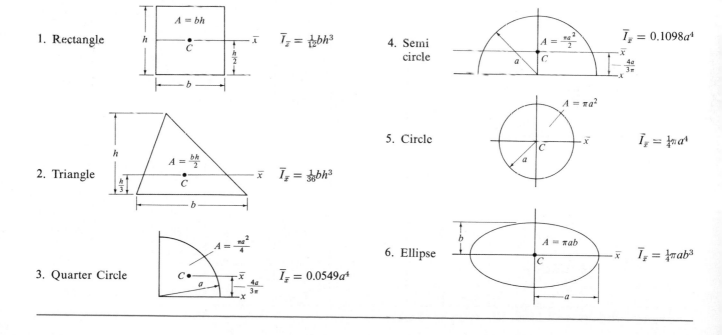

1. Rectangle $A = bh$ $\bar{I}_{\bar{x}} = \frac{1}{12}bh^3$

2. Triangle $A = \frac{bh}{2}$ $\bar{I}_{\bar{x}} = \frac{1}{36}bh^3$

3. Quarter Circle $A = \frac{\pi a^2}{4}$ $\bar{I}_{\bar{x}} = 0.0549a^4$

4. Semi circle $A = \frac{\pi a^2}{2}$ $\bar{I}_{\bar{x}} = 0.1098a^4$

5. Circle $A = \pi a^2$ $\bar{I}_{\bar{x}} = \frac{1}{4}\pi a^4$

6. Ellipse $A = \pi ab$ $\bar{I}_{\bar{x}} = \frac{1}{4}\pi ab^3$

structural elements are tabulated in engineering handbooks and design codes. For purposes here, a representative tabulation, taken from the American Institute of Steel Construction manual, is given in Table 10–2.

The following two example problems illustrate the method for finding the moment of inertia for composite areas using the data in Tables 10–1 and 10–2.

Table 10–2 Properties of Rolled Steel Shapes

Type	Nominal Size	$wt/Length$ (lb/ft)	Area $(in.^2)$	$\bar{I}_{\bar{x}}$ $(in.^4)$	$\bar{y}$ $(in.)$	$\bar{I}_{\bar{y}}$ $(in.^4)$	$\bar{x}$ $(in.)$
Wide Flange (W)	$30 \times 15^*$	210	61.9	9,890	—	757	—
	18×17	60	17.7	986	—	50.1	—
	8×8	67	19.7	272	—	88.6	—
Standard Channel (C)	$15 \times 3\frac{3}{8}$	40	11.8	349	—	9.23	0.778
	12×3	30	8.82	162	—	5.14	0.674
	$10 \times 2\frac{5}{8}$	25	7.35	91.2	—	3.36	0.690
Angle (L)	$4 \times 3 \times \frac{3}{8}†$	8.5	2.48	3.96	1.28	1.92	0.782
	$3 \times 3 \times \frac{1}{4}$	4.9	1.44	1.24	0.842	1.24	0.842
	$2 \times 2 \times \frac{3}{8}$	4.7	1.36	0.479	0.636	0.479	0.636

*First figure is depth; second is width.   †Third figure is thickness.

Example 10-4

Moments of Inertia for an Area   373

Compute the moment of inertia of the composite area shown in Fig. 10-8a about the x axis.

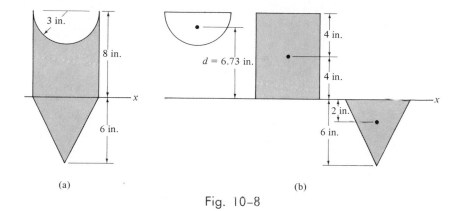

(a)   (b)

Fig. 10-8

Solution

For convenience, the composite area may be obtained by *subtracting* the semicircle from the rectangle and triangle as shown in Fig. 10-8b. The moments of inertia for each of these composite parts about the x axis may be computed using the parallel-axis theorem and the data contained in Table 10-1.

Semicircle:

$$d = 8 - \frac{4(3)}{3\pi} = 6.73 \text{ in.}$$

$$I_x = \bar{I}_x + Ad^2$$

$$= 0.1098(3 \text{ in.})^4 + \frac{\pi(3 \text{ in.})^2}{2}(6.73 \text{ in.})^2 = 649 \text{ in.}^4$$

Rectangle:

$$I_x = \bar{I}_x + Ad^2$$

$$= \tfrac{1}{12}(6 \text{ in.})(8 \text{ in.})^3 + (6 \text{ in.})(8 \text{ in.})(4 \text{ in.})^2 = 1,024 \text{ in.}^4$$

Triangle:

$$I_x = \bar{I}_x + Ad^2$$

$$= \tfrac{1}{36}(6 \text{ in.})(6 \text{ in.})^3 + \tfrac{1}{2}(6 \text{ in.})(6 \text{ in.})(2 \text{ in.})^2 = 108 \text{ in.}^4$$

The moment of inertia for the entire composite area is thus

$$I_x = -649 \text{ in.}^4 + 1,024 \text{ in.}^4 + 108 \text{ in.}^4 = 483 \text{ in.}^4 \qquad \textit{Ans.}$$

Example 10-5

Compute the moment of inertia about the centroidal axis of the composite beam cross section shown in Fig. 10-9a. Neglect the inertia of the rivets.

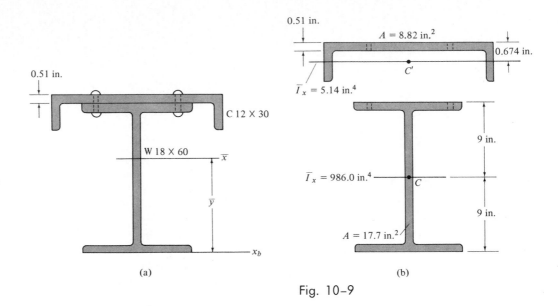

Fig. 10-9

Solution

The necessary geometrical properties for the wide-flange beam and channel, which are listed in Table 10-2, are shown in Fig. 10-9b.

It is first necessary to determine the centroidal distance $\bar{y}$ for the *entire section*, Fig. 10-9a. This is done by using the techniques discussed in Sec. 9-4. With reference to the base axis x_b, the distance $\bar{y}$ is

$$\bar{y} = \frac{\Sigma \tilde{y} A}{\Sigma A}$$

$$= \frac{(9 \text{ in.})17.7 \text{ in.}^2 + (18 \text{ in.} + 0.51 \text{ in.} - 0.674 \text{ in.})8.82 \text{ in.}^2}{17.7 \text{ in.}^2 + 8.82 \text{ in.}^2}$$

$$= 11.94 \text{ in.}$$

Using the parallel-axis theorem, we can now compute the moment of inertia for the wide-flange beam and channel about the $\bar{x}$ axis.

Wide-flange beam:

$$I_{\bar{x}} = \bar{I}_x + Ad^2$$
$$= 986 \text{ in.}^4 + 17.7 \text{ in.}^2(11.94 \text{ in.} - 9 \text{ in.})^2 = 1{,}139 \text{ in.}^4$$

$I_{\bar{x}} = \bar{I}_x + Ad^2$

$= 5.14 \text{ in.}^4 + 8.82 \text{ in.}^2(18 \text{ in.} + 0.51 \text{ in.} - 0.674 - 11.94 \text{ in.})^2 = 312 \text{ in.}^4$

Thus, the moment of inertia for the entire section becomes

$$I_{\bar{x}} = 1,139 \text{ in.}^4 + 312 \text{ in.}^4 = 1,451 \text{ in.}^4 \qquad\qquad \textit{Ans.}$$

Problems

10-16. Determine the moment of inertia of the shaded section with respect to a horizontal axis passing through the centroid.

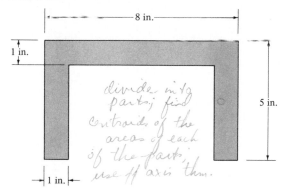

Prob. 10-16

10-17. Determine the radius of gyration k_x of the shaded area about the x centroidal axis.

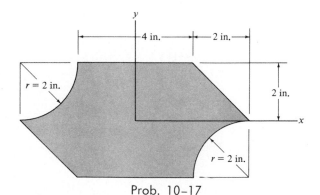

Prob. 10-17

10-18. Determine the moments of inertia of the shaded area with respect to the x and with respect to the y centroidal axes.

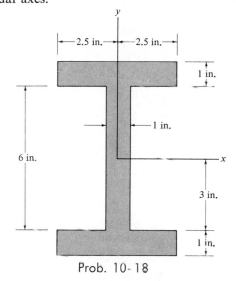

Prob. 10-18

10-19. Determine the moments of inertia of the shaded area with respect to the x and with respect to the y axis.

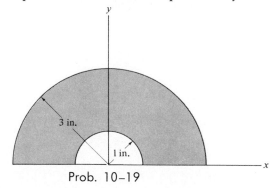

Prob. 10-19

10-20. Determine the moment of inertia of the shaded area with respect to a horizontal axis passing through the centroid of the section.

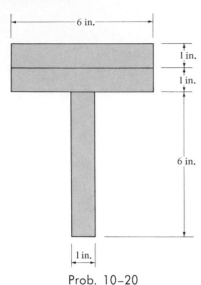

Prob. 10-20

10-21. Determine the moment of inertia of the composite section with respect to a horizontal axis passing through the centroid of the cross section.

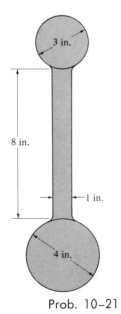

Prob. 10-21

10-22. Determine the moment of inertia of the composite beam cross section with respect to the x centroidal axis. Neglect the inertia of the rivets.

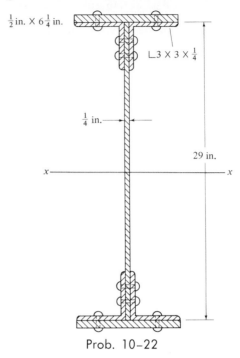

Prob. 10-22

10-23. Determine the moment of inertia of the beam cross section with respect to the x centroidal axis. Neglect the inertia of the rivets.

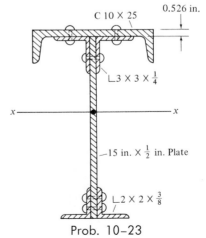

Prob. 10-23

376

10-24. Determine the polar moment of inertia of the shaded area about the origin of coordinates, O, located at the centroid.

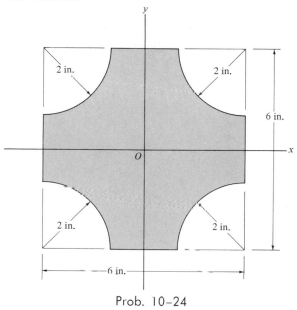

Prob. 10-24

10-25. The cross section of the beam consists of two angles, a wide-flange beam, and a cover plate, all welded together as shown. Determine the moment of inertia of this section with respect to the x centroidal axis.

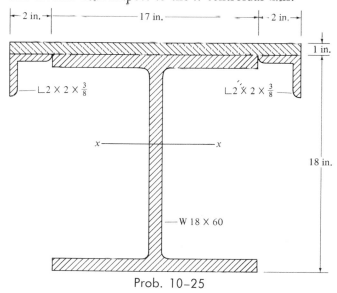

Prob. 10-25

10-26. The composite cross section for the column consists of two cover plates riveted to two channels. Determine the radii of gyration k_x and k_y with respect to the centroidal x and y axes.

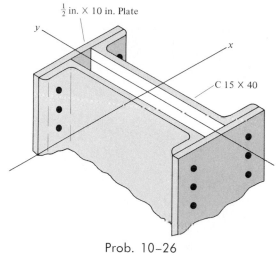

Prob. 10-26

10-27. A column has a builtup cross section as shown. Neglecting the inertia of the lacing and rivets, determine the radius of gyration of the column about the x centroidal axis.

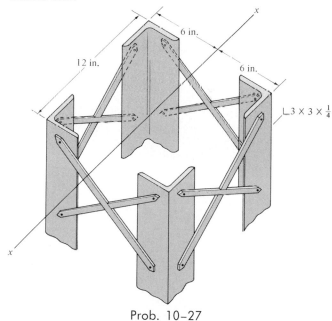

Prob. 10-27

377

10–28. Determine the moment of inertia of the composite area with respect to the x' axis. The area is symmetric with respect to the y axis.

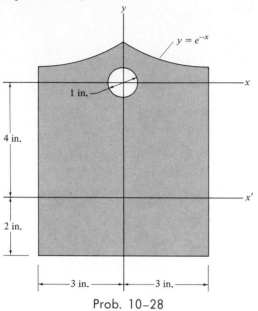

Prob. 10–28

10–29. Determine the moment of inertia of the composite area with respect to the x axis.

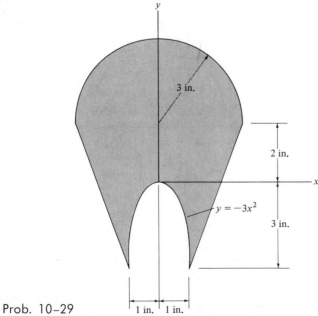

Prob. 10–29

10–30. Determine the moments of inertia of the "Z" section with respect to the x and with respect to the y centroidal axes.

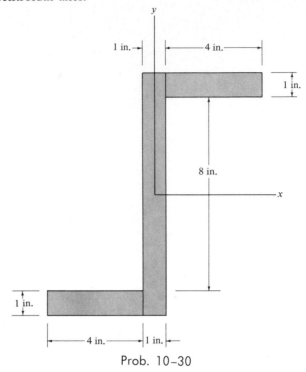

Prob. 10–30

10–31. Determine the moment of inertia of the composite area with respect to the x axis.

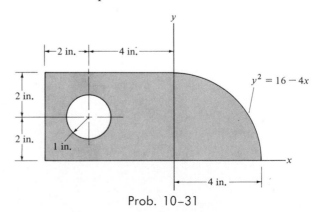

Prob. 10–31

378

The rectangular moment of inertia for a planar area about an axis will usually vary, depending upon how the axis is orientated with respect to the area. In some applications of structural design it is necessary to know the orientation of those axes which give, respectively, the maximum and minimum moment of inertia for the area. Techniques which are used to find these axes will be discussed in Sec. 10–7. To use these techniques it is required that one know the product of inertia for the area as well as its rectangular moments of inertia for a given orientation of the axes.

The *product of inertia* dI_{xy} for an elemental area dA, shown in Fig. 10–10, with respect to the x and y axis, is defined as

$$dI_{xy} = xy \, dA$$

For the total area A, shown in Fig. 10–10, this equation becomes

$$I_{xy} = \int_A xy \, dA \qquad (10\text{–}7)$$

w.r.t.
x & y axis

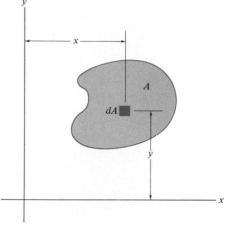

Fig. 10–10

The integration of Eq. 10–7 may be performed by using double or single integration. Although the element of area is more easily established with double integration, there is less confusion in establishing the limits for single integration.

Like the moment of inertia, the product of inertia has units of length raised to the fourth power, e.g., in.^{4} or ft^4. Since x or y may be a negative quantity, while the element of area is always positive, the product of inertia may be positive, negative, or zero, depending upon the location and orientation of the coordinate axes.

The product of inertia I_{xy} for the area will be *zero* if the x or y axis, or both axes are *axes of symmetry* for the area. To show this consider the area given in Fig. 10–11, which happens to be symmetrical with respect to the x axis. As shown in the figure, for every element dA located at the point (x, y) there is a corresponding element dA located at $(x, -y)$. The products of inertia for these elements are respectively $xy \, dA$ and $-xy \, dA$. Since one product of inertia is the negative of the other, the sum of the products of inertia for all of the elements of area which are chosen in this way will cancel each other. Hence, the product of inertia for the total area becomes zero.

The *parallel-axis theorem* for products of inertia of planar areas may be developed in a manner similar to that for rectangular moments of inertia. Consider the shaded area shown in Fig. 10–12, where $\bar{x}$ and $\bar{y}$ represent a set of axes passing through the *centroid C* of the area, and x and y represent a corresponding set of parallel axes. The product of inertia for the elemental area dA, with respect to the x and y axes, is

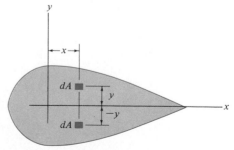

Fig. 10–11

$$dI_{xy} = xy \, dA = (x_C + \bar{x})(y_C + \bar{y}) \, dA$$

Expanding this expression and integrating each term to obtain the total product of inertia yields

$$I_{xy} = \int_A \bar{x}\bar{y} \, dA + x_C \int_A \bar{y} \, dA + y_C \int_A \bar{x} \, dA + x_C y_C \int_A dA$$

or

$$I_{xy} = \bar{I}_{\bar{x}\bar{y}} + x_C \int_A \bar{y} \, dA + y_C \int_A \bar{x} \, dA + x_C y_C A$$

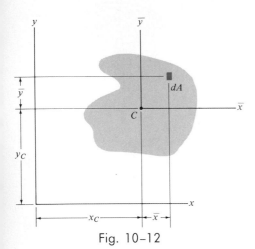

Fig. 10–12

In this expression, $\bar{I}_{\bar{x}\bar{y}}$ represents the product of inertia for the area with respect to the centroidal axes. The integrals in the second and third terms on the right vanish, since the moments of the area are taken about the centroidal axis. Therefore, the parallel-axis theorem for the product of inertia becomes

$$I_{xy} = \bar{I}_{\bar{x}\bar{y}} + A \, x_C y_C$$

In words, the product of inertia I_{xy} is equal to the product of inertia $\bar{I}_{\bar{x}\bar{y}}$, plus the product of the area A, times the perpendicular distances x_C and y_C which lie between the $\bar{x}\bar{y}$ and xy axes. In particular, it is important that the algebraic signs for x_C and y_C be maintained when applying this formula.

*10–7. Principal Moments of Inertia

Consider the planar area A and the coordinate axes xy and uv, shown in Fig. 10–13. In structural mechanics, it is sometimes necessary to calculate the moments and product of inertia I_u, I_v, and I_{uv} for the area with respect to the inclined u and v axes, when the values for θ, I_x, I_y, and I_{xy} are *known*. Referring to Fig. 10–13, we may relate the perpendicular distance from the area element dA to the axes of the two coordinate systems by using the transformation

$$u = x \cos \theta + y \sin \theta$$
$$v = y \cos \theta - x \sin \theta$$

Using these equations, the moments and product of inertia of dA about the u and v axes become

$$dI_u = v^2 \, dA = (y \cos \theta - x \sin \theta)^2 \, dA$$
$$dI_v = u^2 \, dA = (x \cos \theta + y \sin \theta)^2 \, dA$$

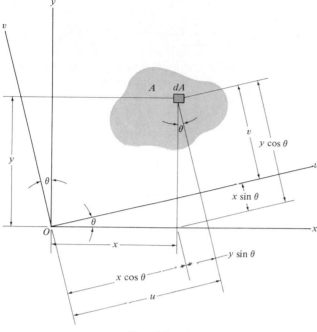

Fig. 10–13

and

$$dI_{uv} = uv \, dA = (x \cos \theta + y \sin \theta)(y \cos \theta - x \sin \theta) \, dA$$

Expanding each of these expressions and integrating, realizing that

$$I_x = \int_A y^2 \, dA, \; I_y = \int_A x^2 \, dA, \; \text{and} \; I_{xy} = \int_A xy \, dA, \; \text{we obtain}$$

$$I_u = I_x \cos^2 \theta + I_y \sin^2 \theta - 2I_{xy} \sin \theta \cos \theta$$
$$I_v = I_x \sin^2 \theta + I_y \cos^2 \theta + 2I_{xy} \sin \theta \cos \theta$$

and

$$I_{uv} = I_x \sin \theta \cos \theta - I_y \sin \theta \cos \theta + I_{xy}(\cos^2 \theta - \sin^2 \theta)$$

Using the trigonometric identities, $\sin 2\theta = 2 \sin \theta \cos \theta$ and $\cos 2\theta = \cos^2 \theta - \sin^2 \theta$, we can reduce the above equations to the form

$$I_u = \frac{I_x + I_y}{2} + \frac{I_x - I_y}{2} \cos 2\theta - I_{xy} \sin 2\theta \qquad (10\text{–}8a)$$

$$I_v = \frac{I_x + I_y}{2} - \frac{I_x - I_y}{2} \cos 2\theta + I_{xy} \sin 2\theta \qquad (10\text{–}8b)$$

and

$$I_{uv} = \frac{I_x - I_y}{2} \sin 2\theta + I_{xy} \cos 2\theta \qquad (10\text{-}8c)$$

If Eqs. 10-8a and 10-8b are added together, we see that the polar moment inertia about the z axis passing through point O is *independent* of the orientation of the u and v axes, i.e.,

$$J_O = I_u + I_v = I_x + I_y$$

From Eqs. 10-8, it may be seen that the moments and product of inertia, I_u, I_v, and I_{uv}, will, in general, have a different value for each value of θ. It is sometimes important to determine the orientation of the axis about which the moments of inertia for the area are maximum and minimum. This particular set of axes is called the *principal axes* of the area through the point O. The corresponding moments of inertia with respect to these axes are called the *principal moments of inertia* at point O. In general, *every point* has its own set of principal axes. However, in structural mechanics, the centroid is important.

The angle $\theta = \theta_p$, which gives the principal moments of inertia for the area, may be found by differentiating Eq. 10-8a with respect to θ, and setting the result equal to zero. Thus,

$$\frac{dI_u}{d\theta} = -2\left(\frac{I_x - I_y}{2}\right) \sin 2\theta - 2I_{xy} \cos 2\theta = 0$$

and therefore,

$$\tan 2\theta_p = \frac{-I_{xy}}{\dfrac{I_x - I_y}{2}} \qquad (10\text{-}9)$$

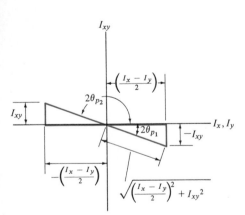

Fig. 10-14

Equation 10-9 has two roots θ_{p_1} and θ_{p_2} which locate the axes for maximum and minimum moments of inertia. Due to the nature of the tangent, the values of $2\theta_{p_1}$ and $2\theta_{p_2}$ are 180° apart, so that θ_{p_1} and θ_{p_2} are 90° apart. Assuming that I_{xy} and $(I_x - I_y)$ are both positive quantities, we can obtain the sine and cosine of $2\theta_{p_1}$ and $2\theta_{p_2}$ from the triangles shown in Fig. 10-14, which are based upon Eq. 10-9.

$$\text{For } \theta_{p_1} \begin{cases} \sin 2\theta_{p_1} = -I_{xy} \Big/ \sqrt{\left(\dfrac{I_x - I_y}{2}\right)^2 + I_{xy}^2} \\[4mm] \cos 2\theta_{p_1} = \left(\dfrac{I_x - I_y}{2}\right) \Big/ \sqrt{\left(\dfrac{I_x - I_y}{2}\right)^2 + I_{xy}^2} \end{cases}$$

$$\text{For } \theta_{p_2} \begin{cases} \sin 2\theta_{p_2} = I_{xy} \Big/ \sqrt{\left(\dfrac{I_x - I_y}{2}\right)^2 + I_{xy}^2} \\[4mm] \cos 2\theta_{p_2} = -\left(\dfrac{I_x - I_y}{2}\right) \Big/ \sqrt{\left(\dfrac{I_x - I_y}{2}\right)^2 + I_{xy}^2} \end{cases}$$

If we substitute these two sets of trigonometric relations into Eq. 10–8a, (or Eq. 10–8b) and simplify, the result reduces to

$$I_{\substack{max \\ min}} = \frac{I_x + I_y}{2} \pm \sqrt{\left(\frac{I_x - I_y}{2}\right)^2 + I_{xy}^2} \qquad (10\text{–}10)$$

Depending upon the sign chosen, this result gives the maximum or minimum moment of inertia for the area. Furthermore, if the above trigonometric relations for θ_{p_1} and θ_{p_2} are substituted into Eq. 10–8c, it may be shown that $I_{uv} = 0$; that is, the *product of inertia with respect to the principal axes is zero.* As shown in Sec. 10–6 the product of inertia is zero with respect to a symmetrical axis; therefore, it follows that *any symmetrical axis represents a principal axis of inertia for the area.*

*10–8. Mohr's Circle for Moments of Inertia

Equations 10–8 through 10–10 have a graphical solution which is convenient to use and generally easy to remember. Squaring Eqs. 10–8a and 10–8c, and adding, we find that

$$\left(I_u - \frac{I_x + I_y}{2}\right)^2 + I_{uv}^2 = \left(\frac{I_x - I_y}{2}\right)^2 + I_{xy}^2 \qquad (10\text{–}11)$$

In a given problem, I_u and I_{uv} are *variables,* and I_x, I_y, and I_{xy} are *known constants.* Thus, Eq. 10–11 may be written in compact form as

$$(I_u - a)^2 + I_{uv}^2 = R^2$$

When this equation is plotted on the $I_u I_{uv}$ plane, the resulting graph represents a circle of radius

$$R = \sqrt{\left(\frac{I_x - I_y}{2}\right)^2 + I_{xy}^2}$$

having its center located at point (a, O), where $a = (I_x + I_y)/2$. The circle so constructed is called *Mohr's circle,* named after the German engineer Otto Mohr (1835–1918).

There are several methods for plotting Mohr's circle as defined by Eq. 10–11. The main purpose in using the circle here is to have a convenient procedure for transforming the moments of inertia I_x, I_y, and I_{xy} into the principal moments of inertia for a given planar area. The following step-by-step procedure provides a method for doing this.

1. Establish an xy axis for the area having the origin located at the point P of interest, and determine I_x, I_y, and I_{xy} (see Fig. 10–15a).

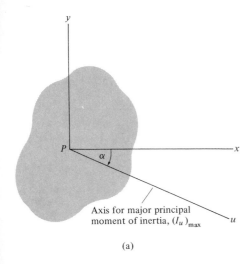

Axis for major principal
moment of inertia, $(I_u)_{max}$

(a)

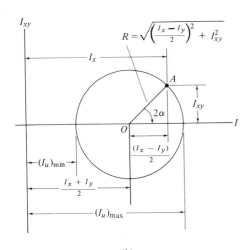

$$R = \sqrt{\left(\frac{I_x - I_y}{2}\right)^2 + I_{xy}^2}$$

(b)

Fig. 10-15

2. Construct a rectangular coordinate system of axes such that the abscissa represents the rectangular moment of inertia, I, and the ordinate represents the product of inertia I_{xy} (see Fig. 10-15b).
3. Determine the location for the center of the circle, O, which is located at a distance $(I_x + I_y)/2$ from the origin (see Fig. 10-15b).
4. Plot the "controlling point" A having coordinates (I_x, I_{xy}). By definition, I_x is always positive, whereas I_{xy} will be either positive or negative (see Fig. 10-15b).
5. Connect the controlling point A found in step 4 with the center of the circle, and determine the distance OA by trigonometry. This distance represents the radius of the circle (see Fig. 10-15b).
6. Draw the circle having the radius found in step 5. The points where the circle intersects the abscissa give the values of the principal moments of inertia $(I_u)_{min}$ and $(I_u)_{max}$. Notice that the *product of inertia will be zero at these points* (see Fig. 10-15b).
7. To find the direction of the major principal axis, determine by trigonometry the angle 2α, *measured from the radius OA to the direction line of the positive abscissa*. This angle represents twice the angle from the x axis of the area in question to the axis of maximum moment of inertia, $(I_u)_{max}$. Both the angle on the circle, 2α, and the angle on the area, α, *must be measured in the same sense*, as shown in Fig. 10-15. The axis for minimum moment of inertia $(I_u)_{min}$ is perpendicular to the axis for $(I_u)_{max}$.

Using trigonometry, we may verify these statements as being in accordance with the equations developed in Sec. 10-7.

Example 10-6

Determine the product of inertia of (a) the rectangle and (b) the triangle, shown in Fig. 10-16a, with respect to both the $\bar{x}$ and $\bar{y}$ centroidal axes, and also with respect to the x and y axes.

Solution
Part (a). Since $\bar{x}$ and $\bar{y}$ are *axes of symmetry* for the rectangle, the product of inertia for the rectangle with respect to these axes is zero. Hence,

$$I_{\bar{x}\bar{y}} = 0 \qquad Ans.$$

Using the parallel-axis theorem, we find that the product of inertia with respect to the x and y axes is

$$I_{xy} = I_{\bar{x}\bar{y}} + A x_C y_C$$

$$= 0 + bh\frac{b}{2}\frac{h}{2}$$

$$= \frac{b^2 h^2}{4} \qquad Ans.$$

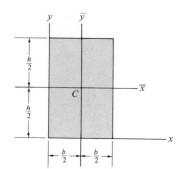

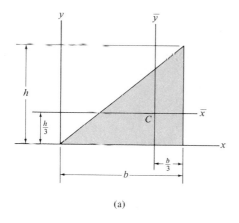

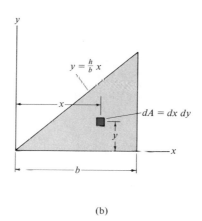

(a)

(b)

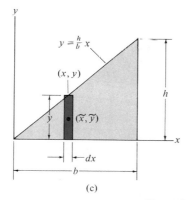

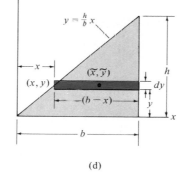

(c)

(d)

Fig. 10–16

Part (b). The product of inertia of the triangle with respect to the x and y axes can be determined by using integration. If a second-order element located at point (x, y) is chosen, as shown in Fig. 10–16b, then

$$dI_{xy} = xy \, dA = xy \, dy \, dx$$

Integrating on y from 0 to $y = (h/b)x$ and then on x from 0 to b we obtain,

$$I_{xy} = \int_A dI_{xy} = \int_A xy \, dy \, dx = \int_0^b \int_0^{(h/b)x} xy \, dy \, dx$$

$$= \int_0^b x \, dx \left[\frac{1}{2} y^2 \right]_0^{(h/b)x}$$

$$= \frac{1}{2} \frac{h^2}{b^2} \int_0^b x^3 \, dx = \frac{b^2 h^2}{8} \qquad \qquad Ans.$$

As a second method, if first-order elements are used for integration, the parallel-axis theorem must be used. The *product of inertia for the differential element* shown in Fig. 10–16c is

$$dI_{xy} = d\bar{I}_{\tilde{x}\tilde{y}} + dA \, \tilde{x}\tilde{y}$$

where $(\tilde{x}, \tilde{y})$ represents the *centroid for the element*. Since $d\bar{I}_{\tilde{x}\tilde{y}} = 0$, (due to symmetry) and $\tilde{x} = x$, $\tilde{y} = y/2$, then

$$dI_{xy} = 0 + (y \, dx) \, x \frac{y}{2} = \left(\frac{h}{b} x \, dx \right) x \frac{h}{2b} x$$

or

$$dI_{xy} = \frac{h^2}{2b^2} x^3 \, dx$$

Integrating with respect to x from 0 to b,

$$I_{xy} = \frac{h^2}{2b^2} \int_0^b x^3 \, dx = \frac{b^2 h^2}{8} \qquad \qquad Ans.$$

As a third method of solution, consider elements having thickness dy and area $dA = (b - x)dy$, as shown in Fig. 10–16d. The centroid is located at point $\tilde{x} = x + (b - x)/2 = (b + x)/2$, $\tilde{y} = y$. Hence,

$$dI_{xy} = d\bar{I}_{\tilde{x}\tilde{y}} + dA \, \tilde{x}\tilde{y}$$

$$= 0 + (b - x) \, dy \left(\frac{b + x}{2} \right) y$$

$$= \left(b - \frac{b}{h} y \right) dy \left(\frac{b + \frac{b}{h} y}{2} \right) y$$

Integrating with respect to y from 0 to h,

$$I_{xy} = \frac{1}{2} \int_0^h y \left(b^2 - \frac{b^2}{h^2} y^2 \right) dy = \frac{b^2 h^2}{8} \qquad \text{Ans.}$$

The product of inertia for the triangle with respect to its centroidal axis, Fig. 10–16a, may be computed using the above result and the parallel-axis theorem.

$$I_{xy} = \bar{I}_{\bar{x}\bar{y}} + A x_C y_C$$

$$\frac{b^2 h^2}{8} = \bar{I}_{\bar{x}\bar{y}} + \frac{1}{2} bh \left(\frac{1}{3} h \right) \left(\frac{2}{3} b \right)$$

Hence,

$$I_{\bar{x}\bar{y}} = \frac{1}{72} b^2 h^2 \qquad \text{Ans.}$$

Example 10–7

Determine the principal moments of inertia for the "Z" section shown in Fig. 10–17a with respect to an axis passing through the centroid C.

Solution

To compute the principal moments of inertia, it is first necessary to determine the moments and product of inertia of the area with respect to the x and y axes shown. This can be done by assuming that the cross-sectional area consists of three rectangles, A, B, and D, as shown in Fig. 10–17b. Using the parallel-axis theorem for rectangles A and D, the computations are as follows:

$$I_x = [\tfrac{1}{12}(1)(3)^3 + (1)(3)(2)^2] + [\tfrac{1}{12}(6)(1)^3] + [\tfrac{1}{12}(1)(3)^3$$
$$+ (1)(3)(2)^2] = 29 \text{ in.}^4$$

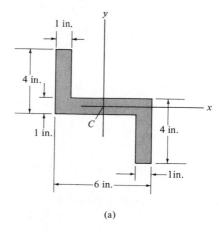

(a)

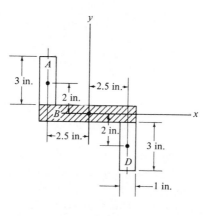

(b)

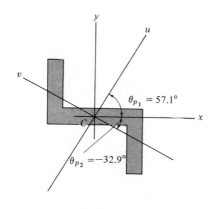

(c)

Fig. 10–17

$$I_y = [\tfrac{1}{12}(3)(1)^3 + (3)(1)(-2.5)^2] + [\tfrac{1}{12}(1)(6)^3]$$
$$+ [\tfrac{1}{12}(3)(1)^3 + (3)(1)(2.5)^2] = 56 \text{ in.}^4$$

$$I_{xy} = [0 + (3)(1)(-2.5)(2)] + [0] + [0 + (3)(1)(2.5)(-2)] = -30 \text{ in.}^4$$

Using Eq. 10–9, the principal axes are orientated as follows:

$$\tan 2\theta_p = \frac{-I_{xy}}{\dfrac{I_x - I_y}{2}} = \frac{30}{\dfrac{29 - 56}{2}} = -2.22$$

$$2\theta_{p_1} = 114.2° \quad \text{and} \quad 2\theta_{p_2} = -65.8°$$

Thus,

$$\theta_{p_1} = 57.1° \quad \text{and} \quad \theta_{p_2} = -32.9°$$

The u and v (principal) axes are therefore orientated as shown in Fig. 10–17c.

The principal moments of inertia with respect to the u and v axes are determined using Eq. 10–10. Hence,

$$(I_u)_{\substack{\max \\ \min}} = \frac{I_x + I_y}{2} \pm \sqrt{\left(\frac{I_x - I_y}{2}\right)^2 + I_{xy}^2}$$

$$= \frac{29 + 56}{2} \pm \sqrt{\left(\frac{29 - 56}{2}\right)^2 + (-30)^2}$$

$$= 42.5 \text{ in.}^4 \pm 32.9 \text{ in.}^4$$

or

$$(I_u)_{\max} = 75.4 \text{ in.}^4, \qquad (I_u)_{\min} = 9.6 \text{ in.}^4 \qquad \textit{Ans.}$$

Specifically, the *maximum moment of inertia* $I_{\max} = 75.4$ in.^{4} occurs with respect to the u axis *since, by inspection, most of the cross-section area is farthest away from this axis*. (To show this mathematically, substitute $\theta = 57.1°$ into Eq. 10–8a.)

Example 10–8

Using Mohr's circle, determine the principal moments of inertia for the "Z" section shown in Fig. 10–18a with respect to an axis passing through the centroid C.

Solution

The problem will be solved using the step-by-step procedure outlined in Sec. 10–8.

Step 1: The moments of inertia and the product of inertia have been determined in Example 10–7 with respect to the xy axis shown in Fig. 10–18a as $I_x = 29$ in.^{4}, $I_y = 56$ in.^{4}, and $I_{xy} = -30$ in.^{4}.

Steps 2, 3, 4, and 5: The I and I_{xy} axes are shown in Fig. 10–18*b*. The center of the circle, O, lies at a distance $(I_x + I_y)/2 = (29 + 56)/2 = 42.5$ in.^{4} from the origin. When the controlling point $A(29$ in.^{4}, -30 in.$^4)$ is connected to point O, the radius OA is determined from the triangle OBA using the Pythagorean theorem.

$$OA = \sqrt{(13.5)^2 + (-30)^2} = 32.9 \text{ in.}^4$$

Step 6: The circle is constructed in Fig. 10–18*c* and intersects the I axes at points (75.4 in.^{4}, 0) and (9.6 in.^{4}, 0). Hence,

$$(I_u)_{\max} = 75.4 \text{ in.}^4 \qquad\qquad Ans.$$
$$(I_u)_{\min} = 9.6 \text{ in.}^4 \qquad\qquad Ans.$$

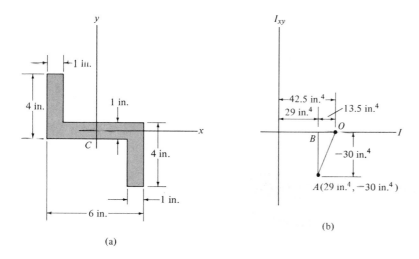

(a)

(b)

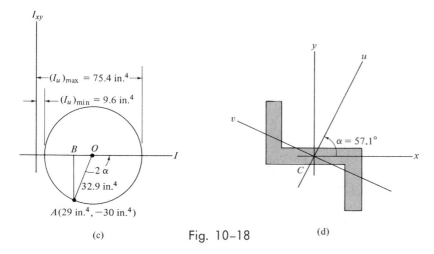

(c)

Fig. 10–18

(d)

Step 7: From Fig. 10–18c, the angle 2α as determined from the circle (*measured counterclockwise* from OA to the direction of the *positive I* axis) is

$$2\alpha = 180° - \sin^{-1}\frac{BA}{OA} = 180° - \sin^{-1}\frac{30}{32.9} = 114.2°$$

The principal axis for $(I_u)_{max} = 75.4$ in.[4] is therefore orientated at an angle $\alpha = 57.1°$ (measured *counterclockwise*) from the *positive x* axis to the *positive u* axis. The v axis is perpendicular to this axis. The results are shown in Fig. 10–18d.

Problems

10-32. Determine the product of inertia of the shaded area with respect to the x and y axes.

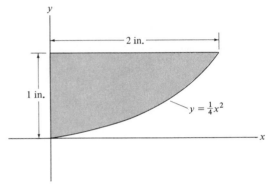

Prob. 10–32

10-33. Determine the product of inertia of the shaded area with respect to the x and y axes.

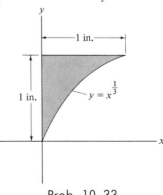

Prob. 10–33

10-34. Determine the product of inertia of the shaded section of the ellipse with respect to the x and y axes.

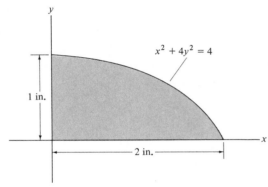

Prob. 10–34

10-35. Determine the product of inertia of the shaded area with respect to the x and y axes.

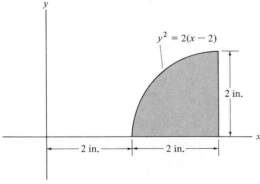

Prob. 10–35

10-36. Determine the product of inertia of the quarter circle with respect to the x and y axes.

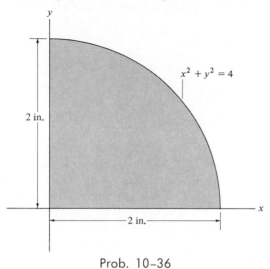

$x^2 + y^2 = 4$

2 in.

2 in.

Prob. 10–36

10-37. Determine the product of inertia of the shaded portion of the parabola with respect to the x and y axes.

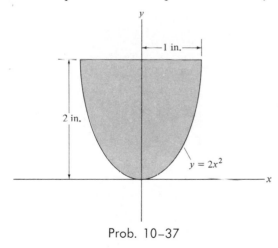

1 in.

2 in.

$y = 2x^2$

Prob. 10–37

10-38. Determine the product of inertia I_{xy} of half the shaded portion of the parabola in Prob. 10–37, bounded by the lines $y = 2$ in. and $x = 0$.

10-39. Determine the product of inertia of the shaded area with respect to the x and y axes passing through the centroid C.

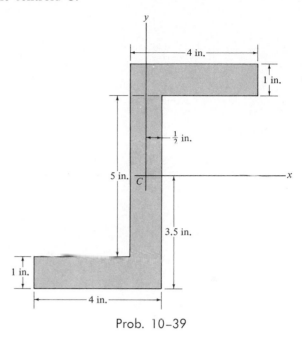

4 in.

1 in.

$\frac{1}{2}$ in.

5 in. C

3.5 in.

1 in.

4 in.

Prob. 10–39

10-40. Determine the product of inertia for the area with respect to the x and y axes passing through the centroid C.

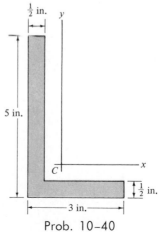

$\frac{1}{2}$ in.

5 in.

C

$\frac{1}{2}$ in.

3 in.

Prob. 10–40

391

10-41. Determine the product of inertia of the "Z" section with respect to the x and y axes passing through the centroid C.

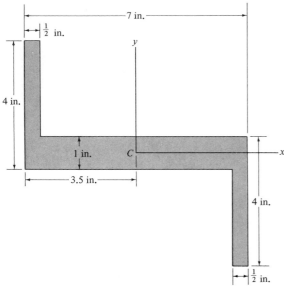

Prob. 10-41

10-42. Compute the moments of inertia of the shaded area with respect to the x' and y' axes.

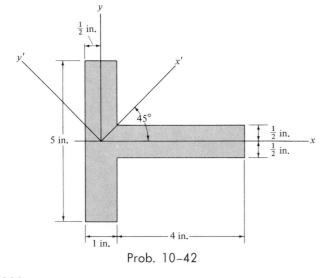

Prob. 10-42

10-43. Determine the orientation of the principal centroidal axis for the composite area. What are the moments of inertia with respect to these axes?

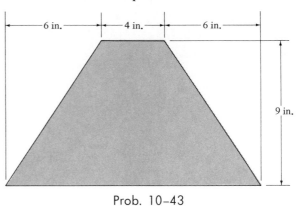

Prob. 10-43

10-44. Determine the moments of inertia and the product of inertia for the rectangular area with respect to the x' and y' axes passing through the centroid C.

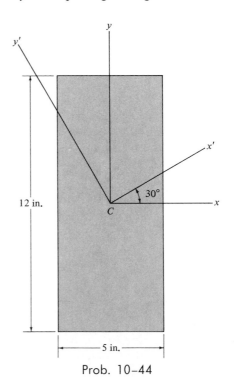

Prob. 10-44

10-45. Compute the moments of inertia for the C 12 × 30 channel section with respect to the inclined x' and y' axes passing through the centroid C.

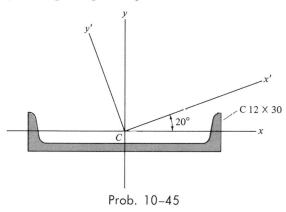

Prob. 10–45

10-47. Determine the product of inertia for the area cross section of the W 18 × 60 beam with respect to the x' and y' axes.

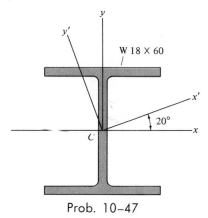

Prob. 10–47

10-46. Determine the principal moments of inertia of the composite area with respect to a pair of axes passing through the centroid C. Use the equations developed in Sec. 10-7. $I_{xy} = -81$ in.[4]

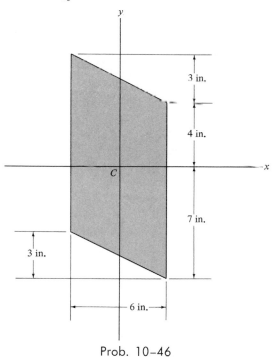

Prob. 10–46

10-48. The "Z" section has an $I_x = 55.53$ in.[4] and $I_y = 13.87$ in.[4]. Determine the principal moments of inertia for axes passing through the centroid C. Use the equations developed in Sec. 10-7. Assume all corners to be square.

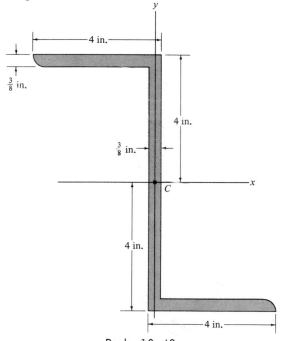

Prob. 10–48

10-49. Determine the moments of inertia and the product of inertia for the semi-circular area with respect to the x' and y' axes.

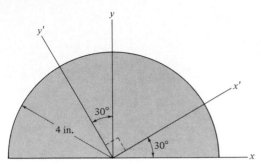

30°

30°

4 in.

Prob. 10-49

10-50. Determine the product of inertia for the angle with respect to the x and y axes, passing through the centroid C. Assume all corners to be square.

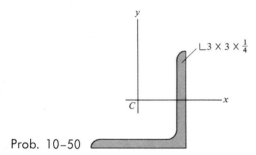

L3 × 3 × ¼

Prob. 10-50

10-51. Compute the principal moments of inertia for the $\llcorner 2 \times 2 \times \frac{3}{8}$ angle with respect to the x and y axes passing through the centroid C. Use the equations developed in Sec. 10-7. Assume all corners to be square.

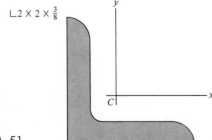

L2 × 2 × ⅜

Prob. 10-51

10-52. Determine the directions of the principal axes acting through point O, and the principal moments of inertia for the rectangular area about this point.

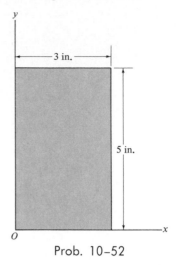

3 in.

5 in.

O

Prob. 10-52

10-53. Construct Mohr's circle for the shaded area in Prob. 10-43.

10-54. Solve Prob. 10-46 using Mohr's circle.

10-55. Solve Prob. 10-52 using Mohr's circle.

10-56. Solve Prob. 10-51 using Mohr's circle.

10-57. Solve Prob. 10-48 using Mohr's circle.

11
Virtual Work

*11-1. Definition of Work and Virtual Work

Up to this point, all equilibrium problems have been solved utilizing the equations of equilibrium and the concept of a free-body diagram. There is, however, another method for solving equilibrium problems which is based on the principles of work and energy. This method, often referred to as *the principle of virtual work,* is found to be very useful in solving certain types of equilibrium problems, particularly those involving a series of connected rigid bodies.

To understand the principle of virtual work, it is first necessary to define the *work done by a force* **F** when the force undergoes an infinitesimal displacement *d*s along a path *s*. This situation is shown in Fig. 11–1a.* If β is the angle made between the tails of the force and displacement vectors, the differential amount of work done by the force **F** is a *scalar quantity* defined by the dot product,

$$dW = \mathbf{F} \cdot d\mathbf{s} = F\,ds\cos\beta \qquad (11\text{-}1)$$

This work may be interpreted in one of two ways, either as the product of the force magnitude F and the magnitude of the component of the displacement vector in the direction of **F**, that is, $ds\cos\beta$, Fig. 11–1b, or as the product of ds times the component of force magnitude in the direction of displacement, $F\cos\beta$, Fig. 11–1c. If **F** $\cos\beta$ and ds are in the same direction, the work is "positive"; if they are in opposite directions, the work is "negative." As seen from Eq. 11–1, if **F** is *perpendicular* to the differential displacement ds, the work done by **F** is zero. For example, the component $F\sin\beta$, shown in Fig. 11–1c, does no work when

*The magnitude of the force is assumed to be constant during the infinitesimal displacement ds. Accounting for a change made in the magnitude of force during the displacement would only result in higher-order terms which would go to zero in the limit.

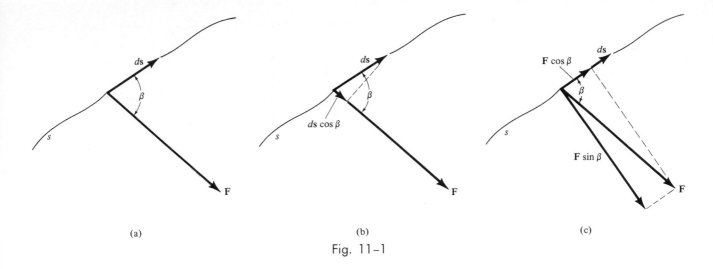

(a)　　　　　　　　(b)　　　　　　　　(c)

Fig. 11-1

the force is displaced a distance $d\mathbf{s}$. The units of work are force times displacement, e.g., ft-lb or in.-lb, the same as those for a moment; however, the two concepts are in no way related. A moment is a vector quantity, whereas work is a scalar.

The two forces of a couple do work only when the couple rotates through an angle in the plane of the couple. Consider, for example, the couple moment $M = Fr$ acting on the rigid body shown in Fig. 11-2a. When the body undergoes a small displacement (shown dashed) the force $-\mathbf{F}$ acting at A moves through a displacement $d\mathbf{s}_A$ to point A', while the force $\mathbf{F}$ at B moves through a displacement $d\mathbf{s}_B$ to B'. To analyze the motion, the displacement of the body is separated into two *independent motions,* consisting of a *translation* and a *rotation.* For example, assume that the entire body is first translated by an amount $d\mathbf{s}_A$, Fig. 11-2b, and then rotated about point A' through an angle $d\theta$. When the motion is separated in this manner, the displacement $d\mathbf{s}_B$ is divided into two components to represent each motion, that is, $d\mathbf{s}_B = d\mathbf{s}_A + d\mathbf{s}_\theta$. Here the force $\mathbf{F}$ acting at B undergoes a *differential displacement,* such that the work done when $\mathbf{F}$ is displaced is independent of the path taken by the force in moving from the beginning to the end of the displacement. Therefore, the work done in displacing $-\mathbf{F}$ along the path $d\mathbf{s}_A + d\mathbf{s}_\theta$ is equivalent to the work done in moving $\mathbf{F}$ along $d\mathbf{s}_B$. The total work done by the couple is the sum of the work done by the two forces during the translation plus the work done during the rotation. During the *translation $d\mathbf{s}_A$,* the work done by force $\mathbf{F}$ is *canceled* by the work of $-\mathbf{F}$ since the forces are equal in magnitude but opposite in direction. When the body is *rotated* about point A', $-\mathbf{F}$ does no work since this point does not move. Force $\mathbf{F}$ moves through a displacement $d\mathbf{s}_\theta$, consequently, the total work is $dW = F\,ds_\theta = F\,r\,d\theta$. Since the product Fr is equal to the

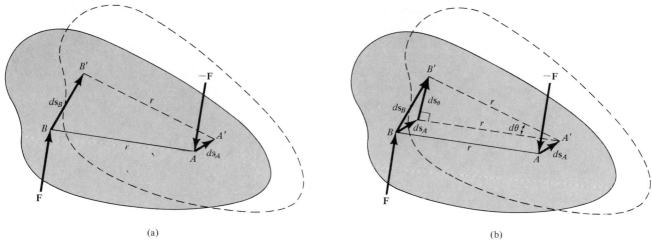

Fig. 11-2

magnitude M of the couple, then

$$dW = M\, d\theta \qquad\qquad (11\text{-}2)$$

Clearly, this result indicates that a *couple does work only* during its *rotation* and *not* during a *translation.*

The definitions of work done by both a force and a couple have been presented in terms of infinitesimal displacements ds or rotations $d\theta$. These differentials represent *actual movements*. On the other hand, a *virtual movement* indicates displacements or rotations which are *assumed* and do not actually exist. These displacements and rotations are first-order differential quantities and will be denoted by the symbols δs and $\delta\theta$, respectively. If a system of forces acts on a body originally at rest, the forces will do work when the body undergoes a virtual movement. The *virtual work* done by a force $\mathbf{F}$ undergoing a virtual displacement δs is

$$\delta W = \mathbf{F} \cdot \delta \mathbf{s} = F \cos\theta\, \delta s$$

When a couple moment $\mathbf{M}$ undergoes a virtual rotation $\delta\theta$, the virtual work is

$$\delta W = M\, \delta\theta$$

where the rotation $\delta\theta$ occurs in the plane of the couple.

★11-2. Principle of Virtual Work for a Particle

The principle of virtual work for a particle initially at rest may be stated as follows: *If the virtual work done by the system of external forces acting on a particle is zero for every independent virtual displacement of the particle, then the particle is in equilibrium.* Mathematically, this principle may be expressed as

$$\delta W = 0$$

where δW represents the virtual work done by *all the external forces* acting on the particle during a virtual displacement. In three dimensions, an unconstrained particle may have three independent virtual displacements, and therefore three independent virtual work equations may be written for the particle. For example, consider the particle P, shown in Fig. 11–3, which has a weight W and is subjected to the action of three forces $\mathbf{F}_1$, $\mathbf{F}_2$, and $\mathbf{F}_3$. Expressing each force in Cartesian vector notation, we have

$$\mathbf{F}_1 = (F_x)_1\mathbf{i} + (F_y)_1\mathbf{j} + (F_z)_1\mathbf{k}$$
$$\mathbf{F}_2 = (F_x)_2\mathbf{i} + (F_y)_2\mathbf{j} + (F_z)_2\mathbf{k}$$
$$\mathbf{F}_3 = (F_x)_3\mathbf{i} + (F_y)_3\mathbf{j} + (F_z)_3\mathbf{k}$$
$$\mathbf{W} = W\mathbf{k}$$

If the particle is given a virtual displacement $\delta x\,\mathbf{i}$, as shown in Fig. 11–3, the virtual work equation for this displacement is

$$\delta W = 0; \qquad \mathbf{F}_1 \cdot \delta x\,\mathbf{i} + \mathbf{F}_2 \cdot \delta x\,\mathbf{i} + \mathbf{F}_3 \cdot \delta x\,\mathbf{i} + \mathbf{W} \cdot \delta x\,\mathbf{i} = 0$$

Substituting the vector components of each force into this equation, and carrying out the dot product operation yields

$$(F_x)_1\,\delta x + (F_x)_2\,\delta x + (F_x)_3\,\delta x = 0$$

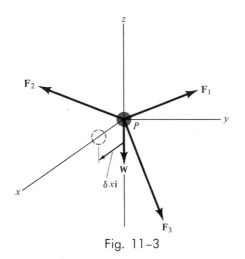

Fig. 11–3

or

$$\left(\sum_{i=1}^{3} (F_x)_i \right) \delta x = 0$$

Since δx has been imposed, this factor cannot be zero; therefore, the sum of the force components in the x direction must equal zero, i.e.,

$$\sum_{i=1}^{3} (F_x)_i = 0$$

This condition is equivalent to writing the *equilibrium equation* $\Sigma F_x = 0$ for the particle. In a similar manner, two other virtual work equations may be written for the particle by assuming virtual displacements $\delta y\,\mathbf{j}$ and $\delta z\,\mathbf{k}$, acting in the y and z directions respectively. Doing this amounts to satisfying the equilibrium equations $\Sigma F_y = 0$ and $\Sigma F_z = 0$ for the particle.

Writing the virtual work equations is therefore another way of stating both the necessary and sufficient conditions of equilibrium for the particle. No real advantage is gained, however, in using this method for the solution of particle equilibrium problems. This is because the virtual displacement in a given direction appears directly in each term of the virtual work equation; hence, when factored, it leaves an equation which is the same as that which would be obtained by using an equilibrium equation written for the particle in the same direction. The only real purpose of applying the method of virtual work to the equilibrium of a single particle as stated here is simply to provide an introduction to the concepts involved.

*11-3. Principle of Virtual Work for a Rigid Body

Since a rigid body does not deform when subjected to a given loading, the total work done by the *internal forces* which hold the particles of a rigid body in equilibrium is *zero*. If the body moves through an arbitrary displacement, each of the internal forces occur in equal and opposite collinear pairs; consequently, the corresponding work done by each pair of internal forces cancels. For equilibrium of the body, therefore, it is necessary that the resultant external force and moment acting on the body be equal to zero. Thus, in a manner similar to that for a particle, the principle of virtual work for a rigid body may be stated as follows: *If the virtual work done by a system of external forces and couple moments acting on the rigid body is zero for every independent virtual displacement of the rigid body, then the rigid body is in equilibrium.*

When applying the principle of virtual work to equilibrium problems involving rigid bodies, it is necessary to take into account *both* translational and rotational movements of the body. A rigid body subjected to a general force system can have *six* independent virtual motions, namely, three coordinate translations δx, δy, and δz, and three rotations $\delta\alpha$, $\delta\beta$, and $\delta\gamma$, about the x, y, and z axes, respectively. An independent virtual work equation may be written for each of these six motions. These equations will then correspond to the *six* scalar equilibrium equations for a body. When the rigid body is subjected to a planar system of forces it has two independent translations on the surface of the plane and one rotation about an axis perpendicular to the plane. These *three* motions will yield *three* independent virtual work equations which correspond to the *three* force and moment equilibrium equations for the body.

Consider, for example, the beam shown in Fig. 11-4a, which has negligible weight. The reactions at supports A and B can be found by *removing the constraining action at each support and allowing the beam to displace in the direction of each reaction.* Thus, to determine the horizontal reaction at B, the roller at B and the pin at A are removed, and the beam is allowed to rotate through an angle $\delta\theta$ about the pin at A. This causes a virtual displacement $\delta\mathbf{b}$ along the direction of $\mathbf{F}_B$ and a movement $\delta\mathbf{c}$ under the 10-lb load, as shown on the free-body diagram (Fig. 11-4b). The support forces at A do no work since the pin at A does

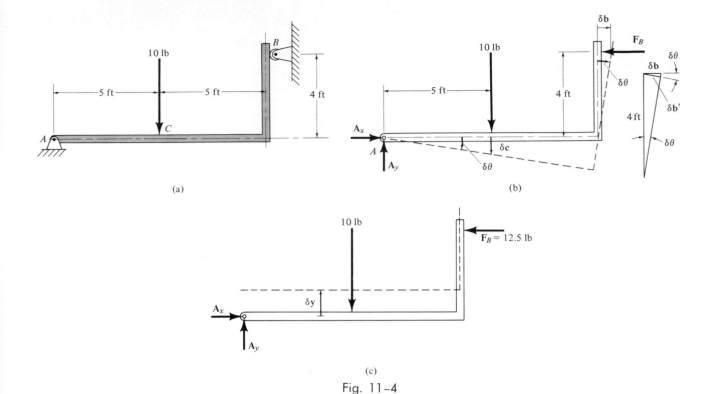

(a)

(b)

(c)

Fig. 11-4

not translate during the motion. The virtual work equation for this movement becomes

$$\delta W = 0; \qquad 10 \text{ lb } \delta c = F_B \, \delta b = 0$$

To solve this equation for the unknown F_B, it is first necessary to relate δc to δb. This can easily be done by relating both of these displacements to $\delta \theta$. From Fig. 11-4b, $\delta c = (5 \text{ ft}) \, \delta \theta$ and $\delta b = (4 \text{ ft}) \, \delta \theta$.* Substituting these expressions into the previous equation, we obtain

$$10 \text{ lb } (5 \text{ ft}) \, \delta \theta - F_B(4 \text{ ft}) \, \delta \theta = 0$$

Factoring out the virtual displacement term yields

$$(50 \text{ lb-ft} - 4 \text{ ft } F_B) \, \delta \theta = 0$$

According to this virtual work equation, the rotation about point A corresponds to computing moments of the forces about point A, as indicated by the term in parentheses. Since $\delta \theta \neq 0$, solution of the above equation requires that

*The displacement acting along the direction of $\mathbf{F}_B$ is $\delta \mathbf{b}$, as shown in Fig. 11-4b. Note, since $\delta \theta$ is a differential of the first order, the actual displacement at B, $\delta \mathbf{b}'$, may be approximated by $\delta \mathbf{b}$.

$$F_B = \frac{50 \text{ lb-ft}}{4 \text{ ft}} = 12.5 \text{ lb}$$

i.e., $\Sigma M_A = 0$.

The vertical reactive force $\mathbf{A}_y$ at A may be determined by *removing the constraints and allowing the entire beam to be translated by an amount δy in the direction of A_y.* This virtual displacement is shown in Fig. 11–4c. The virtual work equation becomes

$$\delta W = 0; \qquad A_y \, \delta y - 10 \text{ lb } \delta y = 0$$
$$(A_y - 10 \text{ lb}) \, \delta y = 0$$

The term in parentheses is equivalent to vertical summation of forces. Since $\delta y \neq 0$, solution requires that

$$A_y = 10 \text{ lb}$$

i.e., $\Sigma F_y = 0$. How would you determine $\mathbf{A}_x$?

As in the case of a particle, no added advantage is gained by solving rigid body equilibrium problems using the principle of virtual work. The above example simply illustrates how the method is applied; and from the results, it can be seen that the solution may be obtained in a more direct manner by using the equations of equilibrium.

*11–4. Degrees of Freedom for a System

The method of virtual work is particularly suited for solving equilibrium problems that involve a series of several *connected* rigid bodies. Since the virtual work done by a force depends upon the direction of displacement, the number of *independent virtual work equations* which can be written for a system of connected rigid bodies will depend upon the number of *independent virtual displacements* which can be made by the system. *For a system of connected bodies the number of independent virtual displacements equals the number of independent coordinates needed to specify completely the location of all members of the system* (provided none of the constraints or supports for the system are removed). Each independent coordinate gives the system a *degree of freedom* which must be consistent with the constraining action of the supports. Thus, an n-degree-of-freedom system requires n independent coordinates to specify its location with respect to a fixed reference point. Furthermore, for this system we may write n independent virtual work equations.

Several examples of connected systems are shown in Fig. 11–5. It is assumed that the *geometry of each system is known.* The piston and crank arrangement shown in Fig. 11–5a is an example of a one-degree-of-freedom system. The independent coordinate θ may be used to specify

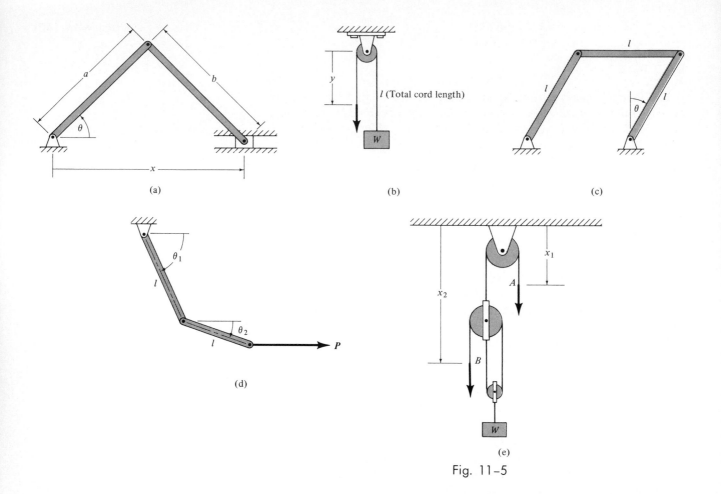

Fig. 11–5

the location of the two connecting links and the piston head. The coordinate x could also be used as the independent coordinate. However, since the piston is constrained to move between the walls, the distance x is *not* independent of θ and can be related to θ using the dimensions a and b of the connecting links. For example, if we use the cosine law, $b^2 = a^2 + x^2 - 2ax\cos\theta$. Other examples of one-degree-of-freedom systems are given in Fig. 11–5b and Fig. 11–5c.

The double pendulum and compound pulley arrangement shown in Figs. 11–5d and 11–5e, respectively, are examples of two-degree-of-freedom systems. To specify the location of each member of the double pendulum, both coordinate angles θ_1 and θ_2 must be known, since a rotation of one link is independent of the rotation of the other. To determine the location of the weight W attached to the rope and pulley arrangement in Fig. 11–5e, it is necessary to know the location of both end points A and B of the ropes. Provided the ropes are inextensible, have known lengths, and do not slip on the pulleys, the independent coordinates x_1 and x_2, Fig. 11–5e, may be used to locate these end points.

As discussed in previous sections, a particle unrestrained to move in space has three degrees of freedom which may be specified by the three coordinate directions $x, y,$ and z. A rigid body free to move in space has six degrees of freedom; three coordinate directions $x, y,$ and z are needed to specify its translation, and three coordinate angles $\alpha, \beta,$ and γ specify its rotation. If a rigid body is constrained to move on a plane, it has three degrees of freedom—two translations on the surface of the plane, and one rotation about an axis perpendicular to the plane.

*11–5. Equilibrium of Multiconnected Rigid Bodies and the Principle of Virtual Work

The principle of virtual work when applied to problems involving the equilibrium of a particle or a rigid body, as discussed in Secs. 11–2 and 11–3, has no real advantage in obtaining the problem solution. This is because after the virtual work equation is applied, the virtual displacement, common to every term, factors out of the equation, leaving an equation which may have been obtained from direct application of the equilibrium equations. The purpose of the previous discussion was to provide an introduction to the concepts used in solving problems by the method of virtual work. The distinct advantage in using the principle of virtual work is realized, however, when solving equilibrium problems involving a series of *ideally connected rigid bodies*. By definition, two bodies are ideally connected provided the connections are frictionless. When an ideally connected system of rigid bodies is given a virtual displacement consistent with the constraints of the system, only the active forces do work during the displacement. *Active forces* are defined as those forces which tend to set the system in motion. Externally applied forces (and couples), weight, and other body forces are examples of active forces. *Reactive forces* tend to prevent motion of the system. These forces occur at the supports and connections. Assuming that the supports do not move, and since the connective forces occur in equal and opposite pairs, the reactive forces do no work during the displacement. In particular, a reactive force becomes an active force when the constraint causing the reaction is *removed*, and the system of connected bodies is given a displacement in the *direction of the force*.

The principle of virtual work may be stated in a form appropriate for ideally connected systems of rigid bodies as follows: *An ideally connected system of rigid bodies is in equilibrium provided the virtual work done by all the active forces acting on the system is zero for all virtual displacements consistent with the constraints imposed by the connections and supports.*

Symbolically, this principle may be stated as

$$\delta W = 0 \qquad (11\text{--}3)$$

where δW represents the total work done by the active forces (and couples) acting on the system during a virtual displacement.

It has been pointed out that if a system has n degrees of freedom it takes n independent coordinates to specify the location of the system. It is thus possible to write a virtual work equation if only *one* of these coordinates undergoes a virtual displacement while the remaining $(n - 1)$ coordinates are held fixed. Hence, for the entire system it is possible to write n independent virtual work equations, one for each independent displacement. In many cases, a system of connected bodies has only one degree of freedom, and therefore only one virtual work equation needs to be written for the (one) virtual displacement.

The method of virtual work, applied to the solution of equilibrium problems of multiconnected bodies, requires more mathematical sophistication (using calculus and trigonometry) than the conventional vector approach (using the equations of equilibrium). However, once the equations of virtual work are established, the equilibrium position for the system may be obtained directly, *without* the necessity for having to dismember the system to obtain relationships between forces occurring at the connections.

When multiconnected rigid bodies are subjected to the effects of *friction* at their connections, or at points of contact, any advantage of using the method of virtual work will generally be lost. The work done by the frictional forces must be included in any equation of virtual work written for the body having a displacement tangent to a surface of contact. This work is negative, since the frictional force always acts in the opposite direction of motion. In any case, if the frictional force is related to the normal force ($F = \mu N$), the system of connected bodies will have to be *dismembered* in order to determine the magnitude of the frictional force.* Since the process of dismembering the system results in analyzing a series of *rigid bodies,* the most expedient way of obtaining the equilibrium forces is by using the equations of equilibrium *directly,* rather than applying the principle of virtual work.

In applying the principle of virtual work to the solution of equilibrium problems, it is *first necessary* to draw a free-body diagram of the entire system of connected bodies. From this diagram one can then determine which forces (or couples) do work (active forces) when the system undergoes a virtual displacement. The virtual work equation is then written

---

*The bodies must be dismembered in order to allow a displacement in the direction of **N**. By writing a virtual work equation in this direction, it is possible to compute the magnitude of **N**, and thereby obtain the value of $F = \mu N$.

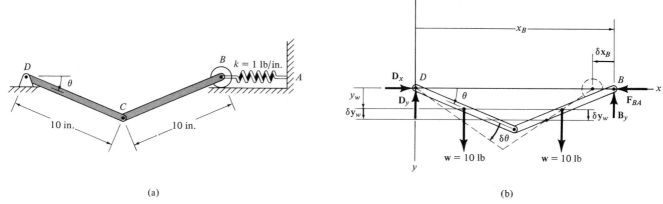

(a)

(b)

Fig. 11-6

for a *displacement* of the system which is made in the *direction of an unknown force*. Using mathematics, the virtual work of all the active forces is computed during this displacement. By relating the virtual displacements of each active force to a common virtual displacement of the system, this common displacement can then be factored out of the virtual work equation. The resulting factor can then generally be solved for the unknown force. The following examples give a detailed treatment of this procedure.

Example 11-1

Using the principle of virtual work, determine the angle θ for equilibrium of the two-member linkage shown in Fig. 11-6a. Each member weighs 10 lb. The spring has a stiffness of $k = 1$ lb/in. and is unstretched when $\theta = 0°$.

Solution

The system has only one degree of freedom, since the location of both links may be specified by the single coordinate θ. As shown on the free-body diagram in Fig. 11-6b, when θ undergoes a virtual rotation $\delta\theta$, only the active forces $\mathbf{F}_{BA}$ and the two 10-lb weights do work. Why? If the origin of an xy coordinate system is established at the *fixed* pin support D, the location of these active forces may be specified by the variables x_B and y_w, as shown in the figure. Expressing these dimensions in terms of the angle θ, we obtain

$$x_B = 2(10 \cos \theta \text{ in.})$$
$$y_w = \tfrac{1}{2}(10 \sin \theta \text{ in.})$$

405

Differentiating to obtain the virtual displacements yields

$$\delta x_B = -20 \sin \theta \; \delta\theta \text{ in.} \tag{1}$$

$$\delta y_w = 5 \cos \theta \; \delta\theta \text{ in.} \tag{2}$$

It is seen by the signs of Eqs. (1) and (2), and indicated in Fig. 11–6*b*, that an *increase* in $\delta\theta$ causes a *decrease* in x_B and an *increase* in y_w.

For the arbitrary angle θ, the spring has been stretched a distance of $\Delta x_B = (20 \text{ in.} - x_B)$, and therefore $F_{BA} = k \, \Delta x_B = (1 \text{ lb/in.})(20 \text{ in.} - x_B) = 20(1 - \cos \theta)$ lb. Since $\mathbf{F}_{BA}$ and $\mathbf{w}$ act in the same direction as $\delta\mathbf{x}_B$ and $\delta\mathbf{y}_w$, respectively, the virtual work equation for the displacement is

$$\delta W = 0; \qquad w \, \delta y_w + w \, \delta y_w + F_{BA} \, \delta x_B = 0$$

Substituting Eqs. (1) and (2), to relate the virtual displacements to the common virtual displacement $\delta\theta$, and expressing F_{BA} in terms of θ,

$$10 \text{ lb } (5 \cos \theta \; \delta\theta \text{ in.}) + 10 \text{ lb } (5 \cos \theta \; \delta\theta \text{ in.})$$
$$+ \; 20(1 - \cos \theta) \text{ lb } (-20 \sin \theta \; \delta\theta \text{ in.}) = 0$$

Factoring out the *common displacement*,

$$[100 \cos \theta - 400(1 - \cos \theta) \sin \theta] \; \delta\theta \text{ in.-lb} = 0$$

Since $\delta\theta \neq 0$, therefore,

$$100 \cos \theta - 400(1 - \cos \theta) \sin \theta = 0$$

or

$$\tan \theta \, (1 - \cos \theta) = 0.25$$

Solving for θ by trial and error, we have

$$\theta = 42.9° \qquad\qquad\qquad \textit{Ans.}$$

If this problem had been solved by using the equations of equilibrium, it would have been necessary to dismember the links and apply three scalar equations to each link. Using the principles of virtual work via calculus, we have eliminated the need for doing this and have arrived at the answer in a very direct manner.

Example 11-2

Using the principle of virtual work, determine the horizontal force **P** required to maintain the equilibrium position of the mechanism shown in Fig. 11–7*a*, when $\theta = 30°$. Neglect the weight of the links.

Solution

The mechanism has one degree of freedom and therefore the location of each member may be specified using the variable θ. When θ undergoes

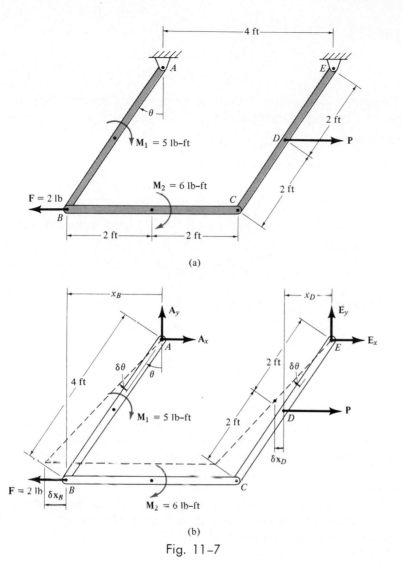

(a)

(b)

Fig. 11-7

a virtual displacement $\delta\theta$, as shown on the free-body diagram in Fig. 11-7b, links AB and EC rotate by the same amount since they have the same length, and link BC only translates. Since a couple does work *only* when it rotates, the work done by $\mathbf{M}_2$ is zero. The reactive forces at A and E do no work since the supports do not translate.

The coordinates x_B and x_D locate the (horizontal) position of the forces $\mathbf{F}$ and $\mathbf{P}$ with respect to the *fixed points* A and E. From Fig. 11-7b,

$$x_B = 4 \sin\theta \text{ ft}$$
$$x_D = 2 \sin\theta \text{ ft}$$

Thus,

$$\delta x_B = 4 \cos \theta \; \delta\theta \text{ ft}$$

$$\delta x_D = 2 \cos \theta \; \delta\theta \text{ ft}$$

Applying the equation of virtual work, noting that **P** is opposite to positive δx_D displacement, and hence does negative work, we obtain

$$\delta W = 0; \qquad M_1 \; \delta\theta + F \; \delta x_B - P \; \delta x_D = 0$$

Relating each of the virtual displacements to the *common* virtual displacement $\delta\theta$, yields

$$5 \text{ lb-ft } \delta\theta + 2 \text{ lb } (4 \cos \theta \; \delta\theta \text{ ft}) - P(2 \cos \theta \; \delta\theta \text{ ft}) = 0$$

$$(5 \text{ ft-lb} + 8 \cos \theta \text{ ft-lb} - 2P \cos \theta \text{ ft}) \; \delta\theta = 0$$

Since $\delta\theta \neq 0$,

$$P = \frac{5 + 8 \cos \theta}{2 \cos \theta} \text{ lb}$$

At the required equilibrium position $\theta = 30°$, therefore,

$$P = \frac{5 + 8 \cos 30°}{2 \cos 30°} \text{ lb}$$

$$= 6.89 \text{ lb} \qquad\qquad\qquad Ans.$$

Example 11–3

Using the principle of virtual work, determine the force which the spring must exert in order to hold the mechanism shown in Fig. 11–8a in equilibrium when $\theta = 45°$. Neglect the weight of the members.

Solution

The *xy* coordinate system has its origin located at the *fixed point A,* as shown on the free-body diagram in Fig. 11–8b. The system has one degree of freedom, defined by the angle θ. Why? The spring stretches when link *AB* undergoes a counterclockwise virtual rotation $\delta\theta$. If the spring is removed, $\mathbf{F}_s$ becomes an active force. Noting that the 20-lb force is directed in the negative δy_B direction, the virtual work equation for the displacement becomes

$$\delta W = 0; \qquad\qquad -20 \text{ lb } \delta y_B - F_s \; \delta x_C = 0 \qquad\qquad (1)$$

Forces $\mathbf{A}_x$, $\mathbf{A}_y$, and $\mathbf{C}_y$ do no work during this movement. Why? From Fig. 11–8b, using the "law of cosines," we have

$$(7 \text{ ft})^2 = (6 \text{ ft})^2 + (x_C)^2 - 2(6 \text{ ft})x_C \cos \theta \qquad\qquad (2)$$

The variation or differential of the above equation is then

$$0 = 0 + 2x_C \; \delta x_C - 12 \text{ ft } \delta x_C \cos \theta + 12 \text{ ft } x_C \sin \theta \; \delta\theta$$

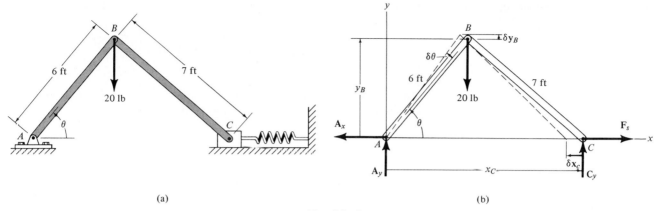

(a)   (b)

Fig. 11-8

Thus,

$$\delta x_C = \frac{12x_C \sin \theta}{12 \cos \theta - 2x_C} \delta\theta \text{ ft} \qquad (3)$$

Also,

$$y_B = 6 \sin \theta \text{ ft}$$

Therefore,

$$\delta y_B = 6 \cos \theta \, \delta\theta \text{ ft} \qquad (4)$$

When Eqs. (3) and (4) are substituted into Eq. (1) this yields,

$$-20 \text{ lb } (6 \cos \theta \, \delta\theta \text{ ft}) - F_s \frac{12x_C \sin \theta \text{ ft}}{12 \cos \theta \text{ ft} - 2x_C} \delta\theta = 0$$

or

$$\left[-120 \cos \theta - \frac{F_s(12x_C \sin \theta)}{12 \cos \theta - 2x_C} \right] \delta\theta \text{ ft-lb} = 0$$

Hence,

$$F_s = \frac{-120 \cos \theta (12 \cos \theta - 2x_C)}{12x_C \sin \theta} \text{ lb}$$

At the required equilibrium position $\theta = 45°$, the corresponding value of x_C can be found by using Eq. (2), in which case

$$x_C^2 - 12 \cos 45° \text{ ft } x_C - 13 \text{ ft}^2 = 0$$

Solving for the positive root, we obtain,

$$x_C = 9.81 \text{ ft}$$

Thus,

$$F_s = \frac{-120 \cos 45° \, [12 \cos 45° - 2(9.81)]}{12(9.81) \sin 45°} \, \text{lb}$$

$$= \quad 11.35 \text{ lb} \qquad\qquad\qquad\qquad \textit{Ans.}$$

The positive sign indicates that $\mathbf{F}_s$ was shown acting in the correct direction in Fig. 11–8b. Hence, the spring must be subjected to a *compressive force* in order to maintain equilibrium of the mechanism.

Example 11–4

Using the principle of virtual work, determine the equilibrium position of the "double" pendulum shown in Fig. 11–9a. Neglect the weight of the links.

Solution

The position for equilibrium may be determined by specifying the angles θ_1 and θ_2 in terms of the applied loading and the dimensions of the pendulum. The system has two degrees of freedom, since both θ_1 and θ_2 must be known to locate the position of both links. Measured from the *fixed point O,* the coordinate x_B may be related to θ_1 and θ_2 by the equation

$$x_B = l \sin \theta_1 + l \sin \theta_2 \qquad\qquad (1)$$

If we hold θ_1 *fixed* and vary θ_2 by an amount $\delta\theta_2$, as shown in Fig. 11–9b, the virtual work equation becomes

$$[\delta W = 0]_{\theta_2}; \qquad\qquad P(\delta x_B)_{\theta_2} - M \, \delta\theta_2 = 0 \qquad\qquad (2)$$

P and M represent the magnitudes of the applied force and couple acting on link AB. The work term for the couple is negative, since $\mathbf{M}$ is directed opposite to the rotation of $\delta\theta_2$. To obtain the variation of δx_B in terms of $\delta\theta_2$ it is necessary to take the *partial derivative* of x_B with respect to θ_2 in Eq. (1) since x_B is a function of θ_1 and θ_2. Hence,

$$\frac{\partial x_B}{\partial \theta_2} = l \cos \theta_2$$

Then

$$(\delta x_B)_{\theta_2} = l \cos \theta_2 \, \delta\theta_2$$

Substituting into Eq. (2), we have

$$(Pl \cos \theta_2 - M) \, \delta\theta_2 = 0$$

Since $\delta\theta_2 \neq 0$, then

$$\theta_2 = \cos^{-1} \frac{M}{Pl} \qquad\qquad\qquad\qquad \textit{Ans.}$$

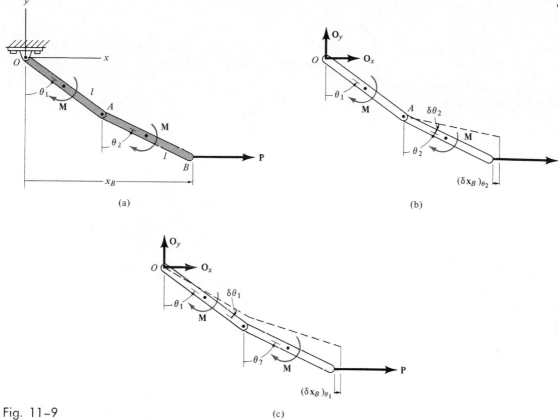

Fig. 11-9   (c)

When θ_2 is held *fixed*, and θ_1 is allowed to vary by an amount $\delta\theta_1$, as shown in Fig. 11-9c, the virtual work equation becomes

$$[\delta W = 0]_{\theta_1}; \qquad -M\,\delta\theta_1 - M\,\delta\theta_1 + P(\delta x_B)_{\theta_1} = 0 \qquad (3)$$

The first two terms are negative since the couples **M** act opposite to the rotation of $\delta\theta_1$. Using Eq. (1), we obtain the variation of x_B with θ_1:

$$\frac{\partial x_B}{\partial \theta_1} = l \cos \theta_1$$

or

$$(\delta x_B)_{\theta_1} = l \cos \theta_1 \,\delta\theta_1$$

Substituting into Eq. (3) yields

$$(-2M + Pl \cos \theta_1)\,\delta\theta_1 = 0$$

Since $\delta\theta_1 \neq 0$, then

$$\theta_1 = \cos^{-1}\frac{2M}{Pl} \qquad\qquad\qquad Ans.$$

Problems

Neglect the weights of the members in the following problems unless specified otherwise.

11–1. Use the method of virtual work to compute the tensions in cables *AB* and *AC*. The lamp weighs 10 lb.

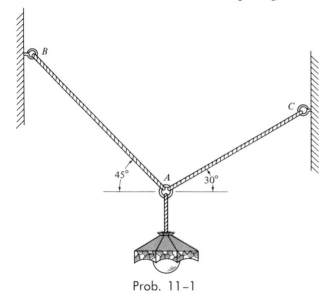

Prob. 11–1

11–2. Block *A* weighs 50 lb and rests on the smooth inclined plane. Determine the maximum weight *w* for equilibrium. The pulley at *B* is frictionless.

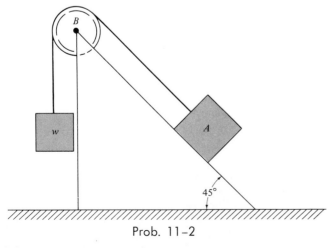

Prob. 11–2

11–3. Determine the vertical force **P** needed to maintain equilibrium of the lever.

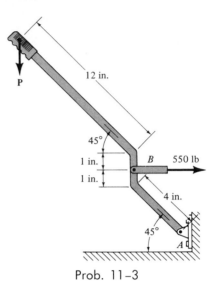

Prob. 11–3

11–4. Determine the angle θ required for equilibrium of the bent lever. The lever weighs 2 lb/ft.

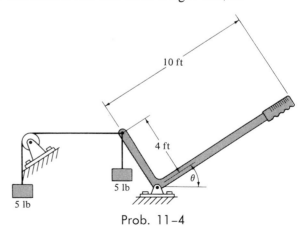

Prob. 11–4

11–5. The uniform rod *AB* weighs 10 lb and has a 100-lb weight attached at its end. If the spring is unstretched when $\theta = 60°$, determine the angle θ for equilibrium.

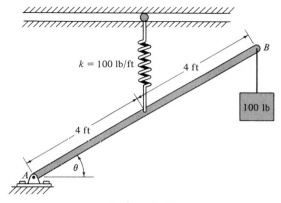

Prob. 11–5

11-6. The uniform links *AB* and *BC* each weigh 2 lb. Determine the horizontal force **P** required to hold the mechanism in the position shown. The spring has an unstretched length of 6 in.

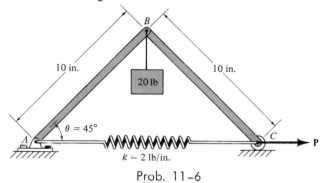

Prob. 11–6

11-7. Calculate the equilibrium position *x* for the 15-lb block. The spring is unstretched when $x = 2$ in. The horizontal plane and pulleys are frictionless.

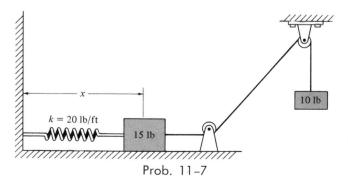

Prob. 11–7

11-8. Compute the force developed in the spring required to keep beam *AB* in equilibrium when $\theta = 35°$.

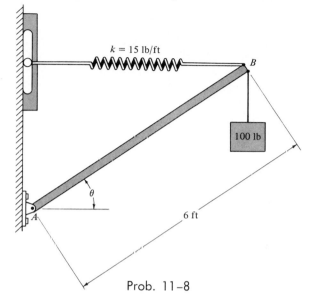

Prob. 11–8

11-9. If small weights w_A and w_B are added to points *A* and *B* of the desk lamp, the lamp will balance at any angle θ. Determine these required weights if the lamp weighs *w* lb.

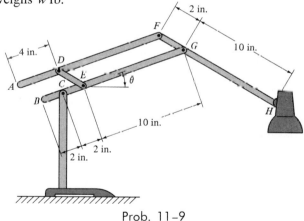

Prob. 11–9

11-10. The pin-connected mechanism is constrained at *A* by a pin and at *B* by a smooth sliding block. If $\theta = 45°$, determine the vertical force **P** which must be applied to block *B* to hold the mechanism in equilibrium.

413

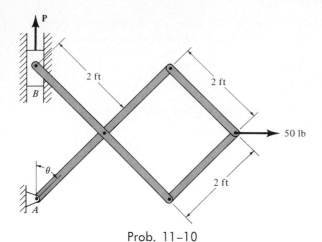

Prob. 11–10

11-11. Each of the three links of the mechanism has a weight of 10 lb. Determine the angle θ for equilibrium. The springs are unstretched when $\theta = 0°$.

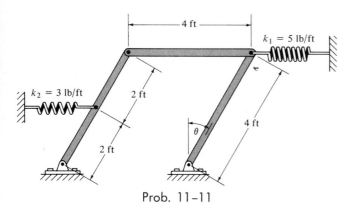

Prob. 11–11

11-12. Determine the vertical reaction at B for the compound beam. The support at C is smooth.

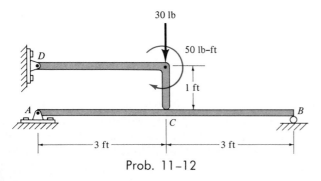

Prob. 11–12

11-13. The uniform rod OA weighs 2 lb, and when the rod is in the vertical position, the spring is unstretched. Determine the position θ for equilibrium.

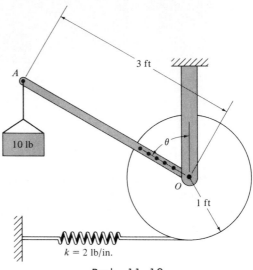

Prob. 11–13

11-14. A force **P** is applied at the handle of the toggle press. Determine the compressive force developed at C for an arbitrary angle θ of the handle.

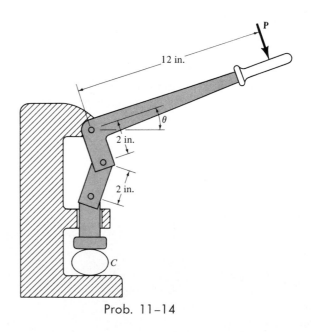

Prob. 11–14

414

11-15. The piston C moves vertically between the two smooth walls. If the spring has a stiffness of $k = 15$ lb/in. and is unstretched when $\theta = 0°$, determine the couple moment **M** which must be applied to the pin at A to hold the mechanism in equilibrium when $\theta = 20°$.

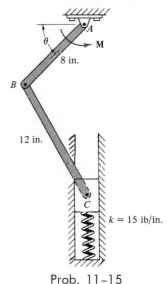

Prob. 11-15

11-16. Determine the vertical force **P** needed to hold the 100-lb block in equilibrium. Pulley A weighs 5 lb. Neglect the weight of the ropes and assume that the inclined plane is smooth.

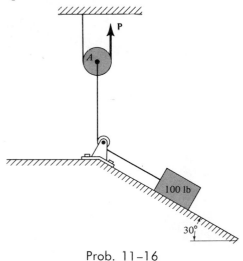

Prob. 11-16

11-17. The members of the mechanism are pin connected. Determine the angle θ necessary to hold the 50-lb horizontal force in equilibrium. The spring is unstretched when $\theta = 90°$.

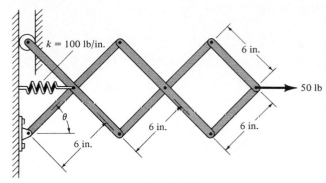

Prob. 11-17

11-18. When $\theta = 20°$, the 50-lb block compresses the two vertical springs 4 in. If the uniform links AB and CD each weigh 10 lb, determine the magnitude of the applied couple moments **M** needed to maintain equilibrium when $\theta = 20°$.

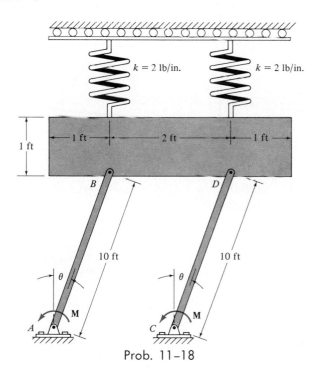

Prob. 11-18

11-19. Each of the uniform beams *AB* and *BC* has a center of gravity located at their midpoints. If all contacting surfaces are smooth and beam *BC* weighs 20 lb, determine the weight of beam *AB* required for equilibrium in the position shown.

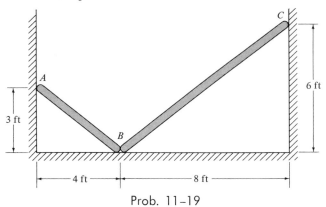

Prob. 11-19

11-20. Determine the force in member *BC* of the truss using the principle of virtual work. (*Hint:* Cut member *BC*, exposing the internal force acting in this member.)

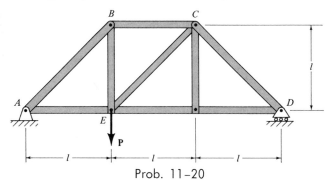

Prob. 11-20

11-21. Determine the vertical force **P** required to maintain equilibrium of the mechanism. The spring has a stiffness $k = 3$ lb/in. and is compressed 2 in. when in the position shown.

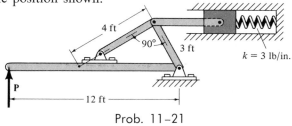

Prob. 11-21

11-22. For the press shown, it takes *n* turns of the worm shaft at *A* to produce one turn of gear *B*. Determine the compression developed at *C* if a load **P** is applied to the handle. The pitch of the screw *s* is *p*.

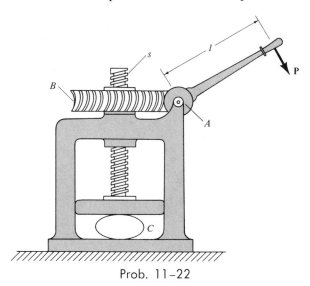

Prob. 11-22

11-23. Determine the load **P** required to lift the 100-lb load using the differential hoist. The lever arm is fixed to the upper pulley and turns with it.

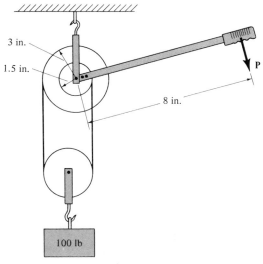

Prob. 11-23

11-24. Determine the horizontal force **F** required to maintain equilibrium of the slider mechanism when $\theta = 60°$.

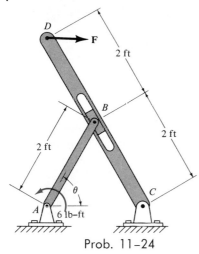

Prob. 11-24

11-25. Determine the angles θ_1 and θ_2 for equilibrium of the two uniform links. Each link has a weight of w lb.

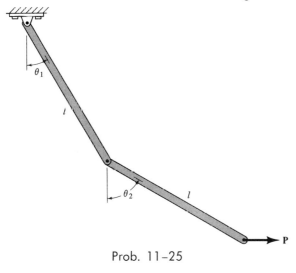

Prob. 11-25

11-26. Replace the 50-lb weight in Prob. 11-28 by a 50-lb *horizontal* force acting to the right, and determine the angle θ for equilibrium. Use the data in Prob. 11-28.

11-27. Determine the horizontal force **P** and vertical force **Q** necessary to maintain the equilibrium position of the two uniform links. Each link weighs 20 lb.

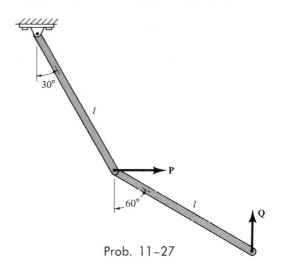

Prob. 11-27

11-28. The spring acting on the mechanism has an unstretched length of 1 ft. Determine the angle θ for equilibrium.

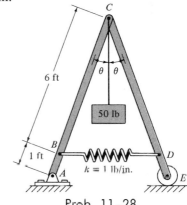

Prob. 11-28

11-29. Determine the reaction at B for the compound beam.

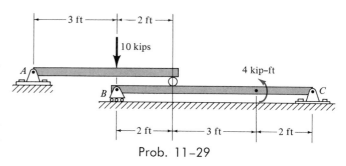

Prob. 11-29

417

*11–6. Definition of Potential Energy

Equation 11–1 defines the work done by a force $\mathbf{F}$ when the force undergoes an infinitesimal displacement $d\mathbf{s}$. If the displacement path has a finite length s, Fig. 11–1a, the total work done is

$$W = \int_s \mathbf{F} \cdot d\mathbf{s} = \int_s F \cos \beta \, ds \qquad (11\text{–}4)$$

The integration is carried out over the entire length of the path, and as a result, in order to evaluate the integral it is necessary to obtain a relation between the force component $F \cos \beta$ and the displacement path s.

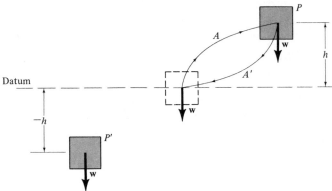

Fig. 11–10

In some instances, however, the work done by a force will be *independent of the path* followed and will depend only upon the initial and final points of the path. A force which has this property is called a *conservative force*. For example, a weight w, initially at some fixed horizontal reference or *datum*, as shown in Fig. 11–10, may be moved to position P, a distance h *above* the datum, along any arbitrary path A. Regardless of this path, the total work W done by the gravitational force w is independent of the path and depends only on the vertical height h. Thus,

$$W = -wh$$

The work is negative since $\mathbf{w}$ acts in the opposite direction of upward displacement. In a similar manner, the work done by lowering the weight w a distance h back to the datum along the arbitrary path A' is

$$W = wh$$

Why is the work positive?

Since the work done by a gravitational force is independent of the path and depends only on the initial and final points of the path, *the gravitational force is called a conservative force.*

The force developed by an elastic spring is also a conservative force. As shown in Fig. 11–11, the work done by a spring force *acting on a body,* such that the spring is elongated or compressed a distance d away from its equilibrium position, is

$$W = \int F \, dx = -\int_0^{-d} kx \, dx = -\int_0^d kx \, dx = -\tfrac{1}{2}kd^2$$

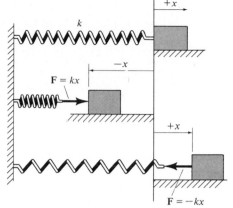

Fig. 11–11

The amount of work done *on the body* is thus dependent only upon the amount of extension *or* compression of the spring and the spring stiffness k. In *both* cases, the work is negative, since the spring exerts a force *on the body* which is opposite to its displacement.

In contrast to a conservative force, consider a *friction force* exerted on a moving object by a fixed surface. The work done by the friction force *depends upon the path*; the longer the path, the greater the work. When the object is slid across a fixed surface to some point and then returned to its original position, the friction force reverses direction when the block is returned, so that instead of recovering the work done during the first displacement, we must again do work on returning the body back to its original position. Thus, *a friction force is a nonconservative force.* The work done by this force is dissipated from the body in the form of heat.

When work is done on a body by a conservative force,* it gives the body *energy*. The energy stored in a body because of its elastic state, or energy measured due to the vertical position of a body, is known as *potential energy*. The total potential energy of a body or system of bodies is therefore the *sum* of its elastic potential energy V_e and its potential energy due to gravitation V_g, i.e.,

$$V = V_e + V_g \qquad (11\text{--}5)$$

Provided the weight w, shown in Fig. 11–10, is *above* the datum at position P, it has a *positive* potential energy,

$$V_g = wh$$

In this position, the gravitational force has a capacity of doing positive work on the body in moving it back to the datum. When the body is at position P', *below* the datum, the potential energy is *negative,* $V_g = -wh$, since work must be done on the body to move the weight back up to the datum level. In the next section it will be shown that the datum can be chosen at any elevation. This is so since the solution of

---

*A detailed discussion of conservative forces is given in *Engineering Mechanics: Dynamics*.

mechanics problems depends only upon a *change* in the potential energy, not the potential energy itself.

The potential energy stored in an elastic spring when the spring is *elongated or compressed* a distance d is

$$V_e = \tfrac{1}{2}kd^2$$

where k is the spring stiffness. In the deformed position, the spring has the capacity of doing work in returning an attached block to its original position. Hence, the elastic potential energy is always positive.

From this discussion, it may be concluded that the *work* done by a weight (gravitational) force is *opposed* to the *potential energy* gained or lost by the weight—for example, a weight force which acts *on the body* does *negative work* when the body is moved above a datum; this, however, causes a corresponding *increase* in the potential energy of the body. In a similar manner, a spring force does *negative work* when it acts *on a body* which compresses or elongates it; however, this causes an *increase* in the potential energy of the body. As a general statement, the total work done by all the conservative forces acting on a system of ideally connected rigid bodies is equal to a corresponding decrease in the potential energy of the system. This statement may be expressed mathematically as

$$W = -V + \text{const} \qquad (11\text{-}6)$$

The constant is needed because the choice of a datum used to measure the potential energy is *arbitrary*. From this equation it may be seen that when the work is a minimum, the potential energy is a maximum and vice versa.

*11-7. Potential Energy Criterion for Equilibrium

When an ideally-connected system of bodies is acted upon by a series of conservative forces, the total potential energy stored in the system will depend upon the positions of each of the bodies relative to some datum or fixed reference position of the bodies. For example, a block of weight w resting on a spring, as shown in Fig. 11-12a, has a total potential energy relative to a datum plane located at the *unstretched length* of the spring of

$$\begin{aligned} V &= V_e + V_g \\ &= \tfrac{1}{2}kx^2 - wx \end{aligned} \qquad (11\text{-}7)$$

Using this equation, we may compute the total potential energy V for any deformed position x of the spring measured from the chosen datum plane.

The potential energy criterion for equilibrium may be formulated by using Eq. 11-6. Taking the derivative of this equation, we obtain

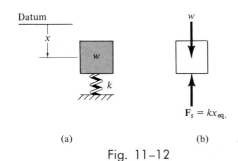

(a)   (b)

Fig. 11-12

$dW = -dV$. If the independent coordinates undergo *virtual displacements* rather than actual displacements, this equation becomes $\delta W = -\delta V$. For equilibrium, the principle of virtual work requires $\delta W = 0$, and therefore, knowing the potential-energy function for the system, we can also require

$$\delta V = 0 \qquad (11\text{-}8)$$

Therefore, when *an ideal system of multiply connected bodies is in equilibrium, the first variation or change in the potential energy function is zero.* Provided the system has only one degree of freedom, this change is computed by taking the *first derivative* of the potential-energy function and setting it equal to zero. For example, to determine the equilibrium position for the spring and block shown in Fig. 11–12a, a differential movement δx of the system causes a change in potential energy δV. Applying the equilibrium criterion to Eq. 11–7, we have

$$\delta V = \frac{dV}{dx}\,\delta x - (kx - w)\,\delta x = 0$$

Since δx is a virtual movement of the system, which is not equal to zero, we require that the term in the parentheses be zero. Hence, the equilibrium position $x = x_{\text{eq.}}$ becomes

$$x_{\text{eq.}} = \frac{w}{k}$$

We may obtain this *same result* by applying the equation of equilibrium $\Sigma F_y = 0$ to the forces acting on the free-body diagram of the block, Fig. 11–12b.

When the ideally-connected system has n degrees of freedom, the total potential energy stored in the system will be a function of n independent coordinates q_n; i.e., $V = V(q_1, q_2, \ldots, q_n)$. Applying the equilibrium criterion $\delta V = 0$ we must compute the total change in potential energy δV by using the "chain rule" of differential calculus; that is, the total variation or total differential of V must be equal to zero. Thus,

$$\delta V = \frac{\partial V}{\partial q_1}\,\delta q_1 + \frac{\partial V}{\partial q_2}\,\delta q_2 + \cdots + \frac{\partial V}{\partial q_n}\,\delta q_n = 0$$

Since the virtual displacements $\delta q_1, \delta q_2, \ldots, \delta q_n$ are independent of one another, it is necessary that

$$\frac{\partial V}{\partial q_1} = 0, \qquad \frac{\partial V}{\partial q_2} = 0, \qquad \ldots, \qquad \frac{\partial V}{\partial q_n} = 0 \qquad (11\text{-}9)$$

As in the case of virtual work, *we can therefore write n independent potential energy equations for a system having n degrees of freedom.*

Provided the potential-energy function for a system is known, the method of obtaining the solution is considerably simplified. All that is required for equilibrium is that the derivative of the total potential energy be equal to zero. It will be shown in the next section that there is an added feature in knowing the potential-energy function for an equilibrium configuration, and that is, the *stability* of the equilibrium position may be studied.

*11–8. Stability of Equilibrium

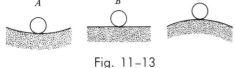

Fig. 11–13

Consider the position of a small sphere resting at one point on each of the paths shown in Fig. 11–13. Each point represents an equilibrium state for the sphere. When the sphere is at point *A*, it is said to be in *stable equilibrium*. The sphere, when given a small displacement up the hill, will always *return* to its original equilibrium position. At point *A*, its total potential energy is a *minimum*. When the sphere is at point *B*, it is in *neutral equilibrium*. A small displacement of the sphere either to the left or right of point *B* will not alter the equilibrium condition of the sphere. It will *remain* in equilibrium in the displaced position. In this case, the potential energy of the sphere is *constant*. When the sphere is at point *C*, it is in *unstable equilibrium*. A small displacement of the sphere will cause its potential energy to be *decreased*, and therefore the sphere will roll further *away* from its equilibrium position. At point *C*, the potential energy of the sphere is a *maximum*.

To summarize, this simple example illustrates three *types of equilibrium* which can occur. *Stable equilibrium* occurs when a small displacement of the system returns the system to its original position. In this case the potential energy stored in the system is a minimum. In *neutral equilibrium*, the system may be displaced by a small amount, in which case the system remains in the displaced state; that is, the potential energy

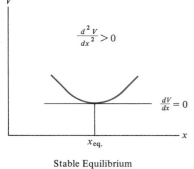

Stable Equilibrium

(a)

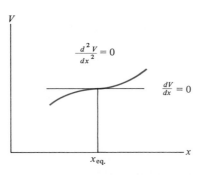

Neutral Equilibrium

(b)

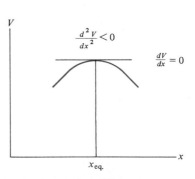

Unstable Equilibrium

(c)

Fig. 11–14

of the system remains constant during a displacement. *Unstable equilibrium* exists when the system is displaced by a small amount and not only does not return to its original equilibrium position but continues to go further away from the equilibrium position. In this equilibrium position, the potential energy is a maximum.

In particular, for *equilibrium* of a system having a single degree of freedom, it has been shown that the *first derivative* of the potential-energy function for the system must be equal to zero. The function V may have zero slope at points where the function is maximum, minimum, or at an inflection point. As shown in Fig. 11–14, each of these points represents an equilibrium position for the system.

Often one is interested in investigating the stability of a particular equilibrium configuration. The *type of equilibrium* may be investigated by computing the *second derivative* of the potential-energy function and substituting in the value of $x = x_{eq.}$ at the equilibrium position. When $d^2V/dx^2 > 0$, Fig. 11–14a, the equilibrium position is stable. When $d^2V/dx^2 = 0$, Fig. 11–14b, the system is in neutral equilibrium. And finally, when $d^2V/dx^2 < 0$, Fig. 11–14c, the equilibrium position is termed unstable.

The criterion for investigating stability becomes increasingly complex as the number of degrees of freedom for the system increases. For a system having two degrees of freedom, with independent coordinates (x, y), it may be verified (using the calculus of functions of two variables) that equilibrium and stability occur at a point $(x_{eq.}, y_{eq.})$ when

$$\frac{\partial V}{\partial x} = \frac{\partial V}{\partial y} = 0$$

$$\left[\left(\frac{\partial^2 V}{\partial x \partial y}\right)^2 - \left(\frac{\partial^2 V}{\partial x^2}\right)\left(\frac{\partial^2 V}{\partial y^2}\right)\right] < 0$$

$$\left[\frac{\partial^2 V}{\partial x^2} + \frac{\partial^2 V}{\partial y^2}\right] > 0$$

at the point. Both equilibrium and instability occur when

$$\frac{\partial V}{\partial x} = \frac{\partial V}{\partial y} = 0$$

$$\left[\left(\frac{\partial^2 V}{\partial x \partial y}\right)^2 - \left(\frac{\partial^2 V}{\partial x^2}\right)\left(\frac{\partial^2 V}{\partial y^2}\right)\right] < 0$$

$$\left[\frac{\partial^2 V}{\partial x^2} + \frac{\partial^2 V}{\partial y^2}\right] < 0$$

at the point.

The following examples illustrate both the procedures for solving equilibrium problems using the method of potential energy and determining the type of equilibrium.

Example 11-5

The uniform link shown in Fig. 11-15a has a weight of $w = 20$ lb and length of 6 ft. The spring is unstretched when $\theta = 0°$. Using the method of potential energy, determine the angle θ for equilibrium and investigate the stability at the equilibrium position.

Solution

The datum is established at the top of the link when the *spring is unstretched,* Fig. 11-15b. (Location of the datum is arbitrary. Why?) The system has one degree of freedom. When the link is located at the *equilibrium position,* defined by the angle θ, the spring increases its potential energy by stretching, and the weight decreases its potential energy since it moves further below the datum plane. The potential-energy function for the system may therefore be written as

$$V = V_e + V_g$$
$$= \frac{1}{2} kx^2 - w\left(x + \frac{l}{2} \cos \theta - \frac{l}{2}\right)$$

The potential-energy function will be expressed in terms of the independent variable θ. Since $l = x + l \cos \theta$ or $x = l(1 - \cos \theta)$, then

$$V = \frac{1}{2} kl^2(1 - \cos \theta)^2 - \frac{wl}{2}(1 - \cos \theta)$$

Computing the first derivative to determine the equilibrium position, we obtain,

$$\delta V = 0; \quad \frac{dV}{d\theta} \delta\theta = \left[kl^2(1 - \cos \theta) \sin \theta - \frac{wl}{2} \sin \theta\right]\delta\theta = 0$$

Since $\delta\theta \neq 0$, then

$$l\left[kl(1 - \cos \theta) - \frac{w}{2}\right]\sin \theta = 0$$

This equation is satisfied provided

$$\sin \theta = 0$$

for which

$$\theta = 0° \qquad\qquad Ans.$$

or

$$kl(1 - \cos \theta) - \frac{w}{2} = 0$$
$$\theta = \cos^{-1}\left(1 - \frac{w}{2kl}\right)$$

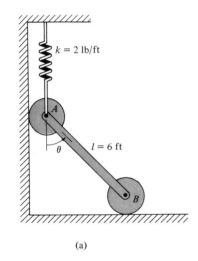

(a)

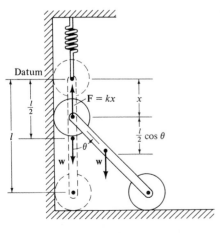

(b)

Fig. 11-15

Substituting in the numerical data for k, l, and w, we have

$$\theta = \cos^{-1}\left[1 - \frac{20\ \text{lb}}{2(2\ \text{lb/ft})(6\ \text{ft})}\right]$$

$$= 80.4° \hspace{4cm} \textit{Ans.}$$

Computing the second derivative of V to determine the type of equilibrium gives

$$\frac{d^2V}{d\theta^2} = kl^2(1 - \cos\theta)\cos\theta + kl^2\sin\theta\sin\theta - \frac{wl}{2}\cos\theta$$

or

$$\frac{d^2V}{d\theta^2} = kl^2(\cos\theta - \cos 2\theta) - \frac{wl}{2}\cos\theta$$

Substituting the values $\theta = 0°$ and $\theta = 80.4°$ and the numerical values of the constants yields

$$\left.\frac{d^2V}{dx^2}\right|_{\theta=0°} = 2\ \text{lb/ft}\ (6\ \text{ft})^2(\cos 0° - \cos 0°) - \frac{20\ \text{lb}\ (6\ \text{ft})}{2}\cos 0°$$

$$\frac{d^2V}{dx^2} = -60\ \text{ft-lb} < 0 \hspace{1cm} (\text{unstable at } \theta = 0°) \hspace{1cm} \textit{Ans.}$$

$$\left.\frac{d^2V}{dx^2}\right|_{\theta=80.4°} = 2\ \text{lb/ft}\ (6\ \text{ft})^2(\cos 80.4° - \cos 160.8°) - \frac{20\ \text{lb}\ (6\ \text{ft})}{2}\cos 80.4°$$

$$\frac{d^2V}{dx^2} = 70.0\ \text{ft-lb} > 0 \hspace{1cm} (\text{stable at } \theta = 80.4°) \hspace{1cm} \textit{Ans.}$$

Example 11-6

Determine the weight w required for equilibrium of the uniform 10-lb rod shown in Fig. 11-16a when $\theta = 30°$. The spring is unstretched when $\theta = 0°$. Investigate the stability at the equilibrium position.

Solution

The potential-energy function for the system may be determined by establishing the datum through point A and measuring the displaced position θ, as shown in Fig. 11-16b. When $\theta = 0°$, the weight is assumed to be suspended $(y_w)_1$ below the datum. In the final position the weight is $(y_w)_2$ below the datum. Thus, when the spring is stretched, the weight moves downward a distance $[(y_w)_2 - (y_w)_1]$ below the datum. The potential energy function is therefore

$$V = V_e + V_g$$

$$= \tfrac{1}{2}(30\ \text{lb/in.})(15\sin\theta\ \text{in.})^2 + 10\ \text{lb}\left(\frac{15\sin\theta\ \text{in.}}{2}\right) - w[(y_w)_2 - (y_w)_1] \hspace{1cm} (1)$$

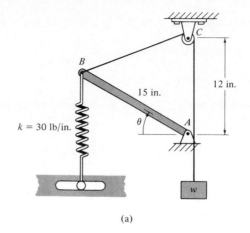

(a)

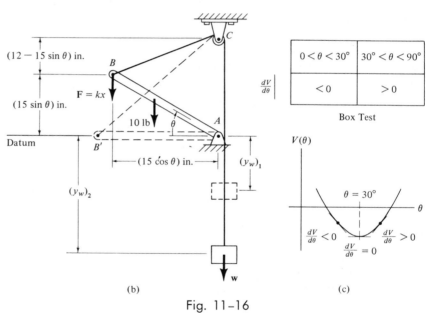

	$0 < \theta < 30°$	$30° < \theta < 90°$
$\dfrac{dV}{d\theta}$	< 0	> 0

Box Test

(b)   (c)

Fig. 11–16

The distance $[(y_w)_2 - (y_w)_1]$ may be related to the variable θ by measuring the difference in cord length $B'C$ and BC. Since

$$B'C = \sqrt{(15)^2 + (12)^2} = 19.21 \text{ in.}$$

and

$$BC = \sqrt{(15\cos\theta)^2 + (12 - 15\sin\theta)^2} \text{ in.}$$
$$= \sqrt{369 - 360\sin\theta} \text{ in.}$$

then

$$[(y_w)_2 - (y_w)_1] = B'C - BC$$
$$= 19.21 \text{ in.} - \sqrt{369 - 360\sin\theta} \text{ in.}$$

Substituting this relation into Eq. (1), we have

$$V = \tfrac{1}{2}(30 \text{ lb/in.})(15 \sin \theta \text{ in.})^2 + 10 \text{ lb}\left(\frac{15 \sin \theta \text{ in.}}{2}\right)$$

$$- w(19.21 \text{ in.} - \sqrt{369 - 360 \sin \theta} \text{ in.}) \qquad (2)$$

For equilibrium we require $\delta V = 0$; hence,

$$\frac{dV}{d\theta} \delta\theta = \left(6{,}750 \sin \theta \cos \theta + 75 \cos \theta - \left(\frac{w}{2}\right)\frac{360 \cos \theta}{\sqrt{369 - 360 \sin \theta}}\right)\delta\theta = 0$$

or

$$\frac{dV}{d\theta} \delta\theta = \frac{15 \cos \theta}{\sqrt{369 - 360 \sin \theta}} [(450 \sin \theta$$

$$+ 5)\sqrt{369 - 360 \sin \theta} - 12 \, w] \, \delta\theta = 0$$

Substituting the value of $\theta = 30°$ into this expression and simplifying, we have

$$\frac{dV}{d\theta}\bigg|_{\theta=30°} \delta\theta = 0.945\,(3{,}162 - 12w)\,\delta\theta = 0$$

Thus,

$$w = \frac{3{,}162}{12} = 264 \text{ lb} \qquad\qquad Ans.$$

Taking the second derivative of Eq. (2) to determine the type of equilibrium, we obtain,

$$\frac{d^2V}{d\theta^2} = 6{,}750 \cos 2\theta - 75 \sin \theta - \frac{w}{4}(369 - 360 \sin \theta)^{-3/2}(360 \cos \theta)^2$$

$$+ 180w \sin \theta\,(369 - 360 \sin \theta)^{-1/2}$$

For the equilibrium position $\theta = 30°$, $w = 264$ lb, hence,

$$\frac{d^2V}{d\theta^2} = 2{,}600 \text{ in.-lb} > 0 \qquad \text{(stable equilibrium at } \theta = 30°) \; Ans.$$

When the first derivative of the potential-energy function becomes complicated, as in this case, the "box test" provides a simplified way for determining whether the *second derivative* is positive, negative, or zero at the equilibrium position. After obtaining $w = 264$ lb, compute $\dfrac{dV}{d\theta}$ using values of θ just to the right and just to the left of $\theta = 30°$, as shown in Fig. 11–16c. From the calculations we can then reason from the behavior of the slope that the curve is concave upward as shown by the corresponding graph. Therefore, $\dfrac{d^2V}{d\theta^2}\bigg|_{\substack{w=264 \\ \theta=30°}} > 0$ (stable equilibrium).

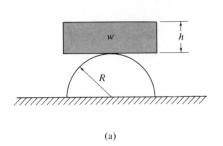

(a)

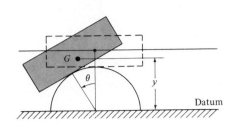

(b)

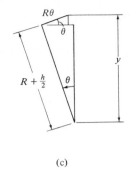

(c)

Fig. 11-17

Example 11-7

A homogeneous block having a weight w rests on the top surface of a smooth cylinder, as shown in Fig. 11-17a. Show that this is a condition of unstable equilibrium.

Solution

The datum is established through the center of gravity, at the equilibrium position of the block. If the block is displaced by an amount θ from the equilibrium position as shown in Fig. 11-17b, the potential-energy function may be written in the form

$$V = V_e + V_g$$
$$= 0 - wy$$

From Fig. 11-17c,

$$y = \left(R + \frac{h}{2}\right)(1 - \cos\theta)$$

Thus,

$$V = -w\left(R + \frac{h}{2}\right)(1 - \cos\theta)$$

For equilibrium,

$$\delta V = \frac{dV}{d\theta}\,\delta\theta = -w\left(R + \frac{h}{2}\right)(\sin\theta)\,\delta\theta = 0$$

Obviously $\theta = 0°$ is the equilibrium position which satisfies this equation.

Taking the second derivative of V, we have

$$\frac{d^2V}{d\theta^2} = -w\left(R + \frac{h}{2}\right)\cos\theta$$

At $\theta = 0°$,

$$\left.\frac{d^2V}{d\theta^2}\right|_{\theta=0°} = -w\left(R + \frac{h}{2}\right) < 0$$

Since all the constants are positive, the block is in unstable equilibrium.

Problems

11-30. If the potential energy for a conservative one-degree-of-freedom system is expressed by the relation $V = 4x^3 - x^2 - 3x + 10$, determine the positions for equilibrium and investigate the stability at each of these positions.

11-31. Work Prob. 11-30 using the potential-energy function $V = 10 \cos 2\theta + 24 \sin \theta$, $0 \le \theta \le 180°$.

11-32. If the potential energy for a conservative two-degree-of-freedom system is expressed by the relation $V = 3y^2 + 2x^2$, determine the position of equilibrium and investigate the stability at each of these positions.

11-33. The spring acting on the mechanism has an unstretched length when $\theta = 30°$. Determine the position θ for equilibrium using the principle of potential energy, and investigate the stability of the mechanism at this position.

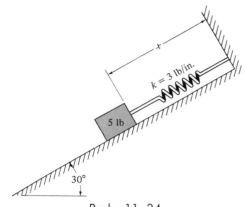

Prob. 11-34

11-35. Solve Prob. 11-7 using the principle of potential energy, and investigate the stability at the equilibrium position.

11-36. Solve Prob. 11-13 using the principle of potential energy, and investigate the stability at the equilibrium position.

11-37. Solve Prob. 11-28 using the principle of potential energy, and investigate the stability at the equilibrium position.

11-38. Using the method of potential energy, determine the angle θ for equilibrium of the 10-lb weight. The spring is unstretched when $\theta = 0°$. Investigate the stability in the equilibrium position.

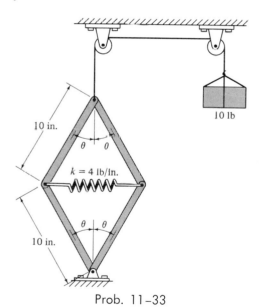

Prob. 11-33

11-34. Using the method of potential energy, determine the equilibrium position x for the 5-lb block. The spring is unstretched when $x = 2$ in. Investigate the stability at the equilibrium position. The inclined plane is smooth.

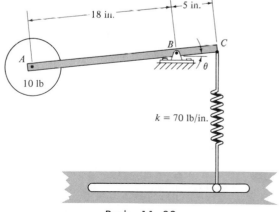

Prob. 11-38

429

11-39. The uniform beam weighs 100 lb. If the contacting surfaces are smooth, determine the angle θ for equilibrium using the principle of potential energy. Investigate the stability of the beam when it is in the equilibrium position. The spring has an unstretched length of 4 ft.

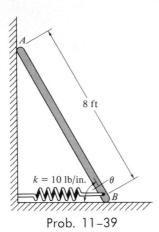

Prob. 11-39

11-41. The two blocks weigh 10 lb each and are suspended from the ends of springs as shown. Using the method of potential energy, determine the deflection of the springs, x_1 and x_2, for both blocks. The springs are unstretched when $x_1 = x_2 = 0$.

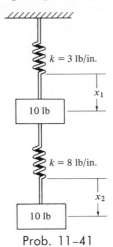

Prob. 11-41

11-40. The uniform rod AB weighs 10 lb. If the spring has an unstretched length when $\theta = 60°$, determine the angle θ for equilibrium using the principle of potential energy. Investigate the stability at the equilibrium position.

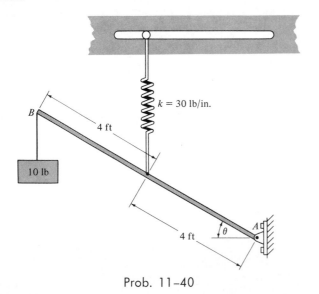

Prob. 11-40

11-42. The uniform beam AB weighs 100 lb. If both springs DE and BC are unstretched when $\theta = 90°$, determine the angle θ for equilibrium using the principle of potential energy. Investigate the stability at the equilibrium position. Both springs always act in the horizontal position because of the roller guides at C and E.

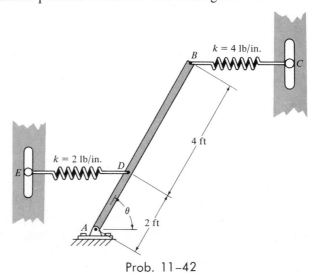

Prob. 11-42

430

11–43. The uniform beam OA weighs 150 lb. Determine the weight w which will hold the beam in equilibrium when $\theta = 30°$. Neglect the size of the pulley at B.

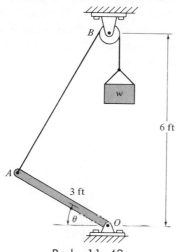

Prob. 11–43

11–44. A block made of homogeneous material rests on top of the cylindrical surface. Derive the relationship between the radius of the cylinder, r, and the dimension of the block, b, for stable, unstable, and neutral equilibrium. (*Hint:* Establish the potential energy function for *small* angle θ; i.e., approximate $\sin\theta \approx 0$, and $\cos\theta \approx 1 - \dfrac{\theta^2}{2}$.)

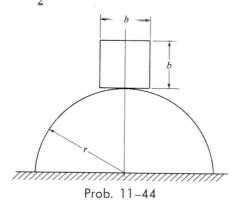

Prob. 11–44

11–45. Using the method of potential energy, determine the weight w required to deform the mechanism so that $\theta = 45°$. The springs are unstretched when $\theta = 60°$. Neglect the weights of the members.

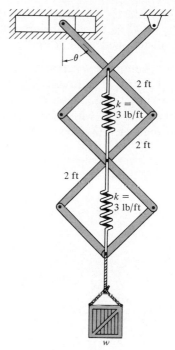

Prob. 11–45

11–46. The uniform 50-lb beam AB is pin-connected at both of its end points. The rod BC, having negligible weight, passes through a swivel block at C. If the spring has a stiffness of $k = 5$ lb/ft and is unstretched when $\theta = 0°$, determine the angle θ for equilibrium of the beam. Investigate the stability at the equilibrium position.

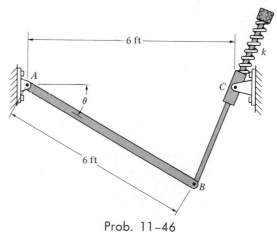

Prob. 11–46

11–47. Determine the spring constant k so that the 50-lb beam in Prob. 11–46 is in equilibrium when $\theta = 45°$. The spring is unstretched when $\theta = 0°$.

11–48. The 60-lb hemisphere supports a cylinder having a density of 311 lb/ft³. If the radii of the cylinder and hemisphere are both 5 in., determine the maximum height h of the cylinder which will produce neutral equilibrium in the position shown.

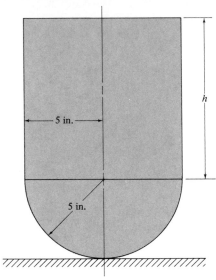

Prob. 11–48

11–49. The cylinder is made of two materials and has a center of gravity at point G. Show that when G lies directly above the centroid C of the cylinder, the equilibrium position is unstable.

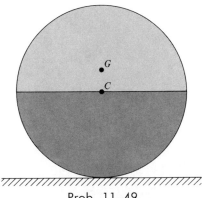

Prob. 11–49

11–50. Determine the position of stable equilibrium for the cylinder in Prob. 11–49.

11–51. A right circular cone is attached to the hemisphere. If both pieces have the same density, $\rho = 50$ lb/ft³, determine the maximum height h of the cone if the configuration is to be in neutral equilibrium at the position shown.

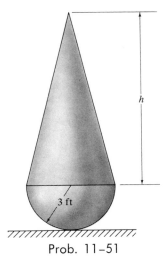

Prob. 11–51

11–52. Using the method of potential energy, establish two equilibrium equations which relate the two angles θ_1 and θ_2. The spring is unstretched when $\theta_1 = \theta_2 = 0°$. The pulley support at P is movable such that it keeps the cord BP horizontal.

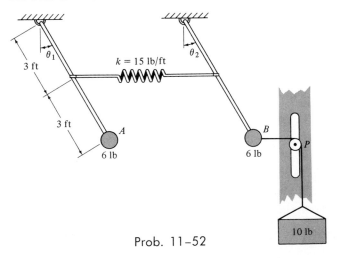

Prob. 11–52

A

Computer Program for the Simultaneous Solution of Linear Algebraic Equations

The application of the equations of static equilibrium or the equations of dynamic motion to the solution of problems involving three-dimensional force systems generally results in the necessity of solving a set of linear algebraic equations. The computer program listed in Fig. A–1 may be used to solve a series of n linear, nonhomogeneous, algebraic equations for n unknowns ($n \leq 21$). These equations are solved numerically using a Gauss elimination procedure. (Refer to a textbook on numerical analysis.)

The program is written in "Fortran IV" computer language, which is commonly used in most computer systems today. In using this program one must supply the *job control language cards (JCL),* the *program statement cards,* and the *input data cards.* Personnel at the computer center should be able to lend assistance both in obtaining the proper *JCL* cards and in arranging these cards in the proper order in the program. *In general, the cards are arranged in the following manner: JCL cards, program statement cards, JCL cards, input data cards, JCL cards.* The *program statement cards* are composed of the program statements listed in Fig. A–1. Each of these statements must be punched on a separate computer card in the proper card columns, as indicated in the figure. The input data is recorded on cards which are contained at the end of the program.

1	2	3	4	5	6	7	Card column

```
C        PROGRAM FOR SOLVING SIMULTANEOUS EQUATIONS
         DIMENSION A(21,21),B(21),X(21),C(21,3)
         READ(5,1)RCH
       1 FORMAT(F10.4)
         N=RCH
         READ(5,2)((A(I,J),J=1,N),I=1,N)
       2 FORMAT(8F10.4)
         READ(5,2)(B(I),I=1,N)
         WRITE(6,3)
       3 FORMAT(35H1SOLUTION OF SIMULTANEOUS EQUATIONS//)
         WRITE(6,4)
       4 FORMAT(//13H THE A MATRIX/)
         DO 5 I=1,N
       5 WRITE(6,6)(A(I,J),J=1,N)
       6 FORMAT(1X,1PE16.7,6(2X,1PE16.7))
         WRITE(6,8)
       7 FORMAT(4X,2HX(,I2,2H)=,1PE16.7/)
       8 FORMAT(//13H THE B MATRIX/)
         DO 9 I=1,N
       9 WRITE(6,6)B(I)
         DO 10 I=1,N
      10 C(I,1)=0.0
         II=0
      11 AMAX=-1.0
         DO 16 I=1,N
         IF(C(I,1))16,12,16
      12 DO 15 J=1,N
         IF(C(J,1))15,13,15
      13 T=ABS(A(I,J))
         IF(T-AMAX)15,15,14
      14 IR=I
         IC=J
         AMAX=T
      15 CONTINUE
      16 CONTINUE
         IF(AMAX)27,32,17
      17 C(IC,1)=IR
         IF(IR-IC)18,20,18
      18 DO 19 J=1,N
         T=A(IR,J)
         A(IR,J)=A(IC,J)
      19 A(IC,J)=T
         II=II+1
         C(II,2)=IC
      20 P=A(IC,IC)
         A(IC,IC)=1.0
         P=1.0/P
         DO 21 J=1,N
      21 A(IC,J)=A(IC,J)*P
         DO 24 I=1,N
         IF(I-IC)22,24,22
      22 T=A(I,IC)
         A(I,IC)=0.0
         DO 23 J=1,N
      23 A(I,J)=A(I,J)-A(IC,J)*T
```

```
24 CONTINUE
   GO TO 11
25 IC=C(II,2)
   IR=C(IC,1)
   DO 26 I=1,N
   T=A(I,IR)
   A(I,IR)=A(I,IC)
26 A(I,IC)=T
   II=II-1
27 IF(II)25,28,25
28 DO 29 I=1,N
   X(I)=0.0
   DO 29 K=1,N
29 X(I)=X(I)+A(I,K)*B(K)
   WRITE(6,30)
30 FORMAT(///10H SOLUTIONS//)
   DO 31 I=1,N
31 WRITE(6,7)I,X(I)
   GO TO 34
32 WRITE(6,33)
33 FORMAT(///27H EQUATIONS CANNOT BE SOLVED)
34 STOP
   END
```

Fig. A-1

Each numerical element of data is punched anywhere within a field of 10 spaces (card columns) on the cards. Since a standard computer card contains 80 spaces, one can put at most *eight elements of input data on a card*. Each element *must* contain a decimal point, and these elements must be rounded off to, at most, four numeric characters after the decimal point.

Consider, for example, solving the following set of four linear algebraic equations for the unknowns x_1, x_2, x_3, and x_4.

$$A_{11}x_1 + A_{12}x_2 + A_{13}x_3 + A_{14}x_4 = B_1$$
$$A_{21}x_1 + A_{22}x_2 + A_{23}x_3 + A_{24}x_4 = B_2$$
$$A_{31}x_1 + A_{32}x_2 + A_{33}x_3 + A_{34}x_4 = B_3$$
$$A_{41}x_1 + A_{42}x_2 + A_{43}x_3 + A_{44}x_4 = B_4$$

The coefficients of these equations may be arranged in the following matrix form

$$[A][x] = [B]$$

or

$$
\begin{bmatrix}
A_{11} & A_{12} & A_{13} & A_{14} \\
A_{21} & A_{22} & A_{23} & A_{24} \\
A_{31} & A_{32} & A_{33} & A_{34} \\
A_{41} & A_{42} & A_{43} & A_{44}
\end{bmatrix}
\begin{bmatrix}
x_1 \\
x_2 \\
x_3 \\
x_4
\end{bmatrix}
=
\begin{bmatrix}
B_1 \\
B_2 \\
B_3 \\
B_4
\end{bmatrix}
$$

To use the computer program for the solution of these equations, the input data (cards) must consist of the following:

1. Card 1 always contains the number of equations. In this case there are four equations, hence, the number 4.0 is punched anywhere within spaces 1 through 10 on the first card.
2. Cards 2 and 3 contain the A-matrix coefficients. (In all there are 16 coefficients.) Since there are 80 columns per card, and each coefficient is to be punched anywhere within a field of 10 spaces, the eight elements A_{11}, A_{12}, A_{13}, A_{14}, A_{21}, A_{22}, A_{23}, and A_{24} are punched *in this order* on the second card. The third card contains the remaining eight elements A_{31}, A_{32}, A_{33}, A_{34}, A_{41}, A_{42}, A_{43}, and A_{44}. (If there were more than 16 elements in the A-matrix, one would continue listing the data on cards 4, 5, etc.)
3. Card 4 contains the B-matrix coefficients. Each of these four elements is punched anywhere within a 10-space field on the card. They are entered in the following order: B_1, B_2, B_3, B_4.

When the program is received back from the computer center, the input data along with the answers (*output*) will be printed on paper. The answers are printed using "E-field" notation. This notation is similar to scientific notation. For example,

$$3.02 \text{ E } 02 = 3.02 \times 10^2 = 302.0$$
$$3.02 \text{ E } 00 = 3.02 \times 10^0 = 3.02$$
$$3.02 \text{ E} - 02 = 3.02 \times 10^{-2} = 0.0302$$

The following example illustrates the use of the program.

Example A–1

Solve the three equations
$$-x_1 - 2x_2 + 3x_3 = 2$$
$$2x_1 + x_2 + x_3 = -3$$
$$x_1 + 3x_2 + 4x_3 = 1$$

Solution:
Arranging the coefficients of three equations in the matrix form $[A][x] = [B]$ yields

$$\begin{bmatrix} -1 & -2 & 3 \\ 2 & 1 & 1 \\ 1 & 3 & 4 \end{bmatrix} \begin{bmatrix} x_1 \\ x_2 \\ x_3 \end{bmatrix} = \begin{bmatrix} 2 \\ -3 \\ 1 \end{bmatrix}$$

The input data is punched on four cards, as shown in Fig. A-2a. The first card contains the number of equations to be solved. The second and third cards contain the coefficients of the A-matrix, and the fourth card contains the B-matrix coefficients.

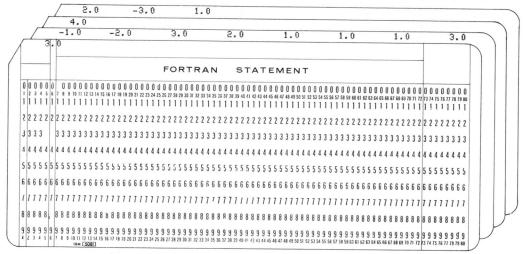

Fig. A–2a

```
SOLUTION OF SIMULTANEOUS EQUATIONS

THE A MATRIX

   -1.0000000E 00    -2.0000000E 00     3.0000000E 00
    2.0000000E 00     1.0000000E 00     1.0000000E 00
    1.0000000E 00     3.0000000E 00     4.0000000E 00

THE B MATRIX

    2.0000000E 00
   -3.0000000E 00
    1.0000000E 00

SOLUTIONS

   X(1)=   -1.9285698E 00
   X(2)=    5.0000006E-01
   X(3)=    3.5714293E-01
```

Fig. A–2b

The printed output is shown in Fig. A-2*b*. Thus, the answers are

$$x_1 = -1.93 \qquad \qquad Ans.$$
$$x_2 = 0.50 \qquad \qquad Ans.$$
$$x_3 = 0.36 \qquad \qquad Ans.$$

B

Centroids of Line, Area, and Volume Elements

Circular arc segment $$\bar{x} = \frac{r \sin \alpha}{\alpha}$$	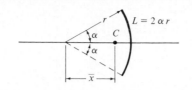
Quarter and semi-circular arcs $$\bar{x} = \bar{y} = \frac{2r}{\pi}$$	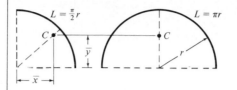
Triangular area $$\bar{y} = \frac{h}{3}$$	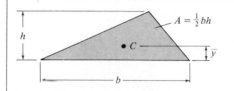
Trapezoidal area $$\bar{y} = \frac{1}{3}\left(\frac{2a + b}{a + b}\right)h$$	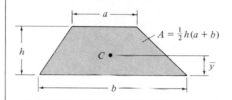
Circular sector area $$\bar{x} = \frac{2}{3}\left(\frac{r \sin \alpha}{\alpha}\right)$$	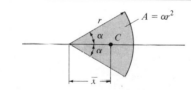
Quarter and semi-circular area $$\bar{x} = \bar{y} = \frac{4r}{3\pi}$$	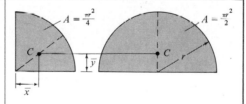
Semiparabolic and parabolic area $$\bar{x} = \frac{2}{5}b, \qquad \bar{y} = \frac{3}{8}a$$	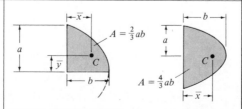

Semiparabolic area $\bar{x} = \dfrac{3}{4}\,b, \qquad \bar{y} = \dfrac{3}{10}\,a$	$A = \dfrac{ab}{3}$
Hemispherical surface $\bar{y} = \dfrac{r}{2}$	$A = 2\pi r^2$
Conical surface $\bar{y} = \dfrac{h}{3}$	$A = \pi r\sqrt{r^2 + h^2}$
Hemispherical volume $\bar{y} = \dfrac{3}{8}\,r$	$V = \dfrac{2}{3}\pi r^3$
Conical volume $\bar{y} = \dfrac{h}{4}$	$V = \dfrac{1}{3}\pi r^2 h$
Paraboloid of revolution volume $\bar{y} = \dfrac{h}{3}$	$V = \dfrac{1}{2}\pi r^2 h$

Table of Conversion Factors (FPS)→(SI)

Fundamental Quantities:

Length 1 foot (ft) = 12 inches (in.) = 0.3048 meter (m) = 30.48 centi-
meters (cm). The centimeter scale shown here approximates its
actual size, and represents a comparison of length with the inch
scale.

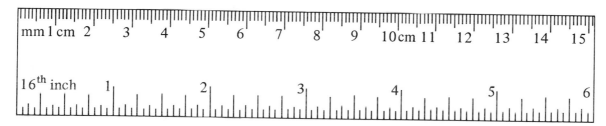

Force 1 pound (lb) = 4.448 newtons (N). A weight equivalent to 1
kilogram (kg) of mass is shown here in comparison to 1 lb of
the same material. $1\ lb_m = 0.454$ kg.

Time The second (sec or s) is the standard unit of time in both
systems of units.

Derived Quantity	Unit of Measurement (FPS)	To Convert (FPS) → (SI) Multiply by	Unit of Measurement (SI)
Moment of a Force Couple Torque	lb-ft	1.3558	N-m
Linear load intensity Linear density	lb/ft	1.4594×10	N/m
Surface load intensity Surface density Pressure (stress)	lb/ft^2	4.7880×10	N/m^2
Volume load intensity Density	lb/ft^3	1.5709×10^2	N/m^3
Area Moment of inertia	ft^4	8.6310×10^{-3}	m^4
Mass Moment of inertia	$ft-lb-sec^2$	1.3558	$kg-m^2$
Velocity	ft/sec	3.048×10^{-1}	m/s
Acceleration	ft/sec^2	3.048×10^{-1}	m/s^2
Work (energy)	ft-lb	1.3558	J
Power	ft-lb/sec	1.3558	W
Impulse Momentum	lb-sec	4.4482	N-s
Frequency	Hz	1.0000	Hz
Angular velocity	rad/sec	1.0000	rad/s
Angular acceleration	rad/sec^2	1.0000	rad/s^2
Angular impulse Angular momentum	lb-ft-sec	3.4380×10	$kg-m^2/s$

Answers to Even-Numbered Problems

2-2. 4.8 lb. $^{11°}\!\!\nearrow$

2-4. 84.6°.

2-6. 400 lb $\rightarrow$, 300 lb.$\uparrow$

2-8. 374 lb. $\searrow^{49°}$

2-10. 82.3°.

2-12. 21.6 ft/sec. $^{88°}\!\!\nearrow$, 4.5 ft/sec $^{4°}\!\!\searrow$, 6.7 ft/sec, $^{79°}\!\!\searrow$

2-14. (a) $F_{AC} = 226$ lb, $F_{AB} = 298$ lb.
(b) 70°.

2-16. 133.1 lb, 52.1°.

2-18. 458 lb, 23.6°.

2-20. (a) 40.3 lb, $\alpha = 75.6°$, $\beta = 51.7°$, $\gamma = 138.1°$.
(b) 26 in., $\alpha = 112.6°$, $\beta = 22.6°$, $\gamma = 90°$.

2-22. $\cos \alpha = 0.226$, $\cos \beta = -0.793$, $\cos \gamma = -0.566$,
8.83 ft.

2-24. (a) 2.24 ft, $\alpha = 153.2°$, $\beta = 63.5°$, $\gamma = 90°$.
(b) 4.82 ft, $\alpha = 78.0°$, $\beta = 58.8°$, $\gamma = 33.9°$.

2-26. $\theta = 38.7°$, $\phi = 59.0°$, $\psi = 36.9°$.

2-28. 374 lb, $\alpha = 48.7°$, $\beta = 138.7°$.

2-30. $\alpha = 69.0°$, $\beta = 74.4°$, $\gamma = 26.6°$.

2-32. 202.4 lb, $\alpha = 106.2°$, $\beta = 78.1°$, $\gamma = 159.7°$.

2-34. $\beta = 115.3°$, $\mathbf{r} = \{8.66\mathbf{i} - 4.27\mathbf{j} + 2.59\mathbf{k}\}$ ft.

2-36. 5.48 in., $\alpha = 68.6°$, $\beta = 79.5°$, $\gamma = 24.1°$.

2-38. $\mathbf{F}_{BA} = \{14.3\mathbf{j} - 4.43\mathbf{k}\}$ lb, $\mathbf{F}_{DC} = \{13.27\mathbf{i} + 14.29\mathbf{j} - 4.42\mathbf{k}\}$ lb.

2-40. 32.4 lb, 2.98 ft.

3-2. $F_D = 1{,}596$ lb, $F_B = 2{,}042$.

3-4. $F_A = 13.08$ lb, $F_B = 9.07$ lb, 36.9°.

3-6. 152 lb, 48.2°. ?

3-8. 11.16 lb.

3-10. $T = 3{,}026$ lb, $F = 2{,}263$ lb.

3-12. 12.25 lb.

3-14. 6.88 in.

3-16. 24.9 in.

3-18. 3.40 ft.

3-20. $N = 2.50$ lb, $W = 4.48$ lb.

3-22. 419 lb.

3-24. 96.6 lb, $\alpha = 138.4°$, $\beta = 131.5°$, $\gamma = 91.9°$.

3-26. 1.79×10^{-3} lb.

3-28. $F_{DE} = 125$ lb, $F_{DF} = 707$ lb. ✓

3-30. (5.05 in., -1.05 in., 0).

3-32. $T_{BD} = 47.1$ lb, $T_{CD} = 60.0$ lb, $W = 67.8$ lb.

3-34. $F_{AB} = 210$ lb, $F_{CB} = 201$ lb, $F_{OB} = 24.3$ lb.

3-36. $P = F = 0$, $R = 200$ lb.

3-38. $F_{OA} = 202$ lb, $F_{OC} = 216$ lb, $F_{OD} = 58.7$ lb.

3-40. 639 lb, $\alpha = 77.2°$, $\beta = 148.2°$, $\gamma = 118.6°$.

4-2. (a) $-48i - 48j - 32k$.
(b) $-38i + 52j - 47k$.

4-6. $\{-176.8k\}$ lb-in.

4-8. $\{119i + 148.8j\}$ lb-ft.

4-10. 310 lb-in., $\alpha = 93.8°$, $\beta = 104.4°$, $\gamma = 14.9°$.

4-12. 31.6 lb.

4-14. $M_A = \{-144.3i - 289k\}$ lb-in.

4-16. (a) $M_D = \{-13.6i - 174.2j + 96.6k\}$ lb-ft.
(b) $M_D = \{-13.6i - 174.2j + 96.6k\}$ lb-ft.

4-18. $F_{AB} = 16.75$ lb C; $F_{AC} = 34.5$ lb T; $F_{AD} = 26.0$ lb C; no: $M_{P'} = \{10i\}$ ft-lb.

4-20. $\alpha = 77.8°$, $\beta = 29.6°$, $\gamma = 63.4°$.

4-22. 909 lb.

4-24. 58.4 lb-in., $\alpha = 142°$, $\beta = 90°$, $\gamma = 52°$, any point.

4-26. $F = 5.00$ lb, $P = 6.67$ lb.

4-28. 40 lb.

4-30. 100 lb.

4-32. 60 lb-in., 10 lb.

4-34. 8.40 ft.

4-36. $M_A = 1,628$ lb-in., $\alpha = 169.4°$, $\beta = 100.6°$, $\gamma = 90°$; $M_O = 2,474$ lb-in., $\alpha = 166°$, $\beta = 104°$, $\gamma = 90°$.

4-38. $F_O = \{25j - 60k\}$ lb, $M_O = \{-487i - 312j - 103.9k\}$ lb-in.

4-40. 200 lb →, 1,000 lb-in.

4-44. $3x + 5y + 6z = 20$.

4-46. 160.0 lb-in. *106*

4-48. 80.3°.

4-50. $M_O = \{152.8i - 40j - 38.2k\}$ lb-ft; $\alpha = 19.9°$, $\beta = 104.2°$, $\gamma = 103.6°$; $M_{OD} = \{152.8i\}$ lb-ft.

4-52. $M_x = \{44.2i\}$ lb-ft.

4-54. (a) $F_x = 10$ lb, $F_y = 48.0$ lb, $F_z = 10$ lb.
(b) Projections are along the same orthogonal coordinate system.

4-56. $F_R = \{2.18i + 3.77j\}$ lb, point O.

4-58. $F_R = \{193i + 100j + 248k\}$ lb, $M_O = \{1,104i - 2,072k\}$ lb-in.

4-60. $F_R = \{-1.94i + 3.24j - 3.20k\}$ lb, $M_A = \{9.71i + 5.83j\}$ lb-in.

4-62. $(-1.39$ ft, -1.24 ft, $0)$.

4-64. 667 lb↓, 1,667 lb-ft.

4-66. 162.5 lb↓, 6.8 ft from A.

4-68. $F_R = 0$, $M_R = 100$ kip-ft.

4-70. 8,013 lb↑, 187,600 lb-ft. Use Appendix B.

4-72. $F_R = \{-31.4k\}$ kips, $M_A = \{114.2i + 200j\}$ kip-ft.

5-2. 3 unknowns, A_x, A_y, T_B.

5-4. 3 unknowns, F_A, F_B, F_C.

5-6. 2 unknowns, T_A, T_B.

5-8. 3 unknowns, A_x, A_y, T.

5-10. 3 unknowns, B_x, B_y, N_A.

5-12. 3 unknowns, A_x, A_y, T_B.

5-14. $T_A = 40$ lb, $T_B = 20$ lb.

5-16. $N_A = N_B = N_C = 47.0$ lb $^{70°}$.

5-18. $A_x = 17.4$ lb →, $A_y = 197.7$ lb↑, $F_B = 50.8$ lb. $^{70°}$

5-20. $T = 112.5$ lb, $F = 187.5$ lb, $\theta = 0°$.

5-22. $T = 74.6$ lb, $A_x = 33.4$ lb →, $A_y = 61.3$ lb.↓

5-24. $A_y = 137.5$ lb↑, $B_x = 0$, $B_y = 137.5$.↑

5-26. $A_x = 52.7$ lb →, $A_y = 49.6$ lb↑, $F_B = 60.8$ lb. $^{30°}$

5-28. $A_x = 69.3$ lb →, $A_y = B_y = 74.8$ lb.↓

5-30. $T = 20.3$ lb, $N = 3.38$ lb.

5-32. $A_x = 760$ lb →, $A_y = 400$ lb↓, $F_B = 990$ lb $^{45°}$.

5-34. $\alpha = 43.5°$, $\beta = 51.5°$, 87.3 lb.

5-36. 1,370 lb.

5-38. $N_A = N_B = W/(2 \cos \alpha)$.

5-40. 195.4 lb, 51.4°.

5-42. $W = 3,000$ lb.

5-44. $F_R = 53.9$ lb, $\alpha = 90°$, $\beta = 68.2°$, $\gamma = 21.9°$; $M_R = 416.7$ lb-ft, $\alpha = 24.2°$, $\beta = 112.6°$, $\gamma = 81.7°$.

5-46. $P = 75$ lb, $A_x = 37.5$ lb, $A_y = 0$, $A_z = 75$ lb; $B_x = 112.5$ lb, $B_z = 75$ lb.

5-48. $A_x = A_y = 0$, $A_z = 2,000$ lb; $M_A = 13,730$ lb-ft, $\alpha = 79.5°$, $\beta = 10.5°$, $\gamma = 90°$.

5-50. $E_x = E_y = 0$, $E_z = 2$ lb, $F_A = F_B = 7$ lb.

5-52. $A_x = 90$ lb, $A_z = 80$ lb; $B_x = 30$ lb, $B_y = 0$, $B_z = 125$ lb, $\Sigma M_z \neq 0$.

5-54. $T_{AB} = 31.4$ lb, $C_x = 13.9$ lb, $C_y = 3.73$ lb, $C_z = 32.2$ lb, $M_{Cy} = 20.9$ lb-ft, $M_{Cz} = 36.2$ lb-ft.

5-56. 900 lb, $A_x = A_y = 0$, $A_z = 600$ lb, $M_{Ax} = M_{Az} = 0$.

5-58. $A_x = 37.5$ lb, $A_y = 0$, $A_z = 37.5$ lb, $T_{BD} = T_{CD} = 70.2$ lb.

5-60. $A_x = A_y = 0$, $A_z = B_z = C_z = 5.33$ lb.

5-62. $P = 6.38$ lb, $A_x = 4.50$ lb, $A_y = 11.9$ lb, $B_x = 4.50$ lb, $B_y = 15.69$ lb, $B_z = 40.0$ lb.

6-2. $F_{AB} = 1,179$ lb, C; $F_{AC} = 833$ lb, T; $F_{CB} = 373$ lb, C.

6-4. $F_{AB} = 978$ lb, C; $F_{AF} = 437$ lb, T; $F_{BC} = 437$ lb, C; $F_{BF} = 875$ lb, T; $F_{CF} = 177$ lb, T; $F_{EF} = 312$ lb, T; $F_{ED} = 312$ lb, T; $F_{CE} = 500$ lb, T; $F_{CD} = 699$ lb, C.

6-6. $F_{CL} = 0.50$ kip, T; $F_{MC} = 1.12$ kips, C; $F_{CD} = 5.00$ kips, T.

6-8. $F_{AG} = 12.26$ kips, C; $F_{GF} = 8.66$ kips, C; $F_{BC} = 7.99$ kips, T.

6-10. $F_{AG} = 10.8$ kips, C; $F_{BF} = 1.20$ kips, T; $F_{CD} = 0$.

6-12. $F_{BC} = F_{BA} = 224$ lb, C; $F_{DB} = F_{EB} = 0$; $F_{DC} = F_{DE} = F_{AE} = 100$ lb, T.

6-14. $F_{AB} = F_{BC} = 0.687P$, T; $F_{AD} = 0.471P$, T; $F_{BD} = 0.333P$, T; $F_{DC} = 0.943P$, C.

6-16. $F_{EB} = 1,077$ lb, C; $F_{ED} = 77.7$ lb, C.

6-18. $F_{GF} = 2,167$ lb, C; $F_{BC} = 1,010$ lb, T.

6-20. $F_{GF} = 6$ kips, C; $F_{FC} = 1$ kip, C; $F_{BC} = 7.33$ kips, T.

6-22. $F_{FE} = 1,000$ lb, T; $F_{FB} = 1,500$ lb, C; $F_{BC} = 2,240$ lb, C.

6-24. $F_{GA} = 100$ lb, T; $F_{FC} = F_{FB} = 0$.

6-26. $F_{HG} = 1,146$ lb, C; $F_{BG} = 105.2$ lb, T.

6-28. $F_{DE} = 7.38$ kips, T; $F_{LE} = 0$.

6-30. $F_{JI} = 12.5$ kips, C; $F_{DM} = 0$.

6-32. $F_{AB} = 220$ lb, C; $F_{CB} = F_{DB} = 312$ lb, T.

6-34. $F_{BC} = F_{AC} = 163$ lb, C; $F_{AB} = 0$; $F_{DC} = 231$ lb, T; $F_{DB} = F_{AD} = 116$ lb, T.

6-36. $F_{AD} = 161.2$ lb, T.

6-38. $F_A = 434$ lb $\measuredangle^{64°}$ $F_C = 220$ lb. $^{30°}\searrow$

6-40. $F_{AB} = 2.36$ kips, $\measuredangle^{45°}$; $C_x = C_y = A_x = A_y = 1.67$ kips. 105

6-42. $F_{BC} = 297$ lb, $D_x = 60.0$ lb, $D_y = 210$ lb.

6-44. $A_x = 138$ lb, $A_y = 185$ lb; $C_x = 138$ lb, $C_y = 585$ lb.

6-46. 5,600 lb.

6-48. $F_A = 45.8$ lb, $F_B = 15.7$ lb, $F_C = 29.2$ lb, $F_D = 13.5$ lb.

6-50. $F_{BC} = 350$ lb, $A_x = 303$ lb, $A_y = 25$ lb.

6-52. $F_B = 83.3$ lb, $\measuredangle^{36.9°}$; $F_C = 83.3$ lb. $^{36.9°}\searrow$

6-54. $T = 20$ lb, $R_{BA} = 10$ lb.

6-56. $B_x = 303$ lb, $B_y = 364$ lb, $F_C = 303$ lb.

6-58. 69.3 lb.

6-60. $A_x = 285$ lb, $A_y = 236$ lb, $B_x = 111.6$ lb, $B_y = 536$ lb, $C_x = 285$ lb, $C_y = 436$ lb.

6-62. $A_x = 137.5$ lb, $A_y = 37.5$ lb, $B_x = 275$ lb, $B_y = 75$ lb, $D_x = 275$ lb, $D_y = 175$ lb, $F_E = 265$ lb. $^{45°}\searrow$

6-64. $A_x = 12.11$ k, $A_y = 2.61$ k, $D_x = 12.11$ k, $D_y = 6.38$ k.

6-66. $A_x = 1,455$ lb, $A_y = 40.0$ lb; $C_x = 1,455$ lb, $C_y = 760$ lb.

6-68. $F_{EF} = 886$ lb, $H_x = 679$ lb, $H_y = 2,079$ lb.

7-2. $A_D = 1.14$ kips, $V_D = 1.00$ kip, $M_D = 1.50$ kip-ft.

7-4. $A_F = 0$, $V_F = 3.33$ kips, $M_F = 10$ kip-ft, $A_E = 0$, $V_E = -0.42$ kip, $M_E = 11.67$ kip-ft.

7-6. $A_D = -300$ lb, $V_D = 100$ lb, $M_D = 200$ lb-ft, $A_E = 0$, $V_E = 50$ lb, $M_E = -25$ lb-ft.

7-8. $A_D = -70.7$ lb, $V_D = 0$, $M_D = -82.8$ lb-ft; $A_E = -50.0$ lb, $V_E = 50.0$ lb, $M_E = -50$ lb-ft.

7-10. $V_x = 0$, $A_y = V_z = 60$ lb, $M_x = -60$ lb-ft, $M_y = 0$, $M_z = -180$ lb-ft.

7-12. $A_E = -12.11$ k, $V_E = 1.61$ k, $M_E = 2.11$ k-ft.

7-14. $V_x = -100$ lb, $A_y = 0$, $V_z = 50$ lb; $M_x = -100$ lb-ft, $M_y = 50$ lb-ft, $M_z = 200$ lb-ft.

7-16. $V_x = 0$, $V_y = 0$, $A_z = 80$ lb; $M_x = 288$ lb-ft, $M_y = -36$ lb-ft, $M_z = 0$.

7-18. $0 \leq x < 5$, $V = 9.5 - 2x$, $M = 9.5x - x^2$;
$5 < x < 8$, $V = -0.5$, $M = 25 - 0.5x$;
$8 < x \leq 10$, $V = -10.5$, $M = 105 - 10.5x$.

7-20. $0 \leq x < 4$, $V = 4.43$, $M = 4.43x$;
$4 < x < 10$, $V = -0.57$, $M = 20 - 0.57x$;
$10 < x < 14$, $V = -5.57$, $M = -5.57x + 70$;
$14 < x \leq 18$, $V = 18 - x$, $M = -x^2/2 + 18x - 162$.

7-22. $0 \leq x < 2$, $V = 3$, $M = 3x - 36$;
$2 < x < 3$, $V = 5$, $M = 5x - 40$;
$3 < x \leq 6$, $V = 5$, $M = 5x - 30$.

7-24. Segment CD:
$0 \leq x < 2$, $V = 0.919$, $M = 0.919x$;
$2 < x \leq 8$, $V = 0.306$, $M = -0.306x + 2.45$.
Segment AB:
$0 \leq x < 12$, $V = -0.15x + 0.875$,
$M = -0.075x^2 + 0.875x$;
$12 < x \leq 14$, $V = -0.15x + 2.1$,
$M = -0.075x^2 + 2.1x - 14.7$.

7-26. $0 \leq x < 4$, $V = 5$, $M = 15 + 5x$;
$4 < x < 34$, $V = 0$, $M = 35$;
$34 < x < 38$, $V = -5$, $M = 205 - 5x$.

7-28. $0 \leq x < 6$, $V = -50x + 83$, $M = 83x - 25x^2$;
$6 < x < 8$, $V = -50x + 500$,
$M = -25x^2 + 500x - 2,500$;
$8 < x \leq 9$, $V = 100$, $M = 100x - 900$.

7-30. $0 \leq x < 3$, $V = \frac{1}{2}x^2 - 3x$, $M = \frac{1}{6}x^3 - \frac{3}{2}x^2$;
$3 < x < 10$, $V = -6.5$, $M = 10.5 - 6.5x$;
$10 < x \leq 13$, $V = 29.7 - x$,
$M = 29.7x - x^2/2 - 301.5$.

7-32. $0 \leq x < 8$, $V = 166.7$, $M = 166.7x$;
$8 < x < 10$, $V = -833.3$, $M = 8,000 - 833.3x$;
$10 < x < 12$, $V = 166.7$, $M = 166.7x - 2,000$;
$12 < x \leq 15$, $V = -333.3$, $M = 5,000 - 333.3x$.

7-34. See Prob. 7-18.

7-36. $0 \leq x \leq 15$, $V = 1506.7 - 200x$,
$M = 1506.7x - 100x^2 - 100$.

7-38. $0 \leq x < 5$, $V = 66.7$, $M = 66.7x$;
$5 < x < 10$, $V = -33.3$, $M = 500 - 33.3x$;
$10 < x \leq 18$, $V = -33.3$, $M = 600 - 33.3x$.

7-40. $x = 0$, $V = 633.3$, $M = 0$; $x = 4^{\mp}$, $V = 633.3, 433.3$,
$M = 2,533.3$; $x = 7^{\mp}$, $V = 433.3, 233.3$,
$M = 3,833.3$; $x = 13$, $V = 0$, $M = 4,633.3$; $x = 24$,
$V = -966.7$, $M = 0$.

7-42. $x = 0$, $V = 0$, $M = 0$; $x = 7.5$, $V = 3.25$.
$M = 18.75$; $x = 15$, $V = 0$, $M = 37.5$.

7-44. $x = 0$, $V = -0.45$, $M = 0$; $x = 6$, $V = -0.75$,
$M = -3.30$; $x = 12$, $V = -1.05$, $M = -9$; $x = 16$,
$V = 0$, $M = -9$.

7-46. $x = 0$, $V = 6$, $M = -19$; $x = 6$, $V = 0$, $M = -1$;
$x = 10$, $V = 0$, $M = -1$.

7-48. 2,320 lb.

7-50. $y = (h/L^3)x^3$, $T_{\max} = (w_oL/2)\sqrt{1 + (L/3h)^2}$.

7-52. 50.2 ft, 184.9 lb.

7-54. 546 ft, 506 lb, 82.1 ft.

7-56. 75.2 lb, 46.3 ft.

7-58. 162.0 ft

7-60. $h/l = 0.141$.

8-2. 22.6°.

8-4. 17.14 lb.

8-6. 17.3 lb, no.

8-8. 4.5 in.

8-10. 8 in.

8-12. 20.3 lb.

8-14. 547 lb.

8-16. 59.7 lb.

8-18. $P = 60.0$ lb, $T = 15.0$ lb.

8-20. 2.31 ft.

8-22. 73.8 lb $\leq P \leq$ 233.8 lb.

8-24. $s = b/\mu_s$

8-26. 306 lb.

8-28. $P = 15.63$ lb, $N_A = 14.66$ lb, $N_B = 89.5$ lb.

8-30. 20.4°.

8-32. Motion of crate impends, $P = 30$ lb.

8-34. 85.4°.

8-36. (a) 574 lb, (b) 1,648 lb.

8-38. $2 \tan^{-1} \mu$.

8-40. 28.1°.

8-42. 33.4°.

8-46. 3,060 lb.

8-48. 98.2 lb-ft.

8-50. 33.6 lb-ft.

8-52. (a) 208 lb, (b) 42.4 lb.

8-54. 1,615 lb.

8-56. $\frac{1}{2}\mu PR$.

8-58. $N = 481$ lb, $F = 101.1$ lb.

8-60. 62.8 ft-lb.

8-62. 3.90 lb.

8-64. 98.0 lb.

8-66. (a) 27.2 lb, (b) 3.68 lb.

8-68. 101.8 lb.

8-70. 16.79 lb.

8-72. 5.34 ft.

8-76. 0.00781 in.

8-78. 78.8 lb.

8-80. 187.5 lb.

9-2. (1.44 ft, 2.22 ft, 2.67 ft).

9-4. (1.57 ft, 2.29 ft).

9-6. (1.30 ft, 2.30 ft, 0).

9-8. (1.08 in., 0.540 in.).

9-10. (2.4 in., 1.5 in.).

9-12. (1.61 in., 2.66 in.).

9-14. (0.587 ft, 0.413 ft).

9-16. (1.13 ft, 3.60 ft).

9-18. (0, 0.833 ft, 0).

9-20. $(\frac{4}{5}a, 0, 0)$.

9-22. (0, 1.64 in., 0).

9-24. (0, 6 in., 1.39 in.).

9-26. (1.54 in., 1.72 in., 0.5 in.).

9-28. 1.55 in.

9-30. (1.12 in., 1.12 in., 1.36 in.).

9-32. (2.11 in., 2.11 in.).

9-34. (1.95 in., 0.904 in.).

9-36. (0, 1.64 in.).

9-38. (0, 8.99 in.).

9-40. (−0.262 in., 0.262 in.).

9-42. (0, 0, 2.34 in.).

9-44. (2.43 in., −0.075 in., 2.36 in.).

9-46. (1.174 in., 0, 1.132 in.).

9-48. 118.4 in.^{2}, 59.2 in.^{3}

9-50. 1.04 lb.

9-52. $A = 5.33$ in.^{2}, $\bar{y} = 0.75$ in., $V = 25.1$ in.^{3}

9-54. 156.1 in.^{2}, 118.8 in.^{3}

9-56. 3,120,000 lb.

9-58. $\mathbf{M}_o = \{-120\mathbf{j} - 20.25\mathbf{k}\}$ lb-ft.

9-60. 250 lb. $\measuredangle^{72.5°}$

9-62. $(4/\pi^2)(p_0\,a\,b)$, $(a/2, b/2, 0)$.

9-64. $F_A = 671$ lb. $\measuredangle^{26.6°}$, $F_B = 8,400$ lb. $\rightarrow$

9-66. $F_A = 1,600$ lb, $F_B = 4,240$ lb.

10-2. 0.1650 in.^{4}

10-4. $I_x = 2.13$ in.^{4}, $I_y = 4.57$ in.^{4}

10-6. $I_x = 3.56$ in^4, $I_y = 1.870$ in.^{4}

10-8. $J_o = 81.6$ in.^{4}, $J_{(2,0)} = 21.9$ in.^{4}

10-10. 18.30 in.^{4}

10-12. (a) $I_{xb} = bh^3/12$, (b) $I_{\bar{x}} = bh^3/36$.

10-14. $I_x = 0.0357$ in.^{4} $I_y = 0.050$ in.^{4}

10-16. $\bar{y} = 1.75$ in. (from top), 36.3 in.^{4}

10-18. $I_x = 141.3$ in.^{4}, $I_y = 21.3$ in.^{4}

10-20. $\bar{y} = 2.33$ in. (from top), 86.0 in.^{4}

10-22. 2,947 in.^{4}

10-24. 92.7 in.^{4}

10-26. $k_x = 6.22$ in., $k_y = 2.66$ in.

10-28. 180.6 in.^{4}

10-30. $I_x = 246$ in.^{4}, $I_y = 61.5$ in.^{4}

10-32. 0.667 in.^{4}

10-34. 0.5 in.^{4}

10-36. 2 in.^{4}

10-38. 0.667 in.^{4}

10-40. $\bar{x} = 0.75$ in., $\bar{y} = 1.75$ in., $I_{xy} = -2.81$ in.^{4}

10-42. $I_{x'} = 20.8$ in.^{4}, $I_{y'} = 20.8$ in.^{4}

10-44. $I_{x'} = 571$ in.^{4}, $I_{y'} = 274$ in.^{4}

10-46. $\theta = 8.70°$, $I_{max} = 727$ in.^{4}, $I_{min} = 186$ in.^{4}

10-48. $I_{max} = 64.1$ in.^{4}, $I_{min} = 5.33$ in.^{4}

10-50. 0.740 in.^{4}

10-52. $\theta = -27.3°$, $62.7°$, $I_{max} = 154.0$ in.^{4}, $I_{min} = 15.98$ in.^{4}

10-54. Center (456.5 in.^{4}, 0), $R = 271$ in.^{4}, $I_{min} = 185.5$ in.^{4}, $I_{max} = 727.5$ in.^{4}

10-56. Center (0.479 in.^{4}, 0), $R = 0.273$ in.^{4}, $I_{min} = 0.206$ in.^{4}, $I_{max} = 0.752$ in.^{4}

11-2. 35.4 lb.

11-4. 65.8°.

11-6. 5.28 lb.

11-8. 142.8 lb.

11-10. 75 lb.

11-12. 23.3 lb.

11-14. 2.5 $P/\sin\theta$.

11-16. 27.5 lb.

11-18. 130.0 lb-ft.

11-20. $(\frac{2}{3})P$

11-22. $2\pi lP/pn$.

11-24. 3.46 lb.

11-26. 90°, 16.6°.

11-28. 6.0°.

11-30. $x = 0.590$, stable; $x = -0.424$, unstable.

11-32. (0, 0), stable.

11-34. 2.83 in., stable.

11-36. $\theta = 0°$, unstable; $\theta = 76.6°$, stable.

11-38. $\theta = 90°$, unstable; $\theta = 5.90°$, stable.

11-40. $\theta = 90°$, unstable; $\theta = 57.6°$, stable.

11-42. $\theta = 90°$, stable; $\theta = 9.47°$, unstable.

11-44. $r > b/2$, stable; $r = b/2$, neutral; $r < b/2$, unstable.

11-46. 39.8°, stable.

11-48. 3.99 in.

11-50. $\theta = 180°$, i.e., G is directly below C.

11-52. $36 \sin\theta_1 + 135 \cos\theta_1 (\sin\theta_2 - \sin\theta_1) = 0$.
$36 \sin\theta_2 + 135 \cos\theta_2 (\sin\theta_2 - \sin\theta_1) - 60 \cos\theta_2 = 0$.

Index